ISSN 0887-3070

Contemporary

Authors

Bibliographical Series

American Novelists

James J. Martine
St. Bonaventure University
Editor

volume 1

A Bruccoli Clark Book
GALE RESEARCH COMPANY
BOOK TOWER
DETROIT, MICHIGAN 48226

Editorial Directors

Matthew J. Bruccoli

Richard Layman

Copyright © 1986 by Gale Research Company
ISBN 0-8103-2225-0
ISSN 0887-3070

Printed in the United States

To

Harrison T. Meserole

who taught most of us how

Contents

Plan of the Work

Contemporary Authors Bibliographical Series (CABS) is a survey of writings by and about the most important writers since World War II in the United States and abroad. *CABS* is a new key to finding and evaluating information on the lives and writings of those authors who have attracted significant critical attention.

Purpose

Designed as a companion to the long-established *Contemporary Authors* bio-bibliographical series, *CABS* is dedicated to helping students, researchers, and librarians keep pace with the already massive and constantly growing body of literary scholarship that is available for modern authors of recognized stature. While this proliferation of literary criticism has provided a rich resource, it has also presented a perplexing problem: in the face of so much material, how does one efficiently find the required information, and how does one differentiate the good from the bad?

The purpose of *CABS* is to provide a guide to the best critical studies about major writers: to identify the uses and limitations of individual critiques, and to assist the user with the study of important writers' works.

Scope

CABS will include American as well as foreign authors, in volumes arranged by genre and nationality. Some of the subjects to be covered in the series include contemporary American dramatists, contemporary British poets, and contemporary American short story writers, to cite only a selection. While there will be a concentration of volumes on American and English writers, the scope of *CABS* is world literature, and volumes are also planned on contemporary European, South American, Asian, and African writers.

Format

Each volume of *CABS* provides primary and secondary bibliographies as well as an analytical bibliographical essay for approximately ten major writers. *CABS* entries consist of three parts:

1. A primary bibliography that lists works written by the author, divided for ease of use into:

   —Books and Pamphlets

   —Selected Other: translations, books edited by the subject of the entry, other material in books in which the subject had some role short of full authorship, and important short works that appeared in periodicals, all separated by rubrics.

   —Editions, Collections

2. A secondary bibliography that lists works about the author, divided into:

   —Bibliographies and Checklists

   —Biographies

   —Interviews

   —Critical Studies, subdivided into:

      Books

      Collections of Essays

      Special Journals and Newsletters

      Articles and Book Sections

3. An analytical bibliographical essay in which the merits and the deficiencies of major critical and scholarly works are thoroughly discussed. This essay is divided into categories corresponding to those in the secondary bibliography.

   Although every effort has been made to achieve consistency in the shaping of the checklists and essays included in this volume, each entry necessarily reflects the output of an author and his or her critics. Thus, if a writer has not published notebooks or translations, these rubrics or subrubrics are omitted from the primary checklist; similarly, if there is no biography or collection of essays on the author, these headings do not appear in the secondary checklist or in the essay.

   CABS also contains a Critic Index, citing critics discussed in the bibliographical essays. For the convenience of researchers, this index will cumulate in all volumes after the first. Beginning with Volume 2, *CABS* will also include a cumulative Author Index, listing all the authors presented in the series.

Compilation Methods

Each *CABS* entry is written by an authority on his subject. The entries are reviewed by the volume editor—who is a specialist in the field—and the accuracy of the bibliographical details is verified at the Bruccoli Clark editorial center. Each bibliographical entry is checked whenever possible against the actual publication cited in order to avoid repeating errors in other printed bibliographies. Full citations are provided for each item to facilitate location and the use of interlibrary loans.

Unlike other study guides which are limited to a small selection of writers from earlier eras or which specialize in studies of individual authors, *CABS* is unique in providing comprehensive bibliographical information for the full spectrum of major modern authors. *CABS* is a map to the published critical appraisals of our most studied contemporary writers. It tells students and researchers what is available, and it advises them where they will find the information they seek about a writer and his works.

The publisher and the editors are pleased to provide researchers with this basic and essential service.

Preface

It will come as no surprise to scholars that over the past several decades there has been an explosion of scholarship and criticism on contemporary American novelists. As the national and international reputations of the novelists discussed in this volume have grown, so has the scholarship, often to an amazing degree. It is instructive to calculate this spiraling rise in critical attention using merely quantitative measures. For example, two decades ago, John Cheever received little or no serious attention from scholars, though he had published four volumes of short stories and two novels; now he is acclaimed widely as one of the most important writers of our time. Twenty years ago, six years after *The Sot-Weed Factor* and ten years after *The Floating Opera,* a single article was published in a year on John Barth's works; in a recent single year sixteen books and articles were published about him. In fifteen years, scholarly essays on John Updike have quadrupled. Perhaps most dramatic, however, are the cases of Eudora Welty and Saul Bellow. In 1966, twenty-three years after *The Wide Net and Other Stories,* twenty years after *Delta Wedding,* and seventeen years after *The Golden Apples,* there were one book and five articles published on Welty; in the intervening years that number has steadily grown so that a check of the most recent year will disclose thirty-one scholarly pieces on Welty and her work. The seven scholarly articles of twenty years ago, when most of Bellow's major novels had already been published, pale beside the over fifty books and articles on his fiction in a typical current year.

If one adds the component of the variety of critical approaches, from the formalist through the sociological to the psychoanalytic, to the quantitative factor and considers the varying quality of individual scholarly criticism, it is then clear that the task facing a contemporary researcher, librarian, scholar, teacher, or student of American literature seeking to locate critical works suitable to his needs is formidable. A reliable guide through the labyrinth of scholarship is a necessity rather than a nicety.

As might be expected, over the years critical responses to individual authors have varied. Donald J. Greiner, for example, traces the shift in emphasis of formal commentary on John Updike's work from an initial focus on style and sensuous lyricism to a later concern with theology and human sexuality. James Smith's essay on James Baldwin encompasses the reawakening of critics to black literature. Since James Baldwin is often seen as a spokesman for Afro-Americans and yet as a highly visible public figure his life-style is frequently at odds with the mainstream of American life, critical opinion of his work is sharply divided and often hostile. The review of scholarship on Norman Mailer by J. Michael Lennon reveals the serious, solid efforts by even the earliest critics through to the successful attempts of the most recent scholars to provide explications of a writer whose tumultuous life and complexity of multi-generic canon present special problems.

Unlike Baldwin and Mailer, John Barth chooses to keep his personal life personal. Joseph Weixlmann delineates the sharp difference between criticism of Barth's early works and that on his later, more complex novels and formal innovations. The chapter covering the enormous critical interest in Nobel laureate Saul Bellow's work follows the scholarly interest in the theme of a religious quest for transcendence and his movement away from the nihilistic assumptions of some modern writers, while pointing new directions of critical attention for the resourceful scholar. Robert Morace's examination of criticism and scholarship on John Cheever discloses a critical interest in the dualism manifest in Cheever's work, a juxtaposition of episodic structure and nearly neoclassical prose, and supports the view of Cheever as the most underdiscussed of major contemporary American writers. James Nagel provides a careful and insightful historical record of the serious study of the life and works of Joseph Heller. Citing the abundance of exegeses on *Catch-22*, this essay invites attention to Heller's other novels.

The critical overview of scholarship on Bernard Malamud indicates the difficulty for those critics who find patterns of development in Malamud's fiction and suggests that criticism of this writer needs revision in light of each subsequent work. Virginia Spencer Carr's chapter on Carson McCullers is informed by Carr's own comprehensive biography of the writer and traces the development of McCullers scholarship. Carr's evaluation of feminist readings of McCullers's work is especially interesting. The scholarship surveyed by Carr substantiates, as do other of the chapters in this volume, the significant contributions of the best feminist literary studies to a richer understanding of American fiction. Finally, the view of Eudora Welty criticism, as seen by an important Welty scholar, is as comprehensive as limitations of space allow and is as readable and dependable as is available anywhere. Much the same may be said for each of the chapters herein.

Experience suggests that the format of a bibliographic essay should be easily and readily usable. The rubrics of the chapters in this volume include a comprehensive if not exhaustive checklist of works by and about the writer being considered and an essay evaluating the most significant secondary material on the author. The accuracy of the information provided in the various checklists and essays is assured by the reputation and responsibility of the individual contributor. For the most part, the scholars who have contributed the chapters included here are recognized authorities who may be editors of scholarly journals devoted to his or her subject and authors of books or articles on the novelists discussed. I am proud of my association with them.

—*James J. Martine*
St. Bonaventure University

Acknowledgments

This book was produced by Bruccoli Clark, Inc. The in-house editor was Jefferson Matthew Brook.

Art supervisor is Patricia M. Flanagan. Copyediting supervisor is Patricia Coate. Production coordinator is Kimberly Casey. Supervisor of Typography is Laura Ingram. The production staff includes Rowena Betts, Kathleen M. Flanagan, Joyce Fowler, Ellen Hassell, Pamela Haynes, Judith K. Ingle, Beatrice McClain, Judith McCray, Mary Scott Sims, Joycelyn R. Smith, James Adam Sutton, and Lucia Tarbox. Jean W. Ross is permissions editor.

Walter W. Ross and Rhonda Marshall did the library research with the assistance of the staff at the Thomas Cooper Library of the University of South Carolina: Lynn Barron, Daniel Boice, Connie Crider, Kathy Edman, Michael Freeman, Gary Geer, David L. Haggard, Jens Holley, Marcia Martin, Dana Rabon, Jean Rhyne, Jan Squire, and Ellen Tillett.

Contemporary Authors

Bibliographical Series

American Novelists

James Baldwin

(1924-   )

James F. Smith
Pennsylvania State University

PRIMARY BIBLIOGRAPHY

Books

Go Tell It on the Mountain. New York: Knopf, 1953; London: Joseph, 1954. Novel.

Notes of a Native Son. Boston: Beacon, 1955; London: Mayflower, 1958. Essays.

Giovanni's Room. New York: Dial, 1956; London: Joseph, 1957. Novel.

Nobody Knows My Name: More Notes of a Native Son. New York: Dial, 1961; London: Joseph, 1964. Essays.

Another Country. New York: Dial, 1962; London: Joseph, 1963. Novel.

The Fire Next Time. New York: Dial, 1963; London: Joseph, 1963. Essays.

Blues for Mister Charlie. New York: Dial, 1964; London: Joseph, 1965. Drama.

Nothing Personal. Photographs by Richard Avedon and text by James Baldwin. New York: Atheneum, 1964; London: Penguin, 1964. Essays.

Going to Meet the Man. New York: Dial, 1965; London: Joseph, 1965. Short stories.

The Amen Corner. New York: Dial, 1968; London: Joseph, 1969. Drama.

Tell Me How Long the Train's Been Gone. New York: Dial, 1968; London: Joseph, 1968. Novel.

A Rap on Race, with Margaret Mead. Philadelphia: Lippincott, 1971; London: Joseph, 1971. Dialogue.

No Name in the Street. New York: Dial, 1972; London: Joseph, 1972. Essays.

One Day, When I Was Lost. A Scenario Based on Alex Haley's "The Auto-

3

biography of Malcolm X." London: Joseph, 1972; New York: Dial, 1973.

A Dialogue, with Nikki Giovanni. Philadelphia: Lippincott, 1973; London: Joseph, 1975. Dialogue.

If Beale Street Could Talk. New York: Dial, 1974; London: Joseph, 1974. Novel.

Little Man, Little Man. A Story of Childhood. Illustrated by Yoran Cazac. New York: Dial, 1976; London: Joseph, 1976.

The Devil Finds Work. An Essay. New York: Dial, 1976; London: Joseph, 1976. Essay.

Just Above My Head. New York: Dial, 1979; London: Joseph, 1980. Novel.

Jimmy's Blues. London: Joseph, 1983. Poems.

Meurtres à Atlanta [English title: *The Evidence of Things Not Seen*]. Paris: Editions Stock, 1985; New York: Holt, Rinehart & Winston, 1985. Essay.

Selected Other

"The Harlem Ghetto: Winter 1948," *Commentary,* 6 (Feb. 1948), 165-170. Essay.

"Too Late, Too Late," *Commentary,* 7 (Jan. 1949), 96-99. Essay.

"Preservation of Innocence," *Zero,* 1 (Summer 1949), 14-22. Essay.

"The Death of the Prophet," *Commentary,* 9 (Mar. 1950), 257-261. Short story.

"Two Protests against Protest," *Perspectives USA,* 2 (Winter 1953), 89-100.

"Paris Letter: A Question of Identity," *Partisan Review,* 21 (July/Aug. 1954), 402-410. Essay.

"The Crusade of Indignation," *Nation,* 183 (7 July 1956), 18-22.

"Mass Culture and the Creative Artist: Some Personal Notes." In *Culture for the Millions?* Taiment Institute. Princeton: Van Nostrand, 1959, 122-123, 176-187. Essay.

"A Word from Writer Directly to Reader." In *Fiction of the Fifties,* ed. Herbert Gold. Garden City: Doubleday, 1959, 18-19. Essay.

"They Can't Turn Back," *Mademoiselle,* 51 (Aug. 1960), 324-326, 351-358. Essay.

"The Dangerous Road before Martin Luther King," *Harper's,* 222 (Feb. 1961), 33-42. Essay.

"The New Lost Generation," *Esquire,* 56 (July 1961), 113-115. Essay.

"They Will Wait No More," *Negro Digest,* 10 (July 1961), 77-82. Essay.

"The Creative Process." In *Creative America*. The National Cultural Center. New York: Ridge, 1962, 17-21. Essay.

"The Negro's Role in American Culture: A Symposium," *Negro Digest*, 11 (Mar. 1962), 80-98. Commentary.

"The Image: Three Views, from Messrs. Shahn, Milhoud, Baldwin; Three Creative Artists Debate the Meaning of a Fashionable Term," *Opera News*, 27 (8 Dec. 1962), 8-13. Conversation/Debate.

"The Negro Writer in America: A Symposium," *Negro Digest*, 12 (June 1963), 54-65. Commentary.

"The Uses of the Blues," *Playboy*, 11 (Jan. 1964), 131-132, 240-241. Essay.

"Liberation and the Negro: A Round-Table Discussion (James Baldwin, Nathan Glazer, Sidney Hook, and Gunnar Myrdal)," *Commentary*, 37 (Mar. 1964), 25-42. Discussion.

"What Price Freedom?," *Freedomways*, 4 (Spring 1964), 191-195. Essay.

"The American Dream and the American Negro," *New York Times Magazine*, 7 Mar. 1965, pp. 32-33, 87-89. Dialogue with William F. Buckley, Jr.

"A Report from Occupied Territory," *Nation*, 203 (11 July 1966), 39-43. Essay.

"Dialog in Black and White: James Baldwin and Budd Schulberg," *Playboy*, 13 (Dec. 1966), 33-36, 282-287. Dialogue.

"Unnameable Objects, Unspeakable Crimes." In *The White Problem in America*, ed. *Ebony*. Chicago: Johnson, 1966, 173-181. Essay.

"Negroes are Anti-Semitic Because They're Anti-White," *New York Times Magazine*, 9 Apr. 1967, pp. 26-27, 135-140.Reprinted in *Black Anti-Semitism and Jewish Racism*. New York: Baron, 1969, 3-14. Essay.

"A Letter to Americans," *Freedomways*, 8 (Spring 1968), 50-58. Essay.

"Sidney Poitier," *Look*, 23 July 1968, pp. 50-58. Essay.

"White Racism or World Community?," *Ecumenical Review*, 20 (Oct. 1968), 371-376.

"The Nigger We Invent," *Integrated Education*, 7 (Mar./Apr. 1969), 15-23. Essay.

"Our Divided Society: A Challenge to Religious Education," *Religious Education*, 64 (Sept./Oct. 1969), 342-346. Essay.

"From Dreams of Love to Dreams of Terror." In *Natural Enemies? Youth and the Clash of Generations*, ed. Alexander Klein. Philadelphia: Lippincott, 1969, 274-279. Essay.

"*A Rap on Race:* Mead and Baldwin," *McCall's*, 98 (June 1971), 84-85, 142-154. Dialogue.

"A Talk to Harlem Teachers." In *Harlem, U.S.A.,* rev. ed, ed. John Henrik Clarke. New York: Collier, 1971, 171-180. Essay.

" 'Let me finish, let me finish . . . ,' a Television Conversation," *Encounter,* 39 (Sept. 1972), 27-33. Conversation with Peregrine Worsthorne and Bryan Magee.

"Compressions: L'Homme et La Machine." In Cesar Baldaccini, *Cesar: Compressions d'or.* Paris: Hachette, 1973, 9-16. Essay.

"Race, Hate, Sex, and Colour: A Conversation," *Encounter,* 25 (July 1975), 55-60. Discussion.

"In Search of a Basis for Mutual Understanding and Racial Harmony." In *The Nature of a Humane Society,* ed. H. Ober Hesse. Philadelphia: Fortress Press, 1976, 165-174. Speech.

"Open Letter to the Born Again," *Nation,* 229 (29 Sept. 1979), 263-264. Essay.

"Dark Days," *Esquire,* 94 (Oct. 1980), 42-46. Essay.

"On Being White . . . and Other Lies," *Essence,* 14 (Apr. 1984), 90-92. Essay.

SECONDARY BIBLIOGRAPHY

Bibliographies and Checklists

Breed, Paul F. and Florence Sniderman. "James Baldwin." In *Dramatic Criticism Index.* Detroit: Gale Research Company, 1972, 63-74. Selected secondary on "Sonny's Blues" and *Amen Corner.*

Dance, Daryl C. "James Baldwin." In *Black American Writers: Bibliographical Essays,* vol. 2, ed. M. Thomas Inge, et al. New York: St. Martin's, 1978, 73-120. Primary & secondary.

Fischer, Russell G. "James Baldwin: A Bibliography, 1947-1962," *Bulletin of Bibliography,* 24 (Jan./Apr. 1965), 127-130. Primary & secondary.

Jones, Mary E. "CAAS Bibliography No. 5: James Baldwin." [Mimeographed] Atlanta: Atlanta University's Center for African and African-American Studies, 1-20. Primary & secondary.

Kindt, Kathleen A. "James Baldwin: A Checklist, 1947-1962," *Bulletin of Bibliography,* 24 (Jan./Apr. 1965), 123-126. Primary & secondary.

Pownall, David. "James Baldwin." In *Articles on Twentieth Century Literature: An Annotated Bibliography, 1954-1970.* New York: Kraus-Thompson Organization Ltd., 1973, 133-140. Secondary.

Rush, Theressa Gunnels, et al. "James Baldwin." In *Black American*

Writers: A Biographical and Bibliographical Dictionary, vol. 1. Metuchen, N. J.: Scarecrow Press, 1975, 44-48. Selected primary & secondary.

Standley, Fred L. "James Baldwin: A Checklist, 1963-67," *Bulletin of Bibliography*, 25 (May/Aug. 1968), 135-137, 160. Primary & secondary.

Standley, and Nancy V. Standley. *James Baldwin: A Reference Guide.* Boston: G. K. Hall, 1980. Primary & secondary.

Biography: Book

Eckman, Fern Marja. *The Furious Passage of James Baldwin.* New York: M. Evans, 1966.

Biographies: Major Articles and Book Sections

Howard, Jane. "Doom and Glory of Knowing Who You Are," *Life*, 24 May 1963, pp. 86B, 88-90.

Morrison, Allan. "The Angriest Young Man," *Ebony*, 16 (Oct. 1961), 23-30.

Steinem, Gloria. "James Baldwin, an Original: A Sharpened View of Him," *Vogue*, 144 (July 1964), 78-79, 129, 138.

Interviews

"At a Crucial Time a Negro Talks Tough: 'There's a bill due that has to be paid,' " *Life,* 24 May 1963, pp. 81-86A.

Auchincloss, Eve, and Nancy Lynch. "Disturber of the Peace: James Baldwin." In *The Black American Writer: Volume I: Fiction*, ed. C. W. E. Bigsby. De Land, Fla.: Everett/Edwards, 1969, 199-216.

Binder, Wolfgang. "James Baldwin, an Interview," *Revista/Review Interamericana*, 10 (Fall 1980), 326-341.

"Black Man in America; an Interview by Studs Terkel," *WFMT Perspectives*, 10 (Dec. 1961), 28-39.

"The Black Scholar Interviews: James Baldwin," *Black Scholar*, 5 (Dec. 1973/Jan. 1974), 33-42.

Bondy, François. " 'Pour Liberer les Blancs . . .' (Propos Recueillis par François Bundy)," *Prévues*, 152 (1963), 3-17.

Clark, Kenneth B. "A Conversation with James Baldwin," *Freedomways*, 3 (Summer 1963), 361-368.

Fares, Nobile. "James Baldwin: Une Interview Exclusive," *Jeune Afrique,* 1 (Sept. 1970), 20-24.

Frost, David. "Are We on the Edge of Civil War?" In *The Americans.* New York: Stein & Day, 1970, 145-150.

Georgakas, Dan. "James Baldwin . . . in Conversation." In *Black Voices: An Anthology of Afro-American Literature,* ed. Abraham Chapman. New York: New American Library, 1968, 660-668.

Gresham, Jewell Handy, ed. "James Baldwin Comes Home," *Essence,* 7 (June 1976), 54-55, 80, 82, 85.

"How Can We Get The Black People to Cool It?," *Esquire,* 70 (July 1968), 49-53.

"An Interview with a Negro Intellectual." In *The Negro Protest: Talks with James Baldwin, Malcolm X, Martin Luther King,* ed. Kenneth B. Clark. Boston: Beacon, 1963, 1-14, 49.

"James Baldwin Breaks His Silence," *Atlas,* 13 (Mar. 1967), 47-49.

"James Baldwin, the Renowned Black American Novelist, Talks to Godwin Matatu," *Africa: International Business, Economic and Political Monthly,* 37 (1974), 68-69.

Lewis, Ida. "Why I Left America. Conversation: Ida Lewis and James Baldwin." In *New Black Voices,* ed. Abraham Chapman. New York: New American Library, 1972, 409-419.

Lottman, Herbert R. "It's Hard to Be James Baldwin: An Interview," *Intellectual Digest,* 2 (July 1972), 67-68.

"Revolutionary Hope: A Conversation between James Baldwin and Audre Lorde," *Essence,* 15 (Dec. 1984), 72-74.

Solet, Sue. "N.Y. Negroes and Bobby—Both Shocked," *New York Herald Tribune,* 26 May 1963, pp. 1, 31. Interview with Kenneth Clark and James Baldwin.

Walker, Joe. "Exclusive Interview with James Baldwin," *Muhammad Speaks,* 8 Sept. 1972, pp. 13-14; 15 Sept. 1972, pp.22,29; 22 Sept. 1972; 29 Sept. 1972.

Critical Studies: Books

Bruck, Peter. *Von der "Store-front Church" zum "American Dream": James Baldwin und der amerikanische Rassenkonflikt.* Amsterdam: Verlag B. R. Grunner, 1975.

Macebuh, Stanley. *James Baldwin: A Critical Study.* New York: Joseph Okpaku, 1973.

Moller, Karin. *The Theme of Identity in the Essays of James Baldwin: An*

Interpretation. Göteborg, Sweden: Acta Universitatis Gothoburgensis, 1975, 1-189.

Pratt, Louis Hill. *James Baldwin.* Boston: Twayne, 1978.

Sylvander, Carolyn Wedin. *James Baldwin.* New York: Ungar, 1980.

Weatherby, W. J. *Squaring Off: Mailer vs. Baldwin.* New York: Mason/Charter, 1977; London: Robson, 1977.

Critical Studies: Collections of Essays

Kinnamon, Kenneth, ed. *James Baldwin: A Collection of Critical Essays.* Englewood Cliffs, N. J.: Prentice-Hall, 1974.

O'Daniel, Therman B., ed. *James Baldwin: A Critical Evaluation.* Washington, D. C.: Howard University Press, 1977.

Critical Studies: Articles and Book Sections

Alexander, Charlotte. "The 'Stink' of Reality: Mothers and Whores in James Baldwin's Fiction," *Literature and Psychology,* 18, no. 1, (1968), 9-26. Collected in Kinnamon, 77-95.

Algren, Nelson. "Lost Man," *Nation,* 183 (1 Dec. 1956), 484.

Allen, Shirley S. "The Ironic Voice in Baldwin's *Go Tell It on the Mountain.*" Collected in O'Daniel.

_____. "Religious Symbolism and Psychic Reality in Baldwin's *Go Tell It on the Mountain,*" *CLA Journal,* 19 (Dec. 1975), 173-199.

Arana, Gregorio. "The Baffling Creator—A Study of the Writing of James Baldwin," *Caribbean Quarterly,* 12 (Sept. 1966), 3-23.

Baker, Houston A., Jr. "The Embattled Craftsman: An Essay on James Baldwin," *Journal of African-Afro-American Affairs,* 1, no. 1 (1977), 28-51.

Barksdale, Richard K. "Alienation and the Anti-Hero in Recent American Fiction," *CLA Journal,* 10 (Sept. 1966), 1-10.

_____. "Temple of the Fire Baptized," *Phylon,* 14 (Third Quarter 1953), 326-327.

Bell, George E. "The Dilemma of Love in *Go Tell It on the Mountain* and *Giovanni's Room,*" *CLA Journal,* 17 (Mar. 1974), 397-406.

Berry, Boyd M. "Another Man Done Gone: Self-Pity in Baldwin's *Another Country,*" *Michigan Quarterly Review,* 5 (Fall 1966), 285-290.

Bigsby, C. W. E. "The Committed Writer: James Baldwin as Dramatist," *Twentieth Century Literature,* 13 (Apr. 1967), 39-48.

_____. "The Divided Mind of James Baldwin," *Journal of American Studies*, 13 (Dec. 1979), 325-342.

Blaisdel, Gus. "A Literary Assessment: James Baldwin, the Writer," *Negro Digest*, 13 (Jan. 1964), 61-68.

Bloomfield, Caroline. "Religion and Alienation in James Baldwin, Bernard Malamud, and James F. Powers," *Religious Education*, 57 (Mar./Apr. 1962), 97-102, 158.

Blount, Trevor. "A Slight Error in Continuity in James Baldwin's *Another Country*," *Notes and Queries*, 13 (Mar. 1966), 102-103.

Bluefarb, Sam. "James Baldwin's 'Previous Condition': A Problem of Identification," *Negro American Literature Forum*, 3 (Spring 1969), 26-29.

Bone, Robert. "The Novels of James Baldwin," *Tri-Quarterly*, 2 (Winter 1965), 3-20. Reprinted in his *The Negro Novel in America*. Rev. ed. New Haven: Yale University Press, 1965, 215-239. Collected in Kinnamon, 28-51.

Bonosky, Philip. "The Negro Writer and Commitment," *Mainstream*, 15 (Feb. 1962), 16-22.

Bradford, Melvin E. "Faulkner, James Baldwin, and the South," *Georgia Review*, 20 (Winter 1966), 431-443.

Braithwaite, Edward. "Race and the Divided Self: *Rap on Race*," *Black World*, 21 (July 1972), 54-68.

Breit, Harvey. "James Baldwin and Two Footnotes." In *The Creative Present: Notes on Contemporary American Fiction*, ed. Nona Balakian and Charles Simmons. Garden City: Doubleday, 1963, 1-23.

Brooks, A. Russell. "James Baldwin as Poet-Prophet." Collected in O'Daniel, 126-134.

_____. "Power and Morality as Imperatives for Nikki Giovanni and James Baldwin: A View of *A Dialogue*." Collected in O'Daniel, 205-209.

Brustein, Robert. "Everybody's Protest Play," *New Republic*, 150 (16 May 1964), 35-37.

Bryant, Jerry H. "Wright, Ellison, Baldwin—Exorcising the Demon," *Phylon*, 37 (1976), 174-188.

Burks, Mary Fair. "James Baldwin's Protest Novel: *If Beale Street Could Talk*," *Negro American Literature Forum*, 10 (Fall 1976), 83-87, 95.

Butterfield, Stephen. "James Baldwin: The Growth of a New Radicalism." In his *Black Autobiography in America*. Amherst: University of Massachusetts Press, 1974, 183-200.

Byerman, Keith E. "Words and Music: Narrative Ambiguity in 'Sonny's Blues,' " *Studies in Short Fiction*, 19 (Fall 1982), 367-372.

Champion, Ernest A. "James Baldwin and the Challenge of Ethnic Literature in the Eighties," *MELUS,* 8 (Summer 1981), 61-64.

Charney, Maurice. "James Baldwin's Quarrel with Richard Wright," *American Quarterly,* 15 (Spring 1963), 65-75.

Clarke, John Henrik. "The Alienation of James Baldwin," *Journal of Human Relations,* 12 (First Quarter 1964), 30-33.

Cleaver, Eldridge. "Notes on a Native Son," *Ramparts,* 5 (June 1966), 51-56. Reprinted in his *Soul on Ice.* New York: McGraw-Hill, 1968, 97-111. Collected in Kinnamon, 66-76.

Coles, Robert. "Baldwin's Burden," *Partisan Review,* 31 (Summer 1964), 409-416.

Collier, Eugenia W. "The Phrase Unbearably Repeated," *Phylon,* 25 (Fall 1964), 288-296. Collected in O'Daniel, 38-46.

_____. "Thematic Patterns in Baldwin's Essays: A Study in Chaos," *Black World,* 21 (June 1972), 28-34. Collected in O'Daniel, 135-142.

Cox, C. B., and A. R. Jones. "After the Tranquilized Fifties: Notes on Sylvia Plath and James Baldwin," *Critical Quarterly,* 6 (Summer 1964), 107-122.

Dance, Daryl C. "You Can't Go Home Again: James Baldwin and the South," *CLA Journal,* 18 (Sept. 1974), 81-90.

Daniels, Mark R. "Estrangement, Betrayal and Atonement: The Political Theory of James Baldwin," *Studies in Black Literature,* 7 (Autumn 1976), 10-13.

Davis, Arthur P. "Integrationists and Transitional Writers: James Baldwin." In his *From the Dark Tower: Afro-American Writers, 1900-1960.* Washington, D. C.: Howard University Press, 1974, 216-226.

DeMott, Benjamin. "James Baldwin on the Sixties: Acts and Revelations," *Saturday Review,* 55 (27 May 1972), 63-66. Collected in Kinnamon, 155-162.

Driver, Tom F. *"Blues for Mister Charlie:* The Review That Was Too True to Be Published," *Black World,* 13 (Sept. 1964), 34-40.

Dupee, F. W. "James Baldwin and the 'Man,' " *New York Review of Books,* 1 (Feb. 1963), 1-2. Collected in Kinnamon, 11-15.

Fabre, Michel. "Pères et Fils dans *Go Tell It on the Mountain* de James Baldwin," *Etudes Anglaises,* 23, no. 1 (1970), 47-61. Reprinted [English translation] in *Modern Black Novelists: A Collection of Critical Essays,* ed. M. G. Cooke. Englewood Cliffs, N. J.: Prentice-Hall, 1971, 88-104. Collected in Kinnamon, 120-138.

Farrison, William Edward. "If Baldwin's Train Has Not Gone." Collected in O'Daniel, 69-81.

Ferguson, Alfred R. "Black Men, White Cities: The Quest for Humanity by Black Protagonists in James Baldwin's *Another Country* and Richard Wright's *The Outsider*," *Ball State University Forum*, 18 (Spring 1977), 51-58.

Fiedler, Leslie A. "Some Footnotes on the Fiction of '56," *Reporter*, 15 (13 Dec. 1956), 46.

Finkelstein, S. W. "Existentialism and Social Demands: Norman Mailer and James Baldwin." In his *Existentialism and Alienation in American Literature*. New York: International Publishers, 1965, 276-284.

Finn, James. "The Identity of James Baldwin," *Commonweal*, 77 (26 Oct. 1962), 113-116.

Flint, Robert W. "Not Ideas But Life: Review of *Notes of a Native Son*," *Commentary*, 21 (May 1956), 494-495.

_____. "The Undying Apocalypse," *Partisan Review*, 24 (Winter 1957), 139-145.

Fontinell, Eugene. "The Identity of James Baldwin," *Interracial Review*, 35 (Sept. 1962), 194-199.

Ford, Nick Aaron. "The Evolution of James Baldwin as Essayist." Collected in O'Daniel, 85-104.

Foster, David E. "Cause My House Fell Down: The Theme of the Fall in Baldwin's Novels," *Critique*, 13, no. 2 (1971), 50-62.

Freese, Peter. "James Baldwin und das Syndrom des Identitatsverlustes: 'Previous Condition' im Lichte des Gesamtwerkes," *Literatur in Wissenschaft und Unterricht*, 4 (Sept. 1971), 73-98.

Gayle, Addison, Jr. "A Defense of James Baldwin," *CLA Journal*, 10 (Mar. 1967), 201-208.

_____. "The Dialectic of *The Fire Next Time*," *Negro History Bulletin*, 20 (Apr. 1967), 15-16.

Gerard, Albert. "James Baldwin et la Religiosité Noire," *Revue Nouvelle*, 33 (Feb. 1961), 177-186.

Gibson, Donald B. "James Baldwin: The Political Anatomy of Space." Collected in O'Daniel, 3-18.

Giles, James R. "Religious Alienation and 'Homosexual Consciousness' in *City of the Night* and *Go Tell It on the Mountain*," *College English*, 36 (Nov. 1974), 369-380.

Gounard, Jean-François. "La Carrière Singulière de James Baldwin: 1924-1970," *Revue de L'Université d'Ottawa*, 44 (1974), 507-518.

Graves, Wallace. "The Question of Moral Energy in James Baldwin's

Go Tell It on the Mountain," *CLA Journal,* 7 (Mar. 1964), 215-223.

Gross, Barry. "The 'Uninhabitable Darkness' of Baldwin's *Another Country:* Image and Theme," *Black American Literature Forum,* 6 (Winter 1972), 113-121.

Gross, Theodore L. "The Major Authors: Richard Wright, Ralph Ellison, James Baldwin." In his *The Heroic Ideal in American Literature.* New York: Free Press, 1971, 148-180.

_____. "The World of James Baldwin," *Critique,* 7 (Winter 1964, 139-149.

Hagopian, John V. "James Baldwin: The Black and the Red-White-and-Blue," *CLA Journal,* 7 (Dec. 1963), 133-140. Collected in O'Daniel, 156-162.

Harper, Howard M., Jr. "James Baldwin—Art or Propaganda." In his *Desperate Faith: A Study of Bellow, Salinger, Mailer, Baldwin, and Updike.* Chapel Hill: University of North Carolina Press, 1967, 137-161.

Hernton, Calvin C. "Blood of the Lamb." In his *White Papers for White Americans.* Garden City: Doubleday, 1966, 105-121.

_____. "A Fiery Baptism." In his *White Papers for White Americans.* Garden City: Doubleday, 1966, 122-147.

Hodges, Louis W. "The Fire Next Time," *Shenandoah,* 14 (Summer 1963), 65-68.

Hoffman, Frederick J. "Marginal Societies and the Novel." In his *The Modern Novel in America.* Rev. ed. Chicago: Regnery, 1963, 246-255.

Howe, Irving. "James Baldwin: At Ease in Apocalypse," *Harper's,* 227 (Sept. 1968), 94-100. Collected in Kinnamon, 96-108.

_____. "Black Boys and Native Sons," *Dissent,* 10 (Autumn 1963), 353-368. Reprinted in his *A World More Attractive.* New York: Horizon, 1963, 98-122.

Hughes, Langston. "From Harlem to Paris," *New York Times Book Review,* 26 Feb. 1956, p. 26. Collected in Kinnamon, 9-10.

Inge, M. Thomas. "James Baldwin's Blues," *Notes on Contemporary Literature,* 2 (Sept. 1972), 8-11.

Isaacs, Harold B. "Five Writers and Their African Ancestors," *Phylon,* 21 (Fourth Quarter 1960), 322-329.

Jacobson, Daniel. "James Baldwin as Spokesman," *Commentary,* 32 (Dec. 1961), 495-502.

Jarrett, Hobart. "From a Region in My Mind: The Essays of James Baldwin." Collected in O'Daniel, 105-125.

Jarrett, Thomas D. "Search for Identity," *Phylon*, 17 (First Quarter 1956), 87-88.

Jones, B. F. "James Baldwin: The Struggle for Identity," *British Journal of Sociology*, 17 (June 1966), 107-121.

Jones, Harry L. "Style, Form, and Content in the Short Fiction of James Baldwin." Collected in O'Daniel, 143-150.

Kazin, Alfred. "Close to Us," *Reporter*, 25 (17 Aug. 1961), 58-60.

Kent, George E. "Baldwin and the Problem of Being," *CLA Journal*, 7 (Mar. 1964), 202-214. Collected in Kinnamon, 16-27 and in O'Daniel, 19-29.

Klein, Marcus. "James Baldwin: A Question of Identity." In his *After Alienation: American Novels in Mid-Century*. New York: World Publishing Company, 1962, 147-195.

Kuster, Dieter. "James Baldwin: Tell Me How Long the Train's Been Gone." In *Amerikanische Erzählliteratur 1950-1970*, ed. Frieder Busch and Renate Schmidt-von Bardelehen. Munich: Fink, 1975, 142-154.

Landrigan, Stephen. "The World That Is Coming Is Not White," *Africa: International Business, Economic and Political Monthly*, 100 (Dec. 1979), 61-62.

Lash, John. "Baldwin beside Himself: A Study in Modern Phallicism," *CLA Journal*, 8 (Dec. 1964), 132-140. Collected in O'Daniel, 47-55.

Leaks, Sylvester. "James Baldwin—I Know His Name," *Freedomways*, 3 (Winter 1963), 102-105.

Lee, Brian. "James Baldwin: Caliban to Prospero." In *The Black American Writer: Volume I: Fiction*, ed. C. W. E. Bigsby. De Land, Fla.: Everett/Edwards, 1969, 169-179.

Lee, Robert A. "James Baldwin and Matthew Arnold: Thoughts on 'Relevance,' " *CLA Journal*, 14 (Mar. 1971), 324-330.

Levin, David. "Baldwin's Autobiographical Essays: The Problem of Negro Identity," *Massachusetts Review*, 5 (Winter 1964), 239-247.

Littlejohn, David. *Black on White: A Critical Survey of Writing by American Negroes*. New York: Grossman, 1966, 72-74, 110-137.

Lobb, Edward. "James Baldwin's Blues and the Function of Art," *International Fiction Review*, 6 (1979), 143-148.

Long, Robert E. "Love and Wrath in the Fiction of James Baldwin," *English Record*, 19 (Feb. 1969), 50-57.

Luce, Philip Abbot. "Communications on James Baldwin," *Mainstream*, 15 (May 1962), 45-48.

Lunden, Rolf. "The Progress of a Pilgrim: James Baldwin's *Go Tell It on the Mountain*," *Studia Neophilologia: A Journal of Germanic and Romance Languages and Literature*, 53, no. 1 (1981), 113-126.

MacInnes, Colin. "Dark Angel: The Writings of James Baldwin," *Encounter*, 21 (Aug. 1963), 22-33.

Major, Clarence. "James Baldwin: A Fire in the Mind." In his *The Dark and Feeling: Black American Writers and Their Work*. New York: Joseph Okpaku, 1974, 73-83.

Malcolm, Donald. "Books: The Author in Search of Himself," *New Yorker*, 37 (25 Nov. 1961), 233-238.

Maloff, Saul. "The Two Baldwins," *Nation*, 195 (14 July 1962), 15-16.

Marcus, Steven. "The American Negro in Search of Identity," *Commentary*, 16 (Nov. 1953), 456-463.

Margolies, Edward. "The Negro Church: James Baldwin and the Christian Vision." In his *Native Sons: A Critical Study of Twentieth-Century Negro American Authors*. Philadelphia: Lippincott, 1968, 102-126.

Mayfield, Julian. "And Then Came Baldwin," *Freedomways*, 3 (Spring 1963), 143-155.

Meserve, Walter. "James Baldwin's 'Agony Way.' " In *The Black American Writer: Volume II: Poetry and Drama*, ed. C. W. E. Bigsby. De Land, Fla.: Everett/Edwards, 1969, 171-186.

Millican, Arthenia Bates. "Fire as the Symbol of a Leadening Existence in *Going to Meet the Man*." Collected in O'Daniel, 170-180.

Mitra, B. K. "The Wright-Baldwin Controversy," *Indian Journal of American Studies 1*, 1 (1969), 101-105.

Molette, Carlton W. "James Baldwin as Playwright." Collected in O'Daniel, 183-188.

Monas, Disney. "Fiction Chronicle: 'No Mommy and No Daddy,' " *Hudson Review*, 6 (Autumn 1953), 466-470.

Moore, John R. "An Embarrassment of Riches: Baldwin's *Going to Meet the Man*," *Hollins Critic*, 2 (Dec. 1965), 1-12.

Morrison, Allan. "The Angriest Young Man," *Ebony*, 16 (Oct. 1961), 23-30.

Mosher, Marlene. "James Baldwin's Blues," *CLA Journal*, 26 (Sept. 1982), 112-124.

Mowe, Gregory, and W. Scott Nobles. "James Baldwin's Message for White America," *Quarterly Journal of Speech*, 58 (Apr. 1972), 142-151.

Murray, Albert. "James Baldwin, Protest Fiction, and the Blues Tradition." In his *The Omni-Americans: New Perspectives on Black Ex-*

perience and American Culture. New York: Outerbridge & Dienstfrey, 1970, 142-170.

Murray, Donald C. "James Baldwin's 'Sonny's Blues': Complicated and Simple," *Studies in Short Fiction,* 14 (Fall 1977), 353-357.

Nelson, Emmanuel S. "James Baldwin's Vision of Otherness and Community," *MELUS,* 10 (Summer 1983), 27-31.

Newman, Charles. "The Lesson of the Master: Henry James and James Baldwin," *Yale Review,* 56 (Oct. 1966), 45-59. Collected in Kinnamon, 52-64.

Nichols, Charles H. "James Baldwin: A Skillful Executioner," *Studies on the Left,* 2 (Winter 1963), 74-79.

_____. "The New Calvinism," *Commentary,* 23 (Jan. 1957), 94-96.

Noble, David. "The Present: Norman Mailer, James Baldwin, Saul Bellow." In his *The Eternal Adam and the New World Garden.* New York: Braziller, 1968, 195-224.

O'Daniel, Therman B. "James Baldwin: An Interpretive Study," *CLA Journal,* 7 (Sept. 1963), 37-47.

Orsagh, Jacqueline E. "Baldwin's Female Characters—A Step Forward?" Collected in O'Daniel, 56-68.

Ostendorf, Bernhard. "James Baldwin, 'Sonny's Blues.' " In *Die amerikanische Short Story der Gegenwart: Interpretationen,* ed. Peter Freese. Berlin: Schmidt, 1976, 194-204.

Patterson, H. Orlando. "The Essays of James Baldwin," *New Left Review,* 26 (Summer 1964), 31-38.

Perry, Patsy Brewington. *"One Day When I Was Lost:* Baldwin's Unfulfilled Obligation." Collected in O'Daniel, 213-227.

Plessner, Monica. "James Baldwin und das Land der Verheissung: Zwischen Farbsymbolik und Farbindifferenz," *Merkur,* 20 (1966), 515-533.

Podhoretz, Norman. "The Article as Art." In his *Doings and Undoings: The Fifties and After in American Writing.* New York: Farrar, Straus, 1964, 126-142.

Prasad, Thakur Duru. "Another Country: The Tensions of Drama and Nightmare in the American Psyche." In *Indian Studies of American Fiction,* ed. M. K. Naik, et al. Dhawar: Karnatak University/Delhi: Macmillan India, 1974, 296-310.

Pratt, Louis Hill. "James Baldwin and 'the Literary Ghetto,' " *CLA Journal,* 20 (Dec. 1976), 262-272.

Ranier, Dachine. "Rage into Order," *Commonweal,* 63 (13 Jan. 1956), 384-386.

Reilly, John M. " 'Sonny's Blues': James Baldwin's Image of Black Community," *Negro American Literature Forum,* 4 (July 1970), 56-60. Collected in Kinnamon, 139-146 and in O'Daniel, 163-169.

Rive, Richard. "Writing and the New Society," *Contrast,* 12, no. 3 (1979), 60-67.

Ro, Sigmund. "The Black Musician as Literary Hero: Baldwin's 'Sonny's Blues' and Kelley's 'Cry for Me,' " *American Studies in Scandinavia,* 7, no. 1 (1975), 17-48.

Rupp, Richard H. "James Baldwin: The Search for Celebration." In his *Celebration in Postwar American Fiction: 1945-1967.* Coral Gables, Fla.: University of Miami Press, 1970, 133-149.

Sayre, Robert F. "James Baldwin's Other Country." In *Contemporary American Novelists,* ed. Harry T. Moore. Carbondale: Southern Illinois University Press, 1964, 158-169.

Schero, Elliot M. *"Another Country* and the Sense of Self," *Black Academy Review,* 2 (Spring/Summer 1971), 91-100.

Schwank, Klaus. "James Baldwin: *Blues for Mister Charlie."* In *Das Amerikanische Drama der Gegenwart,* ed. Herbert Grabes. Kronberg: Athenäum-Verlag, 1976, 169-184.

Scott, Robert. "Rhetoric, Black Power and Baldwin's *Another Country,"* *Journal of Black Studies,* 1 (Sept. 1970), 21-34.

Scruggs, Charles. "The Tale of Two Cities in James Baldwin's *Go Tell It on the Mountain,"* *American Literature,* 52 (1980), 1-17.

Sheed, Wilfrid. "Twin Urges of James Baldwin," *Commonweal,* 104 (24 June 1977), 404-407.

Simmons, H. C. "James Baldwin and the Negro Conundrum," *Antioch Review,* 23 (Summer 1963), 250-255.

Spender, Stephen. "James Baldwin: Voice of Revolution," *Partisan Review,* 30 (Summer 1963), 256-260.

Standley, Fred L. *"Another Country,* Another Time," *Studies in the Novel,* 4 (Fall 1972), 504-512.

_____. "James Baldwin: The Artist as Incorrigible Disturber of the Peace," *Southern Humanities Review,* 4 (Winter 1970), 18-30.

_____. "James Baldwin: The Crucial Situation," *South Atlantic Quarterly,* 65 (Summer 1966), 371-381.

Thelwell, Mike. *"Another Country:* Baldwin's New York Novel." In *The Black American Writer: Volume I: Fiction,* ed. C. W. E. Bigsby. De Land, Fla.: Everett/Edwards, 1969, 181-198.

Traylor, Eleanor. "I Hear Music in the Air: James Baldwin's *Just Above My Head,"* *First World,* 2, no. 3 (1979), 40-43.

Turner, Darwin T. "James Baldwin in the Dilemma of the Black

Dramatist." Collected in O'Daniel, 189-194.

Turpin, Waters E. "A Note on *Blues for Mister Charlie.*" Collected in O'Daniel, 195-198.

Vopat, James B. "Beyond Sociology? Urban Experience in the Novels of James Baldwin." In *Minority Literature and the Urban Experience. Selected Proceedings of the Fourth Annual Conference on Minority Studies, April 1976,* ed. George E. Carter and James R. Parker. Lacrosse, Wis.: Institute for Minority Studies, University of Wisconsin/Lacrosse, 1978, 51-58.

Wasserstrom, William. "James Baldwin: Stepping Out on the Promise." In *Black Fiction: New Studies in the Afro-American Novel since 1945,* ed. Robert Lee. New York: Barnes & Noble, 1980, 74-96.

Watson, Edward A. "The Novels and Essays of James Baldwin: Case-Book of a Lover's War with the United States," *Queen's Quarterly,* 72 (Summer 1965), 385-402.

Werner, Craig. "The Economic Evolution of James Baldwin," *CLA Journal,* 23 (Nov. 1979), 12-31.

Williams, Shirley Anne. "The Black Musician: The Black Hero as Light Bearer." In her *Give Birth to Brightness.* New York: Dial, 1971, 145-166. Collected in Kinnamon, 147-154.

Wills, Antony A. "The Use of Coincidence in 'Notes of a Native Son,' " *Negro American Literature Forum,* 8 (Fall 1974), 234-235.

Wills, Gary. "What Color Is God?," *National Review,* 14 (21 May 1963), 408-417.

Zahorski, Kenneth J. "James Baldwin: Portrait of a Black Exile." Collected in O'Daniel, 199-204.

BIBLIOGRAPHICAL ESSAY

Bibliographies and Checklists

The first attempts to collect bibliographical data on the works of James Baldwin appeared in companion essays published in the January-April 1965 *Bulletin of Bibliography.* Russell G. Fischer's "James Baldwin: A Bibliography, 1947-1962" and Kathleen A. Kindt's "James Baldwin: A Checklist, 1947-1962," when used together, provide fairly complete and accurate information on Baldwin primary and secondary sources for the years indicated. Fred L. Standley's "James Baldwin: A Checklist, 1963-1967" (1968) is an attempt to update the two earlier essays, although this work omits several works by and about Baldwin. An undated mimeographed bibliography by Mary E. Jones, "CAAS Bibliography No. 5: James Baldwin," though flawed by omissions, includes previously unnoted entries as well as a list of the Baldwin manuscript holdings in the Trevor Arnett Library at Atlanta University.

Daryl C. Dance offers an annotated bibliographical essay, "James Baldwin," in *Black American Writers: Bibliographical Essays*, volume 2 (1978), edited by M. Thomas Inge, Maurice Duke, and Jackson R. Bryer. Though Dance is somewhat selective in his listing, this work includes useful commentary on works from the entire scope of Baldwin's canon, including his essays, reviews, discussions, and interviews, as well as on significant secondary material, including biography and criticism of Baldwin and his writing. Dance conveniently groups his treatment of Baldwin criticism into general studies and commentary on Baldwin's individual works in turn. The essay includes pointed comments on those critics who launch personal attacks on Baldwin; and it concludes with an assessment of the future needs of Baldwin criticism, noting that *the* definitive study of Baldwin and his later work has yet to appear.

By far the most ambitious attempt at Baldwin bibliography is Fred L. Standley and Nancy V. Standley's *James Baldwin: A Reference Guide* (1980). The only book-length bibliography, this volume provides an annotated listing of secondary material dealing with Baldwin and his writing in year-by-year listings from 1946 through 1978, although the listings for the last year are preliminary and, therefore, incomplete. The Standleys include a classified listing, without annotation, of primary Baldwin materials, including television appearances, films, and recordings, for the years indicated. The listings for secondary sources include not only material specifically relating to Baldwin but also sections of articles and book chapters dealing with Baldwin in the context of black literature, the civil rights movement, and contemporary literary theory. Selected dissertations dealing with Baldwin are included as well. The annotations of secondary material are generally objective and useful, and even though a few entries are marred by typographical errors or mistakes in citations, this is a resource any serious researcher on Baldwin and his work should consult.

Biography: Book

Undoubtedly, the most reliable and complete biographer of James Baldwin is James Baldwin himself. It is difficult to name a contemporary author who has put more of himself in his writing, both in his fiction and in his essays and articles. He returns again and again to significant events in his life, perhaps seeing them through the lens of fiction on one occasion, later as an essayist writing on the black experience, and again as part of his autobiography. The most enduring autobiographical accounts have been collected in *Notes of a Native Son* (1955), *Nobody Knows My Name* (1961), *The Fire Next Time* (1963), and *No Name in the Street* (1972). In addition, many interviews with Baldwin (see below) focus on details of his life.

To date, only one book-length biographical study of Baldwin has appeared. Fern Marja Eckman's *The Furious Passage of James Baldwin* (1966) draws heavily from interviews with Baldwin as well as his published autobiographical pieces. In fact, this work has been criticized as being more a compilation of quotations and paraphrases from Baldwin than a true biography. Further, Eckman has been seen to give undue emphasis to minute details of Baldwin's personality and behavior. However, Eckman does provide information on Baldwin's life and his career, particularly about his childhood, his friendships, and his formal education, that is not otherwise available. Baldwin is seen as both an artist and a revolutionary, and Eckman notes that being a black artist in America is for Baldwin "a very frightening assignment": he writes with "an accusing finger thrust in the face of white America" and is seen as a critic who has laid bare the "wounds of the nation's conscience." Despite any shortcomings, *The Furious Passage of James Baldwin* is an important biography for a Baldwin scholar to consider when investigating this writer who "embodies the paradoxes and potentials" of Afro-American literature and culture.

Though they are not scholarly biography, articles appearing in popular magazines have added to our understanding of James Baldwin, the man and the artist. Jane Howard's "Doom and Glory of Knowing Who You Are" (1963) is an account of Baldwin's 1963 speaking tour in the South, illustrated with candid photographs, and including observations on his personal habits and public appearances as well as his own comments about his life and the influence of Dostoyevski and Dickens on his writing. Similarly, Allan Morrison's "The Angriest Young Man" (1961) takes readers inside Baldwin's Greenwich Village apartment and through the events of a typical day, while portraying Baldwin as "a spokesman for his generation." Finally, Gloria Steinem's "James Baldwin, an Original: A Sharpened View of Him" (1964) looks at the author when *Blues for Mister Charlie* (1964) was being readied for production. Biographical detail is offered, as well as a discussion of the people who have influenced Baldwin during four stages in his life to that time in the context of "Harlem, the Village, Paris, and now, the struggle for civil rights."

Interviews

As noted above, much insight into the character of James Baldwin as artist and as man can be gleaned from the many published interviews available to scholars. They prove to be a record of Baldwin's progress through the times by which he was shaped and the era which he helped to shape. Often the target of criticism for his homosexuality, for his blunt criticism of American racism, and for his artistic rage, Baldwin unflinchingly speaks his mind in public forums. Through his interviews Baldwin emerges as a very public artist whose influence transcends his art; he has become a spokesman, first for American blacks, then for the oppressed of the world. A visit to a Newark ghetto neighborhood in the late 1970s with Amiri Baraka (LeRoi Jones) provides evidence that even youngsters born after the crest of the American civil rights movement had subsided still recognized Baldwin and were familiar with his writing. In spite of his protracted absences from mainstream America, James Baldwin has certainly managed to have a very well-known "name in the street."

In "At a Crucial Time a Negro Talks Tough" (1963) Baldwin asserts "I represent sin, love, death, sex, hell, terror and other things too frightening for you to recognize." In the role of a celebrity-author, he reminds Americans that "There's a Bill Due That Has to Be Paid." He recognizes that his fiery rhetoric has often angered people, but at the same time he has succeeded in "shaking them up, disturbing their peace, getting them to ask real questions." In Kenneth B. Clark's "A Conversation with James Baldwin" (1963), Baldwin adds that "the great victims [of segregation] are the white people. . . . These people have deluded themselves so long, that they really don't think I'm human . . . and this means that they have become in themselves moral monsters." The racial situation in the United States is also discussed in François Bondy's interview "Pour Liberer les Blancs" (1963), and as noted in his discussion with William F. Buckley, Jr., "The American Dream and the American Negro" (1965), the American dream has been achieved at the expense of blacks. "How Can We Get the Black People to Cool It?" (1968) discusses the progress, or lack of it, made in regard to the situation of blacks in America. Finally, in Eve Auchincloss and Nancy Lynch's "Disturber of the Peace: James Baldwin" (1969), Baldwin responds to charges that he is too hard on white liberals by claiming that "one of the hardest things anyone has to survive in this country is his friends."

"Why I Left America. Conversation: Ida Lewis and James Baldwin" (1972) explores Baldwin's expatriation and reveals his growing awareness of the universal plight of oppressed people. Baldwin comments on his return to America, his sojourn in Hollywood working on the screenplay for the life of Malcolm X, and his subsequent return to Europe. "And I know where I've been. I know what the world has tried to do to me as a black man. When I say me, that means millions of people." Nevertheless, he reminds his white audience, "You created me. You're stuck with me for life."

"The Black Scholar Interviews: James Baldwin" (1973/1974) is a wide-ranging discussion, typical of many Baldwin interviews. He relates events in his own life to the struggle of blacks in America, and ultimately to the struggle of all oppressed blacks. He notes that a cultural shift is taking place with a new generation "[that] has grown up without [the] crippling handicaps of my generation; with certainly different illusions and certainly different dangers, but with a freedom which barely could have been imagined 49 years ago." He reminds us that the black nationalism of the 1960s was not really a new phenomenon and that blacks could never really go back to Africa. "The American black man for the first time may be able to move forward into whatever his future is going to be, which means by changing his present. But he cannot do it by romantic return to the past." He speaks of the process of history, relating it to world events, his family background, and contemporary black culture. He recognizes that to be a writer is to be "political" and comments on black artists such as Lorraine Hansberry. Finally, he offers an apocalyptic vision of western civilization on its deathbed, seeing it as an aberration in the scope of human history, and looks to a world "without policemen, without torture, without rape, where gold [is] an ornament, not the summit of human desire. . . . [We] can change the world, and we have to."

Baldwin visited Riker's Island in order to speak to the female inmates at the correctional facility, most of whom were black. Jewell Handy Gresham compiles significant portions of this question-and-answer session in "James Baldwin Comes Home" (1976). Baldwin recalls his father's rage at being black in Harlem: "His pain was so great that he translated himself into silence, rigidity . . . sometimes into beating us and finally into madness." His mother, he recalls, was very different: "We all thought she was a little too gentle and forgiving, but actually she was very, very strong. To raise nine children under those circumstances she had to be." He tells his audience that, in reality, a black artist stands no better chance of succeeding in Europe than in America, noting that the capacity of one people to oppress another knows no geographical boundaries. He comments on his disagreement with the Hollywood establishment over his scenario for the life of Malcolm X, ending with his walking out with his script. Finally, he reaffirms his global view of the decline of western society and the new day coming for the oppressed: ". . . we'll never be slaves again, although it will be a long time before we're free. But that's something else. The basis—moral or spiritual—on which the Western world was built is gone."

The recent extensive interview with Wolfgang Binder, "James Baldwin: An Interview" (1980), reaffirms the ideas noted in earlier conversations. Beginning with a discussion of his most recent novel, *Just Above My Head* (1979), Baldwin reaches into his personal history, noting the importance of jazz and church music to his psyche—and the collective psyche of blacks in America. "They brought themselves a long way out of bondage by means of that music which *Just Above My Head* is at bottom about. So in a sense the novel is a kind of return to my own beginnings, which are not only mine, and a way of using that beginning to start again." Again, relating the evolution of black culture and art to the process of history, Baldwin asserts that black cultural separatism is impossible because black culture is an amalgam of many things and shares a common history with all mankind. Yet, he restates his apocalypse: "There is nothing which will prop up this system [of western civilization], nothing. It depended on slave labor and it lost its slaves. . . . [T]he power of the western world will be over. It will be chaos, and what we will have to go through will not be pleasant, but it is the price we are going to pay to get something else." Recurring subjects such as other black artists, personal background, Richard Wright, and his own expatriation are discussed. Baldwin states that he never intended to get America "out of his system," nor could he ever succeed. However, he contends that Americans continue to try to avoid "black reality." "Everything Americans do to pretend I did not happen brings them closer to the abyss. . . ."

Critical Studies: Books

Not until the third decade of James Baldwin's literary career did the first full-length critical analysis of his work appear. At that time, the Baldwin canon included four novels, four books of essays, a play, a collection of short stories, and numerous uncollected articles. Baldwin had already been a highly visible public figure for more than a decade. But even more remarkably, the reawakening of critics to black literature was also nearly a decade old, and several serious articles on Baldwin's work had been published before a critic turned to an extensive analysis of this writer already acknowledged as a major literary force, sharing black literary stature with Richard Wright and Ralph Ellison.

Stanley Macebuh's *James Baldwin: A Critical Study* (1973) is the first extended analysis of Baldwin's work, focusing most especially on the novels through *Tell Me How Long the Train's Been Gone*. Macebuh frames his treatment of Baldwin's writing with three basic assumptions, outlined in his first chapter. First, he sees Baldwin as part of a continuous tradition of black literature in America. Second, he assumes a "necessary link between 'politics.' and 'literature,'" and as a result his analysis is "cultural" rather than "practical" criticism. Finally, he asserts that Baldwin's art must be judged according to "the black aesthetic," the record of the black man's inescapable hurt fixed in his unique experience and mythology.

Macebuh then turns his attention to Baldwin's "fear" or "theological terror," a tendency to interpret man as a theological rather than a political animal. This, Macebuh contends, is the lyric inspiration for *Go Tell It on the Mountain*. However, this position gives way to political rage as the Baldwin canon develops. Macebuh believes that a black artist will reach maturity only when he reaches the realization that his own suffering is not unique, but part of a social dilemma. Recognizing a "spiral of rage," culminating in *Tell Me How Long the Train's Been Gone* and *No Name in the Street*, Macebuh notes that the rage is related to Baldwin's sense of structural unity.

Next to be considered is Baldwin's refutation of the church and the theological terror of his youth. This rejection is seen to liberate the artist's imagination, but at the same time it presents Baldwin with another challenge, "both in terms of his uneasiness over the value of employing homosexuality either as symbolic or actual rebellion, and in terms also of the necessity . . . to deal more specifically with his social dilemma." This challenge is confronted in the later works of Baldwin's canon.

Calling *Giovanni's Room* (1956) "one of the few novels in America in which the homosexual sensibility is treated with some measure of creative seriousness," Macebuh writes that the theological terror was not yet completely exorcised. But this novel allowed Baldwin "the time he apparently needed to move toward a more public position in his art." While writing *Another Country* (1962), Baldwin had come to realize his need for a more "comprehensive vision." But the "episodic, disintegrated" success of the novel was the result of an imperfectly structured tale, and Macebuh concludes that so long as Baldwin restricted his consideration to private theological visions, he was capable of producing a viable novel. When Baldwin turned to the more social context, "the psychic effort demanded by this radical change appear[ed] to have led to an unfortunate attenuation of his formal artistic talent."

Macebuh then turns his attention to an historical survey of the development of black literature in America. While this is clearly an attempt to place Baldwin in perspective, readers may easily lose sight of Baldwin in the context of this discussion. Concluding Macebuh's analysis is "From Allegory to Realism" in which Baldwin is finally seen to have moved from private history to a public consciousness in a time of social and political turmoil. Macebuh asserts, "that Baldwin finally came to this realisation is a clear indication of his continued growth as a writer," and that with this new authentic voice Baldwin will "again recapture that mastery of the fictional form" that distinguished *Go Tell It on the Mountain* (1953).

Generally, *James Baldwin: A Critical Study* is a carefully researched work; and readers of Macebuh's book will appreciate his end-of-chapter summaries and the conclusion. These tie together and emphasize the major points of his analysis which may be obscured by the book's tendency toward general discussion.

Peter Bruck's *Von der "Store-front Church" zum "American Dream"* (1975) is published in German, but the author provides an English summary of the major points in an appendix to the book. Bruck begins by noting the increasing politicization of writing by and about black Americans. His own methodology is an attempt to discuss Baldwin's protagonists with respect to their possibilities for action and to interpret classic American myths and literary motifs as they relate to Baldwin's work and Baldwin's role as artist.

Baldwin's "love ethic" leading to the eventual "wedding of the two races" is a focus in Bruck's treatment of Baldwin's essays. Works by Richard Wright, Eldridge Cleaver, and Amiri Baraka are contrasted to Baldwin's work, and Bruck maintains that a chief purpose for Baldwin's essays is the education of the white audience.

Bruck then turns to Baldwin as novelist, interpreting the heroes of the novels as victims of racial suffering who are unable to determine their own lives. John, in *Go Tell It on the Mountain,* is trapped by his conflict with his father and an oppressive religious background, but he must come to terms with his roots in order to become truly free. The failure of love is central to *Giovanni's Room,* and the novel also introduces the major theme of the homosexual as outsider and "symbolic black." The fragmented novel *Another Country* again underscores the failure of love and reveals the "white-Negro"—Eric, the homosexual—living the only viable alternative. Bruck argues that Leo Proudhammer in *Tell Me How Long the Train's Been Gone* is Baldwin's "first non-victimized hero," who lives an "ideally harmonious affair" with a white woman. This novel, Bruck contends, represents Baldwin's changed attitude toward the world, with love as a key to salvation. Bruck sees this novel as a confirmation that Baldwin is a "universal minority writer" rather than simply a black author.

Bruck's analysis of Baldwin's work is a useful addition to Baldwin criticism, if for no other reason than he brings a European perspective to an American situation and to an American writer who felt compelled to flee his homeland for artistic sanctuary in Europe. As Baldwin's concerns and public statements become more global in orientation, an increasing amount of interest in his work can be seen among European scholars.

Karin Moller's *The Theme of Identity in the Essays of James Baldwin: An Interpretation* (1975) is a detailed analysis of each of Baldwin's collections of essays through *No Name in the Street.* Moller contends that Baldwin's nonfiction presents a coherent picture of his major concerns and that the theme of identity is the most pervasive. Moller's analysis of this theme, steeped in Biblical allusion, involves the issues of art, sexuality, race, nationality, and morality; and she sees Baldwin using "polarities and incompatibilities of all kinds," such as struggle vs. inevitability and innocence vs. experience, to discover a synthesis to shape an identity. Each of the five books of essays is discussed in a separate chapter.

Moller identifies several major points central to the volumes of essays. The concept of identity is defined as an Afro-American identity, and the Afro-American experience emerges as a form of "bluesy celebration." Racial history is a key to understanding the American heritage, and a kind of imprisonment may be seen in oppressed blacks forced to accept debasing stereotypical roles in society. Moller asserts that Baldwin defines the role of artist as a public witness who can work toward a better world through his personal responsibility and commitment, bringing the "promise" out of the "chaos" that is America today.

Moller concludes that Baldwin's quest for identity is an effort to dramatize his personal situation as an Afro-American and "to render it universally intelligible by infusing physical reality and concrete facts with myth and metaphysics."

W. J. Weatherby's *Squaring Off: Mailer vs. Baldwin* (1977) is not a scholarly book. Instead it describes the author's acquaintance with Mailer from 1959 and Baldwin from 1961. Derived from discussions and interviews as well as from social situations, Weatherby's reportorial account sees these authors as "reverse sides of the same coin" who share "a common quest in public even though in different directions and styles." Representative figures of the 1960s, Baldwin and Mailer are seen in the context of an age when blacks and whites were struggling creatively to understand one another, and so they become symbolic for many Americans. Scholars will find this highly readable, anecdotal record of Baldwin and Mailer an interesting perspective on two important contemporary writers, especially in the interrelationship of their views on art and social action.

Louis Hill Pratt's *James Baldwin* (1978) for the Twayne U.S. Authors series is a useful addition to the limited book-length scholarship on Baldwin. Pratt claims to present "a more precise delineation of the broader concerns with which Baldwin deals—issues which are drawn *not* in terms of the provincial problems of white versus black, but according to the universal concepts of freedom versus slavery, liberation versus oppression, reality versus illusion . . . ." In the first chapter, "Common Experience, Uncommonly Probed," he begins by discussing Baldwin's artistic philosophy regarding the role of the writer in society. He sees differences as well as similarities between Baldwin's views and the black aesthetic of the 1960s, setting the stage for the analysis to follow.

Pratt then proceeds to analyze Baldwin's works clearly and convincingly, returning to familiar and common themes that thread through the Baldwin canon: the search for love, the discovery of identity, the role of history. "The Fear and the Fury" examines the short stories collected in *Going to Meet the Man* (1965) as they exemplify

27

Baldwin's interest in the alienation of individual characters. The third chapter focuses on the novels in terms of style, theme, and technique, and Pratt contends that the novels demonstrate the need to establish a personal environment where love can "survive and flourish." Baldwin's dramatic rendering of illusion and reality and the search for identity in *Blues for Mister Charlie* and *The Amen Corner* (1968) is the subject of "The Darkness Within."

The fifth chapter, "The Confrontation of Experience," turns to Baldwin's essays and discusses them in terms of both their sociological dimension and their artistic merit. The final chapter provides Pratt's review of Baldwin criticism and concludes that recent critical assessments have gone beyond "the narrow context of sociology" and have moved toward a more comprehensive judgment that acknowledges "the consummate artistic skill which transcends the social value of [Baldwin's] artistry."

Pratt presents a competent and useful review of Baldwin's work, and although he may claim to have the more ambitious purpose of redirecting Baldwin criticism, he has succeeded in adding a general, largely thematic, critical review to the scarce full-length criticism on this significant author.

Carolyn Wedin Sylvander's *James Baldwin* (1980) is the most recent addition to book-length Baldwin criticism. Intended as an introductory work for beginning students, this monograph proceeds methodically through a brief look at Baldwin's life, his nonfiction, novels, plays, and short stories, weaving germaine quotations from interviews and speeches throughout. The book concludes with a look at *Just Above My Head*, Baldwin's most recent novel, which Sylvander contends "repeats, expands upon, and resolves many of the ideas, questions, and conflicts that surface throughout his published work."

Yet, most scholars will find this book a disappointment. There is little by way of recognizable thesis or point of view to be found, and the critical interpretations and analyses offered are not particularly new or insightful. Compared to Pratt's similar book, this study offers less direction and stimulation for further investigation.

It is safe to say, then, that a definitive critical interpretation of James Baldwin's life and work is yet to be written. Baldwin has been the subject of numerous dissertations in recent years, and perhaps one or more of these will be developed into just such a work.

Critical Studies: Articles and Book Sections

In spite of the relative lack of extended scholarly analysis of his work, James Baldwin is clearly ranked as one of America's most significant contemporary writers. The dimensions of his reputation must be found in the many scholarly and review articles dealing with his work, but since Baldwin is very much a *public* artist, often seen as a spokesman for Afro-Americans, critical opinion of him and his work frequently is sharply divided. Comparison with his "artistic father," Richard Wright, and with contemporaries such as Ralph Ellison and Norman Mailer are plentiful. And since his writing, particularly his essays; his views, particularly his condemnation of Western civilization; and his lifestyle as expatriate homosexual are at cross currents with the mainstream, Baldwin is often the target of hostile criticism. Nevertheless, his stature is assured, and he is an artistic force that must be reckoned with objectively in order to understand American literature in the last half of the twentieth century.

The 1950s saw the publication of two Baldwin novels and a collection of essays, but the critical response was limited to brief, but occasionally insightful, reviews. Of all his novels, *Go Tell It on the Mountain* received the warmest critical reception. Richard K. Barksdale in "Temple of the Fire Baptized" (1953) focuses on the religious and ethical questions posed by the novel, rather than seeing the book in terms of race relations or sociology. "The American Negro in Search of Identity" (1953) by Steven Marcus notes that Baldwin tries "to define precisely what [being black in America] is like" and sees John's conversion as an escape from the "outrageously narrow range" of American Negro life. Disney Monas expresses the view of many critics when he claims that *Go Tell It* is a "first novel of unusual promise" in his "Fiction Chronicle" (1953). Michel Fabre offers one of the most perceptive readings of this novel in "Pères et Fils dans *Go Tell It on the Mountain*" (1970), seeing the novel as Baldwin's attempt "to free himself," and at the same time to prove himself as a writer "worthy before Wright."

Langston Hughes treats Baldwin's *Notes of a Native Son* in "From Harlem to Paris" (1956) and concludes that as an essayist, Baldwin is "thought-provoking, tantalizing, irritating, abusing, and amusing." Dachine Ranier, in "Rage into Order" (1956), praises Baldwin as "the most eloquent . . . most perceptive Negro writing today," and contends that the essays in *Notes* "portray in lyrical, passionate, sometimes violent prose the complex, oblique, endless outrages by which a man, particularly a black man, can be made to feel outside the established social order." Unlike most critics confronted by *Giovanni's Room*, Robert W. Flint is not outraged by the homosexuality in the novel, but praises the work as "a compelling book, unmistakably alive" in "The Undying Apocalypse" (1957).

The first attempt at a kind of synthesis among Baldwin's first three published books is Harold B. Isaac's "Five Writers and Their African Ancestors" (1960). Isaacs contends that Baldwin recognizes that a key to his identity must be found in America, so his quest for "a more inclusive view of human culture and his place in it" begins when he returns to the American South. And while Baldwin has regained his sense of American identity, "a dark little African thread" runs through *Go Tell It on the Mountain, Notes of a Native Son,* and *Giovanni's Room.* A later, insightful essay by Daryl C. Dance, "You Can't Go Home Again: James Baldwin and the South" (1974), contends that Baldwin's return to America, particularly his trip through the South, enabled him to appreciate "the positive results" of his origins. However, the trip was taxing for him, and Dance concludes that Baldwin "cannot go home again" because it may mean extinction. Identity is a key consideration in Eugene Fontinell's "The Identity of James Baldwin" (1962), which contends that *Nobody Knows My Name* gives "a new and deeper insight" into human understanding. James Finn's "The Identity of James Baldwin" (1962) considers *Another Country* in the context of Baldwin's canon to date. Finn contends that the novel is "incomplete" compared to the earlier work. Baldwin's fiction is carefully analyzed in "James Baldwin: A Question of Identity," a chapter in Marcus Klein's *After Alienation: American Novels in Mid-Century* (1962). Klein sees "the invisibility of the Negro [as] . . . James Baldwin's underlying metaphor," with *Go Tell It on the Mountain* as the first "dramatic recognition" and the subsequent novels as the development of "a rhetoric of private alienation." In "Baldwin's Autobiographical Essays: The Problem of Negro Identity" (1964), David Levin argues that Baldwin focuses his essays through *The Fire Next Time* on the demand to stop seeing the Negro as an "abstraction" and to begin recognizing the Negro's "full weight and complexity as a human being." In "James Baldwin's 'Previous Condition': A Problem of Identification" (1969), Sam Bluefarb contends that this story, first published in 1948, anticipates Ellison's *Invisible Man* as Baldwin attempts to "find a form of identification in the white world" at the same time he "fails to find even a place for himself in the black world." Baldwin presents a hero who is isolated by his sensitivity and intellectuality, revealing the plight of the black artist-intellectual in both the white and the black world.

Albert Gerard's "James Baldwin et la Religiosité Noire" (1961) again focuses on *Go Tell It on the Mountain* and sees the novel as an expression of the particular role Christianity plays in black literature. He sees intense emotions and convictions in Baldwin's characters, and although the emotional religious aspects of the novel may seem "primitive," they are "essentially human." Caroline Bloomfield's "Religion and Alienation in James Baldwin, Bernard Malamud, and James F. Powers" (1962) argues that *Notes of a Native Son* and *Go Tell It on the Mountain* prescribe religion to "alleviate the pain" of the hero's alienation. Shirley S. Allen writes that Baldwin skillfully blends religious symbolism with Freudian allusions in "Religious Symbolism and Psychic Reality in Baldwin's *Go Tell It on the Mountain*" (1975). This is a thoughtful reading of an important novel that Allen believes "deserves a higher place in critical esteem than it has generally been accorded."

Daniel Jacobson, in "James Baldwin as Spokesman" (1961), treats *Notes of a Native Son* and *Nobody Knows My Name*. Jacobson argues that the former is Baldwin's best book, while the latter is directed at his fellow Americans, stressing the theme that "Negroes are . . . ignored in the North and are under surveillance in the South and suffer hideously in both places." Philip Bonosky's "The Negro Writer and Commitment" (1962) criticizes *Nobody Knows My Name* as "abruptly banal," concerned more with the melodrama of discrimination than with its moral consequences. However, Baldwin is seen as "a fighter for the freedom of the Negro people" and "not content with his place in society" in Philip Abbot Luce's "Communications on James Baldwin" (1962), a rebuttal to Bonosky's criticism and pessimism. Julian Mayfield's "And Then Came Baldwin" (1963) analyzes hostile Baldwin criticism from various "black intellectuals," noting that the attacks are actually superficial. Mayfield argues that Baldwin's enduring achievement is that he has captured in "beautiful, passionate, and persuasive prose the essence of Negro determination to live in [America] . . . as a free man."

Harvey Breit's "James Baldwin and Two Footnotes" (1963) praises Baldwin, whose "dark passion and lighted language has proved a unique description of the Negro's situation in America." Breit sees *Go Tell It on the Mountain* as Baldwin's most creative work and *Notes of a Native Son* as his "most natural and graceful one," while the others through *The Fire Next Time* are less satisfying. Maurice Charney's

"James Baldwin's Quarrel with Richard Wright" (1963) contends that the disagreement, beginning with Baldwin's publication of "Everybody's Protest Novel," centers on the belief that Wright "distorted artistic truth into protest and propaganda." In some ways, Baldwin is like Ellison: hope and love are keys to identity as they "make war on the chaos of despair." This quarrel between a "grown up son, Baldwin, and his spiritual father, Wright" is the center of B. K. Mitra's "The Wright–Baldwin Controversy" (1969). Mitra argues that Baldwin tries "to penetrate and analyze the rage [as seen in Wright's fiction] and convert it into a recognizable human emotion."

John V. Hagopian, in "James Baldwin: The Black and the Red–White–and–Blue" (1963) contends that Baldwin "is one of the most accomplished and sophisticated American writers of today," but laments the fact that Baldwin spends so much of his energy writing protest essays. He praises Baldwin's short story "This Morning, This Evening, So Soon" as "one of the most important short stories written since the war." A somewhat opposite view is found in Irving Howe's "Black Boys and Native Sons" (1963) which argues that Baldwin has "secured his place as one of the two or three greatest essayists this country has ever produced," finding both the fiction and essays to be of high literary caliber. Colin MacInnes, in "Dark Angel: The Writings of James Baldwin" (1963) agrees, predicting that a century from now, Baldwin's works will still be discussed since his style is classic and his theme "one of the most relevant." Therman B. O'Daniel's "James Baldwin: An Interpretative Study" (1963) reinforces the notion that the entire Baldwin canon reveals the talent and versatility of a remarkable author: his literary style consists of a clear and "passionately poetic rhythm." Gus Blaisdel's "A Literary Assessment: James Baldwin, the Writer" (1964) points out Baldwin's "revolutionary attitude to both sex and color," and concludes that "Perhaps, in the future, America will be very proud of having produced a black replica of Camus."

Eugenia W. Collier analyzes *Another Country* in "The Phrase Unbearably Repeated" (1964), noting that it has something to offend everyone. Yet she looks beyond the brutality and sex to find "a hurting compassion" as the novel explores "the individual's lonely and futile quest for love"; and she illustrates the significance of music, notably the blues, in revealing "the victimizing of personal and social forces that one cannot control." The quest for love is at the heart of Charlotte Alexander's "The 'Stink' of Reality: Mothers and Whores in James Baldwin's Fiction" (1968) as she sees physical intimacy as a means to "emotional fulfillment" while at the same time it brings risk and the "stink of reality" as one's innocence is lost. The theme of music is used by George E. Kent in "Baldwin and the Problem of Being" (1964). He contends that Baldwin writes in the same way a musician reflects his innermost feelings and compassion, relying on black folk tradition as well as modern literary practice. H. Orlando Patterson, in "The Essays of James Baldwin" (1964), contends that Baldwin's craftsmanship in *The Fire Next Time* is displayed in a "controlled yet spontaneous vigor of prose," a literary counterpart to the "music of the Modern Jazz Quartet." In " 'Sonny's Blues': James Baldwin's Image of Black Community" (1970), John M. Reilly sees the blues as a key metaphor for Baldwin in "its combination of personal and social significance in a lyric encounter with history." It is an "esthetic linking his work in all literary genres, with the cultures of the Black ghetto." M. Thomas Inge agrees in his "James Baldwin's Blues" (1972); he notes that while the narrator of "Sonny's Blues" has "escaped the sordid environment" of the ghetto, music promises to "save Sonny's life and future." Shirley Anne Williams goes even further in "The Black Musician: The Black Hero as Light Bearer" (1971). She contends that the musician becomes an "archetypal figure whose referent is black lives, black experience and black death" and music is the medium through which he "achieves enough understanding and strength to deal with the past and present hurt." Sigmund Ro's "The Black Musician as Literary Hero: Baldwin's 'Sonny's Blues' and Kelley's 'Cry for Me' " (1975) offers "two case studies of the intellectual and ideological sources" of the black hero in Afro-American fiction. Baldwin presents music's significance as "that of putting himself and his audience in touch with their ancestral past"; and Ro argues convincingly that comparisons with Camus and Sartre are warranted in discussing the story.

Robert F. Sayre, in "James Baldwin's Other Country" (1964), argues that Baldwin has emerged as "a kind of prophet, a man who has been able to give a public issue all its deeper moral, historical and personal significance," seen most in his essays published in *Notes of a Native Son*, *Nobody Knows My Name*, and *The Fire Next Time*. In "The Novels of James Baldwin" (1965), Robert Bone calls Baldwin "the most important Negro writer" of the last decade, but notes that his quality from work to work is not consistent; Baldwin is best as an essayist, weakest as a playwright, and successful as a novelist. Bone goes on to state that Baldwin must continue to mature as an artist and that his future depends on his "ability to transcend the emotional reflexes of his adolescence." Eldridge Cleaver is harsh with Baldwin in his "Notes on a Native Son" (1966) as he acknowledges Baldwin's talent but finds a "hatred of the blacks particularly of himself " and a "shameful, fanatical, fawning" love of whites. Cleaver is also angered at Baldwin's repudiation of Wright's "masculinity" and his veneration of André Gide. Addison Gayle, Jr., however, feels that Bone has misjudged Baldwin. In "A Defense of James Baldwin" (1967) Gayle contends that Bone and Cleaver do not give both extrinsic and intrinsic approaches to Baldwin's work. And Mark R. Daniels adds, in "Estrangement, Betrayal and Atonement: The Political Theory of James Baldwin" (1976), that there is political theory in Baldwin's work. He contends that "Baldwin is led to a universal concept of human estrangement. The historical dehumanization of the black man becomes indivisible from the dehumanization of every man."

Baldwin's short fiction is the focus of John R. Moore's "An Embarrassment of Riches: Baldwin's *Going to Meet the Man*" (1965), though he relates the stories to Baldwin's novels. He believes that Baldwin's characters "believe in love with a primitive intensity that civilization cannot destroy" and that they bear the "burden of racial consciousness, of revolt against social convention, of a guilt that self-righteousness cannot absolve them from." Harry L. Jones also analyzes the stories in "Style, Form, and Content in the Short Fiction of James Baldwin" (1977), noting that they "seem to contain in microcosm the universe that later manifests itself in Baldwin's major works." Donald C. Murray focuses on a most highly regarded short story in "James Baldwin's 'Sonny's Blues': Complicated and Simple" (1977), contending that the story explores "man's need to find his identity in a hostile society." Edward A. Watson's "The Novels and Essays of James Baldwin: Case-Book of a Lover's War with the United States" (1965) weighs the merits of the novels and essays, concluding that Baldwin's fame must rest on "his masterful employment of the essay as a means of examining his own soul and that of the country he loves." Clarence Major writes that Baldwin has become "what many people the world over consider the greatest American essayist since Ralph Waldo Emerson" in "James Baldwin: A Fire in the Mind" (1974); Baldwin has become both "writer" and "preacher" in his work.

Calvin C. Hernton's *White Papers for White Americans* (1966) contains two essays of use to Baldwin scholars. "Blood of the Lamb" discusses Baldwin's popularity, especially among white liberals, and analyzes the "phantom" presence of Baldwin's father, projected into other powerful men in his life, haunting most of his writing. After reaching a level of artistic maturity during his sojourn in Europe, he returns to America at a particularly crucial time for blacks and is seized upon by an eager public. Hernton contends that Baldwin is "the categorical head of the newly emerging young . . . Existential Negroes." The second essay, "A Fiery Baptism," contends that with *Blues for Mister Charlie* Baldwin's writing entered into a new phase: no longer is he "addressing a predominantly white audience." Instead, Baldwin reveals "the raw, brutal, objective facts of the white man's barbarity toward black people."

David Littlejohn's discussion of Baldwin's novels in *Black on White: A Critical Survey of Writing by American Negroes* (1966) sees three stages of development: *Go Tell It on the Mountain* sees Baldwin coming to terms with his childhood experiences and transcending them; *Giovanni's Room*, one of the most subtle novels of the homosexual world, presents Baldwin's personal uncertainty; *Another Country* is characterized by a "screaming, no-holds-barred verbal violence." Littlejohn argues that Baldwin's theory of racism has a "fundamentally sexual character" as seen in these novels. Perhaps the highest praise for *Another Country* can be found in Mike Thelwell's "*Another Country:* Baldwin's New York Novel" (1969). Thelwell contends that, although the book is marred by the faults noted by other critics, "its accomplishments and its importance far outweigh them" and Baldwin has broken through a "dead end of platitudes, sociological clichés, complacent white assumptions . . . which have, since the thirties, just about lost their usefulness." Charles Newman's "The Lessons of the Master: Henry James and James Baldwin" (1966) traces Baldwin's "literary antecedents" to Henry James, noting that both authors share a universal vision: Baldwin's identity quest is reflective of western man's burden. Baldwin's "artistic achievements mesh . . . precisely with his historical circumstances," and he becomes spokesman for a "genuinely visible revolution." Jerry H. Bryant discusses the use of political and social concerns as criteria for judging literary works in "Wright, Ellison, Baldwin—Exorcising the Demon" (1976). Noting that the "hyperactive sixties" produced much of this type of criticism, Bryant contends that this tendency is healthy in that it "connected literature with life," and that both Ellison and Baldwin possess an intense determination "to embrace their blackness as a high value and as a means for changing the face of America."

C. W. E. Bigsby sees Baldwin as an artist "who is also, consciously or not, committed to a specific social problem" in "The Committed Writer: James Baldwin as Dramatist" (1967). There is a need for an artist to see humanity as a whole, escaping the limited vision of a specific racial situation, and Bigsby argues that Baldwin's work is "above the naive absolutism" of other black writers because his experience is "seen in broader context of the human condition." However, Baldwin is less successful as a dramatist than he is as an essayist or a novelist since *Blues for Mr. Charlie* presents essentially the stereotyped characters in protest-oriented situations. Nevertheless, Carlton W. Molette's "James Baldwin as Playwright" (1977) offers production-oriented views of *Blues for Mr. Charlie* and *The Amen Corner*. While this is not precisely literary criticism, Molette argues that Baldwin's work on stage is much more successful than that of other novelists. Darwin T. Turner's "James Baldwin in the Dilemma of the Black Dramatist" (1977) addresses the issues of purpose and audience of black drama. He sees *Blues for Mr. Charlie* as written in the protest tradition for a white audience while *Amen*, an artistically superior rendition, explores the black experience for a black audience. Howard M. Harper, Jr., in "James Baldwin—Art or Propaganda" (1967) notes that as a "spokesman" Baldwin advocates rebellion, but as an "artist" he stresses acceptance. He traces this dual theme in the Baldwin canon, giving more praise than other critics to *Another Country* and concluding that *Blues for Mr. Charlie* is "melodrama masked as social criticism" in its "shrill honesty." Irving Howe's "James Baldwin At Ease in Apocalypse" (1968) sees still further decline in Baldwin's work with the publication of *Tell Me How Long the Train's Been Gone*. Seeing Baldwin "whipping himself into postures of militancy and declarations of racial metaphysics which . . . seem utterly inauthentic," Howe argues that the novel is "full of the clichés of soap opera." Baldwin's "crowning disaster" as a novelist is what Robert E. Long calls *Tell Me How Long the Train's Been Gone* in "Love and Wrath in the Fiction of James Baldwin" (1969). While he could be seen as "the apostle of love" in his earlier work, "Baldwin now seems merely a prophet of despair." Nevertheless, Houston A. Baker, Jr.'s "The Embattled Craftsman: An Essay on James Baldwin" (1977) attempts to define a cycle in the Baldwin canon. Baker contends that Baldwin's "quest" begins and ends with "the black urban masses"; he sees *If Beale Street Could Talk* (1974) reinforcing the concepts of family, of "genuine concern for one another," and of positive male figures.

Edward Margolies's chapter, "The Negro Church: James Baldwin and the Christian Vision" (1968), presents an interesting interpretation of religion in Baldwin's writing, noting that the church was one of the few cultural institutions to survive the Negro's transplantation from the South to the North. It functions as "a political force, drawing together persons of diverse . . . origin and directing them toward goals"; and religious energy translated to political and social causes is a theme of Baldwin's work. Margolies is kinder than most critics to *Blues*, noting that even though the play is clearly propaganda, Baldwin's white southern racists are more believable than his northern liberals.

David Noble's "The Present: Norman Mailer, James Baldwin, Saul Bellow" (1968) argues that Baldwin picks up a thesis found in Mailer—that blacks "remain an uncorrupted band of saints within the general corruption of white society"; but Noble finds Baldwin's "romantic primitivism" so extreme that he cannot deal realistically beyond the situation of a particular character without producing a clearly obvious abstraction. The relationship of the black minority to the dominant culture, and "the terrible complexity of human differences based on race in the United States and the modern mercantilist world" is a major focus of Edward Braithwaite's "Race and the Divided Self: *Rap on Race*" (1972). He sees Baldwin and Margaret Mead becoming the persons through whom the public can understand the "psycho-intellectual forces that exist within a racially plural society."

Stephen Butterfield singles out 1961 as a "dividing line in American history, a time when all the race issues left unsettled by Reconstruction were coming back to the surface" in his chapter "James Baldwin: The Growth of a New Radicalism" (1974). Analyzing Baldwin's essays, Butterfield notes that through the publication of *Nobody Knows My Name*, Baldwin's values were still influenced by Christianity and political liberalism; however, later essays, culminating in *No Name in the Street*, are more openly revolutionary, contending that there is "no hope for peace as long as capitalism exists." Nick Aaron Ford analyzes Baldwin's essays in "The Evolution of James Baldwin as Essayist" (1977). He notes that Baldwin, like Emerson, is best in his use of "unstructured, instinctive, and emotional utterance often unsupported by rational safeguards." Vivid imagery evokes emotional response, and personal examples illustrate general truths. Donald B. Gibson's "James Baldwin: The Political Anatomy of Space" (1977) contends that Baldwin "comes closer to putting himself on the printed page than most contemporary novelists and than any contemporary essayist." Since Baldwin's work is intensely personal, even when he turns his attention to more general issues in later writings, his social analysis is limited and conservative. Focusing on Baldwin's criticism of protest writing, Richard Rive points out "weaknesses" in Baldwin's arguments in "Writing and the New Society" (1979). Rive argues that

"Baldwin feels that the 'new' society which the protest writer hopes to realise cannot embrace that greater freedom for which he should strive." Instead, Rive posits that protest writing must be interpreted in terms of its "time, place, and function." Stephen Landrigan writes about Baldwin's return to America to promote *Just Above My Head* in "The World That Is Coming Is Not White" (1979). He notes that Baldwin's book is about "the end of an era"—the Western world we know; and he observes that while Baldwin must return to America every so often to "try to understand it," he cannot write here.

Craig Werner takes a unique approach to Baldwin in "The Economic Evolution of James Baldwin" (1979). Beginning with the notion that "Baldwin has been de-emphasizing purely spiritual approaches to problems and adopting a perspective stressing social action in the face of an oppressive environment," Werner sees cycles in the Baldwin canon in which the author returns to a "socialist perspective" and relies on "spiritual" sources of change. This essay summarizes a good deal of earlier Baldwin criticism and offers a careful interpretation of Baldwin's work seen from an economic perspective. In "Beyond Sociology? Urban Experience in the Novels of James Baldwin" (1978), James B. Vopat examines the novels through *Beale Street* to find the "compounding effects of racism in an already alienating urban environment." He concludes that "One surely cannot read Baldwin without feeling the weight of his social protest, without feeling the narrowness of his lonely rooms or the insidiousness of his darkened movie theaters. . . . without sensing the focus on improving and changing self rather than society."

Familiar themes in earlier Baldwin criticism reappear in recent discussions. C. W. E. Bigsby turns again to an integration of Baldwin's career in "The Divided Mind of James Baldwin" (1979) after the publication of *Just Above My Head*. This thoughtful appraisal sees Baldwin presenting himself as "suffering black and alienated American, social outcast and native son." His style "at its best captured the cadences of hope and rebellion . . . at its worst degenerated into unashamed posturing of a kind which failed to inspect with genuine moral honesty the realities which he had once exposed with such authority." Emmanuel S. Nelson resurrects the theme of identity-quest in "James Baldwin's Vision of Otherness and Community" (1983) as he contends that to Baldwin "personal as well as collective failures stem from the inability of individuals to confront the 'darker' sides of their human nature." This "divided self" amounts to a denial of part of one's humanity (and therefore robs an individual of a sense of identity) and confounds "fruitful and fulfilling interpersonal and communal experience." Baldwin's work, then, is an attempt to "define the chaos of his experience to achieve an orderly sense of self."

Baldwin's use of the blues reappears as a major focus of recent criticism. Eleanor Traylor's "I Hear Music in the Air: James Baldwin's *Just Above My Head*" (1979) sees the novel as "a gospel tale told in the blues mode." Full of contrasts, the book begins each of its five sections with lines from the songs of the elders. Traylor believes that the lyric beauty in this music and its affirmation of a positive vision built tale-tellers such as Wright, Ellison, and Baldwin: "Perhaps a kind of joy, realized even in our struggle through the abyss of dread reality, is the best an art form can offer us." Marlene Mosher's "James Baldwin's Blues" (1982) notes that the "theme of surviving despite tremendous odds is persistent in Baldwin's writings." The most productive way of dealing with life's disappointments, Mosher argues, is creating—and communicating—through art; not only is this courageous, but it may be helpful to others as well. The blues are seen as a wellspring of understanding and strength throughout the Baldwin canon.

Edward Lobb returns to "Sonny's Blues" in "James Baldwin's Blues and the Function of Art" (1979), noting that this popular story "has never received critical treatment adequate to its complexity." Acknowledging John Reilly's perceptive analysis (see above), Lobb contends that the blues "is part of a larger theme which is conveyed almost wholly through the story's images." Baldwin's art, Lobb states, must include paradoxes—both darkness and light, form and shattered unity, the "roar from the void and the order of music." He concludes that to move toward a promising future, Baldwin and his protagonists must come to terms with their past. In a careful analysis of the same story in "Words and Music: Narrative Ambiguity in 'Sonny's Blues' " (1982), Keith E. Byerman states that the narrative "moves within the tension between its openly stated message of order and a community of understanding and its covert questioning, through form, allusion, and ambiguity, of the relationship between life and art." The story suggests, according to Byerman, that "literary art contributes to deceit and perhaps anarchy rather than understanding and order." One measure of Baldwin's achievement in "Sonny's Blues" is his ability to keep the "tension" so well hidden.

Rolf Lunden returns to Baldwin's most highly regarded novel in "The Progress of a Pilgrim: James Baldwin's *Go Tell It on the Mountain*" (1981). Providing a thorough review of previous criticism of the novel, Lunden takes issue with many earlier assumptions, such as an "ironic" interpretation of the religion in the novel (which he notes did not begin to appear until after Baldwin published *The Fire Next Time).* Distinguishing between a "false" and "true" Christianity, Lunden argues that John "has been set free" after his experience on the Threshing Floor. "John is still in the world but not of the world. . . . his battle is no longer with [the] avenue or with his father, but with [the devil]." He concludes that "John's smile [toward Gabriel] in the last lines of the novel is not a smile of mockery, as critics have suggested, but a smile of holy love which has conquered his father's hatred."

William Wasserstrom's ambitious essay "James Baldwin: Stepping Out on the Promise" (1980) is an attempt to assess the thirty-plus-year career of a writer who "might be said to have invested the arts of literature with Martin Luther King's preachments on the politics of race." Wasserstrom traces Baldwin's life, his career, his critical fortunes, and his artistic evolution as he struggles "to compose a classic black literature in an authentic American grain." Noting the ebb and flow of Baldwin's fashionability over the years, Wasserstrom concludes that "Amid pioneers, progenitors, precursors he is today an ancestral presence . . . whose fervour has left its ineradicable mark on American literature in our time." It is, Wasserstrom argues, in his "Whitmanesque union of self and society that James Baldwin's career is lodged."

Finally Ernest A. Champion, in "James Baldwin and the Challenge of Ethnic Literature in the Eighties" (1981), draws attention to the consistency in Baldwin's message in all his works: "black people must fight the oppressor for equality and respect but . . . in so doing they will also help whites to a better way of life." He answers critics who see Baldwin only in the context of the battles of the 1960s by stressing that Baldwin's demand for "a new morality and a new conscience" from the West will give his writing a "relevance . . . far greater in the '80s than it has been in the '60s." Ethnic literature's role, as Champion paraphrases Nathaniel Hawthorne, is "to cast Adam out of Eden, for Adam's own sake."

Future scholarship on the writings of James Baldwin will surely build on foundations already established. The definitive book-length study of Baldwin is still to be written. Many enduring themes noted in the enormous body of critical articles—art, music, protest, morality, Christianity, apocalyptic vision, folklife, community, racial and personal identity, and the sweep of history—will stand further analysis. Baldwin's canon is diverse enough to encourage a variety of critical approaches, and so long as the social and moral issues he so lucidly and passionately explores remain unresolved, the door is left open for scholarly exploration by critics and for opportunities for creation by this consistent, complex, and continually evolving artist.

John Barth

(1930-)

Joseph N. Weixlmann
Indiana State University

PRIMARY BIBLIOGRAPHY

Books

The Floating Opera. New York: Appleton-Century-Crofts, 1956. Rev. ed. Garden City: Doubleday, 1967; London: Secker & Warburg, 1968. Novel.

The End of the Road. Garden City: Doubleday, 1958; London: Secker & Warburg, 1962. Rev. ed. Garden City: Doubleday, 1967. Novel.

The Sot-Weed Factor. Garden City: Doubleday, 1960; London: Secker & Warburg, 1961. Rev. ed. Garden City: Doubleday, 1967. Novel.

Giles Goat-Boy; or, The Revised New Syllabus. Garden City: Doubleday, 1966; London: Secker & Warburg, 1967. Novel.

Lost in the Funhouse: Fiction for Print, Tape, Live Voice. Garden City: Doubleday, 1968; London: Secker & Warburg, 1969. Integrated short-fiction collection.

Chimera. New York: Random House, 1972; London: Deutsch, 1974. Integrated novella collection.

LETTERS. New York: Putnam's, 1979; London: Secker & Warburg, 1980. Novel.

Sabbatical: A Romance. New York: Putnam's, 1982; London: Secker & Warburg, 1982. Novel.

The Friday Book: Essays and Other Nonfiction. New York: Putnam's, 1984.

SECONDARY BIBLIOGRAPHY

Bibliographies and Checklists

Bryer, Jackson R. "Two Bibliographies," *Critique*, 6 (Fall 1963), 86-94.

Harris, Charles B. "John Barth and the Critics: An Overview," *Mississippi Quarterly*, 32 (Spring 1979), 269-283. Collected in *Critical Essays on John Barth*, ed. Joseph J. Waldmeir. See Collections of Essays.

Vine, Richard Allan. *John Barth: An Annotated Bibliography*. Metuchen, N.J.: Scarecrow, 1977.

Walsh, Thomas P., and Cameron Northouse. *John Barth, Jerzy Kosinski, and Thomas Pynchon: A Reference Guide*. Boston: G. K. Hall, 1977.

Weixlmann, Joseph N. "John Barth: A Bibliography," *Critique*, 13, no. 3 (1972), 45-55.

_____. *John Barth: A Descriptive Primary and Annotated Secondary Bibliography, Including a Descriptive Catalog of Manuscript Holdings in United States Libraries*. New York: Garland, 1976.

Biography

Kennedy, Mopsy Strange. "Roots of an Author," *Washington Post Potomac*, 3 Sept. 1967, pp. 17-19.

Interviews and Public Forums

Bellamy, Joe David. "Algebra and Fire: An Interview with John Barth," *Falcon*, no. 4 (Spring 1972), 5-15.

_____. "Having It Both Ways: A Conversation between John Barth and Joe David Bellamy," *New American Review*, no. 15 (Apr. 1972), 134-150.

Cooper, Arthur. "An In-Depth Interview With: John Barth . . . A Young Novelist With Exciting Ideas," *Harrisburg* [Pa.] *Patriot*, 30 Mar. 1965, p. 6.

Coughlin, Ellen K. "John Barth Takes Inventory," *Books & Arts*, 1 (26 Oct. 1979), 4-7.

Enck, John J. "John Barth: An Interview," *Wisconsin Studies in Contemporary Literature*, 6 (Winter-Spring 1965), 3-14.

Gado, Frank. "John Barth." In his *First Person: Conversations on Writers*

& Writing. Schenectady, N.Y.: Union College Press, 1973, 110-141.

Gerst, Angela. "Letters from John Barth," *Boston Globe Magazine*, 21 Oct. 1979, pp. 14-15, 42, 48-50, 52-53. Excerpt collected in Barth's *The Friday Book.*

LeClair, Thomas, ed. "Hawkes and Barth Talk About Fiction," *New York Times Book Review*, 1 Apr. 1979, pp. 7, 31-33.

LeRebeller, Annie. "A Spectatorial Skeptic: An Interview with John Barth," *Caliban*, 12 (1975), 93-110.

McKenzie, James, ed. "Pole-Vaulting in Top Hats: A Public Conversation with John Barth, William Gass, and Ishmael Reed," *Modern Fiction Studies*, 22 (Summer 1976), 131-151.

Prince, Alan. "An Interview with John Barth," *Prism* (Sir George Williams University, Montreal), Spring 1968, 42-62.

Reilly, Charlie. "An Interview with John Barth," *Contemporary Literature*, 22 (Winter 1981), 1-23.

Rushin, Pat. "John Barth's Love Affair with Literature," *Johns Hopkins Magazine*, Dec. 1982, 11-19.

Shenker, Israel. "Complicated Simple Things," *New York Times Book Review*, 24 Sept. 1972, pp. 35-38.

Strack, David. "Buffalo's Funhouse Revisited: Novelist John Barth Talks about Writing and His Years at UB," *Buffalo* (N.Y.) *Courier-Express Magazine*, 12 Sept. 1976, pp. 8-10, 12, 34.

Suplee, Curt. "Life in the Funhouse," *Washington Post*, 17 June 1982, pp. D1, D12-D13.

Ziegler, Heide. "John Barth." In *The Radical Imagination and the Liberal Tradition: Interviews with English and American Novelists*, ed. Ziegler and Christopher Bigsby. London: Junction, 1982, 14-38.

Critical Studies: Books

Glaser-Wöhrer, Evelyn. *An Analysis of John Barth's* Weltanschauung: *His View of Life and Literature.* Salzburg: Institut für Englische Sprache und Literatur, University of Salzburg, 1977.

Harris, Charles B. *Passionate Virtuosity: The Fiction of John Barth.* Urbana: University of Illinois Press, 1983.

Hergt, Tobias. *Das Motiv der Hochschule im Romanwerk von Bernard Malamud und John Barth.* Frankfurt: Lang, 1979.

Joseph, Gerhard. *John Barth.* Minneapolis: University of Minnesota Press, 1970.

Morrell, David. *John Barth: An Introduction.* University Park: Pennsylvania State University Press, 1976.

Robinson, Douglas. *John Barth's* Giles Goat-Boy: *A Study.* Jyväskylä: University of Jyväskylä, 1980.

Tharpe, Jac. *John Barth: The Comic Sublimity of Paradox.* Carbondale & Edwardsville: Southern Illinois University Press, 1974.

Critical Studies: Collections of Essays

Critique, 6 (Fall 1963). Barth/Hawkes number.

Critique, 13, no. 3 (1972). Barth/Fowles number.

Critique, 18, no. 2 (1976). Barth/Gardner number.

Waldmeir, Joseph J., ed. *Critical Essays on John Barth.* Boston: G. K. Hall, 1980.

Critical Studies: Articles and Book Sections

Aarseth, Inger. "Absence of Absolutes: The Reconciled Artist in John Barth's *The Floating Opera,*" *Studia Neophilologica,* 47, no. 1 (1975), 53-68.

Abádi-Nagy, Zoltán. "The Principle of Metaphoric Means in John Barth's Novels," *Hungarian Studies in English,* 9 (1975), 5-31; 10 (1976), 73-94.

Allen, Mary. *The Necessary Blankness: Women in Major American Fiction of the Sixties.* Urbana: University of Illinois Press, 1976, 14-37.

Appel, Alfred, Jr. "The Art of Artifice," *Nation,* 207 (28 Oct. 1968), 441-442. Review of *Lost in the Funhouse.* Collected in Waldmeir.

Bašić, Sonja. "John Barth's Acrobatic Games: An Analysis of 'Lost in the Funhouse,' " *Studia Romanica et Anglica Zagrebiensia,* 40 (1975), 113-133.

Bean, John C. "John Barth and Festive Comedy: The Failure of Imagination in *The Sot-Weed Factor,*" *Xavier University Studies,* 10, no. 1 (1971), 3-15.

Bergmann, Linda S. " 'The Whys and Wherefore's of't': History and Humor in *The Sot-Weed Factor,*" *Markham Review,* 12 (1983), 31-37.

Betts, Richard A. "The Joke as Informing Principle in *The Sot-Weed Factor,*" *College Literature,* 10 (Winter 1983), 38-49.

Bienstock, Beverly Gray. "Lingering on the Autognostic Verge: John Barth's *Lost in the Funhouse,*" *Modern Fiction Studies,* 19 (Spring 1973), 69-78. Collected in Waldmeir.

Bluestone, George. "John Wain and John Barth: The Angry and the Accurate," *Massachusetts Review*, 1 (May 1960), 582-589. Review of *The End of the Road*.

Bryant, Jerry H. "The Novel Looks at Itself—Again," *Nation*, 215 (18 Dec. 1972), 631-633. Review of *Chimera*. Collected in Waldmeir.

_____. *The Open Decision: The Contemporary American Novel and its Intellectual Background*. New York: Free Press, 1970, 283-303.

Byrd, Scott. "*Giles Goat-Boy* Visited," *Critique*, 9, no. 1 (1966), 108-112.

Cantrill, Dante. " 'It's a Chimera': An Introduction to John Barth's Latest Fiction," *Rendezvous*, 10 (Winter 1975), 17-30.

David, Jack. "The Trojan Horse at the End of the Road," *College Literature*, 4 (Spring 1977), 159-164.

Davis, Cynthia. "Heroes, Earth Mothers and Muses: Gender Identity in Barth's Fiction," *Centennial Review*, 24 (Summer 1980), 309-321.

_____. " 'The Key to the Treasure': Narrative Movements and Effects in *Chimera*," *Journal of Narrative Technique*, 5 (May 1975), 105-115. Collected in Waldmeir.

D'Haen, Theo. "John Barth's *LETTERS*." In his *Text to Reader: A Communicative Approach to Fowles, Barth, Cortázar, and Boon*. Amsterdam: John Benjamins, 1983, 43-68.

Dickstein, Morris. "Fiction Hot and Kool: Dilemmas of the Experimental Writer," *TriQuarterly*, no. 33 (Spring 1975), 257-272.

Dippie, Brian W. " 'His Visage Wild; His Form Exotick': Indian Themes and Cultural Guilt in John Barth's *The Sot-Weed Factor*," *American Quarterly*, 21 (Spring 1969), 113-121.

Diser, Philip E. "The Historical Ebenezer Cooke," *Critique*, 10, no. 3 (1968), 48-59.

Domini, John. "*LETTERS* and Ethics: The Moral Fiction of John Barth," *fiction international*, no. 12 (1980), 247-258.

Ewell, Barbara C. "John Barth: The Artist of History," *Southern Literary Journal*, 5 (Spring 1973), 32-46.

Farwell, Harold. "John Barth's Tenuous Affirmation: 'The Absurd, Unending Possibility of Love,' " *Georgia Review*, 28 (Summer 1974), 290-306. Collected in Waldmeir.

Fiedler, Leslie A. "John Barth: An Eccentric Genius," *New Leader*, 44 (13 Feb. 1961), 22-24. Review of *The Sot-Weed Factor*.

Fraustino, Daniel V. "*The Country Wife* Comes to *The End of the Road*: Wycherley Bewitches Barth," *Arizona Quarterly*, 33 (Spring 1977), 76-86.

Gardner, John. *On Moral Fiction.* New York: Basic Books, 1978, 93-96.

Garis, Robert. "What Happened to John Barth?," *Commentary,* 42 (Oct. 1966), 89-90, 92, 94-95.

Gillespie, Gerald. "Barth's 'Lost in the Funhouse': Short Story Text in Its Cyclic Context," *Studies in Short Fiction,* 12 (Summer 1975), 223-230.

Graff, Gerald E. "Mythotherapy and Modern Poetics," *TriQuarterly,* no. 11 (Winter 1968), 76-90.

_____. "Under Our Belt and Off Our Back: Barth's *LETTERS* and Postmodern Fiction," *TriQuarterly,* no. 52 (Fall 1981), 150-164.

Gresham, James T. "*Giles Goat-Boy:* Satyr, Satire, and Tragedy Twined," *Genre,* 7 (June 1974), 148-163. Collected in Waldmeir.

Gross, Beverly. "The Anti-Novels of John Barth," *Chicago Review,* 20 (Nov. 1968), 95-109. Collected in Waldmeir.

Harris, Charles B. "Paradigms of Absurdity: The Absurdist Novels of John Barth." In his *Contemporary American Novelists of the Absurd.* New Haven: College & University Press, 1971, 100-120.

Hauck, Richard Boyd. "These Fruitful Fruitless Odysseys: John Barth." In his *A Cheerful Nihilism: Confidence and "The Absurd" in American Humorous Fiction.* Bloomington: Indiana University Press, 1971, 201-236.

Hawkes, John. "*The Floating Opera* and *Second Skin,*" *Mosaic,* 8 (Fall 1974), 17-28.

Hinden, Michael. "*Lost in the Funhouse:* Barth's Use of the Recent Past," *Twentieth Century Literature,* 19 (Apr. 1973), 107-118. Collected in Waldmeir.

Hipkiss, Robert A. *The American Absurd: Pynchon, Vonnegut, and Barth.* Port Washington, N.Y.: Associated Faculty Press, 1984, 75-113.

Hirsch, David. "John Barth's Freedom Road," *Mediterranean Review,* 2 (Spring 1972), 38-47.

Holder, Alan. " 'What Marvellous Plot . . . Was Afoot?': History in Barth's *The Sot-Weed Factor,*" *American Quarterly,* 20 (Fall 1968), 596-604. Collected in Waldmeir.

Hyman, Stanley Edgar. "John Barth's First Novel," *New Leader,* 48 (12 Apr. 1965), 20-21. Collected in Waldmeir.

Janoff, Bruce. "Black Humor, Absurdity and Technique," *Studies in the Twentieth Century,* no. 13 (Spring 1974), 39-49.

_____. "Black Humor, Existentialism, and Absurdity: A Generic Confusion," *Arizona Quarterly,* 30 (Winter 1974), 293-304.

Jones, D. Allan. "John Barth's 'Anonymiad,' " *Studies in Short Fiction*, 11 (Fall 1974), 361-366.

Jordan, Enoch P. "*The Floating Opera* Restored," *Critique*, 18, no. 2 (1976), 5-16. Collected in Waldmeir.

_____. " 'A Quantum Swifter and More Graceful': John Barth's Revisions of *The Sot-Weed Factor*," *Proof*, 5 (1977), 171-182.

Karl, Frederick R. *American Fictions 1940-1980: A Comprehensive History and Critical Evaluation.* New York: Harper & Row, 1983, 284-291, 457-487.

Kerner, David. "Psychodrama in Eden," *Chicago Review*, 13 (Winter-Spring 1959), 59-67. Review of *The End of the Road*. Collected in Waldmeir.

Kiernan, Robert F. "John Barth's Artist in the Fun House," *Studies in Short Fiction*, 10 (Fall 1973), 373-380.

Klinkowitz, Jerome. "John Barth: Writing Fiction in an Age of Criticism." In *American Writing Today*, ed. Richard Kostelanetz. Washington, D.C.: Forum Books/Voice of America Editions, 1982, II: 198-209.

Knapp, Edgar H. "Found in the Barthhouse: Novelist as Savior," *Modern Fiction Studies*, 14 (Winter 1968-1969), 446-451. Collected in Waldmeir.

Korkowski, Eugene. "The Excremental Vision of Barth's Todd Andrews," *Critique*, 18, no. 2 (1976), 51-58.

Kostelanetz, Richard. "The New American Fiction." In *The New American Arts*, ed. Kostelanetz. New York: Horizon Press, 1965, 194-236.

Krier, William J. "*Lost in the Funhouse:* 'A Continuing, Strange Love Letter,' " *boundary 2*, 5 (Fall 1976), 103-116.

Kyle, Carol A. "The Unity of Anatomy: The Structure of Barth's *Lost in the Funhouse*," *Critique*, 13, no. 3 (1972), 31-43.

LeClair, Thomas. "Death and Black Humor," *Critique*, 17, no. 1 (1975), 5-40.

_____. "John Barth's *The Floating Opera:* Death and the Craft of Fiction," *Texas Studies in Literature and Language*, 14 (Winter 1973), 711-730.

Lewis, R. W. B. *Trials of the Word: Essays in American Literature and the Humanistic Tradition.* New Haven: Yale University Press, 1965, 220-226.

Lindberg, Gary. "It's Just a Game." In his *The Confidence Man in American Literature.* New York: Oxford University Press, 1982, 280-296.

Lodge, David. "This Way to the Folly," *London Times Literary Supplement*, 30 May 1980, pp. 607-608. Review of *LETTERS*.

McCaffery, Larry. "Barth's *LETTERS* and the Literature of Replenishment," *Chicago Review*, 31 (Spring 1980), 75-82.

McConnell, Frank D. "John Barth and the Key to the Treasure." In his *Four Postwar American Novelists: Bellow, Mailer, Barth, and Pynchon*. Chicago: University of Chicago Press, 1977, 108-158.

McDonald, James L. "Barth's Syllabus: The Frame of *Giles Goat-Boy*," *Critique*, 13, no. 3 (1972), 5-10.

Mackenzie, Ursula. "John Barth's *Chimera* and the Strictures of Reality," *Journal of American Studies*, 10 (Apr. 1976), 91-101.

Majdiak, Daniel. "Barth and the Representation of Life," *Criticism*, 12 (Winter 1970), 51-67. Collected in Waldmeir.

Marta, Jan. "John Barth's Portrait of the Artist as a Fiction: Modernism through the Looking-glass," *Canadian Review of Comparative Literature*, 9 (June 1982), 208-222.

Martin, Dennis M. "Desire and Disease: The Psychological Pattern of *The Floating Opera*," *Critique*, 18, no. 2 (1976), 17-33.

Mercer, Peter. "The Rhetoric of *Giles Goat-Boy*," *Novel*, 4 (Winter 1971), 147-158.

Miller, Russell H. "*The Sot-Weed Factor:* A Contemporary Mock-Epic," *Critique*, 8 (Winter 1965-1966), 88-100.

Morris, Christopher D. "Barth and Lacan: The World of the Moebius Strip," *Critique*, 17, no. 1 (1975), 69-77.

Nadeau, Robert. "John Barth." In his *Readings from the New Book on Nature: Physics and Metaphysics in the Modern Novel*. Amherst: University of Massachusetts Press, 1981, 77-94.

Noland, Richard W. "John Barth and the Novel of Comic Nihilism," *Wisconsin Studies in Contemporary Literature*, 7 (Autumn 1966), 239-257. Collected in Waldmeir.

Olderman, Raymond M. "The Grail Knight Goes to College." In his *Beyond the Waste Land: A Study of the American Novel in the Nineteen-Sixties*. New Haven: Yale University Press, 1972, 72-93.

Pinsker, Sanford. "John Barth: The Teller Who Swallowed His Tale," *Studies in the Twentieth Century*, no. 10 (Fall 1972), 55-68.

Porush, David. "Author as Artificial Intelligence: John Barth's Computer-Generated Texts." In his *The Soft Machine: Cybernetic Fiction*. London: Methuen, 1985, 136-156.

Powell, Jerry. "John Barth's *Chimera:* A Creative Response to the Literature of Exhaustion," *Critique*, 18, no. 2 (1976), 59-72. Collected in Waldmeir.

Pütz, Manfred. "John Barth: The Pitfalls of Mythopoesis." In his *The Story of Identity: American Fiction of the Sixties*. Stuttgart: Metzler, 1979, 61-104.

Rackham, Jeff. "John Barth's Four-and-Twenty Golden Umbrellas," *Midwest Quarterly*, 22 (Winter 1981), 163-175.

Reed, Walter L. "*Felix Krull* and *The Sot-Weed Factor:* The Modernity of the Archaic." In his *An Exemplary History of the Novel: The Quixotic versus the Picaresque*. Chicago: University of Chicago Press, 1981, 232-261.

Rice-Sayre, Laura. "The Lost Construction of Barth's Funhouse," *Studies in Short Fiction*, 17 (Fall 1980), 463-473.

Robbins, Deborah J. "Whatever Happened to Realism: John Barth's *LETTERS*," *Northwest Review*, 19, nos. 1, 2 (1981), 218-227.

Rovit, Earl. "The Novel as Parody: John Barth," *Critique*, 6 (Fall 1963), 77-85. Collected in Waldmeir.

Safer, Elaine B. "The Allusive Mode and Black Humor in Barth's *Giles Goat-Boy* and Pynchon's *Gravity's Rainbow*," *Renascence*, 32 (Winter 1980), 89-104.

_____. "The Allusive Mode and Black Humor in Barth's *Sot-Weed Factor*," *Studies in the Novel*, 13 (Winter 1981), 424-438.

Shloss, Carol, and Khachig Tölölyan. "The Siren in the Funhouse: Barth's Courting of the Reader," *Journal of Narrative Technique*, 11 (Winter 1981), 64-74.

Scholes, Robert. "Fabulation and Epic Vision." In his *The Fabulators*. New York: Oxford University Press, 1967, 133-173.

_____. "Metafiction," *Iowa Review*, 1 (Fall 1970), 100-115.

Schulz, Dieter. "John Barth." In *Amerikanische Literatur der Gegenwart in Einzeldarstellungen*, ed. Martin Christadler. Stuttgart: Alfred Kröner, 1973, 371-390.

Schulz, Max F. "Barth, *LETTERS*, and the Great Tradition," *Genre*, 14 (Spring 1981), 95-115.

_____. "Characters (Contra Characterization) in the Contemporary Novel." In *The Theory of the Novel: New Essays*, ed. John Halperin. New York: Oxford University Press, 1974, 141-154.

_____. "The Metaphysics of Multiplicity; and, The Thousand and One Masks of John Barth." In his *Black Humor Fiction of the Sixties: A Pluralistic Definition of Man and His World*. Athens: Ohio University Press, 1973, 17-42.

_____. "The Thalian Design of Barth's *Lost in the Funhouse*," *Contemporary Literature*, 25 (Winter 1984), 397-410.

Slethaug, Gordon E. "Barth's Refutation of the Idea of Progress," *Critique*, 13, no. 3 (1972), 11-29.

Sloane, Thomas O. "Beauty's Spouse's Odd Elysium: Barth's *Funhouse*." In *Retrospectives and Perspectives: A Symposium in Rhetoric*, ed. Turner S. Kobler, William E. Tanner, and J. Dean Bishop. Denton: Texas Women's University Press, 1978, 57-74.

Smith, Herbert F. "Barth's Endless Road," *Critique*, 6, (Fall 1963), 68-76.

Stark, John O. *The Literature of Exhaustion: Borges, Nabokov, and Barth.* Durham, N.C.: Duke University Press, 1974, 118-178.

Stonehill, Brian. "A Trestle of *LETTERS*," *fiction international*, no. 12 (1980), 259-268.

Stuart, Dabney. "A Service to the University," *Shenandoah*, 18 (Autumn 1966), 96-99. Review of *Giles Goat-Boy*. Collected in Waldmeir.

Stubbs, John C. "John Barth As a Novelist of Ideas: The Themes of Value and Identity," *Critique*, 8 (Winter 1966), 101-116.

Sutcliffe, Denham. "Worth a Guilty Conscience," *Kenyon Review*, 23 (Winter 1961), 181-184. Review of *The Sot-Weed Factor*. Collected in Waldmeir.

Tanner, Stephen L. "John Barth's Hamlet," *Southwest Review*, 56 (Autumn 1971), 347-354.

Tanner, Tony. "Games American Writers Play: Ceremony, Complicity, Contestation, and Carnival," *Salmagundi*, 35 (1976), 110-140.

_____. "The Hoax That Joke Bilked," *Partisan Review*, 34 (Winter 1967), 102-109.

_____. "What is the Case?" In his *City of Words: American Fiction 1950-1970.* New York: Harper & Row, 1971, 230-259.

Tatham, Campbell. "The Gilesian Monomyth: Some Remarks on the Structure of *Giles Goat-Boy*," *Genre*, 3 (Dec. 1970), 364-375.

_____. "John Barth and the Aesthetics of Artifice," *Contemporary Literature*, 12 (Winter 1971), 60-73. Collected in Waldmeir.

_____. "Message [Concerning the *Felt* Ultimacies of One John Barth]," *boundary 2*, 3 (Winter 1975), 259-287.

Tharpe, Jac. "Beauty as Good: A Platonic Imperative in John Barth?," *Southern Quarterly*, 15 (July 1977), 335-344.

Tilton, John W. "*Giles Goat-Boy:* Man's Precarious Purchase on Reality." In his *Cosmic Satire in the Contemporary Novel.* Lewisburg, Pa.: Bucknell University Press, 1977, 43-68.

Towers, Robert. "Return to Sender," *New York Review of Books*, 20 Dec. 1979, pp. 30-33. Review of *LETTERS*.

Trachtenberg, Alan. "Barth and Hawkes: Two Fabulists," *Critique*, 6 (Fall 1963), 4-18.

Trachtenberg, Stanley. "Berger and Barth: The Comedy of Decomposition." In *Comic Relief: Humor in Contemporary American Literature*, ed. Sarah Blacher Cohen. Urbana: University of Illinois Press, 1978, 45-69.

Vickery, John B. "Myths and Fiction in the Contemporary American Novel: The Case of John Barth," *Hungarian Studies in English*, 12 (1979), 89-106.

Vidal, Gore. "American Plastic: The Matter of Fiction," *New York Review of Books*, 15 July 1976, pp. 31-39.

Vitanza, Victor J. "The Novelist as Topologist: John Barth's *Lost in the Funhouse*," *Texas Studies in Literature and Language*, 19 (Spring 1977), 83-97.

Wallace, Ronald. "Dwarfed into Dignity: John Barth's *The Floating Opera*." In his *The Last Laugh: Form and Affirmation in the Contemporary American Comic Novel*. Columbia: University of Missouri Press, 1979, 26-44.

Walter, James F. "A Psychochronology of Lust in the Menippean Tradition: *Giles Goat-Boy*," *Twentieth Century Literature*, 21 (Dec. 1975), 394-410.

Warrick, Patricia. "The Circuitous Journey of Consciousness in Barth's *Chimera*," *Critique*, 18, no. 2 (1976), 73-85.

Weixlmann, Joseph. " ' . . . such a devotee of Venus is our Capt . . .': The Use and Abuse of Smith's *Generall Historie* in John Barth's *The Sot-Weed Factor*," *Studies in American Humor*, 2 (Oct. 1975), 105-115.

Weixlmann, and Sher Weixlmann. "Barth and Barthelme Recycle the Perseus Myth: A Study in Literary Ecology," *Modern Fiction Studies*, 25 (Summer 1979), 191-207.

Westervelt, Linda A. "Teller, Tale, Told: Relationships in John Barth's Latest Fiction," *Journal of Narrative Technique*, 8 (Winter 1978), 42-55.

Winston, Robert P. "Chaucer's Influence on Barth's *The Sot-Weed Factor*," *American Literature*, 56 (Dec. 1984), 584-590.

Ziegler, Heide. "John Barth's 'Echo': The Story in Love with Its Author," *International Fiction Review*, 7 (Summer 1980), 90-93.

_____. "John Barth's *Sot-Weed Factor* Revisited: The Meaning of Form," *Amerikastudien*, 25, no. 2 (1980), 199-206.

_____. Review of *Sabbatical*, *International Fiction Review*, 10 (Winter 1983), 50-53.

Ziolkowski, Theodore. *Fictional Transfigurations of Jesus.* Princeton: Princeton University Press, 1972, 230-234, 256-266, 270-298.

Zivley, Sherry Lutz. "A Collation of John Barth's *Floating Opera,*" *Papers of the Bibliographical Society of America,* 72, no. 2 (1978), 201-212.

BIBLIOGRAPHICAL ESSAY

Bibliographies and Checklists

The contents of the early, and detailed, Barth checklists by Jackson Bryer (1963) and Joseph Weixlmann (1972) were subsumed into Weixlmann's *John Barth: A Descriptive Primary and Annotated Secondary Bibliography, Including a Descriptive Catalog of Manuscript Holdings in United States Libraries* (1976). Though now dated, it is the most comprehensive and reliable bibliographical study of Barth available. Weixlmann's bibliography contains full descriptions of all of the editions and issues of Barth's books and first book contributions through 1974 as well as notes about various impressions. Barth's fictional and nonfictional contributions to the periodical press, including reprints, are cited, and Weixlmann describes, in detail, Barth's manuscripts which reside in the Library of Congress as well as those in the Pennsylvania State University and Johns Hopkins University libraries. Annotations are provided for Barth's recordings and for his interviews and other printed remarks, and Weixlmann lists and annotates 112 biographical and 342 critical entries. Over 200 reviews are cited but not annotated. Access to the book is enhanced by subject, author, title, periodical, and publisher indices.

Richard Allan Vine's 1977 bibliography of Barth is slight compared to Weixlmann's, and the section of the 1977 Walsh and Northouse reference guide devoted to Barth is, on the whole, likely to be of no greater use to the researcher than is Vine's book. Although both works were published more recently than Weixlmann's, they are far less thorough: Vine's 289 secondary entries and Walsh and Northouse's 244 pale in comparison to Weixlmann's 675. Vine's book, moreover, is error-laden, and both of the newer works are minimally indexed. The principal service the books provide is that they contain annotations for the reviews their compilers have uncovered, whereas Weixlmann's book does not.

Notice should, finally, be taken of Charles B. Harris's "John Barth and the Critics: An Overview" (1979). Nominally a review of seven then-recent books dealing in sum or in part with Barth, the essay, written by the person who is arguably Barth's finest interpreter, casts glances at a good bit of article-length work in addition to looking closely at the books and documenting a variety of critical gaffs. Harris's essay provides a useful survey of the state of Barth scholarship in the late 1970s.

Biography

John Barth keeps his personal life private. No extant biography reveals more than the barest details of his life and character, although his career as a writer and teacher is reasonably well documented in the chapter of David Morrell's 1976 book *John Barth: An Introduction* entitled "John Barth in Chiaroscuro, 1969." After describing the tidewater Maryland locale in which Barth was raised, Morrell considers Barth's decision to spend only a summer as an orchestration student at the Julliard School of Music in New York before returning to his native state to study journalism at Johns Hopkins University in the fall of 1947. Barth's efforts as a student writer of fiction, which date from 1949, are discussed in some detail, as is his decision, based on financial need, to discontinue Ph.D. work in 1953 in Johns Hopkins's aesthetics of literature program and begin teaching at Penn State. From there, Morrell sketches Barth's writing career through five published books and two aborted works (his sequence of "Dorchester Tales," begun in the fall of 1953 and terminated about a year later, and the novel "The Seeker" or "The Amateur," parts of which found their way into subsequent works), and Morrell follows Barth's academic trail to the State University of New York at Buffalo, where he eventually became Edward H. Butler Professor of English Literature before leaving, in 1973, for Johns Hopkins, where he is currently Alumni Centennial Professor of English and Creative Writing.

The more personal recollections of Barth's parents, siblings, and former high school English teacher are recorded in Mopsy Strange Kennedy's "Roots of an Author" (1967). Barth's own statement on the impact of his life on his writings, entitled "Some Reasons Why I Tell the Stories I Tell . . . ," introduces *The Friday Book* (1984) and provides information in five areas: Barth's being a fraternal twin, his affinity for tidewater Maryland, the influence of music on his writing, his schooling at Johns Hopkins, and his years as a university professor.

Interviews and Public Forums

Principally from a sense of obligation, and despite misgivings, Barth has frequently granted interviews throughout his career. He feels that writers have a limited number of genuinely valuable comments that they can make about their works, and he is less than enamored of cutting into his writing time to edit the transcripts of each of his interviews, something he feels it necessary to do if he is to avoid having his ideas misrepresented. Certain notions do reappear in interview after interview—for example, discussions of his favorite modern writers (Kafka, Joyce, Mann, Musil, and de Assis; Beckett, Borges, Nabokov, Garcia Márquez, Calvino, Hawkes, Gass, and Barthelme)—but for discussions of Barth's aesthetics and narrative strategy his interviews provide the groundwork on which a critical understanding of his fiction may be built.

Two significant interviews with Barth appeared in 1965. His rather crotchety replies in the earlier, conducted by mail by John J. Enck, suggest Barth's uneasiness with many of the questions asked or with the interview process itself, or perhaps both. He does, nonetheless, provide useful information when he discusses his first books as "a series of three nihilistic amusing novels," examines his use of the heroic monomyth in *The Sot-Weed Factor* (1960) and *Giles Goat-Boy* (1966), and comments on the significance of the surname of his protagonist, Jacob Horner, in *The End of the Road* (1958). Several important aesthetic pronouncements also flavor the interview. As an alternative to the strategy employed by the French New Novelists, Barth indicates that he prefers "to come to terms with the discrepancy between art and the Real Thing" by affirming the artificial element in art, making "the artifice part of your point instead of working for higher and higher fi with a lot of literary woofers and tweeters." And he voices his oft-cited quip that "God wasn't too bad a novelist except he was a Realist."

Barth begins his "In-Depth Interview" with Arthur Cooper (1965) by trodding on ground that becomes well-worn in later interviews, his writing apprenticeship at Johns Hopkins, and he indicates that he has no desire to become a commercially successful writer. Barth expresses disdain for the critical term *black humor*, much in vogue in the mid-sixties, which he associates with social satire; he tells Cooper that his authorial consciousness is far less engaged by social issues than by the "spookiness" of the universe, the simple facts of existence. The interview also finds Barth explaining his compositional practice in some detail, and, in a rare personal aside, he indicates that his being married is congenial, rather than disturbing, to his art.

The interview which reveals more about Barth's aesthetics than any other was conducted by Alan Prince in 1968. Echoing his famous "Literature of Exhaustion" essay of the preceding year, Barth refers to *The Sot-Weed Factor* and *Giles Goat-Boy* as "novels which imitate the form of the novel, by an author imitating the role of Author." He also considers the role that linguistic and structural imitation plays in those works and indicates that he tends to think of his writing "as a kind of orchestration, really; I like to take old literary conventions and re-score them for contemporary purposes." Fiction he regards as "a kind of true representation of the distortion we all make of life . . . not a representation of life itself, but a representation of a representation of life," and he contends that comedy, burlesque, and farce liberate one from the demands of realism. Along the way, Barth discusses the historical research into the *Archives of Maryland* which he did for *The Sot-Weed Factor*, and he comments on his use of love triangles. Of the multimedia and literature-of-exhaustion aspects of *Lost in the Funhouse* (1968), he asserts that "technique in art . . . has about the same value as technique in lovemaking. . . . heartfelt ineptitude has its appeal . . . so does heartless skill; but what you want is passionate virtuosity."

Because Joe David Bellamy's two published interviews with Barth, "Algebra and Fire" and "Having It Both Ways," derive from the same transcript, they may be considered as a unit. Published while *Chimera* (1972) was at press, the interviews find Barth, perhaps predictably, indicating his waning interest in the sort of multimedia experimentation which had characterized *Lost in the Funhouse* and expressing his fondness for reorchestrating "received stories" for new fictional purposes. If one is going to borrow from mythic tales, he says, one should do so directly; he finds it "mythopoeically retrograde . . . to write about our daily experiences in order to point up to the myths." Barth also details his desire to use a sophisticated literary vehicle while being true to his love for plot, comments on the relative absence of autobiographical material in his fiction, and offers an extended description of his writing methodology.

Published shortly after the Bellamy interviews, Israel Shenker's exchange with Barth ("Complicated Simple Things," 1972) is even more overtly focused on Barth's fictional practice in *Chimera*. Barth discourses at length about his penchant for building complex narrative structures around simple subjects, although he says that he admires writers "who can make complicated things simple." He also discusses an informing principle in *Chimera:* the ironic recapitulation of the first half of one's life in the second half.

The most comprehensive interview with Barth from the 1970s is that conducted by Frank Gado (1973). It contains Barth's most extensive discussion of his schooling in Cambridge, Maryland, and at Johns Hopkins; a sustained treatment of the genesis of his Maryland trilogy and his revision of *The Floating Opera* (1956, revised 1967); and considered commentary on his unwillingness to write engagé fiction, which he regards as an aberration in literary history. Other significant issues discussed in the conversation include Barth's use of the frame-tale and the fact that many twentieth-century authors have found the short story a congenial art form. Of particular note is Barth's remark that the kind of person he most admires "is the one who has a so-phisticated awareness of alternatives; who knows the tragic futility of actions, yet doesn't yield to castration by all of his sophistication." This insight into what he elsewhere calls the Tragic View of Life helps to explain the persistence of the theme of paralysis versus action in his work.

Of less worth, though not without interest, are Barth's interviews with Annie LeRebeller ("A Spectatorial Skeptic," 1975), David Strack ("Buffalo's Funhouse Revisited," 1976), and Evelyn Glaser-Wöhrer (1977). LeRebeller questions Barth extensively about the implications of his being an "academic" writer, and though he responds in full he obviously feels somewhat put off by this line of inquiry. Asked about his literary "influences," Barth indicates that he uses other writers' works not as models but as inspiration, and regarding the notion of sociopolitical "progress," he opines that even genuinely enlightened changes in public policy do not insure that significant advancement will occur. Because a number of David Strack's questions are focused on Barth's years at the State University of New York (SUNY) at Buffalo, his interview is relatively narrow in its scope, but Barth does speak revealingly about the positive effects of the community of writers in the Buffalo area on his work as well as about the SUNY at Buffalo experiences having helped to nurture his experimental literary temperament. Barth also cites what he feels to be his strengths as a writer (dramaturgy and "the manipulation of language") as well as his deficiencies ("the rendering of character" and failing to create readily accessible fictions), and he discusses taking on the constraints of the epistolary form in writing *LETTERS* (1979). Evelyn Glaser-Wöhrer appends the transcripts of two conversations with Barth to her *Analysis of John Barth's* Weltanschauung. Many of the issues raised are ones to which she personally wants a response rather than concepts that one would expect to be of general interest. Still, fifty-five pages of questions and answers are bound to bear some fruit. Barth discusses the philosophical movement from naive nihilism, in his early work, to absurdism to the Tragic View of Life ("that is, that there are finally just different [if important] ways to live"). His handling of the concept of love, he feels, has changed too: He's now "mellower," "more sentimental." Barth also comments on his use of "mannered language" and on what he considers to be the compatible nature of English as a literary language, and he earnestly analyzes a number of the meanings of his seminal *Chimera* sentence "The key to the treasure is the treasure."

Printed in the fall of 1979, Angela Gerst's "Letters from John Barth" and Ellen K. Coughlin's "John Barth Takes Inventory" both focus on his then-newly-published novel *LETTERS*. Gerst's interview finds Barth in a warm, chatty mood. He speaks lovingly, though not tellingly, about his new creation and its characters, especially Lady Amherst, and he discusses the pros and cons of life in Boston (where he spent a transitional year before leaving SUNY at Buffalo for Johns Hopkins). Coughlin's interview has fewer joys but more substance. Of particular interest are Barth's comments about returning to the origins of the English-language tradition of the novel in *LETTERS* and his explanation of the way in which he used a "structural map" in the creation of the book. In opposing the "Windex theory" of historical-novel writing, he argues that the locale depicted in one's works need not be portrayed with utter accuracy; setting should be "a kind of metaphor" for one's artistic concerns.

LETTERS is also the focal point of Charlie Reilly's 1981 interview with Barth. Barth indicates to Reilly, as he had to Gerst, that, in his recent work, he has been paying more heed to his potential reader than he had in his early years of authorship, and *LETTERS*, he tells Reilly, is designed to be read in conventional sequential order, although he feels that readers adopting another organizational strategy could understand the book. The date 1969 is central to the *LETTERS* project because it "wraps up the decade" of the sixties. Barth ends by commenting on the violence and ambiguity of the novel's conclusion and discussing his authorship of a television script based on the story "Night-Sea Journey."

Heide Ziegler (1982) has conducted perhaps the freshest and most probing Barth interview of the past dozen years. In it, Barth discusses *The Sot-Weed Factor* as "a comic dramatization of some kind of tragic view of innocence" and *Giles Goat-Boy* as a "comic rendition of a sort of tragic view of . . . mystical or at least transcendental experience," and he examines the Tragic View of Life as it relates to the protagonists—and their partners—in *Chimera*. Also interesting are his remarks on the theme of the "paradoxical re-enactment of the past in the present" in *Chimera* and *LETTERS*, and the way in which his protagonists, from *The Sot-Weed Factor* on, operate within that "unstable equilibrium" of past and present existence. The interview concludes with an examination of the fact-fiction dialectic in *LETTERS*.

In two other 1982 interviews, Barth discusses his most recent novel, *Sabbatical* (1982), with Curt Suplee ("Life in the Funhouse") and a variety of concerns with one of his former creative-writing students, Pat Rushin ("John Barth's Love Affair with Literature"). Barth's "Night-Sea Journey" dramatization for WNET was, he tells Suplee, rejected because it would have been too costly to produce, but it "became the scaffolding for the construction" of *Sabbatical*. Barth also considers the novel's limited autobiographical elements, discusses his use of newspaper accounts from the *Baltimore Sun* in writing the book, and waxes philosophical about the critical animus shown the book. Rushin's questioning leads Barth to shed light on his pedagogical practice: a writing teacher should immerse students in the compositional process, provide extensive feedback, bring student writers into contact with "passionate peers," and introduce them to professionalism. *LETTERS* he describes as "a book for readers who *enjoy* difficult things. . . . Literature *should* be a form of delight, among other things." *Sabbatical*, he says, was written from "a delighted wish to do something simpler," by his standards at least, "something that was an easier read."

Those desiring further authorial comment on Barth's works should consult the printed transcripts of two public forums in addition to the interviews. A 1975 University of North Dakota writers' conference brought Barth together with two of his most respected colleagues: William H. Gass and Ishmael Reed. The trio's comments, edited by James McKenzie and published as "Pole-Vaulting in Top Hats" (1976), both give one a sense of Barth's personality and provide useful information about the complex narrative structure of "Perseid" and the film version of *The End of the Road*. "Hawkes and Barth Talk About Fiction" (1979), edited by Thomas LeClair, resulted from a fiction festival held at the University of Cincinnati in 1978. Hawkes is Barth's favorite American contemporary, and some of the reasons why come out in this conversation, as do Hawkes's very positive feelings about Barth's work (*The Sot-Weed Factor,* says Hawkes, is "the staggering fiction of our century"). While many of the questions raised in the dialogue produce responses familiar to readers of Barth's interviews, the precise formulations that appear here are helpful, if somewhat canned.

Comments on Barth's fictional practice also abound in his fictional and nonfictional works. Tony Tanner, in fact, goes so far as to argue, in "Games American Writers Play" (1976), that, at one level, *Chimera* "makes the critic or commentator completely redundant. Barth puts his sources into the text; he includes letters and statements revealing his ideas about the writing of the novel; and, he lists his pet motifs and favorite themes. There is very little for the critic to trace, interpret or decipher. . . . All a commentator can do is to step back into a different frame of reference and, once again, ask, not what is the book about so much as, what is going on here?" The importance of Barth's nonfiction to an understanding of his fiction is underscored by the author himself when he refers to *The Friday Book* (1984) as "a resumé of my Stories Thus Far and an account of what I believe myself to have been up to in writing them." Of the essays collected there, his "The Literature of Exhaustion" (1967) and "The Literature of Replenishment" (1980) are required reading for any serious student of Barth's canon as are "Mystery and Tragedy: The Twin Motions of Ritual Heroism" (1964) and "Muse, Spare Me" (1965).

Critical Studies: Books

David Morrell's introductory book (1976) provides a useful starting point for one unfamiliar with Barth's fiction. Less sophisticated in its treatment of Barth's canon than the books of Charles B. Harris (1983) and Jac Tharpe (1974), the study provides sensible commentary on Barth's philosophical explorations in *The Floating Opera* and *The End of the Road,* his handling of the theme of innocence versus experience in *The Sot-Weed Factor* as well as the historical research he did for the book, the themes and mythic structure of *Giles Goat-Boy,* the unique multimedia aspects of *Lost in the Funhouse,* and the structure of *Chimera.* But Morrell's book also has special interest for initiates into Barth's fictional world: it provides the only substantial biographical account of Barth and offers the only survey of Barth's juvenilia. Moreover, through Barth's good graces and the kind assistance of his agent and editors, Morrell has been able to reconstruct the genesis of each of Barth's novels, to which he appends a substantial discussion of each book's reception by reviewers.

The most critically aware and intellectually astute study of Barth's oeuvre is Charles B. Harris's *Passionate Virtuosity: The Fiction of John Barth* (1983). Barth's first seven books, argues Harris, concluding with *LETTERS*, mark "a stage in Barth's development as an artist." Each book offers a refutation, or at least a qualification, of philosophical positions taken in its predecessor; the seven, taken as a whole, "achieve the effect of a constant grasping for meaning, on the one hand, balanced by the realization that all meaning is *projected*— invented, rather than discovered, and therefore relative and contingent—on the other." The precise philosophical positions which are portrayed in the novels are of less importance than is Barth's dramatic affirmation of the value of such constructions, his emphasis on man's ability to create alternative "realities." According to Harris, "In Barth's fictions, *the passionate desire to construct meaning*—not meaning itself— assumes the status of a universal value."

Harris's book is the product of nearly a decade's intense study of Barth's canon, and that immersion shows. Every chapter is original in insight. Harris begins by using R. D. Laing's concept of "ontological insecurity" to examine Barth's dramatization, in *The Floating Opera,* of "the aesthetic and metaphorical implications of schizophrenia" in his portrait of Todd Andrews. Todd, at one level "a metaphor for the condition of the artist in modern times," oscillates between wanting genuinely to understand his past and realizing that his rendition of that "reality," even when it is faced and not evaded, will always be a fiction. Jacob Horner, the protagonist of *The End of the Road,* also retreats behind a shield of words, but he does so in following "a conscious therapeutic program," whereas Todd's retreat seems instinctual.

Harris turns from psychological to linguistic theory in examining *The Sot-Weed Factor* and *Giles Goat-Boy.* In *The Sot-Weed Factor,* language usage becomes Barth's vehicle for moving away from referentiality and toward the symbolic, away from signification and toward equivalence and coalescence. Henry Burlingame's cosmophilism provides one example of this tendency; two others are the book's abundant use of catalogs and of characters with multiple personalities. In *Giles Goat-Boy,* Barth permits his protagonist to transcend multiplicity and achieve, if only for a moment, "that ineffable unity toward which his first three novels increasingly pointed."

Art, like sex, makes the world go around—this, opines Harris, is at the thematic core of *Lost in the Funhouse,* the first of Barth's self-conscious explorations of his medium and of myth. Harris's treatment of the feminist level of myth and linguistic usage in *Chimera* is the finest extant. He concludes the chapter by asserting that the book contains "a harmonious blend of Logos and Eros, a *hieros gamos* of masculine and feminine opposites which, if seldom achieved in the 'real' world, at moments flourish in the magic 'as if' of Barth's mytho-poeic fictions."

LETTERS, as a recapitulation of Barth's first six books and as a prolegomenon to works to come, is the last book studied. A novel of process which "acknowledge[s] premodernist and modernist models even as it transcends them," *LETTERS* completes Barth's "return to the world while affirming that it is a *worded* world after all. Language, properly employed, is the mythic though perhaps not mystic ligature connecting man, time, and world in a dynamic unity."

The position taken by Jac Tharpe in *John Barth: The Comic Sublimity of Paradox* (1974) is somewhat akin to Harris's. Although Barth's books, considered as a whole, "comprise a history of philosophy," Barth, writes Tharpe, is primarily an aesthetician; in fact, "form—form itself—*is* the content" of *Lost in the Funhouse* and *Chimera.* Nothing is heartily affirmed or denied in Barth's fiction, aside from the fact that nothing can be heartily affirmed or denied. "Barth's genius," Tharpe contends, "lies in his awareness of magnificent ironies and his ability to dramatize paradox[es]," including those of reproduction and decay, illusion and reality, the fabulous and the ridiculous.

The implications of "performance" and the paradoxical Hamlet question dominate Tharpe's treatment of *The Floating Opera,* whereas, in looking at *The End of the Road,* his primary concerns are *cosmopsis* (cosmic paralysis) and Barth's use of the Adamic myth. The myth also figures prominently in Tharpe's treatment of *The Sot-Weed Factor,* in which the New Eden turns out to be the scene of all human ills. The moral and metaphysical implications of Ebenezer Cooke's attempt to establish his identity in a universe of illusion and seemingly endless possibility as well as Barth's depiction of the complex feminine principle (in the person of Joan Toast) are also given considerable attention. Barth's abundant use of cyclology and paradox as well as his creation of a "phylogenic tragedy" highlight the chapter on *Giles Goat-Boy.* Like many critics, Tharpe feels that the twin themes of art and love dominate *Lost in the Funhouse,* Barth's "portrait of the artist as hero." A brief chapter on *Chimera* focuses on the autobiographical aspect of the book as well as its presentation of the "hero-as-artist" motif. While Tharpe's study is not quite so richly textured as Harris's, it is undeniably important. Especially when discussing *The Sot-Weed Factor,* Tharpe is able to keep the bleakness underlying Barth's expansive humor before us.

Another important, if more narrowly focused book is Douglas Robinson's *John Barth's* Giles Goat-Boy: *A Study* (1980). Considerably broader in scope than its title suggests, the book begins by establishing a theoretical framework within which one may profitably analyze not only Barth's entire canon but much of contemporary American fiction. Through the use of parody (which "comically exaggerates the forms of art," as opposed to satire, a kind of comic realism which "mockingly imitates the forms of life"), postmodern fictionalists, Robinson argues, tend to balance "the pleasurably comic" and "the intellectually serious." More specifically, one dialectical plane may be understood as pitting "delightful metaphor" (aesthetic possibility) against "critical irony" (epistemological skepticism), while a related plane pairs introspection and self-reflexivity (metafiction) with an outward-looking concern for ontology and cosmology (metaphysics). These biplanar dialectics, in turn, suggest the centrality of paradox in Barth's work, including his use of farcical comedy to convey a Tragic View of Life, and help to explain his thematic emphasis on the dialectical pair of love and art.

In ensuing chapters, Robinson applies his framework in analyzing *Giles Goat-Boy* at four levels: language and style (including Barth's metafictional technique, his use of frames, and his handling of narration), the book's use and abuse of historical metaphors (including its roman à clef dimension, Barth's embedding of the historical past in the character of Peter Greene, and his handling of the Boundary Dispute), the hero myth (which, in its self-conscious baroqueness, squints toward the metafictional on one hand, while, in showing the protagonist's earnestness, moves paradoxically toward the metaphysical on the other), and philosophy (including the dialectic that is established between ethics and metaphysics, Barth's paradoxical pairing of disparate characters, and the paradoxical nature of the tasks the hero faces which he need not so much *do* as come to *understand*). To this extended analysis Robinson adds one appendix which establishes the book's dual chronology, another which charts Barth's parodic use of Dante's *Inferno* in his creation of Main Detention, and a glossary of terms and characters. Well organized and well argued throughout, Robinson's book not only presents its ideas effectively; it contains a cogent running critique of virtually all previous criticism of *Giles Goat-Boy*.

Of the three decidedly less valuable books which also merit comment, Gerhard Joseph's pioneering University of Minnesota pamphlet (1970) is the most noteworthy. Frequently cited by Barth's critics, if only in passing, Joseph's study begins with a discussion of some of the things Barth's early works have in common: their debt to the Bildungsroman; their author's fondness for philosophical debates, sexual encounters, doubles, and love triangles; their regional verisimilitude; their blend of realism and fable; and their protagonists' search for values. In turning to the individual works, Joseph praises Barth for his handling of form in *The Floating Opera* and *The End of the Road* but criticizes him for his limited psychological reach. *The Sot-Weed Factor* and *Giles Goat-Boy* appeal more strongly to Joseph; he finds both books emotionally unsatisfactory but acknowledges that "a degree of emotional flatness is the price that the parodist agrees to pay for his knowledgeable artificiality and mannered thoroughness." Joseph concludes by defending *Lost in the Funhouse* against those reviewers who read the book as a literary dead end.

More limited in scope than Joseph's pamphlet is Tobias Hergt's *Das Motive der Hochschule im Romanwerk von Bernard Malamud und John Barth* (1979). The book's uninspired central premise is that Barth's handling of the motif of the university becomes increasingly important and multidimensional between its initial appearance in *The Floating Opera*, in which Todd Andrews's law student days at Johns Hopkins are described, and its blossoming into a central metaphor in *Giles Goat-Boy*. The comparisons which Hergt makes between Barth's and Malamud's treatment of the university seem valid but not especially instructive.

Barth, in his 1960 essay "How to Make a Universe," remarked, "You hear it said that the novelist offers you an attitude toward life and the world. Not so, except incidentally or by inference. What he offers you is not a *Weltanschauung* but a *Welt;* not a view of the cosmos, but a cosmos itself." The significance of this observation appears to have been lost on Evelyn Glaser-Wöhrer, whose *Analysis of John Barth's* Weltanschauung: *His View of Life and Literature* (1977) has little to offer anyone attempting to comprehend Barth's fictional practice. For her, Barth's dramatization of ideological positions is an end in itself rather than a fictional vehicle. Moreover, Glaser-Möhrer's analyses of Barth's novels are, by turns, diffuse, tentative, and wrong-headed; she is overly dependent on previous criticism; her text is dotted with malapropisms; and she is wont to cite American thinkers in German translation rather than in their native English. Glaser-Wöhrer shows some originality in discussing *Lost in the Funhouse* and *Chimera*, but even here she stops short of providing genuine insight.

Critical Studies: Articles and Book Sections

Barth's tightly structured, quasi-realistic novels *The Floating Opera* and *The End of the Road* did little to prepare readers for his subsequent books: the baroquely plotted novels *The Sot-Weed Factor* and *Giles Goat-Boy*, his metafictional collections *Lost in the Funhouse* and *Chimera*, his epistolary extravaganza *LETTERS*, and his romance *Sabbatical*. One result was that his early critics, in particular, were uncertain about his basic orientation as a writer. Was he fundamentally an existentialist, a moralist interested in probing philosophical issues; or was his handling of philosophical issues, as most contemporary critics of his work would contend, preeminently grist for his fictional mill? And if the former were so, wondered philosophically minded critics, what was one to make of his use of humor and parody?

Representative of the early critics who regarded Barth as a moralist are Richard W. Noland and Robert Garis. Noland, in "John Barth and the Novel of Comic Nihilism" (1966), contends that Barth's "most interesting and important achievement" resides in his fictive "embodiment of philosophical ideas in a form both tragic and comic"; his books depict "each of the ways in which Western man has attempted to fill his life with value after the death of the old gods." Yet Noland's ethics demand that a writer, to be worthwhile, must articulate a set of personal beliefs that provide moral meaning. "Barth may use parody as a way of clearing his vision," says Noland, "but he can hardly rest in it if he is to develop at all." Questioning "What Happened to John Barth?" (1966), Garis feels betrayed by the self-indulgence of *The Sot-Weed Factor* and *Giles Goat-Boy*. The basic ethical issues which Barth had, in Garis's view, grappled with so earnestly and successfully in *The End of the Road* had given way to artifice.

Jerry H. Bryant, in his book *The Open Decision* (1970), also maintains that Barth is essentially a moralist, since his novels proceed from the tacit assumption that "it is the nature of the human being to justify his life logically on the premises of value." Unlike Garis, however, Bryant feels that Barth's moral vision *develops* in the course of his first four novels. Whereas the protagonist of *The Floating Opera* ends up a relativist, Jacob Horner of *The End of the Road* learns that relative values cannot carry one through life, since they are detached from the true character of our existence. Finally, the protagonists of *The Sot-Weed Factor* and *Giles Goat-Boy* discover that only by embracing the human condition and living in the paradox of one's own subjectivity can the individual lay a solid foundation for moral action.

More attuned to what has become the dominant strain of Barth criticism is Alan Trachtenberg who, in "Barth and Hawkes: Two Fabulists" (1963), contends that Barth should not be approached as a realist; he is more concerned with man's mind than with social issues. In *The End of the Road* and *The Sot-Weed Factor*, argues Trachtenberg, Barth includes characters who teach us "the limits of our own solemn pretensions to responsible behavior." Earl Rovit and Beverly Gross also offer important early views of Barth's work from outside a moralist context, although neither has as much to praise as does Trachtenberg. In "The Novel as Parody: John Barth" (1963), Rovit likens *The Sot-Weed Factor* to the fiction of other contemporary writers for whom he feels parody has become an end in itself. The book, he feels, despite its author's considerable skill, is little more than "a bewildering plaything"; the fork in the road which Barth and company have taken has landed them in a literary cul-de-sac. Anticipating those critics who were to (mis)read Barth's "Literature of Exhaustion" essay (1967) as predicting the end of prose fiction, Gross, in examining "The Anti-Novels of John Barth" (1968), feels that his first four novels, read in sequence, show Barth's movement toward a repudiation of narrative art. The books provide no answers, only paradoxes. Ultimately, she contends, they wind up attacking themselves, the genre of the novel, the narrative impulse, and even the author himself.

While Barth's fiction also had its defenders and detractors in the 1970s and 1980s, friend and foe alike were disinclined to treat Barth as a novelist of ideas. In his seminal article "John Barth and the Aesthetics of Artifice" (1971), Campbell Tatham asserts that, in Barth's fiction, aesthetic concerns take precedence over a moral imperative. *The Floating Opera, The Sot-Weed Factor*, and *Giles Goat-Boy*, says Tatham, are "commentaries on theories of the novel; insofar as novels are a part of life, Barth's novels are a commentary on a part of life." A kindred spirit, Tony Tanner, insists in his *City of Words: American Fiction 1950-1970* (1971) that "Barth starts with a sense of verbal play that precedes existence and essence." Rooted in the Wittgensteinian proposition that "the world is all that is the case," Barth's fiction produces "a mood or atmosphere of ambiguous freedom, both for the character in his situation and the author in his fiction-making."

Blending the philosophical and irrealist approaches to Barth's canon, Richard Boyd Hauck praises Barth's fiction in *A Cheerful Nihilism: Confidence and "The Absurd" in American Humorous Fiction* (1971). Features of Barth's work which had bothered some previous critics—including the fact that his protagonists' dilemmas are not resolved and that a passionate comedic sensibility is intertwined with the exploration of serious issues—do not upset Hauck, who feels that Barth is extending an American narrative tradition which includes the writings of Mark Twain. In "John Barth's Tenuous Affirmation: 'The Absurd, Unending Possibility of Love'" (1974), Harold Farwell sketches Barth's complex attitude toward love from its first appearance in his M.A. project, "Shirt of Nessus" (1952), through its culmination in "Dunyazadiad" (1972). Farwell concludes that Barth's fiction, especially his most recent work, contains a decided affirmation of the possibility of love—not as an absolute value, but as a value which is precious *because* of its fragility and the inevitability of its loss.

John O. Stark, in *The Literature of Exhaustion: Borges, Nabokov, and Barth* (1974), addresses a number of the formal and stylistic properties in Barth's then-recent work: his use of Chinese boxes, the *regressus in infinitum,* paradox, allusion, metamorphosis, imagery (especially mirrors), and point of view. Barth's use of his medium, Stark contends, reinforces his handling of theme. For Frank D. McConnell, writing in *Four Postwar American Novelists: Bellow, Mailer, Barth, and Pynchon* (1977), Barth's work is characterized by his erudition, his treatment of man's linguistic nature, his sense of intellectual play, and his dramatization of the theme of the individual's inauthenticity. While Barth's singular vision is one of "intense privacy," it is nonetheless "valuable to our public imaginative life."

Other critics, however, from within and without academe, have voiced their active disapproval of Barth's formal innovation. Sanford Pinsker, for example, in "John Barth: The Teller Who Swallowed His Tale" (1972), concludes that Barth's lexical skill is not enough to sustain what Pinsker considers to be his thin narrative line: "Barth is not so much the great destroyer of Modernism—exaggerating its faults through extended parody, etc.—as he is the devourer of his own Art." And John Gardner, in his revisionist book *On Moral Fiction* (1978), damns Barth as "an artist who gets so lost in his gimmickry that he forgets the human purposes it has been invented to serve." From the other end of the literary-political spectrum comes Jerome Klinkowitz's assertion that Barth's fictional practice is *not radical enough.* In "John Barth: Writing Fiction in the Age of Criticism"

(1982), Klinkowitz considers Barth a closet Aristotelian whose seemingly avant-garde aesthetic pronouncements betray an underlying conservatism. Mimesis is, at some level, essential for Barth, insists Klinkowitz, and this distinguishes his work from that of truly experimental fictionalists.

More even-handed is Manfred Pütz's chapter on Barth in *The Story of Identity: American Fiction of the Sixties* (1979). In *The Floating Opera* and *The End of the Road*, says Pütz, Barth effectively dramatizes the "failure of mythopoeic strategies in the service of self-formation," but the books "tend to deal [rather too dispassionately] with . . . issues in the manner of the novel of ideas." By contrast, *The Sot-Weed Factor* integrates issues of identity and philosophy "into a narrative whole." While Barth demonstrates the role of fiction in the creation of historical portraiture, he also develops "a pointed critique of the indiscriminate use of the imagination in pursuit of self-generated coherence." In Barth's recent works, Pütz feels, most notably *Lost in the Funhouse*, Barth has so collapsed the distance between himself and his creations that he is no longer in an advantageous position to evaluate his characters' actions. As a consequence, "what is primarily *told* in *The Sot-Weed Factor* is predominantly *shown* in terms of narrative self-reflection in Barth's later fictions."

Barth has not escaped critics' penchant for categorizing writers into schools. Although he has objected more strenuously to the label *black humorist* than any other, numerous essays examine him within a black humor context. Max F. Schulz, in *Black Humor Fiction of the Sixties: A Pluralistic Definition of Man and His World* (1973), contends that black humor is best regarded as a phenomenon "comprising a group of writers who share a viewpoint and an aesthetics for pacing off the boundaries of a nuclear-technological world intrinsically without confinement." Since black humorists see life as an endless maze, they devise "enormously self-conscious" fictional forms which suggest "unbounded multiplicity." *The Sot-Weed Factor, Giles Goat-Boy,* and especially *Lost in the Funhouse* exemplify this tendency. For Bruce Janoff, writing of "Black Humor, Existentialism, and Absurdity: A Generic Confusion" (1974), the essence of black humor inheres in the writer's struggle, as dramatized in Barth's story "Title" (1968), to negate silence and lifelessness. Akin to Janoff's position is Thomas LeClair's contention in "Death and Black Humor" (1975) that "the fact and awareness of death" are central to the black humorists' aesthetic; death is the event which "gives their fiction both a philosophical ultimacy and an artistic rationale." Finally, Elaine B. Safer, in two related articles ("The Allusive Mode and Black Humor in Barth's *Giles Goat-Boy* and Pynchon's *Gravity's Rainbow*," 1980, and "The Allusive Mode and Black Humor in Barth's *The Sot-Weed Factor*," 1981), maintains that the works of the black humorists are designed to encourage reader frustration and emphasize irrationality. One method is to present the reader with allusions which cannot be fully or accurately plumbed (as often happens in *Giles Goat-Boy*); another is to deflate a sacred notion from the past (e.g., Barth's debunking of the Pocahontas legend in *The Sot-Weed Factor*). Relatedly, the quests which are central to the novels of the black humorists end in failure rather than success; they provide questions rather than offering answers. As a result, argues Safer, the reader is brought toward a truer understanding of the human predicament.

Barth's reader is also a concern of Jeff Rackham's. In "John Barth's Four-and-Twenty Golden Umbrellas" (1981), Rackham contends that fiction such as Barth's demands a reader liberated from a false and limiting realism. We, as readers, need, first, "to rid ourselves of the high seriousness that realist fiction has led us to expect." Secondly, we must immerse ourselves in the *experience* of reading; it is "in the interrelationship between text and reader" that a tale's "reality" resides, not in the external world. "Our job with the new fiction is not to analyze . . . but to synthesize. We must draw together the paradoxes instead of attempting to cut through them."

Two female critics have presented diametrically opposite views of Barth's handling of women characters. Mary Allen, in *The Necessary Blankness: Women in Major American Fiction of the Sixties* (1976), feels that Barth's treatment of his female characters is "exemplary among all writers of the sixties." Only in some of the *Funhouse* stories and when describing the lesbianic actions of Hedwig Sears in *Giles Goat-Boy* are Barth's sympathies for women and their problems absent. Allen finds it noteworthy that Barth, who is "capable of making a joke of almost anything," is "never at his funniest when writing about women. The comic strain gives way to pathos or painful awareness when the focus shifts from a male to a female character." Cynthia Davis, on the other hand, contends in "Heroes, Earth Mothers and Muses: Gender Identity in Barth's Fiction" (1980) that Barth's depiction of women embodies assumptions inherent in a male-centered mythology and that his views "support a myth even more deadening to women" than traditional sex-role typing. Barth's women characters, says Davis, "represent and embody consequence without initiating it. They are not individuals, but forms of the non-individual outer world.

Barth's men, too, are types, but human types, choosers and definers."
While *Chimera* appears to offer the possibility of an antidote to the
acted-upon female characters who populate Barth's earlier works, the
women there remain "extraordinarily passive, by choice or force sub-
jected to male decisions, and they are truly functional only as symbols
of the hero's choices."

Numerous essays, some of them quite valuable, treat individual
novels rather than Barth's entire canon. Basic to an understanding
of Barth's first book is "John Barth's *The Floating Opera:* Death and
the Craft of Fiction" by Thomas LeClair (1973). Todd Andrews,
LeClair argues, is an unreliable narrator, yet he is capable of conning
an unwary reader into accepting his accounts as factual by means of
the earnest tone he assumes. Todd is an artist capable of manipulating
the reader just as surely as he manipulates the law: "His approach to
life and his approach to art are interpenetrable, are one." Barth himself shares this manipulative ability, as do a series of aesthetically adept
characters in his ensuing books.

Novelist John Hawkes and critic Inger Aarseth also focus on
Barth's conscious aestheticism in *The Floating Opera*. Comparing *"The
Floating Opera* and *Second Skin"* (1974), Hawkes maintains that Barth's
novel is a carefully crafted work in which he attempts "to extend fiction
into the realm of pure and lively and fearful paradox, to cloak abstractions of the human voice in the comic clothes of humanity, to
reinvent the world's language." Aarseth, in "Absence of Absolutes:
The Reconciled Artist in John Barth's *The Floating Opera"* (1975),
examines Barth's use of sex and boat building as metaphors for art
and artistic creation and considers the correspondences between
Todd's struggle with his masks and the artist's struggle with his medium. She concludes that, while Barth's subsequent tales are more
overtly metafictional than are *The Floating Opera* and *The End of the
Road*, "the whole of Barth's work belongs to the metafiction tradition
of the 20th-century novel."

Eugene Korkowski and Dennis M. Martin provide more specific
insights into *The Floating Opera*. Korkowski, in "The Excremental Vision of Barth's Todd Andrews" (1976), insists that the novel "offers
a sustained burlesque of Freud's theories about anal retentiveness and
prodigality" and that Todd Andrews is the unwitting target of Barth's
humor, for "he is a little incognizant of how fully the novel's theme—
the excremental 'work' mechanism he sees in the other characters—
is operative in himself." Martin's exploration of "Desire and Disease:
The Psychological Pattern of *The Floating Opera"* (1976) leads him to

posit the medical source for Todd's subacute bacteriological endocarditis and severe prostate trouble: untreated gonorrhea. "The matrix of Todd's art," says Martin, "lies in his attempt to impose a coherent pattern on his life, to reduce it to some kind of meaningful order, thereby defending himself from the objective truth of his history."

Two articles explore the extensive changes which *The Floating Opera* underwent between its initial publication in 1956 and its revision in 1967. Comparing the two main printed versions of the novel in *"The Floating Opera* Restored" (1976), Enoch P. Jordan observes that Barth, by returning in 1967 to the design for the novel which his first publisher had compelled him to alter, eradicates the sentimentality and facile optimism which plague the ending of the 1956 edition. He also succeeds in tightening the book's structure and enhancing its thematic unity. More probing is Sherry Lutz Zivley's "Collation of John Barth's *Floating Opera*" (1978), which is based on evidence drawn from seven holograph and typescript versions of the text as well as five printed versions. With Jordan, Zivley feels that the narrative flow of the 1967 edition is, for the most part, sharper, but she asserts that Barth, in excising a number of Todd's colloquialisms and circumlocutions, "interfered with a style that was better suited to the character of his narrator." She adds that many passages altered prior to the book's publication in 1956 in order to bring it into conformity with the publishing morality of the 1950s were *not* restored by Barth when he revised the novel in 1967.

Daniel Majdiak's "Barth and the Representation of Life" (1970) provides the starting place for anyone wishing to explore Barth's use of parody in *The End of the Road*. Jacob Horner, says Majdiak, uses parody to undermine Joe Morgan's value system. Barth uses it to stress the unreality of literature in order to render "a more creditable picture of reality through a more viable fictional form." Majdiak also comments knowingly on Horner's search for identity, his role playing, and his *cosmopsis* as well as on Barth's use of names and settings and his handling of chronology. Less sophisticated, yet useful, is Herbert F. Smith's essay "Barth's Endless Road" (1963), in which he demonstrates that the book involves a "satiric criticism of the limited goals of existentialism."

Barth's research for *The Sot-Weed Factor* is the subject of Philip Diser's "The Historical Ebenezer Cooke" (1968), which is, in the main, devoted to delineating those historical details about Barth's protagonist which he borrowed and those which he knowingly altered. Joseph Weixlmann's " ' . . . such a devotee of Venus is our Capt . . .': The Use and Abuse of Smith's *Generall Historie* in John Barth's *The Sot-Weed Factor*" (1975) shows that Barth's witty deflation of Smith's account involves more than just the Pocahontas story. At least five other native American characters are comically transformed as well, and Barth makes extensive use of Smith's glossary of the Virginia Indian language.

It is Barth's *conception* of history, however, which has caused the greatest critical stir. An influential early assessment is provided in Alan Holder's " 'What Marvellous Plot . . . Was Afoot?': History in Barth's *The Sot-Weed Factor*" (1968). Holder finds it objectionable that Barth refuses to commit himself to a particular version of historical "truth" in *The Sot-Weed Factor* and that history seems to exist in the novel "primarily as a repository of details and plots that Barth wants to master and outdo." Linda S. Bergmann answers, in " 'The Whys and Wherefore's of't': History and Humor in *The Sot-Weed Factor*" (1983), that Barth was honest *not* to select one from among the many discrepant versions of historical "fact" regarding colonial Maryland. "Holder, like Ebenezer [Cooke], like us all, wants our history to give us meaning, moral direction, a grip on the past to use in the present, while for Barth, as Ebenezer learns and we must admit, the past, like the present, is a 'floating opera,' which we can only see in fragments that evade ultimate meaning." Given the fact that history is devoid of intrinsic meaning, "the historical novelist must provide an extrinsic order for the past; the more artificial this order, the less we will be inclined to mistake the structure necessary for art for the hidden truth of history." Barbara C. Ewell, in "John Barth: The Artist of History" (1973), also opposes Holder's view. *The Sot-Weed Factor,* she feels, provides "serious commentary both on the nature of history and ultimately on the nature of the real." Because the events of the past will always be unverifiable, history can only be a subjective human construct in which art and artifice provide structures that cope with "the overwhelming preposterousness of Being."

For Heide Ziegler, *The Sot-Weed Factor* is, "a, or even *the*, decisive landmark in the development of postmodern fiction," since it marks a "shift in commitment from the realm of reality to the realm of the imagination." In "John Barth's *Sot-Weed Factor* Revisited: The Meaning of Form" (1980), Ziegler insists that, by treating both fictional and "historical" events as *stories*, Barth deconstructs the traditional notion of reality and provides for its reconstruction on his own terms. But he does so at a cost. "Necessity for the author," says Ziegler, "comes to lie in the process of storytelling as such: he must pay for the initial freedom of his imagination with self-imposed constraints. . . ." For Brian W. Dippie (" 'His Visage Wild; His Form Exotick': Indian Themes and Cultural Guilt in John Barth's *The Sot-Weed Factor*," 1969), the importance of the novel resides in its deconstruction of a series of popular myths: that of America as the New World Garden, that of red-white reconciliation as a purgation of cultural guilt, and, most importantly, that of America's attainment of genuine civility and identity.

The most oft-cited critique of *Giles Goat-Boy* is Robert Scholes's chapter on the novel in *The Fabulators* (1967), in which he examines Barth's "sacred book to end all sacred books" as a psychological, historical, sociological, philosophical, mythic, and literary allegory. Theodore Ziolkowski, in *Fictional Transfigurations of Jesus* (1972), sees the novel as a "fifth Gospel" of "moral neutralism" in which Barth "exploits the Bible for the sheer aesthetic fun of structural parody." For Ziolkowski, *Giles Goat-Boy* is not an allegory but an analogue which parodies the Gospels, the relationship between the Old Testament and the New, and the entire tradition of higher criticism of the Bible. Still another approach appears in Raymond M. Olderman's 1972 study *Beyond the Waste Land*. The book's title hints at Olderman's thesis: that Barth seriously employs and consciously parodies Eliot's *The Waste Land* in *Giles Goat-Boy*. George Giles, says Olderman, is a quester who, like Tiresias, "narrates his own failure and is transformed from Grail Knight to wounded Fisher King." Finally, James T. Gresham ("*Giles Goat-Boy:* Satyr, Satire, and Tragedy Twined," 1974) and James F. Walter ("A Psychronology of Lust in the Menippean Satiric Tradition: *Giles Goat-Boy*," 1975) view the book as a Menippean satire. But whereas Gresham's very fine essay attempts, simply, to read the novel in the context of the Menippean satiric tradition (illuminating Barth's use of paradox in the process), Walter calls attention to what he feels to be the book's flatness, diffuseness, and excesses.

John W. Tilton's chapter on *Giles Goat-Boy* in his 1977 study *Cosmic Satire in the Contemporary Novel* asserts that the book, unlike Barth's earlier works, provides "a consistent insight into the condition of man in an absurdly meaningless universe." According to Tilton, each of the novel's three main mythological components—the Hero Myth, the Founder's Hill Myth, and the Boundary Dispute Myth— explores an element of man's psyche, and the three, considered together, dramatize Barth's central concern: "to illuminate mythopoetically the plight of man divided against himself and man divided against man. . . , a universal condition . . . [which] arises from a fragmentation of the psyche witnessed in all myths of all ages and countries."

"The Rhetoric of *Giles Goat-Boy*" (1971) is Peter Mercer's subject. Mercer feels that the prose in the novel consists of "academic" and "goatish" registers as well as "heroic" and "comic" styles and that these, in turn, represent the antithetical pairs rational-animal and heroic-bathetic. As a result, the rhetoric of *Giles Goat-Boy* provides "a structural principle for the entire hierarchy of the book's moral allegory as well as the terms for the stages of the narrative allegory." Although George Giles does not triumph physically within Barth's Revised New Syllabus, he triumphs linguistically through his putative creation of the sacred book. Campbell Tatham, in "The Gilesian Monomyth: Some Remarks on the Structure of *Giles Goat-Boy*" (1970), attempts to demonstrate that Barth has relied more heavily on Joseph Campbell's monomyth in creating the character of George Giles than he has on Lord Raglan's concept of the hero, and Tatham contends that the way in which Barth parodies and otherwise manipulates certain aspects of the monomyth affects the novel's meaning.

One approach to Barth's integrated short-fiction collection *Lost in the Funhouse* is that proposed by Carol A. Kyle, who insists that the book may best be understood as an anatomy ("The Unity of Anatomy: The Structure of Barth's *Lost in the Funhouse*," 1972). The collection, she feels, begins with fictions that demonstrate the absurdity of metaphysical, creative, and sexual journeys before moving on to the Ambrose stories, which parody the American adolescent novel and bring the anatomy to its climax. The stories subsequent to "Lost in the Funhouse" form the book's dénouement, "which approximates an anti-climax with two contrapuntal forms: parody of myth alternates with parody of art until the 'novel' talks itself to death." A different level of parody is the subject of Michael Hinden's "*Lost in the Funhouse*: Barth's Use of the Recent Past" (1973). Hinden maintains that the collection involves "an elaborate parody, revival, and refutation" of James Joyce's *Portrait of the Artist as a Young Man*, especially insofar as the *Funhouse* book "concerns the collapse of credibility of the artist-as-hero theme in modern literature and the question raised as to whether there is 'anything more tiresome, in fiction, than the problems of sensitive adolescents.'" Robert F. Kiernan argues, in "John Barth's Artist in the Fun House" (1973), that the book is a *Künstlerroman*. The key stories, he feels, are those involving Ambrose, which trace the evolution of the boy's artistic calling. The narrator of the stories in the second half of the collection (implicitly Ambrose) develops a feeling of disdain for his early attempts "to understand and master the funhouse of fiction" and learns to relinquish his adolescent sensitivity and to concern himself, instead, with the actual productions of fictional art.

According to Max F. Schulz ("The Thalian Design of Barth's *Lost in the Funhouse*," 1984), the *Funhouse* collection is binary in structure. A largely mimetic rehearsal of conception, birth, and growth marks the book's first half, whereas, in the second, a self-reflexive narrative voice "struggles with the problem of writer's block and the question of fictional form." The book's structure, Schulz maintains, suggests "that Barth is less an exhausted metafictionist trying to free himself from outmoded and worn-out forms than a postmodernist bent on preserving and combining past fictional practices with the distinctive narrative voice of the present. He is not an errant realist guilty of formalist perversions so much as a radical preservationist looking for ways to conserve old and new storytelling."

Jan Marta, in "John Barth's Portrait of the Artist as a Fiction: Modernism through the Looking-glass" (1982), contends that *Lost in the Funhouse* has a "fourfold frame structure"—"circle, dissolving frames, joined poles, and open-ending"—and that this structure mirrors the fourfoldness of the twin pairs of thematic opposites which undergird the stories: fiction-reality and art-love. This multiple dialectic, which is also evident at levels of the book beyond the structural, both unites the work and provides a regenerative force which permits Barth to overcome the potentially deadening effects of narrative exhaustion and silence. In "Lingering on the Autognostic Verge: John Barth's *Lost in the Funhouse*" (1973), Beverly Gray Bienstock describes the book's unifying principle as the individual's search for identity. She also examines Barth's handling of Greek myth, especially as it is evidenced in "Menelaiad," as well as the figure of Ambrose, whom she regards as "a younger, pre-Helen Menelaus." Bienstock concludes her article by explaining Ambrose's relationship to Barth and Barth's relationship to all writers, followed by the writer's relationship, through his artwork, to all readers—an eternal, recurring cycle symbolized by the Moebius strip which begins the *Funhouse* collection.

Victor J. Vitanza's "The Novelist as Topologist: John Barth's *Lost in the Funhouse*" (1977) offers a brilliant analysis of Barth's use of the mathematics of distortion as metaphor and technique in the *Funhouse* book. Each story in the collection, argues Vitanza, is a reflection of all the other stories, garbled and radically translated into various topological forms. And this method is, in turn, wedded to Barth's central subject matter: the desire to compose successfully despite the purported exhaustion of certain fictional forms and plots. Vitanza says, "the task or activity that Barth performs in writing these homeomorphic sections is clearly the same task that the structuralist . . . performs and takes as his own unique activity."

In "Beauty's Spouse's Odd Elysium: Barth's *Funhouse*" (1978), Thomas O. Sloane examines *Lost in the Funhouse* as a novel, the subject of which is "how novels get written." This subject is dramatically expressed, Sloane maintains, in terms of a complex writer-reader continuum which involves an implied author, a protagonist/narrator ("he"), a deuteragonist/narratee ("she"), and an implied reader. At the heart of the book is the narrator-narratee relationship, which Barth as implied author and we as implied readers can both objectify and become engaged in—suggesting that Barth's rhetorical strategy in the book is that of irony. Though risking paralysis and nihilism, the collection finally progresses, however tentatively, toward rhetorical communion.

The subject of potential reader-writer interchange in *Lost in the Funhouse* has received considerable critical attention. William J. Krier, for example, insists that the reader is central to Barth's purpose in the book ("*Lost in the Funhouse*: 'A Continuing, Strange Love Letter,' " 1976). Krier reads the tenuous love relationships depicted in the collection as metaphors for reader-writer union and participation in the literary act, and he argues that Barth's technique leads us to "discover the significance of our being a *part* of the doing of the book." Supportive of this reading is Linda A. Westervelt's "Teller, Tale, Told: Relationships in John Barth's Latest Fiction" (1978), in which she sees Barth engaging the reader as "a more equal partner" in *Lost in the Funhouse* and *Chimera*. The tales' construction induces the one told the story to forge a genuine relationship with the teller. She admits that the sometimes abusive tone of the narration in the *Funhouse* collection places severe limits on this relationship but observes that the gentler, less threatening tone projected in *Chimera* permits writer and reader to "share and participate" willingly. Carol Shloss and Khachig Tölölyan disagree. They argue, in "The Siren in the Funhouse: Barth's Courting of the Reader" (1981), that, while active reader participation is required from anyone confronting the *Funhouse* text, "it would be too optimistic to assert that we are invited to participate in a genuinely cooperative, meaning-bestowing activity. . . ." The book encourages readers to hone their analytical reading skills, but, because Barth continually undercuts and frustrates his stories' messages at a variety of levels, true exchange between reader and writer is blocked. For Shloss and Tölölyan, *Lost in the Funhouse* is not an attempt to achieve new and better communication but a masterfully crafted product of solipsism.

Notable among the essays devoted to individual *Funhouse* tales is Edgar H. Knapp's "Found in the Barthhouse: Novelist as Savior" (1968-1969), which treats the title story in the collection. Knapp's analyses of Barth's use of myth, his handling of point of view, and his debts to the masque and the cinema in the story have been repeatedly cited by subsequent critics. Gerald Gillespie argues in "Barth's 'Lost in the Funhouse': Short Story Text in Its Cyclic Context" (1975) that the title story is a microcosm for the entire *Funhouse* collection, which is, in turn, a microcosm for the body of the world's stories. The first seven tales in the book treat the cyclical nature of human experience in a "preponderantly contemporary, biographical" way, whereas the last seven mirror the first by treating the same subject from a "preponderantly historical and mythical" perspective.

In "The Lost Construction of Barth's Funhouse" (1980), Laura Rice-Sayre examines the changes made in the Ambrose stories between their initial magazine publication (in 1963 and 1967) and their inclusion in the *Funhouse* collection (1968). Unsurprisingly, the most revised story is the earliest, "Ambrose His Mark," and the least revised is the most recent, "Lost in the Funhouse." Barth not only made minor stylistic changes in the tales, but he also altered their content and significantly modified the presentation of his characters, especially Ambrose's Uncle Karl. As a result of the alterations, the stories are more focused; specifically, Ambrose becomes more overtly an artist, and increased emphasis is placed on naming and the importance of the blank.

In "John Barth's *Chimera:* A Creative Response to the Literature of Exhaustion" (1976), Jerry Powell analyzes what he considers to be the central issue in Barth's sixth book, the problem of the exhausted possibilities of narrative art, as well as Barth's handling of three themes which develop from and relate to that issue: writer's block, mythology, and the analogy between lovemaking and writing. Each theme, Powell feels, produces a rich paradox at best and, at worst, a despairing contradiction. Beneath the "playful prose" of *Chimera* lies "a tone of deadly seriousness" which bespeaks Barth's commitment to continue publishing "as if" writing were of great value and despite the fact that literature may have no ultimate meaning. Tony Tanner worries in "Games American Writers Play," (1976) that Barth may have become overly dependent on linguistic structures in *Chimera*. In shifting his narrative ground "from the 'what' of presentation to the 'how' of representation," Barth may be precluding "fictional engagement of historical, political, and social problems."

Cynthia Davis is more sanguine in " 'The Key to the Treasure': Narrative Movements and Effects in *Chimera*" (1975). The narrative complexity of *Chimera*, she insists, is a necessary result of Barth's deliberate attempt "to articulate the unarticulable nature of human consciousness and existence." The book "does not celebrate achievement, it celebrates struggle." Relatedly, John B. Vickery argues in "Myths and Fiction in the Contemporary American Novel: The Case of John Barth" (1979) that Barth's handling of myth, far from being a solipsistic endgame, links him, in the only way it validly can, to external reality. Through the techniques of variation, repetition, and contradiction, Barth presents "facets of the nature of fiction and myth which themselves are narrative mirrors of those concepts, forever changing, recurring, and reconstituting, by which man distances self from both others and objects *in order to think all of them*" (italics added). Parody and myth, then, do not, in Barth's hands, suggest an escape from reality but constitute an engagement with it.

Useful to students is the essay " 'It's a Chimera': An Introduction to John Barth's Latest Fiction" (1975), in which Dante Cantrill provides a literal, diachronic distillation of the events in the complexly structured and framed tales that comprise *Chimera*. Useful to students and scholars alike are Cantrill's extended analyses of the book's title and of Barth's use of numerology in *Chimera*. In "Barth and Barthelme Recycle the Perseus Myth: A Study in Literary Ecology" (1979), Joseph Weixlmann and Sher Weixlmann closely examine Barth's handling of the Perseus legend in the second of the three *Chimera* novellas, "Perseid," and they contrast it with Donald Barthelme's treatment of the same myth in "A Shower of Gold." Barth's direct presentation of mythological characters, his elaborate use of framing, his baroque plotting, his creation of an extended mural conceit based on the Fibonacci series of numbers, and his use of paradox are among the subjects explored in the essay, in which the Weixlmanns attempt to isolate and explain Barth's fictional practice.

Opinions as to the significance of Barth's novel *LETTERS* vary widely. According to Gerald E. Graff, for example, the book is a failure because it has nothing of substance to say about twentieth-century history ("Under Our Belt and Off Our Back: Barth's *LETTERS* and

Postmodern Fiction," 1981). Graff concedes that the book effectively portrays the dizzying paradoxes of modern life, but he feels that these are turned inward and thus fail to comment on external "reality." "Although Barth has revived the art of storytelling," Graff concludes, "he's neglected the point of the story." Writing of "Barth, *LETTERS,* and the Great Tradition" (1981), Max F. Schulz expresses an opposite view. For him, *LETTERS* synthesizes American history and geography as well as Barth's own creative past, and it successfully parodies the European literary tradition—in the process creating something akin to The Great American Novel. "Cervantes managed his stunning narrative assimilation of Spanish social and literary histories using the picaresque tradition as his foil. With *LETTERS* Barth has created a novel in the same vein. It is an imitation (in the Coleridgean sense of the word), however, not a copy, using the narrative conventions of the past several centuries to establish on its own terms a fusion of the American experience and the Anglo-American-European epistolary and confessional novel tradition. It stands in its earned integrity as a twentieth-century literary milestone, as *Don Quixote* marks an earlier century, in the history of 'transactions with individual readers over time, space, and language.' "

Whether Barth succeeds or fails in his handling of epistolary conventions in *LETTERS* is also a matter of debate. In "This Way to the Folly" (1980), British critic David Lodge opines that success eludes Barth on this score and that his novel, moreover, "lacks the narrative thrust" which characterized his earlier "epic-scale" narratives. Deborah J. Robbins, on the other hand, feels that Barth has effectively overcome some of the limitations inherent in the epistolary form, although she observes that his advancements are idiosyncratic ones, unlikely "to be duplicated or copied in any effect" ("Whatever Happened to Realism: John Barth's *LETTERS,*" 1981).

In his book *Text to Reader* (1983), Theo D'Haen maintains that the narrative strategies in *LETTERS* support the book's claim "that the human world is primarily linguistic in nature. They do so by problematizing all conventions pertaining to 'letters'—language and writing, letter-writing, and literature—and by showing that every verbalization points to no reality beyond itself." The characters in *LETTERS* come to understand that language and what commonly passes for reality involve fictionalization. Barth's work, says D'Haen, has a social function insofar as it implies "the extent to which . . . reality . . . is determined by what is *presented as* reality." In other words, "Barth

confronts his society with its own methods of mythologizing and perpetuating itself."

Extremely useful is the examination of Barth's use of the com-
puter as a metaphor for authorship in *Giles Goat-Boy* and *LETTERS*
which appears in David Porush's *The Soft Machine: Cybernetic Fiction*
(1985). Along the way, Porush also provides excellent insights into
Barth's use of linguistic structures as well as his handling of the theme
of love. Barth's genius, argues Porush, resides in his clever use of the
very devices which indicate the mechanical limits of language and
fiction—"paradoxes, ambiguities, blanks and other glosses on phenomenological silence—*inside the machine* where they illustrate the in-
commensurability of the structure of the text and experience of
meaning." On the phenomenological level, "love thrusts through the
screens separating form from narrative, narrative from language, and
even language from the 'world.' But love . . . is also a sign of those
differences." Love is, for Barth, genuinely paradoxical, not a facile
tool used to achieve fictive transcendence and resolution. *LETTERS*,
Porush feels, "shows Barth at his best: loving the world through the
form of his fiction without losing the sense that it [the word] is still
no substitute for IT [the world]."

As this discussion suggests, there are still many critical debates
regarding Barth's canon in which one might profitably engage: his
complex and evolving fictional practice remains, for example, a much
treated but unexhausted subject, and the determination of Barth's
true masterworks awaits sage commentary as well as the passing of
time. Moreover, his most recent novel, *Sabbatical*, has yet to receive
noteworthy scholarly attention. Barth has, on various occasions, indicated that the true measure of his authorial success will not be taken
for decades, even centuries; that his attempt, as a writer, is to rival
Shakespeare and Cervantes rather than his contemporaries. In this
context, Barth scholarship is in its infancy, despite the fact that much
serious critical attention has already been focused on his work. A solid
foundation is being laid on which future generations of Barth scholars
will be able to build.

Saul Bellow

(1915-)

Gloria L. Cronin
Brigham Young University
and
Liela H. Goldman
Michigan State University

PRIMARY BIBLIOGRAPHY

Books

Dangling Man. New York: Vanguard, 1944; London: Lehmann, 1946. Novel.

The Victim. New York: Vanguard, 1947; London: Lehmann, 1948. Novel.

The Adventures of Augie March. New York: Viking, 1953; London: Weidenfeld & Nicolson, 1954. Novel.

Seize the Day. New York: Viking, 1956; London: Weidenfeld & Nicolson, 1957. Novella.

Henderson the Rain King. New York: Viking, 1959; London: Weidenfeld & Nicolson, 1959. Novel.

Herzog. New York: Viking, 1964; London: Weidenfeld & Nicolson, 1965. Novel.

The Last Analysis. New York: Viking, 1965; London: Weidenfeld & Nicolson, 1966. Play.

Mosby's Memoirs and Other Stories. New York: Viking, 1968; London: Weidenfeld & Nicolson, 1969. Short stories.

Mr. Sammler's Planet. New York: Viking, 1970; London: Weidenfeld & Nicolson, 1970. Novel.

Humboldt's Gift. New York: Viking, 1975; London: Secker & Warburg, 1975. Novel.

To Jerusalem and Back. New York: Viking, 1976; London: Secker & Warburg, 1976. Personal account.

The Dean's December. New York: Harper & Row, 1982; London: Secker & Warburg, 1982. Novel.

Him With His Foot in His Mouth and Other Stories. New York: Harper & Row, 1984; London: Secker & Warburg, 1984. Short stories.

Selected Other

"Address by Gooley MacDowell to the Hasbeen's Club of Chicago," *Hudson Review,* 4 (Summer 1951), 222-227.

"Hemingway and the Image of Man," *Partisan Review,* 20 (May-June 1953), 338-342.

"How I Wrote Augie March's Story," *New York Times Book Review,* 31 Jan. 1954, pp. 3, 17.

"Foreword." In F. M. Dostoevsky, *Winter Notes on Summer Impressions,* trans. Richard L. Renfield. New York: Criterion Books, 1955, 9-27.

"Isaac Rosenfeld," *Partisan Review,* 23 (Fall 1956), 565-567.

"Distractions of a Fiction Writer." In *The Living Novel: A Symposium,* ed. Granville Hicks. New York: Macmillan, 1957, 1-20. Reprinted in *New World Writing.* New York: New American Library, 1957.

"The University as Villain," *Nation,* 185 (16 Nov. 1957), 361-363. Reprinted and revised as "The Enemy is Academe," *Publishers' Weekly,* 190 (18 July 1966), 34.

"Deep Readers of the World, Beware!," *New York Times Book Review,* 15 Feb. 1959, pp. 1, 34.

"The Uses of Adversity," *Reporter,* 21 (1 Oct. 1959), 42-45.

"The Sealed Treasure," *Times Literary Supplement* (London), 1 July 1960, p. 414. Reprinted in *The Open Forum: Essays For Our Time.* 2nd ed. New York: Harcourt, Brace & World, 1961.

"Foreword." In *The Age of Enormity: Life and Writing in the Forties and Fifties,* ed. Theodore Solotaroff. New York: World, 1962.

"Facts That Put Fancy to Flight," *New York Times Book Review,* 11 Feb. 1962, pp. 1, 28. Reprinted in *Opinions and Perspectives,* ed. Francis Brown. Boston: Houghton Mifflin, 1964, 235-240.

"Where Do We Go From Here: The Future of Fiction," *Michigan Quarterly Review* (Winter 1962), 27-33. Collected in *Saul Bellow and the Critics,* ed. Irving Malin. See Collections of Essays.

"Recent American Fiction." Unpublished lecture, Washington, D.C., Library of Congress, 21 Jan. 1963.

"The Writer as Moralist," *Atlantic Monthly,* 211 (Jan.-June 1963), 58-62.

"Literature." In *The Great Ideas Today,* ed. Mortimer Adler and Robert M. Hutchins. Chicago: Encyclopaedia Britannica, 1963, 135-179.

"Some Notes on Recent American Fiction," *Encounter,* 21 (Nov. 1963), 22-29.

"My Man Bummidge," *New York Times,* 27 Sept. 1964, pp. 1, 5.

"On Jewish Storytelling," *Jewish Heritage,* 7 (Winter 1965), 65-67.

"The Thinking Man's Wasteland," *Saturday Review of Literature,* 48 (3 Apr. 1965), 20.

"Keynote Address Before the Inaugural Session of the 34th Session of the International Congress of Poets, Playwrights, Essayists, and Editors, 13 June 1966," *Montreal Star* (Canada), 25 June 1966, Special Insert: 2-3.

"Skepticism and the Depth of Life." In *Skepticism and the Depth of Life,* ed. J. E. Miller and P. D. Herring. Chicago: University of Chicago Press, 1967, 13-30.

"The Public and the Writer," *Chicago Sun-Times Book Week,* 15 Sept. 1968, pp. 1-6. Reprinted as "Perils of Pleasing the Public," *Observer,* 8 Dec. 1968, pp. 16, 18.

"Culture Now: Some Animadversions, Some Laughs," *Modern Occasions,* 1 (Winter 1971), 162-178.

"Jewish Writers Are Somehow Different," *National Jewish Monthly,* 85 (Mar. 1971), 50ff.

"Technology and the Frontiers of Knowledge." In *The Frank Nelson Doubleday Lectures—1972-73.* New York: Doubleday, 1973, 3-22.

"Literature in the Age of Technology." In *Technology and the Frontiers of Knowledge, Frank K. Nelson Doubleday Lectures.* New York: Doubleday, 1973, 1-22.

"Foreword." In John Berryman, *Recovery and Delusions.* New York: Delta, 1974, ix-xiv.

"Starting Out in Chicago," *American Scholar,* 44 (Winter 1974), 71-77. Reprinted with minor changes as "Recent American Fiction," *American Studies International,* 15, 3 (1977), 7-18.

"Machines and Storybooks: Literature In An Age of Technology," *Harper's Magazine,* 249 (Aug. 1974), 48-59.

"A Matter of the Soul: Address to the Fourth International Congress of the Institute of Verdi Studies," *Opera News,* 39 (18 Sept. 1974), 26, 28, 29.

"What's Wrong With Modern Fiction," *Sunday Times,* 12 Jan. 1975, p. 3.

"On Boredom," *New York Times Book Review,* 7 Aug. 1975, pp. 22ff.

"Artists on Art: A World Too Much With Us," *Critical Inquiry,* 2 (Autumn 1975), 1-9.

"Americans Who Are Also Jews (condensed)," *Jewish Digest,* 22 (Apr. 1977), 8-10.

"The Nobel Lecture," *American Scholar,* 46 (Summer 1977), 316-325.

SECONDARY BIBLIOGRAPHY

Bibliographies and Checklists

Cronin, Gloria L. "Saul Bellow Selected and Annotated Bibliography," *Saul Bellow Journal,* 4 (Fall-Winter 1985), 80-89. This issue lists criticism from 1980. Subsequent issues will each contain selected annotated bibliographical listings for subsequent years until the listings are current with the final issue of each year.

Cronin, and Blaine Hall. *Saul Bellow: Annotated Bibliography and Checklist 1944-1986.* New York: Garland, forthcoming 1986. This volume will contain an exhaustive checklist of Bellow reviews and criticism. In addition, it will contain a selected, annotated listing of major Bellow criticism.

Field, Leslie, and John Z. Guzlowski. "Criticism of Saul Bellow: A Selected Checklist," *Modern Fiction Studies,* 25 (1979), 149-171.

Galloway, David D. "A Saul Bellow Checklist." In his *The Absurd Hero in American Fiction: Updike, Styron, Bellow, Salinger.* Austin: University of Texas Press, 1966, 210-226. Rev. ed. 1970, 220-239.

Lercangée, F. *Saul Bellow: A Bibliography of Sources.* Brussels: Center for American Studies, 1977.

Nault, Marianne. *Saul Bellow: His Works and His Critics: An Annotated International Bibliography.* New York: Garland, 1977.

Noreen, Robert G. *Saul Bellow: A Reference Guide.* Boston: G. K. Hall, 1977-1978.

Schneider, Harold W. "Two Bibliographies—Saul Bellow/William Styron," *Critique,* 3 (1960), 71-91.

Sokoloff, B. A., and Mark E. Posner. *Saul Bellow: A Comprehensive Bibliography.* Folcroft, Pa.: Folcroft Press, 1971.

Interviews

Bellow, Saul. "Bellow on Himself and America," *Jerusalem Post Magazine*, 3 July 1975, pp. 11-12; 10 July 1975, p. 12.

_____. "Interview With Myself," *New Review*, 2, no. 18 (1975), 53-56.

_____. "On John Cheever: Speech to the American Academy of Arts and Letters," *New York Review of Books*, 30 (17 Feb. 1983), 38.

Boyers, Robert T. "Literature and Culture: An Interview With Saul Bellow," *Salmagundi*, no. 30 (Summer 1975), 6-23.

Bragg, Melvin. "Off the Couch by Christmas, Saul Bellow on His New Novel," *Listener* (London), 94 (20 Nov. 1975), 675-676.

Brandon, Henry. "Writer versus Readers: Saul Bellow," *London Sunday Times*, 18 Sept. 1966, p. 24.

Brans, Jo. "Common Needs, Common Preoccupations: An Interview with Saul Bellow," *Southwest Review*, 62 (Winter 1977), 1-19.

Breit, Harvey. "A Talk With Saul Bellow," *New York Times Book Review*, 20 Sept. 1953, p. 22. Reprinted in his *The Writer Observed*. New York: World, 1956, 271-274.

Bruckner, D. J. R. "A Candid Talk With Saul Bellow," *New York Times Magazine*, 133 (15 Apr. 1984), 2.

Bushinsky, Jay. "Saul Bellow on the Firing Line," *Chicago Daily News Panorama*, 13-14 Dec. 1975, p. 2.

Carroll, Paul. "Q & A—Saul Bellow Says a Few Words About His Critics and Himself," *Chicago Sun-Times—Bookweek*, 9 Nov. 1975, p. 8.

Clemons, Walter, and Jack Kroll. "America's Master Novelist: Interview With Saul Bellow," *Newsweek,* 1 Sept. 1975, pp. 33-35.

Coleman, Terry. "Saul Bellow Talks," *Manchester Guardian*, 23 Sept. 1966, p. 11.

Cook, Bruce. "Saul Bellow: A Mood of Protest," *Perspective on Ideas and the Arts* (Feb. 1963), 46-50.

Cromie, Robert. "Saul Bellow Tells (among other things) the Thinking Behind *Herzog*," *Chicago Tribune—Books Today*, 24 Jan. 1965, pp. 8-9.

Dommergues, Pierre. "Rencontre avec Saul Bellow," *Preuves*, 17 (Jan. 1967), 38-47.

Ellenberg, Al. "Saul Bellow Picks Another Fight," *Rolling Stone*, 4 Mar. 1982, pp. 14ff.

Enck, John. "Saul Bellow: An Interview," *Wisconsin Studies In Contem-*

porary Literature, 6 (Summer 1965), 156-160.

Epstein, Joseph. "A Talk With Saul Bellow," *New York Times Book Review,* 5 Dec. 1976, pp. 3, 92-93.

Galloway, David D. "An Interview With Saul Bellow," *Audit,* 3 (Spring 1963), 19-23.

Gray, Rockwell, Harry White, and Gerald Nemanic. "Interview with Saul Bellow," *TriQuarterly,* 60 (Spring-Summer 1985), 12-34.

Gutwillig, Robert. "Talk With Saul Bellow," *New York Times Book Review,* 20 Sept. 1964, p. 40-41.

Harper, Gordon Lloyd. "Saul Bellow," *Paris Review,* 9 (Winter 1965), 48-73. Reprinted in *Writers at Work: Paris Review Interviews,* ed. Alfred Kazin. 3rd series. London: Viking Press, 1967.

Henry, Jim Douglas. "Mystic Trade: The American Novelist Saul Bellow Talks to Jim Douglas Henry," *Listener* (London), 81 (22 May 1969), 705-707.

Heyman, Harriet. "Q & A With Saul Bellow," *Chicago Maroon,* 80 (4 Feb. 1972).

Hogue, Alice Allbright. "Saul Bellow Revisited at Home and at Work," *Chicago Daily News,* 18 Feb. 1967, Panorama: 5.

Howard, Jane. "Mr. Bellow Considers His Planet," *Life,* 68 (3 Apr. 1970), 57-60.

Illig, Joyce. "An Interview With Saul Bellow," *Publishers Weekly,* 204 (22 Oct. 1973), 74-77.

Kakutani, Michiko. "A Talk With Saul Bellow: On His Work and Himself," *New York Times Book Review,* 48 (13 Dec. 1981), 28-30.

Kulshrestha, Chirantan. "A Conversation With Saul Bellow," *Chicago Review,* 23; 24 (Spring-Summer 1972), 7-15.

"Literature and Culture: An Interview with Saul Bellow," *Salmagundi,* 30 (Summer 1975), 6-23.

Medwick, Cathleen. "A Cry of Strength: The Unfashionably Uncynical Saul Bellow," *Vogue* (Mar. 1982), 368-369, 426, 427.

Nachman, Gerald. "A Talk With Saul Bellow," *New York Post Magazine,* 4 Oct. 1964, p. 6.

Nash, Jay, and Ron Offen. "Saul Bellow," *Literary Times* (Chicago) (Dec. 1964), 10.

Pryce-Jones, David. "One Man and His Minyan," *Daily Telegraph Magazine,* 566 (3 Oct. 1975), 26-30.

Robinson, Robert. "Saul Bellow at 60—Talking to Robert Robinson," *Listener* (London), 93 (13 Feb. 1975), 218-219.

Roudane, Matthew. "An Interview With Saul Bellow," *Contemporary Literature,* 25 (Fall 1984), 265-280.

Sanoff, Alan P. "A Conversation With Saul Bellow—Matters Have Gotten Out of Hand in a Violent Society," *U. S. News & World Report*, 92 (28 June 1982), 49-50.

Saporta, Marc. "Interview avec Saul Bellow," *Le Figaro Littéraine*, 1193 (17 Mar. 1969), 24-25.

Simmons, Maggie. "Free to Feel: Conversation With Saul Bellow," *Quest*, 70 (Feb.-Mar. 1979), 30-36.

"Some Questions and Answers: An Interview With Saul Bellow," *Ontario Review*, 3 (1975), 51-61.

Steers, Nina. "Successor to Faulkner: An Interview With Saul Bellow," *Show*, 4 (Sept. 1964), 36-38.

Steinem, Gloria. "Gloria Steinem Spends a Day in Chicago With Saul Bellow," *Glamour* (July 1965), 98, 122, 125, 128.

Critical Studies: Books

Bakker, J. *Fiction as Survival Strategy: A Comparative Study of the Major Works of Ernest Hemingway and Saul Bellow*. Amsterdam: Rodopi, 1983.

Bradbury, Malcolm. *Saul Bellow*. London & New York: Methuen, 1982.

Braham, Jeanne. *A Sort of Columbus: The American Voyages of Saul Bellow's Fiction*. Athens: University of Georgia Press, 1984.

Clayton, John J. *Saul Bellow: In Defense of Man*. Bloomington: Indiana University Press, 1968. 2nd ed. 1979.

Cohen, Sarah Blacher. *Saul Bellow's Enigmatic Laughter*. Urbana: University of Illinois Press, 1974.

Detweiler, Robert. *Saul Bellow: A Critical Essay*. Grand Rapids, Mich.: Eerdmans, 1968.

Dutton, Robert R. *Saul Bellow*. New York: Twayne, 1971. Rev. ed. 1982.

Fuchs, Daniel. *Saul Bellow: Vision and Revision*. Durham, N.C.: Duke University Press, 1984.

A Garland to Saul Bellow. India: Treveni Publishers Ltd., 1981.

Goldman, L. H. *Saul Bellow's Moral Vision: A Critical Study of the Jewish Experience*. New York: Irvington Publishers, 1983.

Harris, Mark. *Saul Bellow: Drumlin Woodchuck*. Athens: University of Georgia Press, 1980.

Kulshrestha, Chirantan. *Saul Bellow: The Problem of Affirmation*. New Delhi: Arnold-Heineman, 1978.

Levy, Claude. *Les Romans de Saul Bellow: Tactiques Narratives et Strategies Oedipiennes.* Paris: Klincksiech, 1983.

McCadden, Joseph F. *Flight From Women in the Fiction of Saul Bellow.* Lanham, Mo.: University Press of America, 1980.

Malin, Irving. *Saul Bellow's Fiction.* Carbondale: Southern Illinois University Press, 1969.

Newman, Judie. *Saul Bellow and History.* New York: St. Martin's, 1984.

Opdahl, Keith. *The Novels of Saul Bellow: An Introduction.* University Park: Pennsylvania State University Press, 1967.

Porter, M. Gilbert. *Whence the Power? The Artistry and Humanity of Saul Bellow.* Columbia: University of Missouri Press, 1974.

Rodrigues, Eusebio L. *Quest for the Human: An Exploration of Saul Bellow's Fiction.* Lewisburg: Bucknell University Press, 1981.

Rovit, Earl. *Saul Bellow* (University of Minnesota Pamphlets on American Writers No. 65). Minneapolis: University of Minnesota Press, 1967.

Scheer-Schäzler, Brigitte. *Saul Bellow.* New York: Ungar, 1972.

Tanner, Tony. *Saul Bellow.* Edinburgh & London: Oliver & Boyd, 1965; New York: Barnes & Noble, 1965.

Vinoda and Shiv Kumar, ed. *Saul Bellow: A Symposium on the Jewish Question.* Hyderabad, India: Nachson Books, 1983.

Wilson, Jonathan. *On Bellow's Planet: Readings From the Dark Side.* Rutherford: Fairleigh Dickenson Press, 1985.

Critical Studies: Collections of Essays

Howe, Irving, ed. *Saul Bellow: Herzog: Text and Criticism.* New York: Viking, 1976.

Malin, Irving, ed. *Saul Bellow and the Critics.* New York: New York University Press, 1967.

Rovit, Earl, ed. *Saul Bellow: A Collection of Critical Essays.* Englewood Cliffs, N.J.: Prentice-Hall, 1975.

Schraepen, Edmond, ed. *Saul Bellow and His Work: Proceedings of a Symposium.* Brussels: Centrum Voor Taal-En Literatuurwetenschap Vrije Universiteit Brussel, 1978.

Trachtenberg, Stanley, ed. *Critical Essays on Bellow.* Boston: G. K. Hall, 1979.

Critical Studies: Journals and Special Issues

Critique: Studies in Modern Fiction (Saul Bellow Issue), 7 (Spring-Summer 1965).
Journal of English Studies (India) (Saul Bellow Issue), 12 (Nov. 1980).
Modern Fiction Studies (Saul Bellow Issue) (1979).
Modern Jewish Studies Annual II (Saul Bellow Issue) (1978).
Salmagundi (Saul Bellow Issue), 30 (Summer 1975).
Saul Bellow Journal, 2 (Fall-Winter 1982). This journal has been published twice yearly since 1982.
Saul Bellow Newsletter, 1 (Fall-Winter 1981). (Became by the next issue the *Saul Bellow Journal*, 2, no. 1, 1982.)
Studies in American Jewish Literature: Saul Bellow: The Vintage Years, 3, no. 1 (1977).
Studies in the Literary Imagination: Philosophical Dimensions of Saul Bellow's Literary Imagination, 17 (Fall 1984).

Critical Studies: Major Articles and Book Sections

Abbott, Porter. "Saul Bellow and the Lost Cause of Character," *Novel: A Forum on Fiction*, 13 (Winter 1980), 264-283.
Agress, H. "A Review of *To Jerusalem and Back: A Personal Account*," *Contemporary Judaism*, 31 (Fall-Winter 1976-1977), 101-103.
Aharoni, Ada. "The Cornerstone of Bellow's Art," *Saul Bellow Journal*, 2 (Fall-Winter 1982), 1-12.
_____. "Saul Bellow and Existentialism," *Saul Bellow Journal*, 2 (Spring-Summer 1983), 42-54.
_____. "*The Victim:* Freedom of Choice," *Saul Bellow Journal*, 4 (Fall-Winter 1985), 38-43.
_____. "Women in Saul Bellow's Novels," *Studies in American Jewish Literature*, 3 (1983), 99-112.
Alam, Fakrul. "A Possible Source of Augie's Axial Lines," *Notes on Contemporary Literature*, 10, no. 2 (1980), 6-7.
Aldridge, John W. "The Complacency of Herzog." In his *Time to Murder and Create: The Contemporary Novel in Crisis*. New York: McKay, 1966, 133-138. Collected in Howe, 440-444.
_____. "The Society of Three Novels." In his *In Search of Heresy: American Literature in an Age of Conformity*. New York: McGraw-Hill, 1956, 126-148. Reprinted in his *The Devil in the Fire: Retrospective Essays on American Literature and Culture*. New York: Harper, 1972, 131-139.

Alexander, Edward. "Imagining the Holocaust: *Mr. Sammler's Planet* and Others," *Judaism*, 22 (Winter 1973), 288-300.

Alhadeff, Barbara. "The Divided Self: A Laingian Interpretation of *Seize the Day*," *Studies in American Jewish Literature*, 3 (Spring 1977), 16-20.

Allen, Michael. "Idiomatic Language in Two Novels by Saul Bellow," *Journal of American Studies*, 1 (Oct. 1967), 275-280.

Alter, Robert. "Heirs of the Tradition." In his *Rogues Progress: Studies In The Picaresque Novel*. Cambridge, Mass.: Harvard University Press, 1964, 106-132.

_____. "Saul Bellow: A Dissent From Modernism." In his *After the Tradition: Essays on Modern Jewish Writing*. New York: Dutton, 1969, 95-115.

_____. "The Stature of Saul Bellow," *Midstream*, 10 (Dec. 1964), 3-15.

Anderson, David D. "The Novelist As Playwright: Saul Bellow on Broadway," *Saul Bellow Journal*, 5 (Winter 1986) (forthcoming).

_____. "The Room, The City and The War: Saul Bellow's *Dangling Man*," *Midwestern Miscellany* (1983), 49-59.

Atkins, Anselm. "The Moderate Optimism of Saul Bellow's *Herzog*," *Personalist*, 50 (Winter 1969), 117-129.

Atlas, James. "Interpreting The World: A Review of *Dean's December*," *Atlantic Monthly*, 249 (Feb. 1982), 78-82.

Atlas, Marilyn Judith. "The Figurine in the China Cabinet: Saul Bellow and the Nobel Prize," *MidAmerica*, 8 (1981), 36-49.

Axelrod, Steven Gould. "The Jewishness of Bellow's *Henderson*," *American Literature*, 47 (Nov. 1975), 439-443.

Axthelm, Peter M. "The Full Perception: Saul Bellow." In his *The Modern Confessional Novel*. New Haven: Yale University Press, 1967, 128-177.

Bailey, Jennifer M. "A Qualified Affirmation of Saul Bellow's Recent Work," *Journal of American Studies*, 7 (Apr. 1973), 67-76.

Baim, Joseph. "Escape From Intellection: Saul Bellow's *Dangling Man*," *University Review*, 37 (Autumn 1970), 28-34.

Baker, Carlos. "Bellow's Gift," *Theology Today*, 32 (Jan. 1976), 411-413.

Bakker, J. "In Search of Reality: Two American Heroes Compared," *Dutch Quarterly Review of Anglo-American Letters*, 4 (1972), 145-161.

Balbert, Peter. "Perceptions of Exile: Nabokov, Bellow and the Province of Art," *Studies in the Novel*, 14, no. 1 (1982), 95-104.

Bartz, F. K. "*Humboldt's Gift* and the Myth of the Artist in America," *South Carolina Review*, 15 (Fall 1982), 79-83.

Baruch, Franklin R. "Bellow and Milton: Professor Herzog in his Garden," *Critique*, 9, no. 3 (1967), 74-83.

Baumbach, Jonathan. "The Double Vision: *The Victim.*" In his *The Landscape of Nightmare: Studies in the Contemporary American Novel.* New York: New York University Press, 1965, 35-54.

Bayley, John. "By Way of Mr. Sammler," *Salmagundi*, 30 (Summer 1975), 24-33.

Belitt, Ben. "Saul Bellow: The Depth Factor," *Salmagundi*, 30 (Summer 1975), 57-65.

Bell, Pearl K. "American Fiction: Forgetting the Ordinary Truths," *Dissent*, 20 (Winter 1973), 26-34.

Bellamy, Michael O. "Bellow's More or Less Human Bestiaries: Augie March and *Henderson the Rain King*," *Ball State University Forum*, 23 (Winter 1982), 12-22.

Berets, Ralph. "Repudiation and Reality Instruction in Saul Bellow's Fiction," *Centennial Review*, 20 (Winter 1976), 75-101.

Berger, Alan. "Holocaust Responses II: Judaism as a Secular Value System." In his *Crisis and Covenant: The Holocaust in American Jewish Fiction.* New York: State University Press, 1985.

Bezanker, Abraham. "The Odyssey Of Saul Bellow," *Yale Review*, 58 (Spring 1969), 359-371.

Billy, Ted. "The Road of Excess: Saul Bellow's *Henderson the Rain King*," *Saul Bellow Journal*, 3 (Fall-Winter 1983), 8-17.

Bird, Christine. "The Return Journey in *To Jerusalem and Back*," *Melus*, 6, no. 4 (1979), 51-57.

Bolling, Douglass. "Intellectual and Aesthetic Dimensions of *Mr. Sammler's Planet*," *Journal of Narrative Technique*, 4 (Sept. 1974), 188-203.

Bordewyk, Gordon. "Saul Bellow's Death of a Salesman," *Saul Bellow Journal*, 1 (Fall-Winter 1981), 18-21.

Borrus, Bruce J. "Bellow's Critique of the Intellect," *Modern Fiction Studies*, 25 (Spring 1979), 29-45.

Boulot, Elizabeth. "Rupture, revolte et harmonie dans Herzog de Saul Bellow." In *Visages de l'harmonie dans la litterature anglo-americaine.* Reims: University of Reims Centre de Recherche sur l'Imaginaire dans les Litteratures de Langue Anglaise, 1982, 153-166ff.

Bowen, Robert O. "Bagels, Sour Cream and the Heart of the Current Novel," *Northwestern Review*, 1 (Spring 1957), 52-56.

Boyers, Robert. "Attitudes Toward Sex in American High Culture,"

Annals of the American Academy of Political and Social Sciences, 376 (Mar. 1968), 36-52.

_____. "Nature and Social Reality in Saul Bellow's *Mr. Sammler's Planet,*" *Critical Quarterly,* 15 (Autumn 1973), 251-271. Reprinted in *Salmagundi,* no. 30 (Summer 1975), 34-56.

Bradbury, Malcolm. "The It & The We: Saul Bellow's New Novel," *Encounter,* 45 (Nov. 1975), 61-67.

_____. "The Nightmare in Which I am Trying to Get a Good Night's Rest: Saul Bellow and Changing History." In *Saul Bellow and His Work: Proceedings of a Symposium,* ed. Edmond Schraepen, 11-29.

_____. "Saul Bellow and the Nobel Prize," *Journal of American Studies,* 11 (Apr. 1977), 3-12.

_____. "Saul Bellow's *Herzog,*" *Critical Quarterly,* 7, no. 3 (1965), 269-278.

_____. "Saul Bellow's *The Victim,*" *Critical Quarterly,* 5 (Summer 1963), 119-128.

Braham, Jeanne. "The Struggle at the Center: Dostoevsky and Bellow," *Saul Bellow Journal,* 2 (Fall-Winter 1982), 13-18.

Brans, Jo. "The Balance Sheet of Love: Money and Meaning in Bellow's *Herzog,*" *Notes on Modern American Literature,* 4 (Fall 1978), item 29.

_____. "The Dialectic of Hero and Anti-Hero in *Rameau's Nephew* and *Dangling Man,*" *Studies in the Novel,* 16 (Winter 1984), 435-450.

Brustein, Robert. "Saul Bellow on the Drag Strip," *New Republic,* 24 Oct. 1964, pp. 24-25. Reprinted in his *Seasons of Discontent, Dramatic Opinions 1959-1965.* New York: Simon & Schuster, 1965, 172-175.

Bullock, C. J. "On the Marxist Criticism of the Contemporary Novel in the United States: A Re-Evaluation of Saul Bellow," *Praxis,* 1, no. 2 (1975), 189-198.

_____. "A Reevaluation of Saul Bellow," *Praxis,* 5 (Winter 1976), 589ff.

Burns, Robert. "The Urban Experience: The Novels of Saul Bellow," *Dissent,* 24 (Winter 1969), 18-24.

Busby, Mark. "Castaways, Cannibals and the Function of Art in Saul Bellow's *Humboldt's Gift,*" *South Central Bulletin,* 41 (Winter 1981), 91-94.

Butler, Robert J. "The American Quest for Pure Movement in Bellow's *Henderson the Rain King,*" *Journal of Narrative Technique,* 14 (Winter 1984), 44-59.

Campbell, Jeff. "Bellow's Intimations of Immortality: *Henderson the Rain King,*" *Studies in the Novel,* 1 (Fall 1969), 323-333.

Casey, Jane Barnes. "Bellow's Gift," *Virginia Quarterly Review,* 52 (Winter 1976), 150-154.

Chametzky, Jules. "Notes on the Assimilation of the American-Jewish Writer: Abraham Cahan to Saul Bellow," *Jahrbuch fur Amerikastudien,* 9 (1964), 172-177.

Chapman, Sara S. "Melville and Bellow in the Real World: *Pierre* and *Augie March,*" *West Virginia University Bulletin, Philological Papers,* 18 (Sept. 1971), 51-57.

Chase, Richard. "The Adventures of Saul Bellow: Progress of a Novelist." In *Saul Bellow and the Critics,* ed. Irving Malin, 25-38.

Chavkin, Allan. "Baron Humboldt and Bellow's von Humboldt Fleisher: Success and Failure in *Humboldt's Gift,*" *Notes on Contemporary Literature,* 10, no. 2 (1980), 11-12.

_____. "Bellow and English Romanticism," *Studies in the Literary Imagination,* 17 (Fall 1984), 7-18.

_____. "Bellow's Alternative to the Wasteland: Romantic Theme and Form in *Herzog,*" *Studies in the Novel,* 11 (Fall 1979), 326-337.

_____. "Bellow's Investigation of the Social Meaning of Nothingness: Role Playing in *Herzog,*" *Yiddish,* 4 (Winter 1982), 48-57.

_____. "Father and Sons: 'Papa' Hemingway and Saul Bellow," *Papers on Language and Literature,* 19 (Fall 1983), 449-460.

_____. "The Feminism of *The Dean's December,*" *Studies in American Jewish Literature,* 3 (1983), 113-127.

_____. " 'The Hollywood Thread' and the First Draft of Saul Bellow's *Seize the Day,*" *Studies in the Novel,* 14 (Spring 1982), 82-94.

_____. "*Humboldt's Gift* and the Romantic Imagination," *Philological Quarterly,* 62 (Winter 1983), 1-20.

_____. "Ivan Karamazov's Rebellion and Bellow's *The Victim,*" *Papers on Language and Literature: A Journal for Scholars and Critics of Language and Literature,* 16 (1980), 316-320.

_____. "The Problem of Suffering in the Fiction of Saul Bellow," *Comparative Literature Studies,* 21 (Summer 1984), 161-174.

_____. "Recovering the World that is Buried Under the Debris: False Descriptions," *Saul Bellow Journal,* 1 (Spring 1982), 47-56.

_____. "Suffering and Wilhelm Reich's Theory of Character-Armoring in Saul Bellow's *Seize the Day*," *Essays in Literature*, 9 (Spring 1982), 133-137.

Chomsky, Noam. "Bellow, *To Jerusalem and Back*." In his *Towards a New Cold War: Essays on the Current Crisis and How We Got There*. New York: Pantheon, 1982, 299-307.

Clay, George R. "Jewish Hero in American Fiction," *Reporter* (Sept. 1956), 43-46.

Clayton, John J. *"Humboldt's Gift:* Transcendence and the Flight From Death." In *Saul Bellow and His Work: Proceedings of a Symposium*, ed. Edmond Schraepen, 31-48.

_____. "Saul Bellow's *Seize the Day:* A Study in Mid-Life Transition," *Saul Bellow Journal*, 5 (Winter 1986) (forthcoming).

_____. *"The Victim."* In *Saul Bellow: A Collection of Critical Essays*, ed. Earl Rovit, 31-51.

Clurman, Harold. Review of *The Last Analysis*, *Nation*, 19 Oct. 1964, pp. 256-257. Reprinted in his *The Naked Image: Observations on the Modern Theatre*. New York: Macmillan, 1966, 45-47.

Cohen, Joseph. "Saul Bellow Heroes in an Unheroic Age," *Saul Bellow Journal*, 3 (Fall-Winter 1983), 53-58.

Cohen, Sarah Blacher. "Comedy and Guilt in *Humboldt's Gift*," *Modern Fiction Studies*, 25 (Spring 1979), 47-57.

_____. "Saul Bellow's Chicago," *Modern Fiction Studies*, 24 (Spring 1978), 139-146.

_____. "Sex: Saul Bellow's Hedonistic Joke," *Studies in American Fiction*, 2 (Autumn 1974), 223-229.

Cohn, Ruby. *Dialogue in American Drama*. Bloomington: Indiana University Press, 1971, 192-197.

Colbert, Robert E. "Satiric Vision in *Herzog*," *Studies in Contemporary Satire*, 5 (1978), 22-33.

_____. "Saul Bellow's King of Confidence," *Yiddish*, 4 (Winter 1982), 41-47.

Cronin, Gloria L. "Art vs Anarchy: Citrine's Transcendental Experiment in *Humboldt's Gift*," *Indian Journal of American Studies*, 15 (Jan. 1985), 33-43.

_____. "Faith and Futurity: The Case For Survival in *Mr. Sammler's Planet*," *Literature and Belief*, 3 (1983), 97-108.

_____. *"Henderson the Rain King:* A Parodic Expose of the Modern Novel," *Arizona Quarterly*, 39 (Autumn 1983), 266-276.

_____. "Saul Bellow's Quarrel with Modernism in *Seize the Day*," *Encyclia*, 57 (1980), 95-102.

_____. "The Seduction of Tommy Wilhelm: A Post-Modernist Appraisal of *Seize the Day*," *Saul Bellow Journal*, 3 (Fall-Winter 1983), 18-27.

_____. "Through a Glass Brightly: Dean Corde's Escape From History in *The Dean's December*," *Saul Bellow Journal* (Winter 1986) (forthcoming).

Crozier, Robert D. "Theme in *Augie March*," *Critique*, 7 (Summer 1965), 18-32.

Curley, Thomas F. "A Clown Through and Through." *Commonweal*, 17 Apr. 1959, p. 84. Review of *Henderson the Rain King*.

Cushman, Keith. "Mr. Bellow's Sammler: The Evolution of a Contemporary Text," *Studies in the Novel*, 7 (Fall 1975), 425-444.

Davis, Robert Gorham. "The American Individualist Tradition: Bellow and Styron." In *The Creative Present: Notes on Contemporary American Fiction*, ed. Norma Balakian and Charles Simmons. New York: Doubleday, 1963, 111-141.

Demarest, David. "The Theme of Discontinuity in Saul Bellow's Fiction: 'Looking For Mr. Green' and 'A Father-To-Be,' " *Studies in Short Fiction*, 6 (Winter 1969), 175-186.

Detweiler, Robert. "Patterns of Rebirth in *Henderson the Rain King*," *Modern Fiction Studies*, 12 (Winter 1966-1967), 405-414.

Dietrich, Richard F. "The Biological Draft Dodger in Bellow's 'A Father-To-Be,' " *Studies in the Humanities*, 9, no. 1 (1981), 45-51.

Dougherty, David C. "Finding Before Seeking: Theme in *Henderson the Rain King* and *Humboldt's Gift*," *Modern Fiction Studies*, 25 (Spring 1979), 93-101.

Dudar, Helen. "The Graying of Saul Bellow," *Saturday Review*, 9 (Jan. 1982), 17-20.

Ehrenkrantz, L. "Bellow in Jerusalem," *Midstream*, 23 (Nov. 1977), 87-90.

Eisinger, Chester. "Saul Bellow: Love and Identity," *Accent*, 18 (Summer 1958), 179-203.

_____. "Saul Bellow: Man Alive, Sustained By Love." In his *Fiction of the Forties*. Chicago: University of Chicago Press, 1963, 341-362.

Elgin, Don D. "Order out of Chaos: Bellow's Use of the Picaresque in *Herzog*," *Saul Bellow Journal*, 3 (Spring/Summer 1984), 13-22.

Ellison, Ralph. "Society, Morality and the Novel." In *The Living Novel*, ed. Granville Hicks. New York: Macmillan, 1957, 58-91.

Enright, D. J. "Saul Bellow's New Novel: Good Exists and Cannot

Wholly Be Credited to Favourable Weather," *Listener*, 107 (Apr. 1982), 20.

Epstein, Seymour. "Bellow's Gift," *University of Denver Quarterly*, 10, no. 4 (1975), 35-50.

Estrin, Barbara L. "Recomposing Time: *Humboldt's Gift* and Ragtime," *Denver Quarterly*, 17 (Spring 1982), 16-31.

Evanier, David. "Bare Bones: A Review of *The Dean's December*," *National Review*, 34 (Apr. 1982), 364-366.

Fairman, Lynette A. "Finitude, Anxiety and Affirmation in Saul Bellow's Novels," *Saul Bellow Journal*, 3 (Spring-Summer 1984), 40-46.

Fiedler, Leslie. *The Jew in the American Novel.* Herzl Institute Pamphlet No. 10. New York: Herzl Press, 1959, 61-62.

_____. "The Fate of the Novel," *Kenyon Review*, 10 (Summer 1948), 519-527. Review of *Dangling Man*.

Field, Leslie. "Saul Bellow and the Critics—After the Nobel Award," *Modern Fiction Studies*, 25 (Spring 1979), 3-13.

_____. "Saul Bellow: From Montreal to Jerusalem," *Modern Jewish Studies Annual*, 4, no. 2 (1978), 51-59.

Finkelstein, Sidney. "Lost Social Convictions and Existentialism: Arthur Miller and Saul Bellow." In his *Existentialism and Alienation in American Literature.* New York: International Publishers, 1965, 252-269.

Fisch, Harold. "The Hero As Jew: Reflections on Herzog," *Judaism*, 17 (Winter 1968), 42-55.

Flamm, Dudley. "Herzog—Victim and Hero," *Zeitschrift fur Anglistick und Amerikanistik* (East Berlin), 17, no. 2 (1969), 174-188.

Flower, Dean. "Fiction Chronicle," *Hudson Review*, 35 (Summer 1982), 281-286. Review of *The Dean's December*.

Forest, Read. "Notes, Reviews and Speculations," *Epoch* (Fall 1964), 81. Review of *Herzog*.

Fossum, Robert H. "The Devil and Saul Bellow," *Comparative Literature Studies*, 3, no. 2 (1966), 197-208. Reprinted in George A. Panichas, *Mansions of the Spirit.* New York: Hawthorne, 1967, 345-355.

_____. "Inflationary Trends in the Criticism of Fiction: Four Studies of Saul Bellow," *Studies in the Novel*, 2 (Spring 1970), 99-104.

Freedman, Ralph. "Saul Bellow: The Illusion of Environment," *Wisconsin Studies in Contemporary Literature*, 1, no. 1 (1960), 50-65.

Friedman, Alan. "The Jews' Complaint in Recent American Fiction,"

Southern Review, new series 8 (Jan. 1972), 41-59.

Frohock, W. M. "Saul Bellow and His Penitent Picaro," *South West Review,* 53 (Winter 1968), 36-44.

Fuchs, Daniel. *"The Adventures of Augie March:* The Making of a Novel." In *Americana-Austriaca: Beitrage zur Amerikunde,* ed. Klaus Lanzinger. Vienna: Universitäts-Verlags-buchandlung, 1980.

_____. "Bellow and Freud," *Studies in the Literary Imagination,* 17 (Fall 1984), 59-80.

_____. *"Herzog:* The Making of a Novel." In *Critical Essays on Saul Bellow,* ed. Stanley Trachtenberg, 101-121.

_____. "Saul Bellow and the Modern Tradition," *Wisconsin Studies in Contemporary Literature,* 15 (Winter 1974), 67-89.

Galloway, David D. "The Absurd Man as Picaro: The Novels of Saul Bellow," *Texas Studies in Literature and Language,* 6 (Summer 1964), 226-254.

_____. "Moses-Bloom-Herzog: Bellow's Everyman," *Southern Review,* new series 2 (Jan. 1966), 61-76.

_____. *"Mr. Sammler's Planet:* Bellow's Failure of Nerve," *Modern Fiction Studies,* 19 (Spring 1973), 17-28.

_____. "Saul Bellow: The Gonzaga Manuscripts." In *Die Amerikanishe Short Story de Gegenwart: Interpretationen,* ed. Peter Freese. Berlin: Schmidt, 1976, 175-183.

Garret, George. "To Do Right in a Bad World: Saul Bellow's *Herzog,*" *Hollins Critic,* 2 (Apr. 1965), 1-12.

Geismar, Maxwell. "Saul Bellow: Novelist of the Intellectuals." In his *American Moderns: From Rebellion to Conformity.* New York: Hill & Wang, 1958, 210-224.

Gerbaud, Colette. "Adventures et sacre dans *Les Adventures d'Augie March.*" In *Aspects du Sacre dans la litterature anglo-americaine.* Reims: Publications du Centre de Recherche sur l'Imaginaire dans Litteratures de Langue Anglaise, 1979, 107-129.

Gerson, Steven M. "The New American Adam in *The Adventures of Augie March,*" *Modern Fiction Studies,* 25 (Spring 1979), 117-128.

Giannone, Richard. "Saul Bellow's Idea of Self: A Reading of *Seize the Day,*" *Renascence,* 27 (Summer 1975), 193-205.

Gilmore, Thomas B. "Allbee's Drinking," *Twentieth Century Literature,* 28, no. 4 (1982), 381-396.

Gindin, James. "Saul Bellow." In his *Harvest of a Quiet Eye: The Novel of Compassion.* Bloomington: Indiana University Press, 1971, 305-336.

Gindon, James. "The Fable Begins to Break Down," *Wisconsin Studies in Contemporary Literature,* 8 (Winter 1967), 1-18.

Gitenstein, Barbara R. "Saul Bellow and the Yiddish Literary Tradition," *Studies in American Jewish Literature,* 5, no. 2 (1979), 24-46.

_____. "Saul Bellow of the 1970's and the Contemporary Use of History in Jewish-American Literature," *Saul Bellow Journal,* 1 (Spring-Summer 1982), 7-17.

Glenday, Michael K. "The Consummating Glimpse: *Dangling Man's* Treacherous Reality," *Modern Fiction Studies,* 25 (Spring 1979), 139-148.

Glickman, Susan. "The World as Will and Idea: A Comparative Study of *An American Dream* and *Mr. Sammler's Planet,*" *Modern Fiction Studies,* 28 (Winter 1982-1983), 569-582.

Glicksberg, Charles I. "The Theme of Alienation in the American Jewish Novel," *Reconstruction,* 23 (Nov. 1957), 8-23.

Goldberg, Gerald Jay. "Life's Customer, Augie March," *Critique,* 3 (Summer 1960), 15-27.

Golden, Daniel. "Mystical Musings and Comic Confrontations," *Essays on Canadian Writing,* 22 (Summer 1981), 62-85.

Goldfinch, Michael. "A Journey to the Interior," *English Studies,* 43 (Oct. 1962), 439-443.

Goldman, L. H. "Bellow's Moses Herzog," *Explicator,* 37 (Summer 1979), 26.

_____. *"The Dean's December:* A Companion Piece to *Mr. Sammler's Planet,*" *Saul Bellow Journal* (Summer 1986) (forthcoming).

_____. "On the Character of Ravitch in Saul Bellow's *Herzog,*" *American Notes and Queries,* 19, nos. 7 & 8 (1981), 115-116.

_____. "Saul Bellow and the Israeli Critics," *Midstream* (forthcoming 1986).

_____. "Saul Bellow and the Philosophy of Judaism," *Studies in the Literary Imagination,* 17 (Fall 1984), 81-96.

_____. "Saul Bellow's Misuse of Hebrew and Yiddish in *Herzog,*" *Jewish Language Review,* 2 (1982), 75-79.

_____. "The Source for *Mr. Sammler's Planet,*" *American Notes and Queries,* 20 (Mar. 1982), 117-119.

Goldman, Mark. *"Humboldt's Gift* and the Case of the Split Protagonist," *Modern Language Studies,* 11 (Spring 1981), 3-16.

Gollin, Rita K. "Understanding Fathers in American Jewish Fiction," *Centennial Review,* 18 (Summer 1974), 273-287.

Goodheart, Eugene. "Radicalism and Fashions in Culture," *Modern Occasions,* 2 (Winter 1972), 106-112.

Gordon, Andrew. "Pushy Jew: Leventhal in *The Victim*," *Modern Fiction Studies*, 25 (Spring 1979), 129-138.

_____. "Shakespeare's *The Tempest* and Yeats' 'Sailing To Byzantium' in *Seize the Day*," *Saul Bellow Journal*, 4 (Fall-Winter 1985).

Greenberg, Alvin. "The Death of the Psyche: A Way to the Self in the Contemporary Novel," *Criticism*, 8 (Winter 1966), 1-18.

Gross, Theodore L. "Saul Bellow: *The Victim* and The Hero." In his *The Heroic Ideal in American Literature*. New York: Free Press, 1971, 243-261.

Guerard, Albert J. "Saul Bellow and The Activists: On *The Adventures of Augie March*," *Southern Review*, 3 July 1967, pp. 582-596.

Guthridge, George. "The Structure of Twentieth-Century Society: The Concept of the Intellectual in Bellow's *Mr. Sammler's Planet*," *Saul Bellow Journal*, 1, no. 1 (1981), 6-10.

Guttmann, Allen. "Bellow's Henderson," *Critique*, 7 (Spring-Summer 1965), 33-42.

_____. "The Conversion of the Jews." In *The Comic Imagination in American Literature*, ed. Louis D. Rubin, Jr. New Brunswick, N.J.: Rutgers University Press, 1978, 329-338.

_____. "Mr. Bellow's America." In his *The Jewish Writer in America: Assimilation and the Crisis of Identity*. New York: Oxford University Press, 1971, 178-221.

_____. "Saul Bellow's Mr. Sammler," *Wisconsin Studies in Contemporary Literature*, 14, no. 2 (1973), 157-168.

Halio, Jay L. "Contemplation, Fiction, and the Writer's Sensibility," *Southern Review*, new series 19 (Jan. 1983), 203-218.

Hall, James. "Portrait of the Artist as a Self-Creating, Self-Vindicating, High Energy Man: Saul Bellow." In his *The Lunatic Giant in the Drawing Room: The British and American Novel Since 1930*. Bloomington: Indiana University Press, 1968, 127-180.

Hall, Joe. "*The Dean's December*: A Separate Act of a Separatist," *Saul Bellow Journal*, 5 (Summer 1986) (forthcoming).

Halperin, Irving. "Saul Bellow and the Moral Imagination," *Judaism*, 28 (Winter 1979), 23-30. Also in *New England Review*, 14 (1979), 75-88.

Handy, William J. "Saul Bellow and the Naturalistic Hero," *Texas Studies in Literature and Language*, 5 (Winter 1964), 538-554.

Harper, Howard M. "Saul Bellow—The Heart's Ultimate Need." In his *Desperate Faith: A Study of Bellow, Salinger, Mailer, Baldwin, and Updike*. Chapel Hill: University of North Carolina Press, 1967, 7-64.

_____. "Trends in Recent American Fiction," *Wisconsin Studies in Contemporary Literature*, 12 (Spring 1971), 204-229.

Harris, James Neil. "One Critical Approach to *Mr. Sammler's Planet*," *Twentieth Century Literature*, 18 (Oct. 1972), 235-250.

Hassan, Ihab. "Five Faces of a Hero," *Critique*, 3 (Summer 1960), 28-36.

_____. "Quest and Affirmation in *Henderson the Rain King*." In *The Modern American Novel: Essays in Criticism*, ed. Max Westbrook. New York: Random House, 1966, 223-229.

_____. "Saul Bellow: The Quest and Affirmation of Reality." In his *Radical Innocence*. Princeton, N.J.: Princeton University Press, 1961, 290-324.

_____. "The Way Down and Out," *Virginia Quarterly Review*, 39 (Winter 1963), 81-93.

Held, George. "Men on the Moon: American Novelists Explore Lunar Space," *Michigan Quarterly Review*, 18 (Spring 1979), 318-342.

Hermans, Rob. "The Mystical Element in Saul Bellow's *Herzog*," *Dutch Quarterly Review of Anglo-American Letters*, 11, no. 2 (1981), 104-117.

Hewes, Henry. "A Muse of Fire," *Saturday Review*, 17 Oct. 1964, p. 29.

Hicks, Granville. "Saul Bellow." In his *Literary Horizons: A Quarter of a Century of American Fiction*. New York: New York University Press, 1970, 49-63.

Hirsch, David. "Jewish Identity and Jewish Suffering in Bellow, Malamud and Philip Roth." In *Jewish Book Annual*. 29th ed. New York: Jewish Book Council, 1971, 17ff.

Hoffman, Michael J. "From Cohn To Herzog," *Yale Review*, 58 (Spring 1969), 342-358.

Hollahan, Eugene. "Bellow's Affirmation of Individual Value Via Classical Plot Structure," *Saul Bellow Journal*, 2, no. 1 (1982), 23-31.

_____. "Crisis in Bellow's Novels; Some Data and a Conjecture," *Studies in the Novel*, 15 (Fall 1983), 249-264.

Howe, Irving. "Down and Out in New York." In his *Saul Bellow: Herzog*, 391-400.

_____. "Mass Society and Post-Modern Fiction," *Partisan Review*, 26 (Summer 1959), 420-436. Reprinted in his *A World More Attractive*. New York: Horizon, 1963, 77-97.

_____. "Review of *Mr. Sammler's Planet*," *Harper's Magazine*, 240 (Feb. 1970), 106-108.

Hruska, Thomas. "Henderson's Riches," *Journal of English Studies* (India), 12, no. 1 (1980), 779-784.

Hughes, Daniel J. "Reality and the Hero: *Lolita* and *Henderson the Rain King*," *Modern Fiction Studies*, 6 (Winter 1960-1961), 345-364. Collected in *Saul Bellow and the Critics*, ed. Irving Malin.

Hull, Byron D. "*Henderson the Rain King* and William James," *Criticism*, 13 (Fall 1971), 402-414.

Hux, Samuel. "Character and Form in Bellow," *Forum*, 12, 1 (1974), 34-38.

Hymas, Barry. "Letter to Bellow," *Reconstructionist*, 13 Nov. 1964, pp. 13-15.

Jefchak, Andrew. "Family Struggles in *Seize the Day*," *Studies in Short Fiction*, 11 (Summer 1974), 297-302.

Johnson, Diane. "Point of Departure," *New York Review of Books*, 29 Mar. 1982, pp. 6, 8.

_____. "Saul Bellow as Reformer." In her *Terrorists and Novelists*. New York: Knopf, 1982, 134-140.

Jones, D. A. N. "What about the Workers?," *New Statesman*, 3 June 1966, pp. 819-820.

Jones, Roger. "Artistry and the Depth of Life: Aspects of Attitude and Technique in *Mr. Sammler's Planet*," *Anglo-Welsh Review*, 25 (Spring 1976), 138-153.

Josipovici, Gabriel. "Bellow and Herzog," *Encounter*, 37, no. 5 (1971), 49-55. Collected in *Saul Bellow: Herzog*, ed. Irving Howe, 401-415.

_____. "*Herzog*: Freedom and Wit." In his *The World and the Book: A Study On Modern Fiction*. Stanford, Cal.: Stanford University Press, 1971, 221-235.

_____. "Introduction." In *The Portable Saul Bellow*. New York: Viking, 1974, vii-xxiv.

Kaler, Ann K. "Saul Bellow's Use of the Journal/Diary Form in His Development of the Odyssean Myth in his Novel *Dangling Man*," *Saul Bellow Journal*, 5 (Winter 1986) (forthcoming).

Kannan, Lakshmi. "Professor Herzog's Academy," *Journal of English Studies* (India), 12, no. 1 (1980), 785-789.

_____. "That Small Voice in Bellow's Fiction," *Visvabharati Quarterly* (India), 42 (1977), 191-206.

Kaplan, Harold. "The Second Fall of Man," *Salmagundi*, 30 (Summer 1975), 66-89.

Karl, Frederick. "Picaresque and the American experience," *Yale Review*, 57 (Winter 1968), 196-212.

Kazin, Alfred. "The Earthly City of the Jews: Bellow To Singer." In his *Bright Book of Life*. Boston: Little, Brown, 1973, 125-162.

_____. "Psychoanalysis and Literary Culture Today," *Partisan Review*, 26 (Winter 1957), 45-55.

Kegan, Robert. *The Sweeter Welcome: Voice for a Vision of Affirmation: Bellow, Malamud and Martin Buber*. Needham Heights, Mass.: Humanitas Press, 1976.

Kehler, Joel R. "Henderson's Sacred Science," *Centennial Review*, 24, 2 (1980), 402-414.

Kemnitz, Charles. "Narration and Consciousness in *Herzog*," *Saul Bellow Journal*, 1 (Spring-Summer 1982), 1-6.

Kennedy, William. "If Saul Bellow Doesn't Have a True Word to Say He Keeps His Mouth Shut," *Esquire*, 97 (Feb. 1982), 49-54.

Kenner, Hugh. "From Lower Bellowvia: Leopold Bloom With a Ph.D.," *Harper's Magazine*, 264 (Feb. 1982), 62-65.

Kernan, Alvin B. "Mighty Poets in their Misery Dead: The Death of the Poet in Saul Bellow's *Humboldt's Gift*." In his *The Imaginary Library: An Essay On Literature and Society*. Princeton, N.J.: Princeton University Press, 1982, 35-65.

Kerner, David. "The Incomplete Dialectic of *Humboldt's Gift*," *Dalhousie Review*, 62 (Spring 1982), 14-35.

Kindilien, Glenn A. "The Meaning of the Name 'Green' in Saul Bellow's 'Looking for Mr. Green,' " *Studies in Short Fiction*, 15 (Winter 1978), 104-107.

Kistler, Suzanne. "Bellow's Man-Eating Comedy: Cannibal Imagery in *Humboldt's Gift*," *Notes on Modern American Literature*, 2 (1977), item 8.

_____. "Epic Structure and Statement in *Mr. Sammler's Planet*," *Notes on Modern American Literature*, 2 (Fall 1978), item 28.

Klein, Jeffrey. "Armies of the Planet: A Comparative Analysis of Norman Mailer's and Saul Bellow's Political Visions," *Soundings: An Interdisciplinary Journal*, 58 (1975), 69-83.

Klein, Marcus. "A Discipline of Nobility: Saul Bellow's Fiction," *Kenyon Review*, 24 (Spring 1962), 203-206.

Knapp, Josephine Z. "Jewish America: Saul Bellow." In her *The Trial of Judaism in Contemporary Jewish Writing*. Urbana: University of Illinois Press, 1975, 126-156.

Kondo, Kyoko. "Pursuit of One Theme: Saul Bellow's Early Novels, *Dangling Man*, *The Victim* and *Seize the Day*," *Sophia English Studies* (Japan), 3 (1978), 86-98.

Kremer, S. Lillian. "The Holocaust in *Mr. Sammler's Planet,*" *Saul Bellow Journal,* 4 (Fall-Winter 1985), 19-31.
_____. "The Holocaust in *The Victim,*" *Saul Bellow Journal,* 2 (Spring-Summer 1983), 15-23.
_____. "*Seize the Day:* Intimations of Anti-Hasidic Satire," *Yiddish,* 4 (Winter 1982), 32-40.
Kulshrestha, Chirantan. "Affirmation in Saul Bellow's *Dangling Man,*" *Indian Journal of American Studies,* 5 (1976), 21-36.
_____. "The Making of Saul Bellow's Fiction: Notes From the Underground," *American Studies International,* 19, no. 2 (1981), 48-56.
Kumar, P. Shiv. "From Kavanah to Mitzvah: A Perspective on *Herzog* and *Mr. Sammler's Planet,*" *Indian Journal of American Studies,* 10 (July 1980), 30-39.
_____. "*Yahudim* and *Ostjude:* Social Stratification in *Mr. Sammler's Planet,*" *Literary Half-Yearly,* 21, no. 2 (1980), 53-67.
Kunar, F. M. "The European Culture Game: Mr. Bellow's Planet," *English Studies,* 53 (Dec. 1972), 531-544.
Lavine, S. D. "In Defiance of Reason: Saul Bellow's *To Jerusalem and Back,*" *Studies in American Jewish Literature,* 4, no. 2 (1978), 72-83.
Leach, Elsie. "From Ritual to Romance Again: *Henderson the Rain King,*" *Western Humanities Review,* 14 (Spring 1960), 223-224.
Lehan, Richard. "Existentialism in Recent American Fiction: The Demonic Quest," *Texas Studies in Literature and Language,* 1 (Summer 1959), 181-200.
_____. "Into the Ruins: Saul Bellow and Walker Percy." In his *A Dangerous Crossing: French Literary Existentialism and the Modern American Novel.* Carbondale: Southern Illinois University Press, 1973, 107-145.
Lemco, Gary. "Bellow's *Herzog:* A Flight of the Heart," *Saul Bellow Journal,* 3 (Fall-Winter 1983), 38-46.
_____. "Theatrical Elements in *Herzog* or, An Act of the Heart," *Studies in Literature,* 3 (Spring 1977), 7-16.
Lenzner, Robert. "A Novel of Politics, Wit and Sorrow," *New York Times Book Review,* 10 Jan. 1982, pp. 1, 22.
Le Pellec, Yves. "New York in Summer: Its Symbolic Function in *The Victim,*" *Caliban,* 8 (1971), 101-110.
Levenson, J. C. "Bellow's *Dangling Man,*" *Critique,* 3 (Summer 1960), 3-14. Collected in *Saul Bellow and the Critics,* ed. Irving Malin, 39-50.
Lewis, R. W. B. "Recent Fiction: Picaro and Pilgrim." In *A Time of*

Harvest: American Literature 1910-1960, ed. Robert E. Spiller. New York: Hill & Wang, 1962, 144-153.

Libowitz, R. "A Review of *To Jerusalem and Back: A Personal Account*," *Reconstructionist*, 43 (1977), 24.

Lippit, Noriko M. "A Perennial Survivor: Saul Bellow's Heroine in the Desert," *Studies in Short Fiction*, 12 (Summer 1975), 281-283.

Lister, Paul A. "The Compleat Fool in *Seize the Day*," *Saul Bellow Journal*, 3 (Spring-Summer 1984), 32-59.

Lucko, Peter. "*Herzog*—Modell der acceptance Eine Erwiderung," *Zeit für Anglistik un Amerikanistik*, 17 (1969), 189-195.

Lutwack, Leonard. "Bellow's Odyssey." In his *Heroic Fiction: The Epic Tradition and American Novels of the Twentieth Century*. Carbondale: Southern Illinois University Press, 1971, 88-121.

Lyons, Bonnie. "From *Dangling Man* to 'Colonies of the Spirit,' " *Studies in American Jewish Literature*, 4, no. 2 (1978), 45-50.

McConnell, Frank. "Saul Bellow and the Terms of Our Contract." In his *Four Post-War American Novelists: Bellow, Mailer, Barth, and Pynchon*. Chicago: University of Chicago Press, 1977, 1-57.

McSweeney, Kerry. "Saul Bellow and the Life to Come," *Critical Quarterly*, 18 (Spring 1976), 67-72.

Malin, Irving. "Bummy's Analysis." In *Saul Bellow: A Collection of Critical Essays*, ed. Earl Rovit, 115-121.

_____. *Jews and Americans*. Carbondale: Southern Illinois University Press, 1965, 7-8, 23-29, 47-51, 73-75, 95-99, 116-119, 132-134, 149-152, 168-169.

_____. "Seven Images." In his *Saul Bellow and the Critics*. New York: New York University Press, 1967, 142-176.

Maloney, Stephen R. "Half-Way to Byzantium: *Mr. Sammler's Planet* and the Modern Tradition," *South Carolina Review*, 6 (Nov. 1973), 31-40.

Mandra, Mihail. "Saul Bellow's Novel in the Context of European Thought: A Greek World," *Synthesis*, 7 (1980), 191-205.

Markos, Donald. "Life Against Death in *Henderson the Rain King*," *Modern Fiction Studies*, 17 (Summer 1971), 193-205.

Le Master, J. R. "Saul Bellow: On Looking For a Way Through the Cracks." In *American Bypaths: Essays in Honor of E. Hudson Long*, ed. Robert G. Colmer and Jack W. Herring. Waco, Tex.: Baylor University Press, 1980, 109-144.

Mathis, James C. "The Theme of *Seize the Day*," *Critique: Studies in Modern Fiction*, 7 (Spring-Summer 1965), 43-45.

Maw, Joe. "Method in His Madness: Bellow Develops the Theme of

Insanity," *Saul Bellow Journal,* 3 (Spring-Summer 1984), 1-12.

Mellard, James M. "Consciousness Fills the Void: Herzog, History, and the Hero in the Modern World," *Modern Fiction Studies,* 25 (Spring 1979), 75-92.

_____. "*Dangling Man:* Saul Bellow's Lyrical Experiment," *Ball State University Forum,* 15, no. 2 (1974), 67-74.

Meyers, Jeffrey. "Breughel and *Augie March,*" *American Literature,* 49 (Mar. 1977), 113-119.

Michelson, Bruce. "The Idea of Henderson," *Twentieth Century Literature,* 27 (Winter 1981), 309-324.

Montrose, David. "Conventional Wisdom," *New Statesman,* 103 (28 May 1982), 20-21, 22.

Morahg, Gilead. "The Art of Dr. Tamkin: Matter and Manner in *Seize the Day,*" *Modern Fiction Studies,* 25 (Spring 1979), 103-116.

Mosher, Harold F. "Herzog's Quest," *Le voyage dans la littérature anglo-saxonne.* Nice: Didier, 1972, 169-179.

_____. "The Synthesis of Past and Present in Saul Bellow's *Herzog,*" *Wascana Review,* 6, no. 1 (1971), 28-38.

Moss, Judith. "The Body as Symbol in Saul Bellow's *Henderson the Rain King,*" *Literature and Psychology,* 20, no. 2 (1970), 51-61.

Mowat, John. "*Humboldt's Gift:* Bellow's Dejection Ode," *Dutch Quarterly Review of Anglo-American Letters,* 8 (1978), 184-201.

Mudrick, Marvin. "Who Killed Herzog? Or, Three American Novelists." In his *On Culture and Literature.* New York: Horizon, 1970, 200-235.

Nakajima, Kenji. "A Study of Saul Bellow's 'A Sermon by Dr. Pep,' " *Kyushu American Literature,* 17 (1976), 12-19.

Nassar, Joseph M. "The World Within: Image Clusters in *Herzog,*" *Saul Bellow Journal,* 2 (Spring-Summer 1983), 24-29.

Nault, Marianne. "Humboldt the First," *American Notes and Queries,* 15 (Winter 1977), 88-89.

Newman, Judie. "Bellow and Nihilism: *The Dean's December,*" *Studies in the Literary Imagination,* 17 (Fall 1984), 111-122.

_____. "Bellow's Indian Givers: *Humboldt's Gift,*" *Journal of American Studies,* 15 (Aug. 1981), 231-238.

_____. "Bellow's Sixth Sense: The Sense of History," *Canadian Review of American Studies,* 13 (Spring 1982), 39-52.

_____. "*Mr. Sammler's Planet:* Wells, Hitler and the World State," *Dutch Quarterly Review of Anglo-American Letters,* 13, no. 1 (1983), 55-71.

_____. "Saul Bellow and Trotsky: 'The Mexican General,' " *Saul Bellow Journal*, 1 (Fall-Winter 1981), 26-31.

Nilsen, Helge N. "Anti-Semitism and Persecution Complex: A Comment on Saul Bellow's *The Victim*," *English Studies*, 60 (Apr. 1979), 183-191.

_____. "Saul Bellow and Wilhelm Reich," *American Studies in Scandinavia*, 10 (1978), 81-91.

Opdahl, Keith. "God's Braille: Concrete Detail in Saul Bellow's Fiction," *Studies in American Jewish Literature*, 4, no. 2 (1978), 60-71.

_____. "The Mental Comedies of Saul Bellow." In *From Hester Street to Hollywood: The Jewish American Stage and Screen*, ed. Sarah Blacher Cohen. Bloomington: Indiana University Press, 1983, 183-196.

_____. "Stillness in the Midst of Chaos: Plot in the Novels of Saul Bellow," *Modern Fiction Studies*, 25 (Spring 1979), 15-28.

_____. "True Impressions: Saul Bellow's Realistic Style." In *Saul Bellow and His Work: Proceedings of a Symposium*, ed. Edmond Schraepen, 61-71.

Overbeck, Pat T. "The Women in *Augie March*," *Texas Studies in Language and Literature*, 10 (Fall 1969), 471-484.

Overton, Harvey. "Sharing *Mr. Sammler's Planet:* Intellect and ConScience in Science and Technology," *Journal of General Education*, 32 (Winter 1981), 309-319.

Park, Sue S. "The Keystone and the Arch: Another Look at Structure in *Herzog*," *Notes on Modern American Literature*, 2 (Fall 1978), item 30.

Pearce, Richard. "The Ambiguous Assault of Henderson and Herzog." In *Saul Bellow: A Collection of Critical Essays*, ed. Earl Rovit, 72-80.

_____. "Harlequin: The Character of the Clown in *Henderson the Rain King* and John Hawkes' *Second Skin*." In his *Stages of the Clown: Perspectives on Modern Fiction From Dostoevsky to Beckett*. Champaign: University of Illinois Press, 1970, 102-116.

Phillips, Louis. "The Novelist as Playwright: Baldwin, McCullers, and Bellow." In *Modern American Drama Essays in Criticism*, ed. William F. Taylor. De Land, Fla.: Everett/Edwards, 1968, 145-162.

Pinsker, Sanford. "Bellow's *Seize The Day*," *Explicator*, 41 (Spring 1983), 60-61.

_____. "Jerusalem Without Fictions," *Jewish Spectator*, 42 (Spring 1977), 36-37.

_____. "A Kaddish For Valeria Raresh: Dean Albert Corde's

Long Dark Month of the Soul," *Studies in American Jewish Literature*, 3 (1983), 128-137.

_____. "Meditations Interruptus: Saul Bellow's Ambivalent Novel of Ideas," *Studies in Jewish American Literature*, 4, no. 2 (1978), 22-32.

_____. "Moses Herzog's Fall Into the Quotidian," *Studies in the Twentieth Century*, 14 (Fall 1974), 105-116.

_____. "*Rameau's Nephew* and Saul Bellow's *Dangling Man*," *Notes on Modern American Literature*, 4 (1980), item 22.

_____. "Saul Bellow Going Everywhere: History, American Letters and the Transcendental Itch," *Saul Bellow Journal*, 3 (Spring-Summer 1984), 47-52.

_____. "Saul Bellow, Soren Kierkegaard and the Question of Boredom," *Centennial Review*, 24 (Winter 1980), 118-125.

_____. "Sustaining Community of Reality Instructors: The City in Saul Bellow's Later Fiction," *Studies in American Jewish Literature*, 3 (Spring 1977), 25-30.

Podhoretz, Norman. "The Adventures of Saul Bellow." In his *Doings and Undoings: The Fifties and After in American Writing*. New York: Farrar, Straus & Giroux, 1964, 205-227.

_____. "Review of *Henderson the Rain King*," *New York Herald Tribune Book Review*, 22 Feb. 1959, p. 3.

Poirier, Richard. "Herzog, or Bellow in Trouble." In *Saul Bellow: A Collection of Critical Essays*, ed. Earl Rovit, 81-89.

Popkin, Henry. "American Comedy," *Kenyon Review*, 16 (Spring 1954), 329-334.

Porter, M. Gilbert. "*Henderson the Rain King*: An Orchestration of Soul Music," *New England Review*, 1 (Spring 1972), 24-33.

_____. "Hitch Your Agony to a Star: Saul Bellow's Transcendental Vision." In *Saul Bellow and His Work: Proceedings of a Symposium*, ed. Edmond Schraepen, 73-88.

_____. "Is the Going Up Worth the Coming Down? Transcendental Dualism in Saul Bellow's Fiction," *Studies in the Literary Imagination*, 17 (Fall 1984S), 19-38.

_____. "The Scene as Image: A Reading of *Seize the Day*." In *Saul Bellow: A Collection of Critical Essays*, ed. Earl Rovit, 52-71.

Possler, K. E. "Cannibalism in *Humboldt's Gift*," *Gypsy Scholar*, 5 (1978), 18-21.

Radner, Sanford. "The Woman Savior in *Humboldt's Gift*," *Saul Bellow Journal*, 1 (Fall 1981), 22-25.

Rahv, Philip. "Saul Bellow's Progress." In his *Myth and the Powerhouse*.

New York: Farrar, Straus & Giroux, 1965, 218-224. Reprinted in his *Literature and the Sixth Sense*. Boston: Houghton Mifflin, 1969.

Richmond, Lee J. "The Maladroit, The Medico, and The Magician: Saul Bellow's *Seize the Day*," *Twentieth Century Literature*, 19, no. 1 (1973), 15-26.

Rodgers, Bernard F., Jr. "Apologia Pro Vita Sua: Biography and Autobiography," *Kwartalnik Neofilologiczny*, 27, no. 4 (1980), 439-454.

Rodrigues, Eusebio. "Augie March's Mexican Adventures," *Indian Journal of American Studies*, 8, no. 3 (1978), 39-43.

_____. "Bellow's Africa," *American Literature*, 43 (May 1971), 242-256.

_____. "Bellow's Confidence Man," *Notes on Contemporary Literature*, 3, no. 1 (1973), 6-8.

_____. "Beyond All Philosophies," *Studies in the Literary Imagination*, 17 (Fall 1984), 97-110.

_____. "Herzog and Hegel," *Notes on Modern American Literature*, 2 (1978), item 16.

_____. "Koheleth in Chicago: Quest for the Real in 'Looking for Mr. Green,'" *Studies in Short Fiction*, 11 (Fall 1974), 387-393.

_____. "Reichianism in *Henderson the Rain King*," *Criticism*, 15 (Summer 1973), 212-233.

_____. "A Rough-Hewn Heroine of Our Time: Saul Bellow's 'Leaving The Yellow House,'" *Saul Bellow Journal*, 1, no. 1 (Fall-Winter 1981), 11-17.

_____. "Saul Bellow's Henderson as America," *Centennial Review*, 20 (Spring 1976), 189-195.

_____. "Saul Bellow's Henderson as Mankind and Messiah," *Renascence*, 35 (Summer 1983), 235-246.

_____. "The Two Manifestations of Jeremiah: Bellow's Creative Use of a Morsel of Personal Experience," *Notes on Modern American Literature*, 5 (1980), item 6.

Rooke, Constance. "Saul Bellow's 'Leaving The Yellow House': The Trouble With Women," *Studies in Short Fiction*, 14 (Spring 1976), 184-187.

Rosenfeld, Alvin H. "Saul Bellow on the Soul," *Midstream*, 23 (Dec. 1977), 47-59.

Roudane, Matthew. "A cri de coeur: The Inner Reality of Saul Bellow's *The Dean's December*," *Studies in the Humanities*, 11 (Dec. 1984), 5-17.

_____. "Discordant Timbre in Saul Bellow's 'Him With His Foot In His Mouth,' " *Saul Bellow Journal*, 4 (Fall-Winter 1985).

Rovit, Earl. "Bellow in Occupancy," *American Scholar*, 34 (Spring 1965), 292-298. Collected in *Saul Bellow and the Critics*, ed. Irving Malin, 177-183.

_____. "Jewish Humor and American Life," *American Scholar*, 36 (Spring 1967), 237-245. Collected in *Saul Bellow: Herzog*, ed. Irving Howe, 510-519.

_____. "Saul Bellow and Norman Mailer: Secret Sharers." In *Saul Bellow: A Collection of Critical Essays*, ed. Rovit, 161-170.

_____. "Saul Bellow and the Concept of the Survivor." In *Saul Bellow and His Work: Proceedings of a Symposium*, ed. Edmond Schraepen, 89-101.

Rubin, Louis D., Jr. "Southerners and Jews," *Southern Review*, new series 2 (July 1966), 697-713.

Russell, Mariann. "White Man's Black Man: Three Views," *College Language Association Journal*, 17 (Sept. 1973), 93-100.

Samuel, Maurice. "My Friend, The Late Moses Herzog," *Midstream*, 12 (Apr. 1966), 3-25.

Samuels, Charles Thomas. "Bellow on Modernism," *New Republic*, 7 Feb. 1970, pp. 27-30. Review of *Mr. Sammler's Planet*.

Saposnik, Irving S. "*Dangling Man:* A Partisan Review," *Centennial Review*, 26 (Fall 1982), 388-395.

Saposnik, S. "A Review Essay of *To Jerusalem and Back*," *Judaism*, 28 (Winter 1979), 42-50.

Schechner, Mark. "Saul Bellow and Ghetto Cosmopolitanism," *Studies in American Jewish Literature*, 4, no. 2 (1978), 33-44.

Scheer-Schäzler, Brigitte. "Epistemology as a Narrative Device in the Work of Saul Bellow." In *Saul Bellow and His Work: Proceedings of a Symposium*, ed. Edmond Schraepen, 103-118.

Scheffler, Judith. "Two-Dimensional Dynamo: The Female Character in Saul Bellow's Novels," *Wascana Review*, 16 (Fall 1981), 3-19.

Scheick, William J. "Circle Sailing in Bellow's *Mr. Sammler's Planet*," *Essays in Literature*, 5 (Spring 1978), 95-101.

Schorer, Mark. "A Book of Yes and No," *Hudson Review*, 7 (Spring 1954), 136-141.

_____. "Fictions Not Wholly Achieved," *Kenyon Review*, 6 (Summer 1944), 459-461.

Schraepen, Edmond. "*Herzog:* Disconnection and Connection." In *Saul Bellow and His Work: Proceedings of a Conference*, ed. Schraepen, 119-129.

_____. "The Rhetoric of Saul Bellow's Novels." In *Rhetoric et Communication,* ed. Hubert Greven. Paris: Didier, 1979.

Schueler, Mary D. "The Figure of Madelaine in *Herzog,*" *Notes on Contemporary Literature,* 1 (Mar. 1971), 5-7.

Schulz, Max F. "Mr. Bellow's Perigee, Or The Lowered Horizon of *Mr. Sammler's Planet.*" In *Contemporary American-Jewish Literature: Critical Essays,* ed. Irving Malin. Bloomington: Indiana University Press, 1973, 118-133.

_____. "Saul Bellow and the Burden of Selfhood." In his *Radical Sophistication: Studies on Contemporary Jewish-American Novelists.* Athens: Ohio University Press, 1969, 110-153.

Schwartz, Joseph. "Good Guys With No Labels: A Review of *Dean's December,*" *Chronicles of Culture,* 6 (Sept. 1982), 9-10.

Scott, Nathan A., Jr. "Bellow's Vision of Axial Lines." In his *Three American Moralists: Mailer, Bellow, Trilling.* Notre Dame: University of Notre Dame Press, 1973, 109-149, 221-225.

_____. "Sola Gratia: The Principles of Saul Bellow's Fiction." In his *Craters of the Spirit.* Washington, D.C.: Corpus Books, 1968, 235-265. Reprinted in *Adversity and Grace: Studies in Recent American Literature.* Chicago: University of Chicago Press, 1968, 27-57.

Shapiro, Karl. "The Jewish Writer in America." In his *In Defense of Ignorance.* New York: Random House, 1960, 205-217.

Shaw, Peter. "The Tough Guy Intellectual," *Critical Quarterly,* 8 (Spring 1966), 13-28.

Shear, Walter. "*Steppenwolf* and *Seize The Day,*" *Saul Bellow Journal,* 1 (Fall-Winter 1981), 32-34.

Shulman, Robert. "Myth, Mr. Eliot, and the Comic Novel," *Modern Fiction Studies,* 12 (Winter 1966-1967), 395-403.

_____. "The Style of Bellow's Comedy," *Publications of the Modern Language Association,* 83 (Mar. 1968), 109-117. Collected in *Saul Bellow: Herzog,* ed. Irving Howe, 489-509.

Sicherman, Carol M. "Bellow's *Seize the Day:* Reverberations and Hollow Sounds," *Studies in the Twentieth Century,* 15 (Spring 1975), 1-34.

Sieburth, Renée. "*Henderson the Rain King:* A Twentieth Century Don Quixote?," *Canadian Review of Comparative Literature,* 5 (Winter 1978), 86-94.

Siegel, Ben. "Artists and Opportunists in Saul Bellow's *Humboldt's Gift,*" *Contemporary Literature,* 19 (Spring 1978), 143-164.

_____. "Saul Bellow and Mr. Sammler: Absurd Seekers of High

Qualities." In *Saul Bellow: A Collection of Critical Essays*, ed. Earl
　　Rovit, 122-124.

_____. "Saul Bellow and the University as Villain," *Missouri Review*, 6, no. 2 (1983), 167-189.

Simon, John. Review of *The Last Analysis, Hudson Review*, 17 (Winter
　　1964-1965), 556-557.

Siskin, E. E. "Saul Bellow in Search of Himself," *Journal of Reform
　　Judaism*, 25 (Spring 1978), 89-93.

Sloss, Henry. "Europe's Last Gasp," *Shenandoah*, 22 (Autumn 1970),
　　82-86. Review of *Mr. Sammler's Planet*.

Smith, Herbert J. *"Humboldt's Gift* and Rudolph Steiner," *Centennial
　　Review*, 22, no. 4 (1978), 479-489.

Solotaroff, Theodore. "Napoleon Street and After," *Commentary*, 38
　　(Dec. 1964), 63-66. Collected in *Saul Bellow: Herzog*, ed. Irving
　　Howe, 472-480.

Spivey, Ted R. "Death, Love, and Rebirth of Language in Saul Bel-
　　low's Fiction," *Saul Bellow Journal*, 4 (Fall-Winter 1985), 5-17.

Steig, Michael. "Bellow's Henderson and The Limits of Freudian Crit-
　　icism," *Paunch*, 36-37 (Apr. 1973), 39-46.

Stevenson, David. "The Activists," *Daedalus*, 92 (Spring 1963), 238-
　　249.

Stevick, Philip. "The Rhetoric of Bellow's Short Fiction." In *Critical
　　Essays on Saul Bellow*, ed. Stanley Trachtenberg, 73-82.

Stock, Irvin. "The Novels of Saul Bellow," *Southern Review*, new series
　　3 (Jan. 1967), 13-42.

Sullivan, Victoria. "The Battle of the Sexes in Three Bellow Novels."
　　In *Saul Bellow: A Collection of Critical Essays*, ed. Earl Rovit, 101-
　　114.

Sullivan, Walter. "Terrors Old and New: Bellow's Rumania and Three
　　Views of the Holocaust," *Sewanee Review*, 90 (Summer 1982),
　　484-492.

Tackach, James M. "Saul Bellow's Dingbat Einhorn, Nails Nagel and
　　the American Dream," *Saul Bellow Journal*, 2 (Spring-Summer
　　1983), 55-58.

Tanner, Tony. *City of Words: American Fiction 1850-1970.* New York:
　　Harper & Row, 1971, 64-72, 295-310.

Teller, Judd L. "From Yiddish to Neo Brahmin." In his *Strangers and
　　Natives: The Evolution of the American Jew from 1921 to the Present.*
　　New York: Delacorte, 1969, 251-272.

Toth, Susan. *"Henderson the Rain King:* Eliot and Browning," *Notes on
　　Contemporary Literature*, 1 (May 1971), 6-8.

Trachtenberg, Stanley. "Saul Bellow and the Veil of Maya," *Studies in the Literary Imagination*, 17 (Fall 1984), 39-58.

_____. "Saul Bellow's *Luftmenschen:* The Compromise With Reality," *Critique*, 9 (Summer 1967), 36-61.

Trilling, Lionel. "Introduction." In Bellow, *The Adventures of Augie March*. New York: Modern Library, 1965.

Trowbridge, Clinton W. "Water Imagery in *Seize the Day*," *Critique*, 9 (Mar. 1967), 62-73.

Uphaus, Suzanne Henning. "From Innocence to Experience: A Study of *Herzog*," *Dalhousie Review*, 46 (Spring 1966), 65-79.

Vernier, Jean-Pierre. "Mr. Sammler's Lesson." In *Les Americanistes: New French Criticism in Modern American Fiction*, ed. Ira D. Johnson and Christiane Johnson. Port Washington, N.Y.: Kennikat, 1978, 16-36.

Vinoda, Dr. "The Dialectic of Sex in Bellow's Fiction," *Indian Journal of American Studies*, 7 (Jan. 1982), 81-87.

_____. "Saul Bellow and Gustave Flaubert," *Saul Bellow Journal*, 1 (Fall 1981), 1-5.

Vogel, Dan. "Saul Bellow's Vision Beyond Absurdity: Jewishness in *Herzog*," *Tradition*, 9 (Spring 1968), 65-79. Reprinted in *Judaism*, 17 (1968), 42-54.

Walden, Daniel. "Bellow, Malamud and Roth: Part of the Continuum," *Studies in American Jewish Literature*, 5, no. 2 (1979), 5-7.

_____. "The Resonance of Twoness: The Urban Vision of Saul Bellow," *Studies in Jewish American Literature*, 4, no. 2 (1978), 9-21.

_____. "Urbanism and the Artist: Saul Bellow and the Age of Technology," *Saul Bellow Journal*, 2 (Spring-Summer 1983), 1-14.

Walsh, Thomas. "Heroism in Bellow's 'The Mexican General,' " *Saul Bellow Journal*, 1 (Spring-Summer 1982), 31-33.

Weales, Gerald. *The Jumping-Off Place: American Drama in the 1960's*. New York: Macmillan, 1969.

Weber, Ronald. "Bellow's Thinkers," *Western Humanities Review*, 22 (Autumn 1968), 305-313.

Weinberg, Helen. *The New Novel in America: The Kafkan Mode in Contemporary Fiction*. Ithaca, N.Y.: Cornell University Press, 1970, 29-107.

Weinstein, Ann. *"The Dean's December:* Bellow's Plea for The Humanities," *Saul Bellow Journal*, 2 (Spring-Summer 1983), 30-41.

_____. "A Toast To Life, L'Chayim: Saul Bellow's 'A Father-To-

Be,' " *Saul Bellow Journal*, 2 (Fall-Winter 1982), 31-35.

Weinstein, Mark. "Bellow's Imagination-Instructors," *Saul Bellow Journal*, 2 (Fall-Winter 1982), 19-21.

_____. "Charles Citrine: Bellow's Holy Fool," *Saul Bellow Journal*, 3 (Fall-Winter 1983), 28-37.

_____. "Communication in *The Dean's December*," *Saul Bellow Journal*, 5 (Winter 1986) (forthcoming).

_____. "The Fundamental Elements in *Mr. Sammler's Planet*," *Saul Bellow Journal*, 1, no. 2 (1982), 18-26.

Weinstein, Norman. "*Herzog*, Order and Entropy," *English Studies*, 54 (June 1973), 336-346.

Weiss, Daniel. "Caliban on Prospero: A Psychoanalytic Study of the Novel *Seize the Day* by Saul Bellow," *American Imago*, 19 (Fall 1962), 277-306. Collected in *Saul Bellow and the Critics*, ed. Irving Malin.

Wieting, Molly Stark. "The Function of the Trickster in Saul Bellow's Novels," *Saul Bellow Journal*, 3 (Spring-Summer 1984), 23-31.

_____. "The Symbolic Function of the Pastoral in Saul Bellow's Novels," *Southern Quarterly*, 16 (1978), 359-374.

Wilson, Jonathan. "Bellow's Dangling Dean," *Literary Review*, 26 (Fall 1982), 164-175.

Wirth-Nesher, Hana, and Andrea Cohen Malamut. "Jewish and Human Survival on Bellow's Planet," *Modern Fiction Studies*, 25 (Spring 1979), 59-74.

Wisse, Ruth. "Saul Bellow's Winter of Discontent," *Commentary*, 73 (Apr. 1982), 71-73.

_____. "The Schlemiel as Liberal Humanist." In her *Schlemiel as Modern Hero*. Chicago: University of Chicago Press, 1971, 91-107. Collected in *Saul Bellow: A Collection of Critical Essays*, ed. Earl Rovit, 90-100.

Wolcott, James. "Dissecting Our Decline," *Esquire*, 97 (Mar. 1982), 134-136.

Yetman, Michael G. "Who Would Not Sing For Humboldt?," *Journal of English Literary History*, 4 (Winter 1981), 935-951.

Young, James Dean. "Bellow's Vision of the Heart," *Critique*, 7 (Spring 1965), 5-17.

BIBLIOGRAPHICAL ESSAY

Bibliographies and Checklists

Early checklists of Bellow criticism include: Harold W. Schneider's "Two Bibliographies—Saul Bellow/William Styron," 1960; David D. Galloway's "A Saul Bellow Checklist," 1966 and updated in 1970; B. A. Sokoloff and Mark E. Posner's *Saul Bellow: A Comprehensive Bibliography*, 1971; Robert G. Noreen's *Saul Bellow: A Reference Guide*, 1977-1978; and F. Lercangée's *Saul Bellow: A Bibliography of Sources*, 1977.

Superseding these early bibliographies and checklists are Leslie Field and John Z. Guzlowski's "Criticism of Saul Bellow: A Selected Checklist" (1979) (very comprehensive) and Marianne Nault's *Saul Bellow: His Works and His Critics: An Annotated International Bibliography*, 1977. Nault's bibliography contains not only listings of Bellow's works and international criticism, but listings of materials held in special collections. These listings mostly include descriptions of the holdings at the Regenstein Library of the University of Chicago up to 1976.

Forthcoming from Garland Publishing in the Fall of 1986 is the most comprehensive bibliographical tool available to date. Gloria L. Cronin and Blaine H. Hall's *Saul Bellow: Annotated Bibliography and Checklist 1944-86* will supersede and correct previous listings of criticism and provide the most exhaustive annotated international bibliography to date. It will also provide comprehensive listings of special collections as well as listings of editions, essays, interviews, and previous bibliographies.

Most current will be the annual "Saul Bellow Annotated Selected Bibliography" in the *Saul Bellow Journal*. The first of these essays annotating books, periodical articles, and dissertations appearing in 1980 was published in the *Saul Bellow Journal*, 4, no. 1, 1985. Listings for 1981, 1982, and 1983 appear in subsequent issues of the journal. The scope of the listings is international. The aim of editors is to provide the most current annotated checklist possible in each year-end issue of the journal.

Interviews

The gap in the Bellow canon of either an autobiography or a biography is bridged, to some degree, by the many interviews available through the years. They comprise, at this time, a considerable body of information concerning Bellow's thoughts on various subjects as well as on his individual works. They also provide much needed background information. Most interviews cover a variety of subjects from politics to art. They all include discussions of his novels and, therefore, help the reader to gain a better understanding of these works. The bulk of the interviews are novel-related, that is, they usually precede or follow a new work and illuminate it. They are somewhat repetitious as interviewers seem to be interested, even fascinated, by specific subjects: Bellow as a Jewish-American writer; his life in Chicago; his relationship to the academic community; the present state of culture. Also, Bellow usually sees the interviews before they are published. He does not censor the subject matter—that he can do, and has done, by refusing to talk about a particular issue—but he does make sure the language is correct and in the form in which he would like it to be before it appears in print. In addition, readers may sense a certain amount of disdain for the interviewer as well as for the public. This attitude is reflected by the fact that he has his own interview, "An Interview with Myself" (1975), as if to suggest the type of question an interview should deal with—the literary one—and, of course, to make sure that his ideas on this subject go on record; his rather disdainful attitude is also supported by his claim that he reads few critiques of his works: "I don't pay too much attention to them" (cf Bill Kennedy, "If Saul Bellow Doesn't Have a True Word To Say He Keeps His Mouth Shut," 1982). Astute readers may even find contradictions and inaccuracies in some of these interviews. Nevertheless, each interview is important for the singular point(s) it makes on individual novels, specific writers, his own life, as well as his works, and merits the serious attention of students and scholars.

The following sampling of interviews will suggest the variety of subjects discussed. While the recent interview with the staff of *TriQuarterly* magazine, Rockwell Gray, Harry White, and Gerald Nemanic (1984), deals mainly with Chicago—Bellow states that the "old Chicago . . . is one of the larger provinces of my psychic life"—his comments on *The Adventures of Augie March* as a piece of "ethnography," on Augie as an "ethical hedonist," on *Herzog* as a "negative *Bildungsroman*," on his rejection of T. S. Eliot's "traditionalism," and on his defense of Rudolf Steiner's theories are interesting.

Matthew C. Roudane's 1984 interview also queries Bellow about Chicago. Bellow explains that there is no "great good place" for artists—writers and painters—in America. He refers back to his Jewish heritage, to Jewish history, "to the ancient, the millennial Jewish power of accommodation to place." You could live anywhere because your "spirit lived independently. You had no need of a supporting culture." Roudane questions Bellow about his international interests, and Bellow points out that Chicago is a "collection of European communities." Bellow comments on *Herzog* and the foolishness of Moses Herzog; on *Henderson the Rain King* and the influence of the James-Lange theory which he applies to Henderson; on *Seize the Day* and his dislike for the sufferer Wilhelm; and on *The Adventures of Augie March*, which he doesn't think will "wear well" because of the "disingenuousness" of the main character. There is also a lengthy discussion of *The Dean's December*, which Bellow terms a "novel of consciousness" rather than a "protest novel." Roudane perceptively notes that Bellow's writing style has changed in the last decade and questions Bellow about this development. Bellow admits that his writing is "more condensed," that "it hits harder than it used to," and that he "detest[s] superfluous sentences, unwanted paragraphs, needless pages." Likewise, Corde in *The Dean's December* makes demands on language.

D. J. R. Bruckner, editor of the *New York Times Book Review*, in his "A Candid Talk with Saul Bellow" (1984), gives a personal glimpse of Bellow in addition to clarifying some of his ideas. The impetus for the interview was the publication of his newest work, the collection of short stories *Him With His Foot In His Mouth and Other Stories*. The stories that comprise this collection are in a much lighter vein than his most recent novel. Bellow does admit that he had no more axes to grind. The stories are actually affectionate portraits of friends, some of them easily recognizable, such as Isaac Rosenfeld as Zetland in the story by the same name and Harold Rosenberg as Victor Wulpy in "What Kind of Day Did You Have?" Bellow talks about his Jewishness, his upbringing in a religious home, his reading Hebrew at age seven. He states that he could not continue in the orthodox tradition because he felt it suffocating him. However, he does not describe himself as an atheist. He still retains a religious feeling and says that he is "a religious man in a retarded condition and the only way

I can square myself is to write." Bruckner also provides his readers with a view of Bellow's studio in his apartment on the thirteenth floor above Lake Michigan and of Bellow's working habits. It is, as the title states, a "candid" and personal interview, informative but not pedantic.

The interview conducted by Robert Boyers, "Literature and Culture" (1975), deals with general literary/cultural topics: romanticism, classicism, the task of the writer, the problem of originality—for Bellow there is nothing new; only individuals are different—the need of the public to be "interesting." On a more personal level, Boyers queries Bellow on his disassociation with the New York intellectual community and the fact that his work no longer appears in the *Partisan Review*. Bellow, although he finds the subject infuriating, does not hesitate to discuss it. He is also asked about the function of comedy in his work. Bellow says it is something he cannot explain because it comes naturally.

Bellow comments on and clarifies Hannah Arendt's notion of the banality of evil and why he (and Sammler in *Mr. Sammler's Planet*) are so vehemently opposed to this concept. The magnitude of evil, he says, does not change by ascribing the blame for it to civilization or society. Boyers also queries Bellow on the statement Moses Herzog makes concerning language, "I go after reality with language." To what degree are language and reality related for Bellow? Bellow does not answer this question. His only comment is that this passage is "just one of the marvelous things that Herzog felt like saying."

Chirantan Kulshrestha's "A Conversation with Saul Bellow" (1972) deals mostly with *Mr. Sammler's Planet*. At the end of the interview, Kulshrestha asks Bellow if he considers himself a Jewish writer. Bellow, once again, voices his objection to that tag but does admit that at the "most susceptible time of my life I was wholly Jewish. That's a gift, a piece of good fortune with which one doesn't quarrel."

Gordon L. Harper's early interview in *Paris Review* (1966) is still significant for its information concerning Bellow's attitudes toward the literary establishment, toward his craft, and toward his early works. Of particular interest are his comments on his rejection of the WASP establishment and their standards and also his remarks on *Herzog* and his rejection of fashionable ideas.

Critical Studies: Books

Indicative of the enormous critical interest with which Bellow's fiction has met since the 1950s are twenty-seven published volumes, five of which constitute critical essays or collections of essays, and one of which represents a less than satisfactory attempt at a biography. Tony Tanner's *Saul Bellow* (1965), a slim volume published as part of the Oliver and Boyd Writers and Critics series, is a ground-breaking volume that provided the first serious students of the Bellow novel with an insightful introductory survey of themes, style techniques, and ideas. It is still an admirable introduction to the early and middle period of Bellow's writing because it identifies most of the significant trends in Bellow criticism. However, Keith Opdahl's *The Novels of Saul Bellow: An Introduction* (1967) is the first major book on Bellow. Opdahl defines the religious quest for transcendence as the goal of all Bellow heroes and identifies their besetting difficulty as the absurd discrepancy between human aspiration and achievement. Much subsequent Bellow criticism has only succeeded in weaving endless and oftentimes repetitious variations on Opdahl's original critical observations.

Robert Detweiler's *Saul Bellow: A Critical Essay* was published in 1968 as part of Eerdman's Contemporary Writers in Christian Perspective series. Admitting the irony of forcing a Jewish writer into a Christian mold, Detweiler contradicts himself by defining Bellow as a "part of society we now label secular, post-Christian, and pluralistic." This essay's credibility depends entirely on one's willingness to accept Detweiler's diluted and confusing concept of Christianity.

Within the next year came the second in-depth study by John J. Clayton, *Saul Bellow: In Defense of Man* (1968, revised in 1979), which presents Bellow as a frustrated idealist and humanist who "reviles that side of himself which concurs with the prophets of doom and hucksters of the void." Dealing extensively with the psychic patterns of Bellow's fiction, Clayton's study, with its vigorous prose and acute analysis, is a major expansion of ideas stated only in general terms in Tanner's pamphlet and remains a definitive work.

Irving Malin's originally useful but now dated book, *Saul Bellow's Fiction* (1969), deals descriptively rather than critically with theme, character, imagery, and style. However, it does contain one of the few critiques on Bellow's first short story, "Two Morning Monologues." In 1972 Brigitte Scheer-Schäzler produced a small volume entitled *Saul Bellow* for the Ungar Publishing Company's Modern Literature Monographs series. Dealing briefly with each novel, Scheer-Schäzler's monograph reiterates in essay form much that Tanner and Clayton had already done in greater depth and length.

Two new books appeared in 1974. Sarah Blacher Cohen's *Saul Bellow's Enigmatic Laughter* took a new direction in its sophisticated treatment of Bellow's use of humor as a retaliatory device in face of twentieth-century despair. Arguing that the comic ploy is shaky in the early novels and gains strength in the later novels, Cohen asserts that the comic element receiving the most extensive treatment in the Bellow novels is the comedy of character. It is a comedy, Cohen reiterates throughout the book, that "does not abandon the flawed individual but continually looks for his saving manhood or nobility." She essentially sees the Bellow novel as a secular comedy depicting a "sullied world" in which man vacillates between "recidivism and reform." Despite Cohen's pioneering efforts, much remains to be said about Bellow as a comic writer.

The second book to appear in 1974 was M. Gilbert Porter's *Whence the Power? The Artistry and Humanity of Saul Bellow.* Using an avowedly formalist approach, Gilbert Porter's study concerns itself with the intrareferential elements of the books—their themes and forms. He manages this task only as well as can be expected with such a critical method. Bellow's ideas and aesthetics of course defy such methods. The book is useful but does not supersede previous studies or create new frontiers of scholarship.

In 1978 the now deceased Chirantan Kulshrestha published his *Saul Bellow: The Problem of Affirmation.* Challenging some of the earlier work of Tanner and Clayton in particular, Kulshrestha asserts that earlier critics overlook "that affirmation has always been a source of persistent anxiety for Bellow and that his attempts to clarify and define its numerous ramifications have molded his fictional method." This study treats the novels in terms of their dramatizing of the plights of the various protagonists as they struggle with the issue of affirmation. The bulk of the study deals with these problematics and the resulting fictional modes of each work. He employs a threefold division of the novels to reflect the chronological artistic development of the author. It is the first critical attempt to see affirmation as an artistic problem rather than just a philosophical one. Given the unavailability of a good critical biography, it is not surprising that this book raises more questions than it answers.

By 1980 the first attempt at a Bellow biography appeared. Mark Harris's *Saul Bellow: Drumlin Woodchuck* contains an anecdotal record of Harris's abortive attempt at writing a Bellow biography. The picture of Bellow which emerges is an unflattering and partial one of a major literary figure constantly evading the fate of becoming a pawn of the literary establishment. Unfortunately, this book has little or no value as biography and minimal value as a source of previously unrecorded Bellow anecdotes and witticisms.

Flight from Women in the Fiction of Saul Bellow (1980) by Joseph McCadden places Bellow in the misogynistic tradition of male writers who are uninterested in dealing with women as individuals. McCadden sees Bellow using women characters as adjuncts to the hero, describing them exclusively from the point of view of a male protagonist, and depicting them as wives and mistresses who are enemies of love and therefore incapable of surrendering their egotistical designs for men. McCadden's major contribution is his establishment of precisely how the female characters contribute significantly to the psychological drama so important to the success of each novel. The great weakness of the study is that it does not draw on what by 1980 is a significant and sophisticated body of feminist critical theory. Much work remains to be done on the subject of Bellow's female protagonists. McCadden fails to deal with the complicated critical question of how much these female characters are projections of Bellow's misogynistic schlemiels rather than of Bellow himself.

Eusebio L. Rodrigues's *Quest for the Human: An Exploration of Saul Bellow's Fiction* (1981) explores the thesis that Bellow's dominant theme is the journey outward for human values. This school of Bellow criticism originates with the earliest commentators, and yet in his chapters on *Henderson the Rain King* and *Seize the Day* Rodrigues provides superior and insightful exegeses. This volume is a series of loosely linked extended essays on the individual novels. Rodrigues is the first critic to deal with Bellow's vocabulary and grammar as integral to the thematic and structural concerns of the novels. However, he barely scratches the surface of this relatively untouched subject, a fertile field of inquiry for future Bellow critics.

Malcolm Bradbury's *Saul Bellow* (1982) begins with the assumption that literature of the last several decades is radically different from that of the preceding period. This well-written and valuable extended essay begins with a useful if somewhat simplified definition of contemporary literature and then proceeds to fit Bellow into it. The book, which makes no attempt to be thorough, establishes the theory that the form Bellow's contemporary radicalism takes is comic. Bradbury's approach is general and open-ended. This slim volume is the first book-length attempt to place Bellow within the contemporary period as such.

Also published in 1982 was Robert R. Dutton's revised Twayne volume, *Saul Bellow*, originally published in 1971. This introductory survey is perhaps the single most useful volume for the beginning researcher. In addition, it contains valuable material on lesser read works, such as *To Jerusalem and Back: A Personal Account* and some of the short fiction, which have been ignored in most other studies.

J. Bakker's *Fiction as Survival Strategy: A Comparative Study of the Major Works of Ernest Hemingway and Saul Bellow* (1983) represents a definitive study of the relationship between the fiction of these two authors. Exhaustive in its comparative analysis of pairs of Bellow and Hemingway novels, the study at times seems forced. The link between the two writers offered by Bakker is their common need for definitions of identity in a society that no longer provides ready-made answers. Also probed is the extent to which Bellow both rejected and was influenced by Hemingway as a twentieth-century literary forefather. In this latter respect the study is more valuable.

Claude Levy's *Les Romans de Saul Bellow: Tactiques Narratives et Strategies Oedipiennes*, a 1983 study written in French, represents the first extensive structuralist and psychoanalytic examination of the novels. Treating each novel as distinct and not a segment in a saga, Levy perceives each text as an organic entity possessing closure. Refusing to use the text to interpret the author, Levy focuses on the text both as story and discourse. His greatest contribution in this significant work is his examination of the results of conflating "narratorial" voice with that of the hero, a strategy that Levy identifies as hiding all kinds of complexities of interpretation not yet plumbed. This study also employs psychoanalytic techniques to discover the "fantasms" or obsessions that color the narrator's reportage and discourse. It offers the first significant attempt to unravel the knotty critical problem of the relationship of the narrator/hero to his creator. Levy credits Bellow with having created highly complex heroes and having employed great skill in his use of point of view, rather than merely creating thinly disguised personas. This is a major contribution to Bellow criticism.

Perhaps the most original book yet published on Bellow is L. H. Goldman's *Saul Bellow's Moral Vision: A Critical Study of the Jewish Experience* (1982). Refusing to skirt the problematic issue of the influence of Judaism upon the Bellow canon, Goldman provides an alternative and compelling account of the source of humane values in the novels.

Goldman's is perhaps the most penetrating and refreshingly unsentimental account of character and theme found in any single volume of Bellow criticism. She systematically rejects the dominant tradition of romantic and religio-mystical interpretation of individual novels, providing instead a unique window on the Jewish perspective revealed in them. This, too, is a major work of Bellow criticism whose premise is that no work of art is culturally "innocent" and that the author's inherited value system will undoubtedly influence his art. The non-Jewish reader can be grateful for the fine elucidation of Judaism, and particularly its religious and ethical values, which is offered along with the discussions of the novels.

Perhaps the most important book to appear in the last two decades is Daniel Fuchs's brilliant landmark study *Saul Bellow: Vision and Revision* (1984), which is one of the first critical studies to deal with all of the novels to date and to examine unpublished manuscripts, letters, and revisions unavailable to nearly all previous reseachers. By studying the progressive revisions of individual novels, Fuchs is able to arrive at important new conclusions about Bellow's artistic search for voice and form. Fuchs's book will remain the definitive study of its kind as long as the Bellow collections of manuscript materials remain closed, and perhaps longer.

Also published in 1984 is Jeanne Braham's *A Sort of Columbus: The American Voyages of Saul Bellow's Fiction,* an interesting but rather unevenly developed extended essay that attempts to establish how deeply rooted Bellow's work is in the nineteenth- and twentieth-century American literary tradition which, she argues, is dominated by the concept of the journey outward into experience. Essayistic rather than definitive, this study pays too little attention to Jewish and European influences upon Bellow in its assertion that his roots lie with the transcendentalists and the naturalists.

The most recent full-length critical study of Bellow is Judie Newman's *Saul Bellow and History* (1984), which attempts to avoid the transcendental and myth-mystical camps of Bellow criticism. Focusing instead on the differing theories and treatments of history implicit and explicit in the novels, she attempts an alternative reading. Some of the chapter divisions are likely to confuse the reader, the early novels are rather inadequately dealt with, and the book stops short after a rather strained attempt to explicate *Humboldt's Gift.* However, despite these weaknesses this is essentially a sophisticated, central, and welcome addition to Bellow criticism.

The most radical departure in Bellow criticism since L. H. Goldman's examination of the Jewishness of the novels is surely Jonathan Wilson's *On Bellow's Planet: Readings From The Dark Side* (1985). Believing that it is high time for a critical revision, Wilson denies the long-held critical commonplace that Bellow is a life-affirming novelist. This he claims to be a "misreading which has obfuscated Bellow's complexity and misrepresented his true relevance as a contemporary American writer." Wilson's central thesis is that there is a "static dialectic" that informs Bellow's fiction. Oppositions such as order and chaos, limitation or freedom are central to the novels but nothing hangs on their resolution. The heroes themselves suffer "the energy of paralysis" in which they experience fits of vivid insight and excitement. The ambivalence of these heroes, Wilson argues, is rooted in their sexuality and relation to the adult male business world. Possessed by a peculiar law of the heart that is essentially feminine, a law they both affirm and deny, such heroes are doomed to paralysis and unable to solve marital, financial, spiritual, or philosophical problems. Hence their futures are not affirmative but potentially bleak.

Critical Studies: Collections of Essays

Edited by Irving Malin, *Saul Bellow and the Critics* (1967) remains the best single collection of Bellow criticism. Containing twelve essays of varied length and scope on theme, character, imagery, style, and sources, the volume presents many essays now recognized as classics in Bellow scholarship, not the least of which is his own "Seven Images."

By 1975 a number of in-depth and specialized studies on individual Bellow novels had been published. A judicious and balanced selection of specialized studies appeared in Earl Rovit's *Saul Bellow: A Collection of Critical Essays* (1975), one in the prestigious series of critical essays published as "Twentieth Century Views" under Maynard Mack's editorship. The publication of this volume confirmed the general critical consensus of Bellow's major status in twentieth-century letters.

By 1979 the third book of reviews and critical essays appeared, edited by Stanley Trachtenberg. *Critical Essays on Saul Bellow*, part of G. K. Hall's Critical Essays on American Literature series, attempted a broad survey of reviews and landmark essays on specialized topics. As such it is only partially successful. However, its "Introduction" provides some valuable insights into the state of Bellow scholarship at the end of the 1970s. Notable among the essays reprinted are those by Rodrigues, Fuchs, Siegel, and Cohen.

Critical Studies: Major Articles and Book Sections

Saul Bellow's first published novel, *Dangling Man* (1944), was reviewed by every major newspaper and journal, and the consensus of these reviewers was positive. It was generally agreed that he "writes with obvious style and mastery, with a sharp cutting to the quick of language, with a brilliance of thought" and that this first book heralded "a fine literary career." Yet it took twenty years for the first critical studies to appear on this work. Although criticism always lags behind reviews, it seems that Bellow had to prove himself as a writer before he would be given serious attention by scholars. Denis Donoghue's "Commitment and the *Dangling Man*" (1964), which contains a discussion of the essence of "the dangling man" in Bellow's novels to date, i.e., through *Henderson the Rain King*, makes a crucial point: Bellow's fiction "is a search for value, the value is moral responsibility and the search is for the strength to overcome the fear of choice." Early critics have viewed the ending of this work, Joseph's enlistment in the army, in terms of failure of individual freedom—or accommodation to society. As such they lack an understanding of the perspective from which Bellow writes and neglect the value system which he brings to literature. It would take another twenty years before a few critics, most notably, perhaps, L. H. Goldman in her book *Saul Bellow's Moral Vision*, 1983, would properly evaluate and interpret the meaning of freedom, that it "has no meaning . . . separate from its social context," and Joseph's entering the army, "rejoining his fellow men, . . . is the sole way by which he can reassert his freedom." Although *Dangling Man* as well as *The Victim* has not received the critical attention Bellow's other works have, there are a few studies of interest. James Mellard's "*Dangling Man:* Saul Bellow's Lyrical Experiment" points to the lyrical quality of the work, while Richard Lehan's "Existentialism in Recent American Fiction" links *Dangling Man* with French existentialist novels, specifically with Sartre's *Nausea* and Camus's *The Stranger* and *The Plague;* and David D. Anderson in "The Room, the City and the War" sees Joseph as a "grotesque in the *Winesburg, Ohio* manner."

Bellow's second novel, *The Victim* (1947), received more praise from reviewers than his first novel. Most agreed with Leslie Fiedler's appraisal of the young writer's achievement: "surely one of the most complexly moving books in the past ten years." Given the complexity of the work, *The Victim* has received scant critical attention as compared to his later works. Readers will find useful Malcolm Bradbury's article, "Saul Bellow's *The Victim*" (1963), which acknowledges Bellow's debt to the French existentialists as well as to the American naturalists. Noting that "though the novel lacks the width and the largeness of *Augie March* or the exuberance and stylistic force of *Henderson the Rain King*, it is a deep and penetrating tale, remarkable for rather than limited by its concentration." Bradbury presents a fine discussion on Leventhal and his growth during the progress of the work toward "an understanding about the nature of a general responsibility, and this involves a radical change in his view of what constitutes humanity, and of what way the social system works." Andrew Gordon's study of Leventhal in "Pushy Jew: Levanthal in *The Victim*" (1979) is also worthwhile. This article is an insightful examination into the motif of "pushing" as it occurs in the novel. Noting that "push" as a noun or verb appears at least twenty-five times in this work and that there are "numerous other episodes which involve violent, pushing actions," Gordon contends that the pattern relates to Leventhal's "emotional problem": his need to "find a balance between his aggressive and his passive impulses, that is, between pushing and being pushed around," observing that these impulses are sexual as well as aggressive.

For those readers who look for the source of a writer's works in other literature, whether American or European, Allan Chavkin's note, "Ivan Karamazov's Rebellion and Bellow's *The Victim*" (1980), is valuable. Chavkin suggests that the primary source for *The Victim* is not only Dostoyevsky's *The Eternal Husband*—duly recognized by critics—but *The Brothers Karamazov* as well, specifically the chapter entitled "Rebellion." Chavkin, however, points out that Bellow's overall purpose goes further than Dostoyevsky's "eloquent protest against man's unwarranted suffering" in its evaluation of twentieth-century man's ability to cope with his victimization.

Few critics, early as well as late ones, deal with the major problem presented by Bellow in this work: anti-Semitism. Of those critics who do deal with the particular problem of *The Victim*, Helge Nilsen's "Anti-Semitism and Persecution Complex: A Comment on Saul Bellow's *The Victim*" is particularly useful. Her reading of the work is original in that she refuses to go along with earlier critics—and better known ones as well—such as Maxwell Geismar, who, Nilsen states, misreads the work when he states that "Leventhal is the eternal Jew, accepting his moral responsibility for a world he never made" ("Saul Bellow

Novelist of the Intellectuals," *Saul Bellow and the Critics*, ed. Irving Malin, 1969), thereby disregarding "the complexity of the novel," or Sarah B. Cohen, whose flippant remark that "Bellow's treatment of anti-Semitism in *The Victim* is a comic one" (*Saul Bellow's Enigmatic Laughter*, 1974), Nilsen suggests, cannot be taken seriously. Nilsen correctly grasps the psychological climate that creates and sustains anti-Semitism which Bellow portrays: that anti-Semitism, specifically in America, is a "condition of misunderstanding, suspicion, and hostility that can only be created by two 'willing' parties who each fulfill a certain, complementary function or role." Her conclusion is also noteworthy: "The book does not describe any process of psychological rebirth or basic change of attitudes, but shows a series of reactions toward the vicissitudes of life" (disagreeing once again with a well-known critic, John—erroneously noted as "Paul"—Clayton, who in his *Saul Bellow: In Defense of Man* states that Leventhal is "essentially changed" at the conclusion of the novel). Nilsen errs, however, in her statement that "Allbee is not exactly guilty of any real crimes against his unwilling host"—after all, Allbee does attempt a suicide/homicide—and her minimizing Allbee's offensive remarks at the Williston party, remarks meant specifically to offend, are in no way comparable to the light-hearted one Allbee makes to Leventhal at the end of the work, in reference to Mary's pregnancy: "I see you're following orders. Increase and multiply." Nevertheless Nilsen's article is very worthwhile.

Articles of special interest are the ones by S. Lillian Kremer, "The Holocaust in *The Victim*" (1983), and Ada Aharoni, "*The Victim:* Freedom of Choice" (1985). Kremer's essay is a protracted discussion of how Bellow "both subordinates and confronts the Holocaust" in his second novel. Noting that critics have excluded this particular area from their discussions, for whatever reasons, Kremer points out that Bellow's *The Victim* was one of the earliest American novels to confront the "European debacle." Fixing on certain "archetypal images of the Holocaust"—"yellow light, train, and suffocation imagery"—Kremer skillfully indicates how Bellow captures the oppressive mood of the Holocaust in a work dealing with the heinous results of centuries of anti-Semitism. Aharoni continues the trend of thought propounded in her earlier article on *Dangling Man* concerning the relationship of responsibility and choice. She states: "Bellow believes that the individual is capable of choice and that he should actively make use of this capability, but he stresses that choice can only operate within certain limits. Man is not the conductor of the train of life, but he is not at its complete mercy, and he can choose the 'stations' where he wants to alight. The stops represent not only opportunities and experiences in life, but also attitudes, values and morals."

The Adventures of Augie March (1953), as Bellow explains in one of his *Paris Review* interviews with Gordon Lloyd Harper, marks a movement conceptually away from his initial works. Early reviewers, however, after the discipline, tight structure, and sobriety of the first two novels, did not know what to make of this sprawling, seemingly lighthearted novel. One reviewer, indicating its ambiguous reception, termed it "the most interesting and the most exasperating book in years." This longer work, which received the National Book Award in 1954 nevertheless, generated more critical interest than the early novels, and there are a number of valuable critical essays that have appeared and continue to be written. For example, David Stevenson's article, "The Activists" (1963), discusses the emergence of a new fiction since the war and indicates how the postmodern novel differs in style, subject matter, characters, and its view of life from earlier American literature. Stevenson then proceeds to a discussion of both *Augie March* and *Henderson the Rain King* to substantiate his thesis. It is an intelligent essay with much good information in it clarifying the literature that has appeared after the Second World War. Albert Guerard, in "Saul Bellow and the Activists: On *The Adventures of Augie March*" (1967), written a few years later, supports Stevenson's thesis. Guerard seeks to place *Augie March* both in Bellow's canon (i.e., through *Herzog*) and also "in a particular current of modern fiction." While he suggests that Bellow's popularity may be related to the "importance of Jewish-American fiction in the 1950's and 1960's," Guerard does not see Bellow's fiction as rooted in European Jewish traditions. He claims that Bellow espouses an "activist" attitude toward his material, an attitude not politically motivated but "activist" in the sense of a "belief in energy, vitality, sheer activity as moral goods." It negates the popular alienation credo. Activism insists upon encountering life rather than shunning it. Guerard places both *Augie March* and *Henderson the Rain King* in the activist mode of fiction in terms of character, perspective, and rhetoric.

The Adventures of Augie March is generally accepted as a picaresque novel and Augie as a picaro figure, who is for the most part a passive character, the receiver of action not the initiator. In "Theme in *Augie March*," Robert Crozier (1965) disagrees with the notion of Augie as a passive character. Augie does state that he is a man of "opposition." Consequently, Crozier feels that "he exercises as his birthright man's highest privilege—that of contemplative action." Augie struggles with the "conflicts between the freedom of personal choice and the fixities of heredity and environment." Yet a careful reading of the novel indicates that there is little exercising of personal choice on Augie's part, and Crozier is, perhaps, too admiring of Augie. The quality of opposition which Augie possesses allows him to choose not to do something when the decision has already been presented. If there is freedom of choice on Augie's part, it is a limited one. W. M. Frohock, in "Saul Bellow and His Penitent Picaro" (1968), finds it difficult to accept the concept of the Jew as picaro. He does not view Augie March as a picaro nor the novel as picaresque but as "a confession that adapts a picaresque structure." As a character, Frohock maintains, Augie is a "penitent" in the Russian style. For Frohock, *The Adventures of Augie March* is one of the three or four memorable novels that have appeared in the 1950s and 1960s.

Early critics have also attempted to place Bellow within the traditional framework of well-known myths, themes, and concepts. R. W. B. Lewis, in "Recent Fiction: Picaro and Pilgrim" (1962), for example, has suggested that *Augie March* was written in the tradition of the Adamic myth. In a more recent reading, however, Steven M. Gerson in "The New American Adam in *The Adventures of Augie March*" indicates how the novel is a modern redaction of the American Adamic myth and that Augie's youthful exuberance and optimism evolve into a "personality shaped by twentieth-century horrors." Gerson's essay is important because of his untraditional reading that allows for newer and more insightful interpretations of Bellow, interpretations which are cognizant of Bellow's iconoclastic writing.

Also worthy and of special interest is Pat T. Overbeck's "The Women in *Augie March*" (1969). Overbeck attempts to fill the gap in the criticism on this novel. While much attention has been paid to the theme of the novel, to Bellow's stylistic change, to Augie's character, scant if any attention has been given to the women in the work and Augie's relationship with them. Overbeck views the women as "emotional fulcrum[s], a pivot around which to circle in a recurring pattern that gives structural support to the novel. Every straight path Augie takes ... inevitably winds around a woman to whom Augie is drawn. ... The cosmos of the novel consists, as Augie suggests, of circles of love enveloping axial lines." Overbeck's essay is thorough and perceptive, acknowledging the feminist stance when necessary yet eschewing its rhetoric. A few other later critics deal with the female figure in Bellow's works generally and include a discussion of *Augie*

March as well. Judith Scheffler, in "Two-Dimensional Dynamo: The Female Character in Saul Bellow's Novels" (1981), is concerned that the women in Bellow's works are seen through the eyes of the protagonists and, consequently, are "seldom, if ever, pictured in a life apart from them." Therefore, "female characters . . . rank first among the protagonists' anxieties, but remain undeveloped personalities." Nevertheless, Scheffler states, "women figure centrally in Augie's quest for a 'better fate.' " Dr. Vinoda, in "The Dialectic of Sex in Bellow's Fiction" (1982), claims that "one of the weaknesses of Bellow's fiction arises from its failure to make the imaginative leap into the consciousness of its female characters." She is concerned that Bellow's works reveal the cultural notions of his heritage in addition to generally accepted stereotypic ideas of women. "For this reason," she says, "women in Bellow's novels never fare well, in spite of the strong family feeling that the Bellow 'hero' is endowed with." Ada Aharoni, in "Women in Saul Bellow's Novels" (1983), however, presents a refreshingly original reading of Bellow's works. While acknowledging that "Bellow's artistic technique imposes some limitations on his portrayal of women characters," Aharoni notes that throughout his career as a writer Bellow "has given us a vast and rich gallery of convincing and vivid women of all kinds. His female characters are active, alive, creative and outspoken. They are shown for the most part, as forging meaningful lives for themselves, struggling, working, searching, growing and achieving." Aharoni's article is an excellent one as far as it goes. Unfortunately she skips over ten years and moves from *Dangling Man* to *Herzog*, omitting from her discussion *Augie March, Seize the Day*, and *Henderson the Rain King*. One wishes she had done more with the topic.

Michael Allen's article, "Idiomatic Language in Two Novels by Saul Bellow" (1967), about *Augie March* and *Henderson the Rain King*, is also valuable. Allen contends that Augie's use of Jewish idioms "heightens, elaborates, and enriches" while Henderson's language "reflects his moral situation."

When *Seize the Day* first appeared in 1956 it was part of a collection which included the title story—a novella, three short stories, and a one-act play. Bellow, by this time, had already developed a coterie of supporters among the reviewers of journals such as *Atlantic, Harper's, New Republic, Partisan Review, Yale Review*, and the *Nation*, and these welcomed the new work with approbation. The most scathing review of *Seize the Day* upon its appearance was "Bagels, Sour Cream and the Heart of the Current Novel" by Robert O. Bowen in the *Northwest Review*. Bowen, obviously not one of Bellow's admirers, refers to him as the "most ballyhooed urban writer" for "several seasons past." The content of the story, he says, "smacks of the popular Manhattan brand of psychoanalysis wherein bored and shiftless people invent problems." He is unsympathetic with the plight of Wilhelm, whom he terms a "middle-aged adolescent," and claims that "the only real progression in the book is extremely superficial: At the end Wilhelm happens onto a convenient funeral and weeps aloud for himself." Bowen's conclusion about *Seize the Day* is that "the novel demonstrates thoroughly the inability of such a creep as Wilhelm to cause either good or evil, let alone any ramifications of these, and without these or comparable values there is no literature. Ergo: This is not literature; it is a *tour de force* based on subject matter dear to the Urban book reviewer." Some of Bowen's criticism of the novel is well-taken, and future critics will be divided in their attitudes toward Wilhelm and the ending of the novel.

Bowen's review gets to the heart of the problem of *Seize the Day*. Critics either love it or hate it. It is not a novel readers feel ambivalent about. The trend, however, until very recently has been to take a more positive attitude toward the work, including the ending. William J. Handy's "Saul Bellow and the Naturalistic Hero" (1964), for example, traces the traditions of naturalism in the writers who have emerged from the mid-fifties onward, suggesting that the characters they create and the problems they present are far more complex than those of their predecessors in that the struggle for self-discovery and self-definition is not only psychological but religious and ethical as well. Handy sees Bellow—rightly so—as a moral writer. (Bellow, in all his essays and interviews, has made his moralistic stance known.) He asserts that *Seize the Day* is a presentation of man's loss of humanity in a world that admires success, and that of all the characters, only Tommy Wilhelm maintains his humanity, his sense of feeling for others. Consequently, he "does not emerge a defeated man, a pathetic victim of forces beyond his control." Handy feels that in the final scene, Tommy's response of grief to the corpse in the coffin is a "grief for mankind . . . for the human situation." This ability to feel the pain that others suffer is what elevates Tommy to heroic and human proportions.

The bifurcated issues in Handy's essay—Bellow's movement away from the pessimism of his predecessors in American literature, be it naturalism or modernism, and the ending as a source of Wilhelm's transcendence or apotheosis—has been treated by later critics to a varying degree but with little modification. Gloria L. Cronin, in her article "Saul Bellow's Quarrel with Modernism in *Seize the Day*" (1980), notes that Bellow is a key figure in the transition of American literature from modernism with its pessimistic and alienated outlook to a humanistic perspective, and that most critics of the 1960s and 1970s have paid scant attention to Bellow's antimodernist stance. She is concerned that the persistence of a "wasteland" reading is a mis-interpretation of Bellow's writing, which is an "ironic use of alienation formulae" by which the author conducts a "deadly skirmish with the stylistic and philosophical clichés of modern literature, and particu-larly with absurdism and Freudian estimates of man." Cronin reads *Seize the Day* in terms of a Jobian allegory which calls for "salvation through deprivation, triumph by way of defeat, transcendence via descent"; and Tamkin, who functions on the one hand as the devil and on the other as a comic figure, is a "physical grotesque" who preaches nihilism and "tampers with men's minds." Cronin sees the ending of the novel in terms of Tommy's apotheosis, wherein Tommy comes into his "spiritual inheritance." This transcendence of the in-dividual indicates Bellow's movement away from the "urban complaint novel" and his disdain for the "stifling orthodoxies of Modernism." Cronin returns to this theme in an excellent essay on *Henderson the Rain King*.

One of the dissenting voices on the subject of the degree to which the ending of *Seize the Day* inspires optimism is expressed in a perceptive and sophisticated article by Carol Sicherman, "Bellow's *Seize the Day:* Reverberations and Hollow Sounds" (1975). Sicherman focuses on the theme of language as Bellow's major concern in this work, specifically on "the breakdown of language as a common bond among men." In evaluating the characters, poets, and philosophers presented in the work, she indicates how Bellow works out his theme of the debasement of language as a major problem modern man has to confront. Yet Sicherman finds the ending of the novel, the "seeming epiphany at the funeral of an anonymous man," difficult to accept and sees it as undercutting the "delicate and forceful ironies" previ-ously presented.

Of special interest are the articles by Allan Chavkin, " 'The Hol-lywood Thread' and the First Draft of Saul Bellow's *Seize the Day*" (1982)—of particular value since it is the only essay to deal with Bel-low's manuscripts of this novel—which indicates how Hollywood or the world of fantasy affects all the characters in this work, not only Tommy; Daniel Weiss, "Caliban on Prospero: A Psychoanalytic Study of the Novel *Seize the Day*, by Saul Bellow" (1962), which focuses on the theme of the father-son relationships in literature; Andrew Jefchak, "Family Struggles in *Seize the Day*" (1974), which considers the breakup of the entire family unit, not only the father-son relationship; James C. Mathis, "The Theme of *Seize the Day*" (1965), which sees water and the image of drowning as the dominant imagery of the work; and Gilead Morahg, "The Art of Dr. Tamkin: Matter and Manner in *Seize the Day*" (1979), which presents a lengthy and provocative discussion of Tamkin as a "socially involved" individual and a "highly successful literary creation."

In the past decade criticism of *Seize the Day* has largely been focused on Bellow's sources, psychological and literary: Barbara Alhadeff in "The Divided Self: A Laingian Interpretation of *Seize the Day*" (1977) is inspired by R. D. Laing, while Helge N. Nilsen ("Saul Bellow and Wilhelm Reich," 1978), Allan Chavkin ("Suffering and Wilhem Reich's Theory of Character-Armoring in Saul Bellow's *Seize the Day*," 1982), and Eusebio Rodrigues ("Bellow's Confidence Man," 1973) interpret the work in Reichian terms. Walter Shear ("*Steppenwolf* and *Seize the Day*," 1981) finds affinities in Bellow's novel to Hermann Hesse's work. In "Saul Bellow's Death of a Salesman" (1981) Gordon Bordewyk sees the influence of Arthur Miller on both themes and character; and Andrew Gordon notes heretofore unnoticed allusions to two other works, in "Shakespeare's *The Tempest* and Yeats' 'Sailing to Byzantium' in *Seize the Day*" (1985).

Henderson the Rain King (1959), Bellow's fifth novel, marked a distinct departure from his previous novels in many ways, most obviously in its gentile protagonist and his African odyssey. Thomas F. Curley, reviewing *Henderson* for *Commonweal*, notes this departure and sees it as a sign of a "genuine artist." He views Henderson as a clown and the work itself as a "comedy of suffering." This view was supported by Bellow in 1967 during his interview with Gordon Lloyd Harper. Not all the reviewers were ready for this change of mood, place, and pace. Norman Podhoretz, for example, reviewing *Henderson* for the *New York Herald Tribune Book Review*, calls it the "most brilliantly written novel to have come along in years" yet a "curiously unsatisfying book." Podhoretz is not sure what Bellow is trying to say and feels that the affirmation of the ending is unconvincing.

Later critics of the work deal with the problems early reviewers noted. Most are cognizant of the humor of the novel and relate its meaning to its humor. In "Bellow's Henderson" (1964), Allen Guttmann chastises critics for attempting to rewrite the novel in their own form, lamenting Bellow's omission of certain facts or the inconclusiveness of the conclusion. Guttmann points out that "fabulous Henderson's comic quest is ended when he learns to replace one verb (*want*) with two others (*imagine, love*). He cannot tell us what to imagine or whom to love any more than he was able to tell us what it was he wanted. Saul Bellow can tell us how it was that Henderson moved from one verb to another. The movement *is* the book. To want more is to be as Henderson was before he learned to love and to imagine."

Because of the nature of *Henderson the Rain King*, most of the criticism focuses either on Bellow's sources or on the place of this work within the American or English literary tradition. Sometimes these foci overlap as Henderson is generally recognized as a caricature of the American hero. Elsie Leach's "From Ritual to Romance Again: *Henderson the Rain King*" (1960) traces the fertility quest in *Henderson* to Jessie L. Weston's *From Ritual to Romance*, published in 1920; while Jeff Campbell in "Bellow's Intimations of Immortality: *Henderson the Rain King*" (1969) believes that the central metaphor for this novel comes from Wordsworth's "Intimations" ode. After presenting a good plot summary showing how Bellow burlesques modern American literary figures, Campbell proceeds to indicate the parallel to Wordsworth, noting how this parallel provides a "meaningful structural pattern." Susan Toth's "*Henderson the Rain King:* Eliot and Browning" (1971) also locates English sources for this work. She claims that T. S. Eliot's "The Wasteland" and Robert Browning's "Childe Roland to the Dark Tower Came," poems which depict a "recurring contemporary figure, a lost soul who searches for life and meaning in a stony and arid wasteland," implicitly provide the background to Henderson's journey. In "The Road of Excess: Saul Bellow's *Henderson the Rain King*" (1983), Ted Billy expresses his belief that the philosophy of William Blake is a pervasive influence in Bellow's *Henderson* and traces Bellow's use of Blakean proverbs, while Robert Edward Colbert, in "Saul Bellow's King of Confidence" (1982), suggests, in an in-depth study, that *Henderson the Rain King* is a parody of Conrad's *Heart of Darkness*. Richard Pearce, in his *Stages of the Clown* (1970), a book-length study of archetypal clown figures, shows how *Henderson* "explore[s] the modern manifestation of the Harlequin figure." Pearce states that the figure of Henderson is a caricature of the American hero and that in the novel, Bellow "synthesized the hero of the Cooper tall-tale tradition with the hero of the clown tradition to explore the contradictions of man in modern society."

Eusebio Rodrigues, who has written a number of valuable articles on *Henderson the Rain King*, in "Bellow's Africa" (1971) traces the novel to Bellow's knowledge of anthropology, specifically to a work written by his former teacher, Melville J. Herskovits, *The Cattle Complex in East Africa*, as well as to writings of the Reverend John Roscoe published in the *Royal Anthropology Journal*, Frederic E. Forbes, and Sir Richard Burton. In another article ("Reichianism in *Henderson the Rain King*," 1973), Rodrigues, picking up on Bellow's interest on Wilhelm Reich as pointed out by Bellow's friend Richard G. Stern in an early review of the work, presents an in-depth study of Bellow's use of Reich's theory of the pervasive existence of orgone energy in both man and nature in order to indicate how the eruptions of this life-force, bottled up in Henderson, produce "strange behavorial distortions." Henderson's farcical adventures, he says, take on a "meaningful dimension in the light of the ideas and methods of Wilhelm Reich."

Bellow's iconoclastic posture toward the literary tradition has been previously commented upon with regard to his other works. Those critics who see Bellow as an anti-Modernist find much in *Henderson the Rain King* to support their contentions. Two excellent and valuable essays on this subject are presented by Donald W. Markos ("Life Against Death in *Henderson the Rain King*," 1971) and Gloria L. Cronin ("*Henderson the Rain King*: A Parodic Expose of the Modern Novel," 1983). Markos's article shows how Bellow deals with his dissatisfaction with modernism in literature: his presentation of both views—"the modernist version of man's alienation and the tentative offering of a new attitude toward the world and man's conception of himself—a humanism grounded in a kind of intuitive naturalism." Markos's analysis of *Henderson* leads to his conclusion that contrary to the "modernist hostility toward civilization . . . the novel poses the possibility of an integration or accommodation which is not destructive to one's sense of authentic being." Bellow, while recognizing the absurdities of civilized man, contends, nevertheless, that man must "cultivate a positive relationship with society."

Cronin's essay, which is the best to date dealing with Bellow's response to modernism, traces Bellow's critical stance to ideas formulated in his essays and then indicates how these ideas work in *Henderson the Rain King*. In a prose which parallels and forcefully expresses the strength of her convictions, she points out that Bellow uses the device of parody to show the "absurdities of absurdism, the banalities of historicist thinking and the ignominy of postmodern sewer searching." Cronin views Henderson as "more than just a parody on the modern hero. Henderson is a parody of the qualities of

solipsism, morbidity, self-abasement, and self-aggrandizement wher-
ever they appear in literature. . . . But more important than this rat-
tling of the foundations of modern social sciences is Bellow's attack
on the Rousseauistic aggrandizement of the powers of the individual,
the extremist romantic impulse which Bellow believes to lie behind
much of the disappointment and anger in the modern novel." Cronin
sees Dahfu, the "African philosopher," as representative of this mode
of thinking; she also sees that Bellow intended Dahfu's characterization as a parody of the "American quack transcendentalist Wilhelm
Reich." Bellow's parody for Cronin is purposive: "to restore to the
Anglo-American novel a measure of health, sanity, and truth about
human existence."

    Other articles of special interest on *Henderson the Rain King* are
Daniel J. Hughes's, "Reality and the Hero: *Lolita* and *Henderson the
Rain King*" (1960), which suggests that since both novels concern the
quest for reality, reading both works "in conjunction" will illuminate
the meaning of each novel; and Joel R. Kehler's "Henderson's Sacred
Science" (1980), which contends that "Bellow plays off against one
another a variety of concepts drawn from the history of science."
Kehler's is an original and valuable critique.

    Six years after the writing of *Henderson the Rain King*, Saul Bellow
published what has been termed by all critics his "most Jewish novel,"
Herzog. While *Henderson* is Bellow's only novel (until *The Dean's December*) to make use of a gentile protagonist, no critic (except for L. H.
Goldman in her book *Saul Bellow's Moral Vision: A Critical Study of the
Jewish Experience*, 1982) has paid much attention to this point. Indeed,
the trend has been to look for the "Jewish" qualities in Henderson.
This is a misreading of the work. Bellow, himself, takes issue with this
interpretation in a statement made to Chirantan Kulshrestha, "A Conversation with Saul Bellow" (1972): "Henderson is not a Jew, but he
has been accused by some of being some sort of convert. But that's
false; that is simply not the case." If Henderson as a gentile has not
been explored sufficiently, Herzog's Jewish characteristics have been
amply investigated and have produced interesting criticism and an
ongoing agon among the critics.

    Maurice Samuel, a well-known Yiddishist and contemporary
Jewish-American writer, sounded the battle cry. In his article "My
Friend, the Late Moses Herzog" (1966), which is a combination of
straight-forward criticism and mock-heroic fantasy (and readers
should recognize the fictitious nature of his purported meeting with
the Herzog brothers) Samuel draws a parallel between Joyce's *Ulysses*

and Bellow's *Herzog*, declaring that from a certain perspective both may be regarded as "two major modern studies in Jewish assimilation." Both protagonists attempt to come to terms with their "self-identification as Jews while trying to leave their mark on the world." Samuel, briefly and forthrightly, discusses Leopold Bloom's relationship to his society and then, after a terse summary section on Moses Herzog, proceeds to elaborate upon his meeting with the Herzog brothers, Willy, Alexander, and Moses. It is a wonderful piece of fantasy and parody in which Samuel projects the type of Jew drawn by Bellow in both the vignettes of Moses's brothers and in Moses himself. However, Samuel cannot reconcile the religious transcendental ending with the rest of the work. Moses's exclamation of *Hineni* in the isolation of Ludeyville, announcing his reestablished freedom and priestly in its suggestion of his willingness to do God's bidding, seems fantastic to Samuel. He says: "Whom, to use his own words, was he kidding?" Samuel's essay is, perhaps, the most negative of those dealing with the issue of Moses's Jewishness. Dan Vogel, who prefaces his essay "Saul Bellow's Vision Beyond Absurdity: Jewishness in *Herzog*" (1968) with a valuable discussion of "why Jewish fiction in America has come to reflect the emotions and concerns of the non-Jewish scholar and critic," concludes with the thesis that the American-Jewish writer contributes to "contemporary American literature . . . a vision beyond absurdity" and that this is Bellow's achievement in *Herzog*. Vogel suggests that the "best way to understand Moses Herzog as the archetypal American Jew of his generation is to consider him as the progeny of the generation of Abraham Cahan's *David Levinsky*," the fictional representative of the "parent generation that produced the Moses Herzogs of American-Jewish history." And "Bellow's archetype comes to represent the pendular experience of the American Jew." Most important, Vogel indicates, in his conclusion, how Bellow's portrayal of Moses Herzog represents a movement away from a modernist-nihilistic "god is dead" view to an antimodernist, humanistic, theonomous ontology. "Herzog's spiritual journey is Bellow's declaration through his protagonist that God is truly alive; but more," writes Vogel, "that He cares; and still more that He pays individual attention. This is truly a vision beyond absurdity." This antimodernist interpretation heralds the trend of newer or later Bellow criticism. In "The Purgation of Twentieth Century Consciousness" (1985) Gloria Cronin views *Herzog* as she has Bellow's earlier novels, as an anti-modernist work. Her conclusion is that *Herzog*, "while it dramatizes the evils of Modernist thinking also depicts the heroic journey of one individual to recover a meaningful private existence. . . . "

Both Harold Fisch in "The Hero as Jew: Reflections on *Herzog*" (1968) and David Galloway in "Moses-Bloom-Herzog: Bellow's Everyman" (1966) deal with Herzog's Jewishness, and both locate its parallel in Joyce's *Ulysses*. Bellow is annoyed at the comparison and insists "The Joyce thing is purely a coincidence." (Cf Liela Goldman's discussion of the name Moses Herzog both in her note "Bellow's Moses Herzog" (1979) and in the chapter on *Herzog* in her book *Saul Bellow's Moral Vision: A Critical Study of the Jewish Experience*, which deal with Bellow's erroneous information on the source of the name.) Galloway emphasizes the point that Herzog's Jewishness is of particular importance to his character development because the values he espouses later on "grow directly from his Jewish immigrant background rather than from his adult experience as a liberal intellectual." Fisch views the Jew as "Everyman," stating that "all are now outcasts." Yet Herzog's story, he says, is the attempt of man to free himself from alienation, despair, emptiness. Together with a discussion of Herzog qua Jew in the "Hebraic tradition," Fisch presents a valuable discussion of the narrative technique, Bellow's use of the epistolary form. In "From Cohn to Herzog" (1969), Michael J. Hoffman sees Moses Herzog as evolving from Robert Cohn, the "hangdog" Jew in Ernest Hemingway's *The Sun Also Rises*. After comparing the characters, Hoffman states that Moses Herzog is "Bellow's butt just as Cohn is Hemingway's; but he is not an object of scorn, just a poor, absurd, over-educated slob—like the rest of us."

By far the best and most valuable discussion on the subject is presented by Dudley Flamm ("Herzog—Victim and Hero," 1969). Flamm recognizes that Herzog's importance in the novel is not as "Everyman," but as Jew, in the limited, particular sense, for it is this parochial "world of the Jew, not totally assimilated to the surrounding culture," that Bellow explores. Herzog is a "displaced person," a member of a minority that never quite fits into the American cultural mix. As such he is a victim. Yet he is also a hero because he refuses the role of victim. Herzog says: "I hate the victim bit." Flamm includes, in his essay, a discussion of the novel *The Victim* to clarify his point, as well as of the women in *Herzog*, who have brought Herzog to the brink of his personal crisis.

Other worthwhile critical studies of *Herzog* deal with specific aspects of the novel. James Dean Young's "Bellow's Vision of the Heart" (1965) includes an excellent and useful discussion of structure;

Mary D. Schueler ("The Figure of Madeleine in *Herzog*," 1971) traces the literary tradition of the character Madeleine (Magdalen) beginning with the New Testament and examines Madeleine's role as Magdalen, with a proper caveat: Whatever the reader knows about her is from Moses Herzog who, from the first page of the novel, has been established "as an unreliable witness and narrator." Harold F. Mosher ("The Synthesis of Past and Present in Saul Bellow's *Herzog*," 1971) examines the significance of Herzog as historian; Jennifer M. Bailey ("A Qualified Affirmation of Saul Bellow's Recent Work," 1973) is concerned with the ironic tone established at the very beginning, which, she feels, "undermines the rightness of Herzog's sensibility as a dramatic realization." Sanford Pinsker points out in "Moses Herzog's Fall into the Quotidian" (1974) that the word "fall"—found on the first page—is crucial to the entire work, as Moses's dealings are with the "ordinary." Pinsker explains that "In a very real sense the 'quotidian' has always been the naturalist's favorite stomping grounds; Bellow's achievement has been in blending the grit of urban life with an ongoing essay about transcendent values." Jo Brans writes in "The Balance Sheet of Love: Money and Meaning in Bellow's *Herzog*" (1978) about the symbolic significance of money in most of Bellow's novels; Allan Chavkin discusses Herzog's love problems in "Bellow's Alternative to the Wasteland: Romantic Theme and Form in *Herzog*" (1979) and concludes that Herzog comes to recognize that "love is often banal, frustrating, and irrational. . . . What Herzog is unable to establish is a balanced relationship with a woman in the course of the novel but he finally recognizes the cause of his lack of success . . . "; in "The Keystone and the Arch: Another Look at Structure in *Herzog*" (1978), Sue S. Park analyzes the book's chapter divisions and views *Herzog* graphically as an arch wherein the fifth chapter is the most important.

Liela Goldman's article (1982) is the only essay to address fully Bellow's use of Hebrew and Yiddish, specifically in this novel. In a thorough study of Bellow's usage of these languages, Goldman chastises Bellow for not being as fastidious in his employment of Hebrew and Yiddish as he is with other foreign languages or even with English. She concludes that this careless usage reflects upon Bellow himself and not upon Herzog. In a shorter article ("On the Character of Ravitch in Saul Bellow's *Herzog*," 1981), Goldman suggests that the poetic Jewish drunkard is fashioned after the well-known, Canadian Yiddish poet—who was alive at the time of the publication of *Herzog*—Melech Ravitch. Joseph Nassar's article ("The World Within: Image

Cluster in *Herzog*," 1983) deals with Bellow's use of image clusters, especially colors, odors, and natural phenomena. Nassar states that these are of symbolic value and reveal Herzog's progressive and psychological condition and the "ultimate meaning of the novel." Don Elgin claims in "Order out of Chaos" (1984) that Herzog is a traditional picaro, but his roguery is of the mind.

By the time Bellow published his seventh novel, a pattern for reviewers had already been established: Bellowphiles would love a new work and praise it accordingly while Bellowphobics would disparage each new work. Such was the case with *Mr. Sammler's Planet*, which, with the added onus of contemporaneity, commenting—as it does—on the culture and the politics of the 1960s, received a partisan critical reception: liberals applauded it; radicals attacked it. Criticism ranged from *Mr. Sammler's Planet* being "an extremely brilliant novel" to the novel being "a dreadful book." Future works of Bellow's will continue to elicit strong reactions. Nevertheless, with regard to *Mr. Sammler's Planet*, there are some balanced critiques and worthwhile points made by some early reviewers. Irving Howe, a sensitive reader and incisive critic, reviewing the work for *Harper's Magazine*, notes that Bellow has cast himself as an "adversary . . . of the dominant styles of our culture." His point about the locus of the story—Manhattan's Upper West Side—as "exemplifying our condition" and suggesting almost a mythic quality to it—is cogent and has not received adequate attention by critics. Howe also comments on Bellow as a Jewish-American writer, who is "not merely the most gifted by far, but the most serious—and the most Jewish in his seriousness. In him alone, or almost alone, the tradition of immigrant Jewishness, minus the *Schmaltz* and *Schumtz* the decades have stuccoed onto it survives with a stern dignity." Charles Thomas Samuels, in his review of *Mr. Sammler's Planet* for the *New Republic* calls it "an intelligent, beautifully written book," but criticizes it for its discrepancy between the action, which "typically proves the presence of vice," and the rhetoric, which "argues for virtue."

Indeed, *Mr. Sammler's Planet*, for some reason, has generated more criticism on technique than any other Bellow novel. The most interesting in this area is "Mr. Bellow's Sammler: The Evolution of a Contemporary Text" (1975) by Keith Cushman. Cushman's intention is to "illustrate the working method of our most distinguished living novelist." He has delved into the manuscripts as well as the differing versions that have appeared, first in its serialized rendition in the *Atlantic* and then in the Viking Press text. He points out the discrepancies between the two texts and indicates the evolution of *Mr. Samm-ler's Planet* from its earliest to its final form. James Neil Harris ("One Critical Approach to *Mr. Sammler's Planet*," 1972) discusses the use of sardonic humor in this novel; Allen Guttmann ("Saul Bellow's Mr. Sammler," 1973) is concerned with the separation between author and protagonist and shows that in Sammler, Bellow has created "an extraordinary character and not a mouthpiece for the radical right." Guttmann indicates that Bellow does maintain an ironic distance from his fictive creation. Douglass Bolling ("Intellectual and Aesthetic Dimensions of *Mr. Sammler's Planet*," 1974) states that "two major patterns inform the novel": one on the intellectual level; the other on the level of action. He suggests that this "double-edged aesthetic" is analogous to drawing and painting. Roger Jones in "Artistry and The Depth of Life: Aspects of Attitude and Technique in *Mr. Sammler's Planet*" (1976) also points to the allusion of Art, both as an activity and as something valuable, and the "level of artistic organization" in *Mr. Sammler's Planet*. Suzanne F. Kistler in "Epic Structure and Statement in *Mr. Sammler's Planet*" (1978) claims that Bellow employs the classical "epic structure" as used in the *Aeneid* and in *Paradise Lost,* "because it is integrally related to the classical statement of affirmation that he [Bellow] is making." Sammler's journey is from "nineteenth-century blindness to illumination and wisdom." Liela Goldman in suggests in "The Source for Mr. Sammler's Planet" (1982) that this novel is Bellow's only satire and that Bellow draws heavily upon the satire of Solomon's Ecclesiastes for this novel. In addition, the work is a tribute to Bellow's good friend, Isaac Rosenfeld, whose short story, "King Solomon," provided the literary stylistic, and ideational inspiration for the work.

Since *Mr. Sammler's Planet* is Bellow's only novel to deal with the Holocaust in any direct way, a few critics, perhaps too few, have commented on this subject. In "Imagining the Holocaust: *Mr. Sammler's Planet* and Others" (1973), Edward Alexander notes that Sammler's "experience of the Holocaust is the chief determinant of [his] . . . life, because it has been the ultimate reality of twentieth-century life. . . . Having become a symbol himself—of the human will to live and the power of endurance—he is alive to the symbolic nature of reality and to the omnipresence of the angel of death." Judie Newman indicates in "*Mr. Sammler's Planet*: Wells, Hitler and the World State" (1983) how the Holocaust, one of two major historical events in the novel, governs the action of the book. Viewed as a metaphor for the world of another planet, the concentration camp universe, the "Holocaust provides a locus for the discussion of evil in history." Bellow develops, Newman states, the opposition between optimistic and pessimistic vision of global history" in the first chapter of the novel. S. Lillian Kremer, whose "The Holocaust in *Mr. Sammler's Planet*" (1985) is the most extensive on this subject, differentiates between "European Holocaust chroniclers," such as Elie Wiesel and Andre Schwartz-Bart, who confront the Holocaust directly, dramatizing the atrocities of camp life, and Bellow, who evokes the past through the haunting recollection of survivors and examines their current "behavioral and emotional disorders stemming from wartime brutality." Although, Kremer notes, the immediacy of the Nazi horror is sacrificed, the enduring effect of this barbarism, the continual mental torment and anguish of the victims, is powerfully transmitted.

Other essays that are noteworthy include Mariann Russell's "White Man's Black Man: Three Views" dealing with the presentation of the black man in *Mr. Sammler's Planet, Rabbit Redux,* and *The Tenants.* She claims that "the black man becomes a convenient metaphor for the disturbing elements in white society, and is, in the last analysis, not an image of black culture, but a mirror image of the prevailing culture." This is a valuable discussion as far as it goes. Yet the subject of the presentation of blacks in Bellow's works remains undeveloped. Mark Weinstein's article "The Fundamental Elements in *Mr. Sammler's Planet*" (1982) suggests that the "complex material of the novel" is "communicated by means of the most fundamental of all image-patterns—that of four basic elements, earth, air, fire, and water." And Gloria Cronin in "Faith and Futurity: The Case for Survival in *Mr. Sammler's Planet*" (1983) views this novel as a "powerful testimony of Bellow's humanistic credo—that the Self is a creature endowed with the power to divine truth and reach moral maturity."

What differentiates *Humboldt's Gift* (1975), Bellow's eighth novel, from his previous novels, is its portraitures of Bellow's deceased friend, Delmore Schwartz, and its comic treatment of the sacrosanct subject of death with its possibility of transcendence through the anthroposophic theories of Rudolf Steiner. Both subjects have been dealt with amply by the critics. As expected, not all the initial reviewers, or even later critics, liked the work. Nevertheless, most would agree with Carlos Baker in "Bellow's Gift" (1976) that Bellow is "America's leading philosophical novelist," and for all its zaniness and humor, *Humboldt's Gift,* is thoughtful, touching, contemporaneous. Baker views *Humboldt's Gift* as a *roman à clef* and states that "Von Humboldt Fleisher is an exact and loving but also satirical picture" of Delmore Schwartz.

His comparison of Bellow and Schwartz from first-hand observation is most interesting as is his comment that Charlie Citrine "is more or less a self portrait of Bellow from youth to sexagenarian." Sarah Blacher Cohen ("Comedy and Guilt in *Humboldt's Gift*," 1979) claims that in the novel Bellow is working out his feelings of guilt toward friends who are now dead. Cohen examines the fictional treatment of his "private obsessions." She views this novel as mostly a "protracted elegy," comic in conception, "with Citrine weeping for Humboldt and cursing materialistic America for driving the brilliant poet to ruin." What is most disturbing in Cohen's article is her equating Citrine, in his ambiguous relationship with the dead, to the Holocaust survivor. Commentators on Holocaust material would view this as a "trivialization" of the Holocaust. Citrine's equivocation towards the dead is insufficient to warrant the analogy, and Bellow's basically comic perspective rules out such a comparison. David Kerner in "The Incomplete Dialectic of *Humboldt's Gift*" (1982), claims that Bellow's rendition of Delmore Schwartz in the character of Von Humboldt Fleisher as incomplete and deficient is purposive: in order to maintain a "dialectical ideal, which is the aim of a novel of ideas." Kerner explores the extent to which Bellow has achieved this ideal.

Herbert J. Smith notes in "*Humboldt's Gift* and Rudolph Steiner" (1978) that Bellow's use of the philosophy of Rudolf Steiner is humanistic, fostering a "more complete defense of man," exploring, as it does, the "dialectical tension between human ideals and human actuality." Fredrica K. Bartz in "*Humboldt's Gift* and the Myth of the Artist in America" (1982) takes issue with the contentions of other critics concerning what she refers to as "the artist-in-material-America myth," i. e., America's increasing and profuse materialism threatens to suffocate the soul of the artist, and that Rudolf Steiner's theories reveal a new perspective on the destruction of artistic talent. Bartz claims that Humboldt's "tragedy is not that of being a poet in a materialistic America, but of being a poet with too little strength for the development of his soul and too little concern for his mystic mission." Familiarity with Steinerian thought reveals the fallacy of this myth. Allan Chavkin in "*Humboldt's Gift* and the Romantic Imagination" (1983) states that "Steiner's occult anthroposophy should not be considered the key to the novel." Chavkin maintains that Bellow's extensive knowledge of the English Romantics suggests that his "sensibility is fundamentally romantic," and that this romantic sensibility is at the core of the work. Therefore, *Humboldt's Gift* "can best be understood as a product of the nineteenth-century humanistic tradition" which maintains a faith in the individual, particularly that "he can achieve an affirmative orientation to his surroundings by the power of his mind." According to Chavkin, Wordsworth's "Ode: Intimations of Immortality from Recollections of Early Childhood" is the "single most important influence on the novel."

Readers will find Ben Siegel's essay, "Artists and Opportunities in Saul Bellow's *Humboldt's Gift*" (1978), valuable. It is more generalized and highly intelligent, and his prose is easily readable. Siegel emphasizes the point that "despite his intellectual concerns, . . . Bellow is basically a storyteller"; and his characters, despite their "antic involvements," "reassert Bellow's unflagging humanism." Siegel persues the two main themes that he feels compose the essence of *Humboldt's Gift:* "The dangers posed to the artist in America by worldly success . . ." and "the comic pathos of a vain intellectual's efforts to age with style and dignity." He, too, notes that Bellow clearly indicates that the "artist in America bears at least partial blame for his failures." He presents an in-depth study of Fleisher and Citrine as well as discussion of Rudolf Steiner and Bellow's "visionary turn." He compares Bellow's "confidence in the occult" with Isaac Bashevis Singer's acceptance of supernatural. Siegel concludes his essay with a discussion on the much-debated conclusion of the novel itself.

An interesting subject relating to this novel that a few critics have dealt with is that of cannibalism. Suzanne F. Kistler's "Bellow's Man-Eating Comedy: Cannibal Imagery in *Humboldt's Gift*" says that cannibalism is a "metaphor for Bellow's vision of exploitative twentieth-century Western society," and notes the numerous times the term is used in the work. K. E. Possler (1978) points out that "cannibalism illustrates the relationship between Citrine and Humboldt—the death of one that the other might survive, financially and artistically." It is the central theme of *Von Trenck, Caldofreddo* and ultimately the work itself. Mark Busby in "Castaways, Cannibals and the Function of Art in Saul Bellow's *Humboldt's Gift*" relates the cannibal motif to "questions of nature, innocence, art, and society" in this work and suggests that Shakespeare's *The Tempest* is Bellow's source.

Also of interest are the essays by Marianne Nault, Allan Chavkin, Sanford Radner, Barbara L. Estrin and Judie Newman. Nault ("Humboldt the First," 1977) suggests that there are multiple sources for Bellow's Von Humboldt Fleisher, not only Delmore Schwartz; Chavkin ("Baron Humboldt and Bellow's Von Humboldt Fleisher," 1980), contrasts the careers of Von Humboldt Fleisher to Baron Alexander Von Humboldt to uncover the source of Fleisher's failure; Radner

("The Woman Savior in *Humboldt's Gift*, 1981) suggests that psychological movement in the novel provides the focal point and suggests a unifying theme; Estrin ("Recomposing Time: *Humboldt's Gift* and Ragtime, 1982) indicates how the central characters of both works attempt to avert the problems of contemporary history; and Newman ("Bellow's Indian Givers," 1981) deals with the thematic implications of Humboldt's gift-giving by relating it to the gift-giving customs among the Kwakiutl Indians.

Six years after Bellow received the Nobel Prize for Literature he published *The Dean's December*. Reviewers were intent upon seeing whether Bellow suffered the fate—literary decline—of most Nobel recipients, and many were elated to affirm that this indeed was the case. The new novel came in for some harsh criticism, ranging from calling the work an "aberration," or a "jeremiad within a jeremiad," or a "lumpy carryall," or claiming that the "dean never really comes to life," or that the "tone is so tired; the structure . . . patchy." Nevertheless, amidst all the nay-saying, some acknowledged that it was a "superbly written novel," or that "Sentence by sentence . . . Saul Bellow is simply the best writer we have." Allan Chavkin, in his review-article on *The Dean's December*, "Recovering the World That Is Buried Under the Debris: False Descriptions" (1982), points out that understanding Bellow's intention regarding this work makes the common criticisms irrelevant. Bellow set out to write a "meditative novel" wherein the plot is subordinate to the subject matter; the sobriety is intentional and befitting to the subject matter. Unlike *Humboldt's Gift*, Bellow does not make a comedy about death in his latest novel. Certainly Chavkin's lengthy review indicates that *The Dean's December* needs more reflection than given the novel by some of the early reviewers who insisted on judging it according to Bellow's other works rather than on its own merit.

More recent scholarly criticism has been more sympathetic and has noted both the complexity of the issues Bellow deals with as well as the appropriateness of his "elegiac" tone. Sanford Pinsker, for example, notes in "A Kaddish for Valeria Raresh: Dean Albert Corde's Long Dark Month of the Soul" (1983) that "Albert Corde joins a long list of protagonists who brood about Significant Issues," and that his "dreamy meditations are juxtaposed against an unmeditative, brutally quotidian world"; however, what is lacking is the "nuttiness" of the early protagonists. Yet, Pinsker observes, as unsatisfying as the work might be as "fiction," *The Dean's December* "raises central, even brave, questions about American life in the 1980s." Pinsker views this work as "another in a series of death-bed meditations," and the drab city, the crying woman, the murder trial, the winter season, all contribute to the novel's "elegiac tone, its sense of an extended *kaddish.*" He points out that if the "sideshow freaks" are missing, the work is unique in its "gallery of memorable women" including a sympathetically drawn wife. Critics were quick to note this, and Allan Chavkin in another article, "The Feminism of *The Dean's December*" (1983), explores the "feminist consciousness that informs the work." In a well-organized and well-considered essay, he examines first the case against Bellow; then the three major points overlooked by critics—that while women are often seen in an unflattering light, there are some that are the equals of their men (Lily in *Henderson the Rain King* and Demmie of *Humboldt's Gift*), that the men are often worse villains than the women in Bellow's fiction, and that the point of view of his stories is usually that of the male protagonist and does not necessarily reflect Bellow's views—then the complexity of the work which depicts "subsidiary and complementary problems." This leads into a discussion of the humanism of the East European women, a "humanism that is necessary for a regeneration of contemporary society," and their matriarch, Valeria.

In "*The Dean's December:* Bellow's Plea for the Humanities" (1983), Ann Weinstein also sees humanism as Bellow's major concern and notes that "Bellow continues to bellow in defense of man and those American ideals worth preserving and reviving." In "Bellow and Nihilism: *The Dean's December*" (1984), Judie Newman, however, while acknowledging that Corde is a humanist, declares that the central problem of the novel is that of nihilism. She defines nihilism in Nietzschean terms: "That the highest values devalue themselves. The aim is missing. 'Why' finds no answer." She carefully explores Corde's relationship to Nietzsche's ideas as well as the myth of Eros and Psyche in this same context.

Matthew C. Roudané suggests in "A Cri de Coeur: The Inner Reality of Saul Bellow's *The Dean's December*" (1984) that the best way to understand Albert Corde is by examining his responses to certain "key" characters in the novel, who are either antagonistic or sympathetic to him: the Colonel at the hospital in Bucharest, Dewey Spangler, Valerie Raresh, and Minna. Corde's relationships with both Valeria and Minna thematically control the novel. In "Through a Glass Brightly: Dean Corde's Escape from History in *The Dean's December*" (1986) Gloria L. Cronin views Corde's responsibility as "the spiritual sifting of empirical reality for evidence of the transcendent." For

Cronin, Corde serves as Bellow's device for "resolving the oldest of all dichotomies in Western thought—that conflict between empirical and mystical modes of apprehension"; the focus of *The Dean's December* is on "the human knowability of truth," and Dean Corde is both "Bellow's representative twentieth-century fool of philosophy and saint of sensibility." Joe Hall observes in *"The Dean's December:* A Separate Act of a Separatist" that Corde puzzles over his sense of ethical outrage; he finds his sources for judgment in the classical ethical tradition of Western Civilization, but finds at the same time that this tradition and the account of the world which sustained it are dying. L. H. Goldman (*"The Dean's December:* A Companion Piece to *Mr. Sammler's Planet,"* 1986) persists in her thesis despite Bellow's statement that his latest work opens new vistas. She compares his treatment of political and social issues, his treatment of blacks, his statement on the darkened universes and totalitarian states, and concludes that the major difference is in the character of the protagonists, one Jewish and the other Gentile. Mark Weinstein points out in "Communication in *The Dean's December"* that communication is the main subject of the novel; "it pervades nearly all of the incidents . . . unifies the otherwise disparate materials, and becomes a major structural principle."

Although Bellow's first published works were short stories, "Two Morning Monologues" (1941) and "The Mexican General" (1942), his short stories have elicited little attention. There seems to be more interest in his most recent collection, *Him With His Foot In His Mouth and Other Stories* (1984), however, than in his earlier collection, *Mosby's Memoirs* (1968), and only sporadic interest in some of the uncollected stories. Likewise his play, *The Last Analysis* (1965) and his memoir, *To Jerusalem and Back: A Personal Account* (1976), have also generated almost no critical attention. These works remain as fertile grounds for the resourceful scholar.

Critical Studies: Articles and Book Sections

Fourteen years after he published his first work and with the appearance of the novella *Seize the Day,* Bellow had established himself as a writer to be reckoned with, and critics started taking account of his literary output. Articles in journals and sections in books were being devoted to assessing his place in American literature and defining his oeuvre. Given the voluminous body of criticism now available of Bellow's works, one would have to say that the basic approach to Bellow criticism is variety. Yet amidst this diversity certain preferred areas of approach can be discerned: religious/philosophical; sources; style; special interests. These categories or trends are not distinct and intersect each other.

Saul Bellow as a Jewish writer has been a consistent concern of critics. Appearing on the literary scene at a time when this locale was basically a "WASP world," it was inevitable that writers and critics should note this audaciousness and should assess the value of this new author in terms of his heritage. Bellow himself is to blame for fueling this controversy with his remarks on the subject, which appear in his interviews, both denying and affirming his stance. This approach started early and spans Bellow's literary career. Chester Eisinger, in his article ("Saul Bellow: Love and Identity," 1958) and then in his chapter on Bellow in his book (*Fiction of the Forties*, 1963) notes the "undeniable Jewish quality of Bellow's work." In his sketch of the Bellow world from the 1930s to the 1950s, he observes Bellow's humanistic attitude toward life, one which can be encompassed in terms of "freedom, identity, and love." Jewish tradition is reflected in Bellow's works, according to Eisinger, in his declaration of love for man despite his fallibility. Actually Bellow would say because of his fallibility—rather than despite—this is what makes man human. Eisinger, perhaps goes a little too far in suggesting the similarity to the principles of Hasidism or in referring to Bellow as a "secular hasid." Nevertheless his discussion of Bellow's works from *The Victim* through *Seize the Day*, provides a good introduction to the reading of Bellow.

Jules Chametzky in "Notes on the Assimilation of the American-Jewish Writer: Abraham Cahan to Saul Bellow" (1964) deals with Bellow in terms of the genre of American-Jewish literature and follows its line of development from the constricting attitudes prevalent at the turn of the century to the liberating postures of the post-Holocaust period—the period in which Bellow writes. Irving Malin in his book *Jews and Americans* (1965), Allen Guttmann in his book *The Jewish Writer in America* (1971), and Alfred Kazin in his *Bright Book of Life* (1973) present similar studies. Malin and Guttmann attempt to reconcile Bellow within the larger body of American literature, while Kazin indicates Bellow's use of the Jewish experience. Stanley Trachtenberg ("Saul Bellow's Luftmenschen: The Compromise with Reality," 1967) uses a distinct invention of the shtetl—the man of air, the marginal man—the *luftmensch*, to describe numerous Bellow characters. They are the antagonists of the novel, those the heroes must confront, contend, and ultimately compromise with in order to determine the nature of reality. The definitive article on this subject is presented by

L. H. Goldman in her essay "Saul Bellow and the Philosophy of Judaism" (in the special Saul Bellow issue of *Studies in the Literary Imagination*, 1984), which links Bellow's entire canon—*Dangling Man* through *The Dean's December*—with the philosophical principles of Judaism. Another article by Goldman ("The Holocaust and the Novels of Saul Bellow," 1986) deals with a different area of Jewish experience: the Holocaust. In this essay she presents an in-depth study of Bellow's treatment of "twentieth-century's greatest crime, throughout his novels, but with greater emphasis on *Herzog, Mr. Sammler's Planet,* and *Humboldt's Gift.*

Judaism was not the only philosophical principle by which to assess Bellow's works. A number of critics link his ideas with the concepts of Existentialism and Transcendentalism. Howard Harper devotes a chapter of his book, *Desperate Faith* (1967) to the fiction of Saul Bellow, through *Herzog,* and examines these works in terms of the existential dilemma: "Man adrift in a world he never made . . . man's yearning for transcendent power." Harper's lengthy discussion, which is generally worthwhile, suffers at times from a too sympathetic view of the protagonist so that he imbues both Tommy Wilhelm of *Seize the Day* and Henderson of *Henderson the Rain King* with much more integrity and stature than the author does and refers to Henderson with the unfortunate epithet of "super-Jew" explaining that Henderson is "a pariah not because of his race but because of his extraordinary humanity." James Gindin, in the chapter from his *Harvest of a Quiet Eye* (1971) on Saul Bellow covering the novels through *Mr. Sammler's Planet,* perceives in Bellow's works an evolving definition of existentialism, from the definition in *Dangling Man,* which is particularly relevant to World War II, to the psychological definition in *The Victim* and the sociological definition in *The Adventures of Augie March* and *Seize the Day.* In *Henderson the Rain King,* Gindin claims that Bellow attempts to go beyond a definition of existentialism and confronts what existential man must do: make meaningful choices. *Mr. Sammler's Planet* he sees as presenting a deterministic view. Richard Lehan, in *Dangerous Crossing* (1973) which attempts to relate American novelists to the French literary existentialists, devotes a chapter to the works of both Saul Bellow and Walker Percy ("Into the Ruins: Saul Bellow and Walker Percy"). In Lehan's presentation, the relationship between the two authors is tenuous. Also Lehan never clarifies Bellow's link with the French Existentialists, although he does so for Walker Percy. Ada Aharoni, however, in a shorter, less thorough but more precise article, "Saul Bellow and Existentialism" (1983), indicates Bellow's connection with Sartrean existentialism, that view of man as a being free to determine his own destiny regardless of the situation he finds himself in. Aharoni points out that the difference between Sartre's existential man and Bellow's is that the freedom of choice the Bellow individual has operates within certain limits. M. Gilbert Porter in his essay "Is the Going Up Worth the Coming Down? Transcendental Dualism in Saul Bellow's Fiction" (1984), which examines Bellow's works through *Humboldt's Gift* sees in these works a concern with democracy, nature, death, immortality, and art, the same concerns and philosophical perspectives, Porter argues, of the nineteenth-century American transcendentalists, especially Hawthorne, Melville, Emerson, Thoreau, and Whitman.

Other critics view Bellow's works in a variation of these doctrinal terms. James Hall in *The Lunatic Giant in the Drawing Room* (1968) attempts to fit Bellow into the contemporary British and American literary scene. Hall claims that Bellow remains a captive—albeit a resentful one—to modern thought. His heroes, "heirs of modernism," may not be victims of alienation, but they are victims of "aloneness." They are portraits of "Irritable Man," and Bellow is the "poet of self-chosen discomfort." Nathan A. Scott, Jr. argues in *Three American Moralists* (1973) that Bellow should not be linked, as some critics have done, with the social realism of the immediate past—i. e., the American naturalists—as his characters transcend the pressures of their environment and query into their own existence and their own humanity. Porter suggests that Bellow belongs to that line of modern fiction, exemplified by Faulkner, Twain, Melville, Hawthorne, Dostoyevski, Kafka, Svevo, and Sartre, which searches into the "phenomenology of selfhood." Porter recognizes in early Bellow tendencies toward the theistic position—not necessarily dogmatic, but a rendering of experience which is profoundly religious.

Theodore L. Gross notes in *The Heroic Ideal in American Literature* (1971) Bellow's movement away from the negative, nihilistic assumptions of modern writers, those who claim civilization is dead. Affirmation is the hallmark of Bellow's writings. Gross offers a good introductory essay, covering works to *Herzog*, and indicates that Bellow presents his protagonists—"hero manqués"—within a comic framework, as men who believe that existence is "worthful." In his examination of *The Victim*, Gross makes an interesting and largely unexplored point about the breakdown of Christian values. Daniel Fuchs, in what is perhaps a landmark essay ("Saul Bellow and the Modern Tradition," 1974), views Bellow as going "against the grain of modernism" and suggests instead that he is a "postmodern" writer, a tag that future critics adopt and explore. Fuchs first defines modernism and then indicates in what way Bellow attacks this nihilistic, immoral, and aesthetic view. He presents a valuable, well-written discussion on Bellow's novels through *Mr. Sammler's Planet* to support his thesis. Both Ihab Hassan ("Five Faces of a Hero," 1960, and "The Way Down and Out," 1963) and Marcus Klein ("A Discipline of Nobility: Saul Bellow's Fiction," 1962) suggest that the movement in Bellow's novels is from alienation to accommodation or to acceptance of the limitations of self and society.

Critics have always interested themselves in source-seeking, and Bellow criticism has had its share of such questers. The difficulty in this type of criticism is that at times it reveals more of the interest of the critic than the source of the author's work, which involves a fusion of multiple influences. The isolation of a specific source narrowly delimits the author's work. Nevertheless, Peter M. Axthelm in *The Modern Confessional Novel* (1967), basically confining his discussion to *Herzog*, sees Bellow's works as rooted in the European confessional novel of Dostoyevsky, Koestler, and Golding. It is a well-wrought study which divides Herzog's confession into five stages and then fully explores each stage. Of special value is his study of Madeleine Herzog, whom he refers to as "one of the most memorable women to appear in a confessional novel." Malcolm Bradbury ("The Nightmare in Which I Am Trying to Get a Good Night's Rest: Saul Bellow and Changing History," 1977), Mihail Mandra ("Saul Bellow's Novel in the Context of European Thought," 1980), Barbara Gitenstein ("Saul Bellow and the Yiddish Literary Tradition," 1979), Sanford Pinsker ("Saul Bellow, Soren Kierkegaard and the Question of Boredom," 1980), Dr. Vinoda ("Saul Bellow and Gustave Flaubert," 1981), Mark Weinstein ("Bellow's Imagination-Instructors," 1982), and E. Jeanne Braham ("The Struggle at the Center: Dostoyevsky and Bellow," 1982) take similar approaches in their essays.

Bradbury suggests that Bellow's attempt to "reconstitute humanism"—i. e., to redefine it in terms of the changes modern history has wrought—links him with contemporary European writing and also explains his large European appeal. Mandra states that Bellow's works are a culmination of a thorough grounding in European culture and notes that they are anthropocentric. Gitenstein claims that the Yiddish past is all-pervasive in Bellow's works and that it affects his genre, style, characters, and themes. While the essay is interesting in terms of the Yiddish literary tradition, it is superficial in terms of

Bellow's link to this tradition. His grounding in Talmud during his early years in cheder Bellow mentions numerous times. To go from that to the declaration that "there is also that fertile secular tradition of nineteenth-century Yiddish literature" is a leap in logic and would need more definitive research into Bellow's background to validate such a claim. Pinsker takes boredom—that peculiar interest of some of Bellow's protagonists—and suggests the humor behind this Kierkegaardian "influence." Weinstein notes that William Blake appears often in Bellow's later novels. His characters are influenced by Blakean thought, and his most prominent reality-instructor—Tamkin, Dahfu, and Humboldt—are Blakean; yet these instructors are not reality-instructors but "imagination-instructors." Braham discusses Dostoyevsky's influence on Bellow's first two novels not only in the similarity of plot and use of the double but also in terms of the transcendent quality in both authors. Vinoda contends that Bellow's break with Flaubert's aesthetics is due to its incompatability with the Jewish moral passion. She summarizes Flaubert's aesthetic creed and then details Bellow's objections to it, as well as his dissent from both European deconstructionists and American post-modernists.

A few critics have dealt with Bellow's style, but it is an area that is certainly open to much more critical research. Samuel Hux ("Character and Form in Bellow," 1974)—basing his claims on Bellow's own statements in a Hopwood Lecture entitled "Where Do We Go From Here?"—dispels the notion of Bellow's vision of human character as either existentialist or "Greek." He asserts that for Bellow human character is a continual process of discovery. He also suggests that the looseness of Bellow's novels, beginning with *Augie March*, is not a flaw, but a "serious sophisticated literary" device. Ralph Berets ("Repudiation and Reality Instruction in Saul Bellow's Fiction," 1976) analyzes Bellow's works through *Mr. Sammler's Planet* in terms of their dramatic polarities. Keith Opdahl ("God's Braille: Concrete Detail in Saul Bellow's Fiction,"1978) analyzes Bellow's style through his intense use of concrete detail to dramatize the act of seeing. Bellow's details, while pleasurable in themselves, Opdahl cautions, must be viewed in the larger context of tone, plot, and character. H. Porter Abbott notes in "Saul Bellow and the Lost Cause of Character" (1980) that Bellow views character as subject. Porter deals mainly with *Dangling Man*, *Herzog*, and the short stories "Looking for Mr. Green," "Mosby's Memoirs," and "The Old System." A most useful article in this category is Chirantan Kulshrestha's "The Making of Saul Bellow's Fiction: Notes from the Underground" (1981). Kulshrestha goes directly to Bellow's sources, the Saul Bellow papers in the Special Collections Department at the University of Chicago's Joseph Regenstein Library. This short essay provides a view of the author in the process of creation. Kulshrestha peruses manuscripts and holographs and notes their variations in the final publication of the works. Ada Aharoni ("The Cornerstone of Bellow's Art," 1982) isolates six characteristics, closely linked elements, of Bellow's art and shows how these elements form a literary pattern which underlies most of Bellow's fiction. Eugene Hollahan ("Crisis in Bellow's Novels: Some Data and a Conjecture," 1983) examines Bellow's use of the term *crisis* at crucial loci in his novels and suggests that the use of this "quasi-technical" word induces "certain perspectives on the characters and events in his books. Judie Newman ("Bellow's Sixth Sense: The Sense of History," 1982) views historical content as the organizing principle in Bellow's novels.

A number of interesting essays—some trendsetters, others individualistic and distinctive—should prove valuable for the Bellow scholar. An early essay by Maxwell Geismar ("Saul Bellow: Novelist of the Intellectuals," appearing as a chapter in his book *American Moderns: From Rebellion to Conformity*, 1958) deals with the popularity of Saul Bellow among academics and intellectuals and claims that Bellow, in his works, accurately represents the world view of the intellectuals. A generation later, Ben Siegel views another aspect of this issue in "Saul Bellow and the University as Villain" (1983). Siegel presents a well-written and lengthy study of Bellow's carping at the university and its professors. His essay is divided into six sections, each elaborating on Bellow's paradoxical attitude toward the university: he is rooted in academe, yet it is his frequent target. Molly Stark Wieting ("The Function of the Trickster in Saul Bellow's Novels," 1984) focuses her essay on the motif of the pastoral element which forms a pervasive pattern in Bellow's works. Wieting claims that the pastoral denotes a desire for a simpler place, one which affords inner harmony, one which provides a less complicated mode of existence than that of the city. These flights to nature, however, only prepare the characters for their eventual return to their natural urban habitat. Wieting suggests that the urban world is a projection of the protagonists' fragmented lives, while the pastoral motif symbolizes the possibility of their spiritual renewal. Daniel Walden makes the effect of urbanism and technology on art and the artist the theme of his essay, "Urbanism and the Artist: Saul Bellow and the Age of Technology" (1983). Quoting from statements made by Bellow in various reviews and interviews, Walden, as did Wieting, claims that Bellow links the mechanistic urban world with emotional deformity and that Bellow suggests "art has within it the power to heal the fissure that divides society and the schizophrenic individuals that inhabit it."

Robert Gorham Davis (in his essay collected in *The Creative Present*, ed. Balakian and Simmons, 1963) brings together in one essay Saul Bellow and William Styron in order to discuss the strong American individualist tradition present in the works of both authors. Marvin Mudrick makes a more likely union in the essay in his book *On Culture and Literature* (1970) in which he discusses the ficitonal Jew. Unfortunately, he reduces Bellow to the prosaic. His reading of Bellow's works is flippant. Two critics compare Saul Bellow and Mordecai Richler, both of Canadian origin—Richler still lives in Canada. In "Sex: Saul Bellow's Hedonistic Joke" (1974), Sarah Blacher Cohen contrasts the urban humor of both authors using *Humboldt's Gift* to make her point concerning the urbanity of Bellow's urban humor stemming from his position as a "revered member of the literary establishment," as against the crudity of the humor of Richler who is still a "minority writer." Daniel Golden ("Mystical Musings and Comic Confrontations: The Fiction of Saul Bellow and Mordecai Richler," 1981) views both authors as "in and of an ethnic literary tradition." Golden maintains that although both authors share the commonality of a Jewish culture, Bellow's penchant is for the abstract and philosophical, at times mystical and occult, while Richler's mode is more comic.

Lynette Fairman ("Finitude, Anxiety and Affirmation in Saul Bellow's Novels," 1984) analyzes the anxiety the characters experience because of their mortality. Joe Maw ("Method in His Madness: Bellow Develops the Theme of Insanity," 1983) traces the theme of madness—its scope, symbolism, and intensity—in Bellow's novels and suggests that Bellow attempts to answer the questions "Why is there madness?" and "What can be done about it?"

John Cheever
(1912-1982)

Robert A. Morace
Daemen College

PRIMARY BIBLIOGRAPHY

Books

The Way Some People Live. New York: Random House, 1943. Stories.

The Enormous Radio and Other Stories. New York: Funk & Wagnalls, 1953; London: Gollancz, 1953.

The Wapshot Chronicle. New York: Harper, 1957; London: Gollancz, 1957. Novel.

The Housebreaker of Shady Hill and Other Stories. New York: Harper, 1958; London: Gollancz, 1958.

Some People, Places, and Things That Will Not Appear in My Next Novel. New York: Harper, 1961; London: Gollancz, 1961. Stories.

The Wapshot Scandal. New York: Harper & Row, 1964; London: Gollancz, 1964. Novel.

The Brigadier and the Golf Widow. New York: Harper & Row, 1964; London: Gollancz, 1965. Stories.

Bullet Park. New York: Knopf, 1969; London: Cape, 1969. Novel.

The World of Apples. New York: Knopf, 1973; London: Cape, 1974. Stories.

Falconer. New York: Knopf, 1977; London: Cape, 1977. Novel.

The Stories of John Cheever. New York: Knopf, 1978; London: Cape, 1979.

Oh What a Paradise It Seems. New York: Knopf, 1982; London: Cape, 1982. Novel.

Letters and Journals

Hills, Rust. "Introduction: Of Anthologizing." In *Writer's Choice*, ed. Hills. New York: McKay, 1974, ix. Quotes from a Cheever letter.
"An Exchange on Fiction," *New York Review of Books*, 24 (3 Feb. 1977), 44. Letter in response to an article by Elizabeth Hardwick.
Weaver, John D. "John Cheever: recollections of a childlike imagination," *Los Angeles Times*, 13 Mar. 1977, Book Review: 3, 8. Biographical reminiscence; quotes from Cheever's letters.
"Cheever's Letters," *Vanity Fair*, 47 (May 1984), 60-65. Letters (1933-1956) to Elizabeth Ames, Director of the Yaddo artists' colony.

Selected Other Writings

"A Word from Writer Directly to Reader." In *Fiction of the Fifties*, ed. Herbert Gold. Garden City: Doubleday, 1959, 21.
"Introduction." In *The Wapshot Chronicle*. Time Reading Program Special Edition. New York: Time, Inc., 1965, xvii-xix.
"F. Scott Fitzgerald." In *Atlantic Brief Lives*, ed. Louis Kronenberger. Boston: Little, Brown, 1971, 275-276.
"The Novelist," *Newsweek*, 88 (4 July 1976), 36.
"Why I Write Short Stories," *Newsweek*, 92 (30 Oct. 1978), 24-25.
"Fiction Is Our Most Intimate Means of Communication," *U. S. News and World Report*, 86 (21 May 1979), 92. Cheever's remarks here are the closest he ever came to summarizing his artistic credo.
"A 'True Life Novel' of a Murderer Transfigured by Death," *Chicago Tribune*, 7 Oct. 1979, 7: 1. Review of *The Executioner's Song*, by Norman Mailer.
"In Praise of Readers," *Parade*, 28 Dec. 1980, p. 6.
The Shady Hill Kidnapping. Original teleplay aired by the Public Broadcasting Service, 12 Jan. 1982.

Adaptations

Tonkonogy, Gertrude. *Town House*. 1948. Play adaptation of Cheever's "Town House" stories.
Perry, Eleanor. *The Swimmer*. New York: Stein & Day, 1967. Novel adapted from Perry's screenplay.
_____. *The Swimmer*. 1968. Film adaptation of Cheever's story, "The Swimmer."

Gurney, A. R., Jr. *Children.* 1976. Play adaptation of Cheever's story, "Goodbye, My Brother."

_____. *O Youth and Beauty.* 1979. Teleplay adaptation of Cheever's story of the same name for the Public Broadcasting Service.

McNally, Terence. *The Five-Forty-Eight.* 1979. Teleplay adaptation of Cheever's story of the same name for the Public Broadcasting Service.

Wasserstein, Wendy. *The Sorrows of Gin.* 1979. Teleplay adaptation of Cheever's story of the same name for the Public Broadcasting Service.

Editions and Collections

Stories, ed. William Peden. New York: Farrar, Straus & Cudahy, 1956; London: Gollancz, 1957. Stories by Cheever, Jean Stafford, Daniel Fuchs, and William Maxwell.

Dry Martini, trans. Amalia d'Agostino Schanzer. Milan: Loganesi, 1962.

Selected Stories, trans. Tatyana Litvinova. Moscow, 1962.

SECONDARY BIBLIOGRAPHY

Bibliographies and Checklists

Bosha, Francis J. *John Cheever: A Reference Guide.* Boston: G. K. Hall, 1981. Primary and secondary.

Coates, Dennis. "A Cheever Bibliographical Supplement, 1978-1981." Collected in *Critical Essays on John Cheever,* ed. R. G. Collins. Boston: G. K. Hall, 1982, 279-285. See Collections of Essays. Primary and secondary.

_____. "John Cheever: A Checklist, 1930-1978," *Bulletin of Bibliography,* 36 (Jan.-Mar. 1979), 1-13, 49. Primary and secondary.

Lepper, Gary M. *A Bibliographical Introduction to Seventy-Five Modern American Authors.* Berkeley: Serendipity Books, 1976, 111-112. Primary.

Trakas, Deno. "John Cheever: An Annotated Secondary Bibliography (1943-1978)," *Resources for American Literary Study,* 9 (1979), 181-199.

Biography: Book

Cheever, Susan. *Home Before Dark.* Boston: Houghton Mifflin, 1984.
Includes excerpts from Cheever's journals.

Biographies: Major Articles and Book Sections

Bellow, Saul. "On John Cheever," *New York Review of Books*, 30 (17
Feb. 1983), 38.
Carver, Raymond. "The Art of Fiction: LXXVI: Raymond Carver,"
Paris Review, 88 (Summer 1983), 192-221. Interview conducted
by Mona Simpson.
Cowley, Malcolm. "John Cheever: The Novelist's Life as a Drama,"
Sewanee Review, 91 (Winter 1983), 1-16.
Kahn, E. J., Jr. *About the "New Yorker" and Me.* New York: Putnam's,
1979, 49, 134, 144, 160-161, 206, 244-245, 252, 308, 402.
Kornbluth, Jesse. "The Cheever Chronicle," *New York Times Magazine*,
21 Oct. 1979, pp. 26-29, 102-105.
Robb, Christina. "Cheever's Story," *Boston Globe Magazine*, 6 July 1980,
pp. 11-13, 27-31, 35.
Sheed, Wilfrid. "Mr. Saturday, Mr. Monday, and Mr. Cheever," *Life*,
66 (18 Apr. 1969), 39-46.
Weaver, John D. "John Cheever: recollections of a childlike imagination," *Los Angeles Times*, 13 Mar. 1977, Book Review: 3, 8.

Interviews

Allen, Henry. "John Cheever: Capturing the Splendors of Suburbia,"
Washington Post, 8 Oct. 1979, pp. B1, B13.
Bandler, Michael J. ". . . and in a conversation with the storyteller,"
Chicago Tribune, 22 Oct. 1978, Book World: 1, 9.
Brans, Jo. "Stories to Comprehend Life: An Interview with John
Cheever," *Southwest Review*, 65 (Autumn 1980), 337-345.
Breit, Harvey. "In and Out of Books," *New York Times Book Review*,
10 May 1953, p. 8.
Cowley, Susan Cheever. "A Duet of Cheevers," *Newsweek*, 89 (14 Mar.
1977), 61-71.
Gilder, Joshua. "John Cheever's Affirmation of Faith," *Saturday Re-
view*, 9 (Mar. 1982), 16-19. Review of *Oh What a Paradise It Seems*.
Includes interview material.
Grant, Annette. "John Cheever: The Art of Fiction LXII," *Paris Re-*

view, 17 (Fall 1976), 39-66. Reprinted in *Writers at Work: The Paris Review Interviews*, ed. George Plimpton. 5th series. New York: Viking, 1981, 113-135.

Gutwillig, Robert. "Dim Views Through Fog," *New York Times Book Review*, 13 Nov. 1960, pp. 68-69.

Hersey, John. "John Hersey Talks with John Cheever," *Yale Alumni Magazine and Journal* (Dec. 1977), 21-24. Reprinted in part as "John Cheever, Boy and Man," *New York Times Book Review*, 26 Mar. 1978, pp. 3, 31-34.

_____. "Talk with John Cheever," *New York Times Book Review*, 6 Mar. 1977, pp. 1, 24, 26-28.

Janeway, Elizabeth. "Is the Short Story Necessary?" In *The Writer's World*, ed. Elizabeth Janeway. New York: McGraw-Hill, 1969. Reprinted in *Short Story Theories*, ed. Charles E. May. Athens: Ohio University Press, 1976, 94-106.

Lee, Alwyn. "Ovid In Ossining," *Time*, 27 Mar. 1964, pp. 66-72.

Lehmann-Haupt, Christopher. "Talk with John Cheever," *New York Times Book Review*, 27 Apr. 1969, pp. 42-44.

Lurie, Morris. "Afternoon in Ossining." In his *About Burt Britton, John Cheever, Gordon Lish, William Saroyan, Isaac B. Singer, Kurt Vonnegut, and other matters*. New York: Horizon, 1977, 37-43.

Mitgang, Herbert. "Behind the Bestsellers," *New York Times Book Review*, 28 Jan. 1979, p. 36.

Munro, Eleanor. "Not only I the narrator, but I John Cheever," *MS*, 5 (Apr. 1977), 74-77.

Nichols, Lewis. "A Visit with John Cheever," *New York Times Book Review*, 5 Jan. 1964, p. 28.

Tavernier-Courbin, Jacqueline, and R. G. Collins. "An Interview with John Cheever," *Studies in Literary Humor*, 1, 2 (1978), 3-9.

Unger, Arthur. "John Cheever's long view," *Christian Science Monitor*, 24 Oct. 1979, pp. 17-18.

Waterman, Rollene. *Saturday Review*, 41 (13 Sept. 1958), 33.

Critical Studies: Books

Coale, Samuel. *John Cheever*. New York: Ungar, 1977.

Hunt, George. *John Cheever: The Hobgoblin Company of Love*. Grand Rapids, Mich.: William B. Eerdmans, 1983.

Waldeland, Lynne. *John Cheever*. Boston: Twayne, 1979.

Critical Studies: Collection of Essays

Collins, R. G., ed. *Critical Essays on John Cheever.* Boston: G. K. Hall, 1982.

Critical Studies: Major Articles and Book Sections

Aldridge, John W. "John Cheever and the Soft Sell of Disaster." In his *Time to Murder and Create: The Contemporary Novel in Crisis.* Freeport, N.Y.: Books for Libraries Press, 1966, 171-177. Reprinted in his *The Devil in the Fire: Retrospective Essays on American Literature and Culture, 1951-1971.* New York: Harper's Magazine Press, 1972, 235-240.

Allen, Walter. *The Short Story in English.* New York: Oxford University Press, 1981, 367-371.

Auser, Cortland P. "John Cheever's Myth of Man and Time: 'The Swimmer,'" *CEA Critic,* 29 (Mar. 1967), 18-19.

Blythe, Hal, and Charlie Sweet. "Ironic Nature Imagery in 'The Swimmer,'" *Notes on Contemporary Literature,* 14 (Sept. 1984), 3-4.

Bracher, Frederick. "John Cheever: A Vision of the World," *Claremont Quarterly,* 11 (Winter 1964), 47-57.

_____. "John Cheever and Comedy," *Critique,* 6 (Spring 1963), 66-77.

Braudy, Leo. "Realists, Naturalists, and Novelists of Manners." In *Harvard Guide to Contemporary American Writing,* ed. Daniel Hoffman. Cambridge: Belknap Press of Harvard University Press, 1979, 143-144.

Burhans, Clinton S., Jr. "John Cheever and the Grave of Social Coherence," *Twentieth Century Literature,* 14 (Jan. 1969), 187-198. Collected in Collins.

Burt, Struthers. "John Cheever's Sense of Drama," *Saturday Review,* 26 (24 Apr. 1943), 9. Review of *The Way Some People Live.* Collected in Collins.

Chesnick, Eugene. "The Domesticated Stroke of John Cheever," *New England Quarterly,* 44 (Dec. 1971), 531-552. Collected in Collins.

Clemons, Walter. "Cheever's Triumph," *Newsweek,* 89 (14 Mar. 1977), 61-62, 64, 67. Review of *Falconer.*

Collins, R. G. "Fugitive Time: Dissolving Experience in the Later Fiction of Cheever," *Studies in American Fiction,* 12 (Autumn 1984), 175-188.

_____. "From Subject to Object and Back Again: Individual Identity in John Cheever's Fiction," *Twentieth Century Literature*, 28 (Summer 1982), 1-13.

DeMott, Benjamin. "A grand gatherum of some late 20th-century American weirdos," *New York Times Book Review*, 27 Apr. 1969, pp. 1, 40, 41. Review of *Bullet Park*.

Detweiler, Robert. "John Cheever's *Bullet Park*: A World Beyond Madness." In *Essays in Honour of Professor Tyrus Hillway*, ed. Erwin A. Stürzl. Salzburg: Institut für Englische Sprache und Literatur, Universität Salzburg, 1977, 6-32.

Didion, Joan. "Falconer," *New York Times Book Review*, 6 Mar. 1977, pp. 1, 22, 24. Review of *Falconer*.

_____. "The Way We Live Now," *National Review*, 16 (24 Mar. 1964), 237-240. Review of *The Wapshot Scandal*. Collected in Collins.

Donaldson, Scott. "John Cheever." In *American Writers: A Collection of Literary Biographies*, ed. Leonard Ungar. Supplement 1, part 1. New York: Scribners, 1979, 174-199.

_____. "The Machines in Cheever's Garden." In *The Changing Face of the American Suburbs*, ed. Barry Schwartz. Chicago: University of Chicago Press, 1976, 309-322, 336-337. Collected in Collins.

_____. *The Suburban Myth*. New York: Columbia University Press, 1969, 203-208, 248.

Friedberg, Maurice. "The U. S. in the U. S. S. R.: American Literature through the Filter of Recent Soviet Publishing and Criticism," *Critical Inquiry*, 2 (Spring 1976), 519-583.

Gardner, John. "A Cheever Milestone: 61 Elegantly Crafted Stories," *Chicago Tribune*, 22 Oct. 1978, Book World: 1. Review of *The Stories of John Cheever*.

_____. "On Miracle Row," *Saturday Review*, 4 (2 Apr. 1977), 20-23. Review of *Falconer*. Collected in Collins.

_____. *On Moral Fiction*. New York: Basic Books, 1978, 97-98.

_____. "Witchcraft in Bullet Park," *New York Times Book Review*, 24 Oct. 1971, pp. 2, 24. Collected in Collins.

Garrett, George. "John Cheever and the Charms of Innocence: The Craft of *The Wapshot Scandal*," *Hollins Critic*, 1 (Apr. 1964), 1-12. Collected in Collins, and, with an afterword, in *The Sounder Few: Essays from the Hollins Critic*, ed. R. H. W. Dillard, et al. Athens: University of Georgia Press, 1971, 19-41.

Gerlach, John. "Closure in Modern Short Fiction: Cheever's 'The Enormous Radio' and 'Artemis, the Honest Well Digger,' " *Mod-*

ern Fiction Studies, 28 (Spring 1982), 145-152.

Gilbert, Susan. "Children of the Seventies: The American Family in Recent Fiction," *Soundings: A Journal of Interdisciplinary Studies,* 63 (1980), 199-213.

Gilder, Joshua. "John Cheever's Affirmation of Faith," *Saturday Review,* 9 (Mar. 1982), 16-19. Review of *Oh What a Paradise It Seems.* Includes interview material.

Gray, Paul. "Inescapable Conclusions," *Time,* 112 (16 Oct. 1978), 122, 125. Review of *The Stories of John Cheever.*

Greene, Beatrice. "Icarus at St. Botolphs: A Descent to 'Unwonted Otherness,' " *Style,* 5 (1971), 119-137. Collected in Collins.

Griffin, Bryan F. "III. Literary Vogues: Getting Cheever while he's hot," *Harper's,* 258 (June 1979), 90-93.

Gussow, Adam. "Cheever's Failed Paradise: The Short-Story Stylist as Novelist," *Literary Review,* 27 (Fall 1983), 103-116. Review of *Oh What a Paradise It Seems.*

Hardwick, Elizabeth. "Cheever, or The Ambiguities," *New York Review of Books,* 32 (20 Dec. 1984), 3-4, 6, 8. Review of *Home Before Dark.*

Hassan, Ihab. *Contemporary American Literature 1945-1972: An Introduction.* New York: Ungar, 1973, 64, 82.

_____. "Fiction." In *Literary History of the United States: History,* ed. Robert E. Spiller, et al. 4th ed. New York: Macmillan, 1974, 1469-1470.

_____. *Radical Innocence: Studies in the Contemporary American Novel.* Princeton: Princeton University Press, 1961, 187-194, 200.

Irving, John. "Facts of Living," *Saturday Review,* 5 (30 Sept. 1978), 44-46. Review of *The Stories of John Cheever.*

Johnson, Glen M. "The Moral Structure of Cheever's *Falconer,*" *Studies in American Fiction,* 9 (Spring 1981), 21-31.

Kakutani, Michiko. "John Cheever Is Dead at 70; Novelist Won Pulitzer Prize," *New York Times,* 19 June 1982, pp. 1, 17.

Kapp, Isa. "The Cheerless World of John Cheever," *New Leader,* 61 (11 Sept. 1978), 16-17. Review of *The Stories of John Cheever.*

Kazin, Alfred. "O'Hara, Cheever & Updike," *New York Review of Books,* 20 (19 Apr. 1973), 14-18. Reprinted in his *Bright Book of Life: American Novelists and Storytellers from Hemingway to Mailer.* Boston: Little, Brown, 1973, 110-114. Collected in Collins.

Keen, William P. "The American Waste Land—Brought to You by John Cheever's Radio," *Notes on Modern American Literature,* 6 (Winter 1982), item 20.

Kendle, Burton. "Cheever's Use of Mythology in 'The Enormous Ra-*

dio,' " *Studies in Short Fiction,* 4 (Spring 1967), 262-264.

Kiernan, Robert F. *American Writing Since 1945: A Critical Survey.* New York: Ungar, 1983, 16-19.

Lee, Alwyn. "Ovid in Ossining," *Time,* 83 (27 Mar. 1964), 66-72.

Leonard, John. "Cheever to Roth to Malamud," *Atlantic Monthly,* 231 (June 1973), 112-116. Review of *The World of Apples.*

_____. "Crying in the Wilderness," *Harper's,* 254 (Apr. 1977), 88-89. Review of *Falconer.* Collected in Collins.

McElroy, Joseph. "Falconer by John Cheever," *New Republic,* 176 (26 Mar. 1977), 31-32. Review of *Falconer.* Collected in Collins.

Moore, Stephen C. "The Hero on the 5:42," *Western Humanities Review,* 30 (Spring 1976), 147-152. Collected in Collins.

Morace, Robert A. "The Religious Experience and the 'Mystery of Imprisonment' in *Falconer,*" *Cithara,* 20 (Nov. 1980), 44-53.

O'Hara, James. "Cheever's *The Wapshot Chronicle:* A Narrative of Exploration," *Critique,* 22, 2 (1980), 20-30.

_____. " 'Independence Day at St. Botolph's': The Wapshot Saga Begins," *Massachusetts Studies in English,* 7, 3 (1980), 20-25.

Ozick, Cynthia. "America Aglow," *Commentary,* 38 (July 1964), 66-67. Review of *The Wapshot Scandal.*

_____. "Cheever's Yankee Heritage," *Antioch Review,* 24 (Summer 1964), 263-267. Review of *The Wapshot Scandal.* Collected in Collins.

Pawlowski, Robert S. "Myth as Metaphor: Cheever's 'Torch Song,' " *Research Studies,* 47 (June 1979), 118-121.

Peden, William. *The American Short Story: Continuity and Change 1940-1975.* Boston: Houghton Mifflin, 1975.

_____. *The American Short Story: Front Line in the National Defense.* Boston: Houghton Mifflin, 1964.

Reilly, Edward C. "Autumnal Images in John Cheever's 'The Swimmer,' " *Notes on Contemporary Literature,* 10, 1 (1980), 12.

_____. "Cheever's 'The Hartleys' and Its Major Image," *Notes on Contemporary Literature,* 10, 5 (1980), 10.

_____. "Saving Grace and Moral Balance in John Cheever's Stories," *Publications of the Mississippi Philological Association,* 1 (Summer 1982), 24-29.

Rupp, Richard H. *Celebration in Postwar American Fiction: 1945-1967.* Coral Gables: University of Miami Press, 1970, 20, 27-39.

Schickel, Richard. "The Cheever Chronicle," *Horizon,* 21 (Sept. 1978), 28-33.

Sizemore, Christine W. "The Sweeney Allusion in John Cheever's

'Enormous Radio,'" *Notes on Contemporary Literature,* 7 (Sept. 1977), 9.

Ten Harmsel, Henrietta. "'Young Goodman Brown' and 'The Enormous Radio,'" *Studies in Short Fiction,* 9 (Fall 1972), 407-408.

Tyler, Anne. "Books Considered," *New Republic,* 179 (4 Nov. 1978), 45-47. Review of *The Stories of John Cheever.*

Voss, Arthur. *The American Short Story: A Critical Survey.* Norman: University of Oklahoma Press, 1973, 348.

Walkiewicz, E. P. "1957-1968: Toward Diversity of Form." In *The American Short Story, 1945-1980: A Critical History,* ed. Gordon Weaver. Boston: Twayne, 1983, 35-40.

Whitman, Alden. "John Cheever's morality play for moderns," *Los Angeles Times,* 13 Mar. 1977, Book Review: 1, 8. Review of *Falconer.*

BIBLIOGRAPHICAL ESSAY

Bibliographies and Checklists

No descriptive bibliography of Cheever's works has as yet appeared. Nor has anyone compiled a single, entirely comprehensive checklist of writings by and about the author. Nonetheless, Cheever bibliography may be said to be in sound, if somewhat scattered, shape. The brief listing of books by Cheever in Gary M. Lepper's *A Bibliographical Introduction to Seventy-Five Modern American Authors* (1976) has already been superseded by Dennis Coates's "John Cheever: A Checklist, 1930-1978" and Francis J. Bosha's *John Cheever: A Reference Guide* (1981). The Coates checklist is especially valuable for its thorough record of all primary materials: books, essays, articles, and 172 short stories (including reprintings of stories in collections and anthologies). Coates also lists adaptations of Cheever's works and other secondary sources arranged by type: books, dissertations, biographical notices, interviews, criticism, and reviews. His "A Cheever Bibliographical Supplement, 1978-1981," in *Critical Essays on John Cheever* (1982), follows the same format and adds 106 new items. Bosha's *Reference Guide,* which includes a very useful seven-page overview of Cheever's career, with particular emphasis on the "inconsistent critical response" on the part of reviewers, provides annotations for 593 chronologically arranged reviews, books, articles, dissertations, and interviews, including a number of British and foreign-language items. Bosha's checklist of writings by Cheever does not include (as the one by Coates does) a separate and exhaustive listing of all Cheever short stories, but it does record book-length translations. Although far more limited in scope (eighty of the most important items), Deno Trakas's "John Cheever: An Annotated Secondary Bibliography (1943-1978)" (1979) does include a number of previously unrecorded articles about Cheever's fiction.

Biography: Book

Until the publication of a full-scale biography, Susan Cheever's memoir, *Home Before Dark* (1984), will remain the standard biographical source. She divides her father's life into two periods: the years until 1960 or so that he spent striving for stability as a son, husband, father, and writer, followed by the twenty years during which he tried to break free from the very stability he had sought. Beneath the facade of the genial, well-bred country squire, Cheever was not only reserved and intensely individualistic but unpredictable and financially and emotionally insecure as well. Susan Cheever draws an especially vivid picture of her father's marriage, his feelings of guilt, his bouts with alcohol, heart disease, and finally cancer, and his devastating sense of homelessness. She provides the fullest account yet available of Cheever's troubled childhood, problematic relationship with his older brother Fred, financially burdensome dealings with the *New Yorker*, harrowing recovery from alcoholism, ambivalent sexual yearnings, and various homes and sojourns. Susan Cheever fleshes out her story with the kind of telling details that only an insider can provide; however, her major accomplishment is her ability to synthesize previously available information, most of which originally appeared in interviews. The absence of an index and the purposely loose chronological order of the narrative make this a less than ideal work for quick biographical reference. The absence of any documentation whatsoever is a far more serious shortcoming, one which masks the fact that *Home Before Dark* is not nearly the original and entirely personal work it purports to be. Equally troubling is Susan Cheever's failure to distinguish, when quoting from her father's unpublished journals, the author's drafts of his stories and novels from the man's most intimate confidences. Her tactic of turning the author's fiction into grist for the biographer's mill leads the unwary reader to believe, quite mistakenly, that all such passages are autobiographical revelations.

Biographies: Major Articles and Book Sections

Home Before Dark provides the most complete record of Cheever's life. Briefer but still useful, especially for quick reference, are the biographical sketches in the Coale and Waldeland books (discussed below), Alwyn Lee's "Ovid in Ossining" (also discussed below), and R. G. Collins's "Introduction" to his *Critical Essays on John Cheever.* Wilfrid Sheed's "Mr. Saturday, Mr. Monday, and Mr. Cheever" (1969) is worth consulting for Sheed's portrait of a reticent Cheever determined to keep fiction separate from the fiction-writer and the public author separate from the private man. In a feature story for the *New York Times Magazine* published a decade later, Jesse Kornbluth stresses Cheever's "recent equanimity" and generosity, evident, for example, in his approving comments on the work of certain younger writers; Kornbluth presents Cheever not as the suburban squire so many have assumed him to be but instead as a "suburban Surrealist" who sings the greatness of his world. Although not quite so readily available, Christina Robb's "Cheever's Story" (1980) in the *Boston Globe* is the best and certainly the most perceptive of the mini-biographies. Based (as were the Sheed and Kornbluth articles) on an interview with Cheever, Robb's essay covers a broad range of topics, from the author's early life and his love of physical activity to his literary tastes, religious faith, and work-in-progress. Robb, who devotes special attention to the effect Cheever's Boston upbringing had on his personality, claims that his turning away from his homosexual love of his brother Fred toward marriage and family formed "the turning point" of his life, one which he has "contemplated over and over in his mind and his work ever since."

The reminiscences of friends and colleagues shed additional light on Cheever the man and Cheever the author. In "John Cheever: The Novelist's Life as a Drama" (1983), Malcolm Cowley draws on the fifty years he served as Cheever's editor, mentor, and friend; despite several slips in chronology, Cowley's account is invaluable for its portrayal of Cheever's early years as a writer and personal assessment of Cheever's work. In a speech delivered before the American Academy of Arts and Letters in December 1982 (and subsequently published as "On John Cheever" in the *New York Review of Books*, 1983), Saul Bellow, the contemporary writer Cheever most admired, comments on Cheever's candor, generosity, amiable personality, and the development of his art and vision. E. J. Kahn, Jr., in his anecdotal book *About the "New Yorker" and Me* (1979), discusses Cheever's relationship with the *New Yorker,* his stint as a volunteer fireman, love of backgammon, and other topics. Another long-time friend, John D. Weaver, in an article written for the *Los Angeles Times* (1977), quotes extensively from Cheever's letters and from remarks made in conversation on topics such as suburban life, working in Hollywood, Sing Sing prison, Italy, and religion. According to Weaver, Cheever's most salient qualities are his "childlike sense of wonder" and "pervasive sweetness of heart"; Cheever, he adds, "goes through life with a winning lottery ticket in his pocket, confident that at any moment someone will ring him up to check the lucky number." Raymond Carver, on the other hand, in his 1983 *Paris Review* interview, paints a grim picture of the fall 1973 semester he and Cheever spent as writers in residence and as alcoholics at the University of Iowa's Writers Workshop.

Carver has subsequently written a sequel to Cheever's story "The Five-Forty-Eight," which appears under the title "The Train: For John Cheever" in Carver's 1983 collection, *Cathedral.*

Interviews

The interviews that appeared prior to Cheever's recovery from alcoholism in 1975 and the writing of *Falconer* (1977) shortly thereafter are worthy of attention partly because they are so few in number and partly because, for all of Cheever's abruptness and defensive posturing, they include important if brief remarks on the relative merits of the short story and the novel (Breit, 1953; Waterman, 1958; Janeway, 1969), on American life in the 1950s and 1960s (Waterman, 1958; Gutwillig, 1960), and on the structure of the Wapshot novels (Nichols, 1964; Lehmann-Haupt, 1969). In his "Art of Fiction" interview with Annette Grant, Cheever appears reticent, even belligerent at times, but nonetheless willing to speak on a variety of topics, including his reasons for writing (to interest the reader, to make sense of life, and to "enlarge people") and the distinctive features of his fiction (mythic resonance and narrative development based on instinct and the coming together of disparate facts rather than on conventional plot). Cheever also discusses each of his first three novels, his relationship with the *New Yorker* (including editorial revisions of "The Enormous Radio" and "The Swimmer"), and the essentially experimental nature of fiction writing. Although it was not published in the *Paris Review* until 1976, the Grant interview was actually conducted some years earlier, as Cheever explains in Morris Lurie's "Afternoon in Ossining"

(1977). Lurie also quotes Cheever on "The Country Husband," "The Death of Justina," teaching at Sing Sing prison, his not being "a money player," Saul Bellow's *Humboldt's Gift*, and his interest in—or anxiety about—what Bellow thinks of *Falconer*, to be published a few months later. (Lurie also believes that for all his talk of not caring about either money or reputation, Cheever does want to win the Nobel Prize for Literature rather badly.)

In the interviews with Eleanor Munro, Susan Cheever Cowley, and John Hersey which appeared in 1977, Cheever seems much more at ease about himself and his work. He speaks to Munro of his New England years, his delight in the present moment and "the thrust of life," and of writing as an attempt to share his sense of excitement and of life's mysteriousness with others. He also comments briefly but suggestively on his love of ceremony, his writing of "The Swimmer," and the prison metaphor in *Falconer*. The same metaphor is explored more fully in John Hersey's "Talk with John Cheever." He explains the importance of confinement in *Falconer* as well as in the earlier fiction and suggests that the "blurted" quality of his prose may derive from his sense of "spiritual ungainliness." In a second interview with Hersey published in the *Yale Alumni Magazine and Journal* later that year, Cheever traces the laconic aspect of his style back to his New England heritage, discusses the light-dark imagery in *Falconer*, defines nostalgia as an aspiration as well as a memory, and agrees with Cocteau's view of literature as "a force of memory we have not yet understood." Concerning his traumatic adolescence, Cheever wonders whether he is able to talk about it "truthfully." He covers some of the same territory in a revealing yet nonetheless evasive interview with his daughter, Susan Cheever Cowley. Especially noteworthy are his comments on his relationship with his brother Fred, his difficult adolescent years, the biographical facts behind *Falconer*, and his own homosexual longings.

The public's interest in Cheever and his interest in becoming more of a public personality continued with the publication of *The Stories of John Cheever* in 1978 and the bestowal of a steady stream of prizes and honors during the following years. Michael J. Bandler quizzed him about his literary preferences in the "Book World" section of the *Chicago Tribune*, and Jacqueline Tavernier-Courbin and R. G. Collins elicited his opinions about comedy, about innovative fiction in general and experimental writers Barth, Barthelme, Coover, and Gass in particular, about the relationship between literature and literary theory, and about the foreign response both to American writing and more particularly to his own work. As he explained to Herbert Mitgang ("Behind the Bestsellers," 1979), fiction is not *a* means of communication but *the* means; it is an attempt not merely to explain life but to illuminate it, and as such it is far more important than politics, history, or journalism. Not surprisingly, then, Cheever tended to disparage all attempts to adapt his work for stage, screen, or television (see, for example, Henry Allen's "Capturing the Splendors of Suburbia," 1979) although he did come to speak approvingly of the adaptations of three stories which aired on PBS in 1979 and eventually wrote, "as an experiment, as a lark," an original 1982 screenplay of his own, *The Shady Hill Kidnapping* (see the interview with Arthur Unger, 1979). Of these late interviews, the one with Jo Brans (1980) is the longest and most varied and Joshua Gilder's "John Cheever's Affirmation of Faith" (1982) the most moving. With Brans, Cheever speaks about Christianity, Saul Bellow, E. E. Cummings, sex in literature, his "self-destructive" relationship with his brother Fred, the brother motif in his fiction, the romantic myth of the suicidal artist, John Gardner's *On Moral Fiction*, and the fear and loneliness that continue to haunt him. Speaking to Gilder just a few months before his death, Cheever discusses his cancer, "the aspiration to live," and his recently published novel, *Oh What a Paradise It Seems* (1982), which he terms "an ecological romance."

Critical Studies: Books

Although John Cheever began publishing his fiction in 1930, no book-length study of his work appeared until the publication of Samuel Coale's *John Cheever* in 1977. A volume in Frederick Unger's Literature and Life series, the Coale book includes a brief biography, two chapters on selected short stories, individual chapters on each of the (then) four published novels, and a brief concluding section on "Cheever's Art." Coale emphasizes the development of Cheever's style (from realism to mythic fantasy) and of his vision (his increasing concern for the moral issues lurking beneath the surface of middle-class life). Cheever's attitude toward suburbia is, according to Coale, as ambivalent as his suburban settings are ambiguous, at once realistic and symbolic of the protagonist's alienated yet hopeful state. Despite its social pretensions and moral limitations, suburbia serves Cheever's characters as a refuge from the darkness that waits beyond its borders. Coale reads the fictions as versions of paradise lost and subsequently regained in a moment of mystical illumination. In its careful balancing of comedy and tragedy, *The Wapshot Scandal* (1964) may be Cheever's "masterpiece." In *Bullet Park* (1969) style triumphs over the novel's chaotic action, but this triumph is perhaps too facile and therefore unconvincing; as Coale notes, although Cheever's graceful style may be his major achievement as a writer, it may also be his chief limitation. The style is harder and more convincing in *Falconer*, the author's most fully realized novel.

Lynne Waldeland's *John Cheever* (1979) is, like Coale's, another introductory study, this one in the Twayne United States Authors series. Of the two, Waldeland's is broader in scope and more useful in its survey of previous criticism; however, it is also less original and less coherent. Trying to cover so much ground in so limited a space, Waldeland tends either to repeat what previous critics and especially reviewers have already said or alternately to reduce her most interesting points to mere mentions sprinkled throughout her text. Nonetheless, the conclusions Waldeland draws are certainly valid even if not always adequately explained and developed. She reads Cheever as at once a romantic concerned about the individual and a moralist whose stories and novels deal with "the relationships between the inner person and the outer world, the present and the past, the best we dream of being and the compromises we continually make." His style, she adds, is lyrical but not flowery, precise but not coldly analytical.

George Hunt's *John Cheever: The Hobgoblin Company of Love* (1983) is not an introduction to Cheever's work but a penetrating and exhaustive critical study, a synthesis of previous commentary and a long-overdue analysis of Cheever's art, with special emphasis on Cheever's style, novels, and vision. Hunt sees Cheever not as an ironist but instead as a Kierkegaardian humorist whose stories and novels begin in ironic detachment but end in compassionate understanding. Cheever's unique style, which Hunt claims must be heard as well as read, corresponds to his moral vision. As the one became more lyrical and flexible, the other became progressively more expansive and accepting. For Hunt, a Jesuit, Cheever is essentially a religious writer but one whose work is marked by the author's "dialectical intelligence." In Cheever's fiction, Hunt contends, a theme never appears in isolation but always in tension with some other theme; and the same is true of Cheever's characters, images, plots, and even styles. Hunt may be overfond of detecting "dialectical configurations" in Cheever's fiction and far too quick to invoke Cheever's "Christian perspective" in order to resolve matters that cannot be treated quite so reductively (the ending of *Bullet Park,* for example, which Hunt considers entirely free of irony). Nonetheless, Hunt's defense of the structural unity of Cheever's novels on the basis of "poetic" rather than narrative logic is soundly reasoned and thoroughly convincing, even if it leads Hunt to transform Cheever, an intuitive writer, into something of a painstaking constructionist on the order of Joyce and Nabokov. Although Hunt stresses the development of Cheever's art and vision and makes a clear distinction between early and late Cheever, he organizes his lengthy discussion of the short fiction according to setting rather than chronology. In fact, the stories seem to have interested Hunt much less than the novels, perhaps because Cheever's reputation as a novelist is less secure than his reputation as a writer of short stories.

Critical Studies: Collection of Essays

Critical Essays on John Cheever (1982), edited by R. G. Collins, is especially useful for the material it reprints in one convenient volume: fifteen representative reviews of the novels and story collections, interviews with Annette Grant and John Hersey, and critical essays by Clinton Burhans, Jr., Alfred Kazin, Eugene Chesnick, Scott Donaldson, Beatrice Greene, and John Gardner. Of the remaining eleven pieces, three are especially noteworthy: Collins's "Introduction" (pp. 1-22), Dennis Coates's updating of his 1979 bibliographical checklist (discussed above), and Samuel Coale's "Cheever and Hawthorne: The American Romancer's Art" (pp. 193-209). In addition to providing concise summaries of Cheever's life, work, and critical reception, Collins points out that Cheever's having been "loved and hated in extraordinary measure" by reviewers can be attributed to his having served as "our guide, our conscience, our court fool, and our protector" during four decades of unprecedented change in the cultural and personal lives of his readers. Coale approaches Cheever from an entirely different perspective in an essay that will undoubtedly serve as the touchstone of Cheever criticism for some time to come. Coale views Cheever as a romancer rather than as a novelist of manners, one who shares Hawthorne's prose style, his sense of narrative structure, and most importantly, his Manichean vision. Cheever's Manicheanism is especially noticeable, Coale finds, in the stories involving brothers, who are not only psychological opposites but in effect Manichean halves of a single personality. In the novels, Cheever's Manichean theme becomes Manichean structure as well. Cheever's episodic plots mirror "the emblematic form of Hawthorne's romances"; each episode "repeats, comments upon or embroiders the basic vision or structure of Cheever's fictional world." The Manichean dualism manifests itself in other elements of Cheever's work: in the juxtaposing of episodic structure and decorous, nearly neoclassical prose; of mythic and mundane elements; of affirmation and ironic undercutting. Coale also notes one important difference between the two writers. Cheever's mood of romance, he says, appears more fragile than Hawthorne's, more susceptible to "the realities of modern guilt, rootlessness, and disconnection." Not simply a reprise of what Coale already claimed in his *John Cheever*, "Cheever and Hawthorne: The American Romancer's Art" stakes out new territory, making clear both the source of Cheever's dark power and (like Hunt, though on different grounds) the integrity of Cheever's art.

Of the remaining eight essays "written especially for this volume," only one is actually new. Richard Rupp, in "Of That Time, Of Those Places: The Stories of John Cheever" (pp. 231-251), provides a superficial whirlwind tour, arranged chronologically and by setting, of the short fiction. Despite the gradual darkening of his vision, Cheever, essentially a religious writer and a middle-class conservative, never gives in to despair, for (Rupp claims) "the family and marital love are first and last Cheever's subject." The other seven essays are reworkings of previously published material. Frederick Bracher's "John Cheever's Vision of the World," essentially a conflation of his two earlier Cheever essays (1963 and 1964), is the best of the lot. In the distinctly realistic stories of his early period, Cheever affirms man and in doing so also affirms that moral vision of continuity that is the essence of comedy. In the later fiction, realism only serves as a point of departure as Cheever makes greater use of myth in an effort to sustain his comic vision in a world in which the individual feels confused and lost. Although the goal of comedy—continuity—seems unattainable in stories such as "The Embarkment for Cythera," Cheever's point is that it is better to strive for continuity, or to imagine it, than to surrender to the discontinuity of modern experience. Robert B. Slabey, in "John Cheever: The 'Swimming' of America" (pp. 180-191), discusses similarities of setting, subject, and treatment in the work of Cheever and Washington Irving, specifically in "The Swimmer" and "Rip Van Winkle." Cheever's vision, Slabey argues, is the bleaker and more tragic of the two, omitting as it does the comic reconciliation with which "Rip" concludes. Nora Calhoun Graves also deals with the same Cheever story in "The Symptomatic Colors in John Cheever's 'The Swimmer' " (pp. 191-193). According to Graves, Cheever uses certain colors when describing water in order to reflect aspects of Neddy Merrill's past (his extravagance) and his present (loss and emptiness). Much of Frederick R. Karl's "John Cheever and the Promise of Pastoral" (pp. 209-219), which is drawn from his *American Fictions 1940-1980* (1983), deals not with Cheever but with the pastoral mode in general. His inconclusive, nearly incoherent remarks on Cheever's having "boldly challenged the pastoral theme" in the Wapshot books and his having had his pastoral imagination defeated by *Falconer*'s severely circumscribed setting serve the interests of Cheever studies in one significant way: pointing out how much still needs to be done in delineating the precise character of Cheever's contribution to the American pastoral.

Burton Kendle takes a step in the right direction in "The Passion of Nostalgia in the Short Stories of John Cheever" (pp. 219-230). The unifying element in Cheever's short fiction, Kendle argues, is "the passionate attempt to retain and foster an image of the innocent past," a vision of moral purity that entails both the recalling of the lost Eden and a recognition of "the painful reality that motivates the nostalgia." Few of Cheever's characters are as fortunate as Asa Bascomb in "The World of Apples," who achieves a successful balance between past and present and as a result regains his lost paradise. John L. Brown might have benefited from Kendle's insights in his discussion of "Cheever's Expatriates" (pp. 251-257), an essay in which Brown merely surveys the Italian stories and draws the obvious conclusions: that these are not among Cheever's best and that Cheever discovered in Italy what he had already discovered in the American suburbs, the evil lurking behind the pleasant surface of life. Lynne Waldeland's "John Cheever's *Bullet Park:* A Key to His Thought" is nothing more than chapter six of her Twayne book minus a few transitional sentences. Waldeland acknowledges that the novel does pose a number of problems for readers but agrees with John Gardner ("Witchcraft in Bullet Park") that the novel is nonetheless unified, albeit very subtly, by the author's adaptation of style, voice, and plot to his two main characters. Finally, in "John Cheever and the Development of the American Novel" (pp. 272-278), Theo D'haen reads the Wapshot books, *Bullet Park*, and *Falconer* in terms of Richard Chase's theory of the American novel. Predictably, D'haen finds that *The Wapshot Chronicle* and *The Wapshot Scandal* are actually romances, rather than novels, involving the myth of the American Eden, symbolic landscapes, and allegorical characters. And just as the American novel evolved from romance to realism, so too does Cheever's career follow the same pattern, leading to the psychological realism that D'haen detects all too inevitably in *Falconer*, the only one of Cheever's novels in which the reader finds psychological growth rather than mystical epiphany.

Critical Studies: Major Articles and Book Sections

Although it was not until the publication of *Falconer* in 1977 that Cheever began to receive the popular and critical attention that, as many of his supporters have claimed, he had long deserved, it is important to realize (1) that even today Cheever's reputation as a novelist and therefore as a major American writer (and not "merely" a writer of short stories) remains suspect and (2) that the lengthy debate over Cheever and his fiction has in essence focused on just two general issues. Both of these issues can be found in the warning Struthers Burt appended to his approving review of *The Way Some People Live* (1943), Cheever's first collection of short stories: "John Cheever has only two things to fear; a hardening into an especial style that might beome an affectation, and a deliberate casualness and simplicity that might become the same. Otherwise, the world is his." Ihab Hassan raises the same issues, albeit less directly, in his influential book *Radical Innocence: Studies in the Contemporary American Novel* (1961). In his analysis of *The Wapshot Chronicle* (1957), the first academic criticism of Cheever's work, Hassan views Cheever as both a novelist of manners and a fantasist, a writer who portrays the contemporary absurdity yet affirms "the heartiness, the gaminess" of life. Hassan feels, however, that Cheever's mythic subject matter tends to overwhelm his "dramatic resources" in a novel sustained not by plot but instead by the author's ironic and whimsical style.

Cheever's failure to develop plot (and character) is not a weakness, Frederick Bracher argues in "John Cheever and Comedy" (1963), but a sign that his major interest lies elsewhere, in the realm of morality, and that the unity of his fiction, including *The Wapshot Chronicle*, derives from his "assertion of the continuity of human experience." In a follow-up article entitled "John Cheever: A Vision of the World" (1964), Bracher discusses the darkening of Cheever's mood in the more recent fiction—*Some People, Places, and Things That Will Not Appear in My Next Novel* (1961) and *The Wapshot Scandal*—as well as his more critical attitude toward the modern world. In a review of *The Wapshot Scandal* ("America Aglow," 1964), Cynthia Ozick questions whether Cheever is being critical enough, and in a second, longer review of the same work, she claims that Cheever's portrait of St. Botolph's evidences not only the author's nostalgic sentimentality but the baselessness of the entire Yankee heritage upon which that portrait rests. In an age of ethnic literature, especially by blacks and Jews, a WASP writer like Cheever, Ozick contends, has nothing important to say to the American reader (a charge that goes entirely unanswered until 1977 when novelist Joan Didion—like Cheever an Episcopalian—points out that the homelessness that is Cheever's major theme speaks to the condition of the great many nonethnic readers who think of themselves not in terms of cultural heritage but instead in terms of cultural and personal loss). As his title, "John Cheever and the Soft Sell of Disaster" (1966, reprinted 1972), suggests, John W. Aldridge also questions whether Cheever's critique of American life is as incisive as it needs to be. Cheever will remain "one of the most grievously underdiscussed important writers of the present age," Aldridge maintains, until his aesthetic vision becomes less sentimental and "comforting," more "drastic" and disturbing.

The unsigned cover story, "Ovid in Ossining," which appeared in the 27 March 1964 issue of *Time* magazine and which was written by Cheever's friend Alwyn Lee, helped to bring Cheever into national prominence. In addition to providing a very useful and thorough biographical sketch, "Ovid in Ossining" is a seminal work of criticism. Lee was one of the first to read Cheever as essentially a moralist and a fabulist whose middle-class characters are in fact "figures in an Ovidian netherworld of demons"—status seekers transformed into the dignified and archetypal figures of classical drama. Cheever does not view man in modern terms, which is to say as an individual, but instead "as the center of a system of obligations." Metamorphosis—sudden and bizarre change—is the punishment meted out to those who either evade or betray their responsibilities. Cheever's vision is double; he is at once the stern moralist and the lyricist who delights in the natural world. Many of the stories, Lee notes, are drawn from Cheever's actual past, including his strained childhood. The relationship between the fiction and the biography is complicated by the fact that Cheever is not above inventing parts of his own past.

Cheever's rise to the rank of major American writer received an additional boost in the form of a long review-essay by George Garrett in the *Hollins Critic* the same year. Looking over Cheever's entire career, Garrett finds evidence that far from having been limited by his long association with the *New Yorker*, Cheever has in fact subtly managed to transform the typical *New Yorker* story, to make it more flexible—less realistic, more fantastic and more digressive. *The Wapshot Scandal* is clearly a major novel, a nearly religious work concerning apocalypse (as *The Wapshot Chronicle* is about original sin) and the need to distinguish between true love and false. In an afterword to his original essay, "John Cheever and the Charms of Innocence: The Craft of *The Wapshot Scandal*," published seven years later, Garrett finds less to praise in Cheever's more recent fiction, especially *Bullet Park*, which Garrett judges "distorted" and "stylized." Benjamin DeMott (*New York Times Book Review*, 1969) is far more critical in his assessment of Cheever's third—and, according to DeMott, least successful—novel. In a review Cheever later claimed had turned the tide against *Bullet Park*, DeMott acknowledges Cheever's attentiveness to the discontinuity of modern life but otherwise condemns the novel as "broken-backed" in structure and inconsistent in characterization. *Bullet Park* is, in sum, a carelessly written work which raises the question of "story style vs. novel style," of fiction which presents phenomena (according to DeMott, the province of the short story) and fiction which explains the world of phenomena (the sine qua non of the novel according to DeMott). "Heretofore, Cheever was a great respecter of the difference," DeMott adds, rather surprisingly so, given the number of reviewers who faulted the "spit and wire" structure of the earlier Wapshot novels.

While DeMott and other reviewers were busy savaging *Bullet Park* in the popular press, Cheever's fiction came under the thoughtful and largely sympathetic scrutiny of a number of academic critics. In "John Cheever and the Grave of Social Coherence," Clinton S. Burhans, Jr. sees Cheever as a "chronicler of contemporary absurdity" and as a "moralist" who recognizes the gap which exists between man's dreams and what he makes of those dreams. Burhans's Cheever is neither a satirist nor an existentialist; he understands his characters' need for "social coherence" in a rapidly changing world in which man feels more bewildered and isolated than ever before, unable to adapt to a world of his own making. Against man's existential predicament and misguided obsession with progress, Cheever posits the very tradition that modern man has unwisely come to deny. It is this denial that Burhans finds at the heart of Cheever's potentially tragic vision, a vision Cheever has not yet fully explored. In "The Domesticated Stroke of John Cheever" (1971) Eugene Chesnick places Cheever in the Emerson-Thoreau tradition of Transcendental individualism. Cheever's fiction clearly demonstrates a "drastic change in the nature of individualism" from the nineteenth to the twentieth century. In Cheever's world, it is not the few who long to assert their individuality but the many and often for no better reason than a "heightened awareness" of their own mortality. The sudden and usually affirmative reversals that occur at the end of many Cheever fictions are not, as Hassan has claimed, a sign of the author's evasiveness, but instead of Cheever's Emersonian belief that evil is not real. Cheever, Chesnick concludes, is a "writer of some talent . . . who is struggling to make his fictional meanings in an increasingly frantic world"; it is this struggle that makes Cheever's career "inconclusive" and the fiction "difficult to appraise."

Although he confines his discussion to just the two Wapshot books, the conclusions Richard H. Rupp draws in his *Celebration in Postwar American Fiction: 1945-1967* (1970) apply equally well to all of Cheever's stories and novels. Rupp finds in Cheever's "ceremonial style" evidence of the author's "essentially conservative outlook," joyous approach to life, and distaste for the "dehumanized values" of the modern age. Ceremony, Rupp contends, is important not only to Cheever's style and vision but to his sense of narrative structure as well; thus, in the Wapshot novels plot is much less important than Cheever's working out of the action in "formal, ritualized gestures." Rupp's analysis is illuminating, but his term "ceremonial style" is misleading, for Rupp is much less interested in the distinctive features of Cheever's prose style than he is in the thematic content of Cheever's criticism of modern society—its technology, rootlessness, and loss of faith—and nostalgia for the ceremonies of the past. Beatrice Greene, on the other hand, in her "Icarus at St. Botolphs: A Descent to 'Unwonted Otherness' " (1971, reprinted 1982) provides a very thorough analysis of one important feature of the author's style. Cheever's characters, she points out, nostalgically yearn to escape from a present of " 'unwonted otherness' to a past where no one has been, to an ideal where no one can go," created out of language alone. Against the fall to earth, Cheever posits an airy vision based solely on style. It is this juxtaposition of the two extremes that makes Cheever's prose so distinctively Cheeveresque: the juxtaposing of past and present, dream and reality, abstract and concrete, mythic and domestic, sublime and prosaic.

Novelist John Gardner has also added appreciably to both our understanding of Cheever's unique style and our appreciation of his much maligned novel *Bullet Park*. In "Witchcraft in Bullet Park" (1971) Gardner defends the novel against the charges of those critics, especially DeMott, who misunderstood the work (1) because it has no simple message, (2) because it exposes the chance nature of good and evil, and (3) because Cheever shows that magic—the supernatural—

is still possible even in an otherwise existential world. *Bullet Park,* Gardner goes on to say, is not a realistic novel which develops on the basis of a carefully delineated plot but instead a "tale" in which the action is controlled by the narrative voice, a story which develops poetically on the basis of rhythm, imagery, correspondence, and "magical coincidence." *Bullet Park* is an ambiguous but ultimately religious novel—"affirmation out of ashes"—that "towers high above the many recent novels that wail and feed on Sartre." In "John Cheever's *Bullet Park:* A World Beyond Madness" (1977), Robert Detweiler argues that *Bullet Park* is a unified and coherent *postmodernist* novel which, both thematically and structurally, concerns the author's (as well as the narrator's and the main characters') efforts "to find a negotiable position . . . in a world of fluctuating values and accelerating change" (cf. Chesnick above). Cheever seems to be calling for a Nietzschean transvaluation of values in order to bring about the "radical spiritual change" he feels is necessary for modern man's survival. *Bullet Park* evidences not only Cheever's "mastery of artistic form" (especially narrative point of view) but too "a skeptical faith in American resiliency" and a Blakean triumph of the visionary imagination.

The precise character of Cheever's affirmative vision—and conversely of his irony—has long been a matter of much debate among reviewers and critics. John Leonard, in his review of *The World of Apples,* has dubbed Cheever "a Chekhov of the exurbs" who writes clearly, effortlessly, and compassionately about seemingly insignificant matters; he is a writer, Leonard claims, who uses irony "protectively, on behalf of ardor and intelligence and clemency," rather than to belittle these qualities and the people who believe in them. Yet, Leonard adds, Cheever understands how inadequate words such as "clemency" are in a world where, as Gardner has pointed out, chance and evil are real. Alfred Kazin disagrees in "O'Hara, Cheever & Updike" (1973), managing—as so many of Cheever's reviewers and critics have done—to disparage even as he praises. According to Kazin, it is Cheever, not his characters, who master the world, and it is his lucid style, not their anecdotal stories, that engages the reader's attention. But this style, Kazin notes, echoing Aldridge, amounts to nothing more than Cheever's attempt "to cheer himself up." Stephen C. Moore detects considerably less cheerfulness in Cheever's work than he does stoic determination. In an existential reading entitled "The Hero on the 5:42" (1976) Moore (like Garrett before him) argues that Cheever's stories constitute a subtle transformation of the conventions of *New Yorker* fiction; the stories are not in fact realistic fictions but "fables of heroism" in which Cheever's seemingly unheroic suburbanites "must face action, responsibility, anxiety, and failure." The protagonists of "O Youth and Beauty!," "The Swimmer," and "The Scarlet Moving Van" must choose to define themselves in relation to a meaningless world. What matters is not that they fail to accomplish what they set out to but that they are dissatisfied with their absurd world and revolt against it. Scott Donaldson, however, views Cheever not as an existentialist but, along with Burhans, as a deft social critic and trenchant moralist. As Donaldson explains in "The Machines in Cheever's Garden" (1976) Cheever is one of the few important American writers to treat suburbia in his fiction and more especially to explore the undercurrents of suburban living. Far from being the cheerful apologist for the suburbs that so many reviewers have dismissed as a literary lightweight, Cheever is its Jeremiah. He knows that modern man cannot escape back into the pastoral past, but he also understands that man's basic values are nonetheless rooted in the past, especially in "organic communities" such as St. Botolphs. The suburbs, on the other hand, are "artificial" communities where Cheever's rootless suburbanites substitute movement for spiritual affirmation. However, as Donaldson points out in an earlier and much briefer discussion of Cheever's work in *The Suburban Myth* (1969), "the bitch goddess success" has ruined life not just in the suburbs, which are not without their own advantages, but everywhere.

The enthusiastic response on the part of readers and reviewers to Cheever's "prison novel," *Falconer*, in 1971 lends considerable support to Donaldson's conjecture (in *The Suburban Myth*) that Cheever's use of suburban material in his stories and novels of the 1950s and 1960s accounts for (as Donaldson claims) the steady decline in his literary reputation during the same period. Whatever the precise nature of the relationship, Cheever's fourth novel evoked not only reviewers' praise but, more importantly, a reassessment—virtually a rediscovery—of Cheever's fiction. Walter Clemons, for example, hails *Falconer* as "Cheever's Triumph" in a 1977 *Newsweek* cover story, adding that Cheever's earlier fiction was never correctly understood or adequately appreciated; in an age of the novel and of ethnic literature, Cheever has been unfairly dismissed as a short story writer and a WASP. *Falconer* represents a departure from the earlier fiction in matters such as setting and language and in the fact that although Cheever's protagonists have always lived precariously, never has one of them plunged so deeply into the abyss of darkness and suffering. Grim as the novel is, the effect is one of elation. *Falconer* is a religious novel, a masterpiece, "the triumphant work of a man reborn" that Clemons puts into proper biographical perspective. Joan Didion, writing in the *New York Times Book Review* (1977), finds an even higher degree of continuity between *Falconer* and the earlier work. Throughout his career, Didion notes, Cheever has dealt with the theme of homelessness, each time refining it more, getting "closer to the bone." Where the earlier stories are marked by a certain plaintiveness, as if Cheever were blaming the modern world for his characters' homelessness and dissatisfaction, *Falconer* is a novel of nearly "liturgical intensity," a brilliantly written "contemplation in shorthand, a meditation on the abstraction Cheever has always called 'home' but has never before located so explicitly in the life of the spirit."

Joseph McElroy, in the *New Republic* (1977), notes one important similarity and one important difference between *Falconer* and the previous fiction. McElroy reads Farragut's fratricide as the culmination of the antagonism between brothers evident in a number of the earlier stories. What distinguishes the new novel from earlier works is that here Cheever does not seem "to have understood everything in advance"; instead, the novel's style "coincides with Farragut's groping pain and strength and moves as he moves." In a review entitled "On Miracle Row" (1977), John Gardner goes even further in his praise of the book and its author, raising Cheever to the rank of "true artist." Unlike many contemporary novelists, Gardner claims, Cheever does not substitute narrative tricks or philosophical complexity for clarity and truth. "The reason Cheever is a great writer—besides his command of literary form, impeccable style, and unsentimental compassion—is that what he says seems true." And in an essay published the same year and then reprinted in *On Moral Fiction* (1978), Gardner goes on to emphasize Cheever's concern for both his characters and his readers as well as his ability to qualify, without undermining, "his optimistic Christian vision with the necessary measure of irony." Alden Whitman, writing a 1977 review in the *Los Angeles Times*, is similarly impressed with Cheever's adaptation of his Christian message for a secular age and with the difference between *Falconer* and most works of contemporary fiction. The novel, Whitman says, has a clear point: that, as Emerson and the Unitarians believed, man is perfectible and can effect his own redemption "through the miracle of love." The style, mood, and characterizations of *Falconer* affect the reader more profoundly than Cheever's at-times-contrived plot. However, although Cheever's miracles may strain the reader's credulity, they make more sense than the alternatives provided by the popular culture (born-again Christianity, transactional analysis, and so forth). The reader comes to accept Cheever's unfashionable view that "loving kindness is more pervasive in this world than cruelty and hatred."

Not all reviewers proved to be quite so convinced of "Cheever's triumph" in realizing his redemptive vision or in mastering the novel form. John Leonard claims in "Crying in the Wilderness" (1977), that "Sentence by sentence, scene by scene, *Falconer* absorbs and often haunts. As a whole, it confounds." However, Leonard adds—as if in reply to McElroy—that *Falconer* "seems more asserted than felt, more willed than imagined." Whereas John Leonard and others express certain reservations concerning the merits of Cheever's fourth novel, Bryan F. Griffin simply denounces it and in so doing raises once again serious doubts as to Cheever's place among twentieth-century American writers. In "Getting Cheever while he's hot" (1979), the third in his caustic "Literary Vogues" series for *Harper's*, Griffin considers the critical reception of *Falconer* as an obvious illustration of the wild overpraising that characterizes current reviewing practice in the United States. Cheever has always been a very good and especially a very entertaining—but certainly neither profound nor provocative—writer who has dealt with interesting but generally insignificant subjects. In *Falconer*, Griffin maintains, Cheever tried to write a fashionably sordid novel and in doing so lost his literary soul while gaining the favor of reviewers blind to the novel's obvious shortcomings.

Griffin's disparaging view of Cheever's art is far too extreme to be considered representative of anything but its author's spleen and his skewed perspective, yet it is also true that Griffin articulates certain long-held assumptions about Cheever's fiction in general and the novels in particular that are implicit in the treatment Cheever has received in critical surveys of contemporary American fiction. Cheever is not only not discussed, he is not even mentioned in Tony Tanner's highly influential *City of Words* (1971), Charles B. Harris's *Contemporary American Novelists of the Absurd* (1971), and Raymond Olderman's *Beyond the Wasteland* (1972). Ihab Hassan, who devotes a chapter to *The Wapshot Chronicle* in *Radical Innocence*, does not include Cheever among either the two "major" or the twelve "prominent" novelists in his *Contemporary American Writing 1945-1972: An Introduction* (1973), in which he at least does briefly discuss Cheever's benign satire, "sacramental" view of life, and coy representation of despair. Hassan makes many of these same points in his essay on recent "Fiction" for the fourth edition of the *Literary History of the United States* (1974). Leo Braudy discusses Cheever's work briefly but intelligently in the "Realists, Naturalists, and Novelists of Manners" chapter of the *Harvard Guide to Contemporary American Writing* (1979). Braudy finds Cheever less satirical and more sympathetic toward his characters than other *New Yorker* writers, such as John O'Hara. Cheever is chiefly concerned with mood rather than plot and with the compromises his characters make in order to achieve the material success that alienates them from life. Robert F. Kiernan also discusses Cheever under the perhaps misleading heading "Naturalists and Realists" in his *American Writing Since 1945: A Critical Survey* (1983), emphasizing Cheever's role as "a puppeteer of the grotesque." Interestingly, although often described and even dismissed as a novelist of manners, Cheever is not discussed (though he is briefly mentioned) in James W. Tuttleton's comprehensive study of *The Novel of Manners in America* (1972); the omission leads one to suspect that Cheever is something of a writer without a literary country, too much the absurdist to be a realist and vice versa.

Far more useful in summarizing the nature of Cheever's achievement than the reductive comments in the surveys of Hassan, Kiernan, and others are the general essays that have appeared in the *Critical Survey of Long Fiction* (1982) and in several volumes of the *Dictionary of Literary Biography* (1978, 1982, 1983). The lengthy *New York Times* obituary written by Michiko Kakutani also provides a very thorough and at times perceptive overview of Cheever's life and more especially his art. Kakutani emphasizes Cheever's "ability to find spiritual resonance in the seemingly inconsequential events of daily life," his distinctive narrative voice ("generous, graceful, and at times amused, and always preoccupied with the fundamental decencies of life"), the development of his style, and the gradual deepening and darkening of his vision. Cheever was, Kakutani concludes, essentially a moralist concerned with "man's dignity and his failings."

In a review of *Oh What a Paradise It Seems*, published shortly before Cheever's death, Joshua Gilder goes even further, calling Cheever "in many ways one of our most religious writers today." Gilder contends that the author's relationship to his protagonist, Lemuel Sears, is based on Christian empathy rather than biographical fact and that this novel of spiritual purification clearly proves that "our best short-story writer has consummately mastered the somewhat different craft of the novel." In a long review-essay entitled "Cheever's Failed Paradise: The Short-Story Stylist as Novelist" (1983) Adam Gussow analyzes the story-versus-novel issue more thoroughly and arrives at a quite different conclusion. The flawed art of *Oh What a Paradise*, Gussow claims, points to "the single most problematic aspect" of Cheever's career: "his inability, as the preeminent short story stylist of our time, to find a voice and an action that would let him write a successful longer work." In making his large claim that "the novel *as a genre* is fundamentally inimical to Cheever's genius," Gussow considers not only Cheever's last novel but the four earlier ones as well. The problem with the Wapshot books derives from Cheever's having known all the answers in advance. *Bullet Park* is better because the writing evidences Cheever's struggle to solve his own personal demons (alcoholism and homosexuality). Of the first four novels *Falconer* is the most successful because in it the author creates an entirely believable physical and moral world. *Oh What a Paradise It Seems*, on the other hand, is not specific enough; its "euphonious abstractions do not convince." Cheever's art, Gussow notes, depends upon the "mutually empowering" combination of Fitzgerald-like idealism with that Hemingway-ish irony and specificity so conspicuously absent from Cheever's last novel.

In addition to Gussow and Coale (discussed above), other critics have taken a keen interest in the doubleness of Cheever's vision and art. Richard Schickel, for example, claims in "The Cheever Chronicle" (1978) that the "basic tension" in Cheever's fiction "derives from balancing his tragic sense of life with his equally strong appreciation of our sheer circumstantial craziness, which he feels redeems us by reminding us of life's infinite and infinitely unpredictable possibilities." This tension involves a balancing of light and dark, of "sensitivity to loss" and a sense of wonder (which in *Falconer* becomes "an uncharacteristic note of triumph"). The later fiction, Schickel adds, appears less ironic and more forgiving. For Scott Donaldson, "Goodbye, My Brother" and "The Enormous Radio" serve as "the poles of Cheever's dual vision": his detesting mournfulness and his celebration of life, love, and usefulness on the other. As Donaldson explains in his "John Cheever" essay (1979), Cheever is an "enlightened Puritan" and more especially a comic writer whose literary shortcomings are fairly obvious but far outweighed by his narrative strengths: his prose style and (as Joan Didion pointed out in her review of *The Wapshot Scandal*) his ability to "tell us so much about the way we live now." Elizabeth Hardwick is similarly struck by the doubleness of Cheever's art but less convinced of his having successfully reconciled the opposing sides. As Hardwick notes in her 1984 review of Susan Cheever's *Home Before Dark*, Cheever, like Melville's Pierre, is "a study in ambiguity." He is nostalgic yet decidedly contemporary, adept at ironic undercutting yet committed to celebrating his world, an "Episcopalian anarch" whose precise, "effortlessly evocative" language rescues his sentiments from mere sentimentalism. However, along with Gussow and others, Hardwick considers Cheever "a disappointing novelist." Despite the abiding features of his work—the mellifluous style and wistful treatment of dramatic scenes—"the novels fly apart, shred, shed as if some wind of inattention had overtaken them."

Whatever the reservations about Cheever the novelist, there are few doubts about Cheever's accomplishments as a writer of short stories. The promise which Struthers Burt announced in his 1943 review of *The Way Some People Live* has been realized in subsequent collections, as reviewers have noted time and again, especially in their overwhelmingly favorable response to *The Stories of John Cheever* (1978; 1979), a retrospective collection of sixty-one previously published works. The collection proves, Paul Gray notes in *Time Magazine*, that there is no such thing as a "typical" Cheever story. Rereading these fictions, Anne Tyler is impressed by the way in which Cheever develops the affirmative truths (which is what the reader usually remembers) from the often ugly facts of the actual world (that the reader tends to forget). Tyler also notes that the stories narrated from a detached point of view ("The Five-Forty-Eight," for example), often leave the reader feeling bitter, whereas those narrated from the "inside" generally lead to that luminous truth one usually associates with Cheever's art. John Gardner, long an admirer, takes special note of Cheever's development, his "unwavering eye for beauty, elegance, and accuracy," and his ability to combine comedy and tragedy, dream and reality. John Irving goes even further, saying that *The Stories of John Cheever* reads more like a novel than a collection and that its author is the premier storyteller of his age. Irving is especially struck by the very quality that Isa Kapp, in one of the most important and most critical of the negative reviews, claims Cheever lacks: sympathy for his characters. According to Kapp, Cheever is not (as John Leonard and others have claimed), the American Chekhov; although he writes clearly and elegantly, Cheever (unlike Chekhov) lurches wildly from cynicism to exaltation and shows little genuine interest in his "awkward and pathetic" characters.

William Peden, who has been reviewing and extolling Cheever's short fiction ever since the publication of *The Enormous Radio* in 1953, clarifies Cheever's achievement as well as Cheever's standing among modern American writers in his important critical survey, *The American Short Story: Front Line in the National Defense* (1964) and again in the updated version, *The American Short Story: Continuity and Change*

1940-1975 (1975). Of the most important "chroniclers of the commonplace and the unexceptional," such as Hortense Calisher, John O'Hara, Peter Taylor, and John Updike, Cheever is "the most distinguished": a "perceptive and urbane commentator" on contemporary life who is saddened by what he sees but (especially in his *The World of Apples*) not at all somber. His "impressive" first collection, *The Way Some People Live,* typifies the later work in its casual yet disciplined prose style, combination of skepticism, compassion, and humor, and depiction of the complex and often disappointing lives of unheroic characters who (as in *The Housebreaker of Shady Hill*), generally achieve "a partial victory through love or by demonstrating a kind of courage or integrity." *The Enormous Radio* is a major work of the 1950s, and *The Brigadier and the Golf Widow* may be Cheever's finest collection overall. Even though it includes two of his best stories, "The Death of Justina" and "Boy in Rome," *Some People, Places, and Things* seems more a self-parody than an artistic advance. Otherwise, Cheever's art has developed throughout his career; his narrative method has become "more varied, more flexible," as in "The Day the Pig Fell in the Well," a story as rich in character and incident as a novel; "The National Pastime," which combines story and essay forms; and "The Jewels of the Cabots," which Peden calls "a saga in miniature."

    Surprisingly and unaccountably, Arthur Voss devotes just a single perfunctory paragraph to Cheever in his *The American Short Story: A Critical Survey*. Voss disagrees with those who view Cheever as merely a *New Yorker* writer; without bothering to prove his point, Voss claims that the stories "have freshness and genuine interest" and are "often saved from being too depressingly realistic by a leavening of humor and fantasy." Walter Allen, in his *The Short Story in English* (1981), contends that while there may not be a *New Yorker* school of fiction, there are writers who "seem essentially of the *New Yorker*" and Cheever is one. Further, he is a moralist, a writer of fables of the life he sees beneath the suburban facade. Allen considers "World of Apples" a "fable of rebirth that quite transcends the ordinary run of Cheever's stories." Unfortunately, Allen prefers to quote from the stories rather than to analyze them; his remarks are interesting but hardly conclusive. In about the same space, E. P. Walkiewicz provides a very useful introduction to the short fiction in his essay, "1957-1968: Toward Diversity of Form" (1983). Walkiewicz views Cheever as a writer working within the literary tradition who is nonetheless a modernist both in his method and his choice of milieu. Cheever's stories combine realistic details and surrealistic effects; they deal with loneliness, the variety of human desires, and the evil lurking behind the common-place surface. Like Coale, Schickel, and Donaldson, Walkiewicz comments on Cheever's dualistic vision, noting that *The Brigadier and the Golf Widow* (1964) represents one pole, "the reaction to calvinism, the descent into bitterness," while *The World of Apples* (1973; 1974) represents the "other, contrary impulse," involving celebration, transcendence, and light.

As is to be expected in the case of a writer whose work has so frequently been anthologized and taught in college classrooms, Cheever's stories have been the subject of numerous notes and short essays by academic critics. Burton Kendle, Cortland P. Auser, and Robert S. Pawlowski, for example, have all discussed the use of myth in Cheever's fiction. In "John Cheever's Myth of Man and Time: 'The Swimmer,' " (1967), Auser argues that the story's plot takes the form of a mythic journey in which the main character refuses to confront and accept "the harsh truth of time's passage." Neddy Merrill is a modern Ulysses who indulges in pleasure and who mistakenly believes he can control his own destiny; "The Swimmer" is the story of his painful metamorphosis and final awareness of his time-bound nature. Burton Kendle, in "Cheever's Use of Mythology in 'The Enormous Radio' " (1967), detects an ironic reinterpretation of the Eden story in which the Westcotts play the part of Adam and Eve while the radio serves as Cheever's Satan. Although Kendle's interpretation becomes at times rather mechanical and therefore strained, his major point is certainly plausible: that the loss of innocence and the awareness of evil, particularly one's own evil, does not constitute a fortunate fall for they result in "additional difficulties and frustrations" for Cheever's characters. In "Myth as Metaphor: Cheever's 'Torch Song' " (1979), Pawlowski claims that "Torch Song" exemplifies the author's ability to revivify the past, to turn myth into metaphor in order to dramatize his view of "human experience as a continuum," a view which, Pawlowski believes, requires that all the characters be understood as allegorical figures: Joan, for example, is "an inverted Beatrice."

More interesting is Henrietta Ten Harmsel's " 'Young Goodman Brown' and 'The Enormous Radio' " (1972). Ten Harmsel finds her comparison of the Cheever story with Hawthorne's "Young Goodman Brown" more illuminating than Kendle's with the Eden story. As she points out, "It is partly the deceptive facades of their societies . . . that have made honest acknowledgement of evil impossible" for Hawthorne's Brown and for Cheever's Irene Westcott, who eventually discover that evil lurks in both the society and the individual. Examining the same story, Christine W. Sizemore, in "The Sweeny Allusion in John Cheever's 'The Enormous Radio' " (1977), and William P. Keen, in "The American Waste Land—Brought to You by John Cheever's Radio" (1982), detect T. S. Eliot's influence. The allusion to Eliot's poem "Sweeney Agonistes," Sizemore believes, informs the reader that Irene's escape into innocence cannot succeed; for Cheever as for Eliot, human reality involves "a confrontation with Nothingness." Keen acknowledges the "Sweeney" allusion but feels that in language, syntax, and sense of "society's disintegration and personal despair," Cheever's essentially realistic story closely resembles Eliot's dreamlike poem, *The Waste Land.* In two notes of 1980, "Cheever's 'The Hartleys' and Its Major Image" and "Autumnal Images in John Cheever's 'The Swimmer,' " Edward C. Reilly discusses the ways in which Cheever's imagery underscores his theme. The description of skiers resembling people on a beach, searching for something they have lost, arises naturally from the plot and setting of "The Hartleys" and conveys that sense of loss which is the story's subject. The prevalent autumnal imagery in "The Swimmer" is only a "part of a larger pattern" involving the seasons, weather, and time of day; Cheever uses this larger pattern ironically in order to contrast Neddy's reality with his "self-deceived vision." (See also Nora Calhoun Graves's "The Dominant Colors in John Cheever's 'The Swimmer,' " an earlier, slightly different version of a similarly titled note included in *Critical Essays on John Cheever,* discussed above.)

Cheever's stories receive more extended analysis in two other journal articles, both of 1982: Edward C. Reilly's "Saving Grace and Moral Balance in John Cheever's Stories" and John Gerlach's "Closure in Modern Short Fiction: Cheever's 'The Enormous Radio' and 'Artemis, the Honest Well Digger." According to Reilly, the characters in Cheever's stories, having achieved material success, experience a crisis that leaves them feeling betrayed and alienated. The saving grace that restores them to a more balanced state is human rather than divine in origin, a matter of courage, intelligence, understanding, and especially love, as in "The Worm in the Apple" and "The Trouble with Marcie Flint." Reilly concludes that for Cheever "man, and man alone, is either his own destroyer or savior." Gerlach's interest lies in the form, not the content, of Cheever's short fiction and the way that form reflects certain changes in the form of the modern short story in general. At first glance, Gerlach notes, Cheever's stories seem the antithesis of Poe's definition of the well-made tale, which depends upon unified structure and singleness of effect. According to Gerlach, the expectation of closure that Poe demands does indeed shape an early Cheever story such as "The Enormous Radio." "Artemis, the Honest Well Digger," a later work, has a much different though no less unified structure, based upon imagery, wit, and formal patterning rather than casual plot and closure.

Although not entirely conclusive, James O'Hara's " 'Independence Day at St. Botolph's': The Wapshot Saga Begins" (1980) is an especially noteworthy item insofar as O'Hara attends closely to the relationship between Cheever's first novel and the short story from which it apparently developed. The themes are the same in both works—the battle between the sexes and the consequent need for men to leave their homes on journeys of exploration—but the changes Cheever made in revising the story for use in the novel help to clarify the connections between these themes, which serve as the unifying elements in an otherwise "very diverse" novel. O'Hara further develops his argument for the formal integrity of Cheever's first novel in "Cheever's *The Wapshot Chronicle:* A Narrative of Exploration" (1980). Like a dream, Cheever's novel "follows a definite internal logic" involving "the related concepts of sexual antagonism and the male drive to explore," which for Coverly and Moses means exploring that final and "impenetrable" frontier, the female soul. If the novel has a flaw, it is not in its structure but instead in the author's having stereotyped his female characters, rendering them as little more than caricatures of sexual dominance.

A number of articles have already appeared on *Falconer.* In "Children of the Seventies: The American Family in Recent Fiction" (1980), Susan Gilbert looks at several contemporary American novels, including *Falconer,* and finds clear evidence that families that fail to pass on to their children a sense of tradition and values doom their children to madness. *Falconer,* she judges, succeeds as satire and as a parody of confessional writing but fails completely in providing a realistic, workable "redemptive program." Robert A. Morace and Glen M. Johnson find Cheever's vision much more convincing in their analyses of the novel's structural and thematic coherence. The novel's power, Morace claims in "The Religious Experience and the 'Mystery of Imprisonment' in *Falconer*" (1980), derives from the depth of Cheever's moral vision and treatment of his prison metaphor. Literally, Farragut's crime is fratricide, but figuratively it is his retreat into self and away from the possibilities and responsibilities of living in the world. His drug addiction, self-pity, and fratricide are all aspects of his self-imprisonment. Gradually he comes to transcend self, to affirm the natural world, and to perform those simple acts of human kindness that restore him to his proper place in the world of free men. In "The Moral Structure of Cheever's *Falconer*" (1981), Johnson approaches Cheever's fourth novel more systematically. For Johnson, Cheever is not a realist but instead a romancer whose "novels are effective because their plots do not serve 'realistic' expectations." The mood and action of *Falconer* are determined by the author's religious imagination, which claims "the romancer's freedom to employ 'miracles' " in plotting. More specifically, the novel's structure follows "the Christian pattern of redemption." Farragut's redemption is secular, however, for Cheever's concern is with the human world rather than with the divine (cf. Reilly, "Saving Grace and Moral Balance in John Cheever's Stories," above). Although Johnson applies the redemptive pattern a bit too rigidly to a novel which, like most of Cheever's fiction, develops intuitively rather than programmatically, his analysis of *Falconer*'s religious subtext and identification of various literary and biblical allusions is helpful and his overall reading convincing.

In addition to editing the *Critical Essays of John Cheever* volume discussed above, R. G. Collins has contributed two especially fine journal articles to the growing body of Cheever studies. In "From Subject to Object and Back Again: Individual Identity in John Cheever's Fiction" (1982), Collins takes exception to those who have dismissed Cheever as "a toothless Thurber." "The increasing alienation of modern man from a central role to that of a peripheral, almost ignored spectator" is the theme Cheever has developed over the course of his career—a theme which parallels the change in the American personality during the same period. The youthfulness and hopefulness of Cheever's early stories gives way to "the shattering failure of material success" that he develops in each of his novels. In *Falconer*, Farragut must relinquish the middle-class life he has had in order to begin life anew "somewhere near the same creative beginning as the first Ezekiel Wapshot": no longer an object, but a subject free to make his own way. In "Fugitive Time: Dissolving Experience in the Later Fiction of Cheever" (1984), the more ambitious and at times more opaque of the two articles, Collins points out that beginning with the *Wapshot Chronicle*, Cheever, with his passion for nostalgia, becomes increasingly preoccupied with the illusory nature of reality in general and of the present moment in particular. In this later work, Cheever appears torn "between a tragic pessimism and a raptured expectancy" as he chronicles the inhumanness of the present age and his hopes for something better to come. Cheever makes clear in the two Wapshot books that the traditions of the past are no longer able to sustain human life. In the subsequent fiction, Cheever's characters find themselves in an even worse situation, adrift in a present marked by contingency rather than continuity, "a world of capricious time, insubstantial events, and meaningless relationships," where "man finds himself invoking visions."

Despite the efforts of Coale, Collins, Hunt, and others, John Cheever remains in the 1980s what John W. Aldridge said he was in the 1960s: "the most grievously underdiscussed" of the major contemporary American writers. Other than the bibliographical checklists by Bosha and Coates, there is nothing in the way of hard scholarship. Except for Maurice Friedberg's brief discussion of the Russian response to Cheever's work (the Russians view Cheever as a social critic and as a "humanist who sympathizes with the people") and a number of annotations in Bosha's *Reference Guide*, Cheever's foreign reputation remains largely unknown territory. And James O'Hara's " 'Independence Day at St. Botolph's': The Wapshot Saga Begins" proves to be the closest anyone has come to producing a textual study of Cheever's work. The number of substantive books and articles and the slight increase in the number of dissertations suggest, however, that criticism and scholarship may soon begin to approach both the quantity and the quality of Cheever's own achievement.

Joseph Heller

(1923-)

James Nagel
Northeastern University

PRIMARY BIBLIOGRAPHY

Books and Pamphlets

Catch-22. New York: Simon & Schuster, 1961; London: Cape, 1962. Novel.

We Bombed in New Haven. New York: Knopf, 1968; London: Cape, 1969. Play.

Catch-22: A Dramatization. New York: French, 1971. Play.

Clevinger's Trial. New York: French, 1971. Play.

Something Happened. New York: Knopf, 1974; London: Cape, 1974. Novel.

Good As Gold. New York: Simon & Schuster, 1979; London: Cape, 1979. Novel.

God Knows. New York: Knopf, 1984; London: Cape, 1984. Novel.

No Laughing Matter, by Heller and Speed Vogel. New York: Putnam's, 1986. Memoir.

Selected Stories

"Bookies, Beware," *Esquire*, 27 (May 1947), 98.

"Castle of Snow," *Atlantic Monthly*, 181 (Mar. 1948), 52-55.

"Girl From Greenwich," *Esquire*, 29 (June 1948), 40-41, 142-143.

"A Man Named Flute," *Atlantic Monthly*, 182 (Aug. 1948), 66-70.

"Nothing To Be Done," *Esquire*, 30 (Aug. 1948), 73, 129-130.

Selected Screenplays

Sex and the Single Girl. Warner Bros., 1964.
Casino Royale. Columbia, 1967.
Dirty Dingus Magee. M-G-M, 1970.

Selected Essays

"*Catch-22* Revisited," *Holiday,* 41 (Apr. 1967), 45-60, 72, 141-142, 145.
"On Translating *Catch-22* into a Movie." Collected in *A "Catch-22" Casebook,* ed. Frederick Kiley and Walter McDonald, 346-362. See Collections of Essays.

SECONDARY BIBLIOGRAPHY

Bibliographies and Checklists

Keegan, Brenda M. *Joseph Heller: A Reference Guide.* Boston: G. K. Hall, 1978. Secondary.
Nagel, James. "Introduction" to *Critical Essays on Joseph Heller,* ed. Nagel. Boston: G. K. Hall, 1984, 1-25. Bibliographical essay; secondary.
Scotto, Robert M. *Three Contemporary Novelists: An Annotated Bibliography of Works By and About John Hawkes, Joseph Heller, and Thomas Pynchon.* New York: Garland, 1977. Primary and secondary.
Weixlmann, Joseph. "A Bibliography of Joseph Heller's *Catch-22,*" *Bulletin of Bibliography,* 31 (Jan.-Mar. 1974), 32-37.

Interviews

Bannon, Barbara. "Joseph Heller," *Publishers Weekly,* 206 (30 Sept. 1974), 6.
Barnard, Ken. "Joseph Heller Tells How *Catch-18* Became *Catch-22* and Why He Was Afraid of Airplanes," *Detroit News Sunday Magazine,* 13 Sept. 1970, pp. 18-19, 24, 27-28, 30, 65.
Braudy, Susan. "Laughing All the Way to the Truth," *New York,* 1 (14 Oct. 1968), 42-45.
Flippo, Chet. "Checking in with Joseph Heller," *Rolling Stone,* 16 Apr. 1981, pp. 51-52, 57, 59-60.
Gold, Dale. "Portrait of a Man Reading," *Washington Post Book World,* 20 July 1969, p. 2.

Krassner, Paul. "An Impolite Interview with Joseph Heller," *Realist*, 39 (Nov. 1962), 18-26, 28-31.

Lester, Elenore. "Playwright-in-Anguish," *New York Times*, 3 Dec. 1967, II: 1, 19.

Merrill, Sam. "Playboy Interview: Joseph Heller," *Playboy*, 22 (June 1975), 59-61, 64-66, 68, 70, 72-74, 76.

Plimpton, George. "How It Happened," *New York Times Book Review*, 6 Oct. 1974, pp. 2, 3, 30.

Reilly, Charlie. "Talking with Joseph Heller," *Inquiry*, 1 May 1979, pp. 22-26.

Ruas, Charles. *Conversations with American Writers*. New York: Knopf, 1985, 143-179.

Sale, Richard B. "An Interview in New York with Joseph Heller," *Studies in the Novel*, 4 (Spring 1972), 63-74.

Shapiro, James. "Work in Progress; An Interview with Joseph Heller," *Intellectual Digest*, 2 (Dec. 1971), 6, 8.

Shenker, Israel. "Did Heller Bomb on Broadway?," *New York Times*, 29 Dec. 1968, II: 1, 3.

"So They Say," *Mademoiselle*, 57 (Aug. 1963), 234-235.

Weatherby, W. J. "The Joy Catcher," *Guardian* [Manchester, England], 20 Nov. 1962, p. 7.

Whitman, Alden. "Something Always Happens on the Way to the Office: An Interview with Joseph Heller," *Pages*, 1 (1976), 74-81.

Critical Studies: Collections of Essays

Kiley, Frederick, and Walter McDonald, ed. *A "Catch-22" Casebook*. New York: Crowell, 1973.

Nagel, James, ed. *Critical Essays on "Catch-22."* Encino: Dickenson, 1974.

_____. *Critical Essays on Joseph Heller*. Boston: G. K. Hall, 1984.

Scotto, Robert M., ed. *"Catch-22": A Critical Edition*. New York: Delta, 1973.

Critical Studies: Articles and Book Sections

Aldridge, John W. *The American Novel and the Way We Live Now*. New York: Oxford University Press, 1983, 35-46.

Anderson, Don. "Yossarian *Haruspex:* Some Observations on *Catch-22*," Sydney Studies in English, 3 (1978), 59-73.

Balch, Clayton L. "Yossarian to Cathcart and Return: A Personal Cross Country." Collected in Kiley and McDonald, 301-306.

Barasch, Frances K. "Faculty Images in Recent American Fiction," *College Literature*, 10, no. 1 (1983), 28-37.

Bassein, Beth Ann. *Women and Death: Linkages in Western Thought and Literature*. Westport: Greenwood Press, 1984, 155, 171-176.

Berryman, Charles. "Heller's Gold," *Chicago Review*, 32, no. 4 (1981), 108-118.

Billson, Marcus K. "The Un-Minderbinding of Yossarian: Genesis Inverted in *Catch-22*," Arizona Quarterly, 36 (1980), 315-329.

Blues, Thomas. "The Moral Structure of *Catch-22*," Studies in the Novel, 3 (Spring 1971), 64-79.

Bradbury, Malcolm. *The Modern American Novel*. New York: Oxford University Press, 1983, 165-167.

Brewer, Joseph E. "The Anti-Hero in Contemporary Literature," *Iowa English Yearbook*, 12 (1967), 55-60.

Bryant, Jerry H. *The Open Decision: The Contemporary American Novel and Its Intellectual Background*. New York: Free Press, 1970, 156-164.

Burhans, Clinton S., Jr. "Spindrift and the Sea: Structural Patterns and Unifying Elements in *Catch-22*," *Twentieth Century Literature*, 19 (Oct. 1973), 239-250.

Canaday, Nicholas. "Joseph Heller: Something Happened to the American Dream," *CEA Critic*, 40, no. 1 (1977), 34-38.

Costa, Richard Hauer. "Notes from a Dark Heller: Bob Slocum and the Underground Man," *Texas Studies in Literature and Language*, 23, no. 2 (1981), 159-182.

Davis, Gary W. "*Catch-22* and the Language of Discontinuity," *Novel*, 12, no. 1 (1978), 66-77.

Day, Douglas. "*Catch-22:* A Manifesto for Anarchists," *Carolina Quarterly*, 15 (Summer 1963), 86-92.

DelFattore, Joan. "The Dark Stranger in Heller's *Something Happened*." Collected in *Critical Essays on Joseph Heller*, ed. Nagel, 127-138.

Denniston, Constance. "The American Romance-Parody: A Study of Purdy's *Malcolm* and Heller's *Catch-22*," *Emporia State Research Studies*, 14, no. 2 (1965), 42-59.

Dickstein, Morris. "Something Didn't Happen," *Saturday Review*, 6 (31 Mar. 1979), 49-52.

Dodd, Burwell. "Social Commentary and Narrative Technique: Joseph Heller's *Catch-22*." In *Approaches to the Novel*, ed. John Colmer. Adelaide [Australia]: Rigby, 1966, 71-78.

Doskow, Minna. "The Night Journey in *Catch-22*," *Twentieth Century Literature*, 12 (Jan. 1967), 186-193.

Driver, Tom. "Curtains in Connecticut," *Saturday Review*, 51 (31 Aug. 1968), 22-24.

Fetrow, Fred M. "Joseph Heller's Use of Names in *Catch-22*," *Studies in Contemporary Satire*, 1, no. 2 (1975), 28-38.

Frank, Mike. "Eros and Thanatos in *Catch-22*," *Canadian Review of American Studies*, 8, no. 1 (1976), 77-87.

Friedman, Melvin J. "Something Jewish Happened: Some Thoughts About Joseph Heller's *Good As Gold*." Collected in *Critical Essays on Joseph Heller*, ed. Nagel, 196-204.

Frost, Lucy. "Violence in the Eternal City: *Catch-22* as a Critique of American Culture," *Meanjin Quarterly*, 30 (Summer 1971), 447-453.

Gaukroger, Doug. "Time Structure in *Catch-22*," *Critique*, 12, no. 2 (1970), 70-85.

Gelb, Barbara. "Catching Joseph Heller," *New York Times Magazine*, 4 Mar. 1979, pp. 14-16, 42-55.

Gordon, Caroline, and Jeanne Richardson. "Flies in Their Eyes? A Note on Joseph Heller's Catch-22," *Southern Review*, 3 (Winter 1967), 96-105.

Greenberg, Alvin. "Choice: Ironic Alternative in the World of the Contemporary Novel." In *American Dreams, American Nightmares*, ed. David Madden. Carbondale: Southern Illinois University Press, 1970, 175-187.

Grossman, Edward. "Yossarian Lives," *Commentary*, 58 (Nov. 1974), 78-84.

Hartshorne, Thomas L. "From *Catch-22* to *Slaughterhouse V:* The Decline of the Political Mode," *South Atlantic Quarterly*, 78, no. 1 (1979), 17-33.

Hasley, Louis. "Dramatic Tension in *Catch-22*," *Midwest Quarterly*, 15 (1974), 190-197.

Hassan, Ihab. "Laughter in the Dark: The New Voice in American Fiction," *American Scholar*, 33 (Autumn 1964), 636-640.

Heller, Terry. "Notes on Technique in Black Humor," *Thalia*, 2 (1979), 15-21.

Hill, Hamlin. "Black Humor: Its Cause and Cure," *Colorado Quarterly*, 17 (Summer 1968), 57-64.

Hunt, John W. "Comic Escape and Anti-Vision: Joseph Heller's *Catch-22*." In *Adversity and Grace: Studies in Recent American Literature*, ed. Nathan A. Scott, Jr. Chicago: University of Chicago Press, 1968, 91-98.

Janoff, Bruce. "Black Humor, Existentialism, and Absurdity: A Generic Confusion," *Arizona Quarterly*, 30 (Winter 1974), 293-304.

Jones, Peter G. *War and the Novelist: Appraising the American War Novel.* Columbia: University of Missouri Press, 1976, 45-52.

Karl, Frederick R. *American Fictions 1940-1980: A Comprehensive History and Critical Evaluation.* New York: Harper & Row, 1983, 309-313, 492-495.

_____. "Joseph Heller's *Catch-22:* Only Fools Walk in Darkness." In *Contemporary American Novelists*, ed. Harry T. Moore. Carbondale: Southern Illinois University Press, 1964, 134-142.

Kazin, Alfred. *Bright Book of Life: American Novelists and Storytellers from Hemingway to Mailer.* New York: Delta, 1974, 82-86.

Kennard, Jean. "Joseph Heller: At War with Absurdity," *Mosaic*, 4, no. 3 (1971), 75-87.

Klemtner, Susan Strehle. " 'A Permanent Game of Excuses': Determinism in Heller's *Something Happened*," *Modern Fiction Studies*, 24, no. 4 (1979), 550-556.

Klinkowitz, Jerome. *The American 1960s: Imaginative Acts in a Decade of Change.* Ames: Iowa State University Press, 1980, 20-32.

Lasch, Christopher. *The Culture of Narcissism: American Life in an Age of Diminishing Expectations.* New York: Norton, 1978, 85-86, 98, 180.

LeClair, Thomas. "Joseph Heller, *Something Happened*, and the Art of Excess," *Studies in American Fiction*, 9, no. 2 (1981), 245-260.

Lehan, Richard. *A Dangerous Crossing: French Literary Existentialism and the Modern American Novel.* Carbondale: Southern Illinois University Press, 1973, 162-172.

Lehan and Jerry Patch. "*Catch-22:* The Making of a Novel," *Minnesota Review*, 7, no. 3 (1967), 238-244.

Lindberg, Gary. *The Confidence Man in American Literature.* New York: Oxford University Press, 1982, 238-244.

McDonald, James L. "I See Everything Twice! The Structure of Joseph Heller's *Catch-22*," *University Review*, 34 (Spring 1968), 175-180.

McGinnis, Wayne D. "The Anarchic Impulse in Two Recent Novels," *Publications of the Arkansas Philological Association*, 5, no. 2, 3 (1979), 36-40.

Mailer, Norman. "Some Children of the Goddess: Norman Mailer vs. Nine Writers," *Esquire*, 60 (July 1963), 63-69, 105.

Marcus, Fred H., and Paul Zall. "*Catch-22:* Is Film Fidelity an Asset?" In *Film and Literature: Contrasts in Media,* ed. Fred H. Marcus. Scranton: Chandler, 1971, 127-136.

Martine, James J. "The Courage to Defy." Collected in *Critical Essays on Catch-22,* ed. Nagel, 142-149.

Mellard, James M. "*Catch-22: Deja vu* and the Labyrinth of Memory," *Bucknell Review,* 16, no. 2 (1968), 29-44.

_____. *The Exploded Form: The Modernist Novel in America.* Urbana: University of Illinois Press, 1980, 108-124.

_____. "*Something Happened:* The Imaginary, The Symbolic, and the Discourse of the Family." Collected in *Critical Essays on Joseph Heller,* ed. Nagel, 138-155.

Merrill, Robert. "The Rhetorical Structure of *Catch-22,*" *Notes on Contemporary Literature,* 8, no. 3 (1978), 9-11.

Micheli, Linda. "In No-Man's Land: The Plays of Joseph Heller." Collected in *Critical Essays on Joseph Heller,* ed. Nagel, 232-244.

Miller, Wayne C. *An Armed America: Its Face in Fiction.* New York: New York University Press, 1970, 205-243.

_____. "*Catch-22:* Joseph Heller's Portrait of American Culture—The Missing Portrait in Mike Nichols' Movie." Collected in Kiley and McDonald, 383-390.

_____. "Ethnic Identity as Moral Focus: A Reading of Joseph Heller's *Good as Gold,*" *MELUS,* 6, no. 3 (1979), 3-17.

Milne, Victor J. "Heller's 'Bologniad': A Theological Perspective on *Catch-22,*" *Critique,* 12, no. 2 (1970), 50-69.

Monk, Donald. "An Experiment in Therapy: A Study of *Catch-22,*" *London Review,* 2 (Autumn 1967), 12-19.

Mullican, James S. "A Burkean Approach to *Catch-22,*" College Literature, 8, no. 1 (1981), 42-52.

Nagel, James. "*Catch-22* and Angry Humor: A Study in the Normative Values of Satire," *Studies in American Humor,* 1 (Oct. 1974), 99-106.

_____. "The *Catch-22* Note Cards," *Studies in the Novel,* 8, no. 4 (1976), 394-405.

_____. "Joseph Heller and the University," *College Literature,* 10, no. 1 (1983), 16-27.

_____. "Two Brief Manuscript Sketches: Heller's *Catch-22,*" *Modern Fiction Studies,* 20 (Summer 1974), 221-224.

_____. "Yossarian, The Old Man, and the Ending of *Catch-22.*" Collected in *Critical Essays on Catch-22,* ed. Nagel, 164-174.

Nelson, Gerald B. *Ten Versions of America.* New York: Knopf, 1972, 165-182.

Nelson, Thomas Allen. "Theme and Structure in *Catch-22,*" *Renascence,* 23 (Summer 1971), 173-182.

Olderman, Raymond M. *Beyond the Waste Land: A Study of the American Novel in the Nineteen-Sixties.* New Haven: Yale University Press, 1972, 94-116.

Percy, Walker. "The State of the Novel: Dying Art or New Science?," *Michigan Quarterly Review,* 16 (Fall 1977), 359-373.

Pinsker, Sanford. "Heller's *Catch-22:* The Protest of a *Puer Eternis,*" *Critique,* 7, no. 2 (1965), 150-162.

Podhoretz, Norman. *Doings and Undoings.* New York: Farrar, Straus, 1964, 228-235.

Protherough, Robert. "The Sanity of *Catch-22,*" *Human World,* 3 (May 1971), 59-70.

Ramsey, Vance. "From Here to Absurdity: Heller's *Catch-22.*" In *Seven Contemporary Authors: Essays on Cozzens, Miller, West, Golding, Heller, Albee, and Powers,* ed. Thomas B. Whitbread. Austin: University of Texas Press, 1968, 99-118.

Richter, David H. "The Achievement of Shape in the Twentieth-Century Fable: Joseph Heller's *Catch-22.*" In *Fable's End: Completeness and Closure in Rhetorical Fiction.* Chicago: University of Chicago Press, 1974, 136-165.

Ritter, Jesse. "Fearful Comedy: *Catch-22* as Avatar of the Social Surrealist Novel." Collected in Kiley and McDonald, 73-86.

_____. "What Manner of Men are These?" Collected in *Critical Essays on Catch-22,* ed. Nagel, 45-56.

Schulz, Max F. *Black Humor Fiction of the Sixties: A Pluralistic Definition of Man and His World.* Athens: Ohio University Press, 1973, 91-92.

Searles, George J. "*Something Happened:* A New Direction for Joseph Heller," *Critique,* 18, no. 3 (1977), 74-81.

Sebouhian, George. "From Abraham and Isaac to Bob Slocum and My Boy: Why Fathers Kill Their Sons," *Twentieth Century Literature,* 27, no. 1 (1981), 43-52.

Seltzer, Leon F. "Milo's 'Culpable Innocence': Absurdity as Moral Insanity in *Catch-22,*" *Papers on Language and Literature,* 15, no. 3 (1979), 290-310.

Sniderman, Stephen L. " 'It Was All Yossarian's Fault': Power and Responsibility in *Catch-22,*" *Twentieth Century Literature,* 19 Oct. 1973, 251-258.

Solomon, Eric. "From Christ in Flanders to *Catch-22:* An Approach to War Fiction," *Texas Studies in Literature and Language,* 11 (Spring 1969), 851-866.

Solomon, Jan. "The Structure of Joseph Heller's *Catch-22,*" *Critique,* 9, no. 2 (1967), 46-57.

Stark, Howard J. "The Anatomy of *Catch-22*." Collected in Kiley and McDonald, 145-158.

_____. "*Catch-22:* The Ultimate Irony." Collected in *Critical Essays on Catch-22,* ed. Nagel, 130-141.

Stern, J. P. "War and the Comic Muse: *The Good Soldier Schweik* and *Catch-22,*" *Comparative Literature,* 20 (Summer 1968), 193-216.

Swardson, H. R. "Sentimentality and the Academic Tradition," *College English,* 37 (Apr. 1976), 747-766.

Tanner, Tony. *City of Words: American Fiction 1950-1970.* London: Cape, 1971, 72-84.

Thomas, W. K. "The Mythic Dimension of *Catch-22,*" *Texas Studies in Language and Literature,* 15 (Spring 1973), 189-198.

Tucker, L. "Entropy and Information Theory in Heller's *Something Happened,*" *Contemporary Literature,* 25 (Fall 1984), 323-340.

Walden, Daniel. " 'Therefore Choose Life': A Jewish Interpretation of Heller's *Catch-22*." Collected in *Critical Essays on Catch-22,* ed. Nagel, 57-63.

Waldmeir, Joseph J. *American Novels of the Second World War.* The Hague: Mouton, 1969, 161-166.

_____. "Two Novelists of the Absurd: Heller and Kesey," *Wisconsin Studies in Contemporary Literature,* 5, no. 3 (1964), 192-204.

Walsh, Jeffrey. *American War Literature 1914 to Vietnam.* New York: St. Martin's, 1982, 189-195.

Way, Brian. "Formal Experiment and Social Discontent: Joseph Heller's *Catch-22,*" *Journal of American Studies,* 2 (Oct. 1968), 253-270.

BIBLIOGRAPHICAL ESSAY

Introduction

The historical record of the serious study of the life and works of Joseph Heller has been shaped by the development of his career. Although he has published four novels, three plays, and a dozen short stories, and despite the fact that he has been a professional writer for almost thirty years, he is still most widely known as the author of

Catch-22 (1961), a comic masterpiece of tragic seriousness that set the tone for a generation of Americans in the 1960s. His other works, especially *Something Happened* (1974), *Good as Gold* (1979), and *God Knows* (1984), have occasioned a good deal of comment in reviews and scholarly articles, but the fact remains that well over half the important criticism on Heller is addressed to his sensational first novel.

Biographies

The professional study of Heller has been influenced by other factors as well. Perhaps the most serious is that despite the enormous impact that Heller's works have had on American letters over the past two decades, there is still no extended and reliable biographical account. Scholars are still writing about Heller based on fragmentary and often erroneous information, some of which grossly distorts even the most basic facts of his life, and yet critics persist in making easy equations of Heller with various of his characters, their views with his, as though there were a solid body of biographical data on which to draw. Unfortunately, such is not the case. Until an authorized biography is added to the critical canon, scholars will be forced to use the best of the existing documents, cautioned by an awareness that even the most reliable of these are not without problems.

Among the biographical essays that should be consulted are the accounts in *Who's Who in America, Who's Who in the East, Contemporary Authors,* and other standard reference works. Of somewhat greater utility are the comments in *200 Contemporary Authors* and *Current Biography Yearbook* and, especially, the entry in the *Dictionary of Literary Biography,* although all three contain minor errors. Also of value is Barbara Gelb's "Catching Joseph Heller" (1979), a lengthy essay in the *New York Times Magazine* that provides information not available elsewhere, especially with regard to Heller's childhood and family background. By far the most influential biographical essay is one filled with misinformation, Richard Lehan and Jerry Patch's "*Catch-22:* The Making of a Novel" in the *Minnesota Review* in 1967. As Heller has recorded in a letter, in just one paragraph of their account, Lehan and Patch err in Heller's age, when his father died, the sex of his siblings, the influence of the Coney Island Renaissance, and other such matters. Suffice it to say, scholars beginning a study of the life and works of Joseph Heller should not rely on this essay, despite the fact that it has been reprinted in two major collections.

Bibliographies and Checklists

Although there are no definitive lists in primary and secondary bibliographies there are several good ones for students of Heller. An early bibliography of considerable merit was published in *A "Catch-22" Casebook,* edited by Frederick Kiley and Walter McDonald, in 1973. Their secondary listing is broken into useful categories of concern, but it is not annotated. Robert M. Scotto provided another brief listing in his *"Catch-22": A Critical Edition,* also published in 1973. The following year James Nagel included a brief annotated bibliography in his *Critical Essays on "Catch-22."* But all of these were superseded in 1974 by Joseph Wiexlmann, "A Bibliography of Joseph Heller's *Catch-22,*" in the *Bulletin of Bibliography.* Weixlmann limits himself to *Catch-22* criticism, but he lists all known reviews and essays on the novel through 1973 along with a partial list of the primary works. Robert M. Scotto improved on Weixlmann in 1977 with *Three Contemporary Novelists: An Annotated Bibliography of Works by and about John Hawkes, Joseph Heller, and Thomas Pynchon.* Scotto includes a primary and secondary bibliography including Heller's stories, novels, plays, interviews as well as articles, books, dissertations, and bibliographies regarding Heller. Scotto's volume is a major contribution, one which remains useful because of its organization and coverage. Another important Heller bibliography is Brenda M. Keegan, *Joseph Heller: A Reference Guide,* an annotated listing of Heller scholarship from 1961 to 1977. Although there are occasional errors, this is a valuable book: the introduction is a bibliographical essay that is thorough and objective; the annotations are descriptive; the index comprehensive and easy to use. And Nagel's introduction to *Critical Essays on Joseph Heller* in 1984 is in fact a major bibliographical essay covering Heller's career as well as the criticism. In short, in addition to the standard listings in periodical bibliographies of American literature, Heller scholars have been well served by the work of bibliographers.

Interviews

Heller has over the years granted more than fifty interviews, many of them containing valuable biographical information. Although the list is far too long to cover in detail, a few of these deserve special mention. Two of the best on *Catch-22* are Paul Krassner's "An Impolite Interview with Joseph Heller" (1962), which deals largely with technique, and W. J. Weatherby's "The Joy Catcher" (1962), which covers the personal background and literary influences, matters also addressed in "So They Say" in *Mademoiselle* in 1963. Elenore Lester's "Playwright in Anguish" in 1967 provided the same function for *We Bombed in New Haven* (1969). Of more general interest is Susan Braudy, "Laughing All the Way to the Truth" (1968), which is largely biographical and contains the fascinating suggestion that Heller has used humor over the years as a protective shield. Dale Gold's "Portrait of a Man Reading" (1969) is another interview that explores literary influences and his assessment of other writers, whereas Ken Barnard, "Joseph Heller Tells How *Catch-18* Became *Catch-22* and Why He Was Afraid of Airplanes" (1970) is more specifically focused on *Catch-22*, particularly Heller's experiences in World War II. Perhaps the most extensive of the important interviews is Richard B. Sale's piece in *Studies in the Novel* in 1972, in which Heller talks about the art of his fiction, Yossarian's moral responsibility in *Catch-22*, the seriousness of *Something Happened*, and his beginnings as a writer. A number of other interviews have also dealt with *Something Happened*, all of them containing intriguing and enigmatic comments, perhaps the best of which is George Plimpton's for the *New York Times Book Review* in 1974. Another interview of considerable value is Sam Merrill's long piece in *Playboy* in 1975, in which Heller discusses his books, places of writing, his views of current political and social issues, as well as his personal background. The most comprehensive recent interview can be found in Charles Ruas, *Conversations with American Writers* (1985), in which Heller reflects on his military career, his early short stories, his novels, and *God Knows*. Although there are a great many others of merit, the general point is that in the current state of Heller scholarship these interviews provide a valuable source of background information.

Critical Studies: Articles and Book Sections

The existence of three extensive bibliographies dealing largely with *Catch-22* obviates the need for an exhaustive survey of reviews and criticism, but a discussion of selected items can suggest the historical development of response to Heller's first novel. *Catch-22* was published in October of 1961 to what are known in the trade as mixed reviews, none of which recognized the full complexity of the book. The scholarship on *Catch-22* since the early reviews has been largely confined to the concerns of the initial readers: matters of social satire, black humor, war protest, absurdity, and structural organization, with only the occasional foray into comparative analysis, origins and influences, style, and the aesthetics of the novel. However, in what has become a body of several hundred essays, *Catch-22* criticism has steadily developed in depth and sophistication despite its relatively narrow range.

One of the early scholarly landmarks is Frederick R. Karl, "Joseph Heller's *Catch-22:* Only Fools Walk in Darkness," published in 1964, in which he took the provocative posture that the absurdity of life in the novel was not so much literary invention as a devastating portrayal of modern life. Yossarian is thus not so much a comic figure as a character in isolation, the only one who sees life as it is, who must therefore accept total responsibility for his actions. Karl is thus led to the conclusion that Yossarian is justified in his defiance of the military bureaucracy and in his desertion for in both actions he defies "death in the name of reason and life." Norman Podhoretz developed much the same argument in *Doings and Undoings* the same year. He describes the modern world as a "gigantic insane asylum" and *Catch-22* as one of "the bravest and most nearly successful attempts we have yet had to describe and make credible the incredible reality of American life in the middle of the 20th century." Joseph J. Waldmeir's contemplation of these issues, however, lead him to a rather different assessment. His conclusion, in "Two Novelists of the Absurd: Heller and Kesey" (1964), is that the book is a "magnificent failure" in that its "complexity is superficial, that its variety is only apparent, that its apparent repetitiveness is unfortunately all too real." He also finds Yossarian's assertion at the end of the novel that he has been fighting all along for his country "totally unconvincing," a charge echoed by a great many other readers. In one of the very best scholarly essays on Heller, "Laughter in the Dark: The New Voice in American Fiction" (1964), Ihab Hassan regards Black Humor as an affirmation of life through comedy: "The buffoonery of Heller's *Catch-22* settles for nothing less than sanity and freedom."

If Hassan's essay is valuable as representing the definitive statement of the role of Black Humor in the novel, Sanford Pinsker's "Heller's *Catch-22:* The Protest of a *Puer Eternis*" in 1965 was instrumental in provoking a new approach to Yossarian. Pinsker's contention was that Heller's protagonist refuses to mature, unlike other American figures, and he remains a "perennial innocent." Constance Denniston, in "The American Romance-Parody: A Study of Purdy's *Malcolm* and Heller's *Catch-22* (1965), is similarly provocative, although she advances the issue of generic classification. To her, flat characters repeated events, and a chaotic structure, matters often criticized, are all consistent with the standards of the romance-parody. Also of interest is Vance Ramsey's "From Here to Absurdity: Heller's *Catch-22*" (1968), which presents Yossarian as an antihero in a world in which the sane and the insane have switched places. Ramsey echoes Waldmeir in feeling that the book loses its dramatic quality in the last four chapters.

In "An Experiment in Therapy: A Study of *Catch-22*" (1967), Donald Monk argues the somewhat eccentric but nonetheless interesting thesis that given the insanity of modern warfare, Heller's novel functions as an inversion of therapy. Standard therapy, says Monk, consists of stripping away illusion to deal with the facts; by introducing fantastic elements into the conclusion of the novel (Orr's escape; Yossarian's flight to Sweden; the persistence of Nately's whore), "Heller seems explicitly to deny the moral claims of the world of facts." Jan Solomon presented in "The Structure of Joseph Heller's *Catch-22*" (1967) an often-challenged thesis that the chronology of the novel presents an impossible series of events to underscore the theme of absurdity. Caroline Gordon and Jeanne Richardson published an article in the *Southern Review* in 1967 in which they argue that Heller uses a fictional technique borrowed from Lewis Carroll's *Alice in Wonderland* in his play with language and control of absurdity through logic. Minna Doskow's "The Night Journey in *Catch-22*" (1967) is an excellent discussion of the importance of Chapter 39, "The Eternal City," in Yossarian's moral development and final desertion. Of special value is Heller's own article in *Holiday*, "*Catch-22* Revisited" (1967), in which he recounts his return to the scene of his war adventures in Rome, Corsica, and Avignon. His reflections are informative, touching, and of considerable biographical significance in understanding how his personal experiences inform specific scenes in the novel, especially those involving the missions to Poggibonsi and Avignon.

To this growing body of scholarship, several important articles were added in 1968. Brian Way maintained that *Catch-22* is a brilliant novel in the tradition of radical protest with a strong antimilitarist and anticapitalist theme and an endorsement of freedom and justice. His view is that because the object of the satire is nonrational, Heller uses the techniques of the literature of the absurd. James L. McDonald's "I See Everything Twice! The Structure of Joseph Heller's *Catch-22*" is an excellent early study of the formal values of the novel, especially its structure and handling of time. McDonald's point is that the chronology is related to Yossarian's consciousness, which accounts for the interplay between the present narrative and the repetitions of scenes from the past. In *"Catch-22: Deja vu* and the Labyrinth of Memory," James M. Mellard regards déjà vu as not only a device of organization but also a concept central to the sense of reality (disjunctive). He goes on to demonstrate how Yossarian is involved in, and to some extent responsible for, nearly all of the major events. "War and the Comic Muse: *The Good Soldier Schweik* and *Catch-22*," by J. P. Stern, offers an excellent comparison of Heller's novel to Jaroslav Hasek's in their portrayals of war and bureaucracy, twisted logic, sex, death, and a fight for survival. Stern maintains that they both show war as meaningless and death as irrational rather than heroic; however, Stern sees no social protest against war in *Catch-22*. John W. Hunt gave precise formulation to what was becoming a common insight in his "Comic Escape and Anti-Vision: Joseph Heller's *Catch-22*." Hunt's point is that the novel has a classic structure for a comedy based on the absurd, one that compels the realization that it is the modern world that is absurd, not the world of the novel. In related essays, Hamlin Hill in "Black Humor: Its Cause and Cure" (1968), further refined the role of Black Humor, and Max F. Schulz in *Black Humor Fiction of the Sixties* (1973) argued that Colonel Cathcart and Yossarian share "the anxiety that afflicts man faced with his own helplessness and insignificance before the diffusion of twentieth-century mass society."

Scholarship in 1969 produced only two notable contributions, Eric Solomon's "From Christ in Flanders to *Catch-22:* An Approach to War Fiction," in which he discusses Heller's book in the context of novels about war, and the section on *Catch-22* in Joseph J. Waldmeir's *American Novels of the Second World War*, essentially a reprinting of his article from 1964. The following year publication on Heller took on renewed vigor, in part because of the release of the movie of *Catch-22*. The most substantial essay on the film was Ken Barnard's interview with Heller for the *Detroit News Sunday Magazine*, in which Heller talks about the novel and the movie, his war experiences (including a mission to Avignon on which a gunner in his plane was wounded), and other background events. Anyone exploring the relationship of novel to film should read this interview carefully.

There were also several important essays on the novel in 1970, among them Wayne Charles Miller's chapter in *An Armed America: Its Face in Fiction*, in which he discusses *Catch-22* in the tradition of the war novel. His contention is that Pianosa is a mirror of America, a device that allows Heller to satirize justice, romantic love, heroism, the military, and capitalism. Miller feels that the ending rings false and yet Yossarian emerges as a "symbol of humanistic faith." Victor J. Milne took a somewhat different twist in "Heller's 'Bologniad': A Theological Perspective on *Catch-22*," exploring the novel as a conflict between the "Christian ethic of universal benevolence" and the competitive ethic of capitalism. Doug Gaukroger took issue with Jan Solomon's reading of the structure of the novel by countering that the time scheme *does* make sense and by producing a chart to make his point. Alvin Greenberg maintained that Orr's desertion is essentially a withdrawal within himself that inspires Yossarian to a sense "that human possibility is to be found and the possibility of a meaningful life to be explored." Another valuable discussion is by Jerry H. Bryant in *The Open Decision*, particularly with regard to the vagaries of *Catch-22* and Yossarian's desertion. Bryant contends that the theme of the novel is "survival through defiance."

Perhaps the best-known study published the following year is Tony Tanner's *City of Words*, in which he gives *Catch-22* a reading marred by limited research and occasional errors of fact. Tanner is very good on Yossarian's struggle for survival and on the roles of individual characters, but his attempt to interpret distortions of language as the center of the novel is not sustained. Another notable essay is Robert Protherough's "The Sanity of *Catch-22*," in which he makes a case for the sanity and coherent structure and theme of the novel. Protherough outlines a variety of satiric devices in the novel very persuasively and is similarly perceptive on the developing thematic patterns as the novel progresses. An often-reprinted essay is Jean Kennard's "Joseph Heller: At War with Absurdity," a study of *Catch-22* as an "illustration of the absurdity of the human condition itself." To reinforce the sense of absurdity, Kennard argues, Heller interrupts chronological flow, presents contradictory statements, and gives contradictory accounts of events; finally, the only value is the perpetuation of human existence. Thomas Blues contends that Yossarian deserts not because he must to be human but because he hears about Orr; nor does Blues find Yossarian's assertion that he has been fighting for his country all along very compelling because the historical war seems of little consequence save as metaphor. Thomas Allen Nelson contributed to the debate about the structure of the novel in an essay in *Renascence* in which he maintains that the novel contains a "cyclical pattern of action" related to the central issue of responsibility: "Events and characters which may be outrageously funny when first introduced acquire a philosophical significance in the last part of the novel as the degeneration of values increases to alarming proportions." In "Violence in the Eternal City: *Catch-22* as a Critique of American Culture," Lucy Frost advanced what was by then a familiar thesis that *"Catch-22* is a serious critique of the total culture, not just of war." Heller eliminates Germany from the conflict, she says, to focus on a criticism of American society. Her best observation is that "the Army's goals are no longer shaped by a governing civilian society; they are predominately internal and autonomous."

There were two essays of special interest in 1972. Richard B. Sale did a long interview with Heller that touches on Heller's concern for the integrity of his art and his career as a writer from his early short stories to *We Bombed in New Haven* and *Something Happened,* which was at that point in progress. In *Beyond the Waste Land,* Raymond M. Olderman gave *Catch-22* a reading in the tradition of T. S. Eliot, seeing Yossarian as both Fisher King and Grail Knight. The real enemy in the novel is the military-industrial complex, not the Germans. The terror is that social institutions have seized control over individual human life; the quest of the novel is thus for a way to "affirm life against the forces of negation without violating what is human." Olderman's contribution would have been more valuable had he read the previous scholarship on the subject.

In the following year, 1973, several remarkable critical publications appeared, chief among them two collections of criticism. In his *Catch-22: A Critical Edition,* Robert M. Scotto published not only the novel itself but "Love, Dad," a deleted chapter from the manuscript, and eight previously published articles on the novel. Of much greater utility is A *"Catch-22" Casebook,* edited by Frederick Kiley and Walter McDonald. This book contains an excellent collection of reviews, critical articles, interviews, comments on the movie, and an extensive bibliography. And, in addition to reprinted criticism, the volume contains several original pieces, including a transcription of remarks by Heller at the Young Men's Hebrew Association in New York in December of 1970 about the background of the novel and the script for the film (pp. 346-362). Of special interest is Clayton L. Balch's "Yossarian to Cathcart and Return: A Personal Cross Country," a reminiscence by an officer in a bomber group (not Heller's) stationed on Corsica that portrays events and people parallel to those in the novel (pp. 301-306). Balch's general reflection is that the men did not realize the seriousness of the situation, or the meaning of what they were doing, until much later, a sentiment shared by Heller. Also of value is Howard J. Stark's "The Anatomy of Catch-22," an excellent discussion of the concepts of *déjà vu, jamais vu*, and *presque vu* as the basis for the structure of the novel (pp. 145-158). Jesse Ritter's study of *Catch-22* as a "Social Surrealist Novel" is also of interest; he defines this genre as a form that features "outcast heroes of mythical stature, the parody and fusion of conventional literary forms, the structural juxtaposition of unrelated elements, and the bitter mixture of black humor and tragicomedy" (pp. 73-86). In his essay on the film, Wayne Charles Miller argues that Mike Nichols misread the novel and missed important themes; the novel is not only antiwar, as the movie suggests, but a book about American culture and its direction since 1945 (pp. 383-390). Beyond the items in *Casebook*, there were only a few valuable studies in 1973. One of the best was Clinton S. Burhans, Jr., "Spindrift and the Sea: Structural Patterns and Unifying Elements in *Catch-22*," a useful discussion of the chronology and structure of the novel, complete with a time chart. Burhans also identifies the major lines of thematic development and demonstrates that although the surface of the novel is chaotic, there are unifying patterns of development beneath the surface. Another is Richard Lehan's *A Dangerous Crossing*, which is a spirited discussion with some fine psychological insights. As in Lehan's other work on Heller, unfortunately there are also many careless mistakes, as in having Nately rape Michaela rather than Aarfy.

One of the contributions in 1974 was *Critical Essays on "Catch-22,"* edited by James Nagel. This volume contains a selection of reviews and reprinted articles on the novel along with five original essays, an annotated bibliography, and a list of suggested readings. Among the original essays is Jess Ritter's "What Manner of Men are These," a reading of the novel in terms of Northrup Frye's definition of Menippean satire and an insightful analysis of the roles of individual characters (pp. 45-56). Daniel Walden's " 'Therefore Choose Life': A Jewish Interpretation of Heller's *Catch-22*" develops the idea that the values of the book, especially those expressed by Yossarian, grow out of Jewish tradition, particularly the commitment to preserve existence and to lead a moral life (pp. 57-63). In *"Catch-22:* The Ultimate Irony," Howard J. Stark argues that because the world is absurd, all meaning generates from the individual through a revolt against inhumanity. From this perspective, Yossarian is wrong in deserting; he should have stayed with his unit and tried to persevere, as did the chaplain (pp. 130-141). James J. Martine, in "The Courage to Defy," presents a good survey of Heller's short stories as a prelude to discussing the weaknesses of *Catch-22*, especially its verbosity, discursive elements, and Heller's failure to realize that greed and inhumanity are not restricted to capitalistic countries (pp. 142-149). And in "Yossarian, The Old Man, and the Ending of *Catch-22*," James Nagel develops the thesis that the old man of the brothel serves as a guide to the ethic of survival that Yossarian gradually endorses in the novel, especially after his night journey through Rome and his epiphany about the meaning of Snowden's death. Contra Stark, Nagel thus maintains that Yossarian's desertion is emblematic of his growth, his affirmation of moral principle, and his rejection of compromise (pp. 164-174).

In other scholarship in 1974, Alfred Kazin discussed *Catch-22* in *Bright Book of Life* as representing the "hypothesis of a totally rejectable world," a situation expressive of what many Americans felt in the postwar period. Of greater substance is Bruce Janoff's "Black Humor, Existentialism, and Absurdity: A Generic Confusion," in which Janoff argues that the first thirty-eight chapters are a brilliant example of Black Humor but that the novel changes tone during the final four chapters to one of existential optimism, a shift that "severely impede[s] its thematic momentum." David H. Richter's section on *Catch-22* in *Fable's End* is an extensive essay (twenty-nine pages) that relies heavily on paraphrase of the key scenes of the novel. His thesis is that the form of the narrative "represents an achievement towards which contemporary rhetorical fiction had been groping." Richter sees Yossarian's desertion in positive terms as "the only meaningful and sane form of heroism Heller's world allows." James Nagel had two essays in 1974, a note in *Modern Fiction Studies* that contains two manuscript fragments, one of which shows Yossarian to have been Jewish at the earliest stage of composition, and another hospital scene in which Yossarian and Dunbar seem to be writing a novel. In "*Catch-22* and Angry Humor: A Study in the Normative Values of Satire," Nagel attempts to define the shared assumptions of the novel from which all deviation appears ludicrous. His conclusion is that the novel is essentially a Juvenalian satire with a radical, or idealistic, frame of reference, and this perspective serves as a base for a critique of American society.

In the next two years *Catch-22* scholarship abated somewhat, probably because of the interest in *Something Happened*, published in 1974. In Mike Frank's "Eros and Thanatos in *Catch-22*" (1976), his best point is that the enemy is the Protestant ethic, not the Germans, and the conflict is between capitalistic greed allied with war (thanatos) and the forces of sex and life (eros). H. R. Swardson used his article in *College English* ("Sentimentality and the Academic Tradition," 1976) to express his contempt for *Catch-22* as a sentimental novel not worth teaching: "I find it phony on every page." Fred M. Fetrow explored "Joseph Heller's Use of Names in *Catch-22*" (1975) and concluded that the characters have symbolic functions suggested by their names. In *War and the Novelist* (1976), Peter G. Jones discusses *Catch-22* at some length in what is essentially a summary of major critical issues. Jones interprets Yossarian's desertion as a commitment to "his responsibilities as a rational human being." James Nagel once again based his research on the Heller manuscripts for "The *Catch-22* Note Cards" (1976), an essay that discusses the notes Heller made in the planning stages of the novel and their relationship to the published novel. The essay should be a point of reference for all future scholarship on *Catch-22*.

In 1978, in two persuasive studies, Robert Merrill addressed the use of repetition for thematic emphasis in the scene with the Soldier in White and concludes that "*we* contribute to death and dehumanization through our amused tolerance for life's injustices," and Gary W. Davis discussed how the world of the novel reveals "how society's institutions reflect fundamental discontinuities in language, thought, and behavior." He says that Yossarian's search is for a more meaningful discourse, in which language and reality are brought together. In 1979 Leon F. Seltzer published "Milo's 'Culpable Innocence': Absurdity as Moral Insanity in *Catch-22*," the most extensive and most persuasive article thus far on Milo and the capitalistic ethic. Seltzer's thesis is that the absurd world of Pianosa is used as a vehicle to explore the inhumanity of modern society. Also of interest is Thomas L. Hartshorne's discussion in the *South Atlantic Quarterly* (1979) of *Catch-22* and Kurt Vonnegut's *Slaughterhouse V* as expressions of the "left-tending protest movements" of the 1960s, fables, in effect, consisting of antiwar sentiments, Black Humor, and absurdity.

In the 1980s of much greater substance is James M. Mellard's discussion in *The Exploded Form* of Heller's use of "modern lyrical fiction" in the concept of déjà vu, "a term that suggests something of the delusive experience, hallucinatory quality, and disjunctive expression of reality in *Catch-22*." The impact of this structural device is an emphasis on Yossarian's moral growth, his recognition of his mortality and responsibility for his participation in the war, and his development of a new set of values. In *The American 1960s* Jerome Klinkowitz regards Yossarian and Randall Patrick McMurphy of *One Flew Over the Cuckoo's Nest* as "culture heroes for the bold new decade of the

American 1960s." He says they are the "first underground literary heroes of the new activist generation, proclaiming revolutionary new values. . . ." James S. Mullican presented again Jesse Ritter's argument that *Catch-22* can be read as Menippean satire with flat, stylized characters that embody thematic traits. Gary Lindberg takes a promising tack in *The Confidence Man in American Literature* in discussing Yossarian and Milo as con men. And Jeffrey Walsh, in *American War Literature 1914 to Vietnam*, presents an excellent discussion of the concept of the "catch" and the satiric method of the novel. Frederick R. Karl's much heralded book *American Fictions 1940-1980* is marred by factual errors of various kinds that make his other comments suspect. Karl cites "The Eternal City" as "City of Death"; he mistakenly believes that Mudd is the soldier in white, that Wintergreen does not appear, that Nately's whore is the only one who responds to Snowden's death, Orr's disappearance, and Nately's fatal crash and thus misses the impact these events have on Yossarian's motivation in the final chapters.

The scholarship on *Catch-22* thus represents a rich reservoir of insight on many of the major issues of the novel, especially the method of its satire, its relationship to literature of the absurd, its blend of humor and serious themes, and the complexity of its chronology and structure, matters still unresolved. If there is a persistent weakness in this critical record it is that far too many scholars do not do their homework. This lapse has led to a good deal of repetition in the scholarly record and some perpetuation of error of biographical facts. However, the developing critical approaches, especially those involving basic background research and the use of manuscripts, along with a close reading of the text, promise to contribute to the study of the best American novel of the 1960s.

Something Happened received a good deal of attention, largely in the form of interviews with Heller about his work in progress, even before it was published on 16 October 1974. In one of these, Heller spoke with James Shapiro in 1971 about his protagonist, "Joe" Slocum, the basic plot of the novel, and commented that he was almost through with the writing. In another, with Barbara Bannon, Heller again made general remarks about his forthcoming novel and added the comment, "I do not think novels are like life. Novels are better than life." The best of these prepublication interviews is the one with George Plimpton in the *New York Times Book Review* in which Heller explains how he started the novel with a sentence that expanded into a chapter, comments on his working habits, and reflects on *Catch-22* and its relationship to his new novel.

Subsequent comment in scholarly journals and other forums has continued a diversity of opinion, although in general the reputation of the novel has gradually improved over the years, as has Heller's. George J. Searles in 1977 was among the first serious scholars to give the novel extended treatment. His view was that *Something Happened* is a more subtle and sophisticated novel than *Catch-22* in that it works through implication and understatement. A more mature work that captures the American situation, it has not been fully appreciated, Searles maintained, because of its use of an unheroic protagonist, its narrative method, and its pessimistic theme. In "Joseph Heller: Something Happened to the American Dream," Nicholas Canaday portrayed Slocum as the Willy Loman of the 1970s. He sees Slocum's reflections as "efforts to screw down his life so tight that discovery and change and the unknown cannot possibly threaten him." Of value in 1978 are the comments on *Something Happened* by Christopher Lasch in *The Culture of Narcissism* that explore Slocum's narcissism, his relationships with his children, and his daughter's need for punishment. Susan Strehle Klemtner presents some views that are certain to spark controversy in an article in which she concludes that Slocum "deliberately murders his son," the unacknowledged hero of the novel. By so doing "Slocum succeeds in ridding himself of the poignant reminder of his freedom and responsibility" (p. 556). The only article worthy of note in the following year is Wayne D. McGinnis, "The Anarchic Impulse in Two Recent Novels." McGinnis sees *Something Happened* as a "brilliant satire" that will endure; Slocum is a "crazy paranoid" but his voice is enchanting and transcends the limitations of the novel. Perhaps McGinnis's best observation is that the liberating vision of the novel is Slocum's humanity.

The best scholarship on Heller's second novel has appeared in the 1980s, and perhaps the finest essay thus far is Thomas LeClair's "Joseph Heller, *Something Happened*, and the Art of Excess" (1981). LeClair reads the book as a novel of "unsettling massiveness or multiplicity of implication that exceeds the norms of conventional fiction," a form he terms the novel of excess. He regards *Something Happened* as a better work than *Catch-22*, one that shows Heller's growth as an artist in that "a work of excess has the rhetorical advantage of soliciting conventional responses which are then overturned because excess forces the reader to reconsider such notions as proportion, propriety, quantity, and value." In another notable article, George Sebouhian's

"From Abraham and Isaac to Bob Slocum and My Boy: Why Fathers Kill Their Sons," the novel is discussed in the context of American works that examine the "disintegration of the personality" in terms of fathers destroying sons as a rejection of the son's potential for renewal; in this instance, Slocum is regarded as a helpless instrument in his son's death. Another article from 1981 that deserves attention is "Notes from a Dark Heller: Bob Slocum and the Underground Man" by Richard Hauer Costa. His view is that *Something Happened* is "really concerned principally with the forces in man which cause him to be terrified of himself," and he goes on to explore this theme in a comparison of Heller's novel to Dostoyevski's underground man, especially with regard to tonal and rhetorical devices. Despite the problems with the *Catch-22* section in *American Fictions 1940-1980,* Frederick R. Karl's reading of *Something Happened,* with an emphasis on Slocum's narcissism and infantilism, is compelling and worthy of serious study. One item of interest in 1983 is John W. Aldridge, *The American Novel and the Way We Live Now,* a volume in which he comments (pp. 35-41) on Slocum as a narrator, with an emphasis on how Slocum's fantasies distort his sense of reality. Aldridge feels that Slocum is, in at least one sense, realistic: he sees life in entropic terms. L. Tucker developed a similar thesis in "Entropy and Information Theory in Heller's *Something Happened*" the same year. Also worthy of note are the two original essays on *Something Happened* published in Nagel's *Critical Essays on Joseph Heller* in 1984. In "*Something Happened:* The Imaginary, the Symbolic, and the Discourse of the Family," James M. Mellard gives the novel a Lacanian reading with an emphasis on Bob Slocum and his relationship to his family. Joan DelFattore, in "The Dark Stranger in Heller's *Something Happened,*" directs her attention to the meaning of Slocum's dreams, especially those involving a dark stranger with a concealed knife. DelFattore shows how these dreams are related to Slocum's fear of powerlessness, his concern for sexual performance, and his obsession with public speaking. These issues help explain and put into context the conclusion of the novel.

The publication of *Good As Gold* in 1979 was again greeted with a range of opinions from reviewers, many of them negative. Whatever the validity of the individual assessments of the novel, as a body the reviews constitute an important body of information and should be read by all students of Heller's work. In addition to the reviews, there are a few other pieces worthy of consultation. Two interviews are of some substance. In the first, "Talking with Joseph Heller," Heller responded to a question by Charlie Reilly by saying that the idea for

Gold came from a reading in Wilmington, Delaware, during which a woman asked him why he had never written about the Jewish experience. Heller said he then invented Bruce Gold to write such a book. In his interview with Chet Flippo in *Rolling Stone,* Heller talked at length about *Gold* and, to a lesser extent, *Catch-22,* and reflected that capitalism is dead but that socialism will not work either.

Formal scholarship on *Gold* thus far has been extremely limited, but what has been written has been informative and engrossing. In 1979, in "Ethnic Identity as Moral Focus: A Reading of Joseph Heller's *Good as Gold,*" Wayne C. Miller argues that ethnicity is at the heart of the moral vision of the novel and that Bruce Gold finds himself in the values of the American Jewish experience. He contends that Heller portrays several generations of that experience interacting and shows the ethical deterioration as each succeeding generation moves further away from its racial identity. Charles Berryman mounts an energetic attempt in the *Chicago Review* in 1981 to demonstrate that *Gold* is Heller's best novel, that it has the virtues of the first two efforts but not the faults. Where they were rambling and repetitive, he says, *Gold* is structurally unified. It has a more sophisticated humor closely interwoven with the plot and people in the book. "Heller's skill at the craft of fiction has made clear advances in characterization, narrative control, and most of all in, dramatic timing." In "Joseph Heller and the University," James Nagel discusses all of Heller's fiction, including *Gold,* in terms of its portrayal of education as a means of socioeconomic advancement, a matter also explored in Frances K. Barasch, "Faculty Images in Recent American Fiction." In *Women and Death,* Beth Ann Bassein focuses on the portrait of women in *Gold* and finds that Heller "shows no strong commitment to changing the way literature stereotypes women" (p. 172). The best single discussion of *Gold* thus far is Melvin J. Friedman, "Something Jewish Happened: Some Thoughts about Joseph Heller's *Good as Gold,*" in Nagel's *Critical Essays on Joseph Heller.* Friedman draws on his considerable background as a scholar of Jewish writing in America to place *Gold* in that tradition and to explore the ways in which its satire, portrayal of the family, regard for education, and especially its language relate to the traditions of Jewish literature.

Despite the considerable scholarly record that has been compiled on Heller as the writer of fiction, very little has been written on him as dramatist. Of *We Bombed in New Haven, Catch-22: A Dramatization,* and the one-act play "Clevinger's Trial," only the first has received any sustained attention, even with regard to reviews. *We Bombed,* which ran for eighty-six performances on Broadway in 1968, starring Jason Robards and Diana Sands, received the same broad mix of reviews that characterized the reception of Heller's novels. Beyond the reviews, there is very little on the scholarly record to examine. Elenore Lester did an interview for the *New York Times* with Heller at Yale before the opening of the play that is worthy of attention. In it Heller says that in general he does not like the theater, that he does not consider himself to be a writer of Black Comedy, that, in any event, *New Haven* is not comic, and that he is somewhat concerned about the quality of his script. On the other end of the public performances of the play, Israel Shenker did another interview for the *New York Times* on 29 December 1968, the day the play closed its New York run. In "Did Heller Bomb on Broadway?" Heller comments that the play is modeled on Greek tragedies and comedies and that most of all he wanted to move the conscience of the audience. The most substantial discussion of Heller as dramatist, however, is Linda Micheli's "In No-Man's Land: The Plays of Joseph Heller," in Nagel's *Critical Essays on Joseph Heller* in 1984. In her essay Micheli discusses all three of Heller's plays in terms of the art of theater. She concludes that Heller is a dramatist who must be taken seriously, especially for his skill with dialogue and for the drafting of memorable individual scenes. Micheli's essay will always be valuable as the first comprehensive treatment of Heller's controversial but nonetheless remarkable plays.

Conclusion

As a review of the scholarship reveals, a great deal has been written on Heller and a great deal remains to be done. Although *Catch-22* had been examined from numerous perspectives, most of the central issues of the book, and most of the basic technical aspects of it, have yet to receive definitive treatment, and only a few scholarly essays take into account the rich legacy of the manuscripts of the novel. Heller's other novels have been studied in only a preliminary way, and his short stories and plays have received only scant attention. Beyond specific works, a reliable and extended biographical account would be of use to scholars of all persuasions as would a full primary and secondary bibliography. It is perhaps too early to contemplate an edition of Heller's letters, but scholars who seek them out in libraries and private collections will find them fascinating reading and patently quotable for scholarly purposes. At some point a full scholarly study would help to draw together Heller's life with his creative work, but until such time as one is produced, students and scholars will have to rely on the rich body of criticism contained in articles and sections of books, along with the collections of scholarship, to guide their study of one of the most controversial, and one of the finest, contemporary American writers.

Norman Mailer

(1923-)

J. Michael Lennon
Sangamon State University

PRIMARY BIBLIOGRAPHY

Books and Pamphlets

[Note: It has been Mailer's practice every three or four years beginning in 1959 to collect the bulk of his accumulated periodical
writings into miscellanies and thematic collections, and to include
in some of them excerpts from previous books as well as original
work. He has published nine such collections. Because of the
large number of periodical pieces he has reprinted, sometimes
two or three times, only the most important are cross-referenced
in the following listing. All important periodical writings which
have not been collected are listed under the appropriate rubrics,
but those which have been collected—over 150—are not listed.
Citations for the original periodical publication of these items
can be found in the acknowledgments of the nine collections.]

The Naked and the Dead. New York: Rinehart, 1948; London: Wingate,
1949. Novel.

Barbary Shore. New York: Rinehart, 1951; London: Cape, 1952. Novel.

The Deer Park. New York: Putnam's, 1955; London: Wingate, 1957.
Novel.

The White Negro. San Francisco: City Lights, 1957. Reprinted in *Advertisements For Myself.* Essay.

Advertisements For Myself. New York: Putnam's, 1959; London:
Deutsch, 1961. Miscellany.

Deaths for the Ladies (and other disasters). New York: Putnam's, 1962;
London: Deutsch, 1962. Poems.

The Presidential Papers. New York: Putnam's, 1963; London: Deutsch, 1964. Miscellany.

Gargoyle, Guignol, False Closets. Palma de Mallorca: Anthony Kerrigan, 1964. Poems. Limited edition.

An American Dream. New York: Dial, 1965; London: Deutsch, 1965. Novel.

Cannibals and Christians. New York: Dial, 1966; London: Deutsch, 1967. Miscellany.

The Bullfight: A Photographic Narrative with Text by Norman Mailer. New York: CBS Legacy Collection Book, distributed by Macmillan, 1967. Accompanied by record of Mailer reading from text and a poem by Federico Garcia Lorca. Reprinted in *Existential Errands.* Essay.

The Deer Park: A Play. New York: Dial, 1967.

The Short Fiction of Norman Mailer. New York: Dell, 1967; London: Weidenfeld & Nicolson, 1969.

Why Are We in Vietnam? New York: Putnam's, 1967; London: Weidenfeld & Nicolson, 1969. Novel.

The Armies of the Night: History as a Novel, The Novel as History. New York: New American Library, 1968; London: Weidenfeld & Nicolson, 1968. Nonfiction narrative.

The Idol and the Octopus: Political Writings on the Kennedy and Johnson Administrations. New York: Dell, 1968. Selections from *The Presidential Papers* and *Cannibals and Christians.*

Miami and the Siege of Chicago: An Informal History of the Republican and Democratic Conventions of 1968. New York: World, 1968; London: Weidenfeld & Nicolson, 1969. Nonfiction narrative.

Of a Fire on the Moon. Boston: Little, Brown, 1970. Republished as *A Fire on the Moon.* London: Weidenfeld & Nicolson, 1970. Nonfiction narrative.

King of the Hill. Accompanied by photographs. New York: New American Library, 1971. Reprinted in *Existential Errands.* Nonfiction narrative.

Maidstone: A Mystery. New York: New American Library, 1971. Accompanying essay, "A Course in Filmmaking," reprinted in *Existential Errands.* Filmscript.

The Prisoner of Sex. Boston: Little, Brown, 1971; London: Weidenfeld & Nicolson, 1971. Essay.

Existential Errands. Boston: Little, Brown, 1972. Miscellany.

St. George and the Godfather. New York: New American Library, 1972. Nonfiction narrative.

Marilyn: A Biography. Accompanied by photographs. New York: Grosset & Dunlap, 1973; London: Hodder & Stoughton, 1973.

The Faith of Graffiti. Documented (photographs) by Mervyn Kurlansky and Jon Naar. New York: Praeger, 1974. Republished as *Watching My Name Go By.* London: Mathews, Miller, Dunbar, 1974. Reprinted in *Pieces and Pontifications.* Essay.

The Fight. Boston: Little, Brown, 1975; London: Hart-Davis, 1976. Nonfiction narrative.

Some Honorable Men: Political Conventions, 1960-1972. Boston: Little, Brown, 1976. Nonfiction narratives reprinted from previous books.

A Transit to Narcissus. New York: Howard Fertig, 1978. Facsimile of typescript of previously unpublished 1944 novel. Limited edition.

The Executioner's Song. Boston: Little, Brown, 1979; London: Hutchinson, 1979. Nonfiction narrative.

Of a Small and Modest Malignancy, Wicked and Bristling with Dots. Northridge, Cal.: Lord John Press, 1980. Reprinted in *Pieces and Pontifications.* Essay. Limited edition.

Of Women and Their Elegance. Photographs by Milton H. Greene. New York: Simon & Schuster, 1980. Fictional autobiography.

The Essential Mailer. Sevenoaks, Kent: New English Library, 1982. Combines full texts of *The Short Fiction of Norman Mailer* and *Existential Errands.*

Pieces and Pontifications (Pontifications, ed. Michael Lennon). Boston: Little, Brown, 1982; Sevenoaks, Kent: New English Library, 1983. Essays and interviews.

Ancient Evenings. Boston: Little, Brown, 1983; London: Macmillan, 1983. Novel.

Tough Guys Don't Dance. New York: Random House, 1984; London: Joseph Nicolson, 1984.

Selected Other

[Note: For the most part, the following list contains only important, uncollected items not listed in Laura Adams's *Norman Mailer: A Comprehensive Bibliography.*]

"Authors and Humanism," *Humanist* (Oct./Nov. 1951). Reprinted as "Are You a Humanist?," *Humanist* (Mar./Apr. 1981), 23. Symposium contribution.

"Mailer, Norman." In *Twentieth Century Authors*, ed. Stanley J. Kunitz. New York: H. W. Wilson, 1955, 628-629. Autobiographical entry.

"The Boston Trial of 'Naked Lunch,'" *Evergreen Review*, 9 (June 1965), 40-44, 46-49, 87-88. Reprinted in paperback edition of *Naked Lunch* by William S. Burroughs. New York: Grove, 1966, x-xxxvi. Court testimony.

"Democracy Has/Hasn't a Future . . . A Present," *New York Times Magazine*, 26 May 1968, pp. 30-31, 98-104. Account of a symposium in which Mailer participated.

The Tales of Hoffman (The Trial of the Chicago 8), ed. Mark L. Levine, George M. McNamee, and Daniel Greenberg. New York: Bantam, 1970, 204-207. Court testimony.

"Introduction" to paperback edition of *Deaths for the Ladies (and other disasters)*. New York: New American Library, 1971.

"The Capote Perplex: An Open Letter from Norman Mailer," *Rolling Stone*, 19 July 1973, p. 8.

Introduction to "The Time of Her Time." In *Writer's Choice*, ed. Rust Hills. New York: McKay, 1974, 251.

"Gladiators: For Hemingway," *New Republic*, 30 Nov. 1974, p. 22. Poem.

"Preface" to *A Fiction Writer's Handbook* by Hallie and Whit Burnett. New York: Harper & Row, 1975, xvii-xxi.

"The Murder File." In *Marilyn: A Biography*. New York: Warner, 1975, 340-351. Chapter on details of Monroe's death written for this paperback edition.

"The Meaning of Vietnam," *New York Review of Books*, 12 June 1975, pp. 26-27. Symposium contribution.

"Foreword" to *St. Patrick's Day with Mayor Daley And Other Things Too Good To Miss* by Eugene Kennedy. New York: Seabury, 1976, ix-xii.

"Preface" to paperback edition of *The Deer Park*. New York: Putnam's, 1976, v.

"Preface" to paperback edition of *The Presidential Papers*. New York: Putnam's, 1976, vii-ix.

"Norman Mailer on Women, Love, Sex, Politics and All That!," *Cosmopolitan*, 80 (May 1976), 182-185, 235. Self-interview.

"The Search for Carter," *New York Times Magazine*, 26 Sept. 1976, pp. 19-21, 69-70, 72-78, 80-85, 88-92. Profile.

"Trial of the Warlock," *Playboy*, 23 (Dec. 1976), 121-124, 126, 132,

232, 235-236, 240, 243-244, 246, 249-252, 254. Screenplay adaptation of J. K. Huysmans's *La Bas.*

"The CIA and Watergate," *Best of Chic,* 1 (1978), 3-8, 10, 18, 30, 72, 100. Essay followed by conversation with John Erlichman.

"Novelist Shelved," *Boston Magazine,* Sept. 1979, p. 91. Comic auto-obituary.

[Affidavit concerning loyalty of Mailer's father, Isaac Barnett Mailer]. Reprinted in *The Law of the Land: The Evolution of Our Legal System* by Charles Rembar. New York: Simon & Schuster, 1980, 370-375.

"Introduction" to *Soon to be a Major Motion Picture* by Abbie Hoffman. New York: Putnam's, 1980, xii-xv.

"An Appeal to Lillian Hellman and Mary McCarthy," *New York Times Book Review,* 11 May 1980, pp. 3, 33. Open letter.

"Before the Literary Bar," *New York,* 10 Nov. 1980, pp. 27-31, 33-36, 38, 40, 43-46. Self-interview on *Of Women and Their Elegance.*

"Introduction" to *In the Belly of the Beast: Letters from Prison* by Jack Henry Abbott. New York: Random House, 1981, ix-xvi.

"Until Dead: Thoughts on Capital Punishment by Norman Mailer," *Parade,* 8 Feb. 1981, pp. 6-9, 11. Essay.

"A Sinister Occupation," *Book Digest Magazine* (Apr. 1981), 20, 22-24, 27-29. Essay.

"Foreword" to *Dear Muffo: 35 Years in the Fast Lane* by Harold Conrad. New York: Stein & Day, 1982, xix-xxii.

"Marilyn's Sexiest Tapes and Discs," *Video Review* (Feb. 1982), 71-74. Review.

"The Poor American in London," *Esquire* (Oct. 1983), 49-52, 54, 56, 58, 60, 62. Essay on British elections.

"All the Pirates and People," *Parade,* 23 Oct. 1983, pp. 4-7. Profile of Clint Eastwood.

"A Country, not a Scenario," *Parade,* 19 Aug. 1984, pp. 4-9. Essay on Russia.

"Huckleberry Finn, Alive at 100," *New York Times Book Review,* 9 Dec. 1984, pp. 1, 36-37. Essay.

"The Hazards and Sources of Writing," *Michigan Quarterly Review,* 24 (Summer 1985), 391-402. Expanded version of "A Sinister Occupation."

Edited Book

Genius and Lust: A Journey Through the Major Writings of Henry Miller. New York: Grove, 1976. Selections from ten of Miller's books with eighty pages of commentary by Mailer.

Screenplays and Productions

Wild 90. Supreme Mix Inc., 1968. Produced by Mailer and Buzz Farbar and directed by Mailer.

Beyond the Law—Blue. Supreme Mix Inc., 1968. Produced by Mailer.

Maidstone—A Mystery. Supreme Mix Inc., 1970. Produced by Mailer and Buzz Farbar; directed with screenplay by Mailer.

The Executioner's Song. Film Communications Inc. Productions, 1982. Screenplay by Mailer.

Editions and Collections

Manso, Peter, ed. *Running Against the Machine.* Garden City: Doubleday, 1969. Interviews, articles, debates, speeches, position papers, etc., concerning Mailer's 1969 campaign for mayor of New York, including several by Mailer.

Lucid, Robert F., ed. *The Long Patrol: 25 Years of Writing from the Work of Norman Mailer.* New York: World, 1971. Selections from thirteen of Mailer's books.

SECONDARY BIBLIOGRAPHY

Bibliographies and Checklists

Adams, Laura. "Criticism of Norman Mailer: A Selected Checklist," *Modern Fiction Studies,* 17 (Autumn 1971), 455-463. Primary and secondary.

_____. *Norman Mailer: A Comprehensive Bibliography.* Metuchen, N. J.: Scarecrow Press, 1974. Primary and secondary.

Lucid, Robert F. "A Checklist of Mailer's Published Work." In his *Norman Mailer: The Man and His Work.* Boston: Little, Brown, 1971, 299-310.

Shepherd, Douglas. "Norman Mailer: A Preliminary Bibliography of Secondary Comment, 1948-1968," *Bulletin of Bibliography,* 29 (Apr. 1972), 37-45.

Sokoloff, B. A. *A Bibliography of Norman Mailer*. Darby, Pa.: Darby Books, 1969. Primary and secondary.

Biographies: Books

Flaherty, Joe. *Managing Mailer*. New York: Coward-McCann, 1970. Account of Mailer's 1969 campaign for mayor of New York.
Manso, Peter. *Mailer: His Life and Times*. New York: Simon & Schuster, 1985. Oral biography.
Mills, Hilary. *Mailer: A Biography*. New York: Empire Books, 1982.
Weatherby, William J. *Squaring Off: Mailer vs. Baldwin*. New York: Mason/Charter, 1977. Account of Mailer-James Baldwin friendship and fights.

Biographies: Major Articles and Book Sections

Atlas, James. "Life With Mailer," *New York Times Sunday Magazine*, 9 Sept. 1979, pp. 52-55, 86, 88, 90, 92, 94, 96, 98, 102, 104, 107.
Baldwin, James. "The Black Boy Looks at the White Boy." In his *Nobody Knows My Name*. New York: Dial, 1961, 216-241. Collected in *Norman Mailer: A Collection of Critical Essays*, ed. Leo Braudy and in *Norman Mailer: The Man and His Work*, ed. Robert F. Lucid. See Collections of Essays.
Brower, Brock. "In this Corner, Norman Mailer: Never the Champion, Always the Challenger," *Life*, 24 Sept. 1965, pp. 94-96, 98, 100, 102, 105-106, 109-112, 115, 117.
Christian, Frederick. "The Talent and the Torment," *Cosmopolitan*, 155 (Aug. 1963), 63-67.
Cook, Bruce. "Aquarius Rex," *National Observer*, 4 Nov. 1972, pp. 1, 15. Collected in *Will The Real Norman Mailer Please Stand Up?*, ed. Laura Adams. See Collections of Essays.
DeMott, Benjamin. "An Unprofessional Eye: Docket No. 15883," *American Scholar*, 30 (Spring 1961), 232-237.
Land, Myrick. "Mr. Norman Mailer Challenges All the Talent in the Room." In his *The Fine Art of Literary Mayhem*. New York: Holt, Rinehart & Winston, 1963, 216-238. Rev. ed. San Francisco: Lexikos, 1983, 228-244.
Lucid, Robert F. "Prolegomenon to a Biography of Mailer." Collected in *Critical Essays on Norman Mailer*, ed. J. Michael Lennon. See Collections of Essays.
Macdonald, Dwight. "Our Far-Flung Correspondents: Massachusetts

vs. Mailer." In his *Discriminations: Essays & Afterthoughts, 1938-1974*. New York: Grossman (Viking), 1974, 194-209. Collected in *Norman Mailer: The Man and His Work*, ed. Lucid. See Collections of Essays.

Martien, Norman. "Norman Mailer at Graduate School or: One Man's Effort," *New American Review*, no. 1, ed. Theodore Solotaroff. New York: New American Library, 1967, 233-241. Collected in *Norman Mailer: The Man and His Work*, ed. Lucid. See Collections of Essays.

Newfield, Jack. "On the Steps of a Zeitgeist." In his *Bread and Roses Too: Reporting About America*. New York: Dutton, 1971, 385-390. Collected in *Critical Essays on Norman Mailer*, ed. Lennon. See Collections of Essays.

Pell, Edward. "Norman Mailer Remembers Long Branch: His Childhood Was a Happy Time," *Daily Register* (Red Bank, N. J.), 12 Dec. 1966, p. 1.

Plimpton, George. *Shadow Box*. New York: Putnam's, 1979, 66-67, 257-264, 276-280, 318-320, 322-324.

Roddy, Joseph. "The Latest Model Mailer," *Look*, 27 May 1969, pp. 22-28.

Rosenbaum, Ron. "The Siege of Mailer: Hero to Historian," *Village Voice*, 21 Jan. 1971, pp. 1, 40-41.

Sokolov, Raymond A. "Flying High with Mailer," *Newsweek*, 9 Dec. 1968, pp. 84, 86-88.

Soll, Rick. "Norman Mailer: A Man, an Artist, a Cultural Phenomenon," *Living (Chicago Sunday Sun-Times)*, 7 Aug. 1983, pp. 1, 6-7, 12.

Toback, James. "At Play in the Fields of the Bored," *Esquire*, 70 (Dec. 1968), 150-155, 22, 24, 26, 28, 30, 32, 34, 36.

Trilling, Diana. "The Prisoner of Sex." In her *We Must March My Darlings: A Critical Decade*. New York: Harcourt Brace Jovanovich, 1977, 199-210. Collected in *Critical Essays on Norman Mailer*, ed. Lennon. See Collections of Essays.

Truscott, Lucian K., IV. "Mailer's Birthday," *Village Voice*, 8 Feb. 1973, pp. 1, 24-26.

Willingham, Calder. "The Way It Isn't Done: Notes on the Distress of Norman Mailer," *Esquire*, 60 (Dec. 1963), 306-308. Collected in *Norman Mailer: The Man and His Work*, ed. Lucid. See Collections of Essays.

Interviews

Aldridge, John W. "An Interview with Norman Mailer," *Partisan Review*, 47 (July 1980), 174-182.

Auchincloss, Eve, and Nancy Lynch. "An Interview with Norman Mailer," *Mademoiselle*, 52 (Feb. 1961), 76, 160-163.

Begiebing, Robert. "Twelfth Round: An Interview with Norman Mailer," *Harvard Magazine*, 85 (Mar.-Apr. 1983), 40, 42-50.

Bezner, Kevin. "An Interview with Norman Mailer," *San Francisco Review of Books*, Feb. 1980, pp. 6-9, 26-27, 31.

Bragg, Melvyn. "A Murderer's Tale: Norman Mailer Talking to Melvyn Bragg," *Listener*, 15 Nov. 1979, pp. 660-662.

_____. "Norman Mailer Talks to Melvyn Bragg about the Bizarre Business of Writing a Hypothetical Life of Marilyn Monroe," *Listener*, 20 Dec. 1973, pp. 847-850. Transcript of a television interview with Mailer on "Second House" (BBC2).

Breit, Harvey. "Norman Mailer." In his *The Writer Observed*. New York: Collier, 1956, 199-201.

Buckley, William F., Jr. "Crime and Punishment: Gary Gilmore," *Firing Line*, no. 390. Columbia, S.C.: Southern Educational Communications Association, 1979, 1-19. Transcript of "Firing Line" television interview taped 11 Oct. 1979.

Canby, Vincent. "When Irish Eyes Are Smiling, It's Norman Mailer," *New York Times*, 27 Oct. 1968, II: 15.

Cook, Bruce. "Angry Young Rebel With a Cause," *Rogue* (Apr. 1961), 16-18, 76.

Ellison, James Whitfield. "A Conversation with Norman Mailer," *Book-of-the-Month Club News*, Aug. 1973, pp. 4, 24.

Fallaci, Oriana. "Norman Mailer: Why Do People Dislike America?" In her *The Egotists: Sixteen Surprising Interviews*. Chicago: Regnery, 1968, 1-18.

Fulford, Bob, moderator. "Mailer, McLuhan and Muggeridge: On Obscenity," *Realist*, Oct. 1968, pp. 5-12. Transcript of television discussion program entitled "The Way It Is," broadcast in May 1968 on CBLT-TV, Toronto.

Gelmis, Joseph. "Norman Mailer." In his *The Film Director as Superstar*. Garden City: Doubleday, 1970, 43-63.

Grace, Matthew, and Steve Roday. "Mailer on Mailer: An Interview," *New Orleans Review*, 3, no. 3 (1973), 229-234.

Herman, Jan. "Norman Mailer Meets Middle-age and Wins with a

Knockout Book," *Show (Chicago Sunday Sun-Times)*, 14 Oct. 1979, pp. 1, 14.

Howard, Peter E. "Mailer: Tough Guy at Ease in P'town," *Sunday Cape Cod Times*, 12 Aug. 1984, pp. 1, 12, 13.

Isaacs, Stan. "Norman Mailer," *Tropic (Miami Herald)*, 30 Nov. 1975, pp. 30-34, 36.

Kakutani, Michiko. "Mailer Talking," *New York Times Book Review*, 6 June 1982, pp. 3, 38-41.

Kennedy, Eugene. "The Essential Mailer," *Sunday (Chicago Tribune Magazine)*, 9 Sept. 1984, pp. 23-25, 28-29.

_____. "God and Man and Norman Mailer," *Notre Dame Magazine*, 12, no. 3 (1983), 18-21.

_____. "Mailer: 'It's easier to talk of sex than death,' " *Bookworld (Chicago Tribune)*, 10 Apr. 1983, pp. 1, 7.

Kent, Leticia. "The Rape of the Moon: Norman Mailer Talks About Sexual Lunacy and the Wasp," *Vogue*, 1 Feb. 1971, pp. 134-135.

"Light on Orwell," *Listener*, 4 Feb. 1971, pp. 144-145. Summary of *Omnibus* (BBC 1) program in which Mailer participated.

McNeil, Legs. "Norman Mailer," *High Times*, Sept. 1979, pp. 43-47, 49, 51-53, 55, 107-109, 111, 113, 115, 117.

Merrill, Robert, et al. "Norman Mailer," *Brushfire* (Associated Students of University of Nevada at Reno), 23, no. 1 (1973), 7-14, 16, 20.

Monaghan, Charles. "Portrait of a Man Reading," *Washington Post Book World*, 11 July 1970, p. 2.

Plimpton, George. "Unbloodied By The Critical Pounding, Norman Mailer Defends the Egyptian Novel That Took A Decade To Write," *People*, 30 May 1983, pp. 53-54, 59-60.

Rodman, Selden. "Norman Mailer." In his *Tongues of Fallen Angels*. New York: New Directions, 1974, 163-181.

Ross, Lillian. "Rugged Times," *New Yorker*, 23 Oct. 1948, p. 25.

Ruas, Charles. "Norman Mailer." In his *Conversations with American Writers*. New York: Knopf, 1985, 18-36.

Scavullo, Francesco. "Norman Mailer, Writer." In his *Scavullo on Men*. New York: Random House, 1977, 126-129.

Schumacher, Michael. "Modern Evenings: An Interview with Norman Mailer," *Writer's Digest*, 63 (Oct. 1983), 30-34.

Wallace, Mike. "Norman Mailer." In his *Mike Wallace Asks*. New York: Simon & Schuster, 1958, 26-27.

Weber, Bruce. "Mailer's Flight to Ancient Egypt," *Harper's Bazaar*, 114 (May 1984), 160-161, 96, 104.

Winn, Janet. "Capote, Mailer and Miss Parker," *New Republic*, 9 Feb.

1959, pp. 27-28. Account of "Open End" television program moderated by David Susskind.

Wollheim, Richard. "Living Like Heroes," *New Statesman*, 29 Sept. 1961, pp. 443-445.

Young, David. "A Section of An Interview Between Norman Mailer and David Young," *Notre Dame Review*, 115 (Mar. 1974), 5-9. Another portion of this interview is reprinted in Mailer's *Pontifications*.

Documentary Films

Will the Real Norman Mailer Please Stand Up? Grove Press/Evergreen Films, 1970.

Town Bloody Hall. D. A. Pennebaker, 1971.

Norman Mailer: The Sanction to Write. Picture Start, 1982.

Critical Studies: Books

Adams, Laura. *Existential Battles: The Growth of Norman Mailer.* Athens: Ohio University Press, 1976.

Bailey, Jennifer. *Norman Mailer: Quick-Change Artist.* New York: Barnes & Noble, 1979.

Begiebing, Robert J. *Acts of Regeneration: Allegory and Archetype in the Works of Norman Mailer.* Columbia: University of Missouri Press, 1980.

Bufithis, Philip H. *Norman Mailer.* New York: Ungar, 1978.

Cohen, Sandy. *Norman Mailer's Novels.* Amsterdam: Rodopi, 1979.

Ehrlich, Robert. *Norman Mailer: The Radical as Hipster.* Metuchen, N. J.: Scarecrow Press, 1978.

Foster, Richard. *Norman Mailer.* Minneapolis: University of Minnesota Press, 1968. Collected in *Norman Mailer: The Man and His Work*, ed. Lucid. See Collections of Essays.

Gordon, Andrew. *An American Dreamer: A Psychoanalytic Study of the Fiction of Norman Mailer.* Rutherford, N. J.: Fairleigh Dickinson Press, 1980.

Gutman, Stanley T. *Mankind in Barbary: The Individual and Society in the Novels of Norman Mailer.* Hanover, N. H.: University Press of New England, 1975.

Kaufmann, Donald L. *Norman Mailer: The Countdown (The First Twenty Years).* Carbondale: Southern Illinois University Press, 1969.

Leeds, Barry H. *The Structured Vision of Norman Mailer*. New York: New York University Press, 1969.

Merrill, Robert. *Norman Mailer*. Boston: Twayne, 1978.

Middlebrook, Jonathan. *Mailer and the Times of his Time*. San Francisco: Bay Books, 1976.

Poirier, Richard. *Norman Mailer*. New York: Viking, 1972.

Radford, Jean. *Norman Mailer: A Critical Study*. New York: Barnes & Noble, 1975.

Solotaroff, Robert. *Down Mailer's Way*. Urbana: University of Illinois Press, 1974.

Critical Studies: Collections of Essays

Adams, Laura, ed. *Will the Real Norman Mailer Please Stand Up?* Port Washington, N. Y.: Kennikat, 1974.

Braudy, Leo, ed. *Norman Mailer: A Collection of Critical Essays*. Englewood Cliffs, N. J.: Prentice-Hall, 1972.

Lennon, J. Michael, ed. *Critical Essays on Norman Mailer*. Boston: G. K. Hall, 1986. Forthcoming.

Lucid, Robert F., ed. *Norman Mailer: The Man and His Work*. Boston: Little, Brown, 1971.

Modern Fiction Studies, 17 (Autumn 1971). Mailer number.

New Orleans Review, 3, no. 3 (1973). Mailer number.

Critical Studies: Major Articles and Book Sections

Aldridge, John W. "From Vietnam to Obscenity." In his *The Devil in the Fire: Retrospective Essays on American Literature and Culture 1951-71*. New York: Harper's Magazine Press, 1970, 185-194. Collected in Lucid.

_____. "Mailer, Burns, and Shaw: The Naked Zero." In his *After the Lost Generation: A Critical Study of Writers of Two Wars*. New York: McGraw-Hill, 1951, 133-156.

_____. "Norman Mailer: The Energy of New Success." In his *Time to Murder and Create: The Contemporary Novel in Crisis*. New York: McKay, 1966, 149-163. Collected in Braudy.

_____. "The Perfect Absurd Figure of a Mighty, Absurd Crusade," *Saturday Review*, 13 Nov. 1971, pp. 45-46, 48-49, 72. Collected in Lennon.

Alter, Robert. "The Real and Imaginary World of Norman Mailer," *Midstream*, 15 Jan. 1969, pp. 24-35. Collected in *The Politics of*

Twentieth-Century Novelists, ed. George .A. Panichas. New York: Hawthorn, 1971, 321-334.

Bersani, Leo. "The Interpretation of Dreams," *Partisan Review,* 32 (Fall 1965), 603-608. Collected in Braudy and in Lucid.

Berthoff, Warner. "Witness and Testament: Two Contemporary Classics." In his *Fictions and Events: Essays in Criticism and Literary History.* New York: Dutton, 1971, 288-308.

Bloom, Harold. "Norman in Egypt," *New York Review of Books,* 28 Apr. 1983, pp. 3-4, 6.

Bryant, Jerry H. *The Open Decision: The Contemporary American Novel and Its Intellectual Background.* New York: Free Press, 1970, 369-394.

Bufithis, Philip. "Norman Mailer." In *Dictionary of Literary Biography Yearbook: 1983,* ed. Mary Bruccoli and Jean W. Ross. Detroit: Gale Research Company, 1984.

Burgess, Anthony. *99 Novels: The Best in English Since 1939.* New York: Simon & Schuster, 1984, 42-43, 132-133.

Capote, Truman. *Conversations with Capote* by Lawrence Grobel. New York: New American Library, 1985.

Carson, Tom. "The Time of His Prime Time," *Village Voice Literary Supplement,* no. 14 (Feb. 1983), 1, 10-12.

Cowan, Michael. "The Americanness of Norman Mailer." Collected in Braudy, 143-174, in Adams, and in expanded form as "The Quest for Empowering Roots: Mailer and the American Literary Tradition" in Lennon.

Didion, Joan. " 'I want to go ahead and do it,' " *New York Times Book Review,* 7 Oct. 1979, pp. 1, 26-27. Collected in Lennon.

Dienstfrey, Harris. "The Fiction of Norman Mailer." In *On Contemporary Literature,* ed. Richard Kostelanetz. New York: Avon, 1964, 422-436.

Dupee, F. W. "The American Norman Mailer," *Commentary,* 29 (Feb. 1960), 128-132. Collected in Braudy.

Fetterley, Judith. "An American Dream: 'Hula, Hula,' Said the Witches." In her *The Resisting Reader: A Feminist Approach to American Fiction.* Bloomington: Indiana University Press, 1978, 154-189. Collected in part in Lennon.

Finholt, Richard. "Mailer's Cosmology." In his *American Visionary Fiction: Mad Metaphysics as Salvation Psychology.* Port Washington, N. Y.: Kennikat, 1978, 112-127.

Foster, Richard. "Mailer and the Fitzgerald Tradition," *Novel,* 1 (Spring 1968), 219-230. Collected in Braudy.

Gilman, Richard. "Norman Mailer: Art as Life, Life as Art." In his *The Confusion of Realms.* New York: Random House, 1969, 81-153.

Girgus, Sam B. "Song of Him-Self: Norman Mailer." In his *The New Covenant: Jewish Writers and the American Idea.* Chapel Hill: University of North Carolina Press, 1984, 135-159.

Grace, Matthew. "Norman Mailer at the End of the Decade," *Etudes Anglaises,* 24 (Jan.-Mar. 1971), 50-58. Collected in Adams.

Green, Martin. "Mailer's *Why Are We in Vietnam?*" In his *The Great American Adventure.* Boston: Beacon, 1984, 199-215.

_____. "Norman Mailer and the City of New York: Faustian Radicalism." In his *Cities of Light and Sons of the Morning: A Cultural Psychology for an Age of Revolution.* Boston: Little, Brown, 1972, 58-89. Collected in part in Lennon.

Greer, Germaine. "My Mailer Problem," *Esquire,* 76 (Sept. 1971), 90-93, 214, 216.

Gross, Theodore L. "Norman Mailer: The Quest for Heroism." In his *The Heroic Ideal in American Literature.* New York: Free Press, 1971, 272-295.

Guttman, Allen. "The Apocalyptic Vision of Norman Mailer." In his *The Jewish Writer in America: Assimilation and the Crisis of Identity.* New York: Oxford University Press, 1971, 153-172.

Harper, Howard M., Jr. "Norman Mailer—A Revolution in the Consciousness of Our Time." In his *Desperate Faith: A Study of Bellow, Salinger, Mailer, Baldwin and Updike.* Chapel Hill: University of North Carolina Press, 1967, 96-136.

Hassan, Ihab. "Encounter With Necessity, III." In his *Radical Innocence: Studies in the Contemporary Novel.* Princeton: Princeton University Press, 1961, 140-151. Collected in Lennon.

_____. "Focus on Norman Mailer's *Why Are We In Vietnam?*" In *American Dreams, American Nightmares,* ed. David Madden. Carbondale: Southern Illinois University Press, 1970, 197-203.

Hellman, John. "Journalism as Nonfiction: Norman Mailer's Strategy for Mimesis and Interpretation." In his *Fables of Fact: The New Journalism as New Fiction.* Athens: Ohio University Press, 1980, 35-65.

Hendin, Josephine. "American Rebels Are Men of Action." In her *Vulnerable People: A View of American Fiction Since 1945.* New York: Oxford University Press, 1978, 117-144.

Hesla, David. "The Two Roles of Norman Mailer." In *Adversity and Grace: Studies in Recent American Literature,* ed. Nathan A. Scott,

Jr. Chicago: University of Chicago Press, 1968, 211-238.

Hoffa, William. "Norman Mailer: Advertisements for Myself, or a Portrait of the Artist as a Disgruntled Counter-Puncher." In *The Fifties: Fiction, Poetry, Drama,* ed. Warren G. French. De Land, Fla.: Everett/Edwards, 1970, 73-82.

Hollowell, John. "Mailer's Vision: History As a Novel, The Novel As History." In his *Fact & Fiction: The New Journalism and the Non-fiction Novel.* Chapel Hill: University of North Carolina Press, 1977, 87-125.

Horn, Bernard. "Ahab and Ishmael at War: The Presence of *Moby-Dick* in *The Naked and the Dead," American Quarterly,* 34 (Fall 1982), 379-395.

Jameson, Fredric. "The Great American Hunter, or Ideological Content in the Novel," *College English,* 34 (Nov. 1972), 180-199.

Karl, Frederick R. *American Fictions 1940-1980.* New York: Harper & Row, 1983, 12-14, 35-36, 79-80, 95-99, 102-103, 254-255, 267-269, 579-582.

Kazin, Alfred. *Bright Book of Life: American Novelists and Storytellers from Hemingway to Mailer.* Boston: Little, Brown, 1973, 71-77, 149-157, 236-241, 255-257.

_____. "The Trouble He's Seen," *New York Times Book Review,* 5 May 1968, pp. 1-2, 26. Collected in Lennon.

Kernan, Alvin B. "The Taking of the Moon: The Struggle of the Poetic and Scientific Myths in Norman Mailer's *Of A Fire On the Moon."* In his *The Imaginary Library: An Essay on Literature and Society.* Princeton: Princeton University Press, 1982, 130-161.

Langbaum, Robert. "Mailer's New Style." In his *The Modern Spirit: Essays on the Continuity of Nineteenth- and Twentieth-Century Literature.* New York: Oxford University Press, 1970, 147-163.

Lasch, Christopher. "The Anti-Intellectualism of the Intellectuals." In his *The New Radicalism in America, 1889-1963: The Intellectual as a Social Type.* New York: Knopf, 1965, 334-349.

Lennon, J. Michael. "Mailer's Cosmology," *Modern Language Studies,* 12 (Summer 1982), 18-29. Collected in Lennon.

_____. "Mailer's Radical Bridge," *Journal of Narrative Technique,* 7 (Fall 1977), 170-188.

_____. "Mailer's Sarcophagus: The Artist, the Media and the 'Wad,' " *Modern Fiction Studies,* 23 (Summer 1977), 179-187.

Lucid, Robert F. "Norman Mailer: The Artist as Fantasy Figure," *Massachusetts Review,* 15 (Autumn 1974), 581-595.

_____. "Three Public Performances: Fitzgerald, Hemingway,

Mailer," *American Scholar,* 43 (Summer 1974), 447-466.

McConnell, Frank D. "Norman Mailer and the Cutting Edge of Style." In his *Four Postwar American Novelists: Bellow, Mailer, Barth and Pynchon.* Chicago: University of Chicago Press, 1977, 58-107.

Millett, Kate. *Sexual Politics.* New York: Doubleday, 1970, 10-16, 314-335.

Parker, Hershel. "Norman Mailer's Revision of the *Esquire* Version of *An American Dream* and the Aesthetic Problem of 'Built-in Intentionality,' " *Bulletin of Research in the Humanities,* 84 (Winter 1981), 405-430.

Pizer, Donald. "Norman Mailer: *The Naked and the Dead.*" In his *Twentieth Century American Literary Naturalism: An Interpretation.* Carbondale: Southern Illinois University Press, 1982, 90-114.

Podhoretz, Norman. *Breaking Ranks: A Political Memoir.* New York: Harper & Row, 1979, 263-267.

_____. *Making It.* New York: Random House, 1967, 352-356.

_____. "Norman Mailer: The Embattled Vision." In his *Doings and Undoings: The Fifties and After in American Writing.* New York: Farrar, Straus, 1964, 179-204. Collected in Lucid.

Poirier, Richard. "In pyramid and palace," *Times Literary Supplement,* 10 June 1983, pp. 591-592. Collected in Lennon.

Raleigh, John Henry. "History and Its Burdens: The Example of Norman Mailer." In *Uses of Literature,* ed. Monroe Engel. Cambridge: Harvard University Press, 1973, 163-186.

Richardson, Jack. "The Aesthetics of Norman Mailer," *New York Review of Books,* 8 May 1969, pp. 3-4. Collected in Lucid.

Ricks, Christopher. "Mailer's Primal Words," *Grand Street,* 3 (Autumn 1983), 161-172.

Ross, Mitchell S. "Norman Mailer." In his *The Literary Politicians.* Garden City: Doubleday, 1978, 166-211.

Schickel, Richard. *Intimate Strangers: The Culture of Celebrity.* New York: Doubleday, 1985, 108-129, 170-184.

_____. "Stars and Celebrities," *Commentary,* 52 (Aug. 1971), 61-65.

Schrader, George Alfred. "Norman Mailer and the Despair of Defiance," *Yale Review,* 51 (Dec. 1961), 267-280. Collected in Braudy.

Schulz, Max F. "Mailer's Divine Comedy." In his *Radical Sophistication: Studies in Contemporary Jewish-American Novelists.* Athens: Ohio University Press, 1969, 69-109. Collected in Adams.

Scott, Nathan A., Jr. "Norman Mailer—Our Whitman." In his *Three American Moralists: Mailer, Bellow, Trilling.* Notre Dame, Ind.:

University of Notre Dame Press, 1973, 15-97.

Silverstein, Howard. "Norman Mailer: The Family Romance and the Oedipal Family," *American Imago*, 34 (Fall 1977), 277-286.

Stade, George. "Mailer and Miller," *Partisan Review*, 44, no.4 (1977), 616-624.

Steiner, George. "Naked but not Dead," *Encounter*, 17 (Dec. 1961) 67-70. Collected in Lennon.

Styron, William. "Aftermath of 'Aftermath.' " In his *This Quiet Dust And Other Writings*. New York: Random House, 1982, 137-142.

Tanner, Tony. "On the Parapet." In his *City of Words: American Fiction, 1950-1970*. New York: Harper & Row, 1971, 344-371. Collected in Adams.

Taylor, Gordon O. "Of Adams and Aquarius," *American Literature*, 46 (Mar. 1974), 68-82.

Toback, James. "Norman Mailer Today," *Commentary*, 44 (Oct. 1967), 68-76.

Trilling, Diana. "The Radical Moralism of Norman Mailer." In her *Claremont Essays*. New York: Harcourt, Brace & World, 1964, 175-202. Collected in Braudy and in Lucid.

Vidal, Gore. "Norman Mailer's Self-Advertisements." In his *Homage to Daniel Shays: Collected Essays 1952-1972*. New York: Random House, 1972, 75-86. Collected in Lucid.

_____. *Views From a Window: Conversations with Gore Vidal*, ed. Robert J. Stanton and Gore Vidal. Secaucus, N. J.: Lyle Stuart, 1980, 38-42, 155-160, 179-181, 197-198, 212-213.

_____. "Women's Liberation Meets Miller-Mailer-Manson Man." In his *Homage to Daniel Shays*, 389-402.

Vogelgesang, Sandy. *The Long Dark Night of the Soul: The American Intellectual Left and the Vietnam War*. New York: Harper & Row, 1974, 9-10, 131-133, 149-151, 178-179.

Volpe, Edmund C. "James Jones—Norman Mailer." In *Contemporary American Novelists*, ed. Harry T. Moore. Carbondale: Southern Illinois University Press, 1964, 106-119.

Waldron, Randall H. "The Naked, the Dead, and the Machine: A New Look at Norman Mailer's First Novel," *PMLA*, 87 (Mar. 1972), 271-277.

Weinberg, Helen A. "The Heroes of Norman Mailer's Novels." In her *The New Novel in America: The Kafkan Mode in Contemporary Fiction*. Ithaca: Cornell University Press, 1970, 108-140.

Widmer, Kingsley. "Several American Perplexes." In his *The Literary*

Rebel. Carbondale: Southern Illinois University Press, 1965, 175-198.

BIBLIOGRAPHICAL ESSAY

Bibliographies and Checklists

Laura Adams's *Norman Mailer: A Comprehensive Bibliography* (1974) is dedicated to "all of us who needed this book." The need was great; the earlier bibliographies of B. A. Sokoloff (1969) and Douglas Shepherd (1972) are error-filled and incomplete. Robert F. Lucid's 1971 checklist of Mailer's published works, including items from the most obscure periodicals, is much more thorough, although not without errors, many of which are corrected by Adams in her volume. Her ambitious and indispensable volume provides listings of not only the usual primary and secondary sources but also of unpublished manuscripts, dissertations, reviews of work about Mailer, nonprint media and anthologizations. Her separate listing of interviews is also very helpful. There are errors in her volume, but they are minor (page numbers, misspellings, etc.). Given the great range and number of Mailer's publications, it is remarkable that Adams was able to locate and correctly cite so many of them. The same is true of secondary publications.

The number of items by and about Mailer published since Adams's mid-1974 cutoff point, plus items omitted by her, probably comes close to the total listed in her 131-page bibliography. The checklist given here covers some of this ground and corrects some of her errors and omissions, but a new bibliography is sorely needed. An annotated listing of Mailer's periodical publications, which number over 200, would be a welcome addition to such a bibliography.

Biographies: Books

The first biographical study listed in the checklist is concerned with Mailer's unsuccessful 1969 campaign for mayor of New York. Peter Manso's collection of campaign position papers, speeches, etc., *Running Against the Machine* (1969), complements Joe Flaherty's *Managing Mailer* (1970). Flaherty, Mailer's campaign manager, is unsparing in his depiction of the quixotic attempt by Mailer and Jimmy Breslin (who ran for president of the city council) to convince New Yorkers to "vote the rascals in."

W. J. Weatherby's *Squaring Off: Mailer vs. Baldwin* (1977) is an attempt to aggrandize several disagreements between Mailer and James Baldwin into a grandiose cultural confrontation. Weatherby, who conducted a thoughtful interview on violence with Mailer in 1964 (collected in *Pontifications,* 1982), yokes the two writers into conflict with a patchwork of speculation, gossip, supposition, rhetorical questions and liberal borrowings from their writings. His documentation consists of an acknowledgements page; there is no index.

Hilary Mills's *Mailer: A Biography* (1982) is the first serious biography. Written without Mailer's active support (he gave her only one interview—reprinted in *Pontifications*—and that before she announced her biographical intention), and without the cooperation of many of his friends and family, Mills's book is forced to rely on published materials or single sources to reconstruct many of the important events of his life. Nevertheless, she was the first to interview many of Mailer's friends and relatives and their recollections are of considerable value. Mills researched and wrote the book in about eighteen months, however, and could not obtain interviews with many important people in Mailer's life, including several of his wives and secretaries and all of his children. She makes little use of secondary material on Mailer, confining herself largely to quotations from the reviews of his major books. Important critics such as Richard Foster, Robert F. Lucid, and Richard Poirier are not mentioned at all. But the biography's major fault is that Mills has no biographical thesis beyond her unarguable assertion that Mailer is an important, controversial writer who "seems the very embodiment of the time." Finally, her documentation is irregular and there is no bibliography.

Given the tumultuous events of Mailer's life, the complexity of his large, multi-generic *oeuvre* and the bewildering, contradictory array of images of him in highbrow books and periodicals as well as the mass media, it is not surprising that Mills chose the unobjectionable thesis that she did. Determining what images are genuine projections and which are the enlargements of his supporters, the innocent or nasty simplifications of the media or the calculated distortions of satirists and enemies will be one of the key tasks of Mailer's future biographers. It will be complicated by the fact that for most of his career Mailer has collaborated with his admirers in painting "improvements," as he calls them in *The Armies of the Night* (1968), on the "sarcophagus of his image." But the circumstance that will make the biographer's task most difficult is that there may not be a fundamental Mailerian self to which all these chosen avatars and media faces can or cannot be reconciled. Mailer has changed dramatically several times since he burst on the literary scene in 1948 with the publication of *The Naked and the Dead*.

In *Mailer: His Life and Times* (1985), Peter Manso offers no thesis at all, arguing that "there is more truth in a montage than a monolith." His oral biography consists of lightly edited transcripts from interviews with over 200 individuals, a much larger group than that interviewed by Mills, although there are still a few omissions. Because many of Manso's interviewees—George Plimpton, José Torres, Jean Malaquais, Scott Meredith, Roger Donoghue and Charles Rembar, for example—have known Mailer for many years, their reminiscences appear in a number of places throughout this 718-page book. Manso was not primarily interested in the integrity of his interviewees' utterances; what they had to say is cut up and distributed along with Mailer's life line. The fragmentation of much of the testimony is compensated for by the triangulation that it permits. Unlike Mills, Manso gives several versions of important events and periods in Mailer's life, allowing readers to make their own judgments. Manso's book was criticized by a majority of reviewers for not assessing the mountain of memories he amassed, and it does stimulate more than it satisfies. By not advancing even the most provisional of hypotheses, Manso avoids the criticism of superficiality leveled at Mills, but the reader is still without any sort of critical scaffolding, much less an authoritative, reasoned perspective from which to comprehend this huge mass of recollection. His montage of Mailer does not tessellate into a sharp picture. It is more an archive than a mosaic, but his unprecedented collection of testimony will be absolutely vital material for future biographers. Manso's book also includes interviews with a number of important Mailer critics, including Diana Trilling, who is quite penetrating, excerpts from Mailer's letters to his Army friend, "Fig" Gwaltney, stretching from 1948-1964, and excerpts from major reviews of Mailer's books.

Biographies: Articles and Book Sections

Space does not permit much comment on the shorter biographical pieces on the checklist. There are (1) articles or chapters by friends, or former friends; (2) those which examine a particular event; or (3) pieces which give a reliable overview of some moment or aspect of Mailer's career. The articles by James Baldwin (1961), Dwight Macdonald (1974), and Calder Willingham (1963) are the best of the first category. In the second category, those of Bruce Cook (1972), Norman Martien (1967), Jack Newfield (1971), Ron Rosenbaum (1971), and Diana Trilling (1977), all of which describe Mailer at public events, are the most evocative. The best of the third category are Brock Brower's 1965 profile in *Life*, published shortly after *An American Dream* (1965) appeared in book form; Myrick Land's 1963 chapter on Mailer's literary feuds, which features counterpoint by his contemporaries and further rejoinders from Mailer; and Raymond A. Sokolov's 1968 profile in *Newsweek* which captures Mailer shortly after the publication of *The Armies of the Night* and *Miami and the Siege of Chicago* (1968). All three include comment by Mailer. Robert F. Lucid's 1986 overview of his projected, authorized biography constitutes a category unto itself. His "prolegomenon" sketches out a hypothesis that attempts to explain Mailer's complex motives for engaging in what sometimes appears to be self-destructive extra-literary activity, but is really a species of aesthetic calisthenics. Lucid's biography will apparently be an effort in cultural historiography as well as a biographical study.

Interviews

Mailer has been interviewed approximately 200 times, probably more than any other American author. Each of his first four miscellanies contains at least one interview, and the second half of his fifth, *Pieces and Pontifications*, consists of twenty interviews, four of which are excerpted from the interviews reprinted in earlier miscellanies. These four, with Richard G. Stern and Robert F. Lucid (1959), Paul Krassner (1962), Steven Marcus (1963), and Paul Carroll (1967), are loaded with information on a wide range of topics and have been mined by critics, journalists and subsequent interviewers since they were published. The Stern-Lucid interview is the first full articulation of Mailer's personal belief in God "as a warring element in a divided universe," a cosmology, he has said, from which all his ideas derive. In this interview he also forwards the notion of the unconscious possessing a "navigator" which directs human action. The Krassner interview covers many topics, but it is most notable for its presentation of Mailer's iconoclastic views on sex. In the original version (reprinted in *The Presidential Papers*, 1963), Mailer reveals that the characters in *Naked* "for whom I had the most secret admiration, like Croft, were violent people," a remark commented on by many Mailer critics. Mailer speaks at some length in the Marcus interview about the problems he encountered in writing his first three novels, and also discusses the relationship of literary craft and character, culminating in the now well-known story of Harry Greb the boxer and the way his unorthodox training methods parallel his own. This interview is perhaps the most revealing Mailer has ever given on the links between his life and art. The Carroll interview contains his lengthiest discourse on drugs; he also foreshadows his later examination of technology in *Of a Fire on the Moon* (1970). It is important to note that in three of these four interviews (excepting Krassner's) Mailer talks about his vision of an embattled, existential God, his bulwark against pessimism since the mid-1950s.

Of the remaining sixteen interviews, five (four with J. Michael Lennon and one with Anita Eichholz) were excerpted from the transcript of Jeffrey Van Davis's (1982) documentary, "Norman Mailer: The Sanction to Write" and were published for the first time in *Pontifications*. There is no easy way to summarize these five interviews, conducted in Munich in 1980, except to say that they comprise a synopticon of his views. Two of the remaining eleven interviews (with Richard Stratton, 1975; Laura Adams, 1975) also deal with his cosmology; three others (with Buzz Farbar, 1973; Cathleen Medwick, 1970; and Jeffrey Michelson and Sarah Stone, 1981) deal with sex, love, and marriage. David Young's 1974 conversation illumines Mailer's ideas on the primitive sensibility, magic and science, while Paul Attansio's interview (1981) is valuable for the light it sheds on Mailer's continuing admiration for Hemingway. The two final interviews in *Pontifications* are among Mailer's best. The first of these is a 1981 conversation among Mailer, Joseph McElroy, and his creative writing class at Columbia. It stands in marked contrast with the Marcus interview, Mailer having become much more amenable to discussions of literary technique in the nearly two decades which separate the interviews. He explains in great detail why and how he turned to journalism in the 1960s and his chagrin at learning that his audience, at that time, "wanted interpretation. It was those critical faculties that were being called for, rather than one's novelistic gifts." Mailer also discusses his then-unpublished novel, *Ancient Evenings* (1983), as he does in the final interview with Barbara Probst Solomon (1981). The most important topic of the Solomon interview, however, is *The Armies of the Night*, which he explains, was not consciously written under the influence of *The Education of Henry Adams*, even though "it's an absolute take-off, as if I were the great-grandson of Henry Adams."

Of the many remaining uncollected interviews with Mailer, there are thirty–eight listed. Some are included because in them Mailer talks about something previously unremarked on, some because he goes over old ground more thoroughly, others because they reveal him at a crucial point in his career. For example, the interview with Lillian Ross was conducted in 1948 when Mailer was campaigning for Henry Wallace and trying to come to grips with the celebrity resulting from *The Naked and the Dead,* which was still on the best–seller list. The Janet Winn article (1959) recounting Mailer's appearance on David Susskind's television program, "Open End," with Dorothy Parker and Truman Capote appeared just before *Advertisements for Myself* (1959) was published. Mailer doggedly defended Kerouac and the Beat Movement on the program. The interview with Eve Auchincloss and Nancy Lynch (published in February, 1961, conducted in mid-November, 1960), and the one with Richard Wollheim, which took place in September 1961, bracket "The Trouble," as Mailer's friends call his penknife stabbing of his second wife, Adele, on November 20, 1960 (he received a suspended sentence when she refused to press charges). Another early interview of note is Harvey Breit's. It was reprinted in Breit's book, *The Writer Observed* in 1956, but took place in 1951. In it Mailer disavows naturalism ("that terrible word"), and argues that writers must become more intellectual if they are to succeed.

Two important interviews bracket the publication of *The Armies of the Night* in 1968: Bob Fulford's comes just before and Vincent Canby's just after. In Canby's, which is really a profile with long quotations, Mailer discusses his movie-making and explains that he decided to use the third person to describe himself in *The Armies of the Night* only after he had edited his own image in his film, "Wild 90" (1968). This experience enabled him to see himself "as a piece of material, as a piece of yard goods. I'd say: 'Where am I going to cut myself? ' " The Fulford interview took place on the Canadian Broadcasting System program, "The Way It Is." It is a wonderfully free-wheeling conversation (many of the longer interviews with Mailer were edited by him, however slightly) on the affairs of the universe among Fulford, Mailer, and two avuncular figures he admired: Malcolm Muggeridge and Marshall McLuhan, who represent, roughly and respectively, his conservative and radical sides.

Some of the interviews dealing with specific topics are Joseph Gelmis's on filmmaking (1970), Mailer's longest on the topic; Leticia Kent's (1971) on WASPs and *Of a Fire on the Moon;* and Charles Monaghan's (1970), in which Mailer lists some of the books which influenced him—from *Tarzan of the Apes* to *Das Kapital, Studs Lonigan* to *The Decline of the West.*

Melvyn Bragg's two interviews with Mailer (1973 and 1979) deal with *Marilyn* (1973) and *The Executioner's Song* (1979), respectively. Two interviews from the mid-1970s, one with Matthew Grace and Steve Roday (1973) and the other with Stan Isaacs (1975), reveal a more conjectural Mailer. This is made most clear by Mailer's surprising comment to Isaacs that "compared to the champs of the past"—he names Hemingway, Faulkner, Melville and Hawthorne—"I'm like the equivalent of Ezzard Charles, if you will." Mailer discusses *Marilyn* in both interviews and makes perhaps his earliest extended comment on *Ancient Evenings* explaining that "the book starts in Egypt, in the 20th Dynasty—about 1500 B. C. And there's also a portion of it that takes place in a spaceship. There is also a small portion of the book that has to do with a Jewish family about 40 years ago, 50 years ago." Later, of course, Mailer dropped the non-Egyptian material, reserving it for possible future use.

The Legs McNeil interview (1979) is interesting because McNeil was only in his early twenties at the time and Mailer spoke to him in a paternal, but not condescending manner on several matters, rock and roll and the use and abuse of drugs, most notably. The interview with William F. Buckley, Jr. (1979) is the longest and best on *The Executioner's Song.* Mailer not only discusses Gilmore's psychology and capital punishment, he also summarizes the false start he made on the book and compares it to Truman Capote's *In Cold Blood,* noting that Gilmore was "a real convict" while Capote's two killers were "essentially pretty dull fellows . . . punks."

Some of the most recent interviews with Mailer have been among the best. Eugene Kennedy's are certainly in this category; he published two profile interviews in 1983 and one in 1984. Kennedy is positively Jamesian in his ability to capture the mood of each of his conversations with Mailer, who is obviously comfortable and expansive in the presence of his old friend. In the 1984 conversation, Mailer names some of the source materials for *Ancient Evenings.* Mailer names other sources in the 1983 interview with another old friend, George Plimpton, whose short interview belies the claim that Menenhetet, the protagonist of *Ancient Evenings,* is a stand-in for Mailer. A third interview in which Mailer discusses *Ancient Evenings* is that with Charles Ruas (1985). Mailer is extremely lucid in this one, the bulk of which is devoted to his relationship to Jack Abbott, a convict whom Mailer helped get paroled and who subsequently murdered a man in New

York in 1981, shortly after his book of prison letters, *In the Belly of the Beast*, was published by Random House.

One of the longest interviews Mailer has given, and certainly the most comprehensive as far as biographical detail is concerned, is that with Robert Begiebing. In this interview, which was conducted in the fall of 1982 and published the next year in *Harvard Magazine*, Mailer speaks of his childhood in Brooklyn and his relations with his family, his army service, his stint as a screenwriter in Hollywood in 1949-1950 and, appropriately, his years at Harvard (1939-1943). He recalls at some length his professors, his friends, the books he read, and the fiction he wrote. The Begiebing interview would be indispensable for this material alone but Mailer has much to say on other topics as well, including *Ancient Evenings*, which he claims is "the best book about magic that's ever been written." The final interview which requires note is that with Peter Howard (1984), one of the few to date in which Mailer discusses *Tough Guys Don't Dance* (1984).

Critical Studies: Books

Book-length critical studies of Mailer's work began to appear in the late 1960s and have been published at the rate of one a year since then, although none have appeared since 1980. Most of these books have been solid, serious efforts and even some of the oldest are still of value.

Richard Foster's monograph, *Norman Mailer* (1968), is part of the University of Minnesota pamphlet series on American writers. Only forty–six pages in length, it was the longest critical essay on Mailer to that time. Foster stresses his interpretation of Mailer as an "experimentalist," comparing him to Joyce, Lawrence, and, especially, Fitzgerald. Despite the reservations of many "serious literary people," he says, Mailer's accomplishments in fiction, nonfiction, movies, and theater, along with "a great deal of moral, social, and political punditry" make him the most "vivid public figure on the American literary scene." Foster provides capsule summaries of all of Mailer's books through *The Armies of the Night*, relating them to his contention—a fair one—that "life threatened in our time by the forces of death is Mailer's subject everywhere." Foster's subtle dissection of Mailer's "forcing style" and his clear depiction of Mailer as a public writer make his essay useful still as an introduction to the first half of Mailer's work.

Donald L. Kaufmann's *Norman Mailer: The Countdown (The First*

Twenty Years) was published in 1969, the same year that Barry H. Leeds's *The Structured Vision of Norman Mailer* appeared. They vie for the distinction of being the first full-length critical study on Mailer. Kaufmann says in his introduction that his study will "begin at the end . . . from literature as such, to literature as public statement, and finally, to literature as private vision." This is his "countdown" and, accordingly, he numbers his chapters in reverse order. What it amounts to, however, is that his first three chapters discuss Mailer's first four novels; succeeding chapters examine the novels and miscellanies as expressions of various themes: sex, politics, existentialism, etc. His final chapter, "Early Last Words," argues that Mailer will soon drop his various "I" narrators and return to an omniscient authorial voice. Kaufmann was wrong about this, but a bigger criticism is that his mix of thematic and chronological approaches scatters his insights and does not illumine Mailer's development. Also, his exclusion of *Why Are We In Vietnam?* (1967), *The Armies of the Night,* and *Miami and the Siege of Chicago* seems unwarranted. Some of his chapters, however, are more than competently done. The one on *An American Dream,* for example, contains a careful examination of the relationship of manners to morality in the novel culminating in a convincing explanation of Rojack's walk around the parapet.

Leeds's study is well organized and comprehensive; he examines all of Mailer's work through *Miami and the Siege of Chicago.* His announced intention is to trace the development of a "very qualified hope" on social issues in Mailer's work, and he does this, while other matters go begging. He is sound and clear on Mailer's inability to create "a credible first person voice which would fit his prose style" in his first three novels, but is disappointing in his discussion of point of view in *The Armies of the Night,* which he does not relate well to Mailer's earlier books. Leeds is most convincing and penetrating in his chapter on *An American Dream,* by far the longest in his study and devoted largely to a discussion of sex in the novel. This chapter alone makes Leeds's book of continuing value; it is also useful for its discussions of Mailer's volume of poems, *Deaths for the Ladies (and other disasters)* (1962) and the dramatic version of *The Deer Park* (1967), two works rarely discussed by critics.

Although the most recent work treated by Richard Poirier in *Norman Mailer* (1972) is *The Prisoner of Sex* (1971), his book is considered by many to be the finest study of Mailer published to date. Poirier is not much interested in Mailer the social critic, or rather, his ideas about social issues. What absorbs him is Mailer the combative literary performer. Poirier apparently believes that the substantive positions Mailer takes are not absolutely serious but are functions of whatever "game he thinks he is playing." But Poirier is quite thoughtful in his analysis of Mailer's dialectics, as in his discussion of "the minority within" in Mailer's work, which he defines as the element in either or both sides of a dualism "which has been repressed or stifled by conformity to system." For example, a boxing match as described by Mailer is also a form of love-making, and love-making can be a battle, as in Mailer's celebrated short story, "The Time of Her Time" (*Advertisements for Myself*). He shows how crucial these somewhat reversible dualisms are to the overall effect of Mailer's work. Yet his first chapter opens with a disapproving discussion of Mailer's "verbal pugilism" which seems to be at odds with his later celebration of "the minority within." Poirier finds war to be not only Mailer's major topical interest from *The Naked and the Dead* through *The Prisoner of Sex* but also his primary metaphor for experience and art. Without disputing the fact that challenging the status quo is an important activity for Mailer, it still seems that discerning the *relations* among phenomena may be a more fundamental one. This view finds support in "the Metaphysics of the Belly," a self-interview which first appeared in *The Presidential Papers* and was reprinted in *Cannibals and Christians* (1966). Poirier mentions but does not discuss this piece although in it Mailer qualifies considerably the bellicosity Poirier objects to. Mailer says that war is one of a series of relationships which includes "the mood and its occasion, the good rider and his good horse, the blocking back and the line-backer." However much one might disagree with some of Poirier's interpretations, the fact that he has notched discussion of Mailer's work to a much higher level cannot be disputed. His reasoned appreciation of the critical importance of style to Mailer, and a dazzling ability to illumine it by reference to a score of modern writers make his relatively brief (192 pages with biographical note, index and short bibliography) but provocative study crucial for all students of Mailer.

One of the reasons for the relative brevity of Poirier's book is that he does not systematically comment on all major narrative threads, characters, or themes in Mailer's books. In *Down Mailer's Way* (1974), Robert Solotaroff comes close to accomplishing this, covering the same books as Poirier but in greater detail in 301 pages. Solotaroff provides a wealth of information on Mailer's sources to support his careful readings of Mailer's first five novels. He is both comprehensive and penetrating in his elucidation of Mailer's existentialism in relation to the continental philosophers and his reading of "The White Negro" (1957) is masterful. He is less compelling on the nonfiction, however. If there is a significant lack in his study it is that he does not pay enough attention to perspective and voice, especially in his discussion of *The Deer Park*, although his analysis of Eitel's "essentialist" view of human nature is most perceptive. Like Poirier he finds less merit in *An American Dream* than *Why Are We In Vietnam?* and argues that "Mailer's unwillingness to permit his struggling protagonists to be defeated by the societal forces around them gradually ebbs." Both of these interpretations are debatable, but Solotaroff makes a strong case for them. He admires *The Armies of the Night* more than any of the nonfiction narratives that follow it because "Mailer's fictional imagination was eventually more deeply and consistently moved" by the March on the Pentagon than by "anything it contemplated since the imagined events on Anopopei" in the third part of *The Naked and the Dead*. Like most critics and reviewers, he judges part one of *The Armies of the Night* to be superior to part two, not only because of the diminished presence of its semimythic protagonist in the concluding section but because of what Solotaroff calls Mailer's "false prophecy" regarding changes in American hearts caused by the Vietnam War. He is vague, however, about precisely what was false about Mailer's predictions. And after all, the March and similar peace efforts did hasten the end of the war. *The Armies of the Night* played a crucial role in the peace offensive, as Sandy Vogelgesang argues in *The Long Dark Night of the Soul: The American Intellectual Left and the Vietnam War*, which was also published in 1974. Solotaroff spends a good deal of time chiding Mailer for his visions and speculations on the nation's future in *The Armies of the Night* and does not analyze the book's unusual third-person perspective as rigorously as he might. His skepticism, however, is usually more salutary than not.

Despite his title, Stanley T. Gutman's 1975 study, *Mankind in Barbary: The Individual and Society in the Novels of Norman Mailer* does examine some of the nonfiction. Gutman devotes one chapter to "The White Negro" and another, his last, to *The Armies of the Night*. But Mailer's themes are Gutman's chief interest and he is most able, if sometimes redundant, in his summaries and analyses of growth, courage, sex, power, etc. He contends, rightfully, that "The White Negro" "contains and explores the core of Mailer's philosophy" and then goes on to argue in a convincing way that this philosophy is akin to the Hegelian-Marxist principle of definition by opposite. In Mailer's first three novels, he says, "a semi-Marxist, institutional and historical approach to man's conflict prevailed." But after "The White Negro" Mailer became more and more interested in "man's psychic life, his subconscious and unconscious desires and frustrations," or the world of Freud. In his later chapters on *Dream* and *Vietnam*, Gutman demonstrates how Mailer attempts and to some extent succeeds in resolving this Marx-Freud, or political-psychological conflict. Gutman's book is an excellent introduction to the major themes of Mailer's novels, but it has little to say about his narrative strategies and how they are related to his schemes. He also makes scant comment on the early nonfiction, with the exception of his chapter on "The White Negro," and passing comment only on the nonfiction narratives after *The Armies of the Night*.

Also published in 1975 was *Norman Mailer: A Critical Study* by Jean Radford, a British critic. Unlike Gutman she surveys all of Mailer's work through *The Faith of Graffiti* (1974), although her comments mainly parallel those of earlier critics, especially Poirier, whose argument that Mailer is preoccupied by war is echoed by her. Radford says that Mailer is "a talented and interesting minor writer" and concludes her study by claiming that Mailer is in danger of "becoming, like his own literary hero, Hemingway, parasitic on his earlier achievements." While her criticism cannot be rejected out of hand when considering Mailer's books of the late sixties and early seventies, it has little merit in assessing the remainder of his career. Radford's derivative study is also flawed by her belief that aesthetic questions are of little interest to Mailer.

In the introductory chapter of *Existential Battles: the Growth of Norman Mailer* (1976), Laura Adams says that she has tried to write "an adventurous criticism, one which broke new ground." Her discussions of Mailer's thematic concerns, however, follow the same general lines as her predecessors, Solotaroff, in particular. Where she differs from most earlier critics is in her thoughtful examination of the development of a confident narrative voice in Mailer's work and in the addition of descriptions of Mailer's extraliterary activities. Her fourth and final chapter, "In the Center of History," contains accounts of all three of Mailer's movies, his December 1971 fight with Gore Vidal on the Dick Cavett show, his campaign for mayor of New York, his fiftieth birthday party at which he announced the establishment of The Fifth Estate (a sort of people's investigative agency), and other such affairs. She justifies the inclusion of these accounts by noting that as "an American spokesman-hero Mailer is obliged to confront those events which have the capability of influencing our national destiny." Adams's first three chapters deal with the phases of his career as she sees them: the first, culminating in *Advertisements for Myself;* the second, with *An American Dream;* and the third with *The Armies of the Night.* Adams's first (and best) chapter provides a reliable discussion of Mailer's difficulties with his early narrators, leading up to a clear but lengthy explanation of how and why Mailer painted himself into a corner and "could neither write about himself nor not write about himself." Her subsequent chapters are not quite as strong and her discussion of *An American Dream* is weakened by her belief that Mailer did not intend this novel to be realistic. Overall, Adams's sympathetic study of Mailer is a good introduction to Mailer's work through the mid-1970s. As might be expected of the leading Mailer bibliographer, her documentation is excellent.

The other study on Mailer published in 1976, *Mailer and the Times of his Time* by Jonathan Middlebrook, is a rambling essay comparing Mailer with dozens of writers—Milton, William Langland, Keats, Donne, and so on. Quotations from their work and from Mailer's are set off in large type, some in boldface, some in italic. The bizarre typography, lack of an index, and all other documentation make the book difficult to read. The best thing about Middlebrook's book is his opening chapter, a comic account of his first meeting with Mailer, which is memorable for its description of Mailer's charm and the author's understandable anxiety.

Much more thoughtful is the study of Mailer in the Twayne series, Robert Merrill's *Norman Mailer* (1978). His book is clear evidence of the shift in critical opinion on Mailer after the success of *The Armies of the Night* and *Miami and the Siege of Chicago.* He argues that, excepting *The Naked and the Dead* and *The Deer Park,* Mailer's greatest achievements up to 1978 are his works of nonfiction, *The Armies of the Night* in particular. Merrill, unlike many earlier critics, tends to evaluate Mailer's works according to the formal consistency of their structures. Thus, he criticizes the miscellanies for including too great a variety of material and faults *An American Dream* and *Why Are We In Vietnam?* because "they incorporate several fictional strategies without achieving the unity of any single strategy." Merrill argues this point forcefully, but he is even more effective in his discussion of *The Naked and the Dead,* which he examines from three perspectives: as documentary, as social critique, and as dramatic action. He concludes this impressive chapter with the following comment: "it is possible to see all of his subsequent work as an attempt to qualify or even disavow the bleak implications of his first novel." Merrill's chapter on

The Armies of the Night stands in contrast to Solotaroff's on the question of the successes of part two, which he praises. He devotes a number of pages in this chapter to a comparison of *The Armies of the Night* and Capote's 1966 nonfiction novel, *In Cold Blood,* an exercise which is flawed by his assumption that "Capote cannot alter the events or details of his story in order to develop characters or theme." Phillip K. Tomkins's article "In Cold Fact" (*Esquire,* June, 1966) presents strong evidence that Capote altered both, whether consciously or unconsciously. Merrill's study, along with Poirier's, Solotaroff's and Philip H. Bufithis's *Norman Mailer* (1978) comprise the quality quartet of Mailer books in the seventies.

At 174 pages, Bufithis's is the briefest of the four. He devotes a chapter to each of the novels through *Why Are We In Vietnam?*, another to *Advertisements for Myself,* three to the nonfiction from *The Armies of the Night* through *Genius and Lust* (1976), and bookend chapters of introduction (including a brief biography) and conclusion. It is a remarkable performance, although a twelfth chapter on the other miscellanies would have been welcome. Bufithis does not waste words. For example, in his chapter on *Barbary Shore* (1951) he says that its "final effect on the reader is of life argued rather than life lived." His gemlike chapters are linked by his clearly articulated understanding of the slow development of Mailer's narrative voice, and the crucial tension, in Mailer's eyes, between free will and the conditioning forces of technology in modern life. Bufithis agrees with those critics (Poirier and Adams, for example) who believe that the author of *An American Dream* is "a self-delighting fabulist playing with the possibility of language, not a brooding realist" and says that the novel's style and plot "rank it among the finest of contemporary American novels." Yet he seems to rank *Why Are We In Vietnam?* higher because of what he calls *An American Dream*'s "refusal to deal with the ethical nature of man's relation to man." One would have liked to have more from Bufithis on this matter; it is one of the few places where his terseness might be a disadvantage. His analysis of *Armies of the Night* and the nonfiction that followed it is quite sound, and his penultimate chapter on *The Fight* (1975) and *Genius and Lust* is the most thoughtful examination of these books. In sum, Bufithis' slim volume is perhaps the most reliable and clearly written study of Mailer published to date.

Robert Ehrlich's *Norman Mailer: The Radical as Hipster* also appeared in 1978. While the importance of "The White Negro" to an understanding of Mailer's work, even his earlier work, is agreed to by all Mailer critics, Ehrlich is misleading on some of Mailer's work, especially the later nonfiction, in his emphasis on its philosophic derivation from the essay. His book is a serious effort, however, and provides a useful contrast to the views of those who feel Mailer's philosophic utterances are merely playful put-ons in the age of pop culture. Although it was published in 1978, Ehrlich's book was apparently written much earlier. *Marilyn* and *The Faith of Graffiti* are only briefly discussed and *The Fight* and *Genius and Lust* are not mentioned at all.

Neither of the two books on Mailer that appeared in 1979 add anything to an understanding of his work. *Norman Mailer: Quick-Change Artist*, by Jennifer Bailey, is much more mature than Sandy Cohen's *Norman Mailer's Novels*, but it has no real thesis and is only of value for its recapitulation of the positions of earlier critics such as Diana Trilling, John W. Aldridge, and Richard Poirier.

The most recent book-length studies of Mailer are both psychological in orientation—one Freudian, one Jungian. The announced intention of Andrew Gordon's *An American Dreamer: A Psychoanalytic Study of the Fiction of Norman Mailer* (1980) is to "interpret Mailer's fiction in much the same way as Freud analyzed the content of dreams in *The Interpretation of Dreams*." Gordon tries strenuously "not to put Mailer on the couch and attempt therapy thirdhand," but inevitably he does. His working assumption is that the various obsessions and ambivalences of Mailer's characters are ultimately referable to Mailer himself. Nevertheless, his psychoanalytic apparatus does produce new insights on the novels (the most recent book he discusses is *The Armies of the Night*, even though his study appeared twelve years after it was published). He is at his best in his discussion of *Why Are We In Vietnam?* and the alternate wooing and attacking by D. J. of "the reader-as-feces." Even those who are hostile to Freudian analysis will find some merit in Gordon's study, although his attribution of Mailer's stylistic and formal experimentation to "anal ambivalence" will not necessarily be applauded. Perhaps the best thing about his study is its cataloging of the imagery patterns in the novels, an effort which might aid future examinations of *Ancient Evenings*.

Robert J. Begiebing approaches his subject from a Jungian perspective in *Acts of Regeneration: Allegory and Archetype in the Works of Norman Mailer* (1980). His thesis is that Mailer's goal is to awaken "heroic consciousness" in his readers through the conscious or unconscious use of archetypes which depict "the struggle of Life against Death in the contemporary world." Begiebing is not the first, of course, to point to the importance of this struggle for Mailer. As noted earlier, Richard Foster called it "Mailer's subject everywhere," and numerous critics before and after have said much the same. But it bears repeating and Begiebing does so in a crisp, informed manner, only occasionally leaning too heavily on Jung. The only portion of the book that I find unclear is his introduction where he is at pains to rescue allegory from the attacks of the Romantics and to rehabilitate it by dividing it into "rational" (bad) and "true" (good) categories. The latter seems to be what is usually called symbolism. Archetypes get mixed in as well. Indeed, Begiebing's method of interpretation is not that different from Charles Feidelson Jr.'s in *Symbolism and American Literature* (1953). But his earnest defense of allegory warms him to his task: a close reading of most of the major works from *Barbary Shore* to *The Executioner's Song* (*The Naked and the Dead*, in his view, is a realistic-naturalistic novel and so is omitted from consideration). After the introductory chapter, he devotes one chapter to each of the novels from *Barbary Shore* to *Why Are We in Vietnam?*; chapter six, one of his best, discusses Mailer's heroes and heroic consciousness; seven is given over to *Armies of the Night;* and his final chapter examines *Of a Fire on the Moon, The Fight* and *The Executioner's Song.*The miscellanies, *Marilyn* (strange omission) and *Genius and Lust* are discussed only in passing. Because he lays down the terms of the archetypal structure he finds in all of Mailer's work in his chapter on *Barbary Shore,* which he sees as an "artistically consistent and compact" dream vision of rebirth, it may be his most stimulating. But his chapter on *An American Dream,* which he calls "a journey into the unconscious" and "Mailer's boldest use of the allegorical mode," will certainly be his most controversial, especially to those who still believe the novel to be fundamentally realistic.

Critical Studies: Articles and Book Sections

[Note: I have passed over without comment the collections of critical essays on Mailer on the checklist; many of the essays and long reviews in these collections are discussed below, however. I would also call attention to the introductions to the collections of Adams, Braudy, Lennon, and Lucid for their overviews of critical and popular responses to Mailer.]

Although Mailer began publishing in 1941 when his short story, "The Greatest Thing in the World," won *Story* magazine's college contest, nothing of real critical interest on his work appeared in the 1940s, and little in the 1950s beyond reviews. The torrent began in the 1960s and continues unabated. The checklist contains eighty-odd items, essays and book chapters on Mailer, and annotation is limited to about half of these.

The first important comment on Mailer came from John W. Aldridge, still one of Mailer's most important critics. In his pioneering study, *After the Lost Generation: A Critical Study of the Writers of Two Wars* (1951), Aldridge lauds Mailer's "magnificent reportorial sense" and his "potent condemnation of the fascistic military system" in *The Naked and the Dead,* but finds the novel to be seriously flawed. Mailer's original intention, Aldridge believes, was to write a protest novel, but he was true to the real nature of his characters and they are variously defeated, deceived, ridiculed or "ride to victory on an accident." Thus, without a "vestige of hope on which to base protest," *The Naked and the Dead* "descends through a series of reductions to an absolute zero." Norman Podhoretz, in one of the most influential articles on Mailer, "Norman Mailer: The Embattled Vision" included in his 1964 collection *Doings and Undoings,* also praises Mailer's "phenomenal talent for recording the precise look and feel of things" in *The Naked and the Dead,* and also focuses on Mailer's characters, but differs markedly with Aldridge in his contention that Mailer secretly admired the formal villains of *The Naked and the Dead,* Cummings and Croft, and suggests that Mailer's attempted and failed redemption of Hearn "lacks conviction." He looks closely at Mailer's shifting ideologies and was one of the first critics to clearly identify the emergence of his idiosyncratic existentialism.

Gore Vidal's long review of *Advertisements for Myself,* "Norman Mailer's Self-Advertisements" (written in 1960 and included in his 1972 volume of collected essays), is one of the first pieces to discuss Mailer seriously as a literary celebrity. Vidal also discusses *The Naked and the Dead* and *Barbary Shore,* and *Advertisements for Myself,* but most of his remarks are given to the opportunities and dangers of literary self-advancement. His grudging affection for Mailer can be seen in his statement that "Mailer is a Bolingbroke, a born usurper. He will rouse an army anywhere, live off the country as best he can . . . even assisted at brief moments by rival claimants like myself." Vidal's frank ambivalence regarding Mailer is instructive. Ihab Hassan also stresses Mailer's "stance . . . of opposition" in his chapter on *The Naked and the Dead* in *Radical Innocence* (1961). He sees Mailer's depiction of World War II in the novel as "a mirror of vaster social and historical issues" and analyzes the major characters along ideological lines. Departing from most earlier and later critics, Hassan finds Hearn to be the novel's central dramatic and thematic character, the one character who interacts in more than a routine way with both Sergeant Croft and General Cummings. He argues that Hearn's refusal to buy into Cummings's quasi-fascistic "fear ladder" makes him one of the few figures of true dissidence in the novel and concludes that Hearn and perhaps Goldstein are the scapegoats who give *The Naked and the Dead* its ironic form.

The sympathetic portrayal of leftists in *Barbary Shore* and *The Deer Park* did not endear Mailer to certain establishment critics, but the hip existentialism of "The White Negro" resulted in a much stronger reaction. Mailer published two of the rebuttals to his essay (and the essay itself) in *Advertisements for Myself*, but the sharpest response came from George Alfred Schrader in "Norman Mailer and the Despair of Defiance" (1961). Schrader argues that hipsterism is not existentialism at all, but a violent, primitivistic variant of romanticism which finds man's salvation not in nature or serene reflection, but in "the uncorrupted (which means socially untrammeled) vitality of man's libidinal urges." He finds Mailer to be spoiled and "phoney" for not facing "up to the fact that the world is inevitably and hopelessly square." His essay overstates Mailer's position—for example, he says Mailer believes individuals must "blindly" surrender to the forces of the unconscious—but is still of interest for its rigorous disapproval, a fairly typical reaction to Mailer in the early sixties. George Steiner's 1961 review of *Advertisements for Myself* is the obverse of Schrader's essay. "Mailer," he says, "is among the honest men," a figure who approaches the horror of World War II and the dread of nuclear apocalypse with "four principal values. He is by origin a Jew, and by vocation a Socialist, Hipster and Writer." Steiner delineates Mailer's quadruple identity in his penetrating review and, despite strong reservations about "the screeds of polemic and confession" in *Advertisements for Myself*, finds that several pieces in the collection—"The White Negro" and "The Time of Her Time," most notably—give evidence that "Mailer is not through yet, that he will stop being a case and start being a writer again."

The best developed and most intelligent examination of Mailer's work through *Advertisements for Myself* came from Diana Trilling, whose 1962 essay, "The Radical Moralism of Norman Mailer," has been reprinted several times and referred to more often than any other criticism of Mailer with the possible exception of the Podhoretz essay. Her admiration of Mailer's "high political consciousness," "moral affirmation," and the "charismatic charge" of his personality creates a picture of him which accentuates his "messianic impulse." The Blakean, Lawrentian version of Mailer has been reprised by countless critics and reviewers since then; Trilling's negative comments—that he lacks self-discipline, that his God is a fascist, that he is detached from cultural tradition—have also been often repeated. The strength of her essay lies in her sensitive mediation between the extremes of Mailer's sensibility. Installing Mailer at "the forefront of modern writers," she calls his work one of "the braver efforts of culture." Her essay is still indispensable, although many of her conclusions are inapplicable to the Mailer who emerged with *The Armies of the Night.*

Aldridge has written often and well about Mailer. His 1965 review of *An American Dream,* later expanded into an essay, "Norman Mailer: The Energy of New Success" (1966), is his most impassioned piece on Mailer, and perhaps his best. He gives a brisk and trenchant recapitulation of Mailer's career, with special emphasis on how the reading public has seen Mailer and vice versa. Aldridge is not overtly solicitous of Mailer's bruised sensibilities and discusses, for instance, the nonfiction after *The Deer Park* as an effort "to salvage what was left of his career by peddling his megalomania to *Esquire.*" But his fundamental thrust is celebratory and he recommends *An American Dream* as a descendant of the romances of Cooper, Melville and Hawthorne in which "fantasy and fact, witchcraft and melodrama, myth, allegory, and realism" are combined in order to examine "the various ways a man may sin in order to be saved." With *An American Dream* Aldridge concludes, Mailer became the most "remarkable writer of these undistinguished years." Mailer's status in the literary world is further attested to in the 1967 autobiography *Making It* by his then-friend Norman Podhoretz. (The review by Mailer is collected in *Existential Errands,* 1972.) Podhoretz concludes by admitting that he has chosen Mailer for his model in his attempt to ascend the greasy pole of literary fame because "Mailer is the only man in America . . . capable of perfect honesty on the subject of success." In his 1979 book, *Breaking Ranks: A Political Memoir,* Podhoretz describes his later falling-out with Mailer.

Alfred Kazin has been writing about Mailer for over twenty-five years. His most considered estimate is found in his 1973 study, *Bright Book of Life: American Novelists and Storytellers from Hemingway to Mailer,* which is somewhat less enthusiastic or more judicious, as you prefer, than his 1968 review of *The Armies of the Night,* which captures Mailer perfectly at one of the great turning points of his career. Kazin not only recognizes the new form ("diary-essay-tract-sermon") forged by Mailer out of his keen apprehension of the national crisis over Vietnam, he also has his own sharp sense of that crisis and how it parallels the cataclysm of a century before when Mailer's literary ancestors, Whitman and Melville, felt their literary energies revitalized by the Civil War. A New York Jew with mixed feelings about the Old Left like Mailer, Kazin has a confident sense of Mailer's roots ("a nice Jewish boy from Harvard"), achievements (*The Naked and the Dead* in particular, which he finds "as intensely readable as it was in 1948"), liabilities ("his vexing dualities") and strengths ("his particular gift for detecting political deterioration"), and how they coalesced in *The Armies of the Night*. Those interested in Mailer's politics should also consult "The Real and Imaginary World of Norman Mailer" (1969) by Robert Alter, who shares Kazin's high opinion of *The Armies of the Night* and his lower opinion of *An American Dream*. Alter examines most of Mailer's books through *The Armies of the Night* for their political views and is especially good on "the gyrating pyrotechnics of D. J.'s self-delighting rhetoric." Jack Richardson is similarly impressed with D. J.'s "superbly monstrous . . . vernacular fustian," but the major aim of his 1969 essay, "The Aesthetics of Norman Mailer," is to make the case that Mailer is not primarily a polemicist or an ideologue but a "belletrist," specifically "a literary modernist, juggling forms and experimenting with narrative voice." Richardson's essay reinforces and elaborates on the significance of style for Mailer noted earlier in Foster's monograph (see previous section), and foreshadows in its emphasis Robert Langbaum's "Mailer's New Style" (1970), another admiring piece, and the largely disparaging but well-developed essay by Richard Gilman, "Norman Mailer: Art as Life, Life as Art" (1969).

Not so much dissenting from as sidestepping this new belletristic direction in Mailer criticism, Max F. Schulz places all the works through *Cannibals and Christians* (1966) in a Dantesque framework in "Mailer's Divine Comedy," a chapter in *Radical Sophistication: Studies in Contemporary Jewish-American Novelists* (1969). After endorsing the conventional but sound view of how Mailer moved from "agitation for political solution" to society's ills to "the call for an erotic, quasi-religious redefinition of the modern consciousness," Schulz, with only modest procrusteanism, tries to demonstrate that *Barbary Shore, The Deer Park,* and *An American Dream* represent purgatory, hell, and heaven, respectively. His parallels are suggestive but problematic, especially his equating of *An American Dream* with heaven. William Hoffa's overview of Mailer's writing in the 1950s, "Norman Mailer:

Advertisements for Myself, or a Portrait of the Artist as a Disgruntled Counter-Puncher" (1970), provides a useful contrast to the essay of Schulz. The "subjectivism" of *Advertisements,* he says, places it in the tradition of Jonathan Edwards, Emerson, and Whitman, while Mailer's novels of the 1950s derive from the Realistic movement "with its emphasis on the faithful reproduction of physical, social and psychological realities."

Mailer's reemergence as a major literary figure in the middle and late 1960s generated an outpouring of critical studies in the early 1970s. The critical collections of Lucid, Adams, and Braudy were published during this period as were the book-length studies of Leeds, Kaufmann, Poirier, and Solotaroff, not to mention special issues of *Modern Fiction Studies* and the *New Orleans Review.* A number of important and original articles also appeared in the early 1970s, many of them attempts to come to grips with Mailer's shift to nonfiction and his status as a sort of defrocked cultural prophet, a secular Jeremiah. Warner Berthoff's English Institute paper, "Witness and Testament: Two Contemporary Classics" (1971), is one of the most extravagant of these in its praise, calling *The Armies of the Night* and *The Autobiography of Malcolm X* works of "visionary force . . . transforming authority." Berthoff locates *The Armies of the Night* in the tradition of "secular autobiographies" which includes Thoreau's *Walden,* Franklin's *Autobiography,* and Twain's *Roughing It,* and lauds it for its "saving counterforce of personality." Gore Vidal's essay "Women's Liberation Meets Miller-Mailer-Manson Man" (1972) also recognizes Mailer's tendency toward cultural prophecy but, unfortunately and unfairly, lumps Mailer and Henry Miller with the murderer Charles Manson, an act which precipitated Mailer's famous feud with Vidal.

Word for word, nothing ever written on *An American Dream,* is so consistently intelligent and *right* as Tony Tanner's "On the Parapet," a chapter in his 1971 study, *City of Words: American Fiction, 1950-1970.* Far from being restricted by his binary approach to reality, Tanner says that by combining "the documentary and the demonic modes" in *An American Dream,* Mailer is really presenting two opposed methods of coping with "the mystery of America." Barney Kelly's Waldorf Towers penthouse and Shago Martin's Harlem are only two of the dozens of linked opposites around and through which Rojack moves during his thirty–two–hour odyssey, "capitulating neither to . . . the traps of social architecture" nor "the chaotic dissolutions of the pre-social or sub-social dark," and never more boldly than when he walks the parapet around Kelly's terrace. Tanner's chapter, which also examines Mailer's earlier novels and "The White Negro," should be read by everyone interested in Mailer's fiction. Martin Green's examination of Mailer as the embodiment of New York City in the 1960s can be profitably read as a companion to Tanner's work. Entitled "Norman Mailer and the City of New York: Faustian Radicalism," Green's essay is a chapter in his 1972 book, *Cities of Light and Sons of Morning: A Cultural Psychology for an Age of Revolution*. Although his prose may seem a bit breathless in the 1980s, Green's extended comparisons of Mailer with urban figures as diverse as Goethe, Byron, and Kingsley Amis provide a stimulating cross-cultural perspective. Another essay from this period which examines Mailer as a cultural spokesman is Fredric Jameson's "The Great American Hunter, or Ideological Content in the Novel" (1972). His essay is a brief against the notion that Marxist literature is reductive, and along the way he makes some challenging criticisms of Mailer's artistic dependency upon the very diseases and poisons of the technological society that he condemns.

Useful to those interested in Mailer's historical sense is John Henry Raleigh's "History and Its Burdens: The Example of Norman Mailer" (1973). More sympathetic than Jameson, Raleigh is nevertheless dispassionate in his survey of Mailer's indebtedness to his American literary forebears and his remarks on "the rhythm of his historical outlook" (rather than the specific content of Mailer's historical knowledge). His comments on how Mailer uses the small town are particularly informative. Robert F. Lucid also considers Mailer in the company of his literary forebears, specifically Hemingway and Fitzgerald, in two 1974 essays, "Norman Mailer: The Artist as Fantasy Figure" and "Three Public Performances: Fitzgerald, Hemingway, Mailer." In these tandem essays Lucid argues that the public imagination of Americans conjures several types of heroes in a manner "comparable to the process by which an individual creates his own dreams." The artist-figure is one of those hero types and Mailer, he says, one of the most unusual of these in that he did not cooperate in this dream-making until his career was well underway. Finally, in *Advertisements for Myself*, his fourth book, Mailer compares his artistic situation with that of the sensitive individual at large in the culture, offering, even demanding "absolute vicarious identification." Lucid goes on to show how Mailer's perch in the public imagination is like and unlike those of Hemingway and Fitzgerald and also how much more precarious it is. Lucid's meditation on Mailer not only offers an interpretation of how Mailer has avoided oblivion but also a warning that some ghoulish portion of our public imagination may "send our artist hero forth" not to overwhelm the destructive elements, "but to serve as a sacrifice to appease" them. Gordon O. Taylor's 1974 article, "Of Adams and Aquarius," is another exercise in literary genetics, one of the most thoughtful. His examination of the similar "predicaments of understanding and expression" faced by the two authors should be considered in light of Mailer's comments on Adams in his *Pieces and Pontifications* interview with Barbara Probst Solomon.

The first major appraisal of Mailer as a New Journalist, John Hollowell's "Mailer's Vision: History as a Novel, The Novel as History," a chapter in his *Fact & Fiction: The New Journalism and the Nonfiction Novel*, appeared in 1977. Hollowell offers no new insights into Mailer's nonfiction, but his survey is reliable and his study contains an excellent bibliography of the New Journalism. Much more valuable is John Hellman's chapter on Mailer in *Fables of Fact: The New Journalism as New Fiction* (1980). Hellman's thesis is that the works of Mailer and the other New Journalists are neither "dramatized documentaries" nor "absurdist transcriptions of facts" but functional griffins, "fables of fact." He defends this idea vigorously in close readings of *The Armies of the Night, Of a Fire on the Moon,* and *The Executioner's Song.*

Two attacks on Mailer's work, one serious and qualified, the other viciously angry and unreliable were published in 1978. Judith Fetterley's sensitive feminist interpretation of *An American Dream* ranks with the best criticisms of that novel. Her goal is to "exorcise" Mailer by exposing "the twin myths of male powerlessness and female power" which, she argues, undergird the novel and permit power to masquerade as weakness. The other piece is a chapter in Mitchell S. Ross's *The Literary Politicians.* Throughout the entire forty–five–page diatribe, relieved only rarely by tepid praise ("of course Mailer is capable of occasional insights"), Ross is either raging about Mailer's wretchedness or complaining of the tedium of his critical task. He concludes with this thought: "He is a dreadful writer, and deserves oblivion." Ross is a dreadful critic, but as the Babe Ruth of Mailer revilers (a title he would happily accept) his chapter should be read. It contains perhaps the best collection of Mailer's worst passages. As an antidote to Ross, one might consult Joan Didion's 1979 review of *The Executioner's Song* in which she notes that Mailer is "a great and obsessed stylist, a writer to whom the shape of the sentence is a story." Didion's review marks the start of still another Mailer revival; it is also a first-rate appreciation of Mailer's narrative achievement in this "true-life novel." Didion is the first to note what even Mailer apparently failed to notice: that " 'Western Voices,' Book One, are most strongly voices of women, and 'Eastern Voices,' Book Two, voices which are not literally those of Easterners but are largely those of men." *The Executioner's Song*, she concludes, "is an absolutely astonishing book."

Two traditionally executed articles on Mailer appeared in the early 1980s. Hershel Parker's "Norman Mailer's Revision of the *Esquire* Version of *An American Dream* and the Aesthetic Problem of 'Built-in Intentionality' " was published in 1981, and Bernard Horn's "Ahab and Ishmael at War: The Presence of *Moby-Dick* in *The Naked and the Dead*" appeared in 1982. Parker's laborious comparison of the original magazine and the book version of *An American Dream* will be useful to students interested in the problems of literary revision as well as Mailerians, and Horn's tightly written articles, apparently stimulated by Mailer's statement in the 1951 Harvey Breit interview (collected in Breit's *The Writer Observed*, 1956) that "the biggest influence on *The Naked and the Dead* was *Moby-Dick*," will be of considerable use to those interested in Mailer's debt to the American Romantics. J. Michael Lennon's 1982 article, "Mailer's Cosmology" also compares and contrasts Mailer and Melville and delineates the former's "ditheistic cosmology" which, he argues, encompasses "the obliquely opposed principles of human freedom and progress, divine providence and limitation, and cosmic evil."

Little beyond reviews has been published to date about Mailer's controversial novel, *Ancient Evenings*, which was over a decade in the making. Authors of what are probably the two finest books on Mailer, Philip H. Bufithis and Richard Poirier, have written two of the best review-essays on the novel. Both reviews resonate with their authors' detailed knowledge of Mailer's *oeuvre* and both argue that the early reviewers of *Ancient Evenings* made mistakes in judging it. For Poirier, the crucial error is to assume that Mailer effaced himself from it; for Bufithis what has been overlooked is that *Ancient Evenings* is fundamentally a novel about magic.

The final two items on Mailer are markedly different although both are favorable. Richard Schickel, whose 1971 essay on Mailer's moviemaking is still of considerable value, is the author of *Intimate Strangers: The Culture of Celebrity* (1985). In his introduction he acknowledges his indebtedness to "Norman Mailer, whose analyses of the celebrity factor in almost every walk of American public life form the beginnings (and sometimes the end) of everyone's understanding of the subject." Schickel demonstrates this by using Mailer's insights on Marlon Brando, Marilyn Monroe, Hemingway, and John F. Kennedy in the following chapters. Strangely, he never considers Mailer's own celebrity, surely a legitimate inclusion.

Michael Cowan's "The Quest for Empowering Roots: Mailer and the American Literary Tradition" (1986) is a revised and greatly expanded version of his 1972 essay, "The Americanness of Norman Mailer," written for Braudy's critical collection. Mailer, Cowan says, "has been curiously reluctant to acknowledge explicitly his bonds with most nineteenth-century American literature," yet "the buried voices of this indigenous art speak constantly in his own work." Cowan's essay is a brilliantly successful effort to locate these voices. Melville's can be heard most often, as many other commentators have noted. Cowan is the most exhaustive recorder of the Melvillean influence, however, and the only one to note the similarity of Billy Budd and Gary Gilmore. The themes, rhetoric and transcendentalist perception of Emerson, Hawthorne, even Poe, as reflected and maintained in Mailer are examined, and Cowan demonstrates the common "search for a metaphysical structure that will at least bring the illusion of order to the multiplying force fields of modern experience" ·in the nonfiction of Mailer and Henry Adams. To sum up, his article is the most thoroughly documented and persuasive effort to place Mailer in the tradition of American romanticism, the "symbolic essence" of which he defines as "a dream of revolutionary adventure on behalf of an apocalyptic quest for identity, both personal and collective."

Bernard Malamud

(1914-   )

Robert D. Habich

Ball State University

PRIMARY BIBLIOGRAPHY

Books

The Natural. New York: Harcourt, Brace, 1952; London: Eyre & Spottiswoode, 1953. Novel.

The Assistant. New York: Farrar, Straus & Cudahy, 1957; London: Eyre & Spottiswoode, 1959. Novel.

The Magic Barrel. New York: Farrar, Straus & Cudahy, 1958; London: Eyre & Spottiswoode, 1960. Short stories.

A New Life. New York: Farrar, Straus & Cudahy, 1961; London: Eyre & Spottiswoode, 1962. Novel.

Idiots First. New York: Farrar, Straus, 1963; London: Eyre & Spottiswoode, 1964. Short stories.

The Fixer. New York: Farrar, Straus & Giroux, 1966; London: Eyre & Spottiswoode, 1967. Novel.

Pictures of Fidelman: An Exhibition. New York: Farrar, Straus & Giroux/ London: Eyre & Spottiswoode, 1969. Novel.

The Tenants. New York: Farrar, Straus & Giroux, 1971; London: Eyre Methuen, 1972. Novel.

Rembrandt's Hat. New York: Farrar, Straus & Giroux/London: Eyre Methuen, 1973. Short stories.

Dubin's Lives. New York: Farrar, Straus & Giroux/London: Chatto & Windus, 1979. Novel.

God's Grace. New York: Farrar, Straus & Giroux, 1982. Novel.

The Stories of Bernard Malamud. New York: Farrar, Straus & Giroux, 1983.

Uncollected Short Stories

"Benefit Performance," *Threshold*, 3 (Feb. 1943), 20-22.
"The Place Is Different Now," *American Preface*, 8 (Spring 1943), 230-242.
"Steady Customer," *New Threshold*, 1 (May 1943), 13-15, 33.
"An Apology," *Commentary*, 12 (Nov. 1951), 460-464.
"An Exorcism," *Harper's*, 237 (Dec. 1968), 76-89.
"The Model," *Atlantic*, 252 (Aug. 1983), 80-81.
"Alma Redeemed," *Commentary*, 78 (July 1984), 30-34.

Other

"The Writer's Task." In *Writing in America*, ed. John Fisher and Robert B. Silvers. New Brunswick, N.J.: Rutgers University Press, 1960, 173.
"Speaking of Books: Theme, Content, and the 'New Novel,' " *New York Times Book Review*, 26 Mar. 1967, pp. 2, 29.
"Banned Authors Answer Back," *New York Times*, 28 Mar. 1976, XXI: 16 [with Kurt Vonnegut, Jr.].
"Novelist Malamud: 'Living is Guessing What Reality Is,' " *U. S. News and World Report*, 8 Oct. 1979, p. 57.

Collection

A Malamud Reader, ed. Philip Rahv. New York: Farrar, Straus & Giroux, 1967.

SECONDARY BIBLIOGRAPHY

Bibliographies and Checklists

Grau, Joseph A. "Bernard Malamud: A Bibliographical Addendum," *Bulletin of Bibliography*, 37 (Oct.-Dec. 1980), 157-166, 184. Primary and secondary.
_____. "Bernard Malamud: A Further Bibliographical Addendum," *Bulletin of Bibliography*, 38 (Apr.-June 1981), 101-104. Primary and secondary.
Habich, Robert D. "Bernard Malamud: A Bibliographic Survey," *Studies in American Jewish Literature*, 4 (Spring 1978), 78-84.
Kosofsky, Rita N. *Bernard Malamud: An Annotated Checklist*. Kent, Ohio:

Kent State University Press, 1969. Primary and secondary.
Risty, Donald. "A Comprehensive Checklist of Malamud Criticism."
In *The Fiction of Bernard Malamud*, ed. Richard Astro and Jackson
J. Benson. Corvallis: Oregon State University Press, 1977, 163-
190. Secondary. See Collections of Essays.
Sher, Morris. *Bernard Malamud: A Partially Annotated Bibliography Compiled by Morris Sher.* Johannesburg: University of Witwatersrand
Department of Bibliography, Librarianship and Typography,
1970. Primary and secondary.

Interviews

Cadle, Dean. "Bernard Malamud," *Wilson Library Bulletin*, 33 (Dec.
1958), 266.
Field, Leslie, and Joyce Field. "An Interview with Bernard Malamud."
In *Bernard Malamud: A Collection of Critical Essays*, ed. Field and
Field. Englewood Cliffs, N.J.: Prentice-Hall, 1975, 8-17. See Collections of Essays.
Frankel, Haskel. [Interview with Bernard Malamud.] *Saturday Review*,
49 (10 Sept. 1966), 39-40.
Gilroy, Harry. "Malamud Asserts Novel Should Stress a Theme," *New
York Times*, 9 Mar. 1967, p. 42.
Hicks, Granville. "His Hopes on the Human Heart," *Saturday Review*,
46 (12 Oct. 1963), 31-32.
Malamud, Bernard. "Authors' Authors," *New York Times Book Review*,
5 Dec. 1976, p. 4.
Shenker, Israel. "For Malamud It's Story," *New York Times Book Review*,
3 Oct. 1971, pp. 20, 22.
Stern, Daniel. "The Art of Fiction LII: Bernard Malamud," *Paris
Review*, 16 (Spring 1975), 40-64.
Tyler, Ralph. "A Talk with the Novelist," *New York Times Book Review*,
18 Feb. 1979, pp. 1, 31-34.

Critical Studies: Books

Alter, Iska. *The Good Man's Dilemma: Social Criticism in the Fiction of
Bernard Malamud.* New York: AMS, 1981.
Avery, Evelyn G. *Rebels and Victims: The Fiction of Richard Wright and
Bernard Malamud.* Port Washington, N.Y. & London: Kennikat
Press, 1979.

Cohen, Sandy. *Bernard Malamud and the Trial by Love*. Amsterdam:
  Rodopi, N.V., 1974.
Ducharme, Robert. *Art and Idea in the Novels of Bernard Malamud:
  Toward "The Fixer."* The Hague: Mouton, 1974.
Hergt, Tobias. *Das Motiv der Hochschule im Romanwerk von Bernard
  Malamud und John Barth*. Frankfurt: Lang, 1979.
Hershinow, Sheldon J. *Bernard Malamud*. New York: Ungar, 1980.
Meeter, Glen. *Bernard Malamud and Philip Roth: A Critical Essay*. Grand
  Rapids, Mich.: Eerdmans, 1968.
Richman, Sidney. *Bernard Malamud*. New York: Twayne, 1966.

Critical Studies: Collections of Essays

Bernard Malamud: A Collection of Critical Essays, ed. Leslie A. Field and
  Joyce W. Field. Englewood Cliffs, N.J.: Prentice-Hall, 1975.
Bernard Malamud and the Critics, ed. Leslie A. Field and Joyce W. Field.
  New York: New York University Press, 1970.
The Fiction of Bernard Malamud, ed. Richard Astro and Jackson J.
  Benson. Corvallis: Oregon State University Press, 1977.
Linguistics in Literature, 2 (Fall 1977). Malamud number.
Studies in American Jewish Literature, 4 (Spring 1978). Malamud num-
  ber.

Critical Studies: Major Articles and Book Sections

Allen, John A. "The Promised End: Bernard Malamud's *The Tenants*,"
  Hollins Critic, 8 (Dec. 1971), 1-15. Collected in *Bernard Malamud:
  A Collection of Critical Essays*.
Alter, Robert. "Bernard Malamud: Jewishness as Metaphor." In his
  After the Tradition: Essays on Modern Jewish Writing. New York:
  Dutton, 1969, 116-130. Collected in *Bernard Malamud and the
  Critics*.
_____. "A Theological Fantasy: *God's Grace* by Bernard Mala-
  mud," *New Republic*, 20 and 27 Sept. 1982, pp. 38-40.
_____. "Updike, Malamud, and the Fire This Time," *Commentary*,
  54 (Oct. 1972), 68-74.
Astro, Richard. "In the Heart of the Valley: Bernard Malamud's *A
  New Life*." Collected in *Bernard Malamud: A Collection of Critical
  Essays*, 143-153.
Barbour, James, and Robert Sattelmeyer. "*The Natural* and the Shoot-
  ing of Eddie Waitkus," *Midwestern Miscellany*, 9 (1981), 61-68.

Barsness, John A. "*A New Life:* The Frontier Myth in Perspective," *Western American Literature,* 3 (Winter 1969), 297-302.

Baumbach, Jonathan. "All Men Are Jews: *The Assistant* by Bernard Malamud." In his *The Landscape of Nightmare: Studies in the Contemporary American Novel.* New York: New York University Press, 1965, 101-122.

—————. "Malamud's Heroes," *Commonweal,* 85 (28 Oct. 1966), 97-99.

Bellman, Samuel I. "Women, Children, and Idiots First: The Transformation Psychology of Bernard Malamud," *Critique,* 7 (Winter 1964-1965), 123-138. Collected in *Bernard Malamud and the Critics.*

Benedict, Helen. "Bernard Malamud: Morals and Surprises," *Antioch Review,* 41 (Winter 1983), 28-36.

Benson, Jackson J. "An Introduction: Bernard Malamud and the Haunting of America." Collected in *The Fiction of Bernard Malamud,* 13-42.

Bluefarb, Sam. "The Syncretism of Bernard Malamud." Collected in *Bernard Malamud: A Collection of Critical Essays,* 72-79.

Briganti, Chiara. "Mirrors, Windows and Peeping Toms: Women as the Object of Voyeuristic Scrutiny in Bernard Malamud's *A New Life* and *Dubin's Lives,*" *Studies in American Jewish Literature,* new series 3 (1983), 151-165.

Broyard, Anatole. "What Is a Nice Jewish Writer Like Malamud Doing in Italy?," *New York Times Book Review,* 4 May 1969, pp. 5, 45.

Bryant, Earle V. "The Tree-Clock in Bernard Malamud's 'Idiots First,' " *Studies in Short Fiction,* 20 (Winter 1983), 52-54.

Burch, Beth, and Paul W. Burch. "Myth on Myth: Bernard Malamud's 'The Talking Horse,' " *Studies in Short Fiction,* 16 (Fall 1979), 350-353.

Burrows, David J. "The American Past in Malamud's *A New Life.*" In *Private Dealings: Eight Modern American Writers,* ed. Burrows et al. Stockholm: Almquist & Wiksell, 1969, 86-94.

Cuddihy, John M. "Jews, Blacks, and the Cold War on Top," *Worldview,* 15 (Feb. 1972), 30-40.

Desmond, John F. "Malamud's Fixer: Jew, Christian, or Modern?," *Renascence: Essays on Values in Literature,* 27 (Winter 1975), 101-110.

Dickstein, Morris. "*The Tenants,*" *New York Times Book Review,* 3 Oct. 1971, pp. 1ff.

Ducharme, Robert. "Structure and Content in Malamud's *Pictures of*

Fidelman," *Connecticut Review,* 5 (Oct. 1971), 26-36.

Dupee, F. W. "The Power of Positive Sex," *Partisan Review,* 31 (Summer 1964), 425-430.

Epstein, Joseph. "Malamud in Decline," *Commentary,* 74 (Oct. 1982), 49-53.

Featherstone, Joseph. "Bernard Malamud," *Atlantic,* 219 (Mar. 1967), 95-98.

Fiedler, Leslie. "The Commonplace as Absurd," *Reconstructionist,* 21 Feb. 1958, pp. 22-24.

_____. "In the Interest of Surprise and Delight," *Folio,* 20 (Summer 1955), 17-20.

_____. "Jewish-Americans, Go Home!" In his *Waiting for the End.* New York: Stein & Day, 1964, 89-104.

_____. *Love and Death in the American Novel.* New York: Criterion, 1960.

_____. "Malamud's Travesty Western," *Novel: A Forum on Fiction,* 10 (Spring 1977), 212-219.

Field, Leslie. "Bernard Malamud and the Marginal Jew." Collected in *The Fiction of Bernard Malamud,* 97-116.

_____. "Portrait of the Artist as *Schlemiel (Pictures of Fidelman).*" Collected in *Bernard Malamud: A Collection of Critical Essays,* 117-129.

Finkelstein, Sidney. "The Anti-Hero of Updike, Bellow, and Malamud," *American Dialog,* 7 (Spring 1972), 12-14, 30.

Freedman, William. "From Bernard Malamud, With Discipline and With Love." In *The Fifties: Fiction, Poetry, Drama,* ed. Warren French. De Land, Fla.: Everett/Edwards, 1970, 133-143. Collected in *Bernard Malamud: A Collection of Critical Essays.*

Gealy, Marcia. "A Reinterpretation of Malamud's *The Natural,*" *Studies in American Jewish Literature,* 4 (Spring 1978), 24-32.

Gervais, Ronald J. "Malamud's Frank Alpine and Kazin's Circumcised *Italyener:* A Possible Source for *The Assistant,*" *Notes on Contemporary Literature,* 9 (Mar. 1979), 6-7.

Girgus, Sam B. "In Search of the Real America: Bernard Malamud." In his *The New Covenant: Jewish Writers and the American Idea.* Chapel Hill: University of North Carolina Press, 1984, 24-33.

Gittleman, Sol. "The Flight of Malamud's Schlemihls." In his *From Shtetl to Suburbia: The Family in Jewish Literary Imagination.* Boston: Beacon, 1978, 156-164.

Goldman, Mark. "Bernard Malamud's Comic Vision and the Theme of Identity," *Critique*, 7 (Winter 1964-1965), 92-109. Collected in *Bernard Malamud and the Critics*.

Goldsmith, Arnold L. "Nature in Bernard Malamud's *The Assistant*," *Renascence: Essays on Values in Literature*, 29 (Summer 1977), 211-223.

Gollin, Rita K. "Malamud's Dubin and the Morality of Desire," *Papers on Language and Literature*, 18 (Spring 1982), 198-207.

Grebstein, Sheldon N. "Bernard Malamud and the Jewish Movement." In *Contemporary American-Jewish Literature: Critical Essays*, ed. Irving Malin. Bloomington: Indiana University Press, 1973, 175-212. Collected in *Bernard Malamud: A Collection of Critical Essays*.

Greenspan, Ezra. *The "Schlemiel" Comes to America*. Metuchen, N.J.: Scarecrow Press, 1983.

Guttmann, Allen. " 'All Men Are Jews': Bernard Malamud." In his *The Jewish Writer in America: Assimilation and the Crisis of Identity*. New York: Oxford University Press, 1971, 112-120.

Handy, W. J. "The Malamud Hero: A Quest for Existence." Collected in *The Fiction of Bernard Malamud*, 65-86.

Harper, Howard M., Jr. "Trends in Recent American Fiction," *Contemporary Literature*, 12 (Spring 1971), 204-229.

Hassan, Ihab. "Bernard Malamud: 1976. Fictions Within Our Fictions." Collected in *The Fiction of Bernard Malamud*, 43-64.

_____. "The Qualified Encounter." In his *Radical Innocence: Studies in the Contemporary American Novel*. Princeton: Princeton University Press, 1961, 161-168. Collected in *Bernard Malamud and the Critics*.

Hays, Peter L. "The Complex Pattern of Redemption in *The Assistant*," *Centennial Review*, 13 (Spring 1969), 200-214. Collected in *Bernard Malamud and the Critics*.

_____. "Malamud's Yiddish-Accented Medieval Stories." Collected in *The Fiction of Bernard Malamud*, 87-96.

Hicks, Granville. "Bernard Malamud." In his *Literary Horizons: A Quarter Century of American Fiction*. New York: New York University Press, 1970, 65-83.

_____. "Generations of the Fifties: Malamud, Gold, and Updike." In *The Creative Present: Notes on Contemporary American Fiction*, ed. Nona Balakian and Charles Simmons. Garden City: Doubleday, 1963, 213-237.

_____. "One Man to Stand for Six Million," *Saturday Review*, 49 (10 Sept. 1966), 37-39.

Hill, John S. "Malamud's 'The Lady of the Lake'—A Lesson in Rejection," *University Review*, 36 (Winter 1969), 149-150.

Hoag, Gerald. "Malamud's *The Tenants:* Revolution Arrested," *Perspectives on Contemporary Literature*, 2 (Nov. 1976), 3-9.

_____. "Malamud's Trial: *The Fixer* and the Critics," *Western Humanities Review*, 24 (Winter 1970), 1-12. Collected in *Bernard Malamud: A Collection of Critical Essays.*

Hoffer, Bates. "The Magic in Malamud's Barrel," *Linguistics in Literature*, 2 (Fall 1977), 1-26.

Hoyt, Charles A. "Bernard Malamud and the New Romanticism." In *Contemporary American Novelists*, ed. Harry T. Moore. Carbondale: Southern Illinois University Press, 1964, 65-79.

Hyman, Stanley E. "A New Life for a Good Man." In his *Standards: A Chronicle of Books for Our Time.* New York: Horizon, 1966, 33-37.

Inge, M. Thomas. "The Ethnic Experience and Aesthetics in Literature: Malamud's *The Assistant* and Roth's *Call It Sleep*," *Journal of Ethnic Studies*, 1 (Winter 1974), 45-50.

Karl, Frederick R. *American Fictions, 1940-1980: A Comprehensive History and Critical Evaluation.* New York: Harper & Row, 1983.

Kazin, Alfred. "Bernard Malamud: The Magic and the Dread." In his *Contemporaries.* Boston: Little, Brown, 1962, 202-207.

_____. "Fantasist of the Ordinary," *Commentary*, 24 (July 1957), 89-92.

Kellman, Steven G. "*The Tenants* in the House of Fiction," *Studies in the Novel*, 8 (Winter 1976), 458-467.

Kennedy, J. Gerald. "Parody as Exorcism: 'The Raven' and 'The Jewbird,' " *Genre*, 13 (Summer 1980), 161-169.

Kerner, David. "A Note on the Source of 'The Magic Barrel,' " *Studies in American Jewish Literature*, 4 (Spring 1978), 32-35.

Klein, Marcus. "Bernard Malamud: The Sadness of Goodness." In his *After Alienation.* Cleveland: World, 1964, 247-293. Collected in *Bernard Malamud and the Critics.*

Korg, Jacob. "Ishmael and Israel," *Commentary*, 53 (May 1972), 82-84.

Kort, Wesley A. "*The Fixer* and the Death of God." In his *Shriven Selves: Religious Problems in Recent American Fiction.* Philadelphia: Fortress Press, 1972, 90-115.

Leer, Norman. "The Double Theme in Malamud's *The Assistant:* Dostoevsky with Irony," *Mosaic: A Journal for the Comparative Study of Literature and Ideas*, 4 (Spring 1971), 89-102.

_____. "Three American Novels and Contemporary Society,"

Wisconsin Studies in Contemporary Literature, 3 (Fall 1962), 67-86.

Lefcowitz, Barbara F. "The *Hybris* of Neurosis: Malamud's *Pictures of Fidelman,*" *Literature and Psychology,* 20, no. 3 (1970), 115-120.

Leonard, John. "Cheever to Roth to Malamud," *Atlantic,* 231 (June 1973), 112-116.

Lidston, Robert C. "Malamud's *The Natural:* An Arthurian Quest in the Big Leagues," *West Virginia University Philological Papers,* 27 (1981), 75-81.

Lindberg-Seyerstad, Brita. "A Reading of Bernard Malamud's *The Tenants,*" *Journal of American Studies,* 9 (Apr. 1975), 85-102.

Lyons, Bonnie. "Bellowmalamudroth and the American Jewish Genre—Alive and Well," *Studies in American Jewish Literature,* 5 (Winter 1979), 8-10.

Maddocks, Melvin. "Life is Suffering But . . . ," *Atlantic,* 228 (Nov. 1971), 132-136.

Malin, Irving. *Jews and Americans.* Carbondale: Southern Illinois University Press, 1965.

Maloff, Saul. "Loveliest Breakdown in Contemporary Fiction: Malamud's Lives," *Commonweal,* 106 (27 Apr. 1979), 244-246.

Mandel, Ruth B. "Bernard Malamud's *The Assistant* and *A New Life:* Ironic Affirmation," *Critique,* 7 (Winter 1964-1965), 110-122. Collected in *Bernard Malamud and the Critics.*

Mann, Herbert. "The Malamudian World: Method and Meaning," *Studies in American Jewish Literature,* 4 (Spring 1978), 2-12.

May, Charles E. "The Bread of Tears: Malamud's 'The Loan,' " *Studies in Short Fiction,* 7 (Fall 1970), 652-654.

Mellard, James M. "Malamud's Novels: Four Versions of Pastoral," *Critique,* 9, no. 2 (1967), 5-19. Collected in *Bernard Malamud and the Critics.*

Mesher, David R. "Names and Stereotypes in Malamud's *The Tenants,*" *Studies in American Jewish Literature,* 4 (Spring 1978), 57-68.

_____. "The Remembrance of Things Unknown: Malamud's 'The Last Mohican,' " *Studies in Short Fiction,* 12 (Fall 1975), 397-404.

Michaels, Leonard. "Sliding into English," *New York Review of Books,* 30 Sept. 1973, pp. 37-40.

Ozick, Cynthia. "Literary Blacks and Jews," *Midstream,* 18 (June/July 1972), 10-24. Collected in *Bernard Malamud: A Collection of Critical Essays.*

Perrine, Laurence. "Malamud's 'Take Pity,' " *Studies in Short Fiction,* 2 (Fall 1964), 84-86.

Pinsker, Sanford. "A Note on Bernard Malamud's 'Take Pity,' " *Studies in Short Fiction*, 6 (Winter 1969), 212-213.

_____. "The Schlemiel as Moral Bungler: Bernard Malamud's Ironic Heroes." In his *The Schlemiel as Metaphor*. Carbondale: Southern Illinois University Press, 1971, 87-124. Collected in *Bernard Malamud: A Collection of Critical Essays*.

Podheretz, Norman. "The New Nihilism and the Novel," *Partisan Review*, 25 (Fall 1958), 576-590.

Pradhan, S. V. "The Nature and Interpretation of Symbolism in Malamud's *The Assistant*," *Centennial Review*, 26 (Fall 1972), 394-407.

_____. "Spinoza and Malamud's *The Fixer*," *Indian Journal of American Studies*, 5 (Jan. & July 1976), 37-52.

Quart, Barbara K. "Women in Bernard Malamud's Fiction," *Studies in American Jewish Literature*, new series 3 (1983), 138-150.

Raffel, Burton. "Bernard Malamud," *Literary Review*, 13 (Winter 1969-1970), 149-155.

Ratner, Marc. "The Humanism of Malamud's *The Fixer*," *Critique*, 9, no. 2 (1967), 81-84.

Ray, Laura K. "Dickens and 'The Magic Barrel,' " *Studies in American Jewish Literature*, 4 (Spring 1978), 35-40.

Roth, Philip. "Writing American Fiction," *Commentary*, 31 (Mar. 1961), 223-233.

Rovit, Earl H. "Bernard Malamud and the Jewish Literary Tradition," *Critique*, 3 (Winter-Spring 1960), 3-10. Collected in *Bernard Malamud and the Critics*.

Rubin, Stephen J. "Malamud and the Theme of Love and Sex," *Studies in American Jewish Literature*, 4 (Spring 1978), 19-23.

Rudin, Neil. "Malamud's 'Jewbird' and Kafka's 'Gracchus': Birds of a Feather," *Studies in American Jewish Literature*, 1, no. 1 (1975), 10-15.

Samuels, Charles T. "*The Fixer*." In *Critic as Artist*, ed. Gilbert A. Harrison. New York: Liveright, 1972, 291-298.

Saposnik, Irving. "Insistent Assistance: The Stories of Bernard Malamud," *Studies in American Jewish Literature*, 4 (Spring 1978), 12-18.

Scholes, Robert. "Portrait of Artist as 'Escape-Goat,' " *Saturday Review*, 52 (10 May 1969), 32-34.

Schulz, Max F. "Malamud's *A New Life*: The Wasteland of the Fifties," *Western Review*, 6 (Summer 1969), 37-44.

Sharfman, William. "Inside and Outside Malamud," *Rendezvous: Idaho State University Journal of Arts and Letters*, 7 (Spring 1972), 25-38.

Sharma, D. R. "Malamud's 'Jewishness': An Analysis of *The Assistant*," *Literary Criterion*, 11 (Winter 1974), 29-37.

_____. *"The Tenants:* Malamud's Treatment of the Racial Problem," *Indian Journal of American Studies*, 8 (July 1978), 12-22.

Shear, Walter. "Culture Conflict in *The Assistant*," *Midwest Quarterly*, 7 (July 1966), 367-380.

Sheed, Wilfred. "Bernard Malamud: *Pictures of Fidelman.*" In his *The Morning After: Selected Essays and Reviews*. New York: Farrar, Straus & Giroux, 1971, 59-61.

Sheres, Ita. "The Alienated Sufferer: Malamud's Novels from the Perspective of the Old Testament and Jewish Mystical Thought," *Studies in American Jewish Literature*, 4 (Spring 1978), 68-76.

Siegel, Ben. "Through a Glass Darkly: Bernard Malamud's Painful Views of the Self." Collected in *The Fiction of Bernard Malamud*, 117-147.

_____. "Victims in Motion: Bernard Malamud's Sad and Bitter Clowns," *Northwest Review*, 5 (Spring 1962), 69-80. Collected in *Bernard Malamud and the Critics*.

Singer, Barnet. "Outsider Versus Insider: Malamud's and Kesey's Pacific Northwest," *South Dakota Review*, 13 (Winter 1975-1976), 127-144.

Smelstor, Marjorie. "The Schlemiel as Father: A Study of Yakov Bok and Eugene Henderson," *Studies in American Jewish Literature*, 4 (Spring 1978), 50-57.

Standley, Fred L. "Bernard Malamud: The Novel of Redemption," *Southern Humanities Review*, 5 (Fall 1971), 309-318.

Stern, Daniel. "Commonplace Things, and the Essence of Art," *Nation*, 3 Sept. 1973, pp. 181-182.

Stinson, John J. "Non-Jewish Dialogue in *The Assistant:* Stilted, Runyonesque, or Both?," *Notes on Contemporary Literature*, 9 (Jan. 1979), 6-7.

Storey, Michael L. "Pinye Salzman, Pan, and 'The Magic Barrel,' " *Studies in Short Fiction*, 18 (Spring 1981), 180-183.

Sullivan, Walter. " 'Where Have All the Flowers Gone?' Part II: The Novel in the Gnostic Twilight," *Sewanee Review*, 78 (Oct.-Dec. 1970), 654-664.

Tanner, Tony. "A New Life." In his *City of Words: American Fiction 1950-70*. New York: Harper & Row, 1971, 322-343.

Tucker, Martin. *"Pictures of Fidelman,"* *Commonweal*, 27 June 1969, 420-421.

Updike, John. "Cohn's Doom," *New Yorker*, 8 Nov. 1982, pp. 167-169.

Voss, Arthur. *The American Short Story: A Critical Survey.* Norman: University of Oklahoma Press, 1973.

Walden, Daniel. "Bellow, Malamud, and Roth: Part of the Continuum," *Studies in American Jewish Literature,* 5 (Winter 1979), 5-7.

Warburton, Robert W. "Fantasy and the Fiction of Bernard Malamud." In *Imagination and the Spirit,* ed. Charles A. Huttar. Grand Radpids, Mich.: Eerdmans, 1971, 387-416.

Wasserman, Earl. *"The Natural:* Malamud's World Ceres," *Centennial Review,* 9 (Fall 1965), 438-460. Collected in *Bernard Malamud and the Critics.*

Winn, H. Harbour, III. "Malamud's Uncas: 'Last Mohican,' " *Notes on Contemporary Literature,* 5 (Mar. 1975), 13-14.

Wisse, Ruth R. "Requiem in Several Voices." In her *The Schlemiel as Modern Hero.* Chicago: University of Chicago Press, 1971, 110-118.

Witherington, Paul. "Malamud's Allusive Design in *A New Life,*" *Western American Literature,* 10 (Summer 1975), 115-123.

Yevish, Irving A. "The Faculty Novel," *Georgia Review,* 25 (Spring 1971), 41-50.

BIBLIOGRAPHICAL ESSAY

Bibliographies and Checklists

The only book-length attempt at a primary and secondary bibliography of Malamud is Rita N. Kosofsky's *Bernard Malamud: An Annotated Checklist* (1969). Though dated, Kosofsky's book remains valuable for several reasons. Her "primary" section traces first publications of Malamud's short stories, as well as reprints of them in anthologies and textbooks. Her listing of secondary criticism, divided into "Books" and "Periodicals," is followed by a third listing, "Reviews." While those distinctions make it difficult for a reader to find the assembled criticism of individual works (there is often scant difference between a substantial review and a critical article), the separate listing of reviews is useful in tracing the immediate reception of Malamud's works. Kosofsky's annotations are accurate summations, often direct quotes, and she does a creditable job in discovering some of the less likely sources for Malamud criticism: reviews in *Women's Wear Daily* and *Good Housekeeping,* for instance. Yet the listing is limited by the exclusion of doctoral dissertations, periodicals outside the United States and Great Britain, and foreign-language articles. Morris Sher's

Bernard Malamud: A Partially Annotated Bibliography (1970), which includes translations and non-English-language criticism, is idiosyncratically organized, selective in its coverage, and difficult to locate in American libraries.

More current, though not annotated, is Donald Risty's admirable "A Comprehensive Checklist of Malamud Criticism" (1977). Risty includes secondary criticism of Malamud's work through 1975, divided into three sections: books, sections of books, and articles and reviews. Risty picks up dozens of earlier items that Kosofsky missed but reproduces some of her errors as well. Robert D. Habich's "Bernard Malamud: A Bibliographic Survey" (1978) is an attempt to chart the trends in Malamud criticism through the mid-1970s, with the conclusion that "the most pressing task for contemporary scholars is the mature evaluation of Malamud's work in the hierarchy of twentieth-century American fiction," rather than merely as a "Jewish-American, post-war" novelist.

Malamud's bibliography is brought up to date—and supplemented—in Joseph A. Grau's excellent "Bernard Malamud: A Bibliographical Addendum" (1980) and its supplement (1981). Grau lists all translations of Malamud's work, includes dissertations and foreign-language articles of criticism, cites reprintings of Malamud's short stories in anthologies, and supplies a listing of "miscellaneous" items— newspaper articles, reviews of theatrical adaptations of Malamud's fiction, and some nonfiction pieces by Malamud—that have escaped notice elsewhere. With this listing in hand, students of Malamud can indeed "proceed with confidence," as Grau hopes, "that little of substance in the way of Malamud's works and their criticism will escape their notice."

Interviews

There is no full-length biographical study of Malamud, but interviews conducted throughout his career enable readers to understand the connections between his life and his art and the literary influences that have shaped his work. In Dean Cadle's "Bernard Malamud" (1958), the author discusses his childhood in Brooklyn, where his father was a shopkeeper, and the interviewer surveys Malamud's life and career as a writer. More important, he offers his early appraisal of contemporary fiction and the proper role of the artist— opinions which, some readers may believe, he has changed in the past decade. American fiction of the 1950s, Malamud contends, "is loaded with sickness, homosexuality, fragmented man, 'other-directed' man," instead of being "filled with love and beauty and hope." Criticizing the penchant for "journalistic case studies instead of rich personality development," Malamud argues that the writer's task is "to keep civilization from destroying itself. But without preachment."

Granville Hicks, in "His Hopes on the Human Heart" (1963), provides more details about Malamud's life and career, including information about the writing of *A New Life* (1961). (Malamud, then teaching at Oregon State, rented a room in town in order to complete the novel free of distractions.) Haskel Frankel's interview in the *Saturday Review* (1966) is interesting primarily for comments on the genesis and composition of *The Fixer* (1966), a novel that Malamud carefully divorces from the facts of the Mendel Beiliss case on which it is loosely based. In this interview, too, is Malamud's central statement about his art: "My work, all of it, is an idea of dedication to the human. . . . If you don't respect man, you cannot respect my work. I'm in defense of the human."

Despite his contention in "Novelist Malamud: 'Living Is Guessing What Reality Is' " (1979) that artistic creativity should "remain forever a mystery," Malamud's later interviews reveal a great deal about his own methods of composition and his sense of the proper boundaries of fiction. Discussing his work with Israel Shenker in "For Malamud It's Story" (1971), he calls plot "the basic element of fiction" and answers those critics of *The Tenants* who would question a white writer's ability to recreate black experience: "If I'm not afraid to invent God in my fiction . . . I don't see why I shouldn't invent Willie Spearmint." To critics such as Robbe-Grillet, among others, Malamud argues a more traditional definition of the novel: "The existence of theme . . . does not contaminate the work. Theme achieves the formal value in art that only an artist can give it." In sum, says Malamud, novels must be written "as art demands, not definition." The demands of writing *Dubin's Lives* (1979), the novel that interviewer Ralph Tyler calls Malamud's "attempt at bigness, at summing up what he has learned," are the subject of "A Talk with the Novelist" (1979), in which Malamud discusses the composition of the novel, its autobiographical connections (there are none, he claims), and the making of movies from his works.

Revealing though they may be about Malamud's life and craft, his interviews yield relatively little about his intentions in his work. In "An Interview with Bernard Malamud" by Leslie and Joyce Field (1975), he explains why: "People can read; they can read what I say.

That's a lot more interesting than reading what I say I say." Still, the Fields' interview is one of the two most substantial, largely because Malamud so adamantly rejects some of the labels attached to him over the years. The term "Jewish-American writer" he dismisses as "schematic and reductive"; the notion of the academic novel "simply doesn't interest me"; and the "*schlemiel* treatment of fictional characters" is flawed because "it reduces to stereotypes people of complex motivations and fates—not to mention possibilities." Equally as trenchant are his comments on the "prison metaphor" in his fiction: "It's a metaphor for the dilemma of all men throughout history. Necessity is the primary prison, though the bars are not visible to all. Then there are man-made prisons of social injustice, apathy, ignorance. . . . Therefore our most extraordinary invention is human freedom."

The Fields' interview, conducted by mail to allow Malamud the opportunity to modify or reject questions, avoids (by design) personal matters and the issue of sources, concentrating instead on questions about his fiction "asked in one way or another by readers, critics, students." In Daniel Stern's "The Art of Fiction LII: Bernard Malamud" (1975), the most spontaneous and wide-ranging interview available, Malamud looks back over his life and work on his sixtieth birthday. He recalls a childhood of affection but also of "cultural deprivation": "There were no books that I remember in the house, no records, music, pictures on the wall. On Sundays I listened to somebody's piano through the window." Always fond of the movies, he reveals the importance of Charlie Chaplin's influence on his writing: "the rhythm, the snap of comedy; the reserved comic presence—that beautiful distancing; the funny with sad; the surprise of surprise." Though Malamud considers source questions "piddling" ones, he discusses the genesis of some of his work. *The Assistant* (1957) grew out of "my father's life as a grocer, through not necessarily my father," and is a fusion of three of his short stories, "The Cost of Living," "The First Seven Years," and "The Place is Different Now." *The Fixer* owes much, he says, to an abandoned idea for a Sacco and Vanzetti novel, with Yakov Bok conceived initially as a "potential Vanzetti."

Because Malamud prefers "autobiographical essence to autobiographical history," he is more comfortable discussing his work than recounting his life. Readers of the Stern interview will learn much about his method of composition. *Pictures of Fidelman* (1969), for instance, began with the desire to "experiment a little—with narrative structure"; Malamud started with jottings of ideas for a picaresque novel, then worked on the stories at intervals from 1957 to 1968 to see whether the passing of time would influence Fidelman's life. Malamud's novels are generally products of months of note-making, with the final paragraph written first, the rest of the work written in order, and few major divergences from the original plan. In addition, Malamud offers some advice to young writers and old ("Take chances . . . but if you're not a genius imitate the daring"), reveals the process of successive drafts in his novels, and explores the intersection of art and morality: "Morality begins with an awareness of the sanctity of one's life," while art celebrates life and "gives us our measure." Finally, Malamud offers an appraisal of his work that critics and readers alike would do well to heed. In his fiction he strives to create "real qualities in imaginary worlds," a theme he pursues "along the same paths in different worlds." For those who value an author's self-criticism, the Stern interview is indispensable—witty, specific, and forthright in its coverage of Malamud's career.

Critical Studies: Books

Book-length criticism of Malamud's work must be considered in light of two important facts. First, there is no full-length study of any single novel or collection of stories: all of the books written about Malamud purport to survey his complete corpus to date. Second, since Malamud remains an active writer, every book of criticism needs revision in light of his subsequent work. A dilemma for any critic of a living author, this is especially troublesome for those who find patterns of development in Malamud's fiction, since Malamud so easily confounds his readers by changing direction from one novel to the next. The variety and richness of Malamud's work, in short, limit the useful life of any book about him; as Sidney Richman points out in *Bernard Malamud* (1966), book-length studies of Malamud are "doomed to tentativeness" until his last work has been done.

Richman's book, part of the Twayne United States Authors Series, is one of several introductory studies, and despite its age it remains the best. A "novel-by-novel, story-by-story analysis" through *Idiots First* (1963), it begins with a solid biographical chapter, then considers each novel or collection of short stories in turn. What Richman oddly calls the "severest limitation" of his book—the need to confine himself to "a close study of the fiction itself"—in fact constitutes its real strength. The explications of theme, plot, and character are cautious but full, given the limits of the Twayne format, and Richman includes helpful discussions of Malamud's Jewishness and

276

his comic sense. The reader approaching Malamud for the first time will find useful treatment of the major themes; the more expert reader will find little objectionable in Richman's argument that "success in failure, failure in success" is the theme "squarely in the mainstream of Malamud's thought."

More debatable, but still convincingly presented, is Richman's contention about the development of Malamud's fiction. *The Natural* (1952), he writes, is "at one and the same time an excursion into hallucination and a poetic investigation of some of the distinctive sources of modern anxiety" in which myth is used as a "trick of craft." *The Assistant,* on the other hand, shows "only traces of the mythic manner" of *The Natural* and "places the purely psychological drama . . . in a far more real arena." According to Richman, *A New Life* represents a further development, its depiction of an " 'actual' present" the most realistic treatment of the "cycle of redemption" at the heart of Malamud's work. The need to illustrate this development, along with Richman's obvious preference for *The Assistant* ("not only one of the best novels of recent years but perhaps the *very* best"), jeopardizes Richman's objective reading of the fiction at times.

Malamud's thematic development, rather than changes in his craft, is the focus of Robert Ducharme's *Art and Idea in the Novels of Bernard Malamud* (1974). Ducharme's book illustrates the dangers of too closely charting Malamud from novel to novel; subtitled *Toward "The Fixer,"* it actually ends with an appended discussion of *Pictures of Fidelman.* Each chapter considers Malamud's first four novels in relation to a given theme or motif: archetypal patterns, irony and myth, fathers and sons, suffering, and responsibility. One of Ducharme's primary purposes is to trace in the novels "a gradually changing attitude that does not emerge until *The Fixer,*" from the acceptance of suffering to the refusal of it. Ducharme's argument is sensitive and perceptive, bolstered by a wealth of extra-literary material such as Freudian and Jungian psychology and Joseph Campbell's study of primitive myth. But the closing chapter on *Pictures of Fidelman* seems forced, as do the categories under which Ducharme organizes his discussion: suffering and responsibility are so inextricably linked in Malamud's work, for example, that it is distracting to consider them separately.

A third "introductory" study, in fact if not in intent, is *Bernard Malamud and the Trial by Love* (1974). Considering Malamud's work through *The Tenants* (1971), Sandy Cohen examines his blend of myth with reality and attempts to show "how Malamud uses his fiction as a medium and a testing ground for his premises about man's ultimate need for self-transcendence to deliver him from his essentially myth-dominated existence." Unlike Richman and Ducharme, Cohen sees no essential development in Malamud's fiction. "His central theme," Cohen maintains, "is still self-transcendence; his central technique still involves myth." To show that continuity, Cohen treats each novel in turn, along with a selection of short stories that bear some thematic resemblance to it.

What makes Cohen's study finally unconvincing is not its short sentences or its categorical, sometimes simplistic literary judgments: "*The Natural* . . . is not realistic. This is no crime." Instead, the book is compromised by Cohen's apparent inability to define with any precision what is meant by "myth." On the one hand the term refers to "the seasonal cycles and their various attending myths, such as those of the Holy Grail, Thanatos, Easter, Joseph and his brothers, and Passover"; on the other hand, it identifies "the myth of sexuality." At best, Cohen is assuming a much more comprehensive definition of the term than readers usually grant.

If Cohen's study grants the reader too much, Sheldon J. Hershinow's book (1980) grants too little. Part of the Modern Literature Monographs series, Hershinow's *Bernard Malamud* provides the most comprehensive coverage of the fiction (a chapter on each of Malamud's works through *Dubin's Lives*). The readings of individual works are detailed, with enough summary of plot that readers new to Malamud will find Hershinow's survey useful. But even the rankest beginner is likely to be bothered by a gratuitous warning like this one: "To the extent that Malamud's writing romanticizes suffering, it is dangerous and destructive. . . . But Malamud surely never intended anyone to take his metaphoric treatment of suffering literally, as a life model."

The implied danger results from Hershinow's "dark" reading of Malamud. According to Hershinow, the often-cited theme of redemptive suffering is a mere "corollary" to Malamud's "real concern, one that can easily be missed: what he primarily wishes to explore and express is the sheer terror of existence in the twentieth century." Hershinow divides Malamud's fictional treatment of suffering into two types, the "sentimental" and the "hard-headed," and concludes that *The Assistant* and *The Fixer* are Malamud's best novels, exemplars of the second type that "capture most effectively our existential sense of terror." While he acknowledges that Malamud's stories present "the joy as well as the pain" of life, he stresses the latter throughout his book.

A more balanced, and more convincing, treatment of Malamud's "darkness" is Iska Alter's *The Good Man's Dilemma: Social Criticism in the Fiction of Bernard Malamud* (1981). Though Alter wrongly asserts that Malamud's social criticism has been "neglected, ignored, or even declared non-existent" by other critics, the close reading of the canon through *Dubin's Lives* does offer a more developed view of his social vision than any other critic has yet offered. To Alter, the central dilemma in Malamud's work is the paradox of living in an increasingly materialistic America: "to succeed . . . is to lose one's soul; to fail is to preserve one's moral integrity." Throughout his work Malamud has developed a progressively more pessimistic stance toward this dilemma, Alter argues, his fiction presenting "the decline of the American dream into the nightmare of an entire civilization in decay." In the Malamudian world, "affirmation is ambiguous and hope equivocal."

When the book does not descend to cliché (as it does in its coverage of racial issues) or balloon out in overstatement (women characters are minimized, Alter argues, because Malamud's disintegrating fictional world cannot accommodate their "elaborate value system and complicated psychic design"), Alter's study presents much of value. On *A New Life,* for instance, it explores in detail the idea that the myth of an American Eden encourages not purity and nobility but "emotional and psychological escapism." Provocative, too, is the examination of Malamud's many artist characters, whose ability "to discipline chaos is negligible." Some readers will find the depiction of *The Assistant*'s Morris Bober reductive, since to call him "a Lincolnesque figure" who rejects materialism ignores his substantial envy of the moneyed characters in the novel. On the whole, though, Alter remains faithful to the texts, and *The Good Man's Dilemma* resists the easy conclusions that sometimes beset the shorter criticism.

The remaining three book-length studies, comparative treatments of Malamud with some of his contemporaries, show some of the virtues and almost all of the pitfalls of that method. In his brief *Bernard Malamud and Philip Roth* (1968), Glen Meeter has little room to explore his main point: that Roth and Malamud are both "Jewish Romantics" who complement each other, the first writing the more realistic fiction, the second creating "symbolic romance." Tobias Hergt, in *Das Motiv der Hochschule* (1979), has more space but less point. Comparing Malamud with John Barth, Hergt argues that while

Barth's university settings are places to explore existential and literary themes, for Malamud the academy serves as a setting for the treatment of moral and social problems. In *Rebels and Victims* (1979), Evelyn G. Avery explicates the stories and novels of Malamud and Richard Wright, according to the themes of cultural identity and family and social relationships. Wright's "rebels" and Malamud's "victims," she argues, are both restricted by ethnic and racial tradition. But the rebel "forsakes passive suffering and asserts himself violently," while the victim "elevates pain to a moral virtue." Neither Wright nor Malamud is especially illuminated by Avery's conclusion that both writers' heroes "reject conformity . . . [and] affirm the worth of the individual."

Critical Studies: Major Articles and Book Sections

In one of the rare negative appraisals of Malamud's place in American literature, "Malamud in Decline" (1982), Joseph Epstein charges that the author of *God's Grace* (1982) has been "transformed from a central to a now almost negligible figure." That Epstein's is decidedly a minority opinion is nowhere better shown than in the critical attention that Malamud continues to receive some thirty-five years after the publication of his first novel. General appraisals of his canon abound, and the best critical articles on his individual works of fiction shed light on the entire corpus as well.

Some hint of the major issues in Malamudian criticism can be found in Jackson J. Benson's "An Introduction: Bernard Malamud and the Haunting of America" (1977). Ostensibly a response to the other essays in *The Fiction of Bernard Malamud* (1977), Benson's is in fact much more than that—a musing, discursive survey of such problems as Malamud's modernism, his "reversal of the American dream," and his place in American letters. Malamud, Benson decides, is an essentially traditional writer, despite his experiments with form and point of view, an allegorist "vitally concerned with matters of conscience." As a map to the main contours of Malamud's fictional world, Benson's sensitive reading is indispensable, raising questions that in one form or another the better critics have wrestled with since the beginning.

Among the many overviews of Malamud's fiction, the reader would do well to choose Herbert Mann's "The Malamudian World: Method and Meaning" (1978), a survey of Malamud's recurring motifs. In his work, "moral struggle is constantly reflected in physical struggle": motifs of movement and flight, time, and sight/insight are presented in physical terms, Mann argues, to connect the life of the spirit to the "real" world of the senses. Another overview, James M. Mellard's "Malamud's Novels: Four Versions of Pastoral" (1967), examines Malamud's distinctive fictional mode, "a modernization of the pastoral." In the course of analyzing the "archetypal narrative structure" of *The Natural, The Assistant, A New Life,* and *The Fixer,* Mellard also provides an excellent introduction to characterization, symbolism, rhetorical strategy, and use of myth in the novels. Less focused, but suggestive nonetheless, is Sam Bluefarb's "The Syncretism of Bernard Malamud" (1975). Malamud, Bluefarb contends, is a "literary syncretist"—that is, he successfully synthesizes and reconciles "widely differing literary themes and styles." Among those noted by Bluefarb are Malamud's debt to authors from Hawthorne to Joyce, genres from the gothic to the travel narrative, and "schools and styles" from dialect to myth. Broadly conceived, Bluefarb's essay never sufficiently develops any single point, yet for readers new to Malamud it helps to place him in a literary context.

Two of the earliest critics to recognize Malamud's importance were Alfred Kazin and Leslie Fiedler. In "Fantasist of the Ordinary" (1957), Kazin calls Malamud "the poet of the desperately clownish" and suggests that he "writes, a little, the way Chagall paints"—an observation that has become axiomatic. "In the Interest of Surprise and Delight" (1955), Fiedler's review of *The Natural,* contends that Malamud's complex use of the Grail myth, often criticized as contrived, is an integral part of the novel. Fiedler again praises *The Natural* in *Love and Death in the American Novel* (1960), speaking of its "magical universe—in which white witch and black witch struggle for the soul of a secular savior"; but he argues that in *The Assistant* this "lovely, absurd madness" disappears. Among the critics of Fiedler's early criticism, which stresses in part the general "failure of the American fictionist to deal with adult heterosexual love," is F. W. Dupee; in "The Power of Positive Sex" (1964), he argues that in Malamud's work sex is "eminently normal" and distinguishes his fiction from "the Gothic or wacky strain in contemporary novels." Tony Tanner also differentiates Malamud's work from the dominant trends in contemporary fiction. In his valuable *City of Words: American Fiction 1950-70* (1971), Tanner points out the "recurring pattern" in the novels through *Pictures of Fidelman:* "All of his novels are fables or parables of the painful process from immaturity to maturity" that yields regeneration or the "new life." For Tanner, Malamud's fiction is an unusual development in American literature, "which tends to see initiation into manhood as a trauma, a disillusioning shock, a suffocating curtailment of personal potential."

Malamud's stature as a writer seems inextricably bound up with his position in the "Jewish-American literary tradition." As Daniel Walden has rightly pointed out, that tradition extends at least as far back as the work of Abraham Cahan in the 1890s and continues to vitalize writers like Neil Simon and Cynthia Ozick; in "Bellow, Malamud, and Roth: Part of the Continuum" (1979), Walden places Malamud squarely in the tradition. Still, the definitions are slippery, if, as Bonnie Lyons argues in "Bellowmalamudroth and the American Jewish Genre" (1979), the term can refer to "any work in which a writer uses his awareness of himself as an American Jew as a significant theme or aspect of his work." On the one hand, Ezra Greenspan can affirm in *The "Schlemiel" Comes to America* (1983) that Malamud is "a full-blooded Jewish moralist"; on the other, Burton Raffel can claim in "Bernard Malamud" (1969-1970) that Malamud's "warped" viewpoint and the "passionate negatives" who people his books mark such a severe lack of compassion that he cannot be considered a Jewish writer. Leslie Fiedler comes close to begging the question entirely in "Jewish-Americans, Go Home!" (1964), with his claim that "in their very alienation the Jews were always mythically twentieth-century Americans." And Leslie Field, in his carefully argued "Bernard Malamud and the Marginal Jew" (1977), maintains that while Malamud may be a Jewish-American writer, he is among those "intellectual and literary Jews" who have "ignored, skirted, homogenized, or rejected" such key concerns as the holocaust and the creation of the state of Israel.

There is general agreement, however, that Malamud's fictional world is suffused with Jewish themes and symbols, if not with the specific concerns that Field notes. Earl H. Rovit made the point early, in "Bernard Malamud and the Jewish Literary Tradition" (1960), that in its concern with imprisonment, alienation, suffering, and transcendence Malamud's thematic range is "unmistakably Hebraic." But those strengths can also lead to weaknesses, says Rovit, for the "Jewish irony" of Malamud's characters can often be self-deflating. Mark Goldman responds to Rovit's criticism in "Bernard Malamud's Comic Vision and the Theme of Identity" (1964-1965), arguing that while Malamud's "modern anti-heroes" indeed perceive themselves ironically, through their "comic *hubris*" Malamud is able to affirm "the creed of the comic artist: light over darkness, life over death."

It is the metaphor of placelessness, derived from the expulsion from the *shtetl*, that accounts for the Jewish quality of Malamud's fiction, contends Marcus Klein in "Bernard Malamud: The Sadness of Goodness" (1964). A sense of the precariousness of reality thus pervades Malamud's fiction; in a world of uncertainty, Klein says, Malamud's voice is emphatically moral, stressing as it does "the necessity in this world of accepting moral obligation." Robert Alter makes essentially the same point in "Bernard Malamud: Jewishness as Metaphor" (1969), noting further that the immigrant experience, "at once more peripheral and more central" than in other Jewish-American fiction, transforms Jewishness into an ethical symbol. In his analysis of *The Fixer* especially, Alter shows how the complex imagery of imprisonment, rather than the inclusion of nominal Jews as characters, gives Malamud's fiction its religious cast. This escape from psychological as well as physical bondage, which Samuel I. Bellman terms Malamud's "transformation psychology" in "Women, Children, and Idiots First" (1964-1965), is the dominant theme in the fiction, one that leads in Bellman's phrase to a "partial Judaization of society."

The divergent threads of the debate over Malamud's Jewishness are drawn together by Sheldon N. Grebstein in "Bernard Malamud and the Jewish Movement" (1973). A lengthy, perceptive survey of the issue, Grebstein's essay defines the American-Jewish literary movement as a response to the horrors of the holocaust; its central theme is suffering, and the Jew becomes Everyman. In that tradition, exemplified by Bellow, Malamud, and Roth, Malamud is the most representative—"the most solid, the most consistently fulfilled, and . . . the most *Jewish*." Malamud, writes Grebstein, has nearly perfected the theme of suffering, the use of comedy, and the "Jewish style" (an extension of American colloquial dialect). If Grebstein's essay does not put an end to the discussion, it ought at least to define the terms and issues for some years to come.

Part of the difficulty in discussing the Jewishness of Malamud's fiction lies in his characters: as Robert Alter points out in *After the Tradition* (1969), almost all of them are avowedly Jewish, but almost none are animated by religious orthodoxy or the strict observation of Talmudic law. Probably the most useful discussion of these complex, tragic-comic characters is Sanford Pinsker's "The Schlemiel as Moral Bungler: Bernard Malamud's Ironic Heroes" (1971). Pinsker surveys the Malamudian protagonist, tracing the development of the schlemiel from "The Magic Barrel" (where Jewishness is merely "a literary illusion" [*sic*]) through Yakov Bok of *The Fixer*, where the Jewish setting and characterization are more fully realized. Throughout Malamud's work, Pinsker contends, "the schlemiels tended to be moral bunglers moving haphazardly toward redemption. With Yakov Bok, they finally arrived." Ruth R. Wisse, in "Requiem in Several Voices" (1971), examines the demise of the schlemiel figure as a literary hero; for a variety of reasons, she believes—not the least of which was the political turmoil of the American 1960s, in which the schlemiel's dualistic worldview seemed less comic—the moral bungler's popularity as a literary type has waned. *Pictures of Fidelman,* she concludes, is Malamud's "sad requiem for the schlemiel." In "Victims in Motion: Bernard Malamud's Sad and Bitter Clowns" (1962), Ben Siegel overstates the extent to which Malamud's characters are "social misfits" who "can't stand success." But Siegel's later essay, "Through a Glass Darkly: Bernard Malamud's Painful Views of the Self " (1977), demonstrates Malamud's "commitment to absurd man and his comic condition" with an analysis of the main characters and shows how Malamud's stories and novels may be viewed as "parables of possibility and regeneration."

Malamud's delineation of women characters has received little critical attention, though two articles offer some tentative thoughts on the subject. Barbara K. Quart, in "Women in Bernard Malamud's Fiction" (1983), examines the "peculiar obliqueness" of his male characters' relationships toward women. Though Quart is correct in saying that those male protagonists "appear to fear love and women as much as they long for them," not all readers would agree that Malamud is "weak at characterizing women, and at the dynamics of relationship," since the fragility of love is often a dominant theme in his work, rather than an evidence of his weakness as a writer. More satisfactory is Chiara Briganti's "Mirrors, Windows and Peeping Toms" (1983), a discussion of the female character as an "object of voyeuristic scrutiny" in *A New Life* and *Dubin's Lives.* Briganti argues that while Malamud's male characters usually pass through a traumatic crisis in their quest for a "positive identity," the female characters "serve primarily as antagonists and as a means to precipitate the crisis." Whether or not the protagonist succeeds in his quest, Briganti notes, the women characters "never rise above the sexual roles" assigned them.

Articles and chapters devoted to individual works of Malamud's fiction are abundant, and the resiliency of his achievement as a writer is shown by the extent to which critics return to his earlier fiction with the fresh perspective gained from his later books. Malamud's first novel, *The Natural,* continues to attract attention some three decades after it was published, as readers discover in the mythic elements of its plot something more than literary exhibitionism. In "Malamud's *The Natural:* An Arthurian Quest in the Big Leagues" (1981), Robert C. Lidston shows in detail how Malamud mixes the "two legendary realms" of baseball and Arthurian legend to create a modern parable of "initiation, separation, and return." Marcia Gealy presents another reading of the mythic substructure of the novel in "A Reinterpretation of Malamud's *The Natural*" (1978). While the Arthurian parallels are undoubtedly present, Gealy argues that "Roy's quest for himself may also be seen in the not so obvious framework of a Jewish tradition, specifically Hasidism or Jewish mysticism, where the quest for God or the quest for the Father are [*sic*] equated with self-knowledge." To understand that tradition, she concludes, is to recognize in Roy Hobbs the "true *schlemiel* or holy fool" who, like Malamud's other characters, gains dignity from his suffering. Other sources for the novel are the subjects of several short studies. Among these is James Barbour and Robert Sattelmeyer's "*The Natural* and the Shooting of Eddie Waitkus" (1981), which shows how Malamud reshaped the 1949 attack upon the Philadelphia Phillies' first baseman into fictional form.

Unlike *The Natural*, which was largely ignored by the critics when it first appeared, *The Assistant* has never suffered from lack of commentary. Jonathan Baumbach's smart explication in "All Men Are Jews" (1965) divorces the novel's theme of love and redemption from the strictly Jewish-American literary tradition, showing that "the burden and ambivalence of assuming personal responsibility in a world which accommodates evil" is a concern shared by many contemporary writers who are not Jewish. Peter L. Hays calls the novel "a modern parable in the form of a naturalistic novel" in "The Complex Pattern of Redemption in *The Assistant*" (1969). Malamud's sophisticated use of religious allusion, mythology, sacrificial rites, and fertility imagery contributes, Hays argues, to the protagonist's movement from evil to redemption, a spiritual progression that closely parallels Martin Buber's theory of development from "I-it" to "I-thou." While Hays asserts the importance of myth in the novel, Arnold L. Goldsmith maintains that such an approach can distort our reading of it. Instead, he writes in "Nature in Bernard Malamud's *The Assistant*" (1977), it is better to focus on nature imagery and symbolism, which "reinforce mood, provide comic and ironic undertone, and [serve] as a link between the world of dream and reality, fantasy and fact." Goldsmith traces in detail images of weather, seasons, sea and marine life, flowers, and birds, but his conclusion is disappointing: the imagery is too complex, he argues, for us to view the ending of the novel with anything more than "uncertainty" about Frank Alpine's future. Along similar lines, S. V. Pradhan examines the recurring symbols—the store as grave, Helen as a Dantean Beatrice—in "The Nature and Interpretation of Symbolism in Malamud's *The Assistant*" (1972). Ronald J. Gervais discovers a parallel between the novel and an incident in Alfred Kazin's *A Walker in the City,* but he admits that the similarity between the two love stories may merely be due to "the obvious pervasiveness of the issue," in "Malamud's Frank Alpine and Kazin's Circumcised *Italyener*" (1979). M. Thomas Inge, calling for a reevaluation of the "traditional standards by which we judge and teach literature" in "The Ethnic Experience and Aesthetics in Literature" (1974), compares the "literal accuracy and fidelity" of an ethnic novel like Henry Roth's *Call It Sleep* with the metaphorical Jewishness of *The Assistant.* Not really ethnic fiction, and therefore more acceptable to traditional academics, *The Assistant* reveals "the tragic dimensions of everyman's life," Inge contends.

In "A New Life for a Good Man" (1966), Stanley E. Hyman praises *A New Life* as a "novel of consistent excellence" and shows Malamud's third novel, like his first two, to be "a fable of redemption or rebirth." But *A New Life* is more than that. Written during Malamud's years on the faculty at Oregon State University, it is also a roman à clef based upon his experiences there, as Richard Astro explains in "In the Heart of the Valley: Bernard Malamud's *A New Life*" (1975). Beyond its lampoon of academia, Max F. Schulz argues, it presents "a microcosm of the American psyche midway through the twentieth century." In "Malamud's *A New Life:* The Wasteland of the Fifties" (1969), Schulz outlines the novel's creation of "an effective objective correlative for the fear of involvement, the desire for security, the hesitancy and do-nothing attitude" of the decade. And finally, as Paul Witherington shows, its roots in American literature include the works of Thoreau, Hawthorne, Melville, and Twain. In "Malamud's Allusive Design in *A New Life*" (1975), Witherington contends that these sources help to "establish Seymore Levin's basic transcendental ideal."

Probably the most intriguing critical question is where *A New Life* fits, generically, in the American literary tradition. On the one hand, as Sam B. Girgus writes in "In Search of the Real America: Bernard Malamud" (1984), it is an attack upon a complacent culture; thus, Girgus concludes that the novel is "an American jeremiad." On the other hand, Levin's ambiguous recognition that the ennobling West resembles the "corruptive" East leads John A. Barsness to call

A New Life "a new breed of Western novel." According to Barsness, in "*A New Life:* The Frontier Myth in Perspective" (1969), the novel transcends the usual boundaries of the Western genre because it opts for "actuality instead of image." For David J. Burrows, Levin is the archetypal "new man"—in Santayana's terms, "moral, impatient, and enthusiastic." In "The American Past in Malamud's *A New Life*" (1969), he argues for Levin's "pragmatic originality," which places the book "in the tradition of the tragic-comic experiential novels" that began with *Adventures of Huckleberry Finn.* Leslie Fiedler's "Malamud's Travesty Western" (1977) may well be the most thoughtful treatment of the issue. For Fiedler, the Western genre has at its core the archetypal myth of two males in the wilderness, sharing an idyllic love and threatened by the civilizing values of law and order. But in *A New Life,* the schoolmarmish Levin is at once an escapee from those restrictions and, as teacher, an expositor of them; thus, says Fiedler, while *A New Life* begins as a "neo- or meta-Western," it becomes "an anti-Western disguised as a meta-Western . . . a tale about failed Westering." As Fiedler's terminology suggests, the knotty question of genre in *A New Life* is not one easily untied.

Malamud's fourth novel, *The Fixer,* seemed to answer in part Philip Roth's criticism in "Writing American Fiction" (1961) that Malamud lacked "a proper or sufficient backdrop for his tales of heartlessness and heartache, of suffering and regeneration." Based loosely on the turn-of-the-century case of Mendel Beiliss in Czarist Russia, *The Fixer* won both the Pulitzer Prize and the National Book Award. In a representative review, "Malamud's Heroes" (1966), Jonathan Baumbach calls it "a brave book" which, like the earlier novels, is about "the possibilities of heroism—heroism as the fulfillment of one's deepest calling." Marc Ratner also examines the heroic qualities of the protagonist, Yakov Bok. In "The Humanism of Malamud's *The Fixer*" (1967), a sensitive critical appreciation of the novel, Ratner claims that Bok "moves from being 'fixed' by circumstances and events to being the 'fixer.' He begins with the rock of atheism pain, and ends by affirming his faith in an act of moral engagement."

Not all critics agree that Bok is a hero for our time, however. Malamud's story is "not powerful, merely repelling," argues Charles T. Samuels in "*The Fixer*" (1972), and "the plot defeats the theme in the most fundamental way." Samuels laments that Malamud has traded artistry for "a soapbox in the public arena." A more extended, and more thought-provoking, examination of the novel is John F. Desmond's "Malamud's Fixer: Jew, Christian, or Modern?" (1975).

To Desmond, the novel is flawed by the inconsistent development of Bok's moral sense: his dream vision, in which he murders the Czar, represents a regression and "a radical narrowing of the concept of freedom upon which the novel is based." This problem is especially vexing since Bok is paralleled to Christ. If Christic analogies are used, Desmond argues, they must be of a "*whole* Christ, and not a diluted 'Christ figure'" made to conform to modern man's existential crisis of belief.

Criticism of *Pictures of Fidelman*, Malamud's fifth novel, begins with the question of whether it is indeed a novel, since the six episodes in the life of Arthur Fidelman comprise more an "exhibition" than a coherent narrative. Fidelman's artistic and sexual misadventures in Italy constitute a bildungsroman, says Leslie Field in "Portrait of the Artist as *Schlemiel*" (1975); Field's essay, an admirable survey of the criticism on Malamud's schlemiel figures in general, ends with the tentative conclusion that this latest anti-hero "*may* gain salvation in the end." Robert Scholes, in "Portrait of Artist as 'Escape-Goat'" (1969), finds a different thematic link among the episodes. Like other of Malamud's novels, *Pictures of Fidelman* is about the possibility of regeneration. In each of the six episodes, Scholes argues, Fidelman is "frozen in some crucial posture, on his way to an esthetic Calvary"; for the protagonist, salvation comes at last from giving love rather than taking it. Similarly, Martin Tucker contends in "*Pictures of Fidelman*" (1969) that the coherence in the novel rests in the theme of loss and gain; in five of the six episodes, Fidelman must sacrifice something in order to achieve truth or insight. For Walter Sullivan the linking motif is sex and grotesquery, "the easy way out" for Malamud. In "'Where Have All the Flowers Gone?' Part II" (1970), Sullivan finds *Pictures of Fidelman* a "morass of vulgarity" symptomatic of a trend toward the aberrant in contemporary novels.

Robert Ducharme approaches the question of coherence head-on in his valuable explication, "Structure and Content in Malamud's *Pictures of Fidelman*" (1971). Ducharme contends that the six seemingly fragmented episodes are linked not only chronologically but thematically as well. In fact, he sees in the novel "a retrenchment to earlier interests and materials," the familiar Malamudian concerns of suffering and responsibility. Like the heroes of the earlier novels, Fidelman "sorely needs to learn the importance of selflessness," and his adventures are linked by recurring tests of his ability to give of himself and to accept others on moral terms; for Ducharme, Fidelman's bisexuality signals his triumph, for it is evidence of his ability to love others, men and women alike. Through a series of contacts with alter-egos, Ducharme argues, Fidelman undergoes spiritual rebirth. In a less charitable view of these encounters, Barbara F. Lefcowitz sees the linking motif of *Pictures of Fidelman* as the confrontation of a neurotic artist with the public world which tries in vain to shake Fidelman's illusions of artistic superiority. Unlike Ducharme, Lefcowitz in "The *Hybris* of Neurosis: Malamud's *Pictures of Fidelman*" (1970) views Fidelman as both a failed artist and a study in frustrated maturity.

If *Pictures of Fidelman* represented a departure in form, *The Tenants* represented an apparent about-face in theme. As Cynthia Ozick points out in "Literary Blacks and Jews" (1972), Malamud's dark tale of two struggling writers in New York, one black, the other white, signals a shift from "magical brotherhood" in the earlier works to the violent ax-murder in one of the three endings of *The Tenants*. Seen in light of Malamud's entire canon, the novel reflects a necessary "politicization" of his fiction; to Ozick, *The Tenants* is a "claustrophobic fable" that shows racial cooperation (such as that in "The Angel Levine" of *The Magic Barrel*) to be merely illusion. John A. Allen reaches much the same conclusion in "The Promised End: Bernard Malamud's *The Tenants*" (1971), citing the "symbiotic victimization" between races. Compared to Malamud's earlier work, Allen argues, *The Tenants* presents "a vision of evil triumphant, the failure of charity and mercy."

While most readers might agree with Gerald Hoag, who in "Malamud's *The Tenants:* Revolution Arrested" (1976) concludes that *The Tenants* ends "in an unresolved state of tension and stasis," it seems excessive to assign to the white protagonist, Harry Lesser, the stature that Hoag gives him—a "revolutionary hero" fighting for "reintegration with the whole society and the redemption, rebirth, and continuity of his fellows." Nor is it very helpful to read the novel as a sociological artifact, as John M. Cuddihy does in "Jews, Blacks, and the Cold War on Top" (1972). Cuddihy points out that the novel is rooted in two aspects of black-Jewish conflict, social control and cultural status; to Cuddihy, the ambiguous ending still leaves the white Jew triumphant, since even as they hack each other Lesser is both a thinking and a feeling man, while the black writer Willie Spearmint simply *feels*. Steven G. Kellman's dispassionate "*The Tenants* in the House of Fiction" (1976) reminds us that the novel, for all of its violence, also probes "the nature of literature . . . and the social conditions from which it arises." While its message may remain "open-ended," Kellman notes, it is, after all, art, not polemic: "*The Tenants*, faced with composing the unresolved tensions of contemporary society and with fixing the novel's relationship to life, does neither, memorably."

Dubin's Lives, again the story of a writer (this time a biographer of D. H. Lawrence) struggling to create both life and art, has been called Malamud's "most ambitious and richest novel" by Saul Maloff in "Loveliest Breakdown in Contemporary Fiction: Malamud's Lives" (1979). Like the earlier novels, Maloff contends, this one has as its subject "the work of composing enduring lives stroke by stroke against the heaviest odds." In a more extended look at the novel, "Malamud's Dubin and the Morality of Desire" (1982), Rita K. Gollin also connects it to earlier works like *The Assistant* and *A New Life.* Gollin traces in Malamud's fiction two distinct "modes" of desire: the physical (lust) and the spiritual (romantic yearning). Both, she contends, can be positive if they result in "an assumption of moral responsibility for the *other.*" In *Dubin's Lives* physical passion is finally "put in its place," Gollin argues, when Dubin bases it upon a "principled acceptance of commitments." If Gollin's distinctions seem commonplace, they at least remind us that in Malamud's fictional world eros has redemptive possibilities of its own—a useful corrective to those who accuse Malamud of being too ethereal, on the one hand, or too coarse, on the other.

Arguably Malamud's most controversial book, *God's Grace,* his eighth novel, is perhaps the most puzzling as well, for it has received little critical attention beyond reviews. A post-holocaust fantasy peopled by the last living human and an assortment of talking apes, *God's Grace* is, as John Updike notes in "Cohn's Doom" (1982), "less primatological than eschatological," an allegory of man's relationship to God and to history. But, Updike writes, the allegory is confused, and in the context of global annihilation Calvin Cohn's Jewishness seems irrelevant. Robert Alter admires the comedy and Malamud's deft modulation of tone, but he too finds the novel puzzling; Malamud's theological argument, he charges in "A Theological Fantasy: *God's Grace* by Bernard Malamud" (1982), is "schematic, sketchy, lacking weight of experience and density of intellectual texture." Helen Benedict's review-essay, "Bernard Malamud: Morals and Surprises" (1983), is enlivened by excerpts from a telephone interview with Malamud, who discusses the writer's role in a world of nuclear peril: "I feel it is the writer's business to cry havoc, because silence can't increase understanding or evoke mercy." In a sense, Malamud believes, *God's Grace* poses a simple question: "Why does man treat himself so badly?"

Critical articles and chapters on Malamud's short stories are surprisingly rare, especially when one considers that in some quarters he is known primarily as a writer of short fiction. Among the better explications of individual stories are Beth and Paul W. Burch's, "Myth on Myth: Bernard Malamud's 'The Talking Horse' " (1979), an examination of the fusion of Greek myth and Judaic theology in the characters of Goldberg and Abramowitz; Michael L. Storey's "Pinye Salzman, Pan, and 'The Magic Barrel' " (1981), which attempts to account for Salzman's character by showing his parallels to Pan, the mythic goat-god; and David R. Mesher's "The Remembrance of Things Unknown: Malamud's 'The Last Mohican' " (1975), an argument against the view that Susskind is a parasite. (Mesher shows him instead to be a tutor through whom Fidelman progresses from alienation to reconciliation.) Throughout his *Jews and Americans* (1965), Irving Malin explicates many of the stories from *The Magic Barrel* and *Idiots First*; Malin's individual readings are consistently smart and illuminating, though his conclusion that in the short fiction Malamud "affirms the polarities of head and heart" tells the reader very little. A model for the sort of comprehensive treatment that the short stories deserve is Irving Saposnik's "Insistent Assistance: The Stories of Bernard Malamud" (1978). Contrasting the earlier stories to those in *Rembrandt's Hat,* Saposnik claims that "a reading of [Malamud's] recent stories suggests that the ability to provide assistance has been threatened by social reality." While some readers may find Saposnik's interpretation of Malamud's early optimism an oversimplification, his explications of later stories such as "Man in the Drawer" are sound and sensitive.

The need for sustained attention to Malamud's short stories suggests at least one direction that future scholarship may take. We also need solid examinations of his flexible style, of his melding of history and fiction (in *The Natural* and *The Fixer,* for example), and of his process of revision—which will have to await the release of his manuscripts and working drafts. And finally, as Ihab Hassan notes in a dense but suggestive essay, "Bernard Malamud: 1976. Fictions Within Our Fictions" (1977), we need more attempts to place his work within the postmodernist tradition. To the question "How much does Malamud offer us at his best?" Hassan advances several "discomforts" about Malamud's theme of art, his Jewishness, and the relevance of his moral vision. These are, of course, among the very concerns that animated Malamud's earliest critics, and they promise to provoke his future ones as well.

Carson McCullers

(1917-1967)

Virginia Spencer Carr
Georgia State University

PRIMARY BIBLIOGRAPHY

Books

The Heart Is a Lonely Hunter. Boston: Houghton Mifflin, 1940; London: Cresset, 1943. Novel.

Reflections in a Golden Eye. Boston: Houghton Mifflin, 1941; London: Cresset, 1942. Novel.

The Member of the Wedding. Boston: Houghton Mifflin, 1946; London: Cresset, 1947. Novel.

The Member of the Wedding. New York: New Directions, 1951. Play.

The Ballad of the Sad Café: The Novels and Stories of Carson McCullers. Boston: Houghton Mifflin, 1951. Contains *The Ballad of the Sad Café* (novella), "Wunderkind," "The Jockey," "Madame Zilensky and the King of Finland," "The Sojourner," "A Domestic Dilemma" (published for first time), "A Tree. A Rock. A Cloud," *The Heart Is a Lonely Hunter, Reflections in a Golden Eye, The Member of the Wedding.* London: Cresset, 1952 (as *The Shorter Novels and Stories of Carson McCullers*); *The Heart Is a Lonely Hunter* omitted.

The Square Root of Wonderful. Boston: Houghton Mifflin, 1958; London: Cresset, 1958. Play.

Collected Short Stories and the Novel The Ballad of the Sad Café. Boston: Houghton Mifflin, 1961. "The Haunted Boy" added to this edition (later retitled *The Ballad of the Sad Café and Collected Short Stories*).

Clock Without Hands. Boston: Houghton Mifflin, 1961; London: Cresset, 1961. Novel.

As Sweet as a Pickle and Clean as a Pig. Illustrated by Rolf Gerard. Boston: Houghton Mifflin, 1964; London: Cape, 1965. Children's poems.

293

The Mortgaged Heart, ed. Margarita G. Smith. Boston: Houghton Mifflin, 1971; London: Barrie & Jenkins, 1972. Posthumous collection of short pieces (fiction and nonfiction, some published for first time). Introduction by McCullers's sister (Margarita G. Smith).

Recordings

"The Twisted Trinity." Philadelphia: Elkan-Vogel, 1946. Poem set to music by David Diamond (sheet music for piano).

"Carson McCullers Reads from *The Member of the Wedding* and Other Works," ed. Jean Stein vanden Heuvel. 1958. M-G-M 12 " long-play recording (E3619 ARC).

Short Fiction

"Wunderkind," *Story,* 9 (Dec. 1936), 61-73. Collected in *The Mortgaged Heart.*

"Reflections in a Golden Eye," *Harper's Bazaar,* 74 [first installment] (Oct. 1940), 60-61, 131-143; [second installment] (Nov. 1940), 56, 120-139.

"The Jockey," *New Yorker,* 17 (23 Aug. 1941), 15-16.

"Madame Zilensky and the King of Finland," *New Yorker,* 17 (20 Dec. 1941), 15-18.

"Correspondence," *New Yorker,* 17 (7 Feb. 1942), 36-39. Collected in *The Mortgaged Heart.*

"A Tree. A Rock. A Cloud," *Harper's Bazaar,* 76 (Nov. 1942), 50, 96-99.

"The Ballad of the Sad Café," *Harper's Bazaar,* 77 (Aug. 1943), 72-75, 140-161.

"The Member of the Wedding" (Part I), *Harper's Bazaar,* 80 (Jan. 1946), 94-96, 101, 128-138, 144-148.

"Art and Mr. Mahoney," *Mademoiselle,* 28 (Feb. 1949), 120, 184-186. Collected in *The Mortgaged Heart.*

"The Sojourner," *Mademoiselle,* 31 (May 1950), 90, 160-166.

"A Domestic Dilemma," *New York Post Magazine,* 16 Sept. 1951, pp. M10-M11.

"The Pestle," *Botteghe Oscure,* 11 (1953), 226-246; also *Mademoiselle,* 37 (July 1953), 44-45, 114-118 (part of *Clock Without Hands*).

"The Haunted Boy," *Botteghe Oscure,* 16 (1955), 264-278; also *Made-*

moiselle, 42 (Nov. 1955), 134-135, 152-159. Collected in *The Mort-gaged Heart*.

"Who Has Seen the Wind?," *Mademoiselle*, 43 (Sept. 1956), 156-157, 174-188. Collected in *The Mortgaged Heart*.

"Mick," *Literary Cavalcade*, 10 (Feb. 1957), 16-22, 32.

"To Bear the Truth Alone," *Harper's Bazaar*, 94 (July 1961), 42-43, 93-99 (part of *Clock Without Hands*).

"Sucker," *Saturday Evening Post*, 236 (28 Sept. 1963), 69-71. Collected in *The Mortgaged Heart*.

"The March," *Redbook*, 128 (Mar. 1967), 69, 114-123.

"Breath from the Sky," *Redbook*, 137 (Oct. 1971), 92, 228, 230, 233. Collected in *The Mortgaged Heart*.

"Instant of the Hour After," *Redbook*, 137 (Oct. 1971), 93, 194, 196. Collected in *The Mortgaged Heart*.

"Like That," *Redbook*, 137 (Oct. 1971), 91, 166-170. Collected in *The Mortgaged Heart*.

Articles

"Highway Brings Women of West South Georgia More Closely To-gether," *Columbus* (Ga.) *Ledger-Enquirer*, 21 July 1935, p. 7. Signed "Carson Smith."

"Little Girls at Juniper Lake Write Letters on Experiences During Fresh Air Camp Outing," *Columbus* (Ga.) *Ledger-Enquirer*, 28 July 1935, p. 12. Signed "Carson Smith."

"Look Home, Americans," *Vogue*, 96 (1 Dec. 1940), 74-75. Collected in *The Mortgaged Heart*.

"Night Watch Over Freedom," *Vogue*, 97 (1 Jan. 1941), 29. Collected in *The Mortgaged Heart*.

"The Devil's Idler," *Saturday Review*, 23 (15 Mar. 1941), 15. Review of *Commend the Devil* by Howard Coxe.

"Brooklyn Is My Neighborhood," *Vogue*, 47 (Mar. 1941), 62-63, 138. Collected in *The Mortgaged Heart*.

"Books I Remember," *Harper's Bazaar*, 75 (Apr. 1941), 82, 122, 125.

"Love's Not Time's Fool" (signed by "A War Wife"), *Mademoiselle*, 16 (Apr. 1943), 95, 166-168.

"Isak Dinesen: *Winter's Tales*," *New Republic*, 108 (7 June 1943), 768-769. Book review. Collected in *The Mortgaged Heart*.

"Our Heads Are Bowed," *Mademoiselle*, 22 (Nov. 1945), 131, 229. Collected in *The Mortgaged Heart*.

[Letter to the Editor], *Columbus* (Ga.) *Ledger-Enquirer*, 28 Feb. 1948.

Protests the restriction preventing blacks from using the Columbus Public Library.

"How I Began to Write," *Mademoiselle*, 27 (Sept. 1948), 256-257. Collected in *The Mortgaged Heart*.

"Loneliness . . . An American Malady," *This Week Magazine, New York Herald Tribune*, 19 Dec. 1949, pp. 18-19. Collected in *The Mortgaged Heart*.

"Home for Christmas," *Mademoiselle*, 30 (Dec. 1949), 53, 129-132. Collected in *The Mortgaged Heart*.

"The Discovery of Christmas," *Mademoiselle*, 38 (Dec. 1953), 54-55, 118-120. Collected in *The Mortgaged Heart*.

"The Flowering Dream: Notes on Writing," *Esquire*, 52 (Dec. 1959), 162-164. Collected in *The Mortgaged Heart*.

"Author's Note," *New York Times Book Review*, 11 June 1961, p. 4. Discusses *Clock Without Hands*.

"A Child's View of Christmas," *Redbook*, 68 (Dec. 1961), 31-34, 99-100.

"The Dark Brilliance of Edward Albee," *Harper's Bazaar*, 47 (Jan. 1963), 98-99.

"Isak Dinesen: In Praise of Radiance," *Saturday Review*, 46 (Mar. 1963), 29, 83. Collected in *The Mortgaged Heart*.

"A Note from the Author," *Saturday Evening Post*, 236 (28 Sept. 1963), 69.

"A Hospital Christmas Eve," *McCall's*, 45 (Dec. 1967), 96-97. Collected in *The Mortgaged Heart*.

Poetry

"The Twisted Trinity," *Decision*, 2 (Nov.-Dec. 1941), 30.

"The Mortgaged Heart," *New Directions*, 10 (1948), 509; also *Voices*, 149 (Sept.-Dec. 1952), 11-12. Collected in *The Mortgaged Heart*.

"When We Are Lost," *New Directions*, 10 (1948), 509; also *Voices*, 149 (Sept.-Dec. 1952), 12. Collected in *The Mortgaged Heart*.

"The Dual Angel: A Meditation on Origin and Choice," *Botteghe Oscure*, 9 (1952), 213-218; also *Mademoiselle*, 35 (July 1952), 54-55, 108. Poems: "Incantation to Lucifer," "Hymen, O Hymen," "Love and the Rind of Time," "The Dual Angel," "Father, Upon Thy Image We Are Spanned." Collected in *The Mortgaged Heart*.

"Stone Is Not Stone," *Mademoiselle*, 45 (July 1957), 43. Collected in *The Mortgaged Heart*.

"Sweet as a Pickle and Clean as a Pig," *Redbook,* 124 (Dec. 1964), 49-56.

SECONDARY BIBLIOGRAPHY

Bibliographies and Checklists

Bixby, George. "Carson McCullers: A Bibliographical Checklist," *American Book Collector,* 5 (Jan.-Feb. 1984), 38-43; New York: Moretus Press, 1985. Booklet reprint. Primary.

Carr, Virginia Spencer. "Carson McCullers." In *Fifty Southern Writers After 1900,* ed. Robert Bain and Joseph M. Flora. Westport, Conn.: Greenwood, 1986. Primary & secondary.

Carr, and Joseph R. Millichap. "Carson McCullers." In *American Women Writers: Fifteen Bibliographical Essays,* ed. Maurice Duke, Jackson R. Bryer, and M. Thomas Inge. Westport, Conn.: Greenwood, 1981, 297-319. Primary & secondary.

Dorsey, James E. "Carson McCullers and Flannery O'Connor: A Checklist of Graduate Research," *Bulletin of Bibliography,* 32 (Oct.-Dec. 1975), 162-164. Secondary.

Kiernan, Robert F. *Katherine Anne Porter and Carson McCullers: A Reference Guide.* Boston: G. K. Hall, 1976, 95-169, 185-194. Secondary.

Phillips, Robert S. "Carson McCullers, 1956-64: A Selected Checklist," *Bulletin of Bibliography,* 24 (Sept.-Dec. 1964), 113-116. Primary & secondary.

Shapiro, Adrian M., Jackson R. Bryer, and Kathleen Field. *Carson McCullers: A Descriptive Listing and Annotated Bibliography of Criticism.* New York: Garland, 1980. Primary & secondary.

Stanley, William T. "Carson McCullers: 1965-1969, A Selected Checklist," *Bulletin of Bibliography,* 27 (Oct.-Dec. 1970), 91-93. Primary & secondary.

Stewart, Stanley. "Carson McCullers, 1940-1956: A Selected Checklist," *Bulletin of Bibliography,* 22 (Jan.-Apr. 1959), 182-185. Primary & secondary.

Interviews

Balakian, Nona. "Carson McCullers Completes New Novel Despite Adversity," *New York Times,* 3 Sept. 1961, p. 46.

Breit, Harvey. "Behind the Wedding—Carson McCullers Discusses the Novel She Converted into a Stage Play," *New York Times,* 1 Jan. 1950, II: 3.

"Call on the Author," *Newseek,* 18 Sept. 1961, p. 106.

Doar, Harriet. " 'Love . . . Is at the Heart'—Battling Ill Health, Carson McCullers Writes On," *Charlotte Observer,* 5 May 1963, p. 10C.

Gordy, Mary. *"Ledger* Reporter Finds Former Columbus Girl, Now Celebrated Author, Unspoiled by Fame," *Columbus* (Ga.) *Ledger,* 16 Dec. 1940, p. 7.

"An Interview with Carson McCullers," *Literary Cavalcade,* 9 (Feb. 1957), 15.

Kelly, Frank K. " 'Lonely' Miss McCullers Coming Home to Write," *Atlanta Journal,* 16 Nov. 1941, p. 13A.

Lee, Harry. "Columbus Girl Thinks South Is 'Sick'—Carson McCullers Wrote 'The Heart Is A Lonely Hunter,' " *Atlanta Constitution,* 6 Mar. 1941, p. 4.

MacDougall, Sally. "Author, 22, Urges Aid to Refugees," *New York World-Telegram,* 1 July 1940, p. 12.

"The *Marquis* Interviews Carson McCullers," *Marquis* (Lafayette College) (1964), 5-6, 20-23.

Morehouse, Ward. "Broadway After Dark—Carson McCullers Cuts Her Own Hair," *New York World-Telegram and the Sun,* 31 Mar. 1950, p. 36.

Morgan, Nonie. "Carson McCullers, Distinguished Novelist, and Her Mother Visiting Here," *Macon* (Ga.) *News,* 18 Mar. 1949, p. 11.

Patterson, Isabel M. "Turns With a Bookworm," *New York Herald Book Review,* 23 June 1940, p. 11.

Pollock, Arthur. "Theater Time—Carson McCullers Talks About Self and First Play," *New York Daily Compass,* 7 Oct. 1949, p. 18.

Post, Constance. "Three Essentials Cited for Aspiring Novelists by Carson McCullers," *Nyack* (N.Y.) *Journal News,* 13 Aug. 1963, p. 6.

Reed, Rex. " 'Frankie Addams' at 50," *New York Times,* 16 Apr. 1967, II:15.

Rice, Vernon. "A Little Southern Girl Speaks from a Well of Despair," *New York Post,* 29 Jan. 1950, p. 8M.

Sibley, Celestine. "Novelist McCullers Returns for Data on Georgia Story," *Atlanta Constitution,* 12 Dec. 1953.

Watson, Latimer. "Carson McCullers Gets Guggenheim Fellowship," *Columbus* (Ga.) *Enquirer,* 6 Apr. 1942, pp. 1, 3.

"We Hitch Our Wagons," *Mademoiselle,* 33 (Aug. 1951), 248-249.

Weatherby, W. J. "Uh-Huh, Uh-Huh," *Manchester Guardian Weekly,* 29 Sept. 1960, p. 14.

White, Terence de Vere. "With Carson McCullers: Terence de Vere White Interviews the American Novelist at the Home of Her Host, John Huston," *Irish Times* (Dublin), 10 Apr. 1967, p. 12.

Biographies

Carr, Virginia Spencer. *The Lonely Hunter: A Biography of Carson McCullers.* Garden City: Doubleday, 1975; London: Peter Owen, 1976.

Evans, Oliver. *Carson McCullers: Her Life and Work.* London: Peter Owen, 1965. Republished as *The Ballad of Carson McCullers.* New York: Coward-McCann, 1966.

Critical Studies: Books

Cook, Richard. *Carson McCullers.* New York: Ungar, 1975.

Edmonds, Dale. *Carson McCullers.* Austin: Steck-Vaughn, 1969.

Graver, Lawrence. *Carson McCullers.* St. Paul: University of Minnesota Press, 1969.

McDowell, Margaret B. *Carson McCullers.* New York: Twayne, 1980.

Wikborg, Eleanor. *The Member of the Wedding: Aspects of Structure and Style.* Gothenburg Studies in English, 31. Göteborg, Sweden: Acta, Univeritatus Gothoburgensis, 1975; Atlantic Highlands, N.J.: Humanities Press, 1975. Paperback reprint.

Critical Studies: Articles and Book Sections

Albee, Edward. "Carson McCullers—The Case of the Curious Magician," *Harper's Bazaar,* 96 (Jan. 1963), 98.

Allen, Walter. *The Modern Novel in Britain and the United States.* New York: Dutton, 1964, 132-137.

Auchincloss, Louis. "Carson McCullers." In his *Pioneers and Caretakers—A Study of 9 American Women Novelists.* Minneapolis: University of Minnesota Press, 1965, 161-169.

Baldanza, Frank. "Plato in Dixie," *Georgia Review*, 12 (Summer 1958), 151-167.

Beja, Morris. "It Must Be Important: Negroes in Contemporary American Fiction," *Antioch Review*, 24 (Fall 1964), 323-336.

Bluefarb, Samuel. "Jake Blount: Escape as Dead End." In his *The Escape Motif in the American Novel: Mark Twain to Richard Wright*. Columbus: Ohio State University Press, 1972, 114-132.

Bolsterli, Margaret. " 'Bound' Characters in Porter, Welty, McCullers: The Prerevolutionary Status of Women in American Fiction," *Bucknell Review*, 24 (Spring 1978), 95, 103-105.

Box, Patricia S. "Androgyny and the Musical Vision: A Study of Two Novels by Carson McCullers," *Southern Quarterly*, 16 (Jan. 1978), 117-123.

Bradbury, John M. *Renaissance in the South—A Critical History of the Literature, 1920-1960*. Chapel Hill: University of North Carolina Press, 1963, 16, 107, 110-112, 129, 142, 189, 196-197.

Broughton, Panthea Reid. "Rejection of the Feminine in Carson McCullers' *The Ballad of the Sad Café*," *Twentieth Century Literature*, 20 (Jan. 1974), 34-43.

Buchen, Irving H. "Carson McCullers: A Case of Convergence," *Bucknell Review*, 21 (Spring 1973), 15-28.

_____. "Divine Collusion: The Art of Carson McCullers," *Dalhousie Review*, 54 (Autumn 1974), 529-541.

Carpenter, Frederic I. "The Adolescent in American Fiction," *English Journal*, 46 (Sept. 1957), 316-317.

Carr, Virginia Spencer. "Carson McCullers." In *Southern Writers: A Biographical Dictionary*, ed. Robert Blain, Joseph M. Flora, and Louis D. Rubin, Jr. Baton Rouge: Louisiana State University Press, 1979, 290-293.

_____. "Carson McCullers: *The Mortgaged Heart*, ed. Margarita G. Smith," *Choice* (Mar. 1972), 61.

_____. "Carson McCullers and *The Heart Is a Lonely Hunter*: An Introduction." Pamphlet introduction to *The Heart Is a Lonely Hunter*. Southern Classics Library Edition. Birmingham: Oxmoor, 1984, 4-21.

Clark, Charlene. "Male-Female Pairs in Carson McCullers' *The Ballad of the Sad Café* and *The Member of the Wedding*," *Notes on Contemporary Literature*, 11 (Sept. 1979), 11-12.

_____. "Pathos with a Chuckle: The Tragicomic Vision in the Novels of Carson McCullers," *Studies in American Humor*, 1 (Jan. 1975), 161.

_____. "Selfhood and the Southern Past: A Reading of Carson McCullers' *Clock Without Hands*," *Southern Literary Messenger*, 1 (Spring 1975), 15-23.

Clurman, Harold. " 'Member of the Wedding' Upsets a Theory: Director Harold Clurman Says Its Success Calls for a New Definition of an Old Question—What Is a Play?," *New York Herald Tribune*, 29 Jan. 1950, V: 3. Reprinted in his *Lies Like Truth—Theatre Reviews and Essays*. New York: Macmillan, 1958, 62-64.

Cook, Sylvia Jenkins. *From Tobacco Road to Route 66—The Southern Poor White in Fiction*. Chapel Hill: University of North Carolina Press, 1976, 156-158.

Dedmond, Francis B. "Doing Her Own Thing: Carson McCullers' Dramatization of 'The Member of the Wedding,' " *South Atlantic Bulletin*, 40 (May 1975), 47-52.

Dodd, Wayne D. "The Development of Theme Through Symbol in the Novels of Carson McCullers," *Georgia Review*, 17 (Summer 1963), 206-213.

Drake, Robert. "The Lonely Heart of Carson McCullers," *Christian Century*, 85 (10 Jan. 1968), 50-51.

Durham, Frank. "God and No God in *The Heart Is A Lonely Hunter*," *South Atlantic Quarterly*, 56 (Autumn 1957), 494-499.

Dusenburg, Winifred L. "An Unhappy Family." In her *The Theme of Loneliness in Modern American Drama*. Gainesville: University of Florida Press, 1960, 57-85.

Edmonds, Dale. " 'Correspondence': A 'Forgotten' Carson McCullers Short Story," *Studies in Short Fiction*, 9 (Winter 1972), 89-92.

Eisinger, Chester E. "The New Fiction—Carson McCullers and the Failure of Dialogue." In his *Fiction of the Forties*. Chicago: University of Chicago Press, 1963, 243-258. See also pp. 16, 236-237, 259, 283, 380.

Emerson, Donald. "The Ambiguities of *Clock Without Hands*," *Wisconsin Studies in Contemporary Literature*, 3 (Fall 1962), 15-28.

Evans, Oliver. "The Achievement of Carson McCullers," *English Journal*, 51 (May 1962), 301-308.

_____. "The Case of Carson McCullers," *Georgia Review*, 18 (Spring 1964), 40-45.

_____. "The Case of the Silent Singer: A Revaluation of *The Heart Is a Lonely Hunter*," *Georgia Review*, 19 (Summer 1965), 188-203.

_____. "The Theme of Spiritual Isolation in Carson McCullers," *New World Writing*, 1 (Apr. 1952), 297-310.

Felheim, Marvin. "Eudora Welty and Carson McCullers." In *Contemporary American Novelists,* ed. Harry T. Moore. Carbondale: Southern Illinois University Press, 1964, 48-53.

Fiedler, Leslie. *An End to Innocence—Essays on Culture and Politics.* Boston: Beacon, 1952, 149, 202-203.

_____. *Love and Death in the American Novel.* New York: Criterion Books, 1960, 126, 325, 449-451, 453.

Fletcher, Mary Dell. "Carson McCullers' 'Ancient Mariner,'" *South Central Bulletin,* 35 (Winter 1975), 123-125.

Folk, Barbara Nauer. "The Sad Sweet Music of Carson McCullers," *Georgia Review,* 16 (Summer 1962), 202-209.

Ford, Nick Aaron. "Search for Identity: A Critical Survey of Significant Belles-Lettres By and About Negroes Published in 1961," *Phylon,* 23 (Second Quarter 1962), 130-133.

Friedman, Melvin J. *"The Mortgaged Heart:* The Workshop of Carson McCullers," *Revue des Langues Vivantes,* 42 (U. S. Bicentennial Issue, 1976), 143-155.

Gaillard, Dawson F. "The Presence of the Narrator in Carson McCullers' *Ballad of the Sad Café," Mississippi Quarterly,* 25 (Fall 1972), 419-428.

Gannon, B. C. *"The Ballad of the Sad Café," Explicator,* 41 (Fall 1982), 59-60.

Giannetti, Louis D. *"The Member of the Wedding," Literature/Film Quarterly,* 4 (Winter 1976), 28-38.

Ginsberg, Elaine. "The Female Initiation Theme in American Fiction," *Studies in American Fiction,* 3 (Spring 1975), 34-35.

Gossett, Louise Y. "Dispossessed Love: Carson McCullers." In her *Violence in Recent Southern Fiction.* Durham: Duke University Press, 1965, 159-177.

Graver, Lawrence. "Carson McCullers." In *Seven American Women Writers of the Twentieth Century: An Introduction,* ed. Maureen Howard. Minneapolis: University of Minnesota Press, 1977, 265-307.

Gray, Richard J. "Moods and Absences: Carson McCullers." In his *The Literature of Memory—Modern Writers of the American South.* Baltimore: Johns Hopkins University Press, 1977, 265-273.

Griffith, Albert J. "Carson McCullers' Myth of the Sad Café," *Georgia Review,* 21 (Spring 1967), 46-56.

Grinnell, James W. "Delving 'A Domestic Dilemma,'" *Studies in Short Fiction,* 9 (Summer 1972), 270-271.

Hamilton, Alice. "Loneliness and Alienation: The Life and Work of

Carson McCullers," *Dalhousie Review,* 50 (Summer 1970), 215-229.

Hart, Jane. "Carson McCullers, Pilgrim of Loneliness," *Georgia Review,* 11 (Spring 1957), 53-58.

Hassan, Ihab. "Carson McCullers: The Alchemy of Love and Aesthetics of Pain," *Modern Fiction Studies,* 5 (Winter 1959-1960), 311-326. Reprinted in revised form in his *Radical Innocence: Studies in the Contemporary American Novel.* Princeton: Princeton University Press, 1961, 205-229.

_____. "The Character of Post-War Fiction in America," *English Journal,* 51 (Jan. 1962), 1-8. Reprinted in *On Contemporary Literature,* ed. Richard Kostelanetz. New York: Avon Books, 1964, 36-47. Also reprinted in *Recent American Fiction,* ed. Joseph J. Waldmeir. Boston: Houghton Mifflin, 1963, 27-35.

_____. *Contemporary American Literature—1945-1972: An Introduction.* New York: Ungar, 1973, 67-69.

_____. "The Idea of Adolescence in American Fiction," *Atlantic Quarterly,* 10 (Fall 1958), 312-313.

_____. "Laughter in the Dark—The New Voice in American Fiction," *American Scholar,* 33 (Autumn 1964), 636-640.

_____. "The Victim: Images of Evil in Recent American Fiction," *College English,* 21 (Dec. 1959), 140-146.

_____. "The Way Down and Out," *Virginia Quarterly Review,* 39 (Winter 1963), 81-93.

Hendrick, George. " 'Almost Everyone Wants to be the Lover': The Fiction of Carson McCullers," *Books Abroad,* 42 (Summer 1968), 389-391.

Hicks, Granville. "Books," *American Way,* 9 (Aug. 1975), 34-35.

_____. "The Subtler Corruptions," *Saturday Review,* 44 (23 Sept. 1961), 14-15, 49.

Hoffman, Frederick J. "Eudora Welty and Carson McCullers." In his *The Art of Southern Fiction—A Study of Some Modern Novelists.* Carbondale: Southern Illinois University Press, 1967, 51-71.

Huf, Linda. *A Portrait of the Artist as a Young Woman.* New York: Ungar, 1983, 11-12, 104-123, 128.

Johnson, James William. "The Adolescent Hero: A Trend in Modern Fiction," *Twentieth Century Literature,* 5 (Apr. 1959), 3-11.

Joost, Nicholas. " 'Was All For Naught?': Robert Penn Warren and New Directions in the Novel." In *Fifty Years of the American Novel—A Christian Appraisal,* ed. Harold C. Gardiner, S. J. New York: Scribners, 1951, 273-291.

Kahane, Claire. "Gothic Mirrors and Feminine Identity," *Centennial Review*, 24 (1980), 43-64.

Kazin, Alfred. "Heroines," *New York Review of Books*, 16 (11 Feb. 1971), 28-34. Reprinted in his *Bright Book of Life: American Novelists and Storytellers from Hemingway to Mailer*. Boston: Little, Brown, 1973, 51-54.

_____. "We Who Sit in Darkness—The Broadway Audience at the Play," *Commentary*, 9 (June 1950), 525-529.

Klein, Marcus. "The Key Is Loneliness," *Reporter*, 34 (30 June 1966), 43-44.

Knowles, A. S., Jr. "Six Bronze Petals and Two Red: Carson McCullers in the Forties." In *The Forties: Fiction, Poetry, Drama*, ed. Warren French. De Land, Fla.: Everett/Edwards, 1969, 85, 87-98.

Kohler, Dayton. "Carson McCullers: Variations on a Theme," *College English*, 13 (Oct. 1951), 1-8.

Korenman, Joan S. "Carson McCullers' 'Proletarian Novel,' " *Studies in the Humanities* (Indiana University of Pennsylvania), 5 (Jan. 1976), 8-13.

Lawson, Lewis A. "The Grotesque in Recent Southern Fiction." In *Patterns of Commitment in American Literature*, ed. Marston La France. Toronto: University of Toronto Press, 1967, 165-179.

_____. "Kierkegaard and the Modern Novel." In *Essays in Memory of Christina Burleson in Language and Literature by Former Colleagues and Students*, ed. Thomas G. Burton. Johnson City, Tenn.: Research Advisory Council, East Tennessee State University, 1969, 113-125.

Levidova, Inna. "Carson McCullers and Her Last Book." In *Soviet Criticism of American Literature in the Sixties*, ed. Carl R. Proffer. Ann Arbor: Ardis, 1972, 88-95. See also p. xxix. This review appeared originally in Russian in *New World*, no. 10 (1960).

Lubbers, Klaus. "The Necessary Order: A Study of Theme and Structure in Carson McCullers' Fiction," *Jahrbuch fur Americkastudien*, 8 (1963), 187-204.

MacDonald, Edgar E. "The Symbolic Unity of *The Heart Is a Lonely Hunter*." In *A Festschrift for Professor Marguerite Roberts, on the Occasion of Her Retirement from Westhampton College, University of Richmond, Virginia*, ed. Frieda Elaine Penninger. Richmond, Va.: University of Richmond, 1976, 168-187.

McNally, John. "The Introspective Narrator in 'The Ballad of the Sad Café,' " *South Atlantic Bulletin*, 38 (Nov. 1973), 40-44.

McPherson, Hugo. "Carson McCullers: Lonely Huntress," *Tamarack Review*, 11 (Spring 1959), 28-40.

Madden, David. "The Paradox of the Need for Privacy and the Need for Understanding in Carson McCullers' *The Heart Is a Lonely Hunter*," *Literature and Psychology*, 17, nos. 2-3 (1967), 128-140.

_____. "Transfixed Among the Self-Inflicted Ruins: Carson McCullers' *The Mortgaged Heart*," *Southern Literary Journal*, 5 (Fall 1972), 137-162.

Malin, Irving. "The Gothic Family." In *Psychoanalysis and American Fiction*, ed. Malin. New York: Dutton, 1965, 255-277.

_____. *New American Gothic.* Carbondale: Southern Illinois University Press, 1962, 14-15, 21-26, 54-57, 83-86, 111-117, 133-137.

Mathis, Ray. "*Reflections in a Golden Eye:* Myth Making in American Christianity," *Religion in Life*, 39 (Winter 1970), 545-558.

Meeker, Richard K. "The Youngest Generation of Southern Writers." In *Southern Writers—Appraisals in Our Time*, ed. R. C. Simonini, Jr. Charlottesville: University Press of Virginia, 1964, 162-191.

Millichap, Joseph R. "Carson McCullers' Literary Ballad," *Georgia Review*, 27 (Fall 1973), 329-339.

_____. "Distorted Matter and Disjunctive Forms: The Grotesque as Modernist Genre," *Arizona Quarterly*, 33 (Winter 1977), 339-347.

_____. "The Realistic Structure of *The Heart Is a Lonely Hunter*," *Twentieth Century Literature*, 17 (Jan. 1971), 11-17.

Missey, James. "A McCullers Influence on Albee's *The Zoo Story*," *American Notes & Queries*, 13 (Apr. 1975), 121-123.

Montgomery, Marion. "The Sense of Violation: Notes Toward a Definition of 'Southern' Fiction," *Georgia Review*, 19 (Fall 1965), 278-287.

Moore, Jack B. "Carson McCullers: The Heart Is a Timeless Hunter," *Twentieth Century Literature*, 11 (July 1965), 76-81.

Moore, Janice Townley. "McCullers' *The Ballad of the Sad Café*," *Explicator*, 29 (Nov. 1970), item 27.

O'Brien, Edna. "The Strange World of Carson McCullers," *Books and Bookmen*, 7 (Oct. 1961), 9, 24.

O'Connor, William Van. *The Grotesque: An American Genre and Other Essays.* Carbondale: Southern Illinois University Press, 1962, 6, 13, 21.

Paden, Frances Freeman. "Autistic Gestures in *The Heart Is a Lonely Hunter*," *Modern Fiction Studies*, 28 (Autumn 1982), 453-463.

Perrine, Laurence. "Restoring 'A Domestic Dilemma,' " *Studies in Short Fiction*, 11 (Winter 1974), 101-104.

Phillips, Louis. "The Novelist as Playwright: Baldwin, McCullers, and Bellow." In *Modern American Drama: Essays in Criticism*, ed. William E. Taylor. De Land, Fla.: Everett/Edwards, 1968, 145-162.

Phillips, Robert. "Freaking Out: The Short Stories of Carson McCullers," *Southwest Review*, 63 (Winter 1978), 65-73.

Phillips, Robert S. "Dinesen's 'Monkey' and McCullers' 'Ballad': A Study in Literary Affinity," *Studies in Short Fiction*, 1 (Spring 1964), 184-190.

_____. "The Gothic Architecture of *The Member of the Wedding*," *Renascence*, 16 (Winter 1964), 59-72.

_____. "Painful Love: Carson McCullers' Parable," *Southwest Review*, 51 (Winter 1966), 80-86.

Pollock-Chagas, Jeremy E. "Rosalina and Amelia: A Structural Approach to Narrative," *Luso-Brazilian Review*, 12 (Winter 1975), 263-272.

Presley, Delma Eugene. "Carson McCullers and the South," *Georgia Review*, 28 (Spring 1974), 19-32.

_____. "Carson McCullers' Descent to the Earth," *Descant* (Texas Christian University), 17 (Fall 1972), 54-60.

_____. "The Man Who Married Carson McCullers," *This Issue* (McKee Publishing Co., Atlanta), 2, no. 2 (1973), 13-16.

_____. "The Moral Function of Distortion in Southern Grotesque," *South Atlantic Bulletin*, 37 (May 1972).

Rechnitz, Robert M. "The Failure of Love: The Grotesque in Two Novels by Carson McCullers," *Georgia Review*, 22 (Winter 1968), 454-463.

Rich, Nancy B. "The 'Ironic Parable of Fascism' in *The Heart Is a Lonely Hunter*," *Southern Literary Journal*, 9 (Spring 1977), 108-123.

Roberts, Mary. "Imperfect Androgyny and Imperfect Love in the Works of Carson McCullers," *University of Hartford Studies in Literature*, 12 (1980), 73-98.

Robinson, W. R. "The Life of Carson McCullers' Imagination," *Southern Humanities Review*, 2 (Summer 1968), 291-302.

Rubin, Louis D., Jr. "Carson McCullers: The Aesthetic of Pain," *Virginia Quarterly Review*, 53 (Spring 1977), 265-283. Reprinted in his *A Gallery of Southerners*. Baton Rouge: Louisiana State University Press, 1982, 135-151.

_____. *The Faraway Country—Writers of the Modern South*. Seattle: University of Washington Press, 1966, 13, 195, 240.

Schorer, Mark. "McCullers and Capote: Basic Patterns." In *The Creative Present—Notes on Contemporary American Fiction,* ed. Nona Balakian and Charles Simmons. Garden City: Doubleday, 1963, 83-107. Reprinted in his *The World We Imagine: Selected Essays.* New York: Farrar, Straus & Giroux, 1968, 274-296.

Scott, Mary Etta. "An Existential Everyman," *West Virginia University Philosophical Papers* (1981), 82-88.

Sherrill, Rowland A. "McCullers' *The Heart Is a Lonely Hunter:* The Missing Ego and the Problem of the Norm," *Kentucky Review,* 2 (Feb. 1968), 5-17.

Smith, C. Michael. " 'A Voice in a Fugue': Characters and Musical Structure in Carson McCullers' *The Heart Is a Lonely Hunter,*" *Modern Fiction Studies,* 25 (Summer 1979), 258-263.

Smith, Margarita G. "Introduction." In McCullers, *The Mortgaged Heart,* ed., Smith. Boston: Houghton Mifflin, 1971, xi-xix. See also Smith's editor's notes, pp. 3-6, 205-206, 285.

Snider, Clifton. "On Death and Dying: Carson McCullers' *Clock Without Hands,*" *Markham Review,* 11 (1938), 43-46.

Symons, Julian. "Human Isolation," *Times Literary Supplement,* 17 July 1963, p. 460. Reprinted as "The Lonely Heart." In his *Critical Occasions.* London: Hamish Hamilton, 1966, 106-111.

Taylor, Horace. *"The Heart Is a Lonely Hunter:* A Southern Wasteland." In *Studies in American Literature,* ed. Waldo McNeir and Leo B. Levy. Louisiana State University Studies, Humanities Series, no 8. Baton Rouge: Louisiana State University Press, 1960, 154-160, 172-173.

Thorp, Williard. "Suggs and Sut in Modern Dress: The Latest Chapter in Southern Humor," *Mississippi Quarterly,* 13 (Fall 1960), 169-175.

Tinkham, Charles B. "The Members of the Side Show," *Phylon,* 18 (Fourth Quarter 1958), 383-390.

Torrens, James, S. J. "Whatever Will Be . . . Or Will It?," *Today,* 19 (May 1964), 25-28.

Vickery, John B. "Carson McCullers: A Map of Love," *Wisconsin Studies in Contemporary Literature,* 1 (Winter 1960), 13-24.

Vidal, Gore. "Ladders to Heaven: Novelists and Critics of the 1940s," *New World Writing,* 4 (1953), 303-316. Reprinted in his *Rocking the Boat: A Political, Literary and Theatrical Commentary.* Boston: Little, Brown, 1962, 125-146, 178-183.

Walker, Sue B. "The Link in the Chain Called Love: A New Look at

Carson McCullers' Novels," *Mark Twain Journal*, 18 (Winter 1976), 8-12.

Watkins, Floyd C. *The Death of Art: Black and White in the Recent Southern Novel*. Mercer University Lamar Memorial Lectures, No. 13. Athens: University of Georgia Press, 1970, 14, 21, 25, 29, 35, 44, 50, 52, 55-57, 63.

Weales, Gerald. *American Drama Since World War II*. New York: Harcourt, Brace & World, 1962, 175-179.

Westling, Louise. "Carson McCullers' Amazon Nightmare," *Modern Fiction Studies*, 28 (Autumn 1982), 465-473.

_____. "Carson McCullers' Tomboys," *Southern Humanities Review*, 14 (Fall 1980), 339-350.

_____. *Sacred Groves and Ravaged Gardens: The Fiction of Eudora Welty, Carson McCullers, and Flannery O'Connor*. Athens: University of Georgia Press, 1985.

Whittle, Amberys R. "McCullers' 'Twelve Mortal Men' and 'The Ballad of the Sad Café,' " *Answers and Queries* (1980), 14-15.

Williams, Tennessee. "The Author," *Saturday Review*, 44 (23 Sept. 1961), 14-15.

_____. "This Book." Introduction to McCullers's *Reflections in a Golden Eye*. New Classics Series. Norfolk, Conn.: New Directions, 1950, ix-xxi.

Witham, W. Tasker. *The Adolescent in the American Novel—1920-1960*. New York: Ungar, 1964, 16, 19, 25, 42, 59, 60, 61, 80, 98, 145-146, 169, 197, 265, 268, 270, 275.

Young, Marguerite. "Metaphysical Fiction," *Kenyon Review*, 9 (Winter 1947), 151-155.

BIBLIOGRAPHICAL ESSAY

Bibliographies and Checklists

Still the most thorough and helpful bibliography to date is *Carson McCullers: A Descriptive Listing and Annotated Bibliography of Criticism* by Adrian M. Shapiro, Jackson R. Bryer, and Kathleen Field (1980). An update of Shapiro's dissertation, "Carson McCullers: A Descriptive Bibliography" (Indiana University, 1977), Part I contains a chronological list and description of all of McCullers's books, plays, and separate publications, including all first printings of American and English editions, detailed descriptions of all subsequent printings and editions, a chronological list of McCullers's writings in magazines and newspapers (each entry designated according to genre), adaptations of McCullers's works, recordings by McCullers, and English language foreign editions of her works. (Shapiro's dissertation also lists foreign translations of her works.) Part II, compiled by Bryer and Field, is an annotated bibliography of writings about McCullers, published essays and periodical articles, reviews of McCullers's books and plays in performance, dissertations, foreign language material, and many local and regional newspaper and magazine pieces about McCullers and her work. The materials are categorized and arranged alphabetically by author's name.

The first annotated list of criticism and other writings about McCullers was *Katherine Anne Porter and Carson McCullers: A Reference Guide* by Robert F. Kiernan (1976). The spine of the book identifies it as *Carson McCullers and Katherine Anne Porter: A Reference Guide*, which may confuse readers since the Porter material is listed first. (A subsequent edition should correct the inconsistency.) Kiernan's checklist, comprehensive through 1973, is arranged chronologically, which allows the reader to survey easily the development of McCullers criticism. A five-page introduction summarizes the critical reception of each of McCullers's books upon publication, indicates the scope and thrust of most of the academic essays, and makes valid recommendations of the books and articles thought to contain the best critical assessments of McCullers's writings.

Kiernan's book updates and corrects earlier checklists published in the *Bulletin of Bibliography:* Stanley Stewart's "Carson McCullers, 1940-1956, A Selected Checklist" (1959), Robert S. Phillips's "Carson McCullers, 1956-1964" (1964), and William T. Stanley's "Carson McCullers: 1965-1969" (1970). Also helpful to graduate students, especially, is J. R. Dorsey's "Carson McCullers and Flannery O'Connor: A Checklist of Graduate Research" (1975), which provides a good comparative survey of the graduate writings about these authors.

A helpful recent bibliographical checklist was published by George Bixby in the *American Book Collector* (1984), but is more readily available as a Moretus Press booklet reprint (1985). It is designed primarily to help the book collector.

The most comprehensive bibliographical essay on McCullers to date is "Carson McCullers" by Virginia Spencer Carr and Joseph R. Millichap in *American Women Writers; Fifteen Bibliographical Essays* (1981). The five-part essay annotates the bibliographical materials, supplements the printing history of McCullers's books found in the Shapiro, Bryer, and Field bibliography, surveys the publishing history of foreign editions, and tells which short stories and nonfiction pieces have been anthologized most often. It describes the various collections of McCullers's manuscripts, letters, and other materials by or pertaining to McCullers housed in public repositories and reveals succinctly where most of the materials lie. It also provides insight into the research and writing of the two major biographical studies of McCullers, *The Lonely Hunter: A Biography of Carson McCullers* (1975) by Carr and *Carson McCullers: Her Life and Work* (1965) by Oliver Evans. The final section defines trends in McCullers criticism and surveys and annotates selected representative pieces about her work through 1980.

More current than the essay by Carr and Millichap, but less comprehensive as a bibliographical survey, is Carr's "Carson McCullers" in *Fifty Southern Writers After 1900* (1986), which includes an extensive biographical section and a discussion of the major themes in McCullers's writings, as well as a survey of selected criticism and a primary bibliography.

Interviews

McCullers gave few interviews of substance, though she was sought out often for them. The early interviews are interesting, but fairly inaccessible. Sally MacDougall spoke with her upon the publication of *The Heart Is a Lonely Hunter* for the *New York World-Telegram* (1 July 1940) and described the New York apartment she shared with Reeves, her husband, and spoke of her sympathy for European refugees. MacDougall also got McCullers to talk about her next novel, her schooling and creative writing teachers in New York, and her favorite authors. Mary Gordy, writing for the *Columbus* (Ga.) *Ledger* (16 December 1940), found McCullers "unspoiled by fame" and recuperating in her parents' home from what a Manhattan doctor called a "slightly tubercular" condition and "dormant grippe." McCullers's concern for America's European allies, enhanced by close friendships with several exiled writers, prompted her to write that winter two patriotic pieces, "Look Homeward, Americans" and "Night Watch Over Freedom."

Harry Lee's "Columbus Girl Thinks South Is 'Sick' " in the *Atlanta Constitution* (6 March 1941) raised the hackles of Southern readers, and Frank Kelly's " 'Lonely' Miss McCullers Come Home to Write" in the *Atlanta Journal* (16 November 1941) is also a lively interview. Of greater interest regarding McCullers's early success, however, is

Latimer Watson's "Carson McCullers Gets Guggenheim Fellowship" (6 April 1942). Though Watson, as woman's editor of the *Columbus Ledger*, had been insulted by McCullers when she worked briefly for the *Ledger* ("I'd starve to death before I'd do what you do," McCullers told her), Watson gamely interviewed her. Columbus was still smarting from the stir that McCullers's second novel had caused when Watson visited the young celebrity in the Smith home in which she had been reared. Watson described McCuller's bedroom as Spartan, with "nothing to turn her thoughts from work," and concluded that even if Columbus "doesn't always understand her," it is "proud of Carson and would like to know her better."

Harvey Breit's "Behind the Wedding—Carson McCullers Discusses the Novel She Converted into a Stage Play" in the *New York Times* (1 January 1950) is an important interview during which McCullers develops her comments found earlier in the *Playbill* of *The Member of the Wedding* about the play's concern with "identity and the will to belong." Breit, who had known McCullers at Yaddo in 1941, described her now as one who moved with the "awkward hesitancy of a shy, wise, overgrown child, and who in her ways and looks perhaps resembles Frankie most of all."

W. J. Weatherby's interview with McCullers for the *Manchester Guardian Weekly* (29 September 1960) was appropriately entitled "Uh-Huh, Uh-Huh." Although Weatherby had been warned by a friend that McCullers was "brightly shy," he was ill prepared for her unwillingness to "orate." Her "uh-huhs" to his own barrage of observations in an effort to help fill in the silences enabled him finally to frame for McCullers a loose "statement of belief," he said. When she did manage to string together a few thoughts, she told him little that he had not read for himself in such essays as "The Flowering Dream: Notes on Writing," "How I Began to Write," "The Vision Shared," and "The Russian Realists and Southern Literature." Weatherby said that he did not blame her inability to articulate on her illness, as many other visitors were inclined to do. Nonetheless, he charms his readers by an affable portrait and renders deftly McCullers's life in Nyack. Admittedly caught up in her Southern world of the imagination, Weatherby was startled when she admitted being "heart-broken" by Adlai Stevenson's losing the Democratic nomination to John F. Kennedy. "As we talked politics, the life of Nyack outside drew perceptibly closer," he concluded.

Perhaps the three best interviews were in the last decade of her life: "The *Marquis* Interviews Carson McCullers," by the editor of the

Lafayette College (Pennsylvania) *Marquis* (1964); "With Carson Mc-
Cullers: Terence de Vere White Interviews the American Novelist at
the Home of Her Host, John Huston" in the *Dublin Irish Times* (10
April 1967); and Rex Reed's " 'Frankie Addams' at 50" in the *New
York Times* (16 April 1967), reprinted in Reed's *Do You Sleep in the
Nude?*" (New American Library, 1968). In the Reed interview,
McCullers was excited about going to Ireland and despite her serious
ill health spoke of the new book she was writing (*Illuminations and
Night Glare*, which remains unpublished), the filming of *Reflections in
a Golden Eye* (directed by John Huston), and of her work with Mary
Rodgers on a musical version of *The Member of the Wedding*. She also
spoke of Job: "Sometimes I think God got me mixed up with Job.
But Job never cursed God and neither have I. I carry on." Five months
later, McCullers was dead.

Biographies

The first book-length study of the writer was Oliver Evans's
Carson McCullers: Her Life and Work (1965). It was probably most important for having pulled together a good deal of information about
McCullers and her work in one place. Evans analyzes each book in
detail, discusses many of the short stories, and summarizes the most
notable critical responses. His biography is useful, too, for its rendering of McCullers's life and attitudes as a young woman growing
up in Georgia and its comparision to the lives of her most autobiographical characters, Mick Kelly and Frankie Addams, in *The Heart
Is a Lonely Hunter* (1943) and *The Member of the Wedding* (1946). The
book also includes the first publication of McCullers's outline of "The
Mute" (retitled *The Heart Is a Lonely Hunter*), reprinted in Margarita
G. Smith's posthumous collection of her sister's work, *The Mortgaged
Heart* (1971).

Evans's biographical details are less reliable than the insightful
interpretations of her work. Researched and written with McCullers's
cooperation, Evans's book contains a number of errors, which he
might have avoided had he not taken her at her word for facts that
might well have been refuted or verified elsewhere. After McCullers's
death, Evans told Virginia Spencer Carr that he regretted having to
"bend the truth somewhat" in his inability to be totally candid about
her life. All of Evans's resource materials may be found in the Humanities Research Center of the University of Texas, where the bulk
of McCullers's literary estate has been deposited. Overall, the book is

a fair and appreciative introduction to her life and work. Though not widely reviewed, it was generally well received by the critics, who were acquainted with Evans's significant earlier studies of McCullers and his call for a reappraisal of her work.

The only comprehensive biography to date is Carr's 600-page tome, *The Lonely Hunter: A Biography of Carson McCullers* (1975), researched and published without the cooperation of the McCullers literary executors (McCullers's brother cooperated with Carr; her sister did not). Carr was denied permission to quote from any of the hundred of letters from McCullers and members of her immediate family, yet found some five hundred friends, acquaintances, classmates, and other relatives who talked freely about the facets of McCullers that they knew best. Carr discovered that her subject was seldom the *same* person to any two people. With a life both real and fantasized, scars both physical and actual, McCullers herself seldom distinguished between the two, taking a childlike delight in creating and perpetuating for others the tales and myths that abounded about her.

The Lonely Hunter was reviewed in newspapers, magazines, and scholarly journals across the country and widely acclaimed. Most reviewers thought the portrait a sympathetic, yet honest one, and appreciated its being descriptive rather than psychoanalytical and judgemental. Many liked it because Carr seemed to re-create McCullers, allowing the reader to live, as it were, at her elbow and bedside during her troubled and pain-ridden life. Negative reviewers thought the book too long and were disappointed that the biographer did not examine critically McCullers's works and her overall place or rank in twentieth-century American letters.

The introduction to *The Lonely Hunter* ("Some Words Before") is by Tennessee Williams. The book is indexed, has seventy-five photographs, twenty-three pages of footnotes, an appendix of genealogies, a twelve-page chronology of McCullers's life, and a primary bibliography.

A brief biographical sketch by Carr in *Southern Writers: A Biographical Dictionary* (1979) is useful as a first step in interesting readers in McCullers. The dictionary is comprised of many hundreds of such sketches and is the most comprehensive biographical compendium of Southern writers, both living and dead, to date.

A unique look at Reeves McCullers, the author's husband, is Delma Eugene Presley's "The Man Who Married Carson McCullers" (1973), which draws on several biographical sources Carr missed in her research, including a high school classmate of Reeves McCullers and another friend who was, presumably, his lover for a time. Presley's sympathetic portrait of McCullers's husband, who committed suicide in 1953, posits that "without his dynamic presence, without his playful dancing on the grave of despair, Carson seemed to lose touch with the realities of human relationships," and that what she wrote later "bears faint resemblance to the works which emerged from the frustrating, fabulous years when she loved/hated Reeves."

Brief biographical sketches are also found in *Current Biography* (1940) and *Twentieth-Century Authors* (1942). Of the several articles based on interviews with McCullers, perhaps the most memorable is Rex Reed's affectionate portrait, " 'Frankie Addams' at 50" (1967). For details of McCullers's death, Carr's biography is helpful, as are the obituary notices in the *New York Times* (30 September 1967), *Newsweek* (9 October 1967), *Publishers' Weekly* (9 October 1967), *Time* (6 October 1967), and *Contemporary Biography Yearbook* (1967-1968).

Critical Studies: Books

Dale Edmonds's *Carson McCullers* (1969), published in the Southern Writers Series of Steck-Vaughn (Austin, Texas), was one of two pamphlet-length introductions to McCullers's writings to appear in 1969 and is reliable in its biographical essay and plot summaries of the major works and judicious in its interpretations. Edmonds defines McCullers's "slender literary output" as "no mean achievement" and discusses her characteristics as a Southern writer, but insists that she should not be known as a regionalist. In a genre-approach to her work, Edmonds finds *The Heart Is a Lonely Hunter* her most perplexing novel, marred by an overabundance of material and insufficiency of control. He likes *The Ballad of the Sad Café* (1951), which he terms her "most stylized, most nonrealistic work," and believes that the three major plot movements of the novella are analogous to the three stanzas of the Old French *ballade* form, with the concluding "Twelve Mortal Men" passage serving as the envoy of this form. Edmonds sees *The Member of the Wedding* as McCullers's most realistic book. He agrees with the negative critics of *Clock Without Hands* (1961), calls it a "well-intentioned embarrassment" that is lacking in structure and characterization. He finds McCullers's poetry of "negligible artistic value," but of interest for "certain biographical implications," and singles out "Correspondence," "A Tree. A Rock. A Cloud," and "Sojourner" as "distinguished" from a list of half a dozen "good" short stories.

Lawrence Graver's *Carson McCullers* (1969), in the Minnesota Pamphlet Series on American Writers, is an essay that was expanded for the collection edited by Maureen Howard in 1977: *Seven American Woman Writers of the Twentieth Century: An Introduction.* Graver's essay provides a reliable basic introduction to McCullers's life and writings. Graver sees *The Member of the Wedding* as McCullers's "finest achievement" because it remains "complete in itself—a small but undeniably affecting story of adolescent joy and frustration." He faults McCullers for her "flawed control" in *The Heart Is a Lonely Hunter* and discounts her assertion that the novel was meant to be taken as an allegory about fascism. He is also uncomfortable with McCullers's predilection for "the dark night of the soul" and for things going on in her work "that only God can understand." *Clock Without Hands* was "deficient both in psychological intuition and cultural analysis." In summary, Graver posits that McCullers "may eventually rank fourth in this distinguished quarter" (along with Eudora Welty, Katherine Anne Porter, and Flannery O'Connor) for she belongs "by disposition and the solidity of her accomplishment in their company." Graver does not treat the poetry or nonfiction. His bibliography includes primary works by McCullers, current reprints (to 1969), and selected critical studies of McCullers's fiction.

Richard M. Cook's compact *Carson McCullers* (1975) in the Modern Literature Monographs series of Frederick Ungar provides an excellent introduction to McCullers that includes the life, plot summaries, and analytical discussions of her five books, and an objective overview of her literary career. Cook deals more generously with McCullers's later career than do several modern critics who claim that nothing she wrote after *The Ballad of the Sad Café* had significant literary merit.

Cook takes into account the cumulative effect of McCullers's early fame, physical weakness, and an unstable emotional life on her ability to continue the strong pace she set with *The Heart Is a Lonely Hunter* and defends *Clock Without Hands* as her most ambitious novel against the chorus of critics who dismiss it for its lack of artistic continuity. Cook agrees with David Madden that *The Heart Is a Lonely Hunter* is her best novel. The achievement of *The Member of the Wedding* lies in McCullers's success in recreating the feelings of its protagonist through a simple plot and a "highly evocative, poetic style." Cook deals astutely with McCullers's own remarks about her work and her intent in juxtaposition with his own description and interpretation of the work and other critical commentary. His discussion of *The Ballad of the Sad Café* with its ballad characteristic and archetypal, fairy-tale world is especially enlightening. Cook also illustrates how McCullers holds her characters "at arm's length" in *Reflections in a Golden Eye* (1941), that they lack the "warmth of feeling, the humor, the psychological depth that are the result of a more complex, expansive and sympathetic view of human nature," despite her statement: "I become the characters I write about."

Margaret B. McDowell's *Carson McCullers* (1980) remains the best critical overview of McCullers's work to date. A part of the Twayne United States Author Series, McDowell's study provides both an excellent general introduction to the writer and a scholarly analysis of each major work. McDowell underrates *The Heart Is a Lonely Hunter* in calling it "a strong enough first novel to establish her [McCullers] in the very forefront of young American artists." She sees *Reflections in a Golden Eye* with its "portrayal of evil in a small, closed world" as an intermediate step between *The Heart Is a Lonely Hunter* and *The Ballad of the Sad Café*, the best of the three works. In both *Reflections in a Golden Eye* and *The Ballad of the Sad Café*, evil appears as an "unmotivated, irrational or inexplicable phenomenon." McCullers's "ironic humor" employed so successfully in *The Ballad of the Sad Café* and *The Member of the Wedding* was established in *Reflections in a Golden Eye*, which in its technical virtuosity surpasses *The Heart Is a Lonely Hunter*, posits McDowell. She brings fresh insights to the study of *The Member of the Wedding* and explores the range and complexity of critical disagreement over *Clock Without Hands*, which she deems a more important and successful novel than Dale Edmonds, Lawrence Graver, and Richard M. Cook conclude. McDowell's *Carson McCullers* is the first book-length study to treat in depth the short stories and poems. She notes in them the absence of freaks, the handicapped, black characters, Southern setting, and the theme of unrequited love, all prevalent in McCullers's longer works. McDowell's feminist perspective is significant and judicious. She concludes that McCullers's most notable fiction and range of her total work is a substantial and impressive achievement, and that her work "deserves continuing analysis, interpretation, and commentary because of its incisiveness, its comprehensiveness, its sophistication, and its craft."

A unique and convincing study of the author's third novel is Eleanor Wikborg's *The Member of the Wedding: Aspects of Structure and Style* (1975). Wikborg's observations on the explicit and implicit development of symbols and their interaction on the literal and symbolic levels of meaning cast new light on McCullers's achievement. Wikborg isolates the significant structural and stylistic characteristics and discusses their role in the expression of the book's several themes. She also examines a number of recurring words and phrases and tabulates the patterns in rhythm and sound by which McCullers successfully renders the world and point of view of a twelve-year-old girl. Wikborg admits that her "pilot investigation" does not confirm that the novel's "stress patterns exhibited by its sentences make for an unusual degree of rhythmic regularity," yet the prose can be fittingly described as "poetic." Wikborg's appendix of phonemic patterns in *The Member of the Wedding* and excerpts from McCullers's other books, along with samples from a variety of other writings from unspecified authors, is of little interest to most McCullers scholars, yet it illustrates the potential for other linguistic studies of her work.

Critical Studies: Articles and Book Sections

Whereas *The Heart Is a Lonely Hunter* was reviewed enthusiastically as a first novel and its author hailed as a wunderkind, her second novel, *Reflections in a Golden Eye*—published on the heels of the first—was viewed askance, called morbid, bizarre, pretentious. It was to counter these charges that Tennessee Williams, McCullers's friend, wrote an introduction for the second edition of *Reflections in a Golden Eye* (1950), followed a few months later by a Bantam paperback, a reissue triggering a new interest in the author whose popular reputation was established that year with the stage version of *The Member of the Wedding*, which swept the season's major theatrical awards.

To Williams, *Reflections in a Golden Eye* was not her best book ("*The Ballad of the Sad Café* is assuredly among the masterpieces of our language in the form of the novella"), nor was it second best, a niche he reserved for *The Member of the Wedding*, which "combined the heart-breaking tenderness of the first with the sculptural quality of the second." But the playwright saw in *Reflections in a Golden Eye* the one attribute yet to be shown in McCullers's "stunning array of gifts: the gift of mastery over a youthful lyricism." To accusations of morbidity, he spoke of her need to compress the awfulness. "*Reflections in a Golden Eye* is one of the purest and most powerful of those works which are conceived in that Sense of the Awful which is the desperate black root of nearly all significant modern art."

It took the omnibus edition, *The Ballad of the Sad Café: The Novels and Stories of Carson McCullers* (1951), to provoke the attention of serious critics, who addressed the themes of loneliness and longing.

Dayton Kohler's important early study "Carson McCullers: Variations on a Theme" (1951) likens her to such "solitary, midnight haunted novelists" as Hawthorne and Melville, whose worlds were of "half-lights and shadows." He calls her a subjective novelist who disciplined herself to write objectively, whose creative imagination operated simultaneously on two levels: the real and dramatic, the poetic and symbolic. Kohler insists that she employs myth rather than allegory in her works, each a variation of a single theme of loneliness and desire. Oliver Evans's "The Theme of Spiritual Isolation in Carson McCullers's' (1952) strikes a similar chord. In attributing the spiritual aloneness of her characters to the failure of love, Evans cites as evidence the narrator's theory of love in *The Ballad of the Sad Café*.

Jane Hart's "Carson McCullers, Pilgrim of Loneliness" (1957) and Hugo McPherson's "Carson McCullers: Lonely Huntress" (1959) deal also with the author's spiritual isolates, who, in Hart's words, "find for a radiant moment the Thee they are seeking—and are lifted above their own loneliness by a sense of togetherness—of being with others in love, sorrow, or beauty." Yet for each it is a temporary moment in his pilgrimage through loneliness. McPherson treats the inherent incompatibility of the spiritual and physical aspects of McCullers's lonely seekers whose anguish is provoked even more by their ambiguous sexual identities.

Other essays of the 1950s dealing with McCullers's sexually ambiguous characters, especially her adolescents, include Leslie Fiedler's *An End to Innocence: Essays on Culture an Politics* (1952), Frederick Carpenter's "The Adolescent in American Fiction" (1957), Ihab H. Hassan's "The Idea of Adolescence in American Fiction" (1958), and James William Johnson's "The Adolescent Hero: A Trend in Modern Fiction" (1959). For many writers, the fifties was the decade for examining youth in modern fiction.

Fiedler regards Mick Kelly and Frankie Addams as "strange new heroes of our time who stand outside of everything, including their own sex." In their sexual ambiguity, Fiedler finds them kin to Twain's Huck Finn, Faulkner's Ike McCaslin, Bellow's Augie March, and Salinger's Holden Caufield. His theory that a "female homosexual romance" exists between Frankie and Berenice, the family cook and a surrogate mother to Frankie, is pretty much ignored by other critics, but Fiedler returns to it again and again. In *Love and Death in the American Novel* (1960), he declares that McCullers "profited by a *détente* in the middle-class, middlebrow war against homosexuality" (as when Frankie "cuddles in the arms of her black mammy" and comes "oddly, back to the

[Huck's] raft"). In a 1965 essay titled "Come Back to the Raft Ag'in, Huck Honey!" Fiedler likens the affection between Frankie and Berenice to that of Cooper's Natty Bumpo and Chingachgook, Melville's Ishmael and Queequeg, and Twain's Huck and Jim. All are "born of the innocence of childlike ignorance." He sees Frankie's "romance" with Berenice as an "archetypal complex in latter-day writers of a frankly homosexual sensibility." McCullers is "the most accomplished of the neo-Faulknerians," says Fiedler, and her talent "more versatile and durable" than Truman Capote's. Both are descendants of Faulkner in their use of the Southern landscape as a "natural symbol for decay and brooding evil." (See also Fiedler's "From Redemption to Initiation" in *The New Leader,* 26 May 1958).

Frederick Carpenter writes convincingly in "The Adolescent in American Fiction" (1957) of similarities in the writings of McCullers and Salinger in their depiction of adolescence with its inevitable confrontation with the evils of experience. McCullers's characters are handled with greater complexity and realism than Salinger's, says Carpenter, but with "perhaps less art." Carpenter is also one of the first to write about John Singer as a Christ figure. He likens Singer to a Christ-like magnet who attracts the adolescent Mick as well as the other alienated members of her microcosm who crave human love and compassion.

Ihab Hassan makes only passing reference to McCullers in "The Idea of Adolescence in American Fiction," (1958) but writes appreciatively of her treatment of the "cult of adolescence in modern literature embodying our past, a mode of our moral life, and a metaphor of our imagination." In "The Victim: Images of Evil in Recent American Fiction" (1959), Hassan views Singer similarly to Fiedler as a Christ figure, but a "disconsolate and somewhat tawdry" one who is "dumb as confessor and mute as savior." Throughout McCullers's canon, says Hassan, evil is the denial of love and lack of reciprocity. If her fictional people are to survive, they must love without hope of requittal. Hassan develops his concept of Singer as "an unwilling Christ" in "Carson McCullers: The Alchemy of Love and the Aesthetics of Pain" (1959–1960). Like Fiedler, he links McCullers with Faulkner and other major writers of the Southern experience. Upon examining all four of McCullers's novels, Hassan concludes that the "necessary tension" between love and pain in the author's vision is maintained because love tends to "seek its own impediments" by "intensifying the lover's pain, in precluding communion, and in electing outlandish recipients." Hassan finds love handled similarly in Mc-

Cullers's short stories, but deems them "nerveless and contrived." This important essay of Hassan's has been reprinted more often than any other single piece of McCullers criticism.

James William Johnson's 1959 essay on trends in the "adolescent hero" makes brief mention of what he calls McCullers's "myth of adolescence" with its ineffable sense of loss, emphasis on flight, and attempted escape by youths who must discover for themselves their physical and spiritual bondage from which there is little hope for release. Johnson's references are primarily to *The Member of the Wedding*.

Frank Durham in "God and No God in *The Heart Is a Lonely Hunter*" (1957) treats McCullers's first novel as an "ironic religious allegory" that reinforces the author's concept of the "discreteness of human beings" from each other and also from God. Durham views Singer and Antonapoulas as Gods who neither understand their suppliants nor communicate with them. Though the symbolism in the novel is "fuzzy" and the allegory imperfect, says Durham, McCullers has created a sensitive and vivid "iconoclastic religious novel."

Another important essay appearing in the first decade of McCullers criticism is "Plato in Dixie" (1958) in which Frank Baldanza notes significant parallels between the author's "science of love" in "A Tree. A Rock. A Cloud" (one of her most acclaimed short stories) and Plato's dialogues. McCullers's theory, however, is played "an octave lower." Baldanza also sees elements of Plato's *Symposium* and *Phaedrus* (in theory, form, and technique) in each of her major works and likens McCullers to Capote and Welty in their "nearly morbid preoccupation with sublunar imperfection." The physical defects of their characters are merely metaphors for spiritual loneliness, insists Baldanza.

Criticism of McCullers's work in the 1960s was launched by Horace Taylor and John Vickery. In *"The Heart Is a Lonely Hunter:* A Southern Waste Land" (1960), Taylor perceives the "same controlling concept in *The Waste Land*" and in the art of "this important novel," though he admits no direct influence of Eliot upon McCullers. In *The Heart is a Lonely Hunter*, the problem is, ultimately, as with *The Waste Land*, a religious one, both for the individual and society, and the community offers no "psycho-religious bond," for each person is a solipsist. Each is a "kind of universe unto himself, but incomplete to the extent that he needs another person to express himself to, a mirror to reflect against." Taylor writes of each seeker's deep-rooted narcissism and his making of John Singer "a home-made God" as mirror image. Vickery's "Carson McCullers: A Map of Love" (1960) treats her canon in terms of the "total vision of love": "fraternal love" in *The Heart Is a Lonely Hunter*, "convoluted sexual relationships" in *Reflections in a Golden Eye*, "romantic love parodied" in *The Ballad of the Sad Café*, and "familial love" in *The Member of the Wedding*. Biff Brannon, Anacleto, John Henry ("perhaps," conceded Vickery), and Miss Amelia "momentarily grasp" the sum of "human wisdom" when they recognize that "love is a matter of loving unaltered by not being loved" in return, and that the "dream of one's life is a matter of faith not fact."

A decade of critical retribution followed an essentially negative reception of *Clock Without Hands*. In anticipation of such criticism, Tennessee Williams went public once more in McCullers's defense. Four days after publication date, the playwright observed that despite McCullers's great personal adversity, *Clock Without Hands* was "set on paper as indelibly as if it had been carved onto stone. Here was all the stature, nobility of spirit, and profound understanding of the lonely searching heart that make her, in my opinion, the greatest living author of our country, if not of the world." Williams's high praise helped insure a hospitable reception by lay readers who had waited impatiently for fifteen years for another McCullers novel, but reviewers in general were not impressed.

Edna O'Brien in "The Strange World of Carson McCullers" (1961) uses the publication of *Clock Without Hands* as an impetus to reevaluate all of McCullers's books and concludes that she was the "best living woman writer." O'Brien objects to *Clock Without Hands* because it was "written from the outside" in the manner of "cool reportage," but decides that overall, it is a "very worthy book and a sad one."

In an essay for *Phylon* (1962), Nick Aaron Ford calls *Clock Without Hands* the most significant novel of the year in its treatment of race relations, but grants it several general weaknesses, which Donald Emerson describes in detail in "The Ambiguities of *Clock Without Hands*" (1962). Like O'Brien, Emerson finds McCullers at her best in dealing with inward experience and in her comprehension of the human rather than the social condition, but attributes the failure of *Clock Without Hands* to McCullers's unsuccessful attempt to make her characters "stand for the whole South." The "private and symbolic roles" do not fuse, insists Emerson. Moreover, the burden of the old Judge's symbolic role becomes too heavy for him, and as a human being he remains a grotesque. Another reason for its weakness is that there is no central character in whom the others could relate, such as Singer functioned in *The Heart Is a Lonely Hunter*. Also, there is no "tight pattern of antipathy" that inextricably links everyone—including the horse—in *Reflections in a Golden Eye*. There is no single character, such as Frankie Addams, to give the novel a credible viewpoint. Even the title itself and the symbolic role of the clock with its "forceful social reference" weakens the novel, insists Emerson, who concludes that *Clock Without Hands* is "most interesting" within the context of her total work.

Barbara Nauer Folk treats "The Sad Sweet Music of Carson McCullers" (1962) as "architectural framework" and an "extended correlative." McCullers's use of music and musical references and allusions is always "intelligent, functional, and openly reverent," declares Folk. In many instances, music works as a symbol of the ideal. Folk views John Singer as the persona of artist/writer who "sings" for humanity and objects to his being taken for a Christ figure.

In "The Achievement of Carson McCullers" (1962), Oliver Evans extended his earlier argument regarding the author's literary contribution to help counter the negative criticism of *Clock Without Hands*, claiming that she was a controversial and much misunderstood writer because she writes so realistically that most readers miss the point that she is ultimately to be taken as an allegorical writer. Evans argues similarly in "The Case of Carson McCullers" (1964): her theme of unrelieved loneliness and unrequited love is unacceptable to most readers, thus unpopular; the deformities of her characters are seen as real rather than symbolic, thus misunderstood; and her books are taken so literally that readers do not perceive her skillful handling of allegory and symbolism. Though Evans admits flaws in McCullers's first novel in "The Case of the Silent Singer: A Revaluation of *The Heart Is a Lonely Hunter*" (1965), the essay reveals his high regard of her work. Taken collectively, Evans's studies of McCullers's canon comprise the first substantial body of appreciative criticism. Evans's critical biography, *Carson McCullers: Her Life and Work* (1965) caps a fifteen-year critical and personal interest in McCullers and is a significant estimate of her career to date.

Other important studies of McCullers in the 1960s include Irving Malin's discussion in *New American Gothic* (1962) and "The Gothic Family" in *Psychoanalysis and American Fiction* (1965). In the first essay Malin deals with the narcissism of McCullers's characters in her first three books. Like Miss Amelia's crossed eyes, they turn more and more inward to the eventual realization that their own "inseparable love" is the mirror, and they "move in compulsive circles." Malin finds McCullers similar to Capote in their depiction of social isolates who have no place in the "outside world." Rigidity and violence abound in McCullers's major works as demonstrated by Malin, who sees Cousin Lymon as Miss Amelia's double, in a sense, "mutual narcissists." In "The Gothic Family," Malin deals with McCullers's lonely characters whose family tensions become unbearable when they recognize the failure of "any love but self-love." Though each tries to establish meaningful communion with his blood kin or surrogate family, he is destined to live incapsulated only within himself.

Mark Schorer's "McCullers and Capote: Basic Patterns" (1963) includes a comprehensive study of all five of McCullers's books. Schorer treats Singer as a Christ figure, and his reading of *The Heart Is a Lonely Hunter* is similar to Evans's: "For all the realistic detail of the novel, it is at heart a parable that is suggested at once in the legendary style." He finds the tone appropriate "to the retelling of an old myth," a tone combined with "sharply reported vernacular talk and reflection" appropriate to the "social character of her people." In *Reflections in a Golden Eye*, the quality of "fable" recedes, the drama is more concentrated, the tale "more tautly told." McCullers's theme of love and loneliness has been inverted, and in such a world of "static rage and drugged destructiveness," there is "no love to deepen the loneliness." Schorer sees *The Member of the Wedding* as less parabolic than *The Heart Is a Lonely Hunter*, "well within the realistic tradition." *The Ballad of the Sad Café* is McCullers's most successful work. Remote from social realism, the book renders the myth objectively. Moreover, in McCullers's use of the ballad form she has "found the completest consolidation" of her talent. To Schorer, the "lover-beloved interchange" is as patterned as a folk dance, its style the fable of folk tale.

Another notable essay is Chester E. Eisinger's "The New Fiction—Carson McCullers and the Failure of Dialogue" (1963). Eisinger discusses her four novels of the forties as "new fiction" characterized by its "inward-turning and backward-turning" that draws heavily upon the "gothic imagination." Governed by "the aesthetics of the primitive," McCullers is appropriately viewed as an antirealist whose truth is "the truth of the heart." To Eisinger, she has "stacked the deck to guarantee ruptured communion and fruitless love by choosing people . . . whose capacities are crippled." He sees "flight" in her books as "flight from normative behavior, frantic flight of the divided soul between the poles of male and female in the prison of self," with no resolution possible. Unlike those who perceive Singer as God-like,

Eisinger sees him as both Virgin Mary and the Son. "Conceived in a sense as a hermaphrodite, incorporating in one body the male and female principles," Singer has the "potential for universal balm," but is the "false Virgin, the false Son . . . the abysmal zero of the human hope for communion." The limitations of *The Member of the Wedding* are "in its focus on the child's self-centered world in which the macrocosm plays no part," but its contribution as a novel is its statement of the "universal need for human dialogue." To Eisinger, McCullers has created an art form cut off from life . . . depicting "a narrow corner of human existence" and symptomatic of the phenomena of a "disturbed psyche and a disturbed time."

In *Renaissance in the South—A Critical History of the Literature, 1920-1960* (1963), John Bradbury likens McCullers to Faulkner in his partiality for grotesques, but views her concern for the lonely and loveless with their failures to communicate and self-betrayal aligning her more with Porter and Welty, whom he finds superior to McCullers as stylists and in their mastery of the "short form." Like Evans, Bradbury sees her books as variations of a single theme. He views Biff Brannon's suspension "between two worlds" of love and terror at the end of *The Heart Is a Lonely Hunter* as the artist's withdrawal when eros is shown to be "uniformly and terribly defective." Eros is revealed similarly in the short stories, notes Bradbury.

Another period study covering the same forty years is W. Tasker Witham's *The Adolescent in the American Novel, 1920-1960* (1964), which treats McCullers's troubled youths against a literary and cultural background. Witham notes the emergence of the child and adolescent heroes of much important fiction as a "distinctly twentieth-century manifestation" with precedent in British and American fiction. His discussion of Mick and Frankie emphasizes their sexuality, loneliness, ambition, love of music, and rough awakening from dream worlds into "an awareness of reality and responsibility." Witham is particularly impressed by McCullers's psychological soundings of her adolescents through the use of symbolism.

Morris Beja's survey essay, "It Must Be Important: Negroes in Contemporary American Fiction" (1964), examines Sherman Pew (a foundling on a church pew) in *Clock Without Hands* as the "embodiment of two black themes": the search for identity (treated in McCullers's book "ironically but pitifully") and the black man as a Christ martyr ("I have thought often that if Christ was born now he would be colored," said Sherman).

Louis Auchincloss writes appreciatively of McCullers in *Pioneers* and Caretakers: A Study of 9 American Women Novelists (1965). *The Heart Is a Lonely Hunter* lacks the tight control of her art that made *Reflections in a Golden Eye* so memorable, but he found in it all the themes she dealt with later "more particularly." To Auchincloss, the novel's portrayal of Mick served as an "advance study" for *The Member of the Wedding* and is the least successful portion of the book. Also, race relations are handled "less expertly" than in *The Member of the Wedding*, which along with *The Ballad of the Sad Café*, "represents the art of McCullers at its finest." In the history of the American novella one cannot find "more beautifully plotted pieces." Her fame will rest on her novellas, concludes Auchincloss, who notes that McCullers herself insisted that *The Member of the Wedding* be described as a novella since it was "single in its intention." A "memorable book," *Clock Without Hands* lacks structure, but provides a vivid picture of the South in racial crisis. McCullers's credo "explains the curious gentleness with which she handles even her cruelest characters." As Jester Clane concludes, "Better them than nothing. Better them than the blank sky."

Jack B. Moore's "Carson McCullers: The Heart Is a Timeless Hunter" (1965) is a fine reading of a narrow but important aspect of *The Heart Is a Lonely Hunter* and sets the trend for much subsequent McCullers criticism. Moore demonstrates how McCullers successfully employs the myth of initiation to "solve a delicate problem of verisimilitude," yet retells perfectly the myth in "convincingly contemporary terms." McCullers employs the mythic pattern of trial and initiation in describing Mick's sexual adventure, following the traditional pattern of the "hero's, or adolescent's, testing and emergence." Juxtaposing the pattern defined in Joseph Campbell's *The Hero With a Thousand Faces* and McCullers's utilization of the myth in "quite realistic and basically erotic terms," Moore commends the author for her "splendid use of the myth, making it a fresh and immediate experience natural to the world of this particular novel." Moore also likens Mick's journey to the romances and initiation tales of Hawthorne and Poe, but describes Mick's story as "tonally like a fairy tale, with all perils somehow muted and all fears never permitted to destroy an almost idyllic adventure." Mick, a real girl as well as a fairytale princess, learns about sex and faces heroically her difficult entrance into the adult real world.

Important, also, to McCullers scholarship is Louise Y. Gossett's *Violence in Recent Southern Fiction* (1965). In a chapter titled "Carson McCullers: Dispossessed Love," Gossett posits that no matter how distorted a relationship may be, McCullers "has compassion for every

attempt of the human being to became a *we* instead of an *I*. . . . Thus
the author is charitable toward the violence and grotesqueness which
develop when the impulse to love goes astray, and she treats deviations
more with mercy than with horror." Gossett disagrees with Dayton
Kohler, who proposes that outward deformity in McCullers's characters is "simply a reflection of twisted inner lives to express a tragic
vision of life"; instead, McCullers stresses the "accidental rather than
the inevitable nature of this condition." Though the lives of such
physically afflicted as Lymon and Singer are fraught with isolation
and despair, they also "generate love and restrain violence. Within
themselves and in the relationship of others to them they have an
effect similar to Miss Amelia's liquor: it causes joy and suffering but
it reveals the truth and warms the soul." Although the theme of
"dispossessed love" unifies McCullers's work, the "circumstances for
its development" vary to such an extent that they seem new and
original in each book. She allows her adolescents to emerge through
violence to a "healthy measure of maturity," preferring to educate
"rather than to destroy" with violence. Adults in McCullers's fiction
are less fortunate. Sometimes one's capacity for love has been "utterly
twisted," and the result is the "grotesqueness and violence of perv-
ersion and an aggregation of misery such as confounds the characters
in *Reflections in a Golden Eye*." Rather than trying to explain "warped
personalities and twisted loves on the basis of environment or heritage," McCullers simply makes "vivid the violence of the psychological
and physiological illnesses that result from thwarted or abnormal
love."

Marion Montgomery in "The Sense of Violation: Notes Toward
a Definition of 'Southern' Fiction" (1965) sees the "sense of violation
and earned retribution" at the core of so-called Southern fiction, that
is, in a character's willingness to "bear the consequences of his act."
McCullers's characters (and Capote's) do not. Their grotesqueness
"defines them as separate from mankind," and their world is a "dream
world" through which they "float in search of an awakening." To
Montgomery, the fiction of McCullers and Capote bears about the
same relation to true Southern fiction as "a bale of cotton in the Atlanta
Airport Terminal bears to the South." By Montgomery's definition,
McCullers—despite setting—is more a Northern writer than a Southern one.

In *The Faraway Country: Writers of the Modern South* (1966), Louis
Rubin, Jr., asserts that McCullers's fiction is a "poignant exploration
of surfaces," but limited in scope, for it "stopped short of the tragic."

McCullers is best in her treatment of the past when she rejects values that characterize the collective experience of the South. Rubin also makes brief reference to McCullers in *The Curious Death of the Novel: Essays in American Literature* (1967), in which he contrasts McCullers's use of the physically grotesque with Caldwell's. Whereas Caldwell's grotesqueries are tools for low comedy, McCullers's design is not to "provoke amusement" but to convey the sense of loneliness and isolation that accompanies abnormality. Rubin sees pain, not love, as the motif of all of McCullers's fiction.

Robert S. Phillips's important essay "Painful Love: Carson McCullers' Parable" (1966) takes issue with earlier critics who relegated *The Ballad of the Sad Café* to the same Gothic niche of her other novels. Phillips does not see the work as a novel, but as a "parable of painful love," and demonstrates how it is different from conventional Gothic themes and devices (see his "The Gothic Architecture of *The Member of the Wedding*" [1964] for a full discussion). The broad burlesque is "so fantastical and bizarre that it resembles at times the Western tall tale," but it belongs to the tradition of Romance (in the Hawthorne sense). It is McCullers's greatest departure from realism and her most didactic work. In communicating the motif of painful love and isolation in her parable, McCuller utilized symbols rather than fully fleshed characters who are the "physical embodiments of Freudian symbols." Phillips notes that "an unconscious hostility against the phallus is a constant and impelling motive" not only in *The Ballad of the Sad Café* but also in *The Heart Is a Lonely Hunter* and *The Member of the Wedding*. It seems to Phillips that Irving Malin's theory that Amelia and Lymon are to be taken as "mutual doubles" is invalidated by McCullers's use of inversion. Readers may not care for all the Freudian potholes in which Phillips steps, but he argues convincingly. A good comparative study in "literary affinity" is Phillips's "Dinesen's 'Monkey' and McCullers's 'Ballad' " in *Studies in Short Fiction* (1964). Both Isak Dinesen's monkey and McCullers's hunchbacked dwarf, Cousin Lymon, are "small love objects for strong, sexless women" who have several characteristics in common. Dinesen's Boris character has its counterpart in McCullers's Marvin Macy, but Phillips cautions the reader not to construe his remarks as a conjecture that McCullers "deliberately borrowed from the Danish author," whose works she knew well.

In "Carson McCullers' Myth of the Sad Café" (1967), Albert J. Griffith observes that what has been missing in recent discussion of *The Ballad of the Sad Café* is what to "make" of the various elements

in McCullers's tale. Critics have lauded its "quasi-poetic stylistic devices," its fairy-tale atmosphere and aura of legend, its nonliteral
meanings and allegorical structure; but what they have failed to consider, says Griffith, is that these elements are "marks of the mythic
imagination" and in their remarkable combination suggest the "making of a modern myth." McCullers's imagination is "close kin" to that
of certain major ancient writers, and unlike such moderns as Joyce,
Faulkner, Eliot, Welty, and Updike, who created contemporary parallels to various well-known myths, McCullers shaped her own new
myth out of primitive elements. In a careful reading of *The Ballad of
the Sad Café*, Griffith posits that the story is transformed by the "implied presence" of a personal narrator. The characters and events
"have the remoteness, the mystery, the numinousness of myth," concludes Griffith.

Writing for *Literature and Psychology*, David Madden (1967) deals
thematically with McCullers's first novel in "The Paradox of the Need
for Privacy and the Need for Understanding in Carson McCullers'
The Heart Is a Lonely Hunter" (1957). In a discussion of major characters, Madden contends that "if Singer is Christ, Antonapoulos is his
god, and the cruelty of his friend's uncomprehending insanity (though
not really cruel since Singer's illusion is stubbornly firm) suggests an
allegorical statement about illusion." The real dilemma, says Madden,
who traces the subtle patterns of attraction and repulsion among her
characters, is that even the "telling to one person [Singer] does not
destroy the loneliness," for each person is "doomed to be an island
unto himself." The paradox is that everyone craves human understanding "while simultaneously desiring an inviolable privacy."

A rash of critical essays followed McCullers's death in September
1967, many of them appreciative overviews and others condemning
and harsh. Robert Drake in "The Lonely Heart of Carson McCullers"
(1968) wrote of her "kinked-up" *Reflections in a Golden Eye* and the
"ridiculous *The Ballad of the Sad Café* with its fabricated primitivistic
folkishness" in which her "defects become fully evident." Even *The
Heart Is a Lonely Hunter* and *The Member of the Wedding*, which Drake
appraises as her two greatest achievements, suffer from a "considerable degree of incoherence" and occasional "tendentious exploitation of contemporary southern social problems." Although
McCullers's talent was "considerable," Drake is convinced that it never
reached full fruition and that her greatest weakness was an inability
to impose form consistently upon her "one theme of spiritual isolation." Flannery O'Connor and Eudora Welty, with whom she is most

often compared, are better writers, he concludes.

In "Eudora Welty and Carson McCullers" (1964), Marvin Fel-heim ranks the Georgia writer a flagging second to Welty, who was writing consistently "at or near the top of her great talent." McCullers demonstrated no consistent development and her "undeniable abilities" were not realized. To Felheim, *The Member of the Wedding* is her best work, and *The Heart Is a Lonely Hunter* and *Reflections in a Golden Eye* are merely "interesting and readable on a realistic level," but not "distinguished as works of art."

Frederick J. Hoffman in *The Art of Southern Fiction—A Study of Some Modern Novelists* (1967) also compares McCullers with Welty, who he thinks works harder and "more consciously" with form than McCullers and is more subtle. McCullers too often skims the surface of experience, as seen in *Clock Without Hands* and *The Square Root of Wonderful*. Yet the two of them, together with Porter and O'Connor, constitute a "remarkable conjunction of feminine sensibilities in modern American literature," concludes Hoffman.

George Hendrick's important essay, " 'Almost Everyone Wants to Be the Lover': The Fiction of Carson McCullers" (1968), notes that McCullers's reputation has continued to grow in Europe despite scant notice in her own country. Hendrick agrees with Louis Rubin that *Clock Without Hands* is a "confusing book" and is certain that Oliver Evans "overpraised" her in his recent critical biography. Yet he sees justification for the critical and popular successes of *The Ballad of the Sad Café* and *The Member of the Wedding* (both as novel and play), which helped lionize her abroad. In the past, autobiographical elements had served her well, but in *The Square Root of Wonderful* (1958), she failed to transform them into art. Taken collectively, however, McCullers's five books and a handful of good short stories such as "The Jockey" and "A Tree. A Rock. A Cloud" are among the "important artistic achievement of our time." A full-scale reappraisal of her work, new editions of her books, publication of selected letters and her notebooks, a "gathering of fugitive pieces"—all are in order.

W. R. Robinson deals with the creative imagination and the dichotomies in an appreciative essay, "The Life of Carson McCullers's Imagination" (1968). Using the autobiographical "The Flowering Dream: Notes on Writing" as a springboard and frequent reference, Robinson discusses each major work, *The Square Root of Wonderful,* and several notable short stories as a record of the "discipline of her imagination." Whether memory or fiction, says Robinson, the incident McCullers relates of a "wonderful party" going on behind convent walls from which she was distressingly excluded as a child became the "matrix of her art," and thanks to it, readers of McCullers's work today are "heirs to a great knowledge of isolated and suffering man, all illusions stripped away, naked in his own humanity."

In "The Failure of Love: The Grotesque in Two Novels by Carson McCullers" (1968), Robert Rechnitz demonstrates how McCullers's style and content admirably merge in *Reflections in a Golden Eye* and *The Ballad of the Sad Café.* Life is too overpowering and fearsome for her moral cripples, so they shut it out; yet the "limited world" they construct in its stead fails to sustain them. Rechnitz takes issue with critics who find the "coda" of the chain gang in *The Ballad of the Sad Café* a fitting summation of the total work; rather, it is mere rhetoric, not fiction, for it does not grow organically from what preceded it. The real ending, says Rechnitz, is the unbearable despair behind Miss Amelia's boarded-up windows and of the dreary town itself. He approves of McCullers's "childlike style," for the narrator, in treating "matters so frightful," must hide behind a facade of childlike innocence. The style became a "kind of buffer to fend off what would otherwise be unbearable."

Rowland A. Sherrill in "McCullers' *The Heart Is a Lonely Hunter:* The Missing Ego and the Problem of the Norm" (1968) likens the characters in McCullers's first novel to those of Sherwood Anderson, who are dominated by a "single truth foolishly clung to" because the world itself provides no "viable alternative" in the absence of a general norm for conduct. Sherrill views Singer as the Super-ego and Antonapoulos as the Id of a single personality; the absence of a "mediating Ego" reinforces the absence of an "organic center" in the lives of McCullers's characters. The novel is an "ironic document of an age in which the death and disappearance of God is dismally conceded, in which the loneliness of human beings is *a priori,* and in which the responsibility for man's worth is thrust rudely into his own hands."

The motion picture version of *Reflections in a Golden Eye,* along with McCullers's death, stirred new interest in the author and prompted A. S. Knowles, Jr., to compare what her career "looked like" during her most productive decade with her reputation now. He takes the title of his essay "Six Bronze Petals and Two Red: Carson McCullers in the Forties" (1969), from Biff Brannon's freak zinnia, for which he has a penchant, as well as for freaks in general. Like Biff's zinnia, Knowles finds McCullers's art a "kind of hybrid," the familiar and universal mixed with the "strange and personal." Whereas in the 1940s she was viewed as a "Gothic cousin" of Faulkner, today she has achieved in "her own right a legendary status for her cryptically understated works." She handled her themes "with precision and, at her least morbid and most natural, great tenderness." Despite Knowles's praise, he finds her "essentially a minor writer" with a "limited and special vision." One must admit, says Knowles, that the 1940s were dominated by Southern writers and Southern critics, and there was a "good deal of back-scratching and log-rolling in the literary quarterlies that were the official voice of the movement." Knowles also discusses *The Heart Is a Lonely Hunter* as a social document against the backdrop of history. What affects readers most today is that her "ambiguous people moving through their inarticulate, dream-like world come remarkably close to the adolescent sensibility of our own time." He describes *The Member of the Wedding* as a "gentle, bittersweet book" and among its "excellences, its triumph, is the portrait of Berenice." Nonetheless, in 1969 McCullers seems "less important than she once did," Knowles concludes.

McCullers's work provoked more criticism in the 1960s—her most unproductive years when she was plagued by ill health—than in any other decade, yet little of it was born of controversy, unlike the work of her fellow-Georgian, Flannery O'Connor, with whom she was most often compared. Critics continued to mine her writings for their themes of loneliness and alienation and the painful failure and "utter dislocation" of love, for her tendency to myth-make in the absence of religious faith in a chaotic world, for her sympathetic treatment of the underdog, for her use of the South and treatment of the past, for her psychological and social realism, use of violence, the grotesque, and the Gothic, and for her stylistic and structural devices as a symbolist and allegorist. There were overviews and appreciative retrospectives, intensive studies of individual novels—most notably *The Heart Is a Lonely Hunter* and *The Ballad of the Sad Café*— and in the mid-1970s a strong body of feminist criticism emerged. Her short stories also received considerable attention. If there was any ranking of others of her ilk, she usually came off at least two lengths behind.

Major criticism of the 1970s was launched by Alice Hamilton's "Loneliness and Alienation: The Life and Work of Carson McCullers" (1970), which takes a new look at an old and prevalent theme and draws on biographical facts and other gleanings to relate McCullers's life to her work.

Hamilton proposes that radiance is short-lived for McCullers's characters, though it happens, for dreams and love do not endure.

Their search for "interior freedom" and its expression is not only a search for love, but also—in its "greater form"—an act of artistic creation. Hamilton does not discuss *The Member of the Wedding* except to make passing reference to McCullers's affinity to Frankie, but treats in detail the four other major works. In fact, in the 1970s and early 1980s, *The Member of the Wedding* was virtually ignored by most critics except for comparative studies of the novel with the stage version and subsequent screen play, and for its themes and structure when several books were dealt with.

Two fine studies of the dramatic form of *The Member of the Wedding* were published over a quarter of a century after the play opened on Broadway: Francis B. Dedmond's "Doing Her Own Thing: Carson McCullers's Dramatization of 'The Member of the Wedding' " (1975) and Louis D. Giannetti's "The Member of the Wedding" (1976) written for *Literature/Film Quarterly*. Whereas Dedmond judiciously compares the many differences between the novel and the play and explains why he thinks Act Three is inferior to the rest of the play (primarily due to the "exigency of the dramatic form"), Giannetti concentrates on the 1952 Columbia Pictures production (with the original Broadway cast) and its almost exclusive debt to the stage version rather than the novel. Giannetti faults the "surprisingly insensitive" reviewers who complained that the movie was too talky and too restricted spatially. Despite Pauline Kael's enthusiastic review, *The Member of the Wedding* remains one of the "neglected minor masterpieces of the American cinema," concludes Giannetti, who also commends Fred Zinnemann, director, for his techniques in shooting certain memorable scenes to make *The Member of the Wedding* his finest production to date in an already notable career.

The only essay of this period dealing wholly with McCullers's second novel is Ray Mathis's "*Reflections in a Golden Eye:* Myth-making in American Christianity" (1970). Written from a Christian perspective for *Religion in Life,* the article concentrates on the six main characters in terms of their religious experience within the frame of the novel, which Mathis contends reveals McCullers's awareness of modern man's need for a supportive religion and her dissatisfaction with the religions available to him. An example of Mathis's thinking is his view of Alison Langdon, who, with Anacleto, her Filipino houseboy, symbolizes the meeting of Western and Eastern philosophy. Anacleto attempts to Westernize himself by imitating Alison, who fails him by not giving him a sense of self-identity; thus her death leads to his disappearance, and figuratively, to his own death. Alison, who was insane when she died of a heart attack, and Anacleto "might have found comfort sufficient for being had they been able to accept Christianity's Platonism and mythical savior," speculates Mathis. Though McCullers "lampooned several traditional Christian forms," she paradoxically revealed a "touch of sympathy for an undefined religious need and meaning which pointed implicitly toward Christianity." Despite the essay's narrow perspective, Mathis refrains from moralizing in a strict sense and treats rather objectively McCullers's novel as a "series of jokes upon the characters and the readers, especially the 'Christian' middle class."

Alfred Kazin in his *Bright Book of Life: American Storytellers from Hemingway to Mailer* (1973) also discusses McCullers's attraction to myth and calls her a "greater myth-maker than she was a novelist." The chapter gives a splendid overview of the best characteristics of selected Southern writers and singles out McCullers and O'Connor to contrast their unique use of the South and their strengths as writers. McCullers's theme was the "utter dislocation of love 'in our time' and 'in our town.' " Yet in her bleak world, her people have a "sensitiveness that charges other people with magical perceptions," and before they succumb to "earthly damnation," they and their world seem on the verge of some magical transformation. More than anything else, it was McCullers's intuition that enabled her to write as she did, to convert this vision to art. To Kazin, *The Ballad of the Sad Café* is "perfectly controlled art," and his singular theory about the novella is that Miss Amelia's masculine strength comes from her being "past love" and that her battle with Marvin Macy stems from his attempt to "bring her back to his world of passion." *The Heart Is a Lonely Hunter* is "astonishingly alive" despite its bleak solitudes, and *The Member of the Wedding*, its popularity notwithstanding, is second-rate: it "devalues her most familiarly tragic feelings about sex into cuteness," and she imitates herself with an "eye on the audience."

McCullers's *The Mortgaged Heart* (1971), a posthumous collection of miscellaneous writings, provoked David Madden's "Transfixed Among the Self-Inflicted Ruins: Carson McCullers' *The Mortgaged Heart*" (1972), which he labeled "a long look at the mediocre side of the author of *A Member of the Wedding*." Despite Margarita Smith's insistence that her sister's early pieces be thought of as "exercises" and avowal that the collection would appropriately "illustrate the development" of McCullers's talent, Madden suggests that its "main justification" is that the reader can now see the "writer's virtues ineffectively employed in her early work and her early faults put to good use in her later work." Although the best of her early stories compare favorably with the mature work, concedes Madden, it seems "incredible that McCullers could have published articles more trivial than most of those included here." Most of the articles are ridden with clichés and reek of sentimentality, he complains. Moreover, presenting the pieces in the order in which they were written does little for one's appreciation, and Madden suggests a fitting regrouping of the pieces to encourage a study of her use of style, point of view, themes, and certain autobiographical elements in common. Yet for scholars of McCullers, the book remains invaluable. He appreciates her essays in which she comments on the writing process, especially "The Flowering Dream," and notes her ability to describe an "aesthetic concept" that embodies theme. Madden's own irony is remarkable in talking about McCullers's works, such as his statement that "McCullers seems to have achieved a masterful orchestration of her faults to sound a succession of almost perfect notes" in *The Heart Is a Lonely Hunter.* To Madden, radiance is what her style at its best emits. Although most critics feel that *A Member of the Wedding* is her major achievement, he acknowledges that having re-read carefully *The Heart Is a Lonely Hunter*, he finds it the "most re-readable, the most timeless, and among the ten greatest American novels." Madden also likes McCullers's "predilection for the odd-ball detail that cumulatively gave her fiction the density of everyday life, even as an aura of the bizarre overwhelmed it." Madden has done in his essay what he had hoped McCullers's sister had done as an editor: discussed and regrouped the essays and short stories against the backdrop of her life and other works. He writes appreciatively of much of her canon, but does not let her having served admittedly as his "Goddess Muse" of his "creative adolescence" make him pull punches. He calls "Art and Mr. Mahoney" a "very short cruel satire, based on a trite, shallow notion," and its inclusion in *The Mortgaged Heart* serves "only to show another side of McCullers's mind and to demonstrate how poorly a first-rate talent can sometimes function." Madden remains one of McCullers's most judicious critics.

Five additional studies of McCullers's short fiction were published in the 1970s, but there has been nothing devoted exclusively to it in the 1980s to date. Three were published in *Studies in Short Fiction:* James W. Grinnell's "Delving 'A Domestic Dilemma' " (1972) and its response, Laurence Perrine's "Restoring 'A Domestic Dilemma' " (1974), and Dale Edmonds' " 'Correspondence': A 'Forgotten' Carson McCullers Short Story" (1972). Perrine takes sharp issue with Grinnell's interpretation of "A Domestic Dilemma." To Grinnell,

Martin Meadows is a "mechanical, pedestrian businessman" insensitive to his wife's drinking problem, which along with his concern for his public image, were primary causes of her problem; her loneliness and isolation were spinoffs of the true cause. Perrine argues cogently to refute what he considers Grinnell's egregious distortion of the shape and meaning of McCullers's story. He sees Grinnell's "misinterpretation" and exaggeration of the "significance of minor details" making of McCullers's protagonist a caricature that "reduces a round character to a flat one, strips the story of its richness, and emasculates its theme." The Grinnell/Perrine discussions of the tale mark the most explicitly controversial criticism to date.

Dale Edmonds regrets that McCullers's early story, "Correspondence," published in the *New Yorker* in 1942, was omitted from *The Mortgaged Heart* because it reveals, among other things, her "gift for light comedy." He sees Henky Evans, whose four letters to a pen pal in South America go unanswered, as a "way station" between Mick Kelly and Frankie Addams. Whereas Mick is drawn somberly with "scarcely a trace of humor," and not very believable, says Edmonds, Henky's letters with their remarkable idiom of adolescence provide the "essential leavening of humor" that is responsible for much of the success of Frankie. Although Edmonds does not intend for "Correspondence" to be taken for a "stunning achievement," he sees it as "a unified and effective minor work of short fiction" and deserves not to be "virtually forgotten." Edmonds's discussion is a fine reading of the story and of its protagonist's relationships to her close kin in other stories by McCullers, as well as to Salinger's Holden Caulfield, who does not appear until a decade later. As with young Caulfield, Henky's language is "absolutely right."

Mary Dell Fletcher's "Carson McCullers's 'Ancient Mariner' " (1975) treats "A Tree. A Rock. A Cloud" as a modern version of Coleridge's "Ancient Mariner" who detains a wedding guest with his glittering eye and tale of his spiritual voyage. Fletcher acknowledges that Oliver Evans had pointed out the parallel in his *The Ballad of Carson McCullers*, but that they have developed their arguments quite differently. What is most interesting about Fletcher's essay are the many ways that McCullers's tale with its remarkable development of theme and characters are significantly unlike its prototype.

Robert Phillips's "Freaking Out: The Short Stories of Carson McCullers" (1978) is one of the best McCullers essays of the decade. Whereas McCullers's novels abound with freakish characters who feel dissociated by some physical anomaly, her short stories are peopled by spiritual isolates of circumstance, or what Phillips calls "an inner freaking-out." In story after story—there are nineteen—he traces the evolvement of her adults and youths alike who "freak out" and become hardened rebels when they realize they will never "fit in," that they are destined ever to be outsiders. Many of her adolescents are set apart from the world—neither adults nor children—destined to swing suspended between two worlds. Similarly, no conclusion is reached in "A Domestic Dilemma" as the young husband watches his alcoholic wife sleeping, caught up in "the immense complexity of love." In the absence of an outward conflict, he senses merely a vague "threat of undefined disaster." Only in "The Jockey" does the reader encounter "a freakish fellow." With his "diminutive physical stature and his life of mandatory dietary deprivation he is a man-child in the world of men. A Freak," points out Phillips. Although her characters in the short stories are usually absolutely normal in appearance, they are often rendered "symbolically grotesque," as in "Instant of the Hour After," in which a young married couple are seen as two figures in a bottle—like "fleshly specimens in a laboratory."

   The Heart Is a Lonely Hunter provoked five articles in the 1970s. First was Joseph R. Millichap's "The Realistic Structure of *The Heart Is a Lonely Hunter*" (1971). Millichap begins his scholarly insightful look at McCullers's first novel by dissecting the three sections to determine through structural analysis the psychological and social realism of the novel as a means of resolving critical differences. Part One is introductory, acquainting the reader with the Singer-Antonapoulos relationship and the five main characters and bringing into play the basic conflicts between the characters' personal feelings and their social roles. Part Two functions chiefly for plot development. Millichap points out that this section covers one year during which the characters evolve through an elaborate and carefully constructed series of interconnected events, wherein McCullers considers "those particular social ills which plague her characters: Blount provides a connection with economic exploitation, Copeland with racial prejudice, Mick with the alienation of youth." Part Three explores the various characters' reactions to the death of Singer and their own desperate attempts to cope with their personal and social problems. Millichap skillfully reveals how "careful analysis of its structure demonstrates how all elements of the novel—character, plot, style, setting, and symbol—are integrated in the larger purpose of presenting the failure of communication, the isolation, and the violence prevalent in modern society." Moreover, each character through his individual personality demonstrates the "roots of these general conditions." The paradox is that the characters need intercommunication to complete themselves, yet are too self-centered to provide each other with the openness that might help them better reckon with their imperfect society. Millichap points out that to McCullers, man's social world is imperfect because of his own personal failings.

Edgar E. MacDonald in "The Symbolic Unity of *The Heart Is a Lonely Hunter*" (1976) examines the generalizations of recent criticism of the novel (as did Millichap) and concludes that no one has looked carefully at the hagiography or analyzed the structure in terms of the implied sainthood of characters other than Singer. MacDonald also posits that not enough weight has been given to the symbolic value of the numbers *four, twelve,* and *three,* which figure importantly in the novel. Moreover, the unity is intensified by McCullers's "subtle allusions to Gnostic levels of comprehension as well as Judeo-Christian concepts of time and space." To MacDonald, the "cycle of the birth and death of the god [Singer], the central theme of the novel, is a continuous one and the recurring concept is wider in its implications than the human need of the heart." He sees the novel's three parts as "the priesthood culminating in the death of their god, and the dissolution of Singer's priesthood with the emergence of the new god [Biff Brannon]." It is the café owner who illustrates McCullers's "larger thesis," insists MacDonald, who notes that Biff eventually assumes characteristics of both Singer and Antonapoulos, and "with his gift of *gnosis*" attains a "higher degree of divinity than these two." Furthermore, he goes through a "symbolic purification in the relinquishment of physical love." MacDonald sees two climaxes of the novel: Singer's dream (in the exact center of the book) and Biff's "revelation" at the end. Both are mystical experiences with Gnostic implications. MacDonald concludes that in the novel's "rise from darkness to light, from the 'black, sultry night' of the opening action to the 'morning sun' of the final words, in its movement from incomprehension to knowledge," McCullers created a "Divine Comedy whose symbolic architecture and symmetry are everywhere in harmony and which reveals a profound sense of form and artistic completion." The essay is heavily footnoted with Gnostic sources.

Joan S. Korenman points out in "Carson McCullers' 'Proletarian Novel' " (1976) that only Millichap has discussed the social problems presented in *The Heart Is a Lonely Hunter,* though many critics have made reference to it. In her own in-depth study, Korenman contends that all of the novel's "major components" are shaped by the author's

disdain of materialistic values and her "objections to capitalism."
McCullers's most explicit statements about her characters' social and
economic ills are made by Jake Blount and Dr. Copeland, who shares
with Blount an enthusiasm for Marxism and the "desire to enlighten
others." Both men offer bitter indictments of capitalism, but it is Mick
Kelly and her family who best illustrate what happens when capitalism
goes astray, the destructiveness inherent, points out Korenman, who
notes that throughout the novel one's attitude toward money—be it
generosity of greed—"is a reliable index to one's human worth."
McCullers apparently had in mind "an even more political novel than
the one she finally wrote," as the outline for "The Mute" (original
title of *The Heart Is a Lonely Hunter*) indicates. Korenman is intrigued
by McCullers's failure to voice her concerns similarly for the economic
underdog in subsequent novels (except for *Clock Without Hands*, in
which racial prejudice is presented in social rather than economic
terms), a topic she calls for future biographers to address more explicitly than either Oliver Evans or Virginia Spencer Carr do in their
biographies of McCullers.

   Nancy B. Rich addresses *The Heart Is a Lonely Hunter* as the
"Ironic Parable of Fascism" in an essay by the same title (1977), taking
her text from McCullers's own statement and other supportive evidence to conclude that politics was definitely a motive in the genesis
of the novel, and that the book should be read as a parable. In an
extensive discussion of the literal and figurative aspects of the tale,
Rich proposes that Singer and Antonapoulos be viewed as symbols of
the democratic system of government and Mick Kelly, Jake Blount,
Biff Brannon, and Dr. Copeland as "the people." Antonapoulos represents the corruption of the government as he sits in the insane
asylum in his gaudy robes watching cartoon movies. As the "arm of
government," Singer listens to "the people" when they come to him
for help, but each "represents a different faction," and when they
arrive together, each is rude and uncharitable to the others. Rich sees
this situation at the "heart of the pathos in the parable, for all the
characters need Singer, yet he is powerless to help unless they speak
as a majority." Like MacDonald, Rich sees Biff Brannon as the main
character of the novel. The implications of Biff's character suggest
that the "failure of democracy is itself an illusion—that the nature of
the democratic process is like that of Biff, slow, and the condition of
freedom is perseverance," concludes Rich.

   C. Michael Smith's " 'A Voice in a Fugue': Characters and Musical Structure in Carson McCullers' *The Heart Is a Lonely Hunter*" (1979)

is another fine essay focusing on the carefully executed structure of
the novel. He notes McCullers's earlier training in music and finds
her reference to a "fugue pattern" in the outline to "The Mute" the
key to understanding the form of *The Heart Is a Lonely Hunter* and
perhaps to her later work as well. "The book is planned according to
a definite and balanced design," wrote McCullers. "The form is contrapuntal throughout. Like a voice in a fugue each one of the main
characters is an entirety in himself—but his personality takes on a
new richness when contrasted and woven in with the other characters
in the book." The fugue pattern is polyphonic, explains Smith. Multiple, separate voices echo the single theme, voices he identifies as
"imitation, canon, inversion, augmentation, and diminution." Of particular importance are imitation and inversion. Smith demonstrates
each element of a fugue according to its counterpart in the novel and
suggests that McCullers's later books be studied, also, according to
their musical pattern and traces of musical structure.

Frances Freeman Paden takes a unique and convincing approach
to McCullers's first novel in "Autistic Gestures in *The Heart Is a Lonely
Hunter*" (1982). All of the major characters exhibit autistic gestures,
are verbally inhibited, talk with their bodies, and "as their frustration
mounts, their bodily gestures are directed more and more toward
their own person," explains Paden. She notes that just as McCullers
was interested in hands personally, so too did she use hands in the
novel to reveal the spiritual aloneness of her characters in *The Heart
Is a Lonely Hunter* when they fail in their quests for acceptance and
love. Paden agrees with former critics who see Singer at the center
of a narcissistic society. Though he appears to the townspeople to be
a godlike figure, Paden sees him more as a mirror than a god. He
"reflects rather than absorbs" the gestures of his seekers, who in their
frustration become less effective and more autistic, unconsciously directing their gestures toward themselves. Critics continue to comment
on Singer's "pyramid dream" and its symbolic significance; however,
Paden notes that Singer is more fascinated by his god's [Antonapou-
lis's] hands—by the gesture itself—than by the unidentified object he
is holding over his head. Paden distinguished between an unconscious
self-mutilation, characteristic especially of Jake Blount, as an autistic
gesture, and Mick's deliberate self-inflicted hurt when she crouches
among the cedars and, overwhelmed by the music, consciously begins
"hitting her thigh with her fists," as though the "emotions aroused by
the music required a physical expression." At the end of the novel
Biff 's finding his face in the mirror—an autistic gesture—is subverted

and becomes an "epiphanic moment," Paden demonstrates. Biff "confronts his loneliness, and from the confrontation he gathers the courage to turn away, not from the world, as did Singer, nor from ideals," as did Jake, Mick, and Dr. Copeland, but from his own reflection. In the novel's final gesture—not autistic—Biff "seems willing to embrace experience as he steps out to raise the awning and 'to await the sun.' "

The Ballad of the Sad Café had six critical articles devoted almost exclusively to it (one was a comparative study of a work by a Brazilian writer). Janice Townley Moore's page-long essay for *The Explicator*, "McCullers's *The Ballad of the Sad Café*" (1970) concentrates on the bird imagery used to describe Cousin Lymon. Lymon evolves from a "strutting," "hovering," and "goose-stepping" "great chatterer" who picks up "magpie fashion, some detail," his hands "like dirty sparrow claws," to a macabre hawklike character with "clawed little fingers" who sails through the air "as though he had grown hawk wings" to defeat Miss Amelia in the ultimate betrayal. Lymon's progression from apparent innocence to evil is intensified and made more believable by the imagery, concludes Moore.

Three of the essays deal with the narrator of the novella. In "The Presence of the Narrator in Carson McCullers's *The Ballad of the Sad Café* " (1972), Dawson F. Gaillard posits that the voice of the narrator as a member of the community "where changes for the worse have occurred" is central to the power of the novel. Neither "neutral nor ignorant," he takes sides. In his "homey reflections," he is perceptive in his observations and sensitive to the secrets of the human heart and man's common experiences. His empathetic presence makes it impossible for the reader to "distance himself from the emotional impact of the act." The magic of the oral quality of the tale lifts it beyond "the commonplace facts, beyond the immediate, and beyond history." It is his response to the café that lifts it to "mythic proportions." It is the song of the balladeer, the "action of a human mind coming to grips with what has occurred in time, that provides the power of *The Ballad of the Sad Café*."

John McNally in "The Introspective Narrator in 'The Ballad of the Sad Café,' " (1973) is intrigued by the tale as a "grotesque delineation of love's power to destroy," but views its chief significance as a revelation of the character who, in recalling the story, "gives it its shape and who, in reaction to it, finds new meaning in his own existence." Calling *The Ballad of the Sad Café* a "song of the human spirit," McNally likens the narrator to Marlow in Conrad's *Heart of Darkness*, for whom the "meaning of an episode was not inside like a kernel but outside, enveloping the tale which brought it out only as a glow brings out a haze, in the likeness of one of those misty halos that sometimes are made visible by the spectral illumination of moonshine." In McCullers's "beautifully sculptured piece of writing," the reader overhears the "internal monologue of a character whose haunting recollections enable him to overcome his own *ennui* and to resist the atrophying pressures of the familiar world."

Joseph R. Millichap concentrates, too, on the presence and function of the narrator in his "Carson McCullers' Literary Ballad" (1973). He objects to the "bizarre theory of love" offered by the narrator of *The Ballad of the Sad Café* as a key to interpreting all of McCullers's fiction, but does see it as a means of unlocking the novella's "difficulties of literary mode, point-of-view, characterization, and plot structure." The narrator's theory of love is not McCullers's, stresses Millichap, and depicts only "one facet of the love's dynamics." It is this theory, of course, arising out of the "weird triangle of Miss Amelia, Cousin Lymon, and Marvin Macy," that forms the novella's structural center and is Millichap's concern, along with its balladlike characteristics "wrought by a modern, conscious artistry not by the folk mind or by an artless imagination."

Panthea Reid Broughton's "Rejection of the Feminine in Carson McCullers' *The Ballad of the Sad Café* " (1974) is the first significant feminist reading of McCullers's work and gives rise to a number of subsequent studies. Miss Amelia is incapable of manifesting a "healthy femininity" and is left at the novella's close in the "prison of her aloneness because the stereotyped patterns by which she encountered others were exclusively those of dominance or subjugation," says Broughton. Not she nor Marvin Macy nor Cousin Lymon can love without self-abasement because they do not know how to give of themselves without impairing their own integrity or to "take" without assuming an exalted sense of "personal power." Broughton draws on the theories of de Tocqueville, Karl Stern, and Theodore Roszak to conclude that *The Ballad of Sad Café* "may be interpreted as a fable which shows us that rejecting those characters labeled as exclusively feminine bounces back on the rejector and renders men and women alike incapable of love and thereby escaping the prisons of their own spiritual isolation."

Jeremy E. Pollock-Chagas's "Rosalina and Amelia: A Structural Approach to Narrative" (1975), written for the *Luso-Brazilian Review,* interestingly examines Autran Dourado's *Ópera dos Martos* and *The Ballad of the Sad Café* for their musical patterns as "ballad" and "opera," and by its structural nature according to definition finds the Brazilian tale a more complex and intriguing work. In both tales, the linear structure is viewed as a "set of parallels rather than a single line." Pollock-Chagas also notes that each narrative develops around and within a single building with a clear distinction between the atmosphere of the upper and lower floors, and in each tale the building exerts its presence and influence upon the narrative. He sees the "secondary structure" based upon the social/psychological relations of the principals of the triangle. An examination of the "progression" of the narrative (a juxtaposition of the beginning and end to determine to what extent the original situation has changed or remained static) reveals further significant differences. Amelia's final situation is only an intensification of the situation at the beginning. Still another perspective is established by noting that the reader knows only as much as the narrator knows in *The Ballad of the Sad Café* and is not privy to the emotions and thoughts of the protagonists; in the Brazilian tale, the voice swings like the pendulum of a clock. Pollock-Chagas is far more impressed by his countryman's *Ópera dos Martos* than by McCullers's tale; yet *The Ballad of the Sad Café* comes off very well, indeed, in the comparison.

In "Carson McCullers' Amazon Nightmare" (1982), Louise Westling views the sexual dynamics of *The Ballad of the Sad Café* as an "inversion of traditional heterosexual patterns" and posits that the force of the novella lies in its portrayal of the "masculine Amazon whose transgression of conventional sexual boundaries brings catastrophic male retribution." Like Robert S. Phillips, Westling notes McCullers's probable debt to Isak Dinesen's "The Monkey"; yet "unlike Dinesen, who portrayed an uneasy compromise between proud female autonomy and reluctant masculine homage, McCullers sought to deny the feminine entirely and to allow a woman to function successfully as a man." *The Ballad of the Sad Café* serves as an apt vehicle for McCullers's indulgence of the "impulse to appropriate male power and thus escape the culturally inferior role of woman"; McCullers's interpretation of the writing of *The Member of the Wedding* to create her fairy tale played a significant part in Frankie's inexorable move "toward an acceptance of conventional femininity," concludes Westling. The physical proportions of Amelia, a "grown-up tomboy," symbolize her exaggerated masculine self-image.

"Carson McCullers's Tomboys" (1980) was Westling's first feminist criticism of the author's work. Although the motif of sexual ambivalence in *The Heart Is a Lonely Hunter* and *The Member of the*

Wedding had received scholarly attention, the relation between "that ambivalence and the fact that Mick and Frankie are *girls* who share artistic temperaments and serious ambitions" has not, declares Westling, who notes that Mick's great yearning is to become a famous composer and Frankie's interest is in writing plays and becoming a great poet (or "the world's greatest expert on radar"). In her treatment of Mick and Frankie, declares Westling, McCullers "dramatizes the crisis of identity" that ambitious girls face as they "stumble into an understanding" of what is expected of them in young womanhood. What they learn is that a "tomboy is charming" as a girl, but if she persists in her "boyishness" as an adult, she is viewed as a grotesque. The crisis of identity for McCullers's tomboys is accompanied by images of sexual freaks, androgynous longings, homosexuality, and even transvestitism. At the end of *The Member of the Wedding* with Frankie's "deviants" removed from her life, she becomes Frances. Safe conformity triumphs, but "the price for this relief from the tensions of strangeness has been high," notes Westling. She has become a "silly girl" who no longer creates, but "gushes sentimental nonsense about the Great Masters," the "hard edge of her mind gone." Mick and Frankie are McCullers's "most coherent fictional presentation of the problem which warps almost every gifted woman's life." Westling's solid and provocative feminist study, *Sacred Groves and Ravaged Gardens: The Fiction of Eudora Welty, Carson McCullers, and Flannery O'Connor* (1985) convincingly extends her argument of McCullers's "rebellious tomboys" and other androgynous characters and is one of the best feminist literary studies published to date.

Patricia S. Box sets forth a convincing argument in "Androgyny and the Musical Vision: A Study of Two Novels by Carson McCullers" (1978) that only the androgynous Mick and Frankie and Biff (of all the characters in *The Heart Is a Lonely Hunter* and *The Member of the Wedding*) can feel love for all mankind without being inhibited by sexual prejudice. Distinct sexuality, says McCullers, "erects a barrier to human interaction and stifles any attempts at unity and understanding between individuals." Whereas Mick and Frankie evolve from sexual ambivalence to a maturity of sorts, yet as women have no real hope for release from their caught conditions, Biff—the adult male androgyn—"moves from impotent manhood to an androgyny full of hope." Only the androgynes are guided by music, McCullers's metaphor for the ability to elude spiritual isolation, and only they "are capable of lifting themselves out of the world of superficiality and creating a universe in which people genuinely care about one another." But music "fails" both Mick and Frankie as they move into young womanhood and resign themselves to the traditional scheme of things. Biff, on the other hand, accepts his androgyny much later in life, after his wife has died and he can repudiate forever the traditional male role of husband. Music was not a part of Biff's married life, but he remembers that before his marriage he had played the mandolin. As he becomes less polarized toward one sex, music begins to affect him again and his compassion for the plight of mankind is similarly enhanced.

Margaret Bolsterli in "'Bound' Characters in Porter, Welty, McCullers: The Prerevolutionary Status of Women in American Fiction" (1978) posits that the Women's Movement has had sufficient impact in the last twenty years to warrant a review of the treatment of women in fiction writing during the years just preceding the 1960s. The fiction of Porter, Welty, and McCullers reflects a traditional world view of fixed ideas about what a woman should and should not be. McCullers's Miss Amelia appears to be an exception. She looks different and is, yet is pulled down from her liberated perch by the one force she cannot conquer: love. In effect, she is punished for her individuality by losing Lymon's love; without it she cannot function as a complete person. Bolsterli suggests that the Amelias of fiction will remain "imprisoned" in their world until society itself allows real women to be free, whereupon a new world in fiction will reflect a new world in reality, just as the old world is reflected in the fiction of its day.

Charlene Clark offers a feminist reading in "Male-Female Pairs in Carson McCullers' *The Ballad of the Sad Café* and *The Member of the Wedding*" (1979). Linking Frankie with John Henry and Miss Amelia with Cousin Lymon—both pairs cousins—Clark demonstrates that McCullers's aggressive females not only dominate their passive males but also vent their aggression through violence. The irony is that in the more realistic work, *The Member of the Wedding,* the children want to "grow up too fast and join the adult world their behavior mimics" (the precocious John Henry dies before he can enter the real adult world), whereas in the fable, *The Ballad of the Sad Café,* the pair of adults carry on as children. Miss Amelia is an emotional and sexual "adolescent" who refused to consummate her marriage to Marvin Macy, and Cousin Lymon is a petulant and spoiled "crybaby."

Still another feminist reading of McCullers's work is Claire Kahane's "Gothic Mirrors and Feminine Identity" (1980), in which she treats *The Ballad of the Sad Café* and the hermaphroditic Miss Amelia as a "redefined modern Gothic fiction" and places McCullers closer to O'Connor than any of their other contemporaries. A feminist and psychoanalytic critic, Kahane notes that feminist criticism and contemporary psychoanalytic criticism stress the "personal, the individual, the subjective as it shapes both the creative and critical acts," techniques quite different from the "objective practitioners of New Criticism." Her article deals with what she "sees" when she looks at Gothic fiction, treating first several eighteenth-century Gothic romances, then three works by McCullers, O'Connor, and Shirley Jackson.

Mary Roberts's "Imperfect Androgyny and Imperfect Love in the Works of Carson McCullers" (1980) posits that McCullers portrays neither the true androgyne nor the hermaphrodite, but an "incomplete androgyne" unhappily incarcerated with a dualistic nature that he tries desperately to break free of by "imagining a beloved who can make him or her whole." Narcissism is its impetus, insists Roberts, who illustrates her thesis with a careful examination of *The Heart Is a Lonely Hunter, Reflections in a Golden Eye* and *The Member of the Wedding,* as well as several short pieces including McCullers's poetical statement in "Father, Upon Thy Image We Are Spanned." To Roberts, it is McCullers's "supreme achievement to have illuminated, in patterns of extremity, those images of wholeness which haunt the fragmented consciousness."

John Updike

(1932-   )

Donald J. Greiner
University of South Carolina

PRIMARY BIBLIOGRAPHY

Books and Pamphlets

The Carpentered Hen and Other Tame Creatures. New York: Harper, 1958; London: Gollancz, 1959 (as *Hoping for a Hoopoe*). Poems.

The Poorhouse Fair. New York: Knopf, 1959; London: Gollancz, 1959. Novel.

The Same Door. New York: Knopf, 1959; London: Deutsch, 1962. Short stories.

Rabbit, Run. New York: Knopf, 1960; London: Deutsch, 1961. Novel.

Pigeon Feathers and Other Stories. New York: Knopf, 1962; London: Deutsch, 1962. Short stories.

The Magic Flute. New York: Knopf, 1962; London: Deutsch & Ward, 1964. Children's story.

The Centaur. New York: Knopf, 1963; London: Deutsch, 1963. Novel.

Telephone Poles and Other Poems. New York: Knopf, 1963; London: Deutsch, 1964. Poems.

Olinger Stories: A Selection. New York: Vintage, 1964. Short stories.

The Ring. New York: Knopf, 1964. Children's story.

Assorted Prose. New York: Knopf, 1965; London: Deutsch, 1965. Essays and reviews.

Of the Farm. New York: Knopf, 1965; London: Deutsch, 1966. Novel.

A Child's Calendar. New York: Knopf, 1965. Children's poems.

The Music School. New York: Knopf, 1966; London: Deutsch, 1967. Short stories.

Couples. New York: Knopf, 1968; London: Deutsch, 1968. Novel.

Bath After Sailing. Stevenson, Conn.: Country Squire Books, 1968. Poem. Limited edition.

Three Texts from Early Ipswich. Ipswich, Mass.: The 17th Century Day Committee of the Town of Ipswich, 1968. Historical pageant.

The Angels. Pensacola, Fla.: The King & Queen Press, 1968. Poem. Limited edition.

On Meeting Authors. Newburyport, Mass.: Wickford, 1968. Essay. Limited edition.

Midpoint and Other Poems. New York: Knopf, 1969; London: Deutsch, 1969. Poems.

Bottom's Dream. New York: Knopf, 1969. Children's story.

Bech: A Book. New York: Knopf, 1970; London: Deutsch, 1970. Short story cycle.

Rabbit Redux. New York: Knopf, 1971; London: Deutsch, 1972. Novel.

Museums and Women and Other Stories. New York: Knopf, 1972; London: Deutsch, 1973. Short stories.

Warm Wine: An Idyll. New York: Albondocani Press, 1973. Short story. Limited edition.

Six Poems. New York: Aloe, 1973. Poems. Limited edition.

A Good Place. New York: Aloe, 1973. Essay. Limited edition.

Buchanan Dying. New York: Knopf, 1974; London: Deutsch, 1974. Play.

Cunts. New York: Frank Hallman, 1974. Poem. Limited edition.

A Month of Sundays. New York: Knopf, 1975; London: Deutsch, 1975. Novel.

Picked-Up Pieces. New York: Knopf, 1975; London: Deutsch, 1976. Essays and reviews.

Marry Me: A Romance. New York: Knopf, 1976; London: Deutsch, 1977. Novel.

Couples: A Short Story. Cambridge, Mass.: Halty Ferguson, 1976. Short story. Limited edition.

Tossing and Turning. New York: Knopf, 1977; London: Deutsch, 1977. Poems.

Hub Fans Bid Kid Adieu. Northridge, Cal.: Lord John, 1977. Essay. Limited edition.

The Coup. New York: Knopf, 1978; London: Deutsch, 1979. Novel.

From the Journal of a Leper. Northridge, Cal.: Lord John, 1978. Short story. Limited edition.

Too Far to Go: The Maples Stories. New York: Fawcett Crest, 1979. Short story cycle.

Sixteen Sonnets. Cambridge, Mass.: Halty Ferguson, 1979. Poems. Limited edition.

Three Illuminations in the Life of An American Author. New York: Targ, 1979. Short story. Limited edition.

Talk from the Fifties. Northridge, Cal.: Lord John, 1979. Essays and observations. Limited edition.

Problems and Other Stories. New York: Knopf, 1979; London: Deutsch, 1980. Short stories.

The Chaste Planet. Worcester, Mass.: Metacom, 1980. Short story. Limited edition.

Ego and Art in Walt Whitman. New York: Targ, 1980. Essay. Limited edition.

Five Poems. Cleveland: Bits, 1980. Poems. Limited edition.

People One Knows: Interviews with Insufficiently Famous Americans. Northridge, Cal.: Lord John, 1980. Short stories. Limited edition.

Rabbit Is Rich. New York: Knopf, 1981; London: Deutsch, 1982. Novel.

Hawthorne's Creed. New York: Targ, 1981. Essay. Limited edition.

Invasion of the Book Envelopes. Concord, N.H.: Ewert, 1981. Short story. Limited edition.

Bech Is Back. New York: Knopf, 1982; London: Deutsch, 1983. Short story cycle.

The Beloved. Northridge, Cal.: Lord John, 1982. Short story. Limited edition.

Spring Trio. Winston-Salem: Palaemon, 1982. Poems. Limited edition.

Hugging the Shore. New York: Knopf, 1983; London: Deutsch, 1984. Essays and reviews.

The Witches of Eastwick. New York: Knopf, 1984; London: Deutsch, 1984. Novel.

Jester's Dozen. Northridge, Cal.: Lord John, 1984. Poems. Limited edition.

Confessions of a Wild Bore. Newton, Iowa: Tamazunchale, 1984. Short story. Limited edition.

Emersonianism. Cleveland: Bits, 1984. Essay. Limited edition.

Facing Nature. New York: Knopf, 1985; London: Deutsch, 1986. Poems.

Selected Essays

"The Dilemma of Ipswich," *Ford Times,* 65 (Sept. 1972), 8-15.
"Melville's Withdrawal," *New Yorker,* 10 May 1982, pp. 120-147.
"Personal History: A Soft Spring Night in Shillington," *New Yorker,* 24 Dec. 1984, pp. 37-57.

Translation

Borges, Jorge Luis. *Selected Poems 1923-1967,* ed. Norman Thomas
    Di Giovanni. New York: Delacorte, 1972. Three poems trans-
    lated by Updike.

Edited Book

The Best American Short Stories 1984. Boston: Houghton Mifflin, 1984.

Editions and Collections

*Verse: The Carpentered Hen and Other Tame Creatures/Telephone Poles and
    Other Poems.* Greenwich, Conn.: Fawcett Crest, 1965. Poems.
Seventy Poems. Harmondsworth: Penguin, 1972. Poems.
Rabbit Is Rich/Rabbit Redux/Rabbit, Run. New York: Quality Book Club,
    1981. Novels.

SECONDARY BIBLIOGRAPHY

Bibliographies and Checklists

Meyer, Arlin G., and Michael A. Olivas. "Criticism of John Updike:
    A Selected Checklist," *Modern Fiction Studies,* 20 (Spring 1974),
    121-133. Secondary.
Olivas, Michael A. *An Annotated Bibliography of John Updike Criticism
    1967-1973, and A Checklist of His Works.* New York: Garland,
    1975. Primary & secondary.
Roberts, Ray A. "John Updike: A Bibliographical Checklist," *American
    Book Collector,* 1, new series (Jan.-Feb., Mar.-Apr. 1980), 5-12,
    40-44; 39-47. Primary.
Sokoloff, B. A., and David E. Arnason. *John Updike: A Comprehensive
    Bibliography.* Norwood, Pa.: Norwood Editions, 1972. Primary &
    secondary.
Taylor, C. Clarke. *John Updike: A Bibliography.* Kent, Ohio: Kent State
    University Press, 1968. Primary & secondary.

Interviews

Bech, Henry (John Updike). "Henry Bech Redux," *New York Times Book Review,* 14 Nov. 1971, p. 3.

_____. "Updike on Updike," *New York Times Book Review,* 27 Sept. 1981, pp. 1, 34-35.

Burgin, Richard. "A Conversation with John Updike," *John Updike Newsletter,* 10, 11 (Spring-Summer 1979), 1-11 (also in *New York Arts Journal,* nos. 9, 11, 1978).

DeVine, Lawrence. "Updike: Life Meets Paper," *Detroit Free Press,* 26 June 1983, pp. 1C, 4C.

Findlay, William. "Interview with John Updike," *Cencrastus,* 15 (New Year 1984), 30-36.

Gado, Frank. "John Updike." In *First Person: Conversations on Writers and Writing,* ed. Gado. Schenectady, N.Y.: Union College Press, 1973, 80-109.

Howard, Jane. "Can a Nice Novelist Finish First?," *Life,* 4 Nov. 1966, pp. 74-74A, 74C-74D, 79-82.

Kakutani, Michiko. "Turning Sex and Guilt into an American Epic," *Saturday Review,* 253 (Oct. 1981), 14-15, 20-22.

Nichols, Lewis. "Talk with John Updike," *New York Times Book Review,* 7 Apr. 1968, pp. 34-35.

Reilly, Charlie. "A Conversation with John Updike," *Canto,* 3 (Aug. 1980), 148-178.

Rhode, Eric. "Grabbing Dilemmas: John Updike Talks about God, Love, and the American Identity," *Vogue,* 157 (Feb. 1971), 140, 184-185.

Rubins, Josh. "Industrious Drifter in Room 2," *Harvard Magazine,* 76 (May 1974), 42-45, 51.

Samuels, Charles Thomas. "The Art of Fiction XLIII: John Updike," *Paris Review,* 12 (Winter 1968), 84-117.

Seib, Philip. "A Lovely Way Through Life," *Southwest Review,* 66 (Autumn 1981), 341-350.

Sheraton, Mimi. "John Updike Ruminates on Matters Gustatory," *New York Times,* 15 Dec. 1982, pp. 19Y, 21Y.

Vendler, Helen. "John Updike on Poetry," *New York Times Book Review,* 10 Apr. 1977, pp. 3, 28.

Critical Studies: Books

Burchard, Rachael C. *John Updike: Yea Sayings*. Carbondale: Southern
Illinois University Press, 1971.

Detweiler, Robert. *John Updike*. New York: Twayne, 1972. rev. ed.
1984.

Greiner, Donald J. *Adultery in the American Novel: Updike, James, Hawthorne*. Columbia: University of South Carolina Press, 1985.

_____. *John Updike's Novels*. Athens: Ohio University Press, 1984.
Includes primary bibliography.

_____. *The Other John Updike: Poems/Short Stories/Prose/Play*. Ath-
ens: Ohio University Press, 1981. Includes primary bibliography.

Hamilton, Alice and Kenneth. *The Elements of John Updike*. Grand
Rapids, Mich.: William B. Eerdmans, 1970.

_____. *John Updike: A Critical Essay*. Grand Rapids, Mich.: William
B. Eerdmans, 1967.

Hunt, George. *John Updike and the Three Great Secret Things: Sex, Religion, and Art*. Grand Rapids, Mich.: William B. Eerdmans, 1980.

Markle, Joyce B. *Fighters and Lovers: Theme in the Novels of John Updike*.
New York: New York University Press, 1973.

Samuels, Charles Thomas. *John Updike*. Minneapolis: University of
Minnesota Press, 1969.

Tallent, Elizabeth. *Married Men and Magic Tricks: John Updike's Erotic
Heroes*. Berkeley: Creative Arts, 1981.

Taylor, Larry E. *Pastoral and Anti-Pastoral Patterns in John Updike's
Fiction*. Carbondale: Southern Illinois University Press, 1971.

Uphaus, Suzanne Henning. *John Updike*. New York: Ungar, 1980.

Vargo, Edward P. *Rainstorms and Fire: Ritual in the Novels of John Updike*.
Port Washington, N.Y.: Kennikat Press, 1973.

Critical Studies: Collections of Essays

Macnaughton, William R., ed. *Critical Essays on John Updike*. Boston:
G. K. Hall, 1982.

Thorburn, David and Howard Eiland, eds. *John Updike: A Collection
of Critical Essays*. Englewood Cliffs, N.J.: Prentice-Hall, 1979.

Critical Studies: Special Issues of Journals, Newsletters

The John Updike Newsletter (Northridge, Cal.), 1977-1980.
Modern Fiction Studies, 20 (Spring 1974). Updike number.

Critical Studies: Major Articles and Book Sections

Adler, Renata. "Arcadia, Pa.," *New Yorker,* 13 Apr. 1963, pp. 182-188.

Atlas, James. "John Updike Breaks Out of Suburbia," *New York Times Sunday Magazine,* 10 Dec. 1978, pp. 60-61, 63-64, 68-70, 72, 74, 76.

Backscheider, Paula and Nick. "Updike's *Couples:* Squeak in the Night," *Modern Fiction Studies,* 20 (Spring 1974), 45-52.

Barnes, Jane. "John Updike: A Literary Spider," *Virginia Quarterly Review,* 57 (Winter 1981), 79-98.

Barryman, Charles. "The Education of Harry Angstrom: Rabbit and the Moon," *Literary Review,* 27 (Fall 1983), 117-126.

Borgman, Paul. "The Tragic Hero of Updike's *Rabbit, Run,*" *Renascence,* 29 (Winter 1977), 106-112.

Brenner, Gerry. "*Rabbit, Run:* John Updike's Criticism of the 'Return to Nature,' " *Twentieth Century Literature,* 12 (Apr. 1966), 3-14. Collected in Macnaughton.

Burhans, Clinton S., Jr. "Things Falling Apart: Structure and Theme in *Rabbit, Run,*" *Studies in the Novel,* 5 (Fall 1973), 336-351. Collected in Macnaughton.

Cameron, Dee Birch. "The Unitarian Wife and the One-Eyed Man: Updike's *Marry Me* and 'Sunday Teasing,' " *Ball State University Forum,* 21 (Spring 1980), 54-64.

Crowley, Sue Mitchell. "The Rubble of Footnotes Bound into Kierkegaard," *Journal of the American Academy of Religion,* 45, 3, Supplement (Sept. 1977), H: 1011-1035.

Culbertson, Diana. "Updike's 'The Day of the Dying Rabbit,' " *Studies in American Fiction,* 7 (Spring 1979), 95-99.

DeBellis, Jack. "The Group and John Updike," *Sewanee Review,* 72 (July-Sept. 1964), 531-536.

Detweiler, Robert. "Updike's *A Month of Sundays* and the Language of the Unconscious," *Journal of the American Academy of Religion,* 47 (Dec. 1979), 609-625.

——————. "Updike's *Couples:* Eros Demythologized," *Twentieth Century Literature,* 17 (Oct. 1971), 235-246. Collected in Macnaughton.

_____. "Updike's Sermons," *Americana-Austriaca,* 5 (1979), 11-26.

Doody, Terrence A. "Updike's Idea of Reification," *Contemporary Literature,* 20 (Spring 1979), 204-220.

Doyle, Paul. "Updike's Fiction: Motifs and Techniques," *Catholic World* (Sept. 1964), 356-362.

Eiland, Howard. "Play in *Couples."* Collected in Thorburn and Eiland, 69-83.

_____. "Updike's Womanly Man," *Centennial Review,* 26 (Fall 1982), 312-323.

Enright, D. J. "Updike's Ups and Downs," *Holiday,* 38 (Nov. 1965), 162-166.

Falke, Wayne. *"Rabbit Redux:* Time/Order/God," *Modern Fiction Studies,* 20 (Spring 1974), 59-75.

Flint, Joyce. "John Updike and *Couples:* The WASP's Dilemma," *Research Studies,* 36 (Dec. 1968), 340-347.

Galloway, David D. "The Absurd Man as Saint: The Novels of John Updike." In his *The Absurd Hero in American Fiction: Updike, Styron, Bellow, Salinger.* 1966. 2nd rev. ed. Austin: University of Texas Press, 1981, 17-80.

Gindin, James. "Megalotopia and the WASP Backlash: The Fiction of Mailer and Updike," *Centennial Review,* 15 (Winter 1971), 38-52.

Griffith, Albert J. "Updike's Artist's Dilemma: 'Should Wizard Hit Mommy?,' " *Modern Fiction Studies,* 20 (Spring 1974), 111-115.

Hamilton, Alice and Kenneth. "John Updike: Chronicler of the Time of the 'Death of God,' " *Christian Century,* 84 (7 June 1967), 745-748.

_____. "John Updike's Prescription for Survival," *Christian Century,* 89 (5 July 1972), 740-744.

_____. "Metamorphosis Through Art: John Updike's *Bech: A Book,"* *Queen's Quarterly,* 77 (Winter 1970), 624-636. Collected in Macnaughton.

_____. "Theme and Technique in John Updike's *Midpoint,"* *Mosaic,* 4 (Fall 1970), 79-106.

_____. "The Validation of Religious Faith in the Writings of John Updike," *Studies in Religion/Sciences Religieuses,* 5 (1976), 275-285.

Harper, Howard M., Jr. "John Updike: The Intrinsic Problem of Human Existence." In his *Desperate Faith: A Study of Bellow, Salinger, Mailer, Baldwin and Updike.* Chapel Hill: University of North Carolina Press, 1967, 162-190.

Hicks, Granville. "Mysteries of the Commonplace," *Saturday Review,* 17 Mar. 1962, pp. 21-22.

Hoag, Ronald Wesley. "A Second Controlling Myth in John Updike's *The Centaur,*" *Studies in the Novel,* 11 (Winter 1979), 446-453.

Hogan, Robert E. "Catharism and John Updike's *Rabbit, Run,*" *Renascence,* 32 (Summer 1980), 229-239.

Hunt, George W. "Reality, Imagination, and Art: The Significance of Updike's 'Best' Story," *Studies in Short Fiction,* 16 (Summer 1979), 219-229. Collected in Macnaughton.

_____. "Updike's Omega-Shaped Shelter: Structure and Psyche in *A Month of Sundays,*" *Critique: Studies in Modern Fiction,* 19, no. iii (1978), 47-60.

_____. "Updike's Pilgrims in a World of Nothingness," *Thought,* 53 (Dec. 1978), 384-400.

Hyman, Stanley Edgar. "The Artist as a Young Man," *New Leader,* 45 (19 Mar. 1962), 22-23.

Kazin, Alfred. "Professional Observers: Cozzens to Updike." In his *Bright Book of Life: American Novelists and Storytellers from Hemingway to Mailer.* Boston: Little, Brown, 1973, 95-124.

Klausler, A. P. "Steel Wilderness," *Christian Century,* 22 Feb. 1961, pp. 245-246.

Klinkowitz, Jerome. "John Updike since *Midpoint.*" In his *The Practice of Fiction in America: Writers, from Hawthorne to the Present.* Ames: Iowa State University Press, 1980, 85-97.

_____. "John Updike's America," *North American Review,* 265, no. iii (Sept. 1980), 68-71.

Kort, Wesley A. *"The Centaur* and the Problem of Vocation." In his *Shriven Selves: Religious Problems in Recent American Fiction.* Philadelphia: Fortress Press, 1972, 64-89.

La Course, Guerin. "The Innocence of John Updike," *Commonweal,* 88 (7 Dec. 1962), 512-514.

Larsen, R. B. "John Updike: The Story as Lyrical Meditation," *Thoth,* 13, no. i (1972), 33-39.

Lawson, Lewis A. "Rabbit Angstrom as a Religious Sufferer," *Journal of the American Academy of Religion,* 42, 2 (June 1974), 232-246.

Locke, Richard. *"Rabbit Redux,"* New York Times Book Review, 14 Nov. 1971, pp. 1-2, 12-16, 20-24. Collected in Thorburn and Eiland.

Lodge, David. "Post-Pill Paradise Lost: John Updike's *Couples.*" In his *The Novelist at the Crossroads, and Other Essays on Fiction and Criticism.* Ithaca, N.Y.: Cornell University Press, 1971, 237-244. Collected in Thorburn and Eiland.

Lyons, Eugene. "John Updike: The Beginning and the End," *Critique: Studies in Modern Fiction*, 14, no. ii (1972), 44-59.

McCoy, Robert. "John Updike's Literary Apprenticeship on *The Harvard Lampoon*," *Modern Fiction Studies*, 20 (Spring 1974), 3-12.

McFarland, Ronald E. "Updike and the Critics: Reflections on 'A&P,' " *Studies in Short Fiction*, 20 (Spring-Summer 1983), 95-100.

McKenzie, Alan T. " 'A Craftsman's Intimate Satisfactions': The Parlor Games in *Couples*," *Modern Fiction Studies*, 20 (Spring 1974), 53-58.

Matthews, John T. "The World as Scandal: Updike's *A Month of Sundays*," *Arizona Quarterly*, 39 (Winter 1983), 351-380.

Mellard, James M. "The Novel as Lyric Elegy: The Mode of Updike's *The Centaur*," *Texas Studies in Literature and Language*, 21 (Spring 1979), 112-127. Collected in Macnaughton.

Mizener, Arthur. "The American Hero as High School Boy: Peter Caldwell." In his *The Sense of Life in the Modern Novel*. Boston: Houghton Mifflin, 1964, 247-266. Collected in Thorburn and Eiland.

_____. "Behind the Dazzle Is a Knowing Eye," *New York Times Book Review*, 18 Mar. 1962, pp. 1, 29. Collected in Macnaughton.

Muradian, Thaddeus. "The World of John Updike," *English Journal*, 54 (Oct. 1965), 577-584.

Myers, David. "The Questing Fear: Christian Allegory in John Updike's *The Centaur*," *Twentieth Century Literature*, 17 (Apr. 1971), 73-82.

Novak, Michael. "Updike's Quest for Liturgy," *Commonweal*, 10 May 1963, pp. 192-195. Collected in Thorburn and Eiland.

Oates, Joyce Carol. "Updike's American Comedies," *Modern Fiction Studies*, 21 (Autumn 1975), 459-472. Collected in Thorburn and Eiland.

Overall, Nadine. "John Updike's *Olinger Stories: A Selection*," *Studies in Short Fiction*, 4 (Winter 1967), 195-197.

Plagman, Linda M. "*Eros* and *Agape*: The Opposition in Updike's *Couples*," *Renascence*, 28 (Winter 1976), 83-93.

Podhoretz, Norman. "A Dissent on Updike." In his *Doings and Undoings: The Fifties and After in American Writing*. New York: Farrar, Straus, 1964, 251-257.

Regan, Robert A. "Updike's Symbol of the Center," *Modern Fiction Studies*, 20 (Spring 1974), 77-96.

Rosa, Alfred F. "The Psycholinguistics of Updike's 'Museums and Women,' " *Modern Fiction Studies*, 20 (Spring 1974), 107-111.

Rupp, Richard H. "John Updike: Style in Search of a Center," *Sewanee Review,* 75 (Oct.-Dec. 1967), 693-709.

Schopen, Bernard A. "Faith, Morality, and the Novels of John Updike," *Twentieth Century Literature,* 24 (Winter 1978), 523-535. Collected in Macnaughton.

Shurr, William H. "The Lutheran Experience in John Updike's 'Pigeon Feathers,' " *Studies in Short Fiction,* 14 (Fall 1977), 329-335.

Standley, Fred L. "*Rabbit, Run:* An Image of Life," *Midwest Quarterly,* 8 (Summer 1967), 371-386.

Steiner, George. "Scarlet Letters," *New Yorker,* 10 Mar. 1975, pp. 116-118. Collected in Thorburn and Eiland.

Strandberg, Victor. "John Updike and the Changing of the Gods," *Mosaic,* 12 (Fall 1978), 157-175. Collected in Macnaughton.

Stubbs, John C. "The Search for Perfection in *Rabbit, Run,*" *Critique: Studies in Modern Fiction,* 10 (Spring-Summer 1968), 94-101.

Suderman, Elmer F. "The Right Way and the Good Way in *Rabbit, Run,*" *University Review,* 36 (Oct. 1969), 13-21.

Tanner, Tony. "A Compromised Environment." In his *City of Words: American Fiction, 1950-1970.* New York: Harper & Row, 1971, 273-294.

Turner, Kermit. "Rabbit Brought Nowhere: John Updike's *Rabbit Redux,*" *South Carolina Review,* 8 (Nov. 1975), 35-42.

Uphaus, Suzanne. "*The Centaur:* Updike's Mock Epic," *Journal of Narrative Technique,* 7 (Winter 1977), 24-36. Collected in Macnaughton.

_____. "The Unified Vision of *A Month of Sundays,*" *University of Windsor Review,* 12 (Spring-Summer 1977), 5-16.

Vickery, John B. "*The Centaur:* Myth, History, and Narrative," *Modern Fiction Studies,* 20 (Spring 1974), 29-43.

"View from the Catacombs," *Time,* 26 Apr. 1968, pp. 66-75.

Waldmeir, Joseph. "It's the Going That's Important, Not the Getting There: Rabbit's Questing Non-Quest," *Modern Fiction Studies,* 20 (Spring 1974), 13-27.

Waldron, Randall H. "Rabbit Revised," *American Literature,* 56 (Mar. 1984), 51-67.

Waller, G. F. "Updike's *Couples:* A Barthian Parable," *Research Studies,* 40 (Mar. 1973), 10-21.

Ward, John A. "John Updike's Fiction," *Critique: Studies In Modern Fiction,* 5 (Spring-Summer 1962), 27-40.

Waxman, Robert E. "Invitations to Dread: John Updike's Metaphysical Quest," *Renascence,* 29 (Summer 1977), 201-210.

Wyatt, Bryant N. "John Updike: The Psychological Novel in Search of Structure," *Twentieth Century Literature*, 13 (July 1967), 89-96.

BIBLIOGRAPHICAL ESSAY

Bibliographies and Checklists

There is no definitive primary or secondary bibliography of John Updike. Of the several available, Ray Roberts's is indispensable. His "John Updike: A Bibliographical Checklist" (1980) includes the information necessary to identify the first American and English editions of Updike's separate publications through 1979. Roberts lists the various states as well as the colors of bindings and statements of limitation for Updike's numerous rare, limited editions.

Two book-length annotated bibliographies survey primary and secondary materials. C. Clarke Taylor's *John Updike: A Bibliography* (1968) is now dated, but its special value is the listing of Updike's uncollected work from 1949 through July 1967. Thus unlike other bibliographies, it includes information about Updike's contributions to *Chatterbox* (Shillington, Pennsylvania) during his senior year in high school as well as about his appearances in the *Harvard Lampoon*. Annotations of the secondary material are brief, and not every entry is annotated. Michael A. Olivas's *An Annotated Bibliography of John Updike Criticism 1967-1973, and A Checklist of His Works* (1975) is designed to supplement Taylor's bibliography. Olivas provides a generally accurate annotated checklist of primary and secondary materials through 1973, but he is especially helpful with his lists of Updike's uncollected poems, short stories, reviews, and essays. Annotations of the secondary material are discriminating and are divided into headings of "general" and "specific."

Although B. A. Sokoloff and David E. Arnason include many reviews and essays in *John Updike: A Comprehensive Bibliography* (1972), they do not annotate the entries. In addition, their list of the primary material is incomplete, for they omit *Bottom's Dream* (1969). An especially helpful section of their bibliography is the checklist of Updike's uncollected poetry and prose.

Donald J. Greiner's "Selected Checklist" in *The Other John Updike* (1981) lists the original place and date of publication of individual poems, short stories, reviews, and essays that Updike has collected through *Tossing and Turning* (1977), but Greiner, too, cannot locate every source.

Interviews

Since there are as yet no formal biographies, authorized or otherwise, the reader will need to draw upon interviews and critical studies for biographical data.

Although published relatively early in Updike's career, Charles Thomas Samuels's interview with Updike remains the most comprehensive of the author's recorded conversations. Full of information about his life and work, "The Art of Fiction XLIII: John Updike" (1968) has comments about his apprentice years as a writer for the *Harvard Lampoon:* "I began as a cartoonist, did a lot of light verse, and more and more prose. . . . I do have a romantic weakness for gags." Updike also talks about his long association with the *New Yorker:* "From the age of twelve when my aunt gave us a subscription for Christmas, the *New Yorker* has seemed to me the best of possible magazines." Especially useful, however, are Updike's observations on the relationships among his youth near Shillington, Pennsylvania, his maturity in Ipswich, Massachusetts, his family, and his writing. Shillington becomes Olinger in the fiction, just as Ipswich develops into Tarbox, and Updike describes the shift in emphasis as a significant part of his life and art: "The difference between Olinger and Tarbox is much more the difference between childhood and adulthood than the difference between two geographical locations. They are stages on my pilgrim's progress." Commenting on his work through *Couples* (1968) and *Midpoint* (1969), he supplies information that aids all readers: *Rabbit, Run* (1960) was originally subtitled "A Movie"; *The Centaur* (1963) explores the conflict between self-sacrifice and private agony; *Couples* has a happy ending. Perhaps the most revealing comment in the interview is Updike's description of his canon: "My work is meditation, not pontification."

Not as comprehensive but equally as interesting is the interview with Jane Howard. "Can a Nice Novelist Finish First?" (1966) is a valuable source for Updike's thoughts on his penchant for mimesis and domestic topics. Defining his focus as the Protestant small-town middle class, he tells Howard: "I like middles. It is in middles that extremes clash, where ambiguity restlessly rules." He goes on to confirm his interest in the "despair of the daily," and he points to the theology of Kierkegaard and Karl Barth as helping him contest an overwhelming sense of doubt. Despite his statement to Howard that he is "still running on energy laid down in childhood," Updike hints that Barth will become more important to his life and art. This change of emphasis may be seen in *Couples,* a novel that Updike discusses with Lewis Nichols in "Talk with John Updike" (1968). Explaining that after *Of the Farm* (1965) he wanted to leave Pennsylvania "fictionally," Updike points to *Couples* to illustrate his move from small town to suburbia. This interview will help the reader interested in Updike's notion that sex is the "motive force of the new humanism," the substitute when the religion of the preceding generation loses its power to convince, its ability to counter despair.

One of the interesting features about Updike's interviews is his willingness occasionally to make fun of the format. In "Bech Meets Me," also known as "Henry Bech Redux" (1971), Updike in the guise of his own character, Bech, interviews himself upon the publication of *Rabbit Redux* (1971). Parodying the form of the interview by asking such questions as "are you happy?," he then confesses his frustration with reviews of his work: "All the little congruences and arabesques you prepared with such delicate anticipatory pleasure are gobbled up as if by pigs at a pastry cart." This rather sharp retort is aimed at reviewers and critics who are unable to read a book without imposing their definitions of what they think fiction should be. Yet the tone of the short interview with Henry Bech is light, as when Bech mistakenly calls *Rabbit Redux* "Rabbit Rerun."

Ten years later, upon the publication of *Rabbit Is Rich* (1981), Updike consented to another mock interview with Bech. In "Updike on Updike" (1981), he again describes the frustration of having his books noted by reviewers who "don't read more than they have to," but he also confesses that he takes "considerable satisfaction" in the reviews that he himself writes. For all the jaunty tone, however, this interview is significant because of Updike's definition of the novelist's chore. Once again insisting that humanity must rest content with the typical instead of the noble, he reiterates his commitment to the mysteriousness of the mundane: "I distrust books involving spectacular people, or spectacular events. . . . let literature concern itself, as the Gospels do, with the inner lives of hidden men."

Between the publication of the two talks with Henry Bech, Updike consented to several significant interviews. Perhaps the most useful is his conversation with Frank Gado (1973) in which he discusses his early fascination with J. D. Salinger's short stories. Defining Salinger's tales as "very open to the tender invasions," he compares Salinger's "retreat into silence" and Bech's writer's block. This interview will be especially important to readers curious about Updike's opinions on other twentieth-century American authors. With perception and patience, he talks about Jack Kerouac, John Barth, John O'Hara, Bernard Malamud, Philip Roth, and James Gould Cozzens, as well as Hemingway and Fitzgerald. Most telling is his contrast between the generation of the 1920s with its "authentic literary environment," and his own world of publishing which seems dominated by the "academic sphere." This interview also contains many observations about *Rabbit, Run.*

Although not as far-reaching as the discussion with Gado, Updike's interview with Eric Rhode contains revealing general information about the canon. In "Grabbing Dilemmas" (1971), Updike defines his fictions: "they are all meant to be moral debates with the reader. . . . The question is usually 'What is a good man?' or 'What is goodness?' " Because such questions are impossible to answer definitively, Updike's books often end on what he calls a "hesitant or ambiguous note." He also talks with Rhode about specific novels: *The Centaur* is a partial record of his father; *Of the Farm* is about "moral readjustment"; *Couples* suggests that sex is the "emergent religion." Rhode does not ask about the poems, but Helen Vendler does. In "John Updike on Poetry" (1977), Updike remembers the sources of his fascination with light verse. Youthful appreciation of Phyllis McGinley, Ogden Nash, and Morris Bishop gave way to apprentice verse for the *Harvard Lampoon,* and Updike found the germ for his first book, *The Carpentered Hen* (1958), in the puns and rhymes of comic poets. Confessing that "it is always at the back of my mind to be a poet," he indirectly reveals one of the origins of his intricate, often lyrical, prose style: "I feel more at sea writing a novel than a poem, and often re-read my poetry and almost never look at my old novels."

The final important interview with Updike in the 1970s is Richard Burgin's "A Conversation with John Updike" (1979). After expressing appreciation of contemporary writers more formally experimental than himself, writers such as John Barth and Donald Barthelme, Updike answers questions about his own fiction and the public response to it. He reveals, for example, that he thought of James Joyce's *Ulysses* when he wrote *The Centaur* and that the novel illustrates how "all our childhoods are mythological to a degree." He also suggests a parallel between *Couples* and *A Month of Sundays* (1975) when he comments that the latter is about the "deep alliance between the religious impulse and the sexual. Both are a way of perpetuating our lives, of denying our physical limits." Equally important is his singling out Norman Podhoretz, John Aldridge, and Alfred Chester as reviewers who have tried to "puncture" his career. As he notes, nothing is to be gained by trying to placate such predictably disappointed readers.

Two interviews in the 1980s merit notice. In "Turning Sex and Guilt into an American Epic" (1981), Updike tells Michiko Kakutani that he is "no longer as adept at short stories and poems as I was." Part of the loss results from the tremors of middle age, and in this interview Updike says a great deal about both writing, now that he has passed the midpoint of his life, and the advancing years of Harry "Rabbit" Angstrom, his most famous character. Readers interested in *Rabbit Is Rich* and the Rabbit series in general should consult this interview for Updike's sympathetic description of the aging runner: "he's a compound of physical urgencies and spiritual illusions. . . . he's kind of good-natured and accepting. . . . A certain hardness of heart is also true of him; he is kind of callous at times." Finally, in "Interview with John Updike" (1984), Updike talks with William Findlay about the echoes of Scotland in *Bech Is Back* (1982) and *Buchanan Dying* (1974). Declaring his preference for Hume over Locke, and discussing his own understanding of Scots Protestantism, Updike muses on the "fun" he had meditating "about Scottishness" in his unusual but little read play about President Buchanan. He also reveals that just as he had Carlos Fuentes's *The Death of Artemio Cruz* in mind when he wrote *Buchanan Dying*, so he recalled Gabriel Garcia Marquez's *One Hundred Years of Solitude* when he began *The Coup* (1978). Pertinent to the interview is his comparison of his own relatively quiet career and the flamboyant successes of Norman Mailer. The entire discussion with Findlay is important to readers with more than a cursory interest in the Updike canon. One should remember, however, that Updike normally reserves the right to edit his interviews; thus his published responses to the questions are not always spontaneous.

Critical Studies: Books

While one cannot yet say that book-length studies of John Updike have reached the proportions of a critical industry, one nevertheless realizes that Updike's achievement is the subject of some penetrating analysis. The first extended study was written by Charles Thomas Samuels. A forty-six page pamphlet rather than a fully developed book, Samuels's *John Updike* (1969) is designed to introduce Updike to the reader who knows little about the author. Discussing

Updike's books through *Couples* (1968), and providing a short checklist of primary and secondary sources, Samuels declares that Updike should be understood as a "prodigy" because of his expertise in a variety of genres. One understands Samuels's sense of appreciation, for when his study was published, Updike had taken only a decade to blitz the reading public with acclaimed novels, unusual short stories, light verse, reviews, sketches, parodies, essays, children's books, and a pageant. As Samuels tells the reader new to Updike, the author is a force to be reckoned with.

Samuels defends Updike's "supple" prose. Although he concedes that the exquisite style occasionally calls attention to itself, he also insists that it is well adapted to "fine emotional nuance and the painterly objectivity with which he limns the external world." The style seems especially suited to the short stories of which, says Samuels, Updike is a modern master: "At his best, Updike is the detailed realist, filling his stories with facts that guarantee belief." Samuels's Updike is a traditionalist, eschewing apocalypse and arcane symbolism to make the familiar fresh and the unknown familiar.

Following brief but acute glimpses at the poems and essays, Samuels sketches what is known of Updike's biography to illustrate the loose connection between the author's life and the Olinger stories. Understandably, Samuels focuses on the short stories and novels, first cautioning the reader that since Updike believes human behavior to be ambiguous, he "wants his stories to reflect this fact." Discussion of the more autobiographical writing is followed by analysis of what Samuels calls "fiction of wider range," and in some cases he is clearly disappointed. The reader may disagree with the following examples of his judgments, but he realizes that they illustrate one critical perspective: the end of "In Football Season" (1964) is "incongruous"; the mythic parallels in *The Centaur* (1963) are "pretentious and confusing," and the novel itself is "technically a sport." Commenting on the novels that he does like, Samuels offers acceptable introductions. Since he names *Rabbit, Run* (1960) Updike's "masterpiece" and *Of the Farm* (1965) "the most irreducible of his works," he seems more eager to evaluate their nuances. In short, Samuels's pamphlet is occasionally useful but largely dated, the more recent and comprehensive criticism understandably having passed it by.

Readers looking for a source book of allusions and symbols in Updike should consult Alice and Kenneth Hamilton's *The Elements of John Updike* (1970). The first full-length book on the canon, it burgeons with information, some insignificant and some substantial, until it becomes a kind of grab bag of sources. The organization of the book is inconsequential until the Hamiltons focus on individual novels in the second half of their study, but they approach every aspect of Updike's achievement with something close to awe. Indeed, at the end of the preface they explain, "We do not apologize for our enthusiasm. It is with the most intense excitement that we have in the course of our investigation suddenly realized the implications of apparently simple statements in Updike's work."

Their eager approval and their determination to find significance in every corner of Updike's writing lead them to suggest interpretations that even the most initiated critic might not accept, but beyond the source-hunting the value of their analysis is that it prods the reader to consider reverberations, echoes, and allusions unnoticed before *Elements* was published.

Of Peter's black mistress in *The Centaur*, for example, the Hamiltons write, "In making Peter's mistress a Negress, Updike indicates Peter's wish to explore the dimension of life that keeps wholly to the human level without awareness of the divine—to explore, in Kierkegaard's terminology, *the pagan*." This may be so, but other readers might suggest that the black girlfriend is another example, along with living in a New York loft and painting second-rate abstract expressionist pictures, of Peter's rather self-conscious rebellion. All the citing of sources and allusions has its value, however, and the Hamiltons unify their discussions with a resolutely religious framework. They are particularly successful in rebutting those who dismiss Updike's concern for mundane details as superficial, and they counter such charges with the general interpretation that nothing "can be trivial in a universe ordered by truth and justice."

Their religious perspective shapes the analyses of the poems, tales, and novels through *Couples*. Calling *Couples* "the most ambitious of Updike's novels" in terms of technique (one might nominate instead *The Centaur*), the Hamiltons offer the first developed defense of that complicated and controversial book. Although the reader will finally question the insistent, religious point of view and the unceasing search for allusions, he will benefit from consulting *The Elements of John Updike*.

Much less beneficial is Rachael C. Burchard's *John Updike: Yea Sayings* (1971). Although she claims that "Updike reaches his highest range of accomplishment" in the short stories, she devotes only one short chapter to a superficial discussion of them. The following comment about the tales indicates Burchard's elementary approach to the entire Updike canon: "Illustration of the goodness of man is supported in Updike's short stories by another theme. Life is good in little things."

Like the Hamiltons, Burchard reads Updike from the perspective of affirmative Christianity, but she discusses very little of the complexity that the Hamiltons elucidate in such detail. Thus the reader must endure such conclusions as Updike "is a searcher of integrity, one who accepts no for an answer when no is the answer. Accordingly, the yes aspects of his assertions are valid too." For Burchard the "most important of John Updike's 'yea sayings' " is that God exists. Such a limited perspective all but ignores the intricacy of Updike's fiction and essays, and the reader is left with a short book that does little to sort out the difficulties.

Thus while the bulk of Burchard's study focuses on the novels through *Couples,* the reader does not learn much beyond her insistence on religious affirmation. In *The Poorhouse Fair* (1959), for example, "the author seems to suggest that the missing ingredient could be found in the religious point of view." Similarly, the disturbing and complex *Rabbit, Run* is distilled to a short account of a morally naive man who gives "up all guidance other than intuition" to achieve at the end "a sudden unreasonable but optimistic lift." Finally, in a long chapter on *Couples,* Burchard defends the novel against what she perceives are readers who believe Updike wrote the book only to upset them. Somehow she finds *Couples* incorporating "multidimensional media" to stress a message that "sex *is* important to write about." That is undoubtedly true, but the reader looking for a discussion of the theological, esthetic, and social ambiguities with which Updike frames his account of sexuality will not find it in *John Updike: Yea Sayings.*

The reader will learn a great deal, however, from Larry E. Taylor's *Pastoral and Anti-Pastoral Patterns in John Updike's Fiction* (1971). Defining the pastoral tradition from 300 B.C., Taylor shows the development of the theme in American literature from the Puritans to the twentieth century, and he suggests that Updike is the foremost contemporary pastoral writer in the United States: Updike is always conscious of the contrast between "pastoral Olinger" and the anti-pastoral big city. Implying a difference between the early stories and *The Poorhouse Fair* on the one hand, and *Rabbit, Run* on the other, Taylor illustrates how the elements of satire and fable in the latter make it an antipastoral novel.

His most convincing chapter concerns *The Centaur.* Arguing that Updike's rewriting of the Chiron myth is his best effort, Taylor discusses how Updike combines pastoral elegy and epic. The four short chapters in *The Centaur* that illuminate the legend of Chiron both reflect the conventions of the pastoral tradition and prepare the reader to regard modern Olinger as ancient Olympus. Taylor insists, correctly, that while the novel is often comic it is rarely satiric. The formal pastoralism of the four short chapters reminds the reader of the seriousness of the elegy. Theocritus's *Idyls* and Milton's *Lycidas* are distant echoes: "The chapters become the formal structural clues for reading the whole book. Idyl, hymn, obituary, love lyric, lament, epitaph—these recognizable forms within the pastoral elegy form give the novel its coherence, its dignity, its eloquence as a universal statement." Taylor adds a bonus when he translates the Greek passage at the conclusion of *The Centaur.* His entire study is a serious extension of Updike criticism.

Joyce B. Markle's *Fighters and Lovers: Theme in the Novels of John Updike* (1973) is another perceptive reading of the novels through *Rabbit Redux* (1971). Devoting a chapter to each novel, she organizes her general discussion around her definition of Updike's primary concerns: the journey from death, the necessity for lovers (characters who make others feel special), the impact of individuals on the world, the consideration of man's sense of importance, and the difficulty of relating to society. Markle explicitly declares her thesis to be "that not only does Updike deal with essentially the same problems in each of the serious novels (i.e. excluding *Bech*) but that as a group all demonstrate a progression of approach."

Of the themes that Markle defines and discusses, the most significant is Updike's understanding of the need for "specialness" and the resulting pursuit of it when a character senses that he lacks stature. Markle's analysis of *The Poorhouse Fair* is particularly helpful because she does not undervalue it as a first novel. She argues that except for the centrality of sexuality—which is no longer a pressing need in this novel of old people—*The Poorhouse Fair* "contains a surprisingly complete spectrum of Updike's thematic motifs." The opposition of Conner and Hook, for example, gives way to the conflict between Eccles and Rabbit in *Rabbit, Run,* and the Rabbit who rejects the "social corporation" develops by contrast into Caldwell in *The Centaur* who "makes the opposite choice." This kind of thematic approach can be useful, especially when Markle fills in her discussions with commentary on such varied topics as the role of children, the "decreasing force" of a moral framework from novel to novel, the complex system of imagery, and the use of painting and cinema to achieve special effects.

Markle's discussion of *Couples* is by far the most extended in her study primarily because she interprets the novel from the perspective of Denis de Rougemont's *Love in the Western World,* a seminal book that Updike knows well. The other chapters are also good, and the reader may derive special benefit from her interpretation of the psychologically intricate *Of the Farm.* Correctly identifying Mrs. Robinson as lover, mythmaker, and antagonist, for example, Markle shows that while the mother is central to the novel, Joey is central to the reader: "*She* is the focus of attention . . . but *he* is the focus of concern." Markle understands that Joey's inability to grow up is exacerbated by his visit to the farm which the novel shows to be a place of death. *Fighters and Lovers* has this kind of charity and insight throughout; a short checklist is appended.

The reader concerned with such concepts as sacredness and transcendence might examine Edward P. Vargo's *Rainstorms and Fire: Ritual in the Novels of John Updike* (1973). Vargo attributes Updike's fascination with mundane details to his sense of a "sacramental understanding" in the universe between the physical and the spiritual. Thus sports and sex in *Rabbit, Run,* for instance, offer opportunities for transcending the limitations of matter. Vargo's thesis leads him to such rhetorical flourishes as his comment on *The Centaur:* the characters create a "sacralized universe through the paradigmatic use of myth, and consequently are able to go on living in a desacralized milieu."

Vargo argues that Joey Robinson in *Of the Farm* meets a different fate. Unable to find a "sacralized universe," Joey accepts "the values of the modern world" against the wishes of his mother who understands and reveres the sacred forms of life. Thus the restless son "has practically made it impossible for himself to achieve any transcendent communion through ritual." Only Joey's awareness of his wife's earthiness offers him hope for at least sexual transcendence, and his thoughts of her while mowing the field make "it possible for Joey to attempt a harmonization of the farm with his marriage later in the novel." Sticking to his thesis throughout, Vargo suggests that "the significance of ritual is less obtrusive and more subtle in *Of the Farm* than in any of the previous novels."

More valuable is Robert Detweiler's *John Updike* (1972; 1984), a well-written introduction to the fiction. Part of the Twayne United States Authors Series, the book offers a thoughtful analysis of the relation between myth and reality in Updike, with special emphasis on the author's elegiac tone. As Detweiler explains in his preface to the revised edition, he celebrates Updike the stylist and thus has both examined the "texture and structure of his writing" and "paid special attention to the metaphoric language, above all the image patterns, that mark his style." He also focuses on Updike's status as a "literary chronicler of American marital-sexual mores and trends."

At the end of a short biographical chapter, Detweiler summarizes the Updike he will investigate in the body of his study: "a formidable and influential literary-critical force" who, as a combination of "troubling flaws" and genius, reflects the contradictions of the very society he chronicles. The flaws, for example, are evident in *Buchanan Dying* (1974), which Detweiler dismisses as "tedious" and "pedantic," whereas the genius is seen in the conclusion of *Rabbit Redux* where Updike takes the slangy word "OK" and converts "the gimmick into fine art." Detweiler unfortunately elects to discuss the Rabbit novels according to their individual positions in the chronology of Updike's canon, and thus he loses the opportunity for an overview of Updike's most famous character. Yet his short analysis of each novel rewards the reader, and one appreciates his summation of the intricacies of *Rabbit Redux:* "Updike has erected almost flagrantly difficult obstacles for himself in this novel and has overcome them, not merely for the sake of meeting the challenge . . . but to create the superior literature resulting from the imaginative realignments that his risks generate."

Detweiler's discussion of the later short story collections is too cramped to do justice to their complexities; indeed, he covers both *Problems* (1979) and *Too Far to Go* (1979) in only ten pages. But his general point about these tales of marriage and its dissolution persuades the reader to rethink them: "The reader is made to experience this disorder even as the ordering power of expert narrative writing subdues and channels it." In other words, Updike's command of image patterns, the technique that Detweiler has stressed throughout, enables him to create harmony from chaos and to convince the reader of its legitimacy. One wishes for more from Detweiler, but one benefits from his perceptiveness.

Another short but helpful introduction to Updike's novels through *The Coup* (1978) is Suzanne Henning Uphaus's *John Updike* (1980). Using her understanding of Updike's technique, particularly his style and narrative voice, as a frame, Uphaus details the theme of each novel in chronological order. Her Updike is clearly Updike the novelist, the writer who achieves "a breathtaking lyricism" that lifts the longer fiction beyond what she considers to be his "amiable" criticism, his "urbane" short stories, and his "struggling" poems.

One can disagree with Uphaus's dismissal of the rest of the canon and yet appreciate her exceptional ear for Updike's "descriptive power." She is particularly good at detailing the distinctions among his "sustained lyric intensity," his skill at "comic denouement," and his various and authentic voices. She declares that Updike's "greatest gift is the profound sympathy for his characters that his narrative voice conveys," and she correctly suggests that his combination of "verbal talent" and compassion for his characters distinguishes his novels. She uses most of her introduction to illustrate these qualities and to outline such familiar themes as the dichotomy between physical desire and spiritual yearning, the tension between ethical action and religious faith, and the preference for the theology of Karl Barth over that of Paul Tillich.

The remainder of the book is a series of short chapters, usually eight to ten pages, detailing the plot, theme, and technique of each novel. Given this introductory format, Uphaus offers insightful discussions for the beginning reader. Of *The Poorhouse Fair*, for instance, she notes "Conner's failure to recognize the animal streak of malicious and instinctive cruelty in human nature." Commenting on the responses to *Rabbit, Run,* "so varied that it is difficult to believe that critics are writing about the same novel," she shows how the reader's "uncomfortable ambivalence" mirrors Rabbit's own dilemma. Discussing Elellou's sense of uncertainty in *The Coup*, she observes that "his faith has that element of doubt that is always constant in Updike's fiction." Uphaus's most convincing chapter is on *A Month of Sundays* (1975), which she argues is the one novel that shows Updike uncharacteristically accepting a "balanced harmony" of mundane and spiritual. One would like less outlining of plot and more analyzing of theme, but within the constraints of the arrangement allowed her, Uphaus has written a satisfying study.

George Hunt's (S. J.) *John Updike and the Three Great Secret Things: Sex, Religion, and Art* (1980) ventures far beyond the introductory level to probe in detail three major themes in the Updike canon. Taking his title from Updike's autobiographical essay "The Dogwood Tree: A Boyhood" (1962), Hunt offers the most informed treatment to date of the importance of Kierkegaard and Karl Barth to Updike's fiction. Dismissing such simplistic notions that Updike affirms Christianity, Hunt discusses how the rigorous and difficult theologies of Kierkegaard and Barth shape "a religious conviction" that "buttresses" Updike's investigation of sex and art.

In so doing, Hunt arranges Updike's career into three stages in which religion dominates the early phase, sex the middle, and art the later. Yet Hunt knows that each of the three touches on the others, and thus he demonstrates that sex, religion, and art interweave and complement rather than divide and define. Such unity of theme carries over into Hunt's organization of his book, and he correctly urges the reader to "begin at the beginning" rather than read individual chapters: "For some, the immediate dive into the chilly waters of Kierkegaard and Barth might seem a formidable prospect, but I believe they present important illustrations of Updike's sophisticated intelligence."

Those who follow Hunt's advice will find an intellectually stimulating first chapter on *The Poorhouse Fair* and *Rabbit, Run*, followed by good studies of the novels through *The Coup* and of the stories "The Astronomer" (1962) and "Leaves" (1966). Using his opening chapter to document Updike's long interest in Kierkegaard and Barth, he discusses such issues as "Kierkegaard and the Dread of Nothingness" and Barth and "the Power of Nothingness." Hunt shows, for instance, that Updike takes many of his references to Barth from the theologian's "dogmatic" chapter on "Nothingness" in which Barth comments on the nature of evil. Insisting that some acquaintance with Barth is mandatory for the reader of Updike, Hunt clarifies how Barth's concept of Nothingness is a "drastic departure from the philosophic analysis of Nothingness offered by such Existentialists as Sartre or the early Heidegger."

Hunt's sophisticated analysis benefits the initiated reader who is looking for more than superficial commentary on such troubling novels as *Couples* and *A Month of Sundays*. Hunt may be disappointed by the "defects" of *Rabbit Redux*, but he argues that the flaws are "redeemed" in *A Month of Sundays*. His defense of the latter, surely one of the most unusual books by Updike, is important because, as he notes, Updike's novels subsequent to *Couples* have not been adequately treated. *A Month of Sundays* is a milestone because "it capsulizes humorously so much thematic material found in Updike's previous fiction." Readers still hesitant about this "religious" novel should consult Hunt's chapter, which is written by a Jesuit and which analyzes Updike's portrait of a wayward Protestant minister who knows Karl Barth as thoroughly as the Updike who creates him. Sex, religion, and art merge comically in this story of the Reverend Tom Marshfield, and

Hunt carefully takes the reader through the intricate merger. *John Updike and the Three Great Secret Things* is a rewarding book.

When read together, Donald J. Greiner's three books on Updike provide an in-depth overview of the canon through *Rabbit Is Rich* (1981) and suggest Updike's place in the American literary tradition. The earliest of these studies, *The Other John Updike: Poems/Short Stories/ Prose/Play* (1981), examines all of the major volumes through 1977 except the novels. Thus the reader will find the first sustained analysis of four collections of poetry, five of short fiction, two of essays and reviews, and the play *Buchanan Dying*.

Greiner briefly surveys the commentary that greeted the collections in order to show how each has been received. He then groups the books according to genre and offers close readings of individual poems, tales, and essays. Discussing the poetry, for example, he notes that the generally rhymed "verbal acrobatics" of the early poems in *The Carpentered Hen* (1958) are "couched in traditional stanza and metric patterns with amusing twists" to induce a smile, but he also shows that Updike's sense of the gaiety of words is part of his celebration of language itself and thus central to the prose style that has generated so much comment. In other words, Updike's comic poetry is not merely a literary sidelight. Tracing Updike's noticeable de-emphasis of light verse in other volumes, Greiner discusses how such poems as "Seven Stanzas at Easter," "Telephone Poles," "Midpoint," and "My Children at the Dump" point to the significantly darker tone in *Tossing and Turning* (1977), a collection that expresses the losses and hesitations of "a man past midpoint graying toward middle age."

Examining the short story collections through *Museums and Women* (1972), Greiner finds that Updike has moved from nostalgia through lyrical meditation toward irony. Updike's glance over his shoulder in "The Happiest I've Been" (1959) and "Flight" (1962) results in traditionally structured tales written in Updike's distinctive style, but even as early as *Pigeon Feathers* (1962) Updike begins to advance the form of the short story with such innovative meditations as "Wife-wooing" and "Lifeguard." The shock of familial loss and the unavoidance of marital discord propel many of the later short stories toward an irony that challenges the earlier spell of nostalgia. Greiner nominates "The Music School" (1966) as Updike's finest story.

A close reading of Updike's essays, observations, and reviews reveals two general concerns in *Assorted Prose* (1965) and *Picked-Up Pieces* (1975): a sense of America's fall from innocence during the decade between 1955 and 1965, and a commitment to mimesis in fiction. Greiner's chapters will help both those curious about Updike's sense of the nation when he wrote the "Talk of the Town" column for the *New Yorker* and those who want to examine the development of his ideas about the art of fiction. A final chapter on the play *Buchanan Dying* discusses how Updike abandoned a novel to write a closet drama, how Kierkegaard's *Journals* shape Updike's understanding of President Buchanan, and how Updike struggles to present Buchanan "as Hamlet instead of Polonius."

Greiner's *John Updike's Novels* (1984) analyzes the novels through *Rabbit Is Rich.* Rather than impose a thesis on the canon or discuss each book in chronological order, Greiner arranges the novels according to theme. Thus the chapter "Why Rabbit Should Keep on Running" offers the first fully developed commentary on Harry Angstrom's desires and dilemmas through three novels and twenty years. Remarking that "Updike's Rabbit chronicles reflect the post-1950 United States with a combination of realistic and metaphorical accuracy" that exposes "national bungling and personal disaster," Greiner suggests that Angstrom is a character "worthy of joining the long line of fictional American questers from Natty Bumppo to Augie March. The list is a kind of honor roll of American culture."

Throughout *John Updike's Novels* Greiner provides a sense of the critical reception of each book. In the chapter "Faltering Toward Divorce," he joins some critics in expressing minor reservations about *Couples* and *Marry Me* (1976), but unlike many commentators he argues the importance of *A Month of Sundays:* "Marshfield's trouble with his narrative is a metaphor for his difficulty in determining his relationship with God." Greiner also touches on the importance of Hawthorne to *A Month of Sundays* and *Marry Me,* discusses the necessity of understanding the term "Romance" when reading *Marry Me,* and looks at Bech in a concluding chapter that analyzes Updike's sense of the novelist's predicament. A checklist of the various editions of the novels is included.

In *Adultery in the American Novel: Updike, James, Hawthorne* (1985), Greiner takes his observations of Hawthorne's presence in *Marry Me* and, in a full-scale discussion of Updike's place in the American literary tradition, investigates the author's contribution to the persistent theme of sexual infidelity. Pointing out Updike's numerous published comments about James and Hawthorne, he shows how Updike varies the tradition first established in *The Scarlet Letter* and *The Marble Faun* and later in *The Golden Bowl.* Whereas Hawthorne's characters respond to adultery from a religious or moral perspective, and James's react from a concern for social harmony, Updike's find themselves bereft of religious and social guidelines. Their responses are nearly always individual: "Both social harmony and moral surety seem impossible if the transgression persists, but neither force is strong enough in Updike's world to provide definition of right and proper action."

Thus, Greiner notes, Updike's spiritually fearful adulterers live in a "post-pill paradise" that traps them in a paradoxical dilemma: "Freed in the late twentieth century from the constrictions of a socially agreed on set of conventions, but longing for the peace that ceremonial and contractual obligations allow, Updike's adulterer finds himself pursuing the self-definition that transgression invites while looking over his shoulder at the security that constancy promises."

Noting that Updike himself has defined the central question of most fiction as "Who loves whom?" Greiner first discusses "Updike and James" and "Updike and Hawthorne" before examining Updike's variations on the theme of love and transgression in *Couples, A Month of Sundays,* and *Marry Me.* He finds that the Updike adulterer feels caught between a "religiously blessed ceremony" (marriage) and a "religiously defined sin" (infidelity) and that he drifts into adultery as part of his drive for immortality. Love recreates the self, but love "often conflicts with sacrament." One of Greiner's points is that Updike accepts James's "mandate for sexuality" in *The Golden Bowl* but frames it in Hawthorne's concept of guilt in *The Marble Faun.*

Critical Studies: Major Articles and Book Sections

Formal commentary on Updike's work has shifted its emphasis since significant essays began appearing in the early 1960s. While critics of his first books focus on style and the question of what to make of his unusually sensuous lyricism, later commentators are concerned with his intellectually rigorous union of theology and fiction and with his suggestion that sex is a kind of emerging religion in the suburban enclaves of the middle class. Most writers with large critical and popular readerships attract snipers at the flanks, and Updike is no exception. Negative evaluations of his canon appear periodically, and the debate about his current eminence continues at a lively pace.

With the publication of *Rabbit, Run* (1960) and *Pigeon Feathers* (1962), his fourth and fifth books, Updike began to be treated as a writer who might become a major author. Suggesting that Updike has a prophetic voice, for example, A. P. Klausler in "Steel Wilderness" (1961) notes how the foundation of Christian theology supports the accounts of bewildered struggle in *The Poorhouse Fair* (1959) and *Rabbit, Run*. Klausler's notion of Updike's growing importance to American literature was developed by Granville Hicks, Arthur Mizener, and Stanley Edgar Hyman. In "Mysteries of the Commonplace" (1962), Hicks calls Updike's style and command of figurative language "astonishing," and he points to the stories in *Pigeon Feathers* as heralding a breakthrough in fiction: "the achievement of a new attitude and hence a new method." Mizener agrees. Naming Updike "the most talented writer of his age in America . . . and perhaps the most serious," Mizener praises *Pigeon Feathers* as the book in which Updike's style stops "pirouetting" because of delight in its own motion and begins to serve the author's "deepest insight" ("Behind the Dazzle Is a Knowing Eye," 1962). Mizener alludes to a recurring concern in early Updike criticism, the question of whether style overwhelms subject matter and theme. In "The Artist as a Young Man" (1962), Stanley Edgar Hyman also agrees that Updike is the most gifted young writer in the United States. He even compares Updike's language with James Joyce's. But unlike Hicks and Mizener, Hyman worries about the contrast between stories that have the weight of Kafka because of a successful use of style to resolve and deepen, and stories that have the weight of cotton candy because of an unsuccessful reliance on style to show off.

Guerin La Course expresses a similar concern but from a different point of view. In "The Innocence of John Updike" (1962), he notes that the style serves Updike's interest in nostalgia, innocence, and the elusiveness of love, and he wonders whether Updike will have to abandon innocence to achieve the position of major author predicted for him by Hicks and Mizener. Michael Novak was one of the first commentators to respond to critics who seem puzzled by Updike's unexpected combination of self-conscious style and religious sensibility. Titling his essay "Updike's Quest for Liturgy" (1963), Novak focuses on *Pigeon Feathers* and argues that Updike's theological musings may not be what critics want to hear but are nevertheless central to a populace bereft of purpose and direction.

Growing critical interest in the general Updikean conflict between the yearning for religious sureties and the incessant demands of a mundane world caused a slight shift of emphasis away from focus on the dazzling style. Paul Doyle's "Updike's Fiction: Motifs and Techniques" (1964) follows Novak in describing Updike not as a boy wonder with glittering prose but as a searching writer seriously concerned with questions of morality in an anonymous age. From the perspective of today, one understands that the theology of Kierkegaard and Karl Barth helped to shape the tensions in Updike's fiction, but David D. Galloway was the first to explore the connection in a manner thorough enough to do justice to its complexity. In "The Absurd Man as Saint" (1966; 1981), Galloway offers a comprehensive study of Updike's first novels in terms of the existential absurdity facing the man who longs for goodness despite his own serious shortcomings. Galloway suggests that *The Poorhouse Fair* is a Utopian novel and that the saintly but absurd heroes of *Rabbit, Run* and *The Centaur* (1963) must set out on quests to confront the very dilemma that would ensnare them.

Renata Adler discusses *The Centaur* at length to illustrate the care with which Updike balances otherworldly and mundane concerns. In "Arcadia, Pa." (1963), Adler defends the role of Greek myths in *The Centaur*. One of the first early commentators to appreciate Updike's elaboration of the Chiron legend, she points to how the author "modulates" the "key of myth" with the keys of the quotidian. At the end of the first decade or so of Updike criticism, Alice and Kenneth Hamilton summarized the theological urgency in the short stories and novels. The title of "John Updike: Chronicler of the Time of the 'Death of God' " (1967) suggests the overview that earlier analysts had been working toward: that contemporary boredom and aimlessness cause first a loss of spiritual certainty and then a crisis for the Updike character who requires a religious framework to anchor his life.

The Hamiltons' appreciation of Updike reflects the general approval of most commentators between 1958 and 1967, but negative critics have also had their say. One of the most vocal, not to say most persistent, is Norman Podhoretz. First sounding his battle cry in a short review of *The Poorhouse Fair*, Podhoretz later positioned himself so that readers might see him as taking on the entire critical establishment in "A Dissent on Updike" (1964). Podhoretz wants Updike to write about serious political or social issues, but since Updike prefers to focus on little people leading mundane lives, Podhoretz dismisses him as a self-conscious writer who lacks brilliance. Calling Updike's style "mandarin and exhibitionistic," Podhoretz decides that the many commentators who admire Updike are mistaken while he alone is unmistakenly correct: "in the list of the many inflated literary reputations that have been created in recent years, Updike's name belongs somewhere very near the top."

Other negative critics are more temperate and thus more worthy of consideration. John A. Ward, for example, appreciates Updike's careful writing, but he is not convinced that *Rabbit, Run* succeeds. In a fully developed overview titled "John Updike's Fiction" (1962), Ward blames a close association with the *New Yorker* for inhibiting the development of Updike's themes. D. J. Enright is much more haughty than Ward. Calling his essay on *Of the Farm* (1965) "Updike's Ups and Downs" (1965), Enright confesses that he would not be inclined to leave Updike's name off a "dirty-laundry list," that *Of the Farm* is "a sophisticated exercise in naivete," and that while Updike writes well he "doesn't seem to have found something to write about." Enright condescendingly reminds Updike, however, that "he still has time." Richard H. Rupp advises that Updike's dilemma is just the opposite: not the inability to say something but the way he says it is the problem. In "John Updike: Style in Search of a Center" (1967), Rupp dismisses "Wife-wooing" (1962) as "Browning gone wild," *Pigeon Feathers* as exposing a "gap between style and emotion," and *Of the Farm* as lacking "a moral center." Given such failings, says Rupp, Updike's style becomes "mannered and hollow." Bryant N. Wyatt disagrees with both Rupp and Enright and decides that Updike fails because his novels lack structure. Revealing himself to be a reader with traditional tastes in "John Updike: The Psychological Novel in Search of Structure" (1967), Wyatt looks for the safeties of resolved plot and rounded characterization. When he does not find such staples, he declares that "ultimately too many strands are left untied."

Although Alfred Kazin undervalues Updike in *Bright Book of Life* (1973) as too closely tied to the *New Yorker* and thus incapable of creating characters who struggle with anything more than "the reflections in their minds of a circumscribing reality that seems unalterable," most critics in the second decade of Updike's career believe that he has fulfilled the promise predicted for him by Hicks and Mizener. Updike's novels received searching critical analysis, and the more general appraisals turned from style to theological-philosophical perspectives.

Robert A. Regan, for instance, calls on Bergson, Emerson, and Kant in "Updike's Symbol of the Center" (1974) to support his argument that Updike's characters can find unity despite the disunity implied by the eye/I dichotomy. By way of contrast, Alice and Kenneth Hamilton are, as usual, more oriented toward orthodox Christianity in their readings of Updike. In "The Validation of Religious Faith in the Writings of John Updike" (1976), the Hamiltons correctly point to *The Poorhouse Fair* as Updike's first extended investigation of the clash between humanism and faith, and they also insist that Updike continues the investigation in *Couples* (1968). According to them, *Cou-*

ples is the novel in which Updike attacks the humanistic shallowness of the 1960s. Reading the Hamiltons on *Couples,* one might keep in mind Updike's observation in the interviews that he has considered sex to be the emerging religion.

Sue Mitchell Crowley adds Kierkegaard to the echoes of orthodox Christianity, Emerson, and Kant that the Hamiltons and Regan hear in Updike. Her stimulating essay, "The Rubble of Footnotes Bound into Kierkegaard" (1977), suggests that Updike finds in Kierkegaard's philosophy a possibility for unifying the splintered self. His characters' quests for the freedom of infinity while stuck in the quagmire of the finite become a Kierkegaardian leap toward hope out of despair. Crowley's reading of "The Astronomer" (1962) in these terms is intriguing. Equally stimulating, although not as far-reaching, is George W. Hunt's "Updike's Pilgrims in a World of Nothingness" (1978). Hunt agrees that religious concerns undergird much of the fiction, but he argues that the primary issue is not a moral conflict of right and wrong but an ontological discourse on the reality of God. This debate, says Hunt, informs the dialogue and development of the novels. Victor Strandberg's thought-provoking "John Updike and the Changing of the Gods" (1978) suggests that Christianity is but one way that Updike's characters resist the finality of death. The despair of confronting a final nothingness animates Updike's ordinary people, and they turn to what Updike calls the "three great secret things"— art, sex, and religion—to hold back the night. Terrence A. Doody concurs, but in "Updike's Idea of Reification" (1979) he focuses on *A Month of Sundays* (1975) to argue that reification—Updike's theological concern for a revealed God—informs both theme and style in that oddly comic yet always serious novel.

Finally, Robert Detweiler urges the reader to consider Updike's religious concerns in the form of sermons as more than theology dressed up as fiction. In "Updike's Sermons" (1979), Detweiler posits the interesting notion that the sermons pronounced by ministers and religiously oriented characters are meant not so much to convert as to indicate "that the boundary between fiction and nonfiction is blurring increasingly." Thus in an age of declining belief, Updike's readers and characters can turn to the imagination. If Detweiler is correct— and he makes a convincing case—then Updike is closer to postmodernism than many critics have noticed.

Jerome Klinkowitz makes a similar point. In a far-reaching essay titled "John Updike since *Midpoint*" (1980), Klinkowitz takes the occasion of Updike's formal announcement in "Midpoint" (1969) of his arrival at middle age to call for a re-evaluation of the canon. Acknowledging that George Hunt would disagree, he suggests that Updike's new preference for Paul Tillich's theology rather than Karl Barth's parallels an emphasis on postmodernist theories of fiction: "Updike has found the way of animating his own act of writing shared by his more innovative contemporaries—Sukenick, Federman, and Katz." Klinkowitz correctly argues that *A Month of Sundays* will thus become an increasingly important novel for Updike's critics.

Much of the analysis in the second decade of Updike's career concentrates on in-depth discussions of individual parts of the achievement. R. B. Larsen, for example, surveys the short stories to determine Updike's stylistic contribution to the genre. In "John Updike: The Story as Lyrical Meditation" (1972), Larsen points out that Updike's innovative short fiction resembles not the traditional tale but the sketch. Updike establishes a primary image or idea and then uses his glittering style to work variations.

Larsen's calmly stated essay is one of the few concerned with the short stories. More popular with critics is the Rabbit saga. Elmer F. Suderman's "The Right Way and the Good Way in *Rabbit, Run*" (1969) suggests that Rabbit is "enigmatic" and thus cannot be judged in such simple terms as right or wrong. Calling attention to Angstrom's final flight from the cemetery, Suderman shows that Angstrom is caught in a net of the good conflicting with the right: "he is just as helpless in discovering the good, for his society is unaware that the good exists." Clinton S. Burhans, Jr., offers an equally perceptive analysis. In "Things Falling Apart: Structure and Theme in *Rabbit, Run*" (1973), Burhans points to the pattern of circles in the novel, disagrees with Galloway, and says that Rabbit is "less an absurd saint than a wasted victim." Showing that Updike sets up Rabbit so that he and his society "mirror" each other, Burhans correctly praises Updike for the very quality that Podhoretz mistakenly deplores: that Updike refuses to blame his character, that he "demands not blame but understanding."

Wayne Falke takes a similar approach with *Rabbit Redux*. In "*Rabbit Redux:* Time/Order/God" (1974), he names *Redux* as Updike's most mature novel because while it reveals the author's interest in such social issues as the cost of the moon-shot, civil rights, and Vietnam, it also illustrates how Updike rejects both weak Christianity and questionable humanism. One might contrast Falke's point with that of the Hamiltons in "The Validation of Religious Faith in the Writings of John Updike." Lewis A. Lawson also finds Rabbit rejecting traditional Christianity. Arguing in "Rabbit Angstrom as a Religious Sufferer"

(1974) that Angstrom's failure has ontological overtones, Lawson shows how Rabbit dismisses the widely-accepted requirement that he admit his sins while searching for a "Benevolent Dictator" who will make decisions for him. Paul Borgman acknowledges Rabbit's failings but argues persuasively that Angstrom is heroic. In "The Tragic Hero of Updike's *Rabbit, Run*" (1977), Borgman calls attention to the epigraph with its contrast between the "motions of Grace" and the "hardness of the heart," and he discusses how only Rabbit responds to Grace. Eccles is a compromiser who hopes to "demythologize" both religion and Rabbit's imagination. Without "confirmation from a community," Angstrom's quest to transform Grace into Word will tragically fail.

David Myers insists that Christianity is just as important to *The Centaur* as to the Rabbit novels. The title of his analysis makes the point: "The Questing Fear: Christian Allegory in John Updike's *The Centaur*" (1971). Suggesting that the Greek myth of Chiron is more in the service of allusion than of theme, Myers shows that George Caldwell is both "just plain" Caldwell and "a messianic figure": "It is far rather the tragic allegory of a Christian soul crying *de profundis*, struggling for truth and love in a world which is filled with indifference, hate and death." John B. Vickery's excellent "*The Centaur*: Myth, History, and Narrative" (1974) emphasizes the importance of the epigraph from Karl Barth and discusses the ethical frame of the narrator and his tale. Like Chiron and Caldwell, the narrator gives up identity to gain freedom. *The Centaur* is not so much about George Caldwell as "it is a tale about the modern writer's drive, efforts, and need 'to keep an organized mass of images moving forward.'" Suzanne Uphaus's equally fine "*The Centaur*: Updike's Mock Epic" (1977) discusses the relationship in the novel between classical mythology and realistic detail: "the thematic loss of Christianity parallels the artistic loss of classical faith." Thus the artist Peter Caldwell fails, as he himself admits, because he lacks what Uphaus terms "a framework of belief, a metaphoric vision, whether Christian or classical." James M. Mellard directs the reader of *The Centaur* to the importance of mutability. In "The Novel as Lyric Elegy: The Mode of Updike's *The Centaur*" (1979), Mellard focuses on Peter as narrator and writes that "one of the major concerns in *The Centaur* is with time." Peter must examine a past with his father in order to step toward a future with his art: "The novel thus represents Peter's effort to recapture through the lyricist's power of language an image made resonant by his father."

In recent years, *Couples* has begun to attract the scrutiny that has long been the case with *The Centaur* and the Rabbit novels. Nearly everything that Robert Detweiler writes about Updike stimulates the informed reader, and his "Updike's *Couples:* Eros Demythologized" (1971) is no exception. Suggesting that *Couples* should be read in light of a relativistic universe and Denis de Rougemont's analysis of Tristan-Iseult and Don Juan, Detweiler argues that Updike "works with myth to demythologize it." This intelligent essay should calm the hoopla about *Couples* created by readers who get steamed-up while perusing Updike's near-clinical descriptions of adultery. Although not as rigorous, Paula and Nick Backscheider's "Updike's *Couples:* Squeak in the Night" (1974) will help those interested in Piet's journey from the greenhouse of his parents to the hardness of the world. The Backscheiders observe that Piet latches onto a series of bogus gods. His exit with Foxy does not redeem him, but neither does it totally neutralize his Calvinism. Readers may want to compare this article with those that elucidate Rabbit's inability to express his fuzzy religious beliefs. Finally, Linda M. Plagman denies that Piet finds a satisfactory religious framework, disputes Detweiler's "demythologizing concept," and declares that *Couples* ends *un*happily. Her overall essay is spirited, and in "*Eros* and *Agape:* The Opposition in Updike's *Couples*" (1976) she points to the necessity of considering *Couples* in light of characters who dismiss Christian *agape,* which accepts death, and pursue secular *eros,* which seeks death.

Detweiler has also contributed a searching analysis of *A Month of Sundays.* In "Updike's *A Month of Sundays* and the Language of the Unconscious" (1979), he interprets Marshfield's dilemma from the point of view of Jacques Lacan's structuralist psychoanalysis. He correctly argues that not morality but language is the issue and that Marshfield is an artist figure struggling to control an "intractable" medium: "language is used at last to confess its inadequacy and yet to point beyond itself." This excellent essay should convince unbelievers that Updike is much more than a traditional novelist of manners. Suzanne Uphaus reads *A Month of Sundays* from a different perspective. In "The Unified Vision of *A Month of Sundays*" (1977) she notes that whereas Rabbit (and other Updike characters) suffers the opposition of apprehending this world through sensation and longing for the other world through faith, Marshfield comes closer to a reconciling unity. Thus the novel is a thematic and technical "breakthrough," for Updike reinterprets the American religious tradition.

Similarly, in "Faith, Morality, and the Novels of John Updike" (1978), Bernard A. Schopen reads *A Month of Sundays* in the context of Updike's religion-haunted heroes and insists that one must consider the author's views on faith, morality, and Karl Barth when discussing his fiction. As Schopen correctly observes, erroneous interpretations result when the reader confuses Updike's notion of God with "good will and a worldly humanism." George W. Hunt underlines this general argument, and in his thoughtful "Updike's Omega-Shaped Shelter: Structure and Psyche in *A Month of Sundays*" (1978) he shows how Marshfield's unusually shaped motel reflects the curious development of his journal. Hunt also joins Detweiler in pointing to the self-reflexive quality of *A Month of Sundays* as Updike's bow to fictional techniques made current by John Hawkes and John Barth.

Criticism during the third decade of Updike's career has yet to assume a noticeable pattern. Negative evaluations have been toned down in the face of wide-spread agreement that Updike has achieved the stature of major author, and penetrating studies of individual novels continue to be the rule. With all the critical emphasis on Christianity, Karl Barth, and Kierkegaard in Updike's fiction, the reader may benefit from Robert E. Hogan's "Catharism and John Updike's *Rabbit, Run*" (1980). Taking a hint from Updike's essay on Denis de Rougemont's *Love in the Western World,* Hogan suggests that Rabbit's drive for a perfect life may reflect the tenets of a medieval heretical sect.

Especially helpful are the more comprehensive essays that examine part of the canon to evaluate the whole. Klinkowitz's "John Updike's America" (1980) is such an article. Focusing on Updike's two paperback originals, *Olinger Stories* (1964) and *Too Far to Go* (1979), Klinkowitz argues that Updike's language and rearranging of his central characters' stories "all bespeak a self-conscious artistry. Their lives, it seems, are Updike's own life of fiction." *Olinger Stories* is, in effect, an indirect comment on the themes of the earliest novels, and *Too Far to Go* serves the same function for the novels following *Rabbit, Run.* Concluding with a shrewd observation, Klinkowitz notes that "Death and immortality have been the contrary poles of his writing career."

The most indispensable of the recent articles on Updike is Jane Barnes's "John Updike: A Literary Spider" (1981). Although Barnes emphasizes *Too Far to Go* and *Problems* (1979), she does not so much discuss individual stories as argue that the new collections "round out" a phase of Updike's fascination with the theme of family life. In so doing she shows that "the tension in these stories derives from the conflict between the illusions fueling the adult from the past and the demands made on him as a parent and husband in the present." As family life frustrates his current desires, the Updike narrator turns to the past in search of "childhood's glory"—though, as Barnes observes, he does so less and less. "Domestic Life in America" is Barnes's sensible choice for the "culmination of the art the author has evolved through his hero's quest." Serious readers of Updike should consult this essay to consider Barnes's general position that *Problems* marks Updike's growth as an artist.

Predictions about the direction of future scholarship on Updike are risky, but it seems likely that five areas will emerge as primary: the Rabbit saga will become increasingly important as a contemporary extension of the American Adam figure; *A Month of Sundays* will be recognized as a seminal text; *The Witches of Eastwick* (1984) will be examined as Updike's contribution to "magical realism"; the short stories will receive additional study as illustrations of Updike's mastery of the genre; and the reviews and essays will be identified as the most perceptive body of criticism written by an American novelist since Henry James.

Eudora Welty

(1909-   )

W. U. McDonald, Jr.
University of Toledo

PRIMARY BIBLIOGRAPHY

Books and Pamphlets

A Curtain of Green. With an introduction by Katherine Anne Porter. Garden City: Doubleday, Doran, 1941; London: John Lane/Bodley Head, 1943. Short stories.

The Robber Bridegroom. With drawings by James Holland [English edition only]. Garden City: Doubleday, Doran, 1942; London: John Lane/Bodley Head, 1944. Novelette.

The Wide Net and Other Stories. New York: Harcourt, Brace, 1943; London: John Lane/Bodley Head, 1945. Short stories.

Delta Wedding. New York: Harcourt, Brace, 1946; London: Bodley Head, 1947. Novel.

Music from Spain. Greenville, Miss.: Levee Press, 1948. Short story. Limited edition.

The Golden Apples. New York: Harcourt, Brace, 1949; London: Bodley Head, 1950. Short story cycle.

Short Stories. New York: Harcourt, Brace, 1950. Essay. Limited edition.

The Ponder Heart. With drawings by Joe Krush. New York: Harcourt, Brace, 1954; London: Hamish Hamilton, 1954. Novelette.

The Bride of the Innisfallen and Other Stories. New York: Harcourt, Brace, 1955; London: Hamish Hamilton, 1955. Short stories.

Place in Fiction. New York: House of Books, 1957. Essay. Limited edition.

Three Papers on Fiction. Northampton, Mass.: Smith College, 1962. Essays.

The Shoe Bird. With illustrations by Beth Krush. New York: Harcourt, Brace & World, 1964. Children's story.

A Sweet Devouring. New York: Albondocani, 1969. Autobiographical
   essay. Limited edition.
Losing Battles. New York: Random House, 1970; London: Virago,
   1982. Novel.
A Flock of Guinea Hens Seen from a Car. New York: Albondocani, 1970.
   Poem. Limited edition.
One Time, One Place: Mississippi in the Depression, A Snapshot Album. New
   York: Random House, 1971. Photographs with author's fore-
   word.
The Optimist's Daughter. New York: Random House, 1972; London:
   Deutsch, 1973. Novelette.
A Pageant of Birds. New York: Albondocani, 1974. Essay with author's
   photographs. Limited edition.
Fairy Tale of the Natchez Trace. Jackson: Mississippi Historical Society,
   1975. Essay. Limited edition.
The Eye of the Story: Selected Essays and Reviews. New York: Random
   House, 1978. Essays and reviews.
Women!! Make Turban in Own Home! Winston-Salem, N. C.: Palaemon,
   1979. Essay. Limited edition.
Acrobats in a Park. Northridge, Cal.: Lord John, 1980. Short story with
   author's introduction. Limited edition.
Bye-Bye Brevoort. Jackson, Miss.: New Stage Theatre/Palaemon Press,
   1980. Dramatic skit. Limited edition.
The Collected Stories of Eudora Welty. New York: Harcourt Brace Jovanovich, 1980; London: Boyars, 1981. Short stories with author's
   preface.
Twenty Photographs. Winston-Salem, N.C.: Palaemon, 1980. Photographs with author's prefatory note. Limited edition.
Retreat. Winston-Salem, N.C.: Palaemon, 1981. Short story. Limited
   edition.
One Writer's Beginnings. Cambridge, Mass.: Harvard University Press,
   1984. Autobiographical essays.

Selected Other

"José de Creeft," *Magazine of Art,* 37 (Feb. 1944), 42-47. Essay.
"Afterword" and "About the Author." In E. P. O'Donnell, *The Great
   Big Doorstep.* Carbondale & Edwardsville: Southern Illinois Uni-
   versity Press, 1979, 355-366. Criticism.
"Looking Back at the First Story," *Georgia Review,* 33 (Winter 1979),
   751-755. Essay.

"Foreword." In Virginia Woolf, *To the Lighthouse*. New York: Harcourt
Brace Jovanovich, 1981, vii-xii. Criticism.

"Seventy-Nine Stories to Read Again," *New York Times Book Review*, 8
Feb. 1981, pp. 3, 22. Review of *The Collected Stories of Elizabeth
Bowen*.

"Jackson: A Neighborhood." In *Jackson Landmarks*. Jackson: Junior
League of Jackson, Miss., 1982, 1-5. Autobiographical essay.

"A Note about New Stage." In *Standing Room Only: A Cookbook for
Entertaining*. Jackson: New Stage Theatre, 1983, 9-11. Autobiographical essay.

"Finding the Connections." In *Inward Journey: Ross Macdonald*, ed.
Ralph Sipper. Santa Barbara, Cal.: Cordelia Editions, 1984, 154-
158. Essay.

Editions and Collections

Selected Stories. New York: Modern Library, 1954. Reprint of *A Curtain
of Green* and *The Wide Net*. Short stories.

Thirteen Stories. Selected with an introduction by Ruth M. Vande Kieft.
New York: Harcourt, Brace & World, 1965. Short stories.

Welty, ed. Patti Carr Black. Jackson: Mississippi Department of Archives and History, 1977. Photographs and quoted passages
from works.

Ida M'Toy, ed. with foreword by Charles Shattuck, George Scouffas,
and Daniel Curley. Urbana: University of Illinois Press, 1979.
Essay with letters and photographs by Welty.

Eudora, ed. Patti Carr Black. Jackson: Mississippi Department of Archives and History, 1984. Photographs, some by Welty, with her
captions and with quotations from *One Writer's Beginnings*.

SECONDARY BIBLIOGRAPHY

Bibliographies and Checklists

"Checklist of Welty Scholarship, 1975-   ," *Eudora Welty Newsletter*
(Summer 1977-present). Compiled by O. B. Emerson, 1982,
1984-1985; W. U. McDonald, Jr., 1983; Noel Polk, 1977-1979;
V. H. Thompson, 1980-1981. Secondary.

Givner, Joan. "The Eudora Welty Collection, Jackson, Mississippi,"
Descant: the Texas Christian University Literary Journal, 23 (Fall
1978), 38-48.

McDonald, W. U., Jr. "Checklist of Revisions in Collected Welty Stories: Phase I," *Eudora Welty Newsletter,* 7 (Winter 1983), 6-10. [Errata, *EuWN,* 7 (Summer 1983), 8.] Primary.

_____. "Eudora Welty Manuscripts: An Annotated Finding List," *Bulletin of Bibliography,* 24 (Sept./Dec. 1963), 44-46. Primary.

_____. "Eudora Welty Manuscripts: A Supplementary Annotated Finding List," *Bulletin of Bibliography,* 31 (July/Sept. 1974), 95-98, 126, 132. Primary.

_____. "Eudora Welty Manuscripts: A Second Supplement," *Eudora Welty Newsletter,* 2 (Winter 1978), 4-5. Primary.

_____. *"The Eye of the Story:* Bibliographic Notes on the Contents," *Eudora Welty Newsletter,* 2 (Summer 1978), 1-5. Primary.

_____. "Works by Welty: A Continuing Checklist," *Eudora Welty Newsletter,* 1 (Winter 1977-present). Primary.

Polk, Noel. "Eudora Welty: A Bibliographical Checklist," *American Book Collector,* new series, 2 (Jan./Feb. 1981), 25-37. Primary.

_____. "A Eudora Welty Checklist," *Mississippi Quarterly,* 26 (Fall 1973), 663-693. Primary & secondary.

Prenshaw, Peggy W. "Eudora Welty." In *American Women Writers: Bibliographical Essays,* ed. Maurice Duke, Jackson R. Bryer, and M. Thomas Inge. Westport, Conn. & London: Greenwood Press, 1983, 233-267. Secondary.

Swearingen, Bethany C. *Eudora Welty: A Critical Bibliography, 1936-58.* Jackson: University Press of Mississippi, 1984. Primary & secondary.

Thompson, V. H. *Eudora Welty: A Reference Guide.* Boston: G. K. Hall, 1976. Secondary.

Interviews

Brans, Jo. "Struggling Against the Plaid: An Interview with Eudora Welty," *Southwest Review,* 66 (Summer 1981), 255-266.

Bunting, Charles T. " 'The Interior World': An Interview with Eudora Welty," *Southern Review,* new series, 8 (Autumn 1972), 711-735.

Ferris, Bill. "A Visit with Eudora Welty." In *Images of the South: Visits with Eudora Welty and Walker Evans.* Southern Folklore Reports, no. 1. Memphis, Tenn.: Center for Southern Folklore, 1977, 11-26.

Freeman, Jean Todd. "An Interview with Eudora Welty." In *Conversations with Writers II,* ed. Richard Layman. Detroit: Gale Research Company, 1978, 284-316.

Gretlund, Jan Norby. "An Interview with Eudora Welty," *Southern Humanities Review*, 14 (Summer 1980), 193-208.

"An Interview with Eudora Welty," *Comment: The University of Alabama Review*, 4 (Winter 1965), 11-16.

Jones, John Griffin. "Eudora Welty." In *Mississippi Writers Talking*. Jackson: University Press of Mississippi, 1982, 3-35.

Kuehl, Linda. "The Art of Fiction XLVII: Eudora Welty," *Paris Review*, 55 (Fall 1972), 72-97.

Maclay, Joanna. "A Conversation with Eudora Welty," *Literature in Performance: A Journal of Literary and Performing Art*, 1 (Apr. 1982), 68-82.

Petty, Jane Reid. "The Town and the Writer: An Interview with Eudora Welty," *Jackson Magazine* [Jackson, Miss.], 1 (Sept. 1977), 28-31, 34-35.

Price, Reynolds. "Eudora Welty in Type and Person," *New York Times Book Review*, 7 May 1978, pp. 42-43.

Van Gelder, Robert. "An Interview with Miss Eudora Welty," *New York Times Book Review*, 14 June 1942, p. 2.

Van Noppen, Martha. "A Conversation with Eudora Welty," *Southern Quarterly*, 20 (Summer 1982), 7-23.

Walker, Alice. "Eudora Welty: An Interview," *Harvard Advocate*, 106 (Winter 1973), 68-72.

[All the above interviews are collected in *Conversations with Eudora Welty*, ed. Peggy Whitman Prenshaw. Jackson: University Press of Mississippi, 1984.]

Critical Studies: Books

Appel, Alfred, Jr. *A Season of Dreams: The Fiction of Eudora Welty*. Baton Rouge: Louisiana State University Press, 1965.

Bryant, J. A., Jr. *Eudora Welty*. Pamphlets on American Writers No. 66. Minneapolis: University of Minnesota Press, 1968. Reprinted and revised in *Seven American Women Writers of the Twentieth Century: An Introduction*, ed. Maureen Howard. Minneapolis: University of Minnesota Press, 1977, 166-213.

Devlin, Albert J. *Eudora Welty's Chronicle: A Story of Mississippi Life*. Jackson: University Press of Mississippi, 1983.

Evans, Elizabeth. *Eudora Welty*. New York: Ungar, 1981.

Howard, Zelma Turner. *The Rhetoric of Eudora Welty's Short Stories*. Jackson: University and College Press of Mississippi, 1973.

Isaacs, Neil. *Eudora Welty.* Southern Writers Series No. 8. Austin, Tex.: Steck-Vaughn, 1969.

Kreyling, Michael. *Eudora Welty's Achievement of Order.* Baton Rouge: Louisiana State University Press, 1980.

Manning, Carol S. *With Ears Opening Like Morning Glories: Eudora Welty and the Love of Storytelling.* Westport, Conn. & London: Greenwood Press, 1985.

Manz-Kunz, Marie-Antoinette. *Eudora Welty: Aspects of Reality in her Short Fiction.* Swiss Studies in English. Bern: Francke Verlag, 1971.

Randisi, Jennifer Lynn. *A Tissue of Lies: Eudora Welty and the Southern Romance.* Washington: University Press of America, 1982.

Vande Kieft, Ruth M. *Eudora Welty.* New York: Twayne, 1962.

Westling, Louise. *Sacred Groves and Ravaged Gardens: The Fiction of Eudora Welty, Carson McCullers, and Flannery O'Connor.* Athens: University of Georgia Press, 1985.

Critical Studies: Collections of Essays

Delta (Centre d'Etude et de Recherches sur les Ecrivains du Sud aux Etats-Unis, de l'Université Paul Valéry à Montpellier), no. 5 (Nov. 1977). Welty issue.

Desmond, John E., ed. *A Still Moment: Essays on the Art of Eudora Welty.* Metuchen, N.J. & London: Scarecrow, 1978.

Dollarhide, Louis, and Ann J. Abadie, eds. *Eudora Welty: A Form of Thanks.* Jackson: University Press of Mississippi, 1979.

Mississippi Quarterly, 26 (Fall 1973). Welty issue.

Prenshaw, Peggy Whitman, ed. *Eudora Welty: Critical Essays.* Jackson: University Press of Mississippi, 1979.

_____. *Eudora Welty: Thirteen Essays.* Jackson: University Press of Mississippi, 1983. Reprinted from Prenshaw, *Eudora Welty: Critical Essays.*

Shenandoah, 20 (Spring 1969). Welty issue.

Southern Quarterly, 20 (Summer 1982). Welty issue.

Critical Studies: Newsletter

Eudora Welty Newsletter (University of Toledo), 1977- .

Critical Studies: Major Articles and Book Sections

Aldridge, John W. "Eudora Welty: Metamorphosis of a Southern Lady Writer," *Saturday Review*, 11 Apr. 1970, pp. 21-23, 35-36.

Allen, John A. "Eudora Welty: The Three Moments," *Virginia Quarterly Review*, 51 (Autumn 1975), 605-627. Collected in Desmond.

_____. "The Other Way to Live: Demigods in Eudora Welty's Fiction." Collected in *Eudora Welty: Critical Essays*, ed. Prenshaw, 26-55.

Arnold, Marilyn. "Eudora Welty's Parody," *Notes on Mississippi Writers*," 11 (Spring 1978), 15-22.

_____. "Images of Memory in Eudora Welty's *The Optimist's Daughter*," *Southern Literary Journal*, 14 (Spring 1982), 28-38.

Boatwright, James. "Speech and Silence in *Losing Battles*," *Shenandoah*, 25 (Spring 1974), 3-14.

Bradford, M. E. "Fairchild as Composite Protagonist in *Delta Wedding*." Collected in *Eudora Welty: Critical Essays*, ed. Prenshaw, 201-207.

Brooks, Cleanth. "The Past Reexamined: *The Optimist's Daughter*," *Mississippi Quarterly*, 26 (Fall 1973), 577-587.

Brown, Ashley. "Eudora Welty and the Mythos of Summer," *Shenandoah*, 20 (Spring 1969), 29-35.

Bryant, J. A., Jr. "Seeing Double in *The Golden Apples*," *Sewanee Review*, 82 (Spring 1974), 300-315.

Cooley, John R. "Blacks as Primitives in Eudora Welty's Fiction," *Ball State University Forum*, 14 (Summer 1973), 20-28.

Curley, Daniel. "Eudora Welty and the Quondam Obstruction," *Studies in Short Fiction*, 5 (Spring 1968), 209-224.

Davenport, F. Garvin. "Renewal and Historical Consciousness in *The Wide Net*." Collected in *Eudora Welty: Critical Essays*, ed. Prenshaw, 189-200.

Davis, Charles E. "Eudora Welty's *The Robber Bridegroom* and Old Southwest Humor: A Doubleness of Vision." Collected in Desmond, 71-81.

_____. "The South in Eudora Welty's Fiction: A Changing World," *Studies in American Fiction*, 3 (Autumn 1975), 199-209.

Demmin, Julia L., and Daniel Curley. "Golden Apples and Silver Apples." Collected in *Eudora Welty: Critical Essays*, ed. Prenshaw, 242-257.

Desmond, John F. "Pattern and Vision in *The Optimist's Daughter*." Collected in Desmond, 118-138.

Eisinger, Chester E. "Eudora Welty and the Triumph of the Imagination." In his *Fiction of the Forties*. Chicago: University of Chicago Press, 1963, 258-283.

_____. "Traditionalism and Modernism in Eudora Welty." Collected in *Eudora Welty: Critical Essays*, ed. Prenshaw, 3-25.

Ferguson, Mary Anne. "*Losing Battles* as a Comic Epic in Prose." Collected in *Eudora Welty: Critical Essays*, ed. Prenshaw, 305-324.

Fleischauer, John F. "The Focus of Mystery: Eudora Welty's Prose Style," *Southern Literary Journal*, 5 (Spring 1973), 64-79.

French, Warren. " 'All Things are Double': Eudora Welty as a Civilized Writer." Collected in *Eudora Welty: Critical Essays*, ed. Prenshaw, 179-188.

Glenn, Eunice. "Fantasy in the Fiction of Eudora Welty." In *A Southern Vanguard*, ed. Allen Tate. New York: Prentice-Hall, 1947, 78-91.

Goeller, Allison. "*Delta Wedding* as Pastoral," *Interpretations: a Journal of Idea, Analysis and Criticism*, 13 (Fall 1981), 59-72.

Gossett, Louise Y. "*Losing Battles:* Festival and Celebration." Collected in *Eudora Welty: Critical Essays*, ed. Prenshaw, 341-350.

_____. "Violence as Revelation: Eudora Welty." In her *Violence in Recent Southern Fiction*. Durham: Duke University Press, 1965, 98-117.

Gray, Richard J. "Eudora Welty: A Dance to the Music of Order," *Canadian Review of American Studies*, 7 (Spring 1976), 57-65.

Griffin, Robert J. "Eudora Welty's *A Curtain of Green*." In *The Forties: Fiction, Poetry, Drama*, ed. Warren French. De Land, Fla.: Everett/Edwards, 1969, 101-110.

Gross, Seymour L. "Eudora Welty's Comic Imagination." In *The Comic Imagination in American Literature*, ed. Louis D. Rubin, Jr. New Brunswick, N.J.: Rutgers University Press, 1973, 319-328.

_____. "A Long Day's Living: The Angelic Ingenuities of *Losing Battles*." Collected in *Eudora Welty: Critical Essays*, ed. Prenshaw, 325-340.

Hardy, John Edward. "*Delta Wedding* as Region and Symbol," *Sewanee Review*, 60 (July-Sept. 1952), 397-417.

_____. "Eudora Welty's Negroes." In *Images of the Negro in American Literature*, ed. Seymour L. Gross and John Edward Hardy. Chicago: University of Chicago Press, 1966, 221-232.

_____. "Marrying Down in Eudora Welty's Novels." Collected in *Eudora Welty: Critical Essays*, ed. Prenshaw, 93-119.

Heilman, Robert B. "*Losing Battles* and Winning the War." Collected in *Eudora Welty: Critical Essays,* ed. Prenshaw, 269-304.

Hicks, Granville. "Eudora Welty," *College English,* 14 (Nov. 1952), 69-76. [Also in *English Journal,* 41 (Nov. 1952), 461-468.]

Hinton, Jane L. "The Role of Family in *Delta Wedding, Losing Battles,* and *The Optimist's Daughter.*" Collected in *Eudora Welty: Critical Essays,* ed. Prenshaw, 120-131.

Holland, Robert B. "Dialogue as a Reflection of Place in *The Ponder Heart, " American Literature,* 35 (Nov. 1963), 352-358.

Howard, Maureen. "A Collection of Discoveries," *New York Times Book Review,* 2 Nov. 1980, pp. 31-32.

Howell, Elmo. "Eudora Welty's Comedy of Manners," *South Atlantic Quarterly,* 69 (Autumn 1970), 469-479.

Jones, Alun R. "A Frail Traveling Coincidence: Three Later Stories of Eudora Welty," *Shenandoah,* 20 (Spring 1969), 40-53.

_____. "The World of Love: The Fiction of Eudora Welty." In *The Creative Present: Notes on Contemporary American Fiction,* ed. Nona Balakian and Charles Simmons. Garden City: Doubleday, 1963, 175-192.

Jones, William M. "Name and Symbol in the Prose of Eudora Welty," *Southern Folklore Quarterly,* 22 (Dec. 1958), 173-185.

_____. "The Plot as Search," *Studies in Short Fiction,* 5 (Fall 1967), 37-43.

Kreyling, Michael. "Modernism in Welty's *A Curtain of Green and Other Stories [sic]*," *Southern Quarterly,* 20 (Summer 1982), 40-53.

_____. "Words into Criticism: Eudora Welty's Essays and Reviews." Collected in *Eudora Welty: Critical Essays,* ed. Prenshaw, 411-422.

Landess, Thomas H. "More Trouble in Mississippi: Family Vs. Antifamily in Miss Welty's *Losing Battles,*" *Sewanee Review,* 79 (Fall 1971), 626-634.

McDonald, W. U, Jr. "Eudora Welty, Reviser: Some Notes on 'Flowers for Marjorie,' " *Delta,* no. 5 (Nov. 1977), 35-48.

McFarland, Ronald E. "Vision and Perception in the Works of Eudora Welty," *Markham Review,* 2 (Feb. 1971), 94-99.

McHaney, Thomas L. "Eudora Welty and the Multitudinous Golden Apples," *Mississippi Quarterly,* 26 (Fall 1973), 589-624.

MacKethan, Lucinda H. "To See Things in Their Time: The Act of Focusing in Eudora Welty's Fiction." In her *The Dream of Arcady: Place and Time in Southern Literature.* Baton Rouge: Louisiana State University Press, 1980, 181-206.

McMillen, William E. "Conflict and Resolution in Welty's *Losing Bat-*

tles," Critique: Studies in Modern Fiction, 15, no. 1 (1973), 110-124.

Marrs, Suzanne. "The Making of *Losing Battles:* Jack Renfro's Evolution," *Mississippi Quarterly*, 37 (Fall 1984), 469-474.

_____. "The Making of *Losing Battles:* Judge Moody Transformed," *Notes on Mississippi Writers*, 17, no. 2 (1985), 47-53.

Marshall, Margaret. "Notes by the Way," *Nation*, 169 (10 Sept. 1949), 256.

Masserand, Anne M. "Eudora Welty's Travellers: The Journey Theme in Her Short Stories," *Southern Literary Journal*, 3 (Spring 1971), 39-48.

Meese, Elizabeth A. "Constructing Time and Place: Eudora Welty in the Thirties." Collected in *Eudora Welty: Critical Essays*, ed. Prenshaw, 401-410.

Messerli, Douglas. " 'A Battle with Both Sides Using the Same Tactics': The Language of Time in *Losing Battles*." Collected in *Eudora Welty: Critical Essays*, ed. Prenshaw, 351-366.

_____. "Metronome and Music: The Encounter Between History and Myth in *The Golden Apples*." Collected in Desmond, 82-102.

_____. "The Problem of Time in Welty's *Delta Wedding*," *Studies in American Fiction*, 5 (Autumn 1977), 227-240.

Moreland, Richard C. "Community and Vision in Eudora Welty," *Southern Review*, new series, 18 (Jan. 1982), 84-99.

Nostrandt, Jeanne Rolfe. "Eudora Welty and the Children's Hour," *Mississippi Quarterly*, 29 (Winter 1975-1976), 109-118.

Pawlowski, Robert S. "The Process of Observation: *Winesburg, Ohio* and *The Golden Apples*," *University Review*, 37 (June 1971), 292-298.

Peden, William. "The Incomparable Welty," *Saturday Review*, 38 (9 Apr. 1955), 18.

Pei, Lowry. "Dreaming the Other in *The Golden Apples*," *Modern Fiction Studies*, 28 (Autumn 1982), 415-433.

Phillips, Robert L. "Patterns of Vision in Welty's *The Optimist's Daughter*," *Southern Literary Journal*, 14 (Fall 1981), 10-23.

Pickett, Nell Ann. "Colloquialism as a Style in the First-Person-Narrator Fiction of Eudora Welty," *Mississippi Quarterly*, 26 (Fall 1973), 559-576.

Pitavy-Souques, Danièle. "Technique as Myth: The Structure of *The Golden Apples*." Collected in *Eudora Welty: Critical Essays*, ed. Prenshaw, 258-268.

Polk, Noel. "Water, Wanderers, and Weddings: Love in Eudora Welty." Collected in Dollarhide and Abadie, 95-122.

Prenshaw, Peggy Whitman. "Cultural Patterns in Eudora Welty's *Delta Wedding* and 'The Demonstrators,' " *Notes on Mississippi Writers,* 3 (Fall 1970), 51-70.

_____. "Woman's World, Man's Place: The Fiction of Eudora Welty." Collected in Dollarhide and Abadie, 46-77.

Price, Reynolds. "The Collected Stories of Eudora Welty," *New Republic,* 1 Nov. 1980, pp. 31-34.

_____. "The Onlooker, Smiling: An Early Reading of *The Optimist's Daughter,*" *Shenandoah,* 20 (Spring 1969), 58-73. Reprinted in his *Things Themselves: Essays and Scenes.* New York: Atheneum, 1972, 114-135, with "Postscript," 135-138.

Pugh, Elaine Upton. "The Duality of Morgana: The Making of Virgie's Vision, the Vision of *The Golden Apples,*" *Modern Fiction Studies,* 28 (Autumn 1982), 435-451.

Reynolds, Larry J. "Enlightening Darkness: Theme and Structure in Eudora Welty's *Losing Battles,*" *Journal of Narrative Technique,* 8 (Spring 1978), 133-140.

Rosenfeld, Isaac. "Consolations of Poetry," *New Republic,* 109 (18 Oct. 1943), 525-526.

_____. "Double Standard," *New Republic,* 114 (29 Apr. 1946), 633-634.

Rubin, Louis D., Jr. "Everything Brought Out in the Open: Eudora Welty's *Losing Battles,*" *Hollins Critic,* 7 (June 1970), 1-12.

_____. "The Golden Apples of the Sun." In his *The Faraway Country: Writers of the Modern South.* Seattle: University of Washington Press, 1963, 131-154.

_____. "Two Ladies of the South," *Sewanee Review,* 63 (Autumn 1955), 671-681.

Rupp, Richard H. "Eudora Welty: A Continual Feast." In his *Celebration in Postwar American Fiction 1945-67.* Coral Gables, Fla.: University of Miami Press, 1970, 59-75.

Slethaug, Gordon E. "Initiation in Eudora Welty's *The Robber Bridegroom,*" *Southern Humanities Review,* 7 (Winter 1973), 77-87.

Stuckey, William J. "The Use of Marriage in Welty's *The Optimist's Daughter,*" *Critique: Studies in Modern Fiction,* 17, no. 2 (1975), 36-46.

Swados, Harvey. "Some Old Worlds, and Some New Ones, Too," *Hudson Review,* 8 (Autumn 1955), 456-462.

Trilling, Diana. "Fiction in Review," *Nation,* 157 (2 Oct. 1943), 386-387.

_____. "Fiction in Review," *Nation,* 162 (11 May 1946), 578.

Vande Kieft, Ruth M. "Looking with Eudora Welty." Collected in *Eudora Welty: Critical Essays,* ed. Prenshaw, 423-444.

_____. "The Vision of Eudora Welty," *Mississippi Quarterly,* 26 (Fall 1973), 517-542.

Warren, Robert Penn. "The Love and Separateness in Miss Welty," *Kenyon Review,* 6 (Spring 1944), 246-259.

Weiner, Rachel V. "Eudora Welty's *The Ponder Heart:* The Judgment of Art," *Southern Studies,* 19 (Fall 1980), 261-273.

Young, Thomas Daniel. "Social Form and Social Order: An Examination of *The Optimist's Daughter.*" Collected in *Eudora Welty: Critical Essays,* ed. Prenshaw, 367-385.

BIBLIOGRAPHICAL ESSAY

Bibliographies and Checklists

There is no full-scale descriptive bibliography of Eudora Welty's writings. Of available guides, the most complete to 1973 is Noel Polk's "A Eudora Welty Checklist" (1973). It includes books and pamphlets in all editions and first periodical publication of stories, nonfictional prose, poetry, interviews and some juvenilia. Its bibliographical detail is minimal: place and date of publication, publisher, pagination, the number of copies in limited editions, and the contents of short story collections. For publications in book form (including shorter works in anthologies) through 1980, Polk's "Eudora Welty: A Bibliographical Checklist" (1981) provides bibliographic information sufficient to identify the first English and American editions of books (including shorter works in anthologies) and their dust jackets. W. U. McDonald's "Works by Welty: A Continuing Checklist" in the *Eudora Welty Newsletter (EuWN)* since 1977 cites current publications (including interviews) in all media, with comparable bibliographic information and occasional notes on textual variation. These three checklists record virtually all the published works except letters to Jackson, Miss., newspapers and society notes for the Memphis (Tenn.) *Commercial Appeal* in the 1930s. Noel Polk is presently preparing a full-scale descriptive bibliography.

The bulk of Welty's manuscripts are in the Mississippi Department of Archives and History and the Humanities Research Center at the University of Texas at Austin. McDonald's annotated checklists in the *Bulletin of Bibliography* (1963, 1974) and *EuWN* (1978) record and describe those in public collections as of 1977; the 1963 checklist also includes Welty letters. In "The Eudora Welty Collection, Jackson, Mississippi" (1978) Joan Givner discusses information from letters and clippings about Welty's works and their publication.

For secondary materials until mid-1981, Peggy W. Prenshaw's "Eudora Welty" in *American Women Writers: Bibliographical Essays* (1983) is invaluable. It evaluates bibliographies, biographical material, and published scholarship and criticism on the literature, including general studies, analyses of individual works, and discussions of special topics. The most complete list of scholarship and criticism through 1975 (with brief but generally nonevaluative annotations) is *Eudora Welty: A Reference Guide* (1976) by V. H. Thompson; for its errors, see Ruth Vande Kieft's review, *Mississippi Quarterly*, 30 (Winter 1976-77), 169-178. Polk's 1973 checklist includes selected secondary materials. Updating all these is the "Checklist of Welty Scholarship" (unannotated) in each Summer issue of *EuWN* since 1977. Still useful for its extensive annotation is Bethany C. Swearingen's *Eudora Welty: A Critical Bibliography, 1936-58* (1984), which lists Welty's books in considerable bibliographic detail, first periodical appearances, early criticism and reviews, and selected "local material."

Interviews

Since there is as yet no major biography, the reader will need to draw upon interviews and critical studies for biographical data. Personal biographical information occurs in the interviews rarely and briefly, and much about Welty's early life that did emerge has now been transformed into art in her *One Writer's Beginnings* (1984). But two may be noted: Bill Ferris's "A Visit with Eudora Welty" (1977)— for her travels throughout Mississippi while working for the WPA in the 1930s, real-life triggers for some of the early stories, and her acquaintance with black and white Southern writers—and Jane Reid Petty's "The Town and the Writer: An Interview with Eudora Welty" (1977)—for her relationship to Jackson.

About Welty's writing and literary interests, interviews have been much more informative. Two in 1972 merit extended discussion for comments on writing and on specific works that are reiterated and developed in later interviews. Charles T. Bunting's " 'The Interior World': An Interview with Eudora Welty" (1972) is particularly interesting for its account of the evolution of *The Golden Apples* (1949) ("in a way the closest to my heart of all my books") and *Losing Battles* (1970). Of the former Welty explains that "about halfway through" the stories she realized that she had been writing about the same characters under different names and at different periods in their lives, and the "interconnections" that "gradually" emerged fascinated her. The book, she insists, is not a novel: the stories have "independent lives" but "something additional" comes from them "as a group. . . ." *Losing Battles* began as a short story contrasting "how people thought of " Jack Renfro and "what he was," but "the moment" he got home from the penitentiary, she realized "he was somebody" and "the scope of the thing was a good deal larger" than she had expected. Welty also explains her desire "to *show* everything" through speech and action alone and her choice of time and setting: a year when she could depict people "at the rock bottom . . . which meant the depression" and in "the poorest part of the state"; she "wanted to take away everything and show them naked as human beings." It is not a "novel of despair" but of "admiration for the human beings who can cope with any condition . . . and keep a courage, a joy of life, even, that's unquenchable." For *Delta Wedding* (1946) she needed an "uneventful" year when "all the men could be home and uninvolved" so she could "concentrate on the people without any undue outside influences."

Linda Kuehl's "The Art of Fiction XLVII: Eudora Welty" (1972) is informative not only about *Losing Battles* but also about Welty's writing habits and her response to Chekhov and Woolf. Welty elaborates on her attempt to do "something new for me—translating every thought and feeling into action and speech." Although dialogue is easy for her because she is a listener and remembers, she learned much about making a speech perform multiple functions. About her writing habits, her preference is, she explains, to write a story at one sitting, then revise later with "pins and scissors." Her ear tells her the "exact moment" when it is finished, because she "hears" what she writes. But her earliest stories show weaknesses because she did know about revising. Calling herself a "short story writer who writes novels the hard way, and by accident," she discusses the pleasures of writing. Because a work sets its "form from the idea which is complete from the start," she never knows "how far I can wander and yet come back"; and since life seldom resolves itself, she likes "being able to confront an experience and resolve it as art. . ." The writer's "honesty" begins with truth to time and place, from which imagination can take him anywhere. Welty also describes her sense of a closeness between Chekhov and the South, and the powerful impact of first reading Virginia Woolf, "who opened the door": "When I read *To the Lighthouse*, I felt,

Heavens, *what is this?* I was so excited by the experience I couldn't sleep or eat."

Two wide-ranging interviews—both entitled "An Interview with Eudora Welty"—by, respectively, Jean Todd Freeman (1978) and Jan Norby Gretlund (1980), touch on many of the above topics, sometimes with added details, but also include remarks on her natural, instinctive use of myth and her objection to crusading in fiction, as against revealing moral principles through the characters. To Jo Brans ("Struggling Against the Plaid: An Interview with Eudora Welty," 1981), she comments on Miss Eckhart, Virgie Rainey and Julia Mortimer—all "passionate people" as "[m]ost of my good characters are," and to John Griffin Jones ("Eudora Welty," 1982) she describes changes in Mississippi since the 1960s and their effects on new writers. To both she explains how her feelings and memories become reflected in her writings through a character but not as autobiography.

Almost all of Martha van Noppen's "A Conversation with Eudora Welty" (1982) is devoted to *The Optimist's Daughter* (1972). Welty comments on some specific sentences and more general matters—e.g., that she "tried to give the feeling of support and dependence" between Laurel and her parents and that in Laurel she was "not," as some have suggested, "writing about the South" or "the decay of moral certainty" there. Welty also stresses that as with "anything you use," so with the bird in the house she "tried not to be too specific, but just to suggest" a number of things—"the menace of things, and the presence of something, and the difficulty of an imprisoned spirit." She reveals that she delayed publication of the book version to allow time for revising and hopes she "deepened it in some ways" because "things happened" in the interim so that "she could see it more clearly."

Joanna Maclay's "A Conversation with Eudora Welty" (1982) records Welty's observations about oral readings and dramatic adaptations of her fiction. She would "adore" to write a play because she loves the theater, but writing *Losing Battles* in dialogue showed her the differences in approach of the novelist and dramatist. She was "confounded" by the Broadway dramatization of *The Ponder Heart* (1954) because the narrator's role was no longer central and dialogue was borrowed from other stories: for her, "those lines" existed only for a certain character in a certain situation. The experience taught her that the story "can only be a springboard" for a new thing. Feeling "a certain protectiveness toward" her characters, she allows adaptations only if they remain "true to the spirit," the characters, and the relationships while possibly using different means. She "sees" her characters when creating them, but would be undisturbed by a slight visual discrepancy on stage if the acting were good, since "actors work from the inside like writers."

Critical Studies: Books

The first of the early studies remains the best introduction to Welty's fiction through *The Bride of the Innisfallen* (1955)—Ruth M. Vande Kieft's *Eudora Welty* (1962) in the Twayne United States Authors series (fortunately being revised and updated). It stresses Welty's concern with the "mysteries of the inner life," which Vande Kieft defines as "the enigma of man's being"—his relationship to a universe in which chance is prominent, the competing demands of and desire for love and separateness, and the puzzles and difficulties people have about their feelings, meaning and identity.

After a biographical chapter, Vande Kieft primarily provides close readings of stories from *A Curtain of Green, The Wide Net*, and *The Bride of the Innisfallen* and analyses of *Delta Wedding* and *The Golden Apples*. Almost half the book discusses the first two collections. A brief chapter demonstrates the range of Welty's comic vision—embracing humorous characters of nineteenth century fiction, Southern folk humor, the satiric, ironic and absurdist. Three chapters—"The Mysteries of Eudora Welty," "The Weather of the Mind," and "The Season of Dreams"—for the most part analyze stories from *Curtain* (1941), which as a whole "records the shock of the world on the sensitive, innocent mind and heart," and *The Wide Net* (1943), in which fantasy and actuality are more often blurred and which explores "the primal loneliness—the mystery of identity, the way it is met by the innocent and the way it can hurt. . . ."

But in *Delta Wedding* (1946), Vande Kieft says, there is a recognition that the primal loneliness and isolation are "right and necessary," allowing the individual to feel his "own mystery and that of others" and thus to grow in the potential for love and insight. She focuses on George Fairchild, as the "hero" of the trestle event and the novel, and the responses to him by the other center-of-consciousness characters, particularly Ellen, to elucidate Welty's development of the themes of identity and relationship, love and separateness, through the unit of the family. Through George's stance and the thoughts and actions of the "outsiders," she says, Welty reveals the shortcomings of the Fairchild way of life. Turning to technique, she argues that most of the time Welty successfully fuses "the outer and inner life in the novel," especially by infusing descriptions of the physical world (woods, river, field, house interiors, the texture of day and night) with the emotions of the characters, and she comments on the symbolic functioning of atmosphere, light, and the trestle episode.

Vande Kieft considers *The Golden Apples* Welty's most complex and wide-ranging book (as of 1962), unified by its locale, its limited time span, and its "richly thematic, symbolic, mythical patterns of organization." Focusing on the motif of the wanderer (and his foil) as basic, she argues that each story in sequence contributes to this "human odyssey" which reveals that "the horror and the beauty, the despair and the joy, the frustration and the fulfillment, the separateness and the love, exist in an endless counterpoint. . . ." Vande Kieft discusses only a few stories from *The Bride of the Innisfallen,* which she describes as continuing Welty's vision but with more "[e]laborateness, subtlety and sophistication" in characters and motivation, structure, narrative, and style. They show the same power of feeling, but the job of the reader is more difficult because of the more impressionistic method.

In a wide-ranging conclusion Vande Kieft notes Welty's lack of involvement in "the peculiarly southern preoccupations" (such as race relations), denies even in the early stories the strong gothic tendency implied by some reviewers, and emphasizes Welty's juxtaposition and equal weighting of opposing values and her propensity for seeing her characters with "relentlessly clear vision, which records but does not judge." She also comments on Welty's relationship to other writers concerned with projecting the inner life, including Joyce, Chekhov, Woolf, and especially Elizabeth Bowen. Probably no critical work on Welty's writings has been more influential than Vande Kieft's except Robert Penn Warren's seminal essay on love and separateness (see "Articles and Book Sections").

Although it differs in organization and discusses some works only mentioned there, Alfred Appel, Jr.'s *A Season of Dreams: The Fiction of Eudora Welty* (1965) echoes to a remarkable degree the general conclusions, specific interpretations of many works, and, often, the language itself of Vande Kieft's book. Thus, despite scattered original insights, its chief contribution is its commentary on works slighted by Vande Kieft (most notably "Asphodel," "The Hitch-Hikers," "Powerhouse," and *The Ponder Heart),* and its chapters on technique, particularly the discussion of Welty's "verbal metaphors" and of verbs as "fulcrums" for metaphors and similes, and Welty's black characters. Appel argues that they "withstand and even triumph over their isolation and adversity" as her white characters seldom do and asserts that in her fiction the Negro is both "the survivor of the curse of slavery" and "the reminder of the South's guilt."

Of two much shorter assessments in the late sixties, the more original is *Eudora Welty* (1969) by Neil D. Isaacs (43 pp.). He discusses some works as "performances"—in which Welty adopts a character or persona "clearly removed . . . from her own" and tells the entire story from that point of view, usually first person; but sometimes in second- or third-person narratives the "persona" serves as a filter/ reflector and thus creates a kind of performance (e.g., "Powerhouse," "The Burning," "First Love"). The larger part of the book examines stories in the framework of the myth of the summer king and winter king, who compete for and alternately possess "the female figure, the nine-faced triple goddess." Isaacs also perceptively discusses *Delta Wedding* ("a novel striving to become myth"), emphasizing the theme of renewal, which is "the core of Miss Welty's central, archetypal nature myth," and *The Golden Apples,* which "develops a myth of its own." Partly because he tries more than brevity of treatment will allow, Isaacs seems at times to force categorizations (e.g., "Flowers for Marjorie" as an "ironic, negative, inverted-image" summer-king story) or inadequately justify conclusions (e.g., that "Kin" lacks the "consequential or cumulative effect" of "Why I Live at the P. O." because it lacks a "precisely delineated persona in a precise dramatic context"). But the discussions of both the performances and the mythic implications provide the stimulus for a new look at many familiar works.

J. A. Bryant, Jr.'s brief (48 pp.) *Eudora Welty* (1968, reprinted 1977) is a more general introduction, a chronological survey (with some evaluative and interpretative comment) of the published fiction through "the Demonstrators" in 1966 and brief comments on several essays. (The 1977 text adds paragraphs on *Losing Battles* and *The Optimist's Daughter.*) It does not generally extend the interpretation of the works beyond Vande Kieft, but it is noteworthy for its appreciation of the serious themes in *The Robber Bridegroom* (1942) and of Welty's accomplishment in *The Bride of the Innisfallen,* as well as for some perceptive brief observations, such as noting (in James Justus's phrase) "the intricate linkage of Greek myth, Celtic folklore and Mississippi tradition" in *The Golden Apples* and pointing out that in *The Bride of the Innisfallen* Welty "guides us beyond the frame of the story to a level of understanding that with the characters themselves remains principally a level of feeling."

Two studies (dissertation-derived) of only the short stories have problems of clarity or coherence which seriously limit their value. In *Eudora Welty: Aspects of Reality in Her Short Fiction* (1971), Marie-Antoinette Manz-Kunz, after a needless chapter on Welty's life (using Vande Kieft), the American short story, and her relationship to it, concentrates on *A Curtain of Green, The Wide Net,* and *The Golden Apples.* She discusses the first two by categorizing the protagonists' relationship to reality: those who experience it as the rhythm of the universe with which they are in harmony or "disharmony"; those just beginning to apprehend reality "as an objective entity opposing their existence"; those who, by refusing to enter the world, never know it and eventually lose knowledge even of themselves; and those who evade the "immediacy of the world" through their imagination, with only a few (notably Powerhouse) doing so "without losing sight of their actual situations." Manz-Kunz argues that *The Golden Apples* depicts several relationships to a closed, matriarchal society which determines the "public rank" of the protagonists and screens out "unpleasant sides of life," using talk to make "the hazards of existence" ineffectual. The protagonists struggle for self-identity while trying to understand and evaluate the community's demands on their "objective self." She sees a belief in the need to become part of society as a "specifically American" trait in Welty's writing. Unfortunately, ponderous, opaque, and (too often) unidiomatic prose undercuts the usefulness of even the more perceptive chapters.

The value of Zelma Turner Howard's *The Rhetoric of Eudora Welty's Short Stories* (1973) is minimal. Its stated purpose is to study Welty's use of "four rhetorical devices to convey meaning and to render moral judgment": narrative voice, the archetype and semantics (i.e., words with "affective connotations" and "contextual meaning"), language (including idioms, slang, speech patterns and rhythms used to individualize a character's experience and convey judgments of him), and time. But her concept of *rhetoric,* never defined, remains fuzzy, and discussion is generally elementary and frequently marred by imprecision, inconsistency, and incoherence, even in the "language" chapter with its many examples.

The first critical study of all the books through *The Optimist's Daughter*—and one of the most stimulating—is *Eudora Welty's Achievement of Order* (1980) by Michael Kreyling. It aims to show that her fiction "is not primarily regional writing" but "truly encompasses 'the general consciousness' " and "to locate" its "elusive, irreducible voice." Sympathetic, perceptive, and gracefully written, it is the first study to trace in the canon a consistently developing interrelation between technique and vision—characterized as "connections"—and to discuss each book as a unified artistic entity.

Particularly valuable is the examination of the first two collections and *The Bride of the Innisfallen* from these perspectives. While some stories in *A Curtain of Green* universalize a grotesque to make "a point about the nature of individual human existence," Kreyling argues, most, using "a homemade or natural symbolism and net of suggestion," reveal life and discover "the true nature of life's connections." This "effort toward connection through an exploring technique unifies the stories" and anticipates the methods of the later fiction. In *The Wide Net* this idea of connection, given its "flesh and blood in the meetings of several pairs of human beings," unifies individual stories into "something more than a collection" through the common setting (Natchez Trace), the concern with "the difficulty of love and personal expression," the "echoing words" (*silence, haze, dream, still*), and the movement "from the world of history" into that of dream (art, love) and back again.

Kreyling makes the most sustained case to date for the unity, accessibility and artistry of *The Bride of the Innisfallen,* arguing that Welty "discovers a form more complex than the simple assembling of stories and sheds light in areas of human experience and consciousness not generally illuminated in most novels." The book, he contends, asserts "that there is truth in the life of the heart" which "is daily obscured by a prosaic attitude to life." Constituting the technique and in their rhythm creating the meaning (and unity) of the collection, Kreyling argues, are the journey or pilgrimage, the effects of bodies of water as barriers, and a rhythm "of repeated approaches and retreats," passages over water, and "calls of the heart going unheeded." If occasionally strained, his commentary on these collections is always enriching and stimulating, as in his reading of "Going to Naples" and "The Bride of the Innisfallen."

Also challenging and original is Kreyling's analysis of the serious dimension in the critically neglected *The Ponder Heart.* Treating Edna Earle as a familiar figure in Welty's fiction—a troubled soul caught between the "desire for fulfillment and personal freedom" and the "felt" need to fill society's prescribed role—he perceptively discusses the book as a comic version of the conflict between the "champions" of life (Uncle Daniel) and order (Edna Earle), a conflict "inherent in the human consciousness."

All Kreyling's chapters repay attention. For example, comparing *Delta Wedding* with the unpublished story from which it evolved, he maintains that it records Welty's discovery of her "distance"—"the relationship between herself and experience"—as evidenced particularly by the most "vital" technical fact of the novel—redistribution of the point of view among several distinct characters. And this technique, he says, mirrors the meaning of the novel since the human plight is to constantly rearrange the balance of the basic opposites—clan/self, love/separateness, innocence/experience. While acknowledging the importance of mythological allusions (with Perseus/Atalanta as central) in *The Golden Apples,* Kreyling stresses the natural world as nourishing myth and supplying the major imagery. The book's structure he calls "lyrical": each story contains a challenge to growth and fulfillment through King McLain "and the sharers of his vitality" and an affirmation or denial of that challenge; each repetition deepens meaning by "encompassing . . . more of the world." He refines Vande Kieft's wanderer/foil motif into "adventurer going before the onlooker," which occurs in every major story. A commendably balanced reading of *Losing Battles* demonstrates Welty's wholeness of vision in balancing the mythic consciousness (family) and historical consciousness (Julia Mortimer) through her handling of dialogue, incident, and imagery from the world of natural phenomena (particularly rings, trees, cycles).

Elizabeth Evans's *Eudora Welty* (1981) in the Ungar Modern Literature series will be useful primarily to readers whose acquaintance with the fiction and the scholarship is limited. Its 150 pages succinctly provide much information about Welty's literary career, the content of her works, and their initial reception, and identify important emphases in interpretation that have evolved. An opening chapter on Welty as a woman of letters includes interesting material about early (unpublished) stories and efforts to get her first collection published. But the three chapters on the fiction evince some inconsistency between an apparent effort to reflect major critical emphases and a desire to express the author's own predispositions: The result is more comment on manners, characters, and the comic, less on symbol, myth, and profounder dimensions of meaning.

The first illustrates the similarities between Chekhovian and Southern humor that Welty herself has noted and discusses such devices as exaggeration, comic characters, oddities of dress, speech, and manners, and "comic migrations" ("the mixing of different social levels by moving characters from one region to another"). In the other two chapters (half the book) Evans approaches the fiction through two categories, admittedly arbitrary. That relying heavily on "dialogue, tale telling and external confrontations" includes *A Curtain of Green, The Robber Bridegroom, The Golden Apples,* and *Losing Battles.* She reports the generally accepted views as to Welty's important themes—human relationships, the mystery of human life, and change. But her discussion of *Curtain* is surprisingly brief and superficial; and, while acknowledging the mythic element in *The Golden Apples,* she concentrates on the characters and events, an approach that is more effective with *Losing Battles.*

The other fiction—involving "a sense of mystery," "internal and reflective confrontations," and "characters . . . drawn into vortexes of quiet"—includes *The Wide Net, Delta Wedding, The Bride of the Innisfallen,* and *The Optimist's Daughter.* Evans discusses *Delta Wedding* as a study of the family (*the* institution of Southern life), which is on the brink of change, but largely ignores its exploration of important Welty themes about human relationships and mystery through the inner lives of major characters. Echoing familiar adjectives—"elusive" and "difficult"—about *The Bride of the Innisfallen,* she observes that the climaxes in stories are "inner revelations rather than overt action or explicit statement," but devotes half of her discussion to the comic. Commentary on *The Optimist's Daughter* achieves the best balance between character and theme. Evans's conclusion ("The High Art of Eudora Welty") stresses the presence of concrete Southern materials in the fiction and cites Welty's use of detail as "the single most significant aspect" of her style.

As a consideration of Welty's relationship to the Southern Romance tradition, Jennifer Lynn Randisi's *A Tissue of Lies: Eudora Welty and the Southern Romance* (1982) is disappointing. Essentially Randisi lists eight constituents of the genre and then analyzes their manifestation in each of the following works in turn: *The Robber Bridegroom, Delta Wedding, The Ponder Heart, Losing Battles,* and *The Optimist's Daughter.* But the list is very broad, embracing classical, regional, and family mythology, local legend and folktale, "preoccupation with identity or name in relation to the first families of the South," "acceptance of narrator or story-teller as authority," "repetition of, and preoccupation with incident," and the beliefs that language can "order chaos" and that there is a need to rewrite Southern history. The introduction, which briefly defines these elements and asserts a link between Welty and Civil War diarists, offers no reasons for including in the genre such problematic ones as "acceptance of narrator or story-teller as authority." Although in each chapter Randisi makes interesting comparisons to novels discussed elsewhere, no concluding summary assesses the significance of the tradition to Welty's literary achievement.

On the other hand, Randisi often extends and enriches earlier analyses of the interweaving of Southern regional, geographic and family mythologies as major structural and thematic elements in the individual novels. She is particularly illuminating on the relationship between regional and family myth and the establishment of personal identity in *Delta Wedding, Losing Battles,* and *The Ponder Heart,* which she treats as an "ironic myth." Her detailed analyses of individual works also support her assertion that the circle is "the informing mythical pattern" of the novels. Regrettably, the book omits *The Golden Apples* and exhibits an annoying fondness for unnecessary jargon from other disciplines and certain unidiomatic locutions.

Less informative is Albert Devlin's *Eudora Welty's Chronicle: A Story of Mississippi Life* (1983). Devlin insists that critical emphasis on the "lyrical" Welty has obscured her development of a social vision and "cohesive view of historical reality" and ignored the "primary source" of her "fictional coherence": a chronicle of Mississippi life which helps to unify her fiction and reveals "a complex historical imagination."

Devlin succeeds best in revealing the various segments of the "chronicle" imbedded in certain works, discussed in order of publication. (He ignores *The Ponder Heart* and most stories in *The Bride of the Innisfallen,* barely mentions *Losing Battles.*) The most interesting and persuasive chapters concern the first two collections. Examining several stories (and noting particularly the spatial and temporal imagery), he suggests that *A Curtain of Green* reflects the contemporary world of "restricted personal space and harsh temporality," whose characters are increasingly divorced from nature or the more satisfactory "frontier"/"plantation" past or are threatened by the "imminent collapse" of familiar social, economic, and domestic institutions. Especially informative and perceptive is his detailed analysis of Welty's use of historical sources (even for imagery and language) in "First Love" and "A Still Moment" (*The Wide Net*). His discussion of family portraits, house furnishings and even dialogue in *Delta Wedding* as "imbedded" segments of chronicle is also suggestive.

But the treatment of three longer works as exemplars of Welty's "historic" vision is less satisfactory, partly because of gratuitous discussions of the views or concepts from historians Welty is admittedly not familiar with, sometimes to the neglect of the novels themselves. Although *Delta Wedding,* for example, clearly depicts tensions between the personal and communal realms as in the conventional plantation novel, Devlin is unpersuasive that somehow through Ellen Fairchild Welty resolves "historic" tensions. Similarly, he convincingly illustrates that *The Golden Apples* and *The Optimist's Daughter* reflect the passing of a distinctive Southern culture. But he is not persuasive in his characterization of Virgie Rainey and Laurel Hand as "historians" responding to "bristling social change" who are finally reconciled through memory and imagination to a "southern heritage," or in his contention that the "cluster of human values" they come to perceive "has for Welty distinctive regional significance."

In *Sacred Groves and Ravaged Gardens: The Fiction of Eudora Welty, Carson McCullers, and Flannery O'Connor* (1985), Louise Westling takes another approach to the "southern" qualities. She posits a Southern past in which women were treated with a mixture of veneration and betrayal and a present where "the old image of femininity" has been discredited but no better alternative offered. These three writers, she suggests, found strength in "the matriarchal traditions of the South," which each experienced personally, and in "strong traditions of feminine moral influence and literary accomplishment."

For Welty readers, the book's chief value lies in its discussion of *Delta Wedding, The Golden Apples* and *The Optimist's Daughter*. Westling argues with some persuasiveness that Virginia Woolf's *To the Lighthouse*—particularly the treatment of Mrs. Ramsey—vitally influenced "the celebration of distinctly feminine fertility and community" in *Delta Wedding*. She points to a "similarly fragmented" point of view, to Ellen Fairchild as a "mother figure" equaling Mrs. Ramsey in "sensitivity" and "unifying the family," but particularly to the novel as a "dramatization of the wider network of family life around the central event of the wedding." She also finds "specific echoes," as in the symbolic use of the garnet pin and bees. But Westling acknowledges that the specific development of the maternally sustained family and the handling of point of view and of the "garden paradise" setting are distinctly Welty's. She examines the novel in terms of "feminine rituals of hearth, meadow, wood, labyrinth, beehive and sacred river" which reveal "eternal cycles of fertility" and renewal; she finds recurrent suggestions in characters, events and places of the myths associated with Demeter and Dionysus, particularly the erotic feminine quality of landscape and the Eleusinian mysteries.

Although Dabney and Shelley in *Delta Wedding* suggest some "new assertiveness" against the traditional model of women, Westling sees Virgie Rainey in *The Golden Apples* and Laurel Hand in *The Optimist's Daughter* as better exemplars: the former ultimately frees herself from her obligations to her mother, faces her past, and "reaffirms her essential connection to wider natural powers"; the latter defies her mother to make her own life, but, because she denies neither "her mother's values" nor the "nourishing traditions of the past," can use memory to live in the present.

McCullers and O'Connor, Westling concludes, "only grudgingly accept" a female status their work portrays as a "trap" or "diminishment"; but Welty "embraces her femininity . . . [and] . . . sees the world" through her women characters, "lovingly, reaffirming the old female powers of the land . . . [and] . . . the fruitful alliance of male and female humans. . . ." This generally perceptive study includes, however, an occasional startling and debatable assertion—e.g., that usually in Welty's fiction rape appears to be "a natural, if sometimes inconvenient, sexual encounter," or that Welty seems unable to dramatize Virgie's or Laurel's "independent life at all."

The most extended and readable exploration of "southern" elements is Carol S. Manning's *With Ears Opening Like Morning Glories: Eudora Welty and the Love of Storytelling* (1985). Considering the works in the context of the South's oral culture (and Welty's known delight in it), especially tale-telling and reminiscing, Manning argues that it has shaped most aspects of her art. The fiction "exposes the roles the oral tradition plays for the Southerner" and thereby both depicts and criticizes the people who share it, presenting it as a "ritual and mask, diversion, and sustainer of the past"; as both a "social art" and "social menace," and, most crucially perhaps, a means for making heroes of ordinary men and for romanticizing life. Welty, she maintains, has been influenced by both the actual tradition and its depiction in literature, especially Southern fiction.

After an opening chapter rather dismissing the early stories as apprentice work in which "Welty did not set out to mimic life . . . but to tell a good story," Manning identifies and illustrates aspects of her handling of the oral tradition. One chapter sketches her depiction of families and communities engaged in oral reminiscing about the past to preserve tribal history, glorify a group hero, and reinforce approved values. Welty's approach is distinct, she demonstrates, from that of Faulkner, Porter, and others in range and number of tales, the variety of tellers, the narrating of recent as well as past events, and especially the use of the speaker's words and re-creation of the whole situation of the speech—a method which lets her both characterize the speaker and comment on or even undercut the tale. Manning also illustrates this range of the "oral remolding of events"—

from "sometimes malicious gossip to nostalgic tales about the dead, and from the creation of heroes to formalized rituals." With *Delta Wedding,* she argues, Welty began to depict her Southerners as not merely valuing and romanticizing the past, but actually sculpting a pleasant one by transforming painful, tragic, or reprehensible events into comedy or romance, as in *The Ponder Heart* or *Losing Battles.*

Especially stimulating are two chapters on Welty's use of myths both to mirror Southern society's mythologizing and to reveal the fallible reality behind it. An extended analysis of "Asphodel" provides an example: Welty, Manning says, interweaves allusions to classical mythology (Don McInnis as Dionysian, Miss Sabina as Apollonian) and sentimental Southern storytelling (McInnis as Southern gentleman/Don Juan, Miss Sabina as Southern belle/powerful matriarch) to show how Southerners make ordinary mortals who are somewhat different into superbeings; then she undercuts these portraits by revealing the fallible human being beneath. Manning then examines this kind of hero-making and mythologizing in *Delta Wedding, The Golden Apples,* and *The Ponder Heart.* Of the male characters thus glorified, she says, only George Fairchild and Jack Renfro "transcend the legend to become completely realistic and round characters."

In a provocative but not completely persuasive chapter, Manning discusses *Losing Battles* as the climax to Welty's portrait of the South's oral culture, a "subtle exposure of the romantic view of the South," and a parody of "values often called Southern" (such as family devotion and unity) and the literary conventions that depict them. Particularly interesting is her examination of Welty's use of similes in the narrative and descriptive passages, the epic catalogues, and the comic diminishment of Jack as hero. Manning argues that *The Optimist's Daughter* echoes familiar motifs from Southern literature, notably the theme of an "Old South" (with its sense of community and tradition) "giving way" to a "New South" (with its unconcern for either), but handles them differently. It reflects, for example, the ossifying of traditions into staleness and hypocrisy, as seen in Welty's presentation of such oral-tradition elements as the tale-telling and conversational amenities that are part of funeral etiquette.

Critical Studies: Newsletter

The semi-annual *Eudora Welty Newsletter* publishes checklists of writings by and about Welty, bibliographic notes, collations of texts, and miscellaneous news about her and her work.

Critical Studies: Major Articles and Book Sections

Although she had published two novelettes and a full length novel, much of the formal criticism of Welty's fiction prior to *Losing Battles* in 1970 concerned the short stories and took the form of explications of individual stories, which must be ignored here. But some perceptive essays identified major themes, notably love and separateness, discussed her lyrical imagination and poetic techniques, and assessed her achievement in the first phase of her career. Some of the earliest were provoked by reviews, particularly in certain Eastern publications, charging Welty with false poeticism, obsessive concern with the grotesque and horrible, and subjectivity to the point of obscurity. This reaction began with *The Wide Net* in 1943 and intensified with *Delta Wedding* and especially *The Bride of the Innisfallen*, which mystified even some staunch admirers. With *Delta Wedding* came also objections to her Southern subject matter.

The single most influential critique—Robert Penn Warren's "The Love and Separateness in Miss Welty" (1944)—was, in fact, prompted particularly by Diana Trilling's review of *The Wide Net* (1943) attacking Welty's "extreme infusion of subjectivism and private sensibility," development of "her visions of horror to the point of nightmare," "falsely poetic" technique, and failure to write "real" short stories. His examination of Welty's themes and techniques suggested approaches that have been developed in much subsequent criticism. With "the fact of isolation" as "the basic situation," Warren says, the stories concern either a person's attempt "to escape into the world" or his (or the reader's) discovery "of the nature of the predicament." They involve several contrasts—innocence/experience, love/separateness, dream/reality, individuality/anonymous life force—which, "being basic, are not susceptible to a single standard resolution." The only one possible is in terms of human effort, "for the dream must be carried to, submitted to, the world, innocence to experience, love to knowledge, knowledge to the fact, individuality to communion." Through this effort, which is a "mystery" and " to failure but essential," "the human manifests itself as human." Of Welty's technique,

Warren says that the "symbols . . . emerge from and disappear into" a recognizably realistic "world of scene and action" and that the dreamlike effect results often from her attempt to "squeeze meaning from" a detail or act that "in ordinary realistic fiction" would barely be noticed. Acknowledging occasional obscurity and strained metaphor, he declares that in the best stories the actual and mythical are "superimposed" upon one another.

Mostly citing stories from *A Curtain of Green,* Eunice Glenn in "Fantasy in the Fiction of Eudora Welty" (1947) elaborates on "the interrelationship of the external and the internal—reality and the imagination" in her work, declaring that fantasy (reality magnified) is not an escape from ordinary experience but clarification and interpretation of it; and she praises Welty's "profound search of human consciousness." Glenn compares her to Hawthorne in method ("the conjunction of fantasy with actuality" and "the use of symbols"), concern with "presenting a basic truth, not a moral," and desire for "equilibrium between inner and outer experience" while recognizing man's unutterable loneliness. Welty uses the grotesque, she says, "to make everyday life appear as it often does" to someone with extraordinarily acute feelings. Her characters, although "thoroughly Southern," "transcend" geographical limitations.

Welty's poetic technique is the focus of "Eudora Welty's *A Curtain of Green*" (1969) by Robert J. Griffin. Noting that the truly important action is usually either mental or symbolic, he discusses "the prominence of verbal texture" (often the very structure or essence of the story), the "ingenious connectedness" of metaphor and "fictional 'fact,' " the "unobtrusive allusions" and mythic echoes, the "natural emblems and symbols," and point of view (sometimes a form of metaphor). Despite occasional weaknesses inherent in the poetic story, Griffin considers *Curtain* the best of an excellent canon.

In the earliest overview to include some longer works, "Eudora Welty" (1952), Granville Hicks praises Welty's range of emotion and subject matter in the early stories, and her "beautiful adroitness" and "perfect balance" in slipping between "the objective" and "subjective." He also defends her purposeful use of decadence and violence. *Delta Wedding,* strongly criticized by Trilling and Isaac Rosenfeld for its Southern content, he calls "one of the finest novels of recent years": a "triumph of sensitivity" and technique for its "constant, subtle shifting of the point of view" and insight into the characters' "subtle and complicated emotions," which Welty's "matchless gift" makes the reader share. Both it and *The Golden Apples* prove again that "the deeper one goes into the heart of a region, the more one transcends its geographical boundaries."

Still of major historical and critical value are two mid-1960s assessments of Welty's achievement through *The Bride of the Innisfallen*. In his extensive, perceptive "Eudora Welty and the Triumph of the Imagination" (1963), Chester E. Eisinger calls her work "a major contribution to American literature of the twentieth century"; it "sums up" the new fiction of the 1940s—"inward turning and backward turning" and stressing technique—particularly that which drew heavily on the gothic imagination. He links her to Coleridge in her supreme commitment to "the power and mystery of the imagination," fusion of external and internal experience, and faith in place-born images to embody "imaginative truth." Like other Southern writers she constantly tries "to repossess the past," not through history but legend and myth, believing that mythic patterns are imbedded in the consciousness and thus perennially relevant. Welty does not "take over" myths but relies on association and allusion. Devoting almost half his essay to the first two collections, he says she uses the past, like the present, to juxtapose "various versions of reality" without favoritism, and he stresses her probing of the paradox of love and separateness and the mystery of personality. *The Golden Apples* (her "third novel"), Eisinger calls her most impressive book. Unified by its chronological sequence, recurrent characters or families, and especially the community of Morgana, it reflects the human dilemma: the unsuccessful search for love, "the appetite for life" amidst its restraints, and time as stability and prison. *Delta Wedding* is less successful, because Welty's "attention to delicate nuance" and her "habit of indirection" limit the possibilities for passion and narrow her range.

In "The World of Love: the Fiction of Eudora Welty" (1963), Alun R. Jones also focuses on Welty's "essentially lyric imagination," which, he says, is "strengthened by characteristic wit and shrewdness," to combine the "delicate, introspective refinement" of Chekhov, Woolf, and Mansfield and the "tough, American know-how" of Twain, Stephen Crane, and Lardner. Despite their poetic technique, the earlier stories create "an immediate sense of actuality," strongest in those closest to fantasy; later, longer ones increasingly concern the "significant and mythical" and the legendary. For Jones, too, *The Golden Apples* is her "most complex and satisfying achievement," showing the act of the imagination to be "the act of life itself," which "must begin with an act of love." In effect answering reviewers mystified by the stories, he says that in *The Bride of the Innisfallen* Welty "broadened the scope" and "enriched the texture of her writing."

Richard H. Rupp's "Eudora Welty: A Continual Feast" (1970), published shortly before *Losing Battles* in 1970, confirms the developing portrait of the "lyric" Welty: her poetic style, sensitivity to place, and "reliance on the moment of vision" make her achievement "clearly in the short story." *Delta Wedding*, for example, preoccupied with "private responses to experience," is an unsuccessful "attempt at a sustained lyric moment" that reveals her "essential concern with the validity of different ways of seeing." *The Golden Apples*, "probably" her "finest achievement," celebrates the myth-making process, the shaping power of the imagination, and portrays the duality of experience.

Of the few analyses of the longer works before 1970, John Edward Hardy's "*Delta Wedding* as Region and Symbol" (1952) is of major importance. The basic paradox of the novel, Hardy argues, is that the Fairchild family's ability to support the extraordinary individuality of its members rests on their struggle against it; the basic center of interest is the "single, illuminating, still" acts of "private perception." Welty used the plantation society, he says, for the paradoxical vision it supports. More important, he shows that the order of the book is poetic—"of recurrent themes, symbols and motifs of symbolic metaphor." In one of the first and most perceptive discussions of the trestle incident as central to the novel's design and unity, Hardy suggests how it and its components (the trestle/train) function in the underlying conflicts and symbolize communication or the reverse, becoming part of larger, extended motifs (along with horses, water). Louis D. Rubin, Jr., on the other hand, in "The Golden Apples of the Sun" (1963) stresses theme in both *Delta Wedding* and *The Golden Apples*. He argues that the family of Shellmound and the community of Morgana—and their everyday rituals—function to hide certain harsh realities of human existence. But by the end of *Delta Wedding* Welty has shown, particularly through George Fairchild and Troy Flavin, the inevitability of time, change, and separateness; in *The Golden Apples* the revelation of the "real" world comes through Virgie's estrangement from the community. Both books suggest "that the world can be a very appalling place for those . . . [few who] . . . look at it clearly. . . ."

Two essays by William M. Jones provide early examples of an important concern of later criticism—Welty's use of myth. In his suggestive "The Plot as Search" (1967), he maintains that in *The Golden Apples* the mythic and the real are so integrated that over her characters' realistic action and speech "hovers" a world of "eternal truths that inform" them. In "Name and Symbol in the Prose of Eudora

Welty" (1958) he argues that from modernizing and Southernizing specific myths Welty had progressed in that book to such a complete fusion "that her southern characters take on the basic attributes" of the mythic characters and engage in their kinds of actions.

Although still unduly neglected, *The Bride of the Innisfallen* inspired two useful analyses during this period. In a graceful and perceptive essay, "A Frail Traveling Coincidence: Three Later Stories of Eudora Welty" (1969), Alun R. Jones says that Welty's writing increasingly focuses on man's lonely, elusive search for identity, to be found, if ever, "in moments of love." Each of these three "experimental" stories—"No Place for You, My Love," "The Bride of the Innisfallen," and "Going to Naples"—he argues, literally and figuratively is "a voyage into hitherto unknown and uncharted territory of consciousness." Welty lets each "set its own pace and . . . establish its own rhythm." In "Two Ladies of the South" (1955), which includes a substantial analysis of "Kin," Louis D. Rubin, Jr., finds all the stories to be about time: the structure of each is the character's search for the meaning of the moment of time, for his real self "freed of the distractions of elapsing events."

With the reassessment of Welty's achievement occasioned by publication of *Losing Battles* in 1970, the main focus of formal criticism shifted from the short stories to the longer works. Thematically, this meant discussion of love and separateness within the context of family, an extension of the mythic to include family myth and ritual, and increased attention to her treatment of change, time, and the relationship between past and present.

Some of these developments are foreshadowed in essay-reviews which consider that novel in relation to her previous work. In "Eudora Welty: Metamorphosis of a Southern Lady Writer" (1970), for example, John W. Aldridge describes her as an author with "an extraordinary talent for the short story" whose previous novels were only "extended and obviously attenuated short stories"; but *Losing Battles* exhibits gifts "as impressive as those of any writer" presently at work in the U.S. He praises Welty's skill in catching "the meaning and cadence" of the family's talk, with which they "neutralize the force of evil by explaining it away" or burying it under "story, recollection, gossip, and legend," and her use of Julia Mortimer to gradually reveal the price they have paid for survival and transform the novel from "a lyric celebration of life into a civilized and profound criticism" of it. Louis D. Rubin, Jr., calling Welty "one of the three or four most important" twentieth-century American writers, says the Beachams use talk partly to communicate but partly to hide. He links them to the Fairchild family (*Delta Wedding*) and the community of Morgana (*The Golden Apples*) which exist to help their members ignore the realities of life—the fact of time and death ("Everything Brought Out in the Open: Eudora Welty's *Losing Battles*," 1970).

The polarities touched upon by Aldridge and Rubin— and symbolized by the family vs. Julia Mortimer—are the focus for much subsequent discussion, which defines them in various terms and from a variety of perspectives, with most critics agreeing that Welty favors neither "side." In "More Trouble in Mississippi: Family Vs. Antifamily in Miss Welty's *Losing Battles*" (1971), for example, Thomas H. Landess sees the conflict as between "opposing concepts of group," the traditional group sustained by ties of blood which based its judgments on the evidence of the senses, and the modern "abstractionists" whose "view of life is unconditional and *a priori*." Since Welty's "vision is essentially comic," there is a resolution, most obviously through the lovers. Landess is one of a few critics who charge that the work lacks a "single significant action" which embodies "the entire meaning of the central conflict" and is overloaded with nonfunctional metaphors. William E. McMillen, characterizing the conflict similarly (physical, fruitful/intellectual, barren), sees it as a battle between Julia Mortimer/ Granny Vaughn to keep their own lifeview intact, with Gloria as the prize. His somewhat fuzzy discussion seems mainly concerned with Gloria's struggle to establish and maintain her identity and independence in her life with Jack ("Conflict and Resolution in Welty's *Losing Battles*," 1973).

Considerably more thought-provoking are two approaches to the novel through the significance of language. In "Speech and Silence in *Losing Battles*" (1974), James Boatwright maintains that the book both relies heavily on dialogue and is about speech and silence. The family talks, he argues, to preserve community bonds but, more basically, to survive; the silent characters (Granny, Nathan, Julia Mortimer) have "stripped life down to its core of feeling" and its essential solitude and separateness. The written word is also a form of silence, proceeding from solitude and a "furious need to say the truth," and is feared and hated by all the family except Vaughn. If the voices drown out the silences at the end, says Boatwright, Julia has nevertheless affected their lives. Douglas Messerli argues that the family uses language "as a shield" against time, converting past (and even present) events into spoken language through story-telling and thus controlling them and denying time and change. But Julia Mortimer sees life "historically," as a journey through time (as shown by her metaphors). Ultimately she recognizes that both she and the family have used language "to create perspectives of time in which they could survive." According to Messerli, Welty suggests that the best vision is that of Granny and Vaughn, which incorporates past, present, and future (" 'A Battle with Both Sides Using the Same Tactics': The Language of Time in *Losing Battles*," 1979).

Two impressive essays have explored the artistry of the novel. In a rich, wide-ranging discussion, "*Losing Battles* and Winning the War" (1979), that comments on characters, themes, and techniques, Robert B. Heilman takes issue with critics like Landess to praise the book as "highly ordered." Besides the six basic parts with their "conspicuous 'closers,' " he describes an unobtrusive order built on patterned "personal and thematic relationships": characters and issues gradually introduced and identified, past events woven in to generate present-day emotions, speculations and questions awaiting answers, and random chatter organized around major "thematic concerns." Especially informative is his examination of the language—particularly the use of words and highly ordered syntax to give dialogue "an impressive air of authenticity," verbs implying intention and feeling in natural and "even inanimate" things, and "striking or even thrilling comparisons" which suggest thematic elements. Through her even-handed presentation of the conflict between the family/"historical community" and the outsiders, says Heilman, Welty creates "a wide and deep picture of American life."

In "*Losing Battles* as a Comic Epic in Prose" (1979), Mary Anne Ferguson considers the novel as an ironic epic, with ordinary people as characters and a hero who represents their aspirations, that affirms life, albeit with some tentativeness. Relating the book to the genre rather than any specific epic, she gives an especially interesting discussion of narrative technique, epic catalogues, and metaphor and simile—particularly of dust as a "prevailing metaphor" and underlying structure—and suggests that the "great innovation" is "perhaps" the extent to which women's voices tell the epic story.

Two other critics who approach the novel as an affirmation are Seymour L. Gross ("A Long Day's Living: The Angelic Ingenuities of *Losing Battles*," 1979) and Louise Y. Gossett ("*Losing Battles*: Festival and Celebration," 1979). Gross stresses the intertwining of the two "sides" and Welty's balanced depiction of both; Gossett describes the rituals of the reunion—a "complex assemblage of tensions between male and female, individual and group, past and present, change and permanence"—through which Welty both praises and judges the family.

Some of the most stimulating criticism since 1970 has focused on what many critics consider Welty's masterpiece—*The Golden Apples.* It has received increasing attention, especially its mythic qualities and structure. The most detailed discussion of specific mythological allusions is Thomas L. McHaney's "Eudora Welty and the Multitudinous Golden Apples" (1973). McHaney acknowledges that part of the mythic dimension is "the natural and unplanned perception" of a writer steeped in myth who discerns in her characters' lives "patterns that correspond to the old stories she remembers." But he believes that she intentionally used two prime myths—Aengus and Perseus—"to underscore the principal concerns of the book," which include "the full . . . experience of life," where opposites like beauty/ugliness, hope/despair are close together. The heart of the essay details the mythic allusions associated with events in each story and adverts to their thematic implications. But McHaney also asserts "an almost symphonic orchestration of . . . parallels between old myth and modern reality" and suggests a structure of balances and counterpoints among minor and major stories/movements. (In a footnote he succinctly evaluates previous discussions of the mythic element.)

Rather than a specific myth or system, Elaine Upton Pugh argues in "The Duality of Morgana: The Making of Virgie's Vision, the Vision of *The Golden Apples*" (1982) that Welty works within a "cyclical conception of history and myth" from which "archetypal" dualities emerge: Appollonian (golden apples, sun) and Dionysian (silver apples, moon), associated with, respectively, reason, order, community, etc., and intuition, chaos, individuality, etc. Her discussion of how these familiar dualities inform the imagery, structure, and ultimately the meaning of the book is in many ways fresh. Pugh maintains, for example, that, although the sun/moon symbols reflect qualities in different characters or within one, the book is built not on conflict, but rather on a cycle of paired contrasts involving characters, images, and motifs which move toward association and accommodation. Like other critics, she finds the essential resolution in Virgie, who realizes the "conjunctive nature of existence."

Also taking issue with interpretations "according to a strict mythological system" is Danièle Pitavy-Souques in the most challenging discussion of the mythic in the work, "Technique as Myth: The Structure of *The Golden Apples*" (1979). She argues that it is the three elements of the Perseus myth—Perseus, Medusa, and the mirror-shield—that "correspond to the major themes and techniques" of the book, being present in each story and functioning in each as in the myth. The center of the myth is "fascination—Medusa's deadly gaze" or "fascination defeated" by Perseus's gaze in the mirror, which means death (separateness); she illustrates with "Shower of Gold" and "June Recital."

Douglas Messerli, however, in "Metronome and Music: The Encounter between History and Myth in *The Golden Apples*" (1978), argues that, in stressing myth, McHaney and other critics have ignored an equally important element—the concern with time. Each story and the book itself, he maintains, is structured around the encounter between two perceptions of time—mythic (cyclical, associated with the individual) and historic (linear, associated with the community), presented through mythically oriented characters (like Virgie, Loch, and King MacLain) and the historically oriented majority (like Katie Rainey and Cassie), who increasingly dominate life in Morgana. The central resolution is Virgie's acceptance of life in its fullness (i.e., past, present and future simultaneously) and time as cyclical.

In the most striking primarily thematic study, "Dreaming the Other in *The Golden Apples*" (1982), Lowry Pei argues that the central thematic issues in the books are "how we perceive or constitute reality, how we turn it into language, and how we achieve communication (if at all)" between our "subjectivity" and the "bewildering one . . . over there." He makes the interesting suggestion that such stylistic characteristics as apparently arbitrary and meaningless comparisons, "as if " locutions, and "sudden, at first inexplicable, jumps in narration" are used by Welty to make "another person's subjective state perceptible but . . . impenetrable."

Significant comment on *The Optimist's Daughter* begins with Reynolds Price's essay on the *New Yorker* version, "The Onlooker, Smiling: An Early Reading of *The Optimist's Daughter*" (1969). Identifying the act of vision as the key issue in her "strongest, richest work," Price argues that Welty sustains and clarifies the onlooker stance (merciless here), which he says has dominated her stories from the beginning, by confirming it as "the human stance which can hope for understanding, simple survival." The "aims of participation" are "doomed," but "Laurel's final emotion is joy." He praises the "stripped iron efficiency" of the language, "its avoidance of simile and metaphor." These views, which apparently hold also for the book version, have been challenged explicitly or implicitly by others.

Several first-rate essays illuminate the meaning and artistry of the revised text. In "Pattern and Vision in *The Optimist's Daughter*" (1978) John F. Desmond argues that Welty develops a familiar theme, the battle between order and spontaneity, by exploring the relationship between memory (which patterns experience) and experience (which repeatedly disrupts). He shows that her structural technique—shifting between experience and memory, past and present—and the patterns of images—of ordering, birds, food and feeding, water—correspond to the thematic interaction. Marilyn Arnold, concentrating primarily on the bird imagery, shows how it develops the theme that the dead and the past are saved "by being released into . . . the reinterpreting memory," which also frees the living ("Images of Memory in Eudora Welty's *The Optimist's Daughter*," 1982). In a more thematic approach, Robert L. Phillips in "Patterns of Vision in Welty's *The Optimist's Daughter*" (1981) calls it one of Welty's "most significant and clear statements . . . about the nature of vision," which at its best is "inaccessible to reason." With frequent reference to Welty's revision, he stresses the growth of Laurel's awareness of her parents' failures of vision and her own reborn vision—a realization that "memory, not the past . . . humanizes and makes us feel" and a sensitivity to timeless, "mythical underlayers of consciousness" which Welty suggests through image clusters (birds, water, vegetation, light, food).

The conflict of values, most clearly exemplified in Laurel and Fay, has evoked considerable comment. Cleanth Brooks, for example, in "The Past Reexamined: *The Optimist's Daughter*" (1973) underscores the contrast between Laurel, who comes to accept and understand the past, and Fay, whom he sees as rootless, self-aggrandizing and not fully human because to her the past means nothing; William J. Stuckey in "The Use of Marriage in Welty's *The Optimist's Daughter*" (1975) identifies the "ultimate issues" as "feeling vs. emptiness, love vs. self-love, loyalty vs. self-serving" and shares Brooks's antipathy to Fay. On the other hand, in "Marrying Down in Eudora Welty's Novels" (1979), John Edward Hardy argues that Laurel's failure to understand Fay and "the nature of Judge McKelva's attraction to her" after years of Becky's refinement shows her failure to understand herself—an interpretation not widely shared. A more accurate reflection of Welty's balanced presentation is in "Social Form and Social Order: An Examination of *The Optimist's Daughter*" (1979) by Thomas D. Young, who notes, however, that "Nowhere does Welty present more forcefully . . . the poverty of a life unsupported by a sustaining tradition."

Comment on *Delta Wedding*, overwhelmingly thematic, has mainly concerned Welty's portrayal of the love/separateness dualities through the relationship between individuals and the family, which some critics consider "another name for the South." Opinion continues sharply divided as to whether the presentation favors the individual or family or is balanced. In "Fairchild as Composite Protagonist in *Delta Wedding*" (1979), for example, M. E. Bradford, who sees the family as the South, emphasizes that the point is its survival (despite inevitable change) "as a composite entity which protects and sustains the distinctive and internal lives of its component parts" and that the "numerous evidences of private sensibility" are included "only to demonstrate how well they are contained"; Elmo Howell agrees, claiming that Welty sought to "enshrine" the South's values, which "are in danger of being lost in society at large" ("Eudora Welty's Comedy of Manners," 1970). Richard J. Gray, however, in "Eudora Welty: A Dance to the Music of Order" (1976), points to Welty's belief in the "spontaneity and consequent unpredictability" of the human personality, which can never be contained or expressed even by "the myth of the old plantation," and her habit of maintaining "a balance of loyalties, to make us respond critically and sympathetically . . . at the same time." And Peggy W. Prenshaw says that "the values of the family, of the formal life, are reaffirmed, but only after an honest assessment" and "critical recognition" of its limits; that in life there is "formlessness which the questioning individual must order for himself . . . " ("Cultural Patterns in Eudora Welty's *Delta Wedding* and 'The Demonstrators,' " 1970).

Two of the most interesting essays focus on the isolation created by family love and the internal conflicts experienced by some of the Fairchilds. Douglas Messerli, in "The Problem of Time in Welty's *Delta Wedding*" (1977), argues that the novel concerns "coming to terms with" inner individuality, which involves embracing both separateness and love. Most of the adults live only in the present; Dabney, however, combines the "real" present and "imagined" future but "devalues" the past; Shelley, the past and present, but fears the future; India, unexposed yet to separateness, through imagination embraces all three. Only George, whose love "takes in everything in all of time," including his death, and Ellen connect themselves to the world and "resolve the conflict between man and time." Allison Deming Goeller sees the novel as "a complex American pastoral . . . in the tradition of *Walden* and *Moby-Dick*, where the American garden of Eden is found to be seriously flawed." She argues that the insiders are "outsiders to each other, more isolated, perhaps" than actual outsiders like Robbie, and that the family's own "exclusiveness" is a greater threat than the changing material world around them ("*Delta Wedding* as Pastoral," 1981).

Surprisingly, *The Robber Bridegroom* has attracted far more comment than any other early work. Two notably helpful essays explore the most popular topic—the "doubleness" motif. Gordon E. Slethaug examines the theme of the "inextricability" of good and evil and suggests that Welty combined fairy tale and the ballad "Young Andrew" to make Rosamond more "aware" and complex than previously thought ("Initiation in Eudora Welty's *The Robber Bridegroom*," 1973); Warren French suggests that the book links both the familiar dichotomy of "the marketplace" and "the forest" and two traditions of fantasy—"the primitive fairy tale of ancient rural cultures" and the urban "Newgate pastoral" of eighteenth-century England (" 'All Things are Double': Eudora Welty as a Civilized Writer," 1979). In "Eudora Welty's Parody" (1978) Marilyn Arnold offers the provocative thesis that *The Robber Bridegroom* parodies the fairy tale to demolish the "pat-answer" vision it conveys.

Although most of the criticism has been of individual works, some essays have been more comprehensive. Some of the best and most helpful discuss Welty's vision, with general agreement about its honesty, but not about its implications. Ruth M. Vande Kieft, for example, stresses the meeting of the internal with the external and the paradoxical (and unflinching) quality of Welty's vision, "always faithful to the reality of life's contradictions and complexities" as in "the constant resurgence of joy and hope" even in her darkest work, *The Optimist's Daughter* ("The Vision of Eudora Welty," 1973). But Richard C. Moreland in "Community and Vision in Eudora Welty" (1982) emphasizes the darker view. Alluding to several essays and novels, he maintains that in her works Welty "has submitted her vision of love and community . . . more and more daringly to" reality and "has become more aware (and made us more aware) of the inevitable isolation and limitation of that vision in its repeatedly losing battles with time." In a different approach Lucinda H. MacKethan argues that the major longer works "dramatize the demands made on characters whose main challenge is to perceive, understand and transmit the moments when place yields up" its insights in the battle against time. Through characters who are objects, insiders, outsiders, or seers, MacKethan shows, Welty explores this act of focusing in the major longer works, culminating in the most complex of the "seers," Laurel Hand, who fuses "past and future, the pull of place and the power of time, by her trust in the validity of memory" ("To See Things in

Their Time: The Act of Focusing in Eudora Welty's Fiction," 1980).

If the past is prophetic, continued stress seems likely on four major works—*Delta Wedding, The Golden Apples, Losing Battles,* and *The Optimist's Daughter*—with a strong thematic bias, further exploration of the "southern" qualities, and more analysis from a feminist perspective. Recent publication of the *Collected Stories,* the essays and reviews (*The Eye of the Story*), and the autobiographical *One Writer's Beginnings* should prompt reassessment of the stories in the context of Welty's later career, and study of interrelationships among the life, the fiction, and the prose. As a major writer, Eudora Welty deserves no less.

Critics Index